SCOTLAND'S MUSIC

FRONTISPIECE   DETAIL FROM THE TITLE PAGE OF SIMON FRASER'S *Airs and Melodies*, 1816

SCOTLAND'S
MUSIC

A HISTORY OF THE TRADITIONAL
AND CLASSICAL MUSIC OF SCOTLAND
FROM EARLIEST TIMES TO THE PRESENT DAY

JOHN PURSER

MAINSTREAM
PUBLISHING

EDINBURGH AND LONDON

in conjunction with

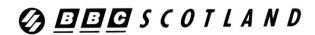 BBC SCOTLAND

For Martin Dalby

First published in Great Britain 1992 by
MAINSTREAM PUBLISHING COMPANY (EDINBURGH) LTD
7 Albany Street
Edinburgh EH1 3UG

ISBN 1 85158 426 9 (cloth)

A catalogue record for this book is available from the British Library.

This publication has been made possible with
generous support from BBC Scotland.

The publishers would like to acknowledge the financial assistance of the
Scottish Arts Council in the production of this volume.

While every effort has been made to trace the copyright owners of
material quoted in this book, it is possible that some have been omitted.
To these we apologise.

Typeset in Perpetua
Music and Text Typeset by Seton Music Graphics Ltd, Co. Cork, Ireland
Book Design by James Hutcheson, Paul Keir, Wide Art, Edinburgh
Printed and bound in Great Britain by Butler & Tanner Ltd, Frome, Somerset

Plates 1 to 64 refer to black and white illustrations
Plates I to XXX refer to colour illustrations
MB refers to *Musica Britannica*

CONTENTS

ACKNOWLEDGMENTS

My chief acknowledgment is to the book's dedicatee, Martin Dalby. Martin commissioned the series *Scotland's Music* for BBC Radio Scotland, and with extraordinary sang-froid accepted its growth from twenty-six thirty-minute programmes to thirty ninety-minute programmes. It is that commitment which essentially funded the research that informs this book. What miracles of budgeting he performed in order to permit the enormous number of special recordings for the series I will never know, but I do know that without those recordings this book could not have covered anything like the ground it does because so much of the material was being performed for the first time in centuries. Only in performance could its true worth be evaluated, and from those performances silent areas of our music history have suddenly become full of sound and hidden works of genius have emerged, as well as all sorts of minor but enlightening curiosities.

The gratitude I feel towards Martin, and that anyone with an interest in Scottish music should also feel, extends to many others at the BBC in Scotland: David Dorward, Hugh Macdonald, Neil Fraser, and many secretaries and sound engineers, patient, kindly and skilful. It also extends to the staff at Mainstream, Judy Moir, Jane Elders, Penny Clarke and Janene Reid, and especially Bill Campbell for taking on a complex project which, as I suppose any perspicacious publisher expects, was both late in delivery and larger than intended.

With one exception I have had nothing but co-operation and encouragement from my fellow scholars. It would be splendid if I could blame all errors on them, but ungrateful I suppose. Those with whom I have had direct communication will, however, have to put up with being publicly named as people who willingly imparted knowledge, whether I was fit to receive it or no. They are as follows:

For early music and related subjects, David Chadd, Warwick Edwards, Kenneth Elliot, Mark Everist, Catherine Fagg, Aloys Fleischmann, Greta-Mary Hair, James Porter, Lewis Purser, James Reid-Baxter, Edward Roesner, James Ross, Nick Sandon, Helena Shire, Jane Stevenson, Peter Walsh and Isobel Woods.

For the seventeenth century to the nineteenth century, Mary Ann Alburger, Ken Barclay, Jeremy Barlow, Brian Boydell, Muriel Brown, Herrick Bunney, Stewart Campbell, Gordon Dodd, Alasdair Hardie, David Johnson, Corky McGuinness, Philip Maund, Heather Melvill, Matthew Spring, Marjorie Rycroft, Heward Rhys, Michael Turnbull, John Ward, Roger Williams.

For traditional music, Alan Beaton, Seoirse Bodley, Alan Bruford, Roderick Cannon, Nicholas Carolan, Peter Cooke, Charles Dunn, Phyllis and Mered Evans, Stewart Eydmann, Anne Lorne Gillies, Charles Gore, Alison Kinnaird, John MacQueen, John MacInnes, Willie Matheson, Allan MacDonald, Eilidh MacKenzie, Morag MacLeod, Joe Miller, Gordon Mooney, David Murray, Ian Olson, Padraig O'Snodaigh, Keith Sanger, Rab Wallace. I also owe much to Stewart Cruikshank and Peter Easton for what I realise is a mere nod in the direction of pop music.

Libraries have been my chief hunting grounds and I have cornered many shy beasts on open shelves as well as musty cellars, thanks to unfailing courtesy and efficient co-operation from staff. First and foremost I must thank the staff of the Scottish Music Information Centre – Ann MacKay and Karen Abbott have been kindness itself. They are in charge of the most important resource for Scottish music in the world and permitted me ex-manager's rights when anyone with a sense of self-preservation would have locked me out.

Glasgow University Library has been an astonishing resource. Rarely have I sought a book that was not there, or asked a question that someone has not eventually answered. To Sheila Craik, knowledgeable guardian of the rich music holdings, I am much indebted.

The National Library of Scotland has also been a happy place to visit, thanks to Patrick Cadell, Roger Duce and Ruzena Wood.

The Bodleian Library, the British Library, Cambridge University Library, Dundee Central Library, Edinburgh University Library, Edinburgh Central Library and the Mitchell Library have also made research a pleasure.

The archaeologists have been generous too. Leslie Alcock, Hugh Cheape, George Dalgleish, Mike King, Ewan MacKie, Roger Miket, Stuart Piggott, Alison Sheridan, Michael Spearman, in this country have suffered many pestiferous probings and been good to me beyond my deserving. In Ireland too, the archaeologists have been wonderfully co-operative. Cormac Bourke, Raighneal O'Floinn, Eamon Kelly, Michael Ryan and John Teahan have given me access to some of the oldest surviving musical artefacts in the world.

The institutions they represent are the Royal Museum of Scotland, the Hunterian Museum, the Perth Museum, the National Museum of Ireland, the Ulster Museum and Skye and Lochalsh District Council.

To musicians I owe special gratitude for learning unfamiliar works, putting up with poor parts, half-realised editions and all the other short-cuts that our profession suffers for love of music and lack of proper funding.

From Ireland, Siomon O'Duibhir, Bronze-Age horn player and impassioned defender of the culture which produced them, and Brendan O'Madagain, expert on the caoine.

From Scotland, chiefly those mentioned below, but many many others who in courageous and obscure publications, recordings and performances have made available material which wealthier institutions have chosen to ignore.

Nigel Boddice, Leon Coates, Heather Corbett, Hilary Dalby, Irene Drummond, Alasdair Hardie and all of Kist of Music, Andy Hunter, David Johnson and all of the McGibbon Ensemble, John Kitchen, Ronald Leith, Allan MacDonald, Ronald Mackie, George MacIlwham, Rhona Mackay, Pat MacMahon, George MacPhee, Ronald Stevenson, Rebecca and Alan Tavener and all of Cappella Nova, Denis Townhill.

The West End of Glasgow deserves mention here. Living in the best-educated constituency in Britain has genuine advantages. A very considerable number of obscure enquiries were answered by chance meetings with academics on the street, or by popping round the corner to beard them in their lairs. Many went to a lot of trouble over all sorts of oddities, phoning me back, sending off-prints, directing me to ever darker corners with little shafts of light which ended up being so numerous that I felt and still feel myself to be in a vast hall of knowledge lit by the brilliance of other people's understanding.

There is, besides Martin Dalby, one person whose understanding exceeds all and that is my wife's. In book after book I note that grateful authors bend the knee before the patient and wise endurance and support of their spouses. I hope the spouses never band together because their power would be terrible: but for my wife, Barbara, I have feelings only of gratitude and love.

PREFACE

They came with so simple and obvious an idea — a history of Scottish music for radio. We had broadcast something of the kind in the early 1970s but this was to be something entirely different. It was to be all-embracing, not just classical music. Any sound in whatever genre created by Scots was to be included. John Purser and Martin Dalby went away to tinker with the idea and developed it from this form to that. They eventually returned with a monster — thirty radio programmes, each nearly ninety minutes long. I think they surprised themselves. The exquisite results of John Purser's intense and painstaking enquiries were a surprise to Scotland's public, a people who, until then, thought they knew something of their own musical treasures. It was a revelation, a history of Scotland in sound.

Now here is that chronicle in these pages and it pleases me and honours me to commend it to you. Purser's writing is inimitable. Its style is lyrical as a poet's. He evokes fun and he evokes sorrow and all other states of the soul which Scotland has sung throughout the centuries. And it is learned too. Within are rich and new discoveries and a story which is a joy to follow.

Now read on.

Neil Fraser
Glasgow, January 1992

FOREWORD

This book is an ambitious undertaking and relies heavily on the labours of others over the centuries. Their names and works are in the Acknowledgments, the Chapter Notes and the Bibliography. Nonetheless, Scotland's music has not had the attention it deserves, and since it is still just possible for one person to present an overall picture of it, that is what the book attempts to do, for general as well as academic readers. A rough guide to the background and approach and a few necessary definitions are required to save explanations later on.

I was determined to bring classical and traditional music together between one set of covers. They have been inseparable in our history and I hope they will remain so. For similar reasons Scottish literature plays an important part and there are many quotations from it. The illustrations serve the same purpose: to give a feel for period and a sense that all our music is an integral part of our whole culture and will be best understood and enjoyed in that knowledge.

The music examples include a number of first publications, but in the case of traditional music there can be many variants, and the same holds true in vocal music from one verse to the next: and just as no extended piece can be fairly represented by brief quotations, so no song or ballad can be appreciated properly without the whole of the text. It is in performance that music lives. In books it merely survives, though mere survival is precious enough. I have deliberately given tempo indications and expression marks only when they were put there by a composer or a normally reticent editor, hoping that those who can read music will use their own sensitivities to find the truths in it.

I have imposed my own definitions on some words. 'Celtic' is used almost exclusively to mean Scotland and Ireland because it is convenient and economical to do so. When it is used to cover the Celts elsewhere in Europe the context should make it clear. 'Gaelic' is used to mean the Gaelic language and culture in Scotland and Ireland, until they began to diverge; and 'Irish' is used for place or nationality, and only serves for the language in that country after divisions become significant. The earliest evidence for even slight divergence from the Gaelic language shared by Scotland and Ireland is early sixteenth-century. Both countries acknowledge a unity of Gaelic culture in general, unbroken for a thousand years and leaving a huge legacy, still actively shared.

For this reason it is legitimate to use Irish sources for information about early Celtic music, Christian or otherwise. If we in Scotland rely heavily on the survival of manuscripts in Ireland and on the continent, the Irish rely heavily on Scotland for the survival in the oral tradition of many of those things to which the manuscripts refer.

Material from the oral tradition is difficult to date. On the one hand it undergoes frequent modification and accepts influences from written sources, themselves influenced sometimes by the oral tradition; on the other hand it can be so conservative that one can reasonably claim some tunes as pre-Christian. But one can never prove it; nor is there any agreed set of criteria for even attempting it. Time can simplify things as well as elaborate them, as church music and book illumination amply demonstrate over extended periods of their histories. Where possible, justifications are given, but the main influence in such matters is instinct, and it is better to be honest about it.

This problem also arises in the written record. A large number of the manuscript sources were produced many centuries later than the events which they purport to relate, and writings attributed to early saints and others may well be by later authors, some of them standing accused of romanticising. That in itself is important evidence, emphasising the perceived significance of earlier events and underlining their tenacity.

Attitudes to manuscripts are frequently far from unbiased. It has taken nearly two hundred years for scholars to relax about James

MacPherson's *Ossian* and restore to him the respect he earned from some of the greatest minds in Europe during his lifetime. His deceits were prompted partly by a desire to enhance the status of Gaelic culture following the 'Forty-Five', partly by artistic ambition – both entirely acceptable motives – and the consequence was the liberation of verse forms throughout Europe, an increased interest in and awareness of Gaelic culture and (amongst his own inventions and distortions) the first publication in English of substantial sections of genuine Gaelic ballad sources.

Dating is also a problem. Doubtful manuscripts and the ascription of influences of one manuscript upon another are themselves often decided by national or other prejudice, or by scientific techniques too readily accepted. One of the most important music manuscripts in the world (see Chapter IV) which also happens to be Scottish, has recently been redated on the evidence of the style of the uncials on a few of its illuminated capital letters. But if we are required to establish our age and identity, we are all going to be in serious trouble if the experts truly believe we can be tracked down by our uncials.

The question of influence relates also to prejudices about 'originality'. It was long the tradition in painting, remains the tradition in classical ballet, and should still be respectable in the other arts, for an artist to copy the work of another and incorporate or imitate the styles of masters of the art. Handel did it regularly and is now accused of filching. Works of art are constantly discussed in comparative terms, article after article trying to discover who did what first. A work can be both derivative and beautiful, unoriginal and a source of enduring pleasure. This history does not, therefore, regard the establishing of chains of influence as a priority. It does not ignore them, but its primary object is to make us aware of and interested in the material itself, leaving us free to sniff the odour of our own comparisons, if sniff we must.

Nor should we sift evidence on the basis of what we individually choose to describe as facts. For millions of educated people the paternity and resurrection of Jesus of Nazareth are facts. If such facts are admissible in rational discussion then so too are the miracles and wonders of much Celtic material (to which Christianity

added its own rich store). Moreover, such material is a proper part of any account that attempts to convey the significance of things as opposed to their mere existence.

The mere existence of much of our music has been ignored. In the process of preparing *Scotland's Music* for Radio Scotland, I had the privilege of arranging for the first modern performances of so many works that the briefest description of them would be a chapter in itself. They include music from Scotland's oldest music manuscript, none of which appears to have been performed in modern times, as well as outstanding compositions from the sixteenth, seventeenth, eighteenth and nineteenth centuries by composers who have been unfairly neglected.

In the field of traditional music there was much to be unearthed, reconstructed or revived, and we were privileged to record for the first time some of the oldest surviving playable instruments in the world. All this involved transcribing music from manuscripts of every period, sometimes making sets of parts and other times liaising with scholars over sources and texts, or with archaeologists, instrumentalists and singers over methods of performance. Since there was no time to work all these researches into articles for appropriate journals, a substantial amount of the material in the series and this book will also be receiving its first serious discussion. This is both exciting and alarming.

Quite apart from the manuscript evidence of the music and the physical evidence of the instruments, the radio series involved a vast quantity of ancillary material, such as poetry, diary entries, correspondence, commentaries and account books – from the seventh century to the present day; and while most of this material was already known, only a proportion of it had been put to use. I have been eclectic in the acceptance of these ancillary sources and ready to consider evidence from the past at its face value and in the spirit in which it was produced.

Most music seeks an emotional response, whether by exciting the body, the intellect or the soul. The only depressing task when researching this book, was having to read scholarly articles in which there was little or no mention of the effect of the music on the author or, indeed, anyone else. There were many of them. This being a history of music, I make no excuse for expressing myself on occasion with feeling and giving credit to others who have done so, trusting that readers will discriminate for themselves between the author's enthusiasms and the raw material.

It is impossible in a work of this size and scope to list even the main sources (they would fill a substantial book), but there are chapter notes giving the sources of supporting material, and a limited bibliography and discography, to which I would like to add the proviso that the scholars and performers of the past deserve at least as much attention as those of the present. We labour under the frequent delusion that the latest reputable publications on a subject represent some kind of final truth about it, when the reality is that they and I will be thrown to the dogs under the table as rapidly as the critics and with as good reason, while the gentle reader will remain, for ever, true commander of the feast.

John Purser
November 1991

THE SCOTTISH IDIOM

Three matchless birds on the chair before the King,
and their minds set on their Creator through all time;
that is their part. The eight hours of prayer, these they
celebrate by praising and acclaiming the Lord, with
chanting of Archangels joining in harmony. The birds
and the Archangels lead the song, and all Heaven's family,
both saints and holy virgins, answer in antiphony.

Gaelic, eleventh century[1]

Birds were the first musicians. There are
those who say their song is purely
functional, designed like human speech
to convey information; but that does
not stop birdsong or speech from giving pleasure,
to birds and to humans. The calls of a raven to
his consort-for-life are no doubt more appealing
to her than those of his brothers. There is a
happy reassurance in such recognition. What
aesthetic value she puts upon his croaks is not
for us to determine any more than we can dictate
musical taste to each other.

Human speech has its own music. Quite
apart from the major linguistic divisions, the
harsher Germanic versus the flowing Romance,
there are many musics to be found within one
language, and we have likes and dislikes for
individual human voices which have little to do
with what they have to say.

Scotland is rich in language variety. Three
languages are still spoken. English, Gaelic and
Scots – the latter a Germanic language of parallel
development and similar antiquity to that of
English, but not a dialect of English. Gaelic belongs
to a different group – the q-Celtic group of
languages which includes Irish. Both English and
Scots are themselves amalgamations of Germanic
and Romance, with Scandinavian influences.

Other languages used to be spoken widely
in Scotland. One was an early form of Welsh – a
p-Celtic language – and was spoken over the
entire southern half of Scotland, surviving as late
as the ninth century AD. The Picts occupying the
rest of Scotland at that time may have spoken a
similar language, but amongst them it is thought

there was a tongue which was not even Indo-
European. The Picts never left. Their culture
became absorbed in that of the Gaelic-speaking
invaders – the Scots from northern Ireland –
and their speech may have influenced the rhythms
and accents of ours, if not our vocabulary and
syntax. There was Norn – a Scandinavian language spoken in the Orkneys and Shetlands until
recently, and still heard on the Scottish mainland
in the early eighteenth century. It influenced
Gaelic, and its surviving influence on speech and
music in the Northern Isles is undisputed.

We should not forget Latin. For many
educated people it was the *lingua franca* of
Europe. Any trained priest from Scotland from
the seventh century on, could sing, converse and
compose in that tongue and, like Sir John Clerk
of Penicuik in the late seventeenth century,
could use it when travelling or corresponding
abroad. Sir John's secular cantatas had Latin texts
written by a Dutchman.

This variety of linguistic and cultural background is reflected in our music and can still be
clearly related to the geography of the country.
One can travel north and west from the Central
Belt where classical music flourishes alongside a
powerful urban and rural tradition of song and
dance, to the Highlands with a Gaelic tradition
stretching back at least 1500 years. During that
journey you would move from mediaeval
cathedrals and abbeys with cathedral choirs and
polyphonic music, through the more sober hymns
and psalms of the regular church of Scotland, to
the far west where many churches are smaller
than a barn and where there are no organs, no
choirs, but a style of singing possibly as old as
Christianity. Or you could start southwards
from the Northern Isles and their Norwegian
influenced fiddle playing to the Borders and
their ballads in Scots, or travel up the east coast
from Fife to Nairn through county after county
rich in ballads and dance music. Yet over the

Plate 1. HARP AND BIRD ON THE SHRINE OF ST MOYNE,
ELEVENTH CENTURY

entire country you would almost always know from the music that you were in Scotland.

Humans, like birds, can be identified by their 'song' – and we will see (Chapter I) that the call of a bird is enshrined in one of Scotland's oldest and most culturally significant melodies. The quotation at the head of this chapter is only one of many that could have been used to show how closely the Celtic people identified with birdsong. The Vision it recounts is attributed by its author to St Adomnan, the seventh-century successor to St Columba on the island of Iona on the west coast of Scotland. A bird is depicted on some of the early Celtic harps (see Plate 1), the harp being the tree from which it sings. What could be more natural since it is made of wood? And when it comes to her own 'bird-call', Scotland, small, classed as remote, and with a mere five million inhabitants, has produced a music which is acknowledged and enjoyed worldwide and which could never be mistaken for anything other than its own. Be it to the bagpipes in New Zealand, *Auld Lang Syne* in Moscow and Hong Kong, Gaelic song in Canada or country dance in the USA, the world still marches, laments, sings farewell and dances to our tune.

Although this book is as interested in music without any national characteristcs as it is in music with them, the prevalence of their influence in Scotland demands that we try to answer the question – what makes Scottish music Scottish? Perhaps at the bottom of it is the love of the Scots for their own land and sea-scape which has encouraged them to retain a vast store of traditional music of every description frequently noticed and appreciated abroad, and which honours nature always.

From an early date music from Scotland seems to have had a clear identity. The chants honouring St Columba in the late thirteenth-century *Inchcolm Antiphoner* (some of which may date back to the seventh to tenth centuries) are as distinctive melodically as were the organisation and practices of the Celtic church. In the fly-leaf of a sixteenth-century book a Scottish folk-tune is written out which uses the double-tonic so typical of Scottish music, and Scotch snaps are found in a mid-seventeenth-century manuscript (see below).

In 1620, music credited to 'Jacopo Re Di Scozia' by the Italian poet, Tassoni, is described as '*una nuova musica lamentevole, e mesta, differente da tutte l'altre*', and Tassoni claims that this unique, plaintive and melancholy style was imitated by the extraordinary Italian madrigalist, Gesualdo.[2] There is confusion as to which king is referred to, James I or James VI and I, and it may be that Scottish music in general has been credited to a Scottish king as a sponsor of it. Plaintive and melancholy are words frequently associated with Scottish music and may relate to our fondness for gapped scales, especially pentatonic ones.

Example 1. MY LADIE LAUDIANS LILT (*Skene Lute Manuscript, c. 1625*)

With the exception of special classes of song, wide-ranging melodies, often with dramatic leaps requiring good voices, are common. But we also have a tendency to build melodies on the interval of a third – an interval which first found favour in part singing among the Welsh-speaking areas of Britain and in the Scandinavian-influenced north.[3] Of frequent occurrence are tunes which seem to end in a different mode from that in which they began, without any loss of coherence – a point which brings conventional modal analysis into question and which requires much further study.

Example 2. THE BLYTHSOME BRIDAL (W. Thomson: *Orpheus Caledonius*, 1733)

The Scots also have their own special ways of decorating melody – in some cases extremely elaborate, particularly in the west where psalm tunes are scarcely identifiable, so richly are they embellished. Music for the Highland bagpipes uses a unique and at times virtuosic handling of melodic variation that is so important to the music that pipers spurn to call it decoration.

These and other characteristics of established popularity are well discussed and illustrated by Francis Collinson and David Johnson,[4] and are considered rather less satisfactorily by Roger Fiske.[5] His book has been influential and is valuable in many respects, but the arguments are flawed by insufficient familiarity with Scottish music and need to be corrected before they take hold. Octave leaps are claimed to be 'unrewarding to sing, and tunes that feature them probably

started life as dances for the fiddle'. This fails to take account of their occurrence in Gaelic song, such as *Tha Mi Sgith*, and in contexts totally unsuited to either the fiddle or to dance, as in this wonderful tune for *Air Faillirinn*.

The suggestion shows an unfamiliarity with traditional Scottish singing styles in general, as instanced by Duncan Williamson's tune for *True Thomas* which is based on the leap of an octave, and John Stickle's for *King Orfeo*, which has an octave leap as its central feature (see Chapter V). *Lovely Molly* starts with an octave leap and, as with all these vocal airs, these leaps have to be repeated over and over for each stanza, so there is no question that they were and are used as tunes for singing.

Example 4. LOVELY MOLLY (Ford: *Vagabond Songs*, 1899)

Many other examples could be given and most musical Scots would not have to think long to provide them. The same author states that snap rhythms were imposed on Scots songs in the eighteenth century, but they appear characteristically in the mid-seventeenth century in the *Companion to The Margaret Wemyss Lute Book* in a tune called *Scotts Man*, so they may be taken as already typical of Scotland.

Example 3. AIR FAILLIRINN (from the singing of Colin Morrison)

Example 5. SCOTTS MAN (*Companion to Margaret Wemyss manuscript*, seventeenth century)

Language plays an important part in much of this, for until relatively recent times most music was vocal music and had to take account of the rhythms, accents and vowel sounds of the words it set. A proper analysis of that relationship has yet to be made, but the Scotch snap may parallel a tendency in Gaelic and Scots to accent first syllables; and the pitch-variation in Gaelic speech could well have influenced the wide range of our melodies. Gaelic psalm-singing (a kind of free heterophony unparallelled in Western Europe) developed partly as a result of a conflict between the Gaelic language and the metrical psalms in English.

Nor should we forget body language. Many of our dance rhythms are instantly recognisable. The smooth-flowing quavers of a reel and the dotted rhythms of a strathspey are quintessentially Scottish, and the dances themselves are Scottish. In the sixteenth century the Scottish branles and jigs were known in France and England[6] for their special character. The jig is quite possibly Scottish in origin: the earliest use of the word in connection with dance anywhere in the world is in a poem by the sixteenth-century Scottish poet-composer, Alexander Scott.[7] A possible predecessor – the mocking jig – is also primarily associated with Scotland. The hornpipe is acknowledged by the eighteenth-century German musicologist, Mattheson, to have come from Scotland and it probably relates to the confusing but widely used term, 'A Scots Measure'. The *Schottische* or *Ecossaise* are terms still in use, though their musical significance is obscure.

Scottish characteristics may also be instrumentally derived. Certain bowing tricks in Scottish fiddle music – ways of breaking up arpeggios,

Example 6.

ways of attacking the string with a powerful flick of the wrist – seem to be unique to the country. An alternative source for the Scotch snap could be a particular style of using the bow in fiddle music, enshrined typically in the strathspey and brought to perfection in the eighteenth century by Niel Gow. The 'double-tonic' which underlies so many Scottish tunes may have its roots in

the scale of the Highland bagpipes, or their precursors.[8] (See Example 7.)

Popularity and distinctiveness were not always welcome. Pepys was puzzled enough to enter in his *Diary* for 28 July 1666: '. . . at supper there played one of their servants upon the viallin some Scotch tunes only; several, and the best of their country, as they seemed to esteem them by their praising and admiring them, but Lord! the strangest ayre that I ever heard in my life, and all of the one cast.'

What was so strange to Pepys was rapidly becoming accepted over the whole of England where it was unmistakable in character and found a ready audience, so that by the eighteenth century Scottish musical mannerisms had become a much imitated commonplace.

A Scottish air is still thought of as a wild thing, but of course our songs and our melodies were highly cultivated. Tunes were frequently composed by known individuals, worked over for long periods and then worked over again countless times by later generations of musicians well versed in the native idiom. They were also cultivated so that they would not seem out of place with their truly wild neighbours, the sounds of the elements and the songs of the birds, or too far removed from the language of the people, whether in Scots, Gaelic or English. Whenever the gap between our music and our native culture has seemed too wide, there has been reaction and protest. Alexander Mollison writing in 1798 in defence of Scottish airs[9] refers interestingly to 'inarticulate language' as the true source of

Example 7. NIEL GOW: LADY LUCY LESSLIE MELVILLE'S REEL
(*Gow, Book V*, 3rd edition)

'simple and pathetic melodies' and objects to modern refinements as too remote from this source: similar things were said by William Tytler.[10] Even in the middle of the nineteenth century, Scottish arrangers show a deep respect for the origins of the music; and it is a measure of our concern for melodic purity that they are nonetheless much criticised for over-elaboration and insensitivity. In this century the Traditional Music and Song Association exists partly to preserve those characteristics, and the use of piano accompaniment, however discreet, still raises hackles.

In pursuit of these ideals, the Scots have been among the greatest pioneers of folk-song collection and arrangement, as well as in folk studies generally. Huge collections of Scottish traditional music were being made in the first half of the eighteenth century by Thomson, Oswald and Ramsay. They were followed by Burns and Johnson and many others. The process has continued unabated and is constantly fed by new compositions written within traditional idioms that seem to be inexhaustible. On the subject of folk studies in general one only has to mention Sir James Frazer and Andrew Lang.

This deep-rooted adherence to native cultural resources had an enormous influence on the development of classical music in Scotland. In the seventeenth century, Scottish ladies in castles and mansions wrote out Scottish airs into their lute books, some taken from the travelling harpists – the clarsach players – others from the folk-songs and ballads that were the shared property of king and commoner. In the eighteenth century our composers adapted the Italian style to the Scottish idiom, often with a sensitivity to both idioms demanding considerable skill, creating whole sonatas out of Scottish tunes, where possible training the harmonic progressions of the Italian figured bass to respect the modal insistences of the native air. In the nineteenth century the Scottish manner was used by Scots to colour their work, occasionally to motivate it. And in the twentieth century the process of adaptation has become increasingly one of absorption rather than imitation.

Much of our music does not come in tartan colours. We have at times been influenced by the French, the Flemish, the Italians, the Germans and the English; and with the Irish we have a traditional musical relationship which amounts to a shared identity. But Scottish music, whatever its sources, is often distinguished by its originality, and its Scottish context is always important. The astonishing riches of the music of Robert Carver do not suggest Scotland to the ear, but aspects of them can only be properly understood in the light of Scottish musical theory in the sixteenth century. The brilliant keyboard music of William Kinloch says more about his dexterity than it does about Scotland; but to understand his remarkable work *The Battel of Pavie* one must look to Scottish politics in the 1580s rather than to continental models. James Oswald's masonic anthems of 1740 have not one Scotticism in them, but their significance lies in the fact that the masonic movement was a Scottish-led one, and it and Oswald's music may well have had something to say to Mozart. The Earl of Kelly, who first brought the exciting new orchestral writing of the Mannheim School to these islands, seems to be almost totally Europeanised; but the liveliness of his style may also be connected with the fact that he was known on his own estates as 'fiddler Tam'. John Thomson, who studied in Europe and adopted the new Romanticism from Weber, Mendelssohn and others, was bringing home in music an approach which Scotland had already exported in its literature; Sir Alexander MacKenzie followed a similar course. In the twentieth century, amongst the plethora of styles and the crowded airwaves of international communications, there is scarcely a single Scottish composer of significance who has not paid a great deal more than lip-service to his or her own musical roots while at the same time showing a lively awareness of international developments; and the many pop groups which have made international reputations for themselves can occasionally be identified by styles which owe something to Scotland.

Much of this music is not yet known, and books on Scottish music are hard to come by. Farmer's magnificent achievement in *A History of Music in Scotland*, published in 1947, is long out of print and out of date. Collinson's impressive *The Traditional and National Music of Scotland*, while filling a serious gap in Farmer, confined itself strictly within the limits of its title. David Johnson's two outstanding books – *Music and Society in Lowland Scotland in the Eighteenth Century* and *Scottish Fiddle Music* – will hold their own for many years yet, as will Alburger's *Scottish Fiddlers and their Music*; but like Collinson and Farmer they are all out of print. Elliott and Rimmer's excellent BBC booklet *A History of Scottish Music* is very small and also out of print. Only Elliott's *Music of Scotland 1500–1700* can still be readily bought. It will always be a standard work but urgently needs to be followed up by further volumes. Put simply, there is a strong case for a new history of Scottish music. Music is indeed an international language; but it is not so airy-fairy that it can be divorced from time, place and personality. As a long established nation in Europe, musically prolific and distinctive, Scotland has an outstanding claim on our attention.

There is a final wretched warning which must be given here and given forcibly. Many students and academics as well as musicians and music lovers will, I hope, want to follow up what appears in these pages; to discover, to enjoy, to verify, to disagree. In the process of searching out sources they will have to look for *The Hymn to St Magnus* under the heading *Early English Part-Songs* in the writings of Dom Anselm Hughes, or under *English Discant* in Richard Hoppin's *Medieval Music*. In the same book, the manuscript W1 – which was written for St Andrews and probably in it – are discussed under the heading *An English Epilogue*, and the same two items are discussed under English headings in Donald Grout, A *History Of Western Music*, though both authors mention Orkney and St Andrews.

You could try the *Sources* section in the *New Groves* to find the location of the Carver choirbook, but though it is Scottish and housed in the National Library of Scotland, you will discover it under an English heading, along with the *Dunkeld Part-books*. If you want to learn about the Earl of Kelly or James Oswald or, if it comes to that, Dublin Theatre Music, you will find relevant material in Roger Fiske's *English Theatre Music in the Eighteenth Century*, and the 'edition' of John Thomson's overtures published by Garland in 1984 appears under the title *The Overture In England, 1800–1840*.

These books are by leading authorities whose works have the status of standard texts. Students throughout the world use them and learn from them. We do not expect them to look up Spain under France or Armenia under Russia, or Canada under the USA. To have to search for Scotland under England – rare in scholarly works written before the First World War – exhibits a profound ignorance of history and culture in Europe and makes a nonsense of basic techniques of reference, rendering research unnecessarily difficult.

This, then, provides the final and, I believe, one of the most pressing justifications for the existence of this book. If the music that is written of here is to be discussed intelligently, then its cultural roots must be understood and its relationship to the music of other countries be approached with that in mind. That so much of that music is beautiful and has yet to be known at home, never mind abroad, is matter for sorrowful reflection and delighted anticipation.

CHAPTER I

BULLS, BIRDS AND BOARS
800 BC–AD 400

Scotland's oldest musical artefact is now nearly three thousand years old (see Plate 2). It is a fragment of a side-blown horn cast in bronze, found in Kirkcudbrightshire, dating from some time before the eighth century BC. The fragment includes part of the rim of the aperture for the mouth, and around it there is a slightly raised decorative line. We can deduce the rest of the instrument from surviving instruments in Ireland and, since some of these are still playable, we can hear what the original instruments sound like.

The nearest in design to the Scottish one comes from Dungannon in County Tyrone. Bronze smiths working in a style similar to that in Ireland were present in the Northern Isles at about this time,[1] so these instruments could also have been produced in Scotland anywhere along the west coast, where such skills would have travelled. The Irish instruments come in two forms, side-blown and end-blown, and their dating is considered absolutely secure (see Plate I). The side-blown instrument is in the shape of a cow's or bull's horn, and buried with the horns discovered in Ireland were bronze rattles – in size, shape and decoration very similar to a bull's scrotum. They are called crotals, produce a delicate tinkle and are varied in pitch (see Plate 3).

The first proper study of the playing potential of these horns was made by Siomon O'Duibhir, and the original horns and rattles were first recorded in 1989 and 1991 when it became clear that the sound world that can be produced from them is extensive and immensely impressive.

The end-blown horns play in the same manner as a didgeridoo, the long hollow wooden straight horn of the Australian aborigines. They produce a powerful rich pedal note (in the bronze horns so flexible in pitch that it extends over the interval of a fifth); and a few harmonics, which require additional effort to produce, especially as the mouth aperture is wide. Although the superficial appearances are quite different, the wide mouthpiece and conical bore of the instruments are so close to those of the didgeridoo that aborigines from Arnhem Land took to a replica of a bronze-age horn without a moment's adjustment being required. In both cases the blowing technique involves circular breathing – a method of drawing in air through the nostrils while still blowing through the lips so that the sound is uninterrupted. A practised musician can continue blowing these instruments for more than an hour without any break in the sound, so naturally are they adapted to the technique, which depends upon a back-pressure to the lungs from the column of air vibrating in the instrument. The wide mouth-piece not only facilitates this but demands it, otherwise breath is exhausted too rapidly.

Side-blown horns can be circular breathed, but the aborigines did not relate to them readily. Their nearest parallels are to be found in West Africa and research comparing West African

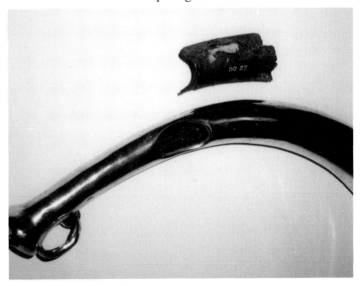

Plate 2. FRAGMENT OF BRONZE SIDE-BLOWN HORN, EIGHTH CENTURY BC

side-blown horns to bronze-age ones has yet to be undertaken. The West African playing techniques may have much to tell us.

Initial attempts to play the side-blown horns were so misguided that they led to the death of Sir Robert Ball in the mid-nineteenth century. This unfortunate man burst a blood-vessel in his brain, probably trying to play the instrument like a trumpet. Subsequent research, cautioned perhaps by this sad tale, has put forward the odd notion that they had separate detachable mouthpieces made of perishable material, and the totally untrue assertion that they were capable of producing only one note.[2]

There is no need for perishable bits — of which no one has pretended to find any trace, anyway. The skill of the craftsmen at this period was such that they could have cast any kind of mouthpiece they chose as an integral part of the instrument. If they did intend to attach a separate mouthpiece it seems extraordinary that they should have made an oval hole — harder to match than a circle — and without any reinforcement. The existing aperture is very comfortable for the mouth; nicely placed when the instrument is held in a playing position, and receiving the lips with an ease which the oval shape clearly suits. Finally, and crucially, the instrument plays perfectly well as it is, so long as you accept the idea that a sound made by buzzing the lips inside the aperture was what was desired.

The side-blown horns are capable of playing any note you choose over a range of about three octaves, some more easily than others. The notes are buzzed by the lips and amplified by the instrument. The voice can contribute also, but the range goes far below that of the singing voice so it cannot be said that the performer is merely singing into a loud hailer. The original horn is much easier to play and makes a much better sound than the replica but, given a chance, modern technology should soon catch up on the casting techniques of three thousand years ago. Cow horns played in the same manner produce similar results but with a very inferior tone quality.

Side-blown and end-blown horns were buried together and there are sufficient buried in one location to suggest that several may well have been played simultaneously. The same mould was used for parts of a pair of instruments, one

Plate 3. BRONZE-AGE CROTALS (RATTLES) FROM THE DOWRIS HOARD

side, the other end-blown; so we have every right to imagine them played in consort, the end-blown providing a drone or drones with a rhythmic pulse related to the players' circular breathing, and the side-blown horns providing a melody, either as solo instruments or supplying different notes from different instruments, perhaps according to some pattern. The rattles could have been used at the same time, possibly at significant moments in some ceremony just as bells were used in the early Christian church.

To return to the shapes of the instruments. The cow or bull horn shape of the side-blown instruments and the bull's scrotum shape of the rattles, suggest that (among other possibilities) the horns and rattles had a cult function. The bull cult was common throughout Europe in the bronze age and survives in places to this day. The Celtic peoples of Ireland and Scotland were cattle people. Their greatest epic — the *Tain Bo Cuailnge* — centres round a cattle-raid and is resolved by a fight between two bulls, one coveted by Queen Maeve who wished to prove herself as powerful as her husband, Aillil, who owned the other. Against Maeve's forces was pitted the strength of a single man — Cuchullain, who had learnt the arts of war from a woman on the island of Skye. Stories of fertility and impotence permeate the epic, so it may be no accident that some of the crotals lack the seed that is necessary to produce a sound — a pebble or ball of clay encased within the bronze husk. A silent musical instrument makes for a powerfully depressing symbol of infertility.

Another cattle-raid — the *Tain Bo Froech* — tells of such wonderful music made by King

Aillil's horn players that thirty of his men died of rapture – but what kind of horns these were is not known for we cannot date the true origins of the epics, only their written sources; and their music is clearly beyond our imagining!

The horns almost certainly had a religious significance. We know they were sometimes ritually destroyed. We know that the only effective way to play them is to learn the trick of circular breathing – itself a kind of magical ritualistic thing as the player never stops blowing, yet never runs out of breath. Add the above to the cult of the bull and the fact that the bronze horns imitate the shape of a bull's horns and can imitate its bellowing, and it seems clear that these instruments would have been of the first importance in society.

There are echoes of that importance at different periods and reaching into modern times. The Picts assembled more than thirty powerfully evocative bull carvings at Burghead in the eighth century AD. Later again, in 1678, to secure the recovery of his wife, Hector Mackenzie and his sons sacrificed a bull on Saint Mael Rubha's island in Loch Maree – notwithstanding the fact that twelve years earlier the presbytery of Dingwall had spoken out against such rites, recognising their ancient origins:

> haveing mett at Appilcross, and finding amongst wyr abominable and heathenishe practizes that the people in that place were accustomed to sacrifice bulls at certaine tyme wppon the 25th of August. wc. day is dedicate as they coneave to St. Mourie, as they call him, . . . That quhosever sall be found to commit such abominations; especiallie sacrifices of ony kind or at ony tyme, sall publickly appeire and be rebuked in sackcloth sex severall lords dayis in sex severall churches, viz. Lochcarron, Appilcross, Contane, Fotterlie, Dingwall and last in Garloch paroch church.[3]

A bull's horn known as the Duthach Mor was used to gather people in Skye in the 1870s to protest at the land grabbers – the granddaughter of the MacPherson who blew it then, still has it in her proud possession. It is perhaps the last survivor of a tradition of horn-blowing that may well go right back to the bronze age, though it is blown through the end by the simple expedient of sawing off the tip of the horn. But every township used to have one, and we shall see in a later chapter how they were sounded at the time of the Battle of Bannockburn.

Ancient traditions associated with cattle management and cattle raids survived well into the nineteenth century, as did the totemic values of clan crests and battle cries. It is not far from the song lines of the Australian aborigines with their Kangaroo and Cockatoo and Lizard dreamings, to the traditional Cat dream of the cat clan – the MacPhersons and MacIntoshs of Clan Chattan, or the Pig dream of the Arcaibh or Pig people of the Orkneys, the Horse dream for the MacLeods.[4] Places as well as peoples had such associations. And horns too, no doubt. The gift of a horn was often used to confirm a land transaction. One such horn – the ivory horn of Leys – was given to the Burnetts at Bannockburn (see Plate IX). But we are not allowed to hear it for whenever it has been sounded a member of the Burnett family has died and they quite rightly refuse to take the risk. In other words the magic of old beliefs still clings to the instrument to this very day.

Nearly two thousand years separate the depositing of the bronze-age horns and rattles from the main written evidence of the epics in which horns are first referred to in Celtic writings – about the same time gap between ourselves and the birth of Christ. However, there is other evidence to suggest that, just as Christianity has sustained its cultural identity over a long period, so too have the Celts. It is possible that the people inhabiting Ireland and Scotland when the horns and rattles were made were already Celtic, speaking basically the same languages that survive to this day and inhabiting two large islands – Ierne and Albion – names from the sixth century BC which still have their modern equivalents.[5] So even at this early stage we should consider the meaning of the word still used by Gaelic speakers to describe that which the English tongue calls 'music'.

Ceol is the Gaelic word for music, but it does not mean the same thing, as it has nothing whatever to do with Greek muses. Ceol means a sound like the sounds that birds make. It relates etymologically to pipolo, pipe, piob, piobaireachd and to pipe like the birds. Many bird sounds have been imitated by humans and there exists in the School of Scottish Studies a remarkable series of recordings of bird imitations in Gaelic[6] in which the dividing lines between bird-song, music and speech are impossible to determine. Some of these calls will have been used to help children identify birds, others to lure birds closer to the hunter, and others just for the fun of it. The lilting musicality of Gaelic is particularly effective in this context.

Connections between bird-song and music and speech and piping cannot be given a time of commencement. But in the European context we can go back far enough to satisfy the sceptics – back to our first visitors some eight thousand years ago. When man first camped on our coasts, to hunt and to fish, if he wanted to catch birds without a gun (though creatures were much tamer then), it helped to cheat them into friendship by imitating their calls – with the voice, or with a pipe. Pipes are as old as man's ability to take a bird bone, which is naturally hollow, and blow through it, perhaps adding a hole in the side to add a note, if there was not one knocked out of it already.

Just such a pipe was found on the coast of Denmark dating from 5000 BC. It was probably used to imitate black guillemots – common enough on the Scottish coast to this day – for the purpose of catching them for food. Other early instruments which might well have been brought here are the naturally hollowed flint flutes found in Jutland.[7] They date from 2000 BC and as flint was a widely traded commodity, something like their strange trumpetings and hootings could have been heard in Scotland.

But in Scotland the connection between bird-song and music goes deeper, for the Picts were reputed to have brought to Ireland 'every spell, charm, sneeze and augury by the voices of the birds, and every omen.'

Augury by the voices of birds probably simply means that they were skilled observers and could predict weather changes and the movement of unseen people and animals by study of the birds (as a later passage in the same source implies).[8] Such observation underlines the associations and bird-imitation which are embedded in what is perhaps our oldest surviving music.

One of the most basic ways of defining a culture from the archaeological record is by its burial customs which tend to be conservative. The same is likely to be true of music associated in the Celtic tradition almost exclusively with funerals. In Ireland and Scotland, there survived until recent times just such a music – the caoine (English 'keen'). The caoine is first referred to in the seventh-century eulogy for St Cummain the Tall. Latterly the church in Scotland and Ireland tried to suppress it, succeeding only in this century. The unequivocal lamentation was

perhaps too much for a religion which preached paradise, though the Celts had their other world and it too seems to have been a happy one. But the caoine is undoubtedly sorrowful.

The music for the caoine, the 'pi-li-li-liu', recorded from the traditional Gaelic singer, Calum Johnston, sounds a bit like a bird. It was quite probably derived from pre-Christian laments, and has its ultimate source in bird-song. The people of Islay used to call one of the seabirds the *caoineteach* or bird of lament, whose cry heard in the night anticipated a death and also represented the cries of the mourners – in particular the women keening. A bird of death is also heard in Jura.[9] The mournful call of the redshank is as near to the cry of pi-li-li-liu as you can ask for, the choice of consonants and vowels matching the bird's evocative cry at the edge of the sea, inhabiting the edge of the land on which man lives, and the ocean which represents the eternal life.

Example 1. REDSHANK CALLS

Example 2. THE CAOINE (from the singing of Mary McMaster)

When Calum Johnston recorded the caoine he said he was imitating bagpipes. He was a piper himself. The connections have come almost full circle. The bird suggests the lament for the voice; the bagpipes take over the function; the voice imitates them and in the process sounds like a bird. The syllables – pi-li-li-liu – were also used in Ireland for the lament,[10] and the tune fits perfectly on the bagpipes so long as you start with the note which to this day is called the note of sorrow by pipers – the high G, a note whose tuning in the bagpipe scale gives it a peculiar and intense quality, especially when it falls to the note below, as it does over and over in this tune known as *The Nameless Lament*, which seems to have inherited, as the bagpipes themselves have done, the function and character of the caoine. It is this kind of music, played by a lone piper at a graveside, that catches the throats even of those for whom the bagpipes normally have little appeal.

Example 3. THE NAMELESS LAMENT (Angus McArthur's setting)

As for bagpipes sounding like birds, Martin Martin, a reporter from the Isle of Skye travelling in the 1690s, tells us: 'The Gawlin is a fowl less than a duck: . . . The Piper of St Kilda plays the Notes which it sings, and hath composed a Tune of 'em which the Natives judg to be very fine Musick.'[11]

There is also a famous piobaireachd – a set of pipe variations – called *The Battle of the Birds*. Some of the more elaborate cuttings – embellishments – in pipe music are very bird-like.

Example 4. CRUNLUATH (MODERN); BARLUDH (Joseph MacDonald, 1760)

The caoine was in three parts: a deep murmuring repetition of the name of the dead: a dirge (in Gaelic, *tuiream*) in which the dead person's character and virtues are evoked and the third part was the goll or cry (in Gaelic, *sesigbhais*) – a chorus using meaningless syllables, perhaps to establish contact with the other world as may have been the case in fairy songs (see Chapter II).

A caoine does not have a fixed tune, but the chorus – the goll – is very similar over a range of sources. It starts high with a semitone and gradually descends the scale. A descending phrase is a natural one to choose for sorrow, as are semitones to suggest intensity of feeling. At the end of each chorus it gives itself a lift back up with an octave leap. There is only one other genre in which all these features are also preserved – in ploughmen's whistles and one ploughman's song.

Why should ploughmen use and preserve the tune of the caoine – the Celtic lament? One could speculate that ploughmen's whistles were a survival from the bull cult, for ploughmen in those days ploughed with oxen – castrated bulls – and ploughing was almost a religious activity. Funerals are also events of religious solemnity. Both are deeply conservative. Ploughing and sowing; digging and burying: they parallel each other as dust to dust. People do not like to be interfered with and told to change their ways on such occasions. Here then you could have an example of religion and work sharing a repertoire – the ploughman whistling the song for burial as he buries his plough in the ground and digs the grave for the seed. It makes sense – and of course whistling is the nearest we can do to birdsong.

Apart from bronze-age horns and birds, there is another source for the music of our ancestors, unexpected but possibly very ancient – the rock gong. Rock gongs or ringing rocks are simply natural rocks which when struck with something hard produce a resonant ringing sound. One at Port Appin was traditionally used for summoning the clans.[12] It is a most unusually shaped rock, full of cups and hollows, which may have been man-made. There is a very resonant ringing rock on Tiree which has ancient cup markings on it, there are two in Aberdeenshire, and there may well be others with traditions attached to them.

No one can say for how long these resonant rocks have been used either for signalling or as musical instruments and the dates of the markings are not easily guessed at either. However, since mankind started with the stone age, making implements out of stone, it would be very surprising if the process had not led to such uses. Two people working at the same site, knocking stone on stone, might well have set up quite complex rhythms, as Nigerian tribesmen do to this day using resonant rocks, sometimes singing through bits of tubing and other items to distort their voices, which are intended to be those of their ancestors speaking from the other world. Just like the Port Appin rock, ringing rocks in

Plate 4. THE DEXFORD CARNYX SEEN FROM ABOVE, *c.* AD 50

Africa have been used for warning and signalling to local people as well as for initiation ceremonies.[13] It may be that our own ringing rocks were played at similar functions. Our kings used to be crowned on the Lia Fail – the Stone of Destiny – which is supposed only to have made a noise when a rightful king sat upon it.[14] This may simply mean that it was only played on such a solemn occasion. When Bernard Fagg started playing a rock gong in the midst of apparently unpeopled territory in Nigeria, an African arrived within minutes to put an end to the sacrilege.[15]

Returning to man-made instruments, as opposed to those obligingly provided by nature, brings us back to the animal kingdom. As well as the bull, our Pictish ancestors regarded the boar as a cult animal. Like the bull, he is powerful and dangerous. Pictish representations of boars are particularly fine, and the boar is raised, literally, to a greater height by its adaptation to form the 'bell' end of the magnificent sheet bronze horn known as the carnyx. The carnyx was held aloft and shaped so that the sound would have carried over the heads of an army,

and we know not only that it was used in a military context but that at least three were played simultaneously on occasion (see Plate II).

The depiction of the carnyx on the famous first-century BC bowl from Gundestrup indicates, along with other representations on Roman and provincial coins, that the instrument was well known in Europe; but the only surviving fragment that gives any idea of its original glory is unequivocally Scottish, unearthed in the nineteenth century near Dexford in Banffshire, and exhibiting magnificent and characteristic Pictish traits[16] in the beautiful flowing lines of its design (see Plate 4). When dug up in 1816 it still had its eyes – presumably of semi-precious stone – and a tongue of wood mounted on springs, which may have modified the sound. The reconstruction of this unique and artistically outstanding instrument is about to be undertaken, but in the meantime what it sounded like and how it impressed its enemies is a matter only for dreams.

The Dexford carnyx is housed in the Royal Museum of Antiquities in Edinburgh and there too you may see a replica of the Caprington horn (see Plate 5). This is the oldest musical instrument in Scotland to survive in playable condition. The museum dates it as mediaeval, but recent research[17] offers good reasons for placing it very much earlier – contemporary with the Roman occupation, if not before. Its closest equivalents are to be found in Germany, Holland and Poland and are all now ascribed to the Roman period; a relief carving at Chiusi of just such an instrument in the hands of a Gaulish cavalryman adds further evidence in support. The traditions associated with its unearthing in the seventeenth century, and passed on in the family which still owns the original, also support this early date. It is said to have been dug out from near the burial mound of King Coilus (from whom the district of Kyle in Ayrshire gets its name) who was supposed to have done battle with the Romans.

The horn is made of cast bronze and appears to have been damaged and repaired with a brass band at some period, for the natural horn-like curve is disturbed where the band appears and there is no reason for this band to have been an original feature. It does not appear on any of the equivalent surviving instruments. Whatever the

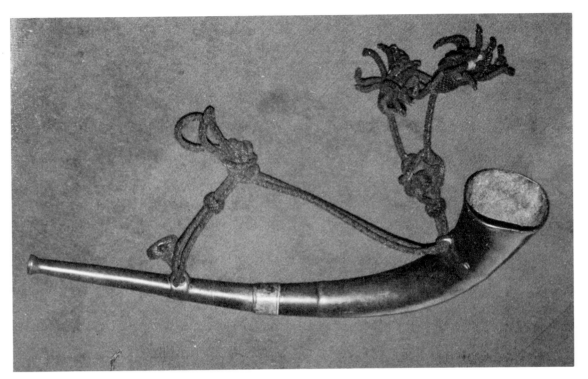

Plate 5. The Caprington Horn, Iron Age

date, the sound is magnificent, but not easy to produce – the mouthpiece, which is an integral part of the casting, is sharp rimmed and hard on the lips of modern players used to a more gentle bed for their mouths. That said, the four or five notes obtainable from it are of a clarity and resonance that no one could criticise (see Example 5), and the instrument is particularly responsive to rapid tonguing – a feature which would make it suitable for signalling.

Example 5. Notes on Caprington Horn

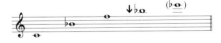

Of course, no music survives for any of these instruments so we must use the instruments themselves to teach us. But there are clues to be had from the various depictions and the two sources have to be taken together. Clearly an instrument used in battle, as the carnyx was and as the Caprington horn probably was, is going to be played with volume and vigour and may be called upon for practical purposes, as trumpets and horns have been through the centuries, using rhythm and pitch to create distinctive

signals. The much older bronze-age horns are far less suited to such tasks, for their mouthpieces do not encourage articulation and the pitch of the end-blown horns is limited and of the side-blown ones undefined, because within three octaves or so the range is infinite. In the rigours of battle any note might come out of a side-blown horn, and signalling requires guaranteed precision.

From an eighth-century AD Hiberno-Saxon Psalter we can be certain that horn players used one hand to modify the sound by placing it over the end of the 'bell' just as a jazz trumpeter uses a felt hat or a wah-wah mute (see Plate III). If we are prepared to extrapolate backwards then we can add this technique to that of the Caprington horn, which is short enough for this to be a natural thing to do; and if we allow that the sprung wooden tongue in the mouth of the carnyx had a rasping effect on the sound, then we can reasonably speculate that it would have been imitated on the contemporary Caprington horn by the self-explanatory technique known as 'flutter-tonguing'. These techniques, and others, were successfully tried out on the Caprington horn by Nigel Boddice, principal trumpet of the BBC Scottish Symphony Orchestra, at my request; and, as with the bronze-age horns, faith in the instrument produced outstanding results. To its owner, Captain Fergusson-Cunningham, we are deeply indebted, as we are to the National Museum of Ireland, the Ulster Museum and the Royal Museum of Scotland for allowing us to handle and record where possible, the bronze-age horns and rattles. From these instruments, beautifully made, happily preserved, astonishingly revealed in performance, we have recaptured some of the most precious and thrilling echoes from a past which might otherwise never have rung in our ears.

CHAPTER II

BRITON, PICT AND SCOT
600–800

In Welsh, as in Gaelic, the words for music and poetry are the same, and although the two languages are mutually incomprehensible, there are many cultural links. A few of these are musical and may go back to the days when the two were neighbours in Scotland, which they were for at least four hundred years. It was during these years, from the fifth century to the ninth century, that Scotland was Christianised. This chapter looks at the kind of music that the Christians might have encountered and, in some cases, adapted.

As far as the Welsh-speaking people are concerned, we can only guess at their music from what has survived in Wales. Wales was that part of the territories of the Britons of southern Scotland to which they were eventually confined. The oldest poem in Welsh – *The Gododdin* – was written in Edinburgh in the seventh century AD. It is an epic roll-call of the dead, and it was sung, but no tune survives. An Arthurian lay – *Am Bron Binn* – persists in the Gaelic tradition: its language is not Welsh and there is no reason for supposing that its music is either, but it is an interesting melodic line with (at the end of the third phrase) an emphatic augmented fourth, an unusual interval in traditional music. Since the words tell of a beautiful girl who cuts off Arthur's head having enchanted him with her harp music (his head on her lap), it is appropriate that the tune should have something a little uncanny about it. Arthur, Merlin and Guinevere all have many associations south of the Highland line in

Scotland where they probably lived a fair part of their lives.

There are other echoes, however. In *The Gododdin* there is a charming interpolation. It is a lullaby. 'Dinogad's coat is of many colours, many colours. I made it of the skins of pine-martens. Phew, Phew – a whistling! Let us sing to him – the eight slaves sing to him . . .'

Again no tune survives; but a Welsh lullaby, collected in the eighteenth century, has words and music which could well have been heard in Scotland as long ago as the seventh century – 'hoo-ee, hoo-ee, little child, hoo-ee hoo-ee, poor little thing'.[1]

Example 2. HWI HWI (from Edward Jones: *Musical and Poetical Relicks*, 1794)

Hwi - hwi____; plen - tyn bach, hwi - hwi____; dru - an bach.

Another kind of song that may have been heard in those days is the wren-hunt song which survived into this century all over the British Isles, though in Scotland only in the extreme north (in fact as a lullaby) and the extreme south-west. These songs have ancient roots. The killing of wrens (the king of all birds) on St Stephen's day, is symbolic of pre-Christian mid-winter rituals to ensure fertility and the return of the sun. The poetic metre of this example is one of the oldest and the tune is very typical of narrow-compass Welsh tunes, using just five notes. These are not the notes of the pentatonic scale and the tune sounds completely different from most Scottish tunes, with its two little motives repeated over and over, matching the repeated question and answer form of the words: 'Where are you going says Dibbin to Dobbin . . . where are you going . . . where are you going? . . . to the woods to catch the wren.'

Example 1. AM BRON BINN (from the singing of Kate MacCormick)

Labh - air Fios Fal - aich gu fì - al, "Théid mis - e' ga h-iarr - aidh dhut,

Mi fhìn 's mo ghill - e 's mo chù Na còmhr - adh fir mar bha e fhéin.

Example 3. WELSH WREN SONG (from an old man in Flintshire, collected by Phyllis and Mered Evans)

It is not such an odd thing that this genre should have survived as a lullaby in Shetland, though the original words for wren songs were very cruel. Like fairy songs and the wren song, lullabies often feature a refrain of meaningless syllables. Lulla-lullaby. Sheo hu leo, sheo hu leo. Hwi hwi. Ba-loo, ba-loo. Of course they help soothe the child, but it seems likely that these were originally protective spells.[2] Nearly all the wren songs have refrains of the kind Milder-Molder: Dibbin-Dobbin or Tozie-Mozie as in this Shetland lullaby where the wren song refrain is turned into something soothing.

Example 4. SHETLAND LULLABY / WREN SONG (from William Huchison, Whalsay, collected by Dr Peter Cooke)

Why should lullabies have spells in them? One reason would be to prevent the child from being stolen by the fairies as in the famous lullaby, *An Cubhrachan*, but in the equally beautiful *A Phiutrag 's a Phiuthar* it is the mother who has been stolen and she uses the lullaby to pass on the message that will lead to her rescue. The refrain is completely integrated into the lullaby,

Example 5. A PHIUTRAG 'S A PHIUTHAR (from the singing of Flora McNeill)

rhythmically and melodically. The tune rocks to and fro as one would rock a child to sleep, the motion casting its own spell.

This kind of song goes deep into racial subconsciousness. It also reflects the ancient association of music and magic. The fairies often bestow the gift of musicianship (particularly on pipers) and in the Orpheus story the musician communicates with the other world. Perhaps that is part of the function of the meaningless refrains. To communicate with the other world you must use a different and secret language – just as the Nigerian tribesmen distort their voices to represent their ancestors.

Belief in fairies has survived uneasily alongside Christianity, though at the height of the repression of superstition in the seventeenth century, the Reverend Robert Kirk wrote, without any hint of censure, that a woman in childbirth would have a piece of bread, a Bible or a lump of iron in her bed to prevent her from being stolen. But Kirk was unusual in encouraging superstition, on the grounds that it helped develop the spiritual rather than the carnal side of our natures. No doubt he would have approved of *The Bressay Lullaby* from Shetland which starts with expelling the fairies but ends with a chorus of angels. Like *A Phiutrag 's a Phiuthar*, it is pentatonic but its range is much more limited and its outline much closer to that of the Welsh lullaby, built round the interval of a major third and repeating its phrases. It has its own beauty, and the comparison shows how the pentatonic scale, used intelligently, can generate a variety of tunes, each with its own character.

Example 6. THE BRESSAY LULLABY (from the singing of Elizabeth Barclay)

God and pagan magic are also found side-by-side in the *Charm Against a Hail Shower* which expresses sentiments all Scots must share, but which survived in the tradition as a charm, not just a prayer. The repetition round the interval of the major third that it shares with two of the lullabies suggests that this pattern may have been a basic one in chants of protection.

Example 7. Charm Against a Hail Shower (from the singing of Calum Johnston)

Clach mhin mheal-lain san to-bar ud thall⎯ thall⎯ Am buach-ail-le bochd Ri sgàth nan cnoc 'Sa bha-ta fo uchd 'S a dhealg 'na bhroit 'S e 'g iarr-aidh air Dia⎯ Tur-adh is grian a chur ann.

Smooth hailstones in yonder well;
The poor herd in the lee of the hills,
With his stick under his chest,
And his pin in his bosom
Praying God to send dry weather and sun.

There were other ancient magics that survived. Fire in particular marks man's command over nature and must be preserved above all. In every household, last thing at night, the peat fire was smoored (smothered) by the women who accompanied the ritual with a chant to ensure the embers kept warm till morning. *Righ na Duil* was collected by Marjory Kennedy-Fraser, who is not a reliable source (see Chapter XVII). But no one has claimed it for other words or purposes, so we may trust her for once. The words are Christian – God, Jesus and Mary are invoked – but the ritual has its roots in older times and the tune uses hypnotic repetitions.

Example 8. Peat-fire Smooring Prayer (collected by Marjory Kennedy-Fraser)

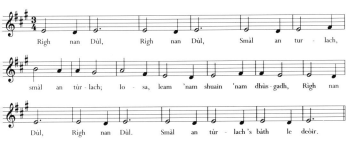

Righ nan Dùl, Righ nan Dùl, Smàl an tur-lach, smàl an tùr-lach; Io-sa, leam 'nam shuain 'nam dhùs-gadh, Righ nan Dùl, Righ nan Dùl. Smàl an tùr-lach 's bàth le deòir.

How old these tunes are no one can say. They have a place at this early stage of our history because the songs are all simple, serve functions as old as humanity, and because they illustrate the progress of adjustment between

Plate 6. Pictish Clarsach, on the Nigg Stone, eighth century

Paganism and Christianity and the extraordinary extent to which the former has survived the cultural pressures of the latter.

Of Pictish lullabies we have no trace. The chief memorials by which the Picts are known are their stone carvings, and a remarkable feature of these is the number of musical instruments and musicians included among them. Most frequent in appearance are various harps, all, except one, triangular framed (see Plate 6). The source of this interest has been said to be the David story as depicted in psalters, for which continental and southern examples are given. But how likely is it that the Picts were copying?

The psalms (and hence the David story) were as vital a part of the Celtic church as any other. The Celts had their own psalters and gospels, illustrated in their own unmistakeable style; and as far as influence goes, it is now thought that the *Book of Kells* was influenced by the Pictish stones. But what really settles the matter is that some of the stones are older than the oldest psalter that could possibly be relevant.[3]

Plate 7. PICTISH STONE CARVING AT ALDBAR, NINTH CENTURY

The Picts show a high quality of technique and observation in their carvings, and the simple fact is that the largest body of evidence from the eighth century to the tenth century for the existence of triangular framed harps comes from the Pictish stones, so the natural conclusion is that this form of harp originated among them.[4]

A triangular framed harp appears on a stone at Nigg which belongs to the second half of the eighth century. St Martin's cross has one too and St Oran's has a quadrangular one. Both are dated to the same period on Iona when crosses are thought to have been influenced or sculpted by Pictish craftsmen.[5] There is one on the Aldbar stone (eighth century/ninth century) (see Plate 7) and its curved forepillar is characteristic of later Celtic harps; another at Dupplin (ninth century) shows the musician sitting on a zoomorphic chair, and the tenth-century Monifieth stone also has the player seated. Other triangular harps appear at Lethendy (tenth century) and possibly Aberlemno (eighth century), Ardchattan and St Andrews. These last three are too worn or damaged to be certain that the instruments have forepillars.

The triangular frame was important. The addition of a pillar so strengthened the structure that more strings could be added, extending the range; and the tension of the strings could be greater, making the sound clearer and more resonant. To assist the resonance harps have sound boxes. These could be carved out of a single piece of willow and early harps may have had the actual sounding board of the box made of leather. The strings were probably of various materials according to the type of instrument. Horse-hair strings were commonly employed by the Welsh[6] and as the Picts and Welsh-speaking Strathclyde Britons were in close contact, that is a type they may have used. Metal and gut are also traditionally employed and there are references to gold, silver and bronze strings being used for the cruit.[7]

The number of strings shown on the Aldbar and Nigg carvings is seven and on the Monifieth stone, eight. These may represent some kind of diatonic scale, or the number may have a symbolic meaning — it is not easy to fit a substantial number of strings on to a small stone carving, given the nature of the material, so it is quite possible that many more strings were used, particularly on the Monifieth No. 4 and Dupplin stones where the harps shown are clearly large instruments — too large to rest on the player's knee (see Plate 8).

The name of the instrument has been long, learnedly and inconclusively discussed.[8] There are two basic terms available — 'cruit' and 'tiompan'. The word 'harp' comes a little later and is Anglo-Saxon and probably at first referred to a lyre such as that discovered at Sutton Hoo. One source refers to a nine-stringed cruit, implying a harp-like instrument and the Gaelic term used nowadays for the Celtic harp — 'clarsach' — first appears in the fifteenth century. Neither 'cruit' nor 'tiompan' is Pictish, for no Pictish survives in interpretable form. Broadly one might opt for the word 'cruit' as a generic term for stringed

Plate 8. PICTISH CLARSAIR, ON MONIFIETH NO. 4 STONE, LATE NINTH CENTURY

instruments and the word 'tiompan' as referring to a three or more stringed lyre, quadrangular in form, the pitch of the strings being altered by stopping them from behind by the left hand, the right hand plucking them (see Plate III). Plectrums may well have been used and there are later references to a 'wand', which is generally taken to mean a bow. The oldest technique was plucking with the nails, though finger tips and knuckles were also used. The tiompan's strings seem to have been metal, and it was a relatively delicate instrument, played among the aristocracy and by women as well as men. Its sound was constantly referred to as 'sweet' and it was common in Scotland and Ireland as late as 1328 when the best tiompan player, in both countries, Maelruanaid MacCerbaill, was killed.[9]

Apart from harps there are long, straight wind instruments described by commentators as trumpets. Cymbals feature on the Nigg stone, and triple pipes (blown by the one player) are clearly shown on St Martin's Cross, as well as the Lethendy and Ardchattan stones (see Plate 9). One of the three pipes will possibly have been a drone, being longer than the others to produce a deeper note – but though they will have sounded like bagpipes, they are blown directly from the mouth with no bag for an air reservoir. Beside the piper on the Lethendy

Plate 9. Pictish Clarsair and Triple Pipe Player on the stair lintel, Lethendy Tower, Perthshire, tenth century

stone, there is a long barrel-shaped drum, which would have been deep in pitch.

In the 'trumpet' section of the Pictish musical world the players seem to be in pairs. On the Aberlemno stone they play long straight instruments, pointing them upwards over the heads of horsemen in a hunting scene. On the Hilton of Cadboll stone there is a similar pair, also accompanying a hunt; and on Sueno's stone (tenth century) there are three of them blowing away in the midst of a battle scene. Beside the harp on the Aldbar stone there is an object described as a staff but which could be a wind instrument with some kind of enclosed reed, for the bottom end seems shaped more for a mouth than a hand.

By this time the Christians among the Picts, Scots and British had bells (see Chapter III) and the Christian chants were already making an impression for the saints were not above using vocal magic to achieve conversions.

Take this account of St Columba who founded the monastery at Iona and brought Christianity to the northern Picts. It was written by St Adomnan in the late seventh century. Adomnan knew people who had known Columba and his account, miracles and all, deserves the closest attention. This story refers to a fortress near Inverness belonging to the Pictish King Brude whom Columba had converted to Christianity, to the dismay of the Druids:

> When the saint himself was chanting the evening hymns with a few of the brethren, as usual, outside the king's fortifications, some Druids, coming near to them, did all they could to prevent God's praises being sung in the midst of a pagan nation. On seeing this, the saint began to sing the 44th psalm, and at the same moment so wonderfully loud, like pealing thunder, did his voice become, that king and people were struck with terror and amazement.

'What is stranger still,' writes Adomnan of other occasions, 'to those with him in the church his voice did not sound louder than that of others; and yet at the same time persons more than a mile away heard it so distinctly that they could mark each syllable.'

A ninth-century text[10] states that Columba had a carrying voice heard at 1500 paces and that it was like a melodious lion. Mere fancy, one might say. And Adomnan admits Columba rarely did this, and only when he was inspired. But it is quite possible Columba had mastered some esoteric vocal techniques such as emphasising the harmonics that exist in everyone's voice. The lower harmonics can be used to give a lion-like sound to the voice, at the same time giving the impression that the singer has two voices, for the ordinary sung note is heard at the same time as the harmonic an octave below – a remarkable sound which might create in others the frightening impressions that Adomnan describes. The higher harmonics sound as though they emanated from somewhere far above the singer's head; and as for voice projection, it is a commonplace in the vocal technique of singers and actors. The bad ones shout, the good ones, though no louder than their neighbours, are heard at the back of the largest assemblies. The miracle of Columba's voice and the credulousness of hagiographers need be no more nor less than the kind of appreciation any remarkable performer evokes from our own lips today. Teenagers literally swoon to pop songs (remember the warriors who died of rapture to the sound of the horns), and the tears stream down the most po-faced of middle-class faces as Rudolfo and Mimi burst into impossible song.

It seems likely that the Gaelic-speaking people made use of a very wide variety of singing techniques: the *Book of Lismore* (compiled in the fifteenth century) and *Cormac's Glossary* (which dates from as early as the eighth to ninth centuries) mention these:

Dord – murmuring sounds
Dordan (diminutive of dord) – brighter lighter murmur
Fodhord – under-murmur low murmuring
Dord-fiansa – martial chant with clash of spears, or a hunting song (= Crann-dord = tree music = trees of spears.)
Cronan – a 'purring' kind of music produced in the throat
Abran – a song
Fead – whistling with the mouth
Coicetul – singing together
Duchand – a chant or melody
Logaireacht – a funeral cry
Cepoc – a chorus
Esnad – a chant (not a sung poem) such as the Fianna (a standing army of selected warriors) sang round their leather cauldrons

A ninth-century eulogy of Columba says of the Fianna: '. . . at that time the Fianna had a strange peculiarity: the first man of them who went into a house would start chanting the beginning of the song, and the last man would answer him, and then they all would chant together . . . they used to drink a pleasant ale out of the cauldron and the nine best men of the company were still singing a melody around it, while the others were chanting the poem.'

Interpretation of these early texts is rarely straightforward, but this does strongly suggest

both antiphonal (the music alternating between groups and individuals) and part-singing.

Columba forbade male choral singing in large groups[11] – perhaps because it represented the music of the wrong religion. But he was a friend to the bards, defending their order from abolition at the council of Drumcet. He himself went to heaven with two songs – harmonic singing perhaps – or maybe something more conventional like two choirs of angels.

He is said to have written a number of poems. One that is accepted as being genuinely by him and transmitted uncorrupted, is his remarkable abecedarian hymn in which the stanzas start each with a different letter of the Latin alphabet, the first with *Altus Prosator* and the twenty-third and last with *Zelus Ignis*. It is a syllabic as well as a rhyming poem – each line has eight syllables. *Altus Prosator* was written towards the end of the sixth century. Some four to five hundred years later – eleventh to twelfth century – someone wrote a preface to the hymn, stating that Columba composed it as a penance for his involvement in the battle of the book (see below). Others said that it was composed while working a quern – a rotary hand mill. This was not usually a man's job, certainly not an abbot's, and the labour evoked the somewhat penitential hymn which he is supposed to have extemporised while grinding the quern. One does not have to believe this story – though it is by no means an impossible one – to accept that the poem was associated with a quern song – for of course the poem was sung – it was a hymn.[12]

Quern songs are thought to be particularly ancient.[13] As it happens there is a recording of a quern song with traces of an octosyllabic structure to the verse, and with a chant-like melody in character as dark as the original hymn.[14] It praises the quern and the man who

Example 9. QUERN SONG (from the singing of Peter Morrison)

'Si mo bhrà fhin	as fheàrr gu min a thionn-dadh mach à gràn, cha bhi 'n t-ac-ras

air mo chloinn	's na lea-can seo a-bhos ri m' làimh.	Chaidh a gear-radh le fear-ceàird,

on char-ragh ghlas 'n taobh thall a' chnoic-Shrac e i-le òrd_ is cruaidh 's tha i dear-bhadh sin a-nochd.

crafted it from the grey rock with hammer and steel and it was sung by Peter Morrison.

It takes scarcely any adjustment to fit this melody to St Columba's poem. It is a speculative reconstruction, but it works extremely well in performance and may give some clue as to how *Altus Prosator* was originally sung. The hymn is basically concerned with the last judgment – it foreshadows the famous *Dies Irae* poem, and indeed this tune has much of the *Dies Irae* character to it – but Columba is not without a more human touch, remembering love and desire:

Example 10. ALTUS PROSATOR, set to a quern song tune

Day of the King most righteous, the day is nigh at hand,
The day of wrath and vengeance, and darkness on the land.

Day of thick clouds and voices, of mighty thundering,
A day of narrow anguish and bitter sorrowing.

The love of women's over, and ended is desire,
Men's strife with men is quiet, and the world lusts no more.

The last lines of the poem refer to the books of conscience open before us and may be a reference to Columba's original sin – the copying by stealth of a precious book. When the High King ordered him to give back the copy as well – 'to every cow its calf, to every book its copy' (books were made of calf-skin) – Columba went to war and the guilt later oppressed him. But the poem ends with a vision of thousands of angels chanting hymns, where no doubt Columba hoped to find a place with his splendid voice which had so terrorised the Picts.

It is interesting, that judgment about the book. The cattle people had come a long way to herdsmen on Iona who could fashion the vellum pages of the world's most beautiful book, the *Book of Kells*. Those calf-skins hold the ink and the colour, even the blue made from lapis lazuli imported from Afghanistan, after hundreds of years. Columba was regularly invoked in Scotland to protect cattle, right up into this century, and he was also a noted scribe. A book brought those two attributes together. The author of this poem attributed it to Columba, who might well have agreed with its sentiments.

My hand is weary with writing.
My sharp-nibbed slender pen gives out a stream of beetle coloured ink
A steady spring of wisdom flows from my neat hand inking the page with ink from the green-skinned holly.
I send my little pen dripping unceasingly over a collection of books of great beauty to enrich men of learning: hence my hand is weary with writing.

Columba's illegal copy may indeed survive. It is called *The Cathach* and is a part of the psalter. The initial letters are decorated with red dots. But what was so precious about the psalter he copied from – psalters must have been common enough? Perhaps the clue is in the little red dots. This is their first appearance in Western manuscripts. Before this book the style is only found in Coptic manuscripts. If the book he copied was a precious and decorated Coptic psalter, that would make it especially valuable. What else came with those books? The influence of the desert fathers?

The word desert came to mean any lonely place of retreat for those early Scottish Christians. Dysart in Fife thus gets its name, for St Servanus made his retreat there. St Kentigern, Glasgow's St Mungo, likewise sought the desert – *heremi deserta*. It was thus that he met Merlin (see Chapter III).

Books, the eremetic life of retreat . . . what about music? Most people, asked to put a name to early Christian chant would call it Gregorian chant. But Gregory merely put his name to a centralising which had already occurred in many places. He was twenty years Columba's junior and the body of Roman chant he promoted was altered by the Spanish Mozarabic chant, the French Gallican chant and by the Celtic chant. The Celtic chant is said not to exist at all, but we shall see in the next chapter that this is untrue.

There is, however, quite separate from the above, a musical coincidence which has struck so many people that it cannot be ignored. It is the similarity of the style of Gaelic psalm-singing with that of Middle Eastern chanting. Two recordings in particular underline this for solo and congregational singing[15] – from a Coptic

Christian enclave in Ethiopia and from the West Highlands. These two cultures have had no direct or indirect contact worth speaking of for several hundred years, if at all. The two solo chants use the same pentatonic scale, in exactly the same layout. The manner of the decorations of the main notes is almost identical and the pace of delivery is the same. The two are even at the same pitch, except that the Gaelic one is an octave higher as the singer is a woman. The embellishments are so fluid and rich that they are only poorly represented on paper.

Example 11. GAELIC AND COPTIC CHANTING, Gaelic above

These recordings are so much closer to each other than anything in Western Europe is to Gaelic solo or congregational singing that they call for explanation. The best that can be suggested is that the Gaelic-speaking people, whether the church wanted it or not, retained a style of singing with roots in very ancient Christian chant. The Ethiopian church services have been isolated for centuries and are thought to retain the oldest Christian music in the world, possibly derived from Syrian sources, though these Ethiopians are Coptic. But given the connection with the Coptic psalter and Egyptian/Palestinian influences in the Irish liturgy[16] it is perhaps not so surprising after all.

Hundreds of years ago sea travel was the easiest way to get around. The west of Scotland was therefore at little disadvantage. Coming out of the Mediterranean and round Spain, you would reach it as easily as London and more rapidly than York. Sailing and rowing were the best means and the missionaries from Iona and Bangor will have been well used to it. One of them, Columbanus, not to be confused with Columba – wrote a poem in the mood of a rowing song for his

monks rowing up the Rhine to convert the heathen: 'See how the greased keel slips over the seas and through the flood of twin-horned Rhine, cutting through the woods. Heave men! And let resounding echo sound our "heave".'

Rowing songs belong to a group known as work-songs. There were work-songs for every kind of labour from milking to spinning, from grinding corn to fulling cloth (known as 'waulking'). But the rowing songs are no longer functional though they are as effective as, and a lot more beautiful than, the coarse yellings of a cox on the Thames. Some of the iorrams (rowing songs) have survived in waulking songs in which the rhythm of beating the tweed to shrink it is not dissimilar to that of rowing. This one, in common with others, has an extra beat in one bar so as to throw the accent on to alternate beats each time round, thus giving the rhythm even more life. The words praise the boat and her crew, but those of the chorus have no meaning.

Example 12. ROWING SONG (from the singing of Colin Morrison)

We have seen then that when Christianity came to Scotland it encountered and embraced a culture rich in music which it has permitted to survive if not helped to preserve. But the Christians in Scotland produced their own music too, developing for their mysteries extended melodic lines which they structured with great skill. Whether such things existed already in the community we shall never know. The material selected above might give the impression that the indigenous music was short-winded and repetitive. But the selection reflects modern assumptions that the oldest music to survive is probably the simplest. It could be that there was a repertoire of more sophisticated material which was forgotten for that very reason and the variety and beauty produced within the limitations of length and scale of these tiny lullabies and charms, are themselves indicators of a musical subtlety and sensitivity not to be underrated.

CHAPTER III

THE BELL AND THE CHANT
500–1100

Christianity came to Scotland with its own peculiar noises – bells of many different sizes and pitches, and monks singing; hour after hour, day after day, year upon year, tirelessly singing. The sounds came from two separate directions, from the south and from Ireland. We can hear how it must have sounded making its way from island to island and up the long sea-lochs and glens in the west, for we have some of the actual bells they rang and, thanks to the *Inchcolm Antiphoner*, can sing some of the chants they sang.

In the fifth century AD after a brief visit to Rome, St Ninian arrived in Whithorn in south-west Scotland on a Christianising mission. The people spoke his own language – British – and were already at least partly Christianised. Other important saints from southern Scotland who came from this British-speaking culture include Patrick (fifth century), and Mungo and Gildas (sixth century). North of the central belt, where Pictish was spoken, came the great Irish mission to the west of Scotland, led by Columba and Moluag in the sixth century, and in the seventh century by Maelrubha and Adomnan, amongst many others.

The arrival of Christianity produced some musical confrontations. Merlin is said to have 'disturbed St Kentigern and his clergy with horrifying shrieks, as they were singing the divine office',[1] and it is not clear whether Kentigern (better known as Mungo) succeeded in truly converting him. It is one of the profoundest tragedies of the history of Scottish music that a manuscript from the eleventh to twelfth century containing chants for an Office of St Kentigern was lost in the 1920s.[2] (But also see end of chapter.)

But the connections of the missionaries with pre-Christian religion were frequently carefully established rather than the reverse. St Ninian's bull, which he protected from cattle-raiders by confining them within a magic circle so that the bull could finish them off himself, indicates close ties with the bull cult of former times (see Chapter I). The line was drawn with his crozier – an object of magical power like a Druid's wand. St Serf's crozier had similar powers, and the early Christian bells were also magical and, along with other important objects such as psalters, gospels and breviaries, were under the special care of hereditary guardians known as dewars.

The name 'dewar' derives from the Gaelic 'deoradh', meaning stranger, or pilgrim – perhaps because they carried the cult objects on missionary pilgrimages. The title has become a surname as well as surviving in its original use, for there are still dewars of the bells, in unbroken succession, though the duties are now passed on from minister to minister in the appropriate churches, rather than from father to son.

The connections and confrontations between Christian and pre-Christian remained long current. As late as the twelfth century, Jocelin, Bishop of Glasgow, was happy to relate that Mungo founded a monastery on a site chosen by a white boar on the top of a little hill – possibly a fairy mound[3] – just as the site of Glasgow cathedral was chosen by a pair of oxen. The power and divine intuition of these creatures seems to have been cheerfully borrowed from older religions and used to reconcile the people who had followed the trumpeting boar's head of the carnyx, or the curved cattle-horn shape of the Caprington horn, to the new ways of the missionaries of Christ. Mungo also had a bell. It was rung in memory of the dead, features on Glasgow's coat of arms, and was replaced in 1641, perhaps worn out with ringing.

Bells are a vital part of religious music in many cultures. The tinkling crotals of the Bronze Age were bell-like and may have been used for religious ceremonies (see Chapter I) and the importance of bells in the Christian religion is scarcely diminished from earliest times. They are used in early Gaelic texts alongside Christian chant, as unwelcome symbols of the new religion:

> Patrick of the closed-up mind . . . Patrick of the joyless clerks and of the bells . . . the rough voice of the bells has deafened me . . . I have no liking for clerks, their music is not sweet to me . . . I have heard music sweeter than your music, however much you are praising your clerks: the song of the blackbird in Leitir Laoi . . . the very sweet thrush of the Valley of the shadow, or the sound of the boats striking the strand.[4]

The lover of the song of the thrush was Oisin (Ossian) who had been in the land of youth and returned to find all his companions of the great warrior troupe – the Fianna – long gone and a new religion and a new music to confront him. As we have seen, he had more than the music of the thrush to remember, but his Christian commentator imagines him hearing it as the ideal of music, perhaps because it is his ideal too, though actual worship of birds was not approved.[5] Maybe it found a too-ready echo in the minds of the Picts (see Chapter I).

The conversations between Patrick and Oisin were worked up by scholars much later than the days of Patrick, but they reflect genuine confrontations between the peoples of Scotland and Ireland and those wishing to Christianise them. The fact that the chants and bells are fixed upon as symbols of the new religion shows that Christianity's musical influence was important.

There were two types of bells, both quad-rangular, one type of sheet iron, the other of cast bronze. The iron hand-bells may date from as early as the seventh or eighth century and are intimately associated with the Iona mission and therefore with Ireland.[6] One, known as St Adomnan's, may well date from his time. It is still housed at a site long associated with the saint at the eastern edge of his missionary activities. There are other bells, iron and bronze, similarly sited, proclaiming their territorial significance. The iron bells are made by bending, lapping and riveting sheet iron. They were originally coated in bronze – perhaps even in gold[7] – and have suffered from corrosion, but those which can be rung produce a melancholy clanging sound not dissimilar to that of large cow- or sheep-bells. Saints themselves were supposed to have made them, which adds to their magical skills the deep-rooted magic of the smith (see Plate IV).

The bells have interesting connections with rock-gongs. Gildas, a sixth-century saint from Strathclyde, reputedly used a rock-gong rather than a bell to summon the faithful in Brittany,[8] though he was credited with the manufacture of at least one bell himself. His rock-gong has been recorded and is so resonant that its sound is not far removed from that of an iron bell: the process of smelting ore and refining it into iron which can be fashioned into a bell can be seen as a releasing of the sound in the rock; and the use of a rock-gong for purposes of Christian assembly is a straightforward continuation of the pre-Christian functions these ringing rocks are assumed to have fulfilled.

Bells were given a form of baptism[9] and their magical powers include those of banishing, of healing, of flight and of speech. Bells are still used to exorcise evil spirits (hence the phrase 'bell, book and candle'); they were frequently employed for healing purposes in Scotland, and the power of flight may be a magical extension of the power of the sound of a bell to travel over long distances and draw people to it: in any case they often travelled with their owners. Their power of speech also had a symbolic source, the hollow of the bell representing the preacher's mouth, the clapper his tongue. We still speak of the iron tongue of a bell. The round towers of Ireland, of which there are two examples in Scotland, were, among other things, bell towers from the top of which a hand-bell would have been rung (see Plate VI). Indeed this seems to have been their primary function for their name in Gaelic is 'cloictech' – bell-house.[10] As the round towers were also refuges, the bells may have been used in times of danger as well as, naturally enough, to call monks to prayer.

We may imagine a monk on Iona stumbling out of his cell on a wild night to the call of the bell to sing the twelve prescribed psalms[11] and this hymn – *Mediae Noctis* – which

Example 1. MEDIAE NOCTIS

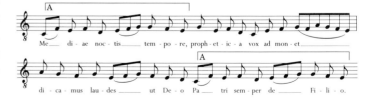

we know the monks of Bangor used to sing at midnight.

St Moluag and St Maelrubha came from the great religious centre at Bangor in Northern Ireland and Christianised much of the north and west of Scotland, just as one of their colleagues from Bangor – St Columbanus – carried his great and influential mission across Europe.

But with the bronze bells of Scotland, thought to be of slightly later date,[12] we enter a different order of musicality, for these bells can each individually play three different notes. I made this discovery only after ringing the Little Dunkeld bell (see Plate V) for several minutes, allowing the clapper to strike each of its four faces. A bell produces a complex sound, rich in harmonics and combination tones and it only gradually dawned on me what I was actually hearing. Once heard, never again mistaken. Two of the faces produced the same note, but the others were different from it and each other. They covered a minor third.

Example 2. PITCHES OF SCOTTISH BRONZE BELLS

Subsequent ringing of other bronze bells of similar design (quadrangular, flared, and with a curved flange where the bell opens out) produced similar results. As far as I can determine, this is a characteristic unique to this design. Irish bronze bells, which are generally less flared, hint at it but do not achieve it. It seems likely that the effect was deliberate and it may be that the different notes could have been used to indicate different times of day or of the hour, just as clock chimes do, or to accompany chanting and to indicate moments of special importance in church services – Christ's presence at the Mass is announced by the Sanctus bell. Pitched bells were certainly used in the Middle Ages to accompany singing; and the Scottish bronze bells, which produce a lovely clear sound capable of soft as well as very loud playing, could well be the earliest surviving musical instruments worthy of that function.

Two of the bronze bells may have been commissioned by Kenneth MacAlpin in 848–49.[13] He was the first king of Scotland to unite the Picts

and the Scots and he built a church at Dunkeld to house the relics of St Columba, perhaps to save them from Viking raiders but also to move the focus of Scottish religious life from the remote west to as near the dead centre of his country as could be managed. His country now included Pictland and covered more of Scotland than any previous monarch had controlled.

What did these early Christians bring by way of chant? In a rare attempt to identify Celtic elements from hints and scraps in non-Celtic sources, one scholar identified two chants as Celtic, largely because of their interest in formal balance, less evident in chant from other sources.[14] One of those scraps was sung by a dying Irish monk in the seventh century in far away Bobbio, in Italy. After he had received the last rites, surrounded by his fellow brothers, Theodaldus intoned an old Celtic antiphon – *Ibunt Sancti* – 'Thy saints shall go from strength to strength' and after he had sung the melody to its end, he was 'blessed with the sleep of the Lord'.[15] This is what he sang.

Example 3. IBUNT SANCTI

It is clear that it starts and ends with the same phrase. A very similar tune with words and music of Celtic origin became widespread throughout Europe and it is more highly structured. Square brackets and letters identify the repeated phrases.

Example 4. CRUCEM SANCTAM

Fortunately we can do much better than this in rediscovering early Celtic chant, by studying the *Inchcolm Antiphoner* which is one of the most

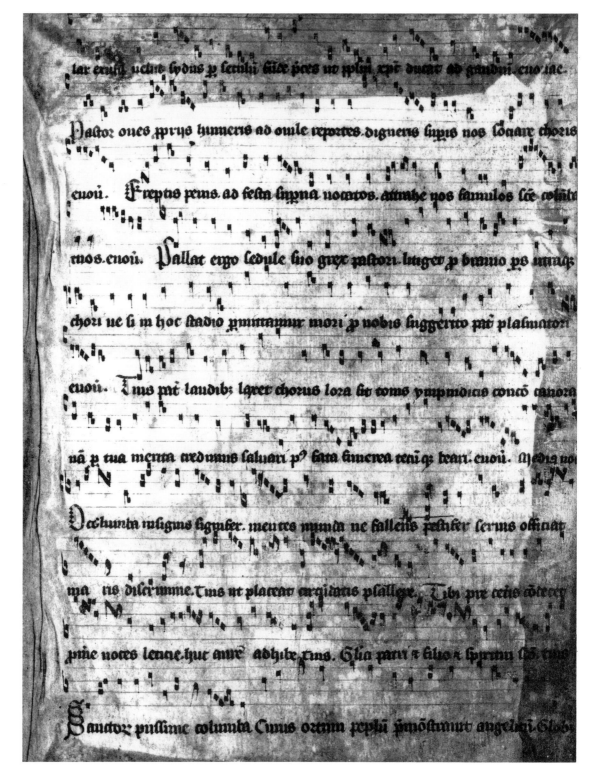

Plate 10. *Inchcolm Antiphoner,* THIRTEENTH CENTURY

important and neglected manuscripts in the history of plainchant (the unaccompanied chant of the western church). It contains the only definitive remnants of the music of the Celtic church, which was responsible for Christianising substantial portions of Europe. It is neglected because only one exploratory study has been made of it.[16] A properly edited transcription of the music and text is not available and the following comments therefore break new ground but are also open to much revision. If they find support then they are certainly exciting discoveries in the history not only of the music of Scotland, but of early Christian chant in general (see Plate 10).

The manuscript was written either at the end of the thirteenth century or beginning of the fourteenth century, probably on the island of Inchcolm in the river Forth from which one looks across the Firth to Edinburgh. One might expect an establishment so accessible from the North Sea and so close to Edinburgh to be wholly devoted to Gregorian chant. After all, in the eleventh century a Scottish Benedictine and musical theorist – Aaron Scotus – had decreed to his monks in Cologne that they sing the latest Office in Gregory's honour.[17] But amongst other things, the *Inchcolm Antiphoner* contains plainchant for a service in memory of the distant St Columba of Iona, for on Inchcolm there was a monastery dedicated to Columba which may have inherited material originally sung and perhaps housed in older manuscript form in Iona itself (see Plates 11 and 12).

> About the year of the Lord 1123, in a way no less strange than marvellous, was founded the monastery of St Columba of the island of Aemonia near Inverkeithing. For when the noble and most Christian king, the lord Alexander, the first of that name, by reason of state affairs, was crossing at Queensferry, there suddenly arose a violent gale from the south-west, which, almost with a comet's speed, compelled the boat with its crew to put in at the island . . . where dwelt a certain hermit who, dedicated to the service of St Columba and supported by a slender diet, consisting of the milk of a single cow and mussels and small fish taken from the sea, zealously devoted himself to a tiny chapel there. On such food the king and his considerable retinue subsisted for three days while storm bound.
>
> But when . . . in the greatest peril of the sea and tossed by the fury of the gale, he despaired of his life, he made a vow to St Columba that if they were brought in safety to the island he would leave to St Columba's praise such a memorial as would afford shelter and comfort to sailors and the shipwrecked.

Walter Bower, who wrote that account in the 1440s, was himself an abbot of Inchcolm and will probably have sung the music in the *Inchcolm Antiphoner*. The manuscript is unpublished, so a lot of space is devoted to transcriptions. The music is all plainsong, and as plainsong manuscripts give no clear duration for the notes, they are all assumed to have much the same length. In modern performance each note is given roughly the value of a quaver, and that is how they are transcribed here; but the notation should not be taken too literally as nobody knows how plainchant was really sung. In the manuscript the chants are strung out along the staves, using every

Plate 11.   INCHCOLM PRIORY FROM THE AIR

bit of space available and with no attempt to show any structure. In the transcriptions, where the music sets a poem, it is laid out as a poem. In this way the relationship between words and music can be easily seen.

Plate 12.   IONA ABBEY FROM THE AIR

Many chants were shared commonly throughout Europe, and parts of the manuscript draw on widely shared material. But all the texts referring to Columba are unique, and for five of these the music is unique also. Five further chants share only their first musical phrase with other sources.

Among the unique chants are settings of texts which in form and character show an intimate connection with early Celtic Latin, and in content a close relationship with Adomnan's *Life of Columba* written in the late seventh century. It is perfectly possible that these texts originated in some cases from as early as the seventh to the ninth centuries.[18] If a structural relationship between texts and music can be established then there is a likelihood that the two were conceived together. This was the common practice, there being no word in Gaelic for a tune without words, and these Latin texts share their characteristics with the poetic styles in Gaelic.

Such a relationship exists, in various forms. For example, in *Salve Splendor* (for which the words and music are unique) the rhymes in the text are very frequently matched by the musical equivalent of rhymes – phrase-endings of identical or almost identical shape. This is a particularly beautiful chant which rises to great heights of feeling as the name of Columba is invoked. It is an 'Antiphon to the Magnificat' which means it was a chant sung immediately before the song of the Blessed Virgin Mary, normally heard at the evening service of Vespers. The words of *Salve Splendor* are very firmly in a syllabic pattern with rhyming to match – a kind of poetry much favoured by the monks of Bangor, who had close links with Iona and whose famous Antiphoner dates from the seventh century. But it has no music in it. To discover that the *Inchcolm Antiphoner* has similar poetry with music and musical rhymes matching and elaborating on the structure of the poems, adds a fascinating dimension.

As above, recurring phrases are indicated by square brackets and identifying letters, A, B, etc. Where the same phrase appears at a different pitch it is given the same letter plus a cross, A+, B+, etc. The line lengths are those of the poetry, so it should be easy to relate the music to the syllabic and rhyming structure of the poem. Sometimes the starts as well as the ends of lines are marked by repeating musical motifs. One phrase only has little in common with the rest of

the chant. It is the setting of the words 'orthodox teacher', dutifully acknowledging the repeated note boredom of orthodoxy!

Example 5. SALVE SPLENDOR (*Inchcolm Antiphoner*)

In *O Columba Insignis Signifer* (also unique) the musical structure expands and contracts the central motifs with a balance of shapes and a dramatic use of different vocal registers that make it one of the loveliest melodic lines in the vast repertoire of plainsong. 'O Columba, proud standard-bearer, cleanse our minds least fear of death hinder your servants, that it may please your followers gathered round to hymn you. For you before all others we should know of our imminent joy. Hear us – your adherents.'

There are similar musical rhymes in *Os Mutorum*, but what is interesting here is that it shares its *incipit* – its opening phrase – with a Salisbury chant. Queen Margaret, the English wife of Malcolm Canmore, had got rid of most of the old Celtic practices in favour of those of Rome by the end of the eleventh century. A hundred years later even Iona had so forsaken its old Irish traditions, when taken over by the Benedictines in 1203, that the archbishops of Armagh and Derry razed the monastery to the ground the following year. During this period from the eleventh century to the thirteenth century most of the major Scottish churches followed the order of service and used the chants which had been established at the great cathedral of Salisbury.

In *Os Mutorum*, as in *Salve Splendor*, the structures are complex, and when the name of Columba is invoked with the words 'O Columba, hope of the Scots', the music rises in pitch and intensity of feeling. Both chants display two other marked features – their wide vocal range and their tunefulness in which little reliance is placed on intoning on one note and in which most of the non step-wise motion is by intervals of a third. Many of the phrases are bounded by the same interval, as is the case in Gaelic songs.[19] It seems that if the Salisbury chant was the starting point, it has been radically altered on principles of construction with their roots in earlier days. The other possibility is that the Salisbury version is altered from an original Celtic one: 'Mouth of the dumb, light of the blind, foot of the lame, proffer a hand to the fallen, strengthen the vain and cure the mad. O Columba, hope of the Scots, make us through the intervention of your merits, associates of the blessed angels. Alleluia.'

The text of another of the unique chants presents a touching picture of the community holding on to what hope it may in a wild world: 'O Columba most pious of Saints, whose noble birth prefigured your holiness. You restore your tired brothers on their journey with drops of comfort. You foresee our household under the power of Rome. You sweeten bitter apples. You renew the dead with life. You govern the winds. You clear the skies and dispel plagues. You draw water from the rock. You are protector of church and country. Look down on this choir, O most pious of the saints, whether they are all worthy or not, and pray that in this place which has been dedicated to you, your goodness may serve Christ.'

Mention of Rome may offer a clue to the date. St Adomnan was the first to attempt to bring the Celtic church into line with Roman practice in the seventh century. Iona reluctantly lowered its neck to that yoke not long after his death. The word 'Romani' is set to the lowest note in the chant, but on the emotive words 'you sweeten bitter apples' the music sweeps to

Example 6. O COLUMBA INSIGNIS SIGNIFER (*Inchcolm Antiphoner*)

Example 7. OS MUTORUM (*Inchcolm Antiphoner*)

its highest note. What more bitter apple could the monks of that ancient seat of Christianity have had to chew upon than that of obedience to Rome? And what more passionate expression of their dilemma could be found?[18]

The text also speaks of 'this place which has been dedicated to you'. Inchcolm was founded by Alexander I in 1123. But since these chants show signs of being much older, the reference could be to an older church from whose service for Columba this was copied. Dunkeld, the patron of Inchcolm, was founded in 849 and will have needed an 'Office' or service for its dedicatee St Columba; and so will Iona itself, following the death of its founder. Given the mention of Rome and the imagery surrounding it, it seems quite possible that this chant was composed not long after Adomnan's death, in final submission to Rome alongside assertion of the Columban tradition.

In *Sanctorum Piissime Columba*, the relationship between music and text is not always so direct as in other chants, but both are still structured. Much early Gaelic writing mixed ornate prose with passages of verse, both of which used alliteration and assonance to give music to the sound of the words. In the centre of this prose chant, there is a section of short rhyming syllabic phrases used for a special purpose – that of the charm. Where Columba is credited with commanding the winds, clearing the skies, dispelling disease and drawing water from a rock, the music matches the short phrases. It centres around the interval of a major third, just as it did for the charms of the lullabies referred to in Chapter II. '*Ventis imperas*', '*serenas*', '*et pestem fugas*' and '*extricas*' all turn around the same three notes like an incantation. Detail like this is matched by a sense of the overall shape. Where the words '*sanctorum piissime*' occur at start and end of this extended chant, so the music repeats with only slight modification.

But the music does not necessarily shadow the text and has its own echoes and shapes. The effect is one of extraordinary subtlety and refinement. Two similar types of structure interweave. It must be sung to be appreciated, for only then do the sounds of the words intermingle with the sounds of the music. The result is as rich in detail and overall control as are the great illuminated pages of the *Book of Kells*. The Celtic love of formal patterning, immensely sophisticated but far from

rigid in fact or effect, is well known in other art forms. The *Book of Kells* (generally accepted as having been made on Iona) and the Pictish crosses in Scotland are obvious examples (see Plates VII and VIII). It should not surprise us that something similar emerges in their church music.

Example 8. SANCTORUM PIISSIME COLUMBA (*Inchcolm Antiphoner*)

Sadly, the hospitality which Alexander I intended the Abbey of Inchcolm to provide was regularly abused by English pirates, so the Augustinian monks had to move their living quarters from ground to first floor to provide some kind of defence. *Pater Columba* prays for deliverance from the incursions of the English and was therefore written on Inchcolm. Again, it is carefully structured so that rhyming words are matched by short rhyming musical phrases – but in this one the music for the second-last line is repeated wholesale for the last line where it prays also for deliverance from the insults of jealous imitators. It is as pointed a way of mocking imitation as could be found: 'Father Columba . . . preserve this choir, which praises you, from the incursions of the English and from insolent imitators.'

Example 9. PATER COLUMBA (*Inchcolm Antiphoner*)

Similar things can be said of the chants not discussed here. *Psallat Ergo* and *Tuis Pater* are both tightly structured, the former sharing its *incipit* with a Salisbury chant, the latter unique. The music for the Inchcolm chants is not alone in its structural organisation, but the close relationship with verse structures associated with the early Celtic church is undoubtedly of great significance, as is the sweeping melodic confidence of these lovely chants.

Let us leave the *Inchcolm Antiphoner* with a picture of the loyalty of its users to their beloved St Columba, for the Augustinians of Inchcolm were loyal to him and to their own body of chant, as was their patron church of Dunkeld. The Charters of the Abbey for 1256 tell us: 'The Dean and Chapter of Dunkeld confirm Bishop Richard's donation of twenty shillings annually for twenty lighted candles at the high altar on the vigil and day of St Columba.'

The twenty candles must have looked pretty there, burning through the summer night as the monks kept the vigil on the eve of 9 June – Columba's feastday – singing through the night. This would have been an appropriate chant for

such an occasion: 'O wondrous clemency of Christ the king! The whole church gleams with the signs and wondrous portents of Columba. The people vie with full voices in blessed remembrance and prayers to the devoted father . . .'

Example 10. O MIRA REGIS (*Inchcolm Antiphoner*)

The Celtic love of patterning also finds expression in a particularly interesting verse-form known as the 'lorica' or 'breastplate'. Many readers will have sung one of these in translation, using a traditional Irish tune – the famous *St Patrick's Breastplate*. The loricae get their name from the belief that singing them would protect the singer from harm. In some of them all the parts of the body are specifically mentioned as though harm might come to any part not named. Such ideas are likely to have had pagan origins, but it is possible that the form had an important influence on later church music.

How the form of the loricae may or may not have affected the sequence is one of the most contentious and difficult problems in musicology and, as the *Inchcolm Antiphoner* has some bearing upon it and the Celtic church as a whole, we should not leave it without asserting the Celtic Christian identity; for the importance of the *Inchcolm Antiphoner* lies not only in the supreme beauty of the music and the interest of the texts, but in its significance as an additional pointer to the special characteristics of the Celtic church.

The distinctive features are as follows. A loose system of organisation based on monastic centres rather than bishops' sees; a particularly strong interest in the eremitic tradition derived from North Africa; a separate date for Easter; a unique form of tonsure possibly imitated from the Druids; certain peculiarities in the order of service and the division of the day and choice of appropriate prayers; and a use of the vernacular – Gaelic – long before any other language culture in Europe, both for secular poetry and prose, divine poetry and prose, commentary and many other functions.

This early use of the vernacular matches a readiness to accommodate the old religion and its symbolism – with only a few exceptions. To all these are related the Pelagian heresy which was the kindly notion that a new-born baby does not come into the world with the name-tag 'original sinner' and that heaven could be attained by living a life of virtue without having to be given a ticket at the door marked 'an act of special grace'. Pelagius came from the same cultural background as Gildas and Patrick, and some of these ideas may have been derived from Druidism. But they did not suit the Roman way and Pelagius is still considered a heretic while the Irishman, Scotus Eriugena, was declared a heretic on similar grounds. Centuries later Duns Scotus (from Duns in the Scottish Borders) echoes their faith in the power of human will, and he too was marginalised philosophically to such an extent that the word 'dunce' is derived from his name, though he was a brilliant philosopher.[20]

In summary, the Celtic church was distinct in philosophy, organisation, cultural bias, language use, literary style, order of service, calendrical calculation and the physical appearance of its

monks, to which we may add the distinctive appearance of its script and, now, the distinctive character of its music in so far as it has survived in the *Inchcolm Antiphoner*.

With that character established, we can approach the origins of the sequence. Sequences are important because they are the first Christian compositions independent textually and musically from the rest of the service, being insertions more than extensions. There is argument over the defintion and status of the sequence – there always will be – but it need not detain us. What matters is that it was one of the most popular forms of the Middle Ages and marks a break from strict control of the artistic content of Christian worship.

The text and chant of *Rex Caeli* form what is called, by most people, a sequence, and it has been suggested that the early sequences had their source in Celtic texts and music,[21] because sequences are highly organised poems with syllabic structures and music equally organised to match, usually with every line repeated and with mostly one note to a syllable. Their French equivalents include rhyme. Much early Celtic poetry anticipates that kind of organisation, in particular the loricae – breastplate poems. One such poem is attributed by some to St Gildas, another to St Patrick, another to St Adomnan; and Columba's *Altus Prosator* (see Chapter II) has close associations with the group. The four poems mentioned here were not contemporary with their 'authors' – they were written down later and if they have anything of those two Strathclyde and two Iona saints in them, maybe it is an old association rather than direct authorship. But the associations are important because they stress a compact geographical area, the loricae being associated with saints from Scotland and Ireland.[22] The form survived into modern times in the traditional prayers of the West Highlanders.[23]

Altus Prosator (see Chapter II) prefigures one of the most famous of all sequence poems – the *Dies Irae* – and a number of the *Vision* texts (one of which recounts a dream attributed to St Adomnan) relate to it and ultimately to Dante with their apocalyptic visions of the end of the world.[24] But these are textual relationships with one sequence only, albeit an important one. If there is to be any connection established, it has to be less tenuous.

The structure of *Rex Caeli* has been likened to that of *St Patrick's Breastplate* – itself likened to that of St Gildas.[25] The music for these does not survive, but in *Rex Caeli* we have perhaps a dim echo of what it might have been. One of the interesting connections is the way in which *Rex Caeli* returns to its opening music. It is a feature of early Gaelic writing to return to its opening line, just as the elaborately intertwined creatures in Celtic art are frequntly biting their own tails. The ninth-century *Amra Columcille* (a eulogy of St Columba) does this, and it was the declared practice of the bards.[26] Music and words belong closely to each other, as they do in the *Inchcolm Antiphoner*, and there is a Celtic feeling for nature: 'King of Heaven, Lord of the roaring sea, of the shining sun and the dark earth, Thy humble servants, by worshipping with pious phrases, beg Thee to free them – at Thy command – from their sundry ills.'

Example 11. REX CAELI

The importance of the harp in Scotland and Ireland may also have a place in this relationship if the text of *Rex Caeli* is anything to go by, 'cithara' meaning either harp or lyre: 'The cithara is the song of the wise; to thee O Creator, may it be pleasing. Having obtained the whole service of praise of the devoted, receive also the harmony of our prayer . . . With sounding strings, we servants devoted to thee attend the humble offering of the prayers of King David. These gifts had come to him from heaven that he might check Saul's anger with pleasant melodies. And so may these our songs be pleasing to thee, O God.'

The sequences were sung just before the act of communion and were joyous celebrations accompanied by the ringing of bells (in Scotland perhaps the beautiful bronze hand-bells), and this sequence actually speaks of the harp as the proper instrument for praising God.

We know that the harp or lyre was used to accompany plainsong from a Gaelic text of the eighth century. Describing the singing of psalms, it defines 'psalmus' as 'what was invented for the cithara and is practised on it'. 'Canticum' was 'What is practised by the choir and sung with the cithara' and 'canticum psalmi' as 'What is taken from the choir to the cithara'.[27] It was only natural. King David, who wrote the psalms, was a musician who played a stringed instrument. That the Scots were the masters of the harp is attested to by Giraldus Cambrensis – Gerald of Wales – though he writes very much later, in the 1170s. He says: 'In the opinion, however, of many, Scotland has by now not only caught up on Ireland, her instructor, but already far outdistances and excels her in musical skill. Therefore people now look to that country as to the fountain of the art.'

The missionary activities of the Celtic monks, prompted partly by Viking raids, provide us with the method by which they might have spread their musical and poetic influence. Monks from Scotland and Ireland moved south and east on great journeys extending to Northumbria, Germany, Switzerland, Northern Italy – even Russia. Perhaps some of them were driven off by Magnus Barelegs and his press-ganged crews, including poor St Magnus himself. Many went in a spirit of self-denial[28] – wandering into what was for them the cultural desert of Europe, just as their exemplars, the desert fathers, had gone into exile in the Sahara. To Europe those monks brought their music, and they also brought their harps with them, for several Gaelic sources mention clerics as carrying a small eight-stringed harp attached to their girdles.[29] They also brought a wide knowledge of classical Latin authors, and a familiarity with Greek the extent of which is much discussed. Certainly many of the early translations of Greek and Latin texts were made by Celtic monks or their pupils, especially the treatise, *The Fundamentals of Music* by Boethius, which was to form the basis of all mediaeval music theory.[30]

Boethius's *Fundamentals of Music* is mostly dry as dust, and that is something the Celts, however scholarly, could not be accused of. They loved patterning and were able to control their ideas with sophisticated structures, whether on metal, on stone, in book illumination, poetry or music. But the ideas themselves were always lively and vigorous, demanding great skill in handling. No wonder then that Notker the Stammerer, 'the least of the monks of St Gall' (an Irish foundation), went to his teachers for help in writing sequences. One of these was Marcellus, the Latin name for Moengal, who was an Irishman. Notker was simply writing new words to match existing music which had been brought to St Gall by a monk from Jumieges (another Celtic foundation).

When Richard Crocker exclaims over the melodic qualities of the early sequence, he could be writing of the chants in the *Inchcolm Antiphoner*, had he but known them: '. . . melodic exuberance [is] everywhere apparent in this repertory. How bright they sound, how gratefully they sing! They combine forceful direction in melodic profile with gracefully animated detail, discretely proportioned and positioned. They combine a clear sense of tonal locus with an easy kind of motion capable of spanning great distances. The early sequence is an extraordinary adventure in lyricism . . . fresh, and different, sui generis, a major accomplishment in the history of music.'[31]

It is not that the Inchcolm chants selected above are sequences: they do not have the characteristic structure of paired lines, though a similar structure was certainly present in early Celtic poetry; but in character they have much in common with sequences – expressive melody and a sensitive balance of form and feeling. The Inchcolm chants come from that same Celtic world of the stone crosses and the *Book of Kells* and the early poetry in Gaelic and Latin, in which nature and human organisation lose their shyness of each other and, in their coming together, discover the kind of beauty which allows one to believe that old Polixenes in *The Winter's Tale* was right to say that 'The art itself is nature'.

Since completing this chapter I have made the very important discovery that the late thirteenth-century Sprouston Breviary, housed in the National Library of Scotland, contains a set of offices for St Kentigern, the rhymed portions of which are sung in plainchant. It appears that this music has not been commented upon, transcribed or sung in modern times, though the text has been published in A.P. Forbes's *Lives of St Ninian and St Kentigern*, Edinburgh 1874.

The rhymed and syllabic verse appears to tell a different version of St Kentigern's life than that of the spoken part which may be older in origin, though the whole service is written out in the one hand. Kenneth Jackson (in N.K. Chadwick (ed.), *Studies in the Early British Church*, Cambridge 1958) believes the rhymed sections to be derived from Jocelin's *Life* – which is reproduced and translated in A.P. Forbes (see above). Neither of these commentators makes any mention of the existence of notation in the manuscript, though it is basically a music book! It was probably written for use in Glasgow Cathedral as the offices for St Kentigern appear in the section of the manuscript which contains all the offices for the main feast days, whereas the offices for all other saints are placed together in a later section. This gives to Kentigern a position of unique importance and, though Glasgow Cathedral is by no means the only church dedicated to him, it is the one under which he is buried and the one most likely to have commissioned such a book.

The bulk of the material in the Breviary is derived from the Salisbury rite and its chants, so whether the music for St Kentigern shares any Celtic characteristics with the chants from the *Inchcolm Antiphoner*, or with the few but significant unique features of the Office for St David's Day, (Owain Tudor Edwards, *Matins, Lauds and Vespers for St David's Day*, D.S. Brewer, Cambridge 1990) remains to be seen. It also remains to be seen whether there are not other manuscripts containing sung offices for Scottish saints, lurking in libraries or, perhaps, known to all except the people of Scotland and the musicologists who should be working on their behalf.

CHAPTER IV

CATHEDRAL VOICES
800–1300

The music of the western world is distinguished from all other music by the discovery and development of part-writing. Scotland's role in this, the greatest evolutionary shift in the history of music, may not be quite as peripheral as one might expect; and, since the origins of polyphony – music of many sounds – are still sunk in a pool of muddy obscurities which show no sign of clearing, one can be forgiven for stirring them a little.

The first book of polyphony is called *Musica Enchiriadis*. It dates from the ninth century and is a theory book. It comes from the kingdom of the West Franks at a time when Celtic influence was still significant in those parts, and it has been suggested by more than one scholar that it was Celtic in origin.[1] From it we can hear how part-writing began – very simply – by a second person singing the tune (the *vox principalis*) at a different pitch (the *vox organalis*). These simple techniques of singing in parallel intervals are called *organum*.

Example 1. PARALLEL ORGANUM (*Musica Enchiriadis*)

How or why should such a practice have started? There are various ideas, but one of them would be that people naturally sing at their own preferred pitch and if a tune were too high or too low for some voices, they would automatically sing it at a pitch that suited them.

Four notes, five notes and eight notes apart were the chosen intervals. Seven notes or two notes apart would be very unpleasant and difficult to sing, but the most natural of all to modern ears would be singing three or six notes apart. The curious thing is that in most of Europe for several centuries it seems they did not think much of that. However, the people in the West Country are described as singing in thirds and there is, from Orkney, the famous *Hymn to Saint Magnus*[2] which is sung almost entirely in parallel thirds.

Example 2. HYMN TO SAINT MAGNUS (*Uppsala manuscript*)

We have seen that the interval of a third is significant in the *Inchcolm Antiphoner*; Roesner[3] has pointed out its significance in the main section of the *St Andrews Music Book* that is unique to Scotland (see below) and this significance holds for Gaelic song also.[4] But using thirds harmonically is first encountered in the *Hymn to Saint Magnus*. St Magnus was originally a pirate – no doubt like Columbanus and all the other sea-going saints he will have joined in many a rowing song when the wind died down (see Chapter II) – but he turned Christian and, after some years as a press-ganged crew member for Magnus Barefoot, he escaped to the court of King Malcolm III of Scotland. When Magnus Barefoot died, St Magnus returned to help his cousin Haakon run the Orkneys, but they fell out and Haakon had Magnus murdered. The *Hymn to Saint Magnus* was written in the twelfth century not long after his murder. He had accepted his martyrdom as a sacrifice and prayed for his murderers and seems to have exhibited other qualities of restraint that most of us would be unwilling to match:

'Noble, humble Magnus, steadfast martyr. You lived courageously, suppressing carnal passions, that the spirit may rule in the prison of the body. Your royal wife was brought to you a virgin, chaste was joined with chaste, and so you both remained for ten years, inviolate. The bush was not consumed in the fire.'

That there has been a northern influence expanding the repertoire of permissible intervals to include thirds, also encouraging their melodic use in plainsong, is a notion that still finds support.[5] If it has even a small element of truth in it, then it is clear that music from Scotland deserves careful consideration in that context.

One of the other theories as to how part-singing evolved is through the use of instruments. A little harp with few strings can only manage parallel thirds and because its structure is weak it could not be made to take any more strings. But in Scotland the addition of the pillar that allowed the harp to develop into the wide-ranging and resonant instrument we think of today (see Chapter II) would have made possible parallel fourths, fifths, sixths and octaves. This potential may have contributed to the growth of part-singing or have further encouraged an existing practice among Gaelic-speaking people (see Chapter II), for however pleasing the lyre and the tiompan may have been, they were too small to be much use when it came to writing and singing music in parts. The triangular harp would have been much better suited, with both hands equally free to pluck its greater number of strings.

Hands naturally move in parallel motion. For a beginner at the piano it is hard to get them to do anything else, so it is natural that they should produce parallel intervals on a harp. A more powerful instrument would make these parallel intervals audible even when a choir was singing. We may guess that the Celtic monks who carried harps with them of only eight strings, slung from their belts, did so for reasons of portability rather than lack of awareness of a larger instrument – for which we have evidence on the Monifieth No. 4 stone. Nor would this next quotation from Giraldus Cambrensis make much sense if the harpists of Scotland and Ireland had not been long practised in the use of instruments with many more strings than eight. It is clear too from Giraldus that the Scottish and Irish harpists used *organum* and other techniques implying more elaborate music:

It is wonderful how, despite the great rapidity of the fingers, musical proportion is preserved. By their faultless art, the melody is sustained through the most complicated arrangements of notes – with a velocity that charms, and a varied rhythmic pattern, and a judicious use of elements of concord and discord. Whether harmonising at intervals of the fourth and the fifth, they always start from B flat and return to it, so that everything may be rounded with the sweetness of pleasing sonority. They glide so subtly from one mode to another, the grace notes of the shorter treble strings freely sporting with abandon and bewitching charm around the steady tone of the bass notes, that the perfection of their art seems to lie in their concealing it.

It is immediately following this passage that Giraldus Cambrensis, writing in the twelfth century, states that the Scots are regarded as far excelling the Irish in musical science and skill.[6] Alas, nothing of that music survives.

One other instrument that might have had the same effect as the harp on part-singing was the organ – an instrument probably introduced into Scotland not later than the twelfth century when Ailred of Rievaulx complained, with querulous peevishness, in his book *The Mirror of Charity,* which he wrote in 1142:

But now that the Church has outgrown the stage of types and figures, what are we doing, I often wonder, with the thunder of organ music, the clash of cymbals, and elaborate part-singing for different voices? The simple folk may well be impressed by the organ music, but they cannot help laughing as they see such a ridiculous show going on in the choir. They are in fact more likely to think that they are watching a stage play than praying in church.

Good players on the harp and the organ would soon learn to move their hands in opposite directions and *Musica Enchiriadis* has examples of that too, using the sequence *Rex Caeli* (see Chapter III). Simple as it may seem to us now, it was important at the time because instead of one part being a mere image of the other, parts began to become independent.

Rex Caeli may have been a significant choice as an exemplar, if we accept that its structure has Celtic origins, as suggested in the previous chapter, and that the *Musica Enchiriadis* was Celtic too. But we must leave these speculations in the hope that they will at least provoke some more research in this fascinating field.

Example 3. FREE ORGANUM (*Musica Enchiriadis*)

We have been following Scottish musical culture developing in the middle of a sandwich of Celtic and Nordic cultures. With Celtic and Nordic peoples marrying into the artistically gifted Picts and using two different styles of singing or playing in parts – thirds as well as fourths and fifths – we need not be surprised to learn that the single most important manuscript of early part-music was compiled and written in Scotland in the thirteenth century.

The bulk of the manuscript contains French music from the magnificent Notre-Dame school of Perotin and Leonin, for which it is the first major source; and this Parisian music, cultivated in Scotland, is regarded as the truly significant move away from the early rigidities of *organum* into the complete independence of several parts, not just two, but three or four.

But there is also a substantial amount of music in this manuscript written specifically for St Andrews, by then the religious centre of Scotland, a place of pilgrimage of European significance, and the provider of our patron saint. *Vir Perfecte* is one of those pieces. It was composed in honour of St Andrew – *Vir Perfecte*, perfect man – and is an example of a kind of *organum* more elaborate than anything we have seen so far. In this music the upper voice has many notes, the lower one sustaining the basic chant much more slowly underneath, but the idea of the old parallel *organum* is still lurking in the background of it, for whenever the lower part changes note, the upper one tends to follow it either an octave or a fifth above.

Example 4. VIR PERFECTE (*St Andrews Music Book*, W.1 f 22v)

The manuscript from which that music came should be known as the *St Andrews Music Book*, but it was taken from St Andrews to Wolfenbuttel in the sixteenth century and the scholars have attached that name to it instead. It was probably compiled in the mid-thirteenth century by someone who knew all the latest developments in Paris and was able to imitate and modify them. There are three main candidates: the Norman Scot, Bishop Mauvoisin; the theoretical Scot, Simon Tailler, whose treatises on music are all lost and of whom we know little or nothing; and the very real Scot, David Bernham, Mauvoisin's successor as Bishop of St Andrews.

The manuscript has connections with Paris, Glasgow and St Andrews. Bernham had been a precentor in Glasgow. This means that he was probably a good singer, was in charge of the choir, and organised the music and music library. He had a degree from either Oxford or Paris – possibly the latter as he supported his nephew as a student there. He was a member of Mauvoisin's *familia* – his entourage of secretaries and administrators – and as such will have travelled with him, almost certainly to France. In any case we know Bernham went to France when he became Bishop of St Andrews, and he must have spent some time there as he had to cut Rome out of his itinerary because of Mediterranean pirates. The earliest date suggested for this manuscript (based on flimsy calligraphic evidence) is the 1230s – just when Bernham was in charge at the Glasgow choir school. If, as has been suggested recently, Mauvoisin commissioned the manuscript, it seems odd that he should have waited thirty years to do so, having become Bishop in 1202 and the Parisian music in the manuscript being dated to that period or earlier.[7] All in all, Bernham remains the most likely person to have brought the music over and commissioned its organisation to suit the needs of his cathedral.

If we could identify the 'Walter' who copied much of the *St Andrews Music Book* we might find out its exact date; but of Walter we know nothing whatever except that when he finished his laborious business at the end of the tenth fascicle of the manuscript on the verso side of folio number 191 Walter signed his name in music (see Plate 13): 'May Walter, the writer of this book, be blessed.'

Plate 13. SCRIBE'S SIGNATURE-TUNE, *St Andrews Music Book*, (W1) *c.* 1250

Let us hope he is. He might have been the Walter who, as one of Bernham's clerks, witnessed a grant to the friars of Scotlandwell in 1250.

Example 5.   QUI LIBER (*St Andrews Music Book*, W1 f191v)

Not only is the manuscript not definitively dated, but the original date of the music in it is impossible to determine. There is, however, one piece which seems likely to date from between 1164 and 1170. It is a *planctus* or lament – *In Rama Sonat Gemitus* – and when Walter wrote it out, he shaped the initial letter 'I' into the form of a bishop's staff (see Plate 14). That was because the lament was for the Archbishop Thomas à Becket's exile in France. Maybe Becket (who was a Norman) had a colleague in France with Scottish connections who wrote this piece that appears uniquely in the manuscript. Another closely related Scottish manuscript appears to be the only insular source for a history of the Office for Thomas à Becket,[8] so Becket may have had Scottish connections.

Plate 14. IN RAMA SONAT GEMITUS, *St Andrews Music Book*, (W1) *c.* 1250

Example 6.   IN RAMA SONAT GEMITUS (*St Andrews Music Book*, W1 f185v)

Scotland's King William the Lion was captured the same day as Becket was scourged in 1174, a coincidence which so impressed the king that he founded the priory of Arbroath and dedicated it to Becket. The lament is a sort of biblical allegory for the relationship between Becket and King Henry II of England, which was not a good one. The church is Rachel; Henry is Herod. The sinuous beauty of the descending phrases and the perfect placing of the intense climax of the lament make this one of the most deeply felt vocal lines from any time or place. 'In Rama the English Rachel weeps, for a descendant of Herod has covered her in ignominy. Behold, her first-born, the Joseph of Canterbury is exiled to the Egypt of France.'

It was never easy, being a bishop. The status of the Archbishop of Canterbury was matched in Scotland by the Bishop of St Andrews who was almost as powerful as the king whom he enthroned on the stone of Scone. In that capacity Bernham took a nationalist line during the minority of Alexander III, and he also secured the canonisation of Queen Margaret of Scotland. But he had to contend with the young king's advisers to maintain the rights of the church, just as Thomas à Becket had to do. Although Bernham was regarded as a '*vir per omnia commendabilis*' – a man altogether praiseworthy – he was also 'harsh and exacting' towards his community of canons and did the unforgiveable in chosing to be buried in Kelso where he presumably expected the Benedictines to sing for his soul more fervently than his fellow Augustinians in St Andrews.

Plate 15. BISHOP BERNHAM FROM HIS PONTIFICAL, THIRTEENTH CENTURY

The bischope David of Bername
past of this warlde til his lange hame.
As he did here sa fande he thar;
Off hyn I bid to spek na mare.
He cheyssit his laye in to Kelsow
Noucht in this Kyrk of Sancte Androw.

Thus Andrew Wyntoun in his *Orygenale Cronykil*, written in the 1420s. Bernham's troubles may have begun before him. Mauvoisin, for instance, deprived Dunfermline Abbey of its presentations to two churches because they hadn't given him enough wine in 1203. The monks' protest, that the wine ran out because Mauvoisin's company had been drinking it on the sly, got them nowhere; so there may well have been other petty squabbles in the episcopal legacy. There is a portrait of Bernham in his pontifical. He has a beard and moustache and a quizzical, critical look on his thin face, though not without kindness and humour (see Plate 15).

Whether he himself added Scottish music to the great riches encountered in Paris will never be known, but this is the kind of music he would certainly have been involved with in St Andrews. It is part of a Kyrie trope – *Kyrie Virginitatus Amator* – and is deeply expressive of the purity and mystery of Mary's virginity. There are nine verses and it was probably sung at the Saturday Lady Mass. The balanced use of fifths, thirds and

octaves at points of rest is a beautiful feature of this poised and lovely music.

Example 7. KYRIE VIRGINITATUS AMATOR (*St Andrews Music Book*, W1 f177v)

A trope is an elaboration of an existing chant. The Mass begins with the old tripartite cry for mercy – *Kyrie Eleison, Christe Eleison, Kyrie Eleison*. It is the only part of the Mass still sung in Greek. In a mass for a special feast day it might well be preceded by other music using a single line. So we can imagine the two-part Kyrie tropes in the *St Andrews Music Book* providing the first sound of polyphony in a world in which this kind of sound was new. As the music changed from the single melody and divided into two parts, it must have transformed the whole aural experience of the Mass. Properly sung it should be a moment both intense and ethereal, an exquisite blend of decoration and simplicity calling for two expert singers, the upper male alto voice floating high above, making use of the resonance of the cathedral for which it was intended. Churches were built big for better reasons than impressing the credulous. Among other things, they were built for sound. Virtually everything that happened in them was sung.

Composers in the early thirteenth century were already moving on to three and four part music – music that had to have more exact rhythms if the singers were to keep together. For this, new forms of notation were invented. The system of notation that developed in Western Europe was crucial to the development of polyphony. Firstly, with the addition of lines to fix the precise pitch of the notes, singers knew exactly what to aim for. Secondly, by altering the shapes of the notes themselves it was possible to give them a defined length in proportion to other notes of different shape. But in the initial stages it cannot have been particularly accurate and transcribing music from this period remains a conundrum.[9]

For how long this music remained in regular use we cannot say. What it establishes is that Scotland, far from being peripheral, was thoroughly aware of the musical world around it. But it was a nation battling for its existence against the English and it was some sixty years after the compilation of the *St Andrews Music Book* before the Battle of Bannockburn gave Scotland a brief opportunity to turn its energies away from politics and fighting.

The victory at Bannockburn must have given great impetus to Scottish culture generally, one of the high points of which was the completion of St Andrews Cathedral by Bishop Lamberton. Walter Bower (in his *Scotichronicon* written in the 1440s) describes it: 'With splendour he equipped the beams of the great church with polished tabula and bas-reliefs, and costly red vestments woven with figures, together with a bishop's mitre and pastoral staff, and he left very many good books.'

Wyntoun also recalls the completion and the great day of celebration.

> A thowsand thre hundyr and awchtene
> Fra Cryst had borne the Madyne clene,
> Off the moneth of July
> The fyft day, full solemply
> The Byschape Willame of Lambertown
> Made the dedicatyown
> Off the newe kyrk Cathedrale
> Off Saynct Andrewys conventuale.
> The Kyng Robert honorably
> Wes thare in persown bodyly;
> And sevyn Byschapys were sene,
> And Abbotis als ware thare fyftene,
> And mony othir gret gentill men
> Ware gaddryd to that assemble then.

On such an occasion the choir might well have sung with particular energy the three-part *Haec Dies*, a motet in which selected words of the plainchant are set polyphonically. Motets get their name from the French word '*mot*', so to be a motet, there should, strictly speaking, be separate words for the added part, which there are not. But *Haec Dies* is certainly in motet style, with independent and lively rhythms in the parts. This makes it one of the most advanced Scottish works in the manuscript. It is based on the jubilant words of Psalms 106 and 118 – 'This is the day which the Lord hath made.

O give thanks unto the Lord'. Both psalms celebrate the deliverance of the children of Israel from the Egyptian overlords; and there was Bishop Lamberton with the man – Robert Bruce – whom he had crowned King of Scots. But at the dedication of the new cathedral, Bruce would have been kneeling in the cathedral he had just endowed with a hundred marks annually 'for the illustrious victory which St Andrew had afforded him at Bannockburn'.

Example 8. HAEC DIES (*St Andrews Music Book*, W1 f81)

An even more positive Scottish work from the *St Andrews Music Book* was written to be sung at the New Year as a kind of New Year's resolution.

> On this threshold of the year
> In this month of January
> Let us turn to our work
> Assisted by our virtues.
> Joys are mutual,
> Vice has been silenced
> The evil ways of wicked men
> are reproved.
>
> Circumcision of the flesh
> was not without mystery
> even for the son of God –
> giving us an apt meaning:
> to remove all superfluity
> by rooting out vice
> on this threshold of the year.

The music is in three parts, romping along together, dance-like and confident. It is in the form of a *conductus* – music originally used for the entrance of the priest or of a character in a liturgical drama to conduct him on his way. It was the first music used in churches in which none of the parts owed anything to plainsong. *Hac In Anni Janua* is a '*conductus habens caudam*' which means that the composer took a little extra trouble finishing it off with some fun on the last vowel.

Example 9. HAC IN ANNI JANUA (*St Andrews Music Book*, W1 f71)

re - pro - bo - rum fa - tu - a   re - pro - ba - tur   a - cti - o

(o)

The joy and the self-confidence were all to be short-lived. The English continued raiding – on one occasion sacking southern abbeys such as Dryburgh and Melrose from which, in 1322, they stole the bell, only to lose it in the river Tweed. Then came the Black Death. The king and the court, including the Bishop of St Andrews, escaped it by moving up to Morayshire. But the bishop did go on pilgrimage to Spain – though St Andrews boasted a bigger cathedral than St James's of Compostella.

Although St Andrews at least followed on the heels of the continental composers, other parts of Scotland kept faith with older traditions. The rite of the cathedral at Salisbury had been widely adopted throughout Scotland, but apart from the lost manuscript of an Office for St Kentigern (see Chapter III) there are traces of another office for him in a manuscript recently identified as Scottish and housed in Paris.[10] And though the *Inchcolm Antiphoner* was written down at the end of the thirteenth century, it too contained material harking back five or six hundred years, to the eighth and ninth centuries; and the chant inveighing against the incursions of the English, which is likely to be a thirteenth-century one,[11] is composed within the style of the other Columban chants. On the other hand this same manuscript has chants for the feast of Corpus Christi, instituted in 1264, and it has been shown that the abbey at Inchcolm kept well abreast of the latest liturgical developments.[12] The overall picture is that of a lingering affection for the past combined with a readiness to accept ideas from elsewhere.

In the Gaelic-speaking world too, they were recording material even older than that. Many of the great Gaelic manuscripts were written in the twelfth to fourteenth centuries. They contained poems and tales of pre-Christian heroes and heroines which have survived in Scottish oral tradition. Emphasis has been placed on manuscripts in the music of the cathedrals and abbeys, but oral transmission will also have played an essential role in the church. Manuscripts may well be a record of what was improvised or remembered rather than what was composed – an echo of St Augustine's explanation of 'jubilation' when commenting on the shouts of joy in Psalm 32: 'It is the realisation that words cannot express the inner music of the heart. For those who sing in the harvest field, or vineyard, or in work deeply occupying the attention, the words fail to express their emotion, they drop into vowel sounds – the vowel sounds signifying that the heart is yearning to express what the tongue cannot utter.'

This instinctive music-making became extended into vocal technique. We have noted Columba's magical vocal powers and the shapely range of chants in the *Inchcolm Antiphoner*, but there was also a type of singing, much more extravagant than the *Inchcolm Antiphoner* chants and the balanced phraseology of the sequences, and yet not without control and form. It is represented at its most elaborate in the *St Andrews Music Book* and comes from one of the sections of it which is accepted as being Scottish in origin.[13]

What is remarkable about this type of singing is its extraordinary virtuosity, its vast range, its demands on vocal flexibility in scale passages, sequential phrases, repeated notes and breath control, and its frequent use of thirds. It carries the practice of elaborating on plainchant to amazing lengths. It is a Sanctus 'trope', which means that the usual 'Holy, Holy, Holy, Lord God of Hosts', sung by the choir, has been added to with these words for a soloist:

'The blessed reign of Christ, the presence of the Lord of hosts, the strength, the life, the path, the complete wisdom of the Father, for whom the melody shall resound, the cherub singeth the songs in heaven. Receive the prayers of those who praise thee with a full voice.' (See Plate 16.)

Aural tradition may have had an influence on these elaborate chants and though it was indeed notated, the lack at that time of a precise

Example 10. SANCTUS IERARCHIA (*St Andrews Music Book*, f186)
[Sanctus: Holy One for whom melody resounds as the cherub sings the song of heaven]

Plate 16. SANCTUS TROPE, *St Andrews Music Book* (W1) *c.* 1250

miserable-mindedness of Ailred you have to have heard chants such as that quoted above properly sung. Fortunately two of them have been superbly recorded.[14] The effect is electrifying; an outpouring of feeling contained nonetheless within its own obvious vocal patterns and set rapturously within the context of the more sober plainchant that is sung by the choir in the intervening sections and other parts of the service. The combined effect is eloquent and must be among the most virtuosic solo vocal writing from the European Middle Ages. We can but hope that Ailred is being converted to it by the angelic choirs and saintly soloists in heaven.

More significant than any amount of bravura however, is the beauty of the part-writing in this great collection. The Scottish contribution to it does not make any technical advances on the Parisian material in the *St Andrews Music Book*, but that does not diminish its attractions and we shall end this chapter with a brief section from a trope on the *Agnus Dei*, the parts crossing and re-crossing, weaving a two-stranded thread of subtle loveliness that reaches out to us across seven hundred years.

rhythmical indication allows the singer the freedom which keeps the music alive. There are scholars who would say that the notes should skip along in the ubiquitous rhythm of lah-di-dah-di-dah-di-dah. Happily there is another band of scholars and they say freedom should rule, and performances in this manner are persuasive.

Nothing, however, is above criticism. It is possibly this sort of singing that Ailred of Rievaulx complained about in *The Mirror of Charity*. Ailred came from Yorkshire but his formative years were spent in the south of Scotland attached to the court of King David I so he had ample opportunity to hear what was being sung in Scotland and northern England:

> For what end is this contraction and dilation of the voice? We hear monks doing all sorts of ridiculous things, plaguing us with womanish falsettos, spavined bleating and tremolos. I myself have seen monks with open mouths, not so much singing, as doing ludicrous feats of breathing, so that they looked as if they were in their last agony or lost in rapture. Their lips are contracted, their eyes roll, their shoulders are shaken upwards and downwards, their fingers move and dance to every note. And this ridiculous behaviour is called religion for they think they are giving God a greater honour than if they sang without all this fuss.

Well, no sooner does a tree mature than someone wants to cut it down. To appreciate the

Example 11. AGNUS DEI (*St Andrews Music Book*, W1 f197)

CHAPTER V

BALLADS, BARDS AND MAKARS

1100–1500

That a tune should in the midst of the twentieth century be recovered for this whisper from the Middle Ages was as little to be expected as that we should hear 'the horns of Elfland faintly blowing.'[1]

Thus the great American scholar, Bertrand Harris Bronson, when he entered the text and tune of *King Orfeo* in his collection of the *Child Ballads*. His wonderment is all the more appealing and meaningful, given that his life's work had been spent on recovering ballad tunes from books and oral tradition, so he should have been used to this sort of thing. The recovery of such tunes in Scotland is made especially significant because between the mid-thirteenth century and the early sixteenth century there does not survive one single Scottish music manuscript, unless it be a few scraps and trimmings cut up in the sixteenth century and used for binding other books. Cause, one might think, for despair and resulting in a treatment here that is unavoidably fragmentary. But what we can resurrect from later manuscripts and from the oral tradition is of outstanding interest – and with the echoes of the Caprington horn we can even hear the horns of Elfland themselves.

The story of Orpheus is both old and international – Greeks, Manchurians, Polynesians, American Indians and Celts all have versions. Like the earliest Greek versions, the Celtic one allows Orpheus to return safely with his wife, but he plays a harp, not a lyre; and because the other world of the Celts is not a place of darkness and death, shadows and sorrows but a place of joy, life and youth, the nature of the loss and the rescue is different. It is an abduction, not a death, and the return of Orpheus's wife is not a favour but a right. An early Scottish version of the story

has recently been discovered[2] but it is in our oral tradition only that the tune has survived, the words for which were first collected in Unst in Shetland in 1880 and the tune, again in Unst, from John Stickle in 1947. In his version the music is played on the pipes, and the 'notes of joy' and the 'notes of noy' which Orpheus plays, recall the ancient Celtic division of music into three types: joyous, noyous – which means unhappy – and sleep music. The Elphin King asks Orpheus what is the price of his playing. It is of course the return of his lady so that he will be 'king over all his own' as the Elphin King puts it.

This is an hypnotic pentatonic tune of simplicity and power. It uses, as a central feature, an octave leap which gives it a sense of command; as though it encompassed a wide expanse of emotional experience, which is indeed what it does. The story expresses every kind of feeling from loneliness and desperation to pride and joy, and this tune, over and over, is able to support all that variety. The two short and perfectly balanced phrases could be played on bagpipes, altering one note only, but its essential function and character is vocal. The strange lines of the refrain are Scandinavian.

And first he played da notes o noy,
Scowan urla grun
An dan he played da notes o joy.
Whar giorten han grun oarlac.

Norn was spoken on mainland Scotland right into the eighteenth century, and it is thought that the mediaeval ballads were transmitted to northern Scandinavia via Scotland. If so, this ballad repays the debt. Translated, the refrain reads: 'The wood is green early where the stag goes yearly'. It points to the vigilance of the stag as an example for Orpheus and probably echoes the belief that spring only returns with the annual release of Euridice from Hades, though in this Celtic/Nordic version she is wholly freed.

The twelfth century to the fourteenth century was the age of troubadours from the south of

Example 1. KING ORFEO (from the singing of John Stickle)

And first he played da notes o - noy, Scow - an ur - la grun An
dan he played da notes o joy Whar gior - ten han grun or - lac.

France, *trouvères* from the north of France, and minstrels and *jongleurs*, who performed the music of these aristocratic classes, extending the repertoire in dance and song, including the *chansons de geste* – stories told in song. In

Scotland it is represented largely by ballads and romances which have survived in the tradition rather than on vellum. Where traditional texts can be compared with early manuscript evidence, it is clear that much has been preserved, and in many instances we can accept this of the tunes. But what is most valuable as regards the tradition is the fact that the method of survival is oral. This means that not only may words and tunes have survived in their essentials, but the manner of performance may also be recorded through centuries of human memory. The flexibility of rhythm, the clarity of enunciation, the unaffected directness, the superb focusing of the voice by the use of a more nasal tone (a vocal timbre which can be sustained over long periods of singing), the unwavering control of pitch and intonation: all these contribute to the effectiveness of the ballads in performance and, until recently, have been at odds with the way in which mediaeval

Plate 17. DUNCAN WILLIAMSON, 1985

song has been performed by classically trained singers. At the heart of that tradition is language.

The language we know as Scots only began to emerge as a widely used one in the twelfth century, and the records of it in verse only in the thirteenth century. Among the oldest surviving Scots poems is one by Thomas of Ercildoune (1219–99) and it may well have been sung. If so, we have no music for it, but his marvellous tale – *Thomas the Rhymer* – has survived in the tradition as a living thing in which both music and words have been reworked over seven hundred years without losing their essential truthfulness to their originals. So, at any rate, the faithfulness of the words to the period would indicate. As for the music, the singing of Duncan Williamson and the tune he has inherited and modelled to his needs, suit the words so well that they seem made for each other. Duncan Williamson is one of the travelling folk, and their respect for their traditions is such that any modelling he has undertaken has probably been done in the same way it would have been in the thirteenth century when this material first drew breath.[3]

True Thomas, or *Thomas the Rhymer* deals with the other world – a world we encountered in the lullabies which were associated with charms against abduction by fairies. Thomas of Ercildoune was known as True Thomas because of his powers of prophecy which are referred to by his contemporary, Barbour, and which he acquired in Elphinland having been taken there by the Queen of the Fairies.

Example 2. THOMAS THE RHYMER (from the singing of Duncan Williamson)

Of the many versions of the words, Duncan Williamson's (see Plate 17) is one of the finest, preserving the deep symbolism rooted in Celtic mythology. The tune also contains, within its own structure, a sense of the marvellous. It is largely confined to the interval of a minor third, but the middle section is sung up an octave, and the tessitura (or average pitch) is high, which gives

an eerie effect so that the voice enters another world in each stanza.

Thomas of Ercildoune lived during the reign of Alexander III. It was a reign that started with disputes, but had great hopes – amongst which was the marriage of his daughter Margaret to Eric II of Norway in 1281. This was the occasion for a more formal song than that of *True Thomas* – more formal partly because *Ex Te Lux Oritur* is in Latin, partly because it is a hymn as well as a *trouvère* song, but chiefly because it is highly organised, repeating each musical phrase in the manner of the sequence (see Chapter III) but with recurring musical phrases throughout. In church it would have been sung by priests, perhaps accompanied by an organ, in the simple and eloquent style of plainsong. But it can also be sung in a regular metre, interpreting the plain-song notation according to the proportional values that had been slowly developing, and these same values give the hymn the character of a *trouvère* song, perhaps accompanied by clarsach. Into what formal category, if any, *Ex Te Lux Oritur* can be fitted has yet to be established. This is its first publication in full.[4]

The word 'trouvère' derives from the idea of something found rather than composed, but that is more a reflection of the romance of the period than the reality of this composition which is carefully thought out. The central section is distinguished by a higher register which matches the description of the enthronement of Eric and Margaret, and the final notes of the phrases give it a tonal shape. At first it alternates between F and G (which, harmonised on the clarsach, would produce the 'double-tonic' effect). The central section phrases all end on A and G, except for the highest pitched section in which there is also a shift of tonality to C. The piece ends with its own opening phrase. This formal control has not inhibited the melodic invention. The tune is one of the loveliest of the mediaeval repertoire, unfolding itself over beautifully shaped sections and with a romance, a gentleness and a generosity of character which suits the eloquent words. Out of the loss of Margaret to Norway, *Ex Te Lux Oritur* makes a gift both spiritual and carnal. It epito-mises all the best ideals of the Middle Ages and we should be proud of it.

Although all the music referred to here is vocal, instruments were regularly involved in its

Example 3. Ex Te Lux Oritur

Wedding Song for Princess Margaret of Scotland
and King Eric II of Norway
(1281)

11. Re — gi — na re — si — — det In re — gni so — li — — o
12. In cul — tu pre — si — — det Di — gna fa — sti — gi — — o

In — jun — cta pos — si — — det Co — ro — nam re — gi — — o.
Sit qui sic pro — vi — — det Laus De — i fi — li — — o.

13. O quam lau — — da — bi — lis Hec re — gis so — ci — a
14. Cun — ctis dat hu — mi — lis Pol — let fa — cun — di — a

Mi — tis af — fa — — bi — lis Ple — na pru — den — ci — a.
Ve — nu — stat no — bi — lis Quam con — ti — nen — ci — a.

15. Vi — ro sit ut fu — — it Ra — chel a — ma — bi — lis
16. Ut Ly — — a ge — nu — it Sit pro — le fer — ti — lis

1)

Ut re — gi pla — cu — — it E — ster pla — ca — bi — lis.
De — gat ut de — gu — — it Su — san — na sta — bi — lis.

17. Ma — nen — tes ju — gi — — ter De — i ser — vi — ci — o
18. Ut vi — te la — bi — — lis De — cur — so sta — di — o

Se — ne — scant ta — li — — ter Fe — li — ci se — ni — o.
Sem — per du — — ra — bi — — lis Sint di — gni bra — vi — o.

19. Ex te pro — gre — di — tur O dul — cis Sco — ci — a

Qua la — te spar — gi — tur Lau — dis ma — te — — ri — a.

1) *Perhaps best changed to correspond with verses 17 and 18*

Ex te lux oritur is preserved in Uppsala University Library, MS Upsalensis C 233. The original notation conveys no information about the melody's rhythmic values, and the transcription is designed to preserve the rhythmic flexibility that implies. Dotted barlines precede suggested articulating accents. They may occur at regular time intervals or be performed 'rubato'. Within this metrical framework individual notes may assume a variety of durations without altering the basic shape of the melody. Simple regular rhythms, like those suggested above the staves, are appropriate if the mood is to be light and dance-like, more sophisticated ones if contemplative. The short stem attached to some notes represents an ornament called a 'plica' (literally 'folded' note). It should probably be interpreted as a gliding towards the note following, where applicable on the second vowel of a diphthong or on an end-consonant.

performance. Thomas of Ercildoune himself refers to a number of musical instruments including the harp:

Harpe and fethill both thay fande,
Getterne and als so the sawtrye;
Lute, and rybybe, bothe gangande,
And all manere of mynstralsye.

The fiddle of those days was a cruder ancestor of what we play now, but it was played with the bow, which latter probably came to Europe from the Middle East following the Crusades. The cittern was a sort of guitar, the psaltery rather like a dulcimer, but plucked, whereas the rebec was bowed, though rybybe may refer to the trump or jew's harp. These were indoor instruments mostly, but the outdoors had its music too – trumpets, drums, horns. Indoors or outdoors, these instruments were widespread throughout Europe; but what consolation to a king could be his attendant trumpeters and minstrels or his harper Elyas when their trip to London in 1278 was only to pay a doubtful homage to the English king? And though the marriage of Margaret and Eric was blessed with a child – another Margaret – her mother died bringing her into the world. Then Alexander lost his wife and when, in 1285, he married again, their only child was stillborn. Indeed, the marriage ceremony itself was ominous.

The music does not survive for the dance of death, but that is probably what was performed by an unexpected troupe of players at the festivities in Melrose, the skeletal figure of death drawing partners out of the company to dance with him, while the official musicians, of whom there were many, fell into horrified silence. The culmination of all these tragedies was ironic indeed. Eager to produce a male heir by his new wife, Yolande, Alexander raced ahead of his escort on a wild night at Kinghorn and fell to his death when his horse stumbled.

Quhen Alexander our kynge was dede,
That Scotland lede in lauche and le,
Away was sons of alle and brede,
Of wyne and wax, of gamyn and gle.
Our golde was changit in to lede.
Crist, borne in virgynyte,
Soccoure Scotlande, and ramede,
That is stade in perplexite.

The baby Margaret, the Maid of Norway, whose birth killed her mother, herself died aged seven. There is a famous ballad often thought to refer to her drowning on her journey back to assume, precariously, the throne of Scotland. But she died of sea-sickness and the ballad probably refers to the drowning of Bernard de Mowat and the Abbot of Balmerino on their return from Norway. It is called *Sir Patrick Spens*, after the captain of the ship, and two tunes survive that are traditionally associated with it, both first published in 1818.[5] Of these the one which was later learnt by Ewan MacColl from his father seems to fulfil all the expectations one might reasonably have, for it to be the original air.

On stylistic grounds it would be hard to criticise it. The tune divides itself into two sections, the first high, the second low with a prominent octave leap – a structure similar to that of *King Orfeo*, as is the tonal relationship of the two phrases. *King Orfeo* is ambiguous. If it has a tonal centre, is it C or G? *Sir Patrick Spens* is ambiguous – does it centre on D or A? The ambiguity serves to impel the music forwards through many repetitions. A sense of completion is provided only by the story.

Example 4. SIR PATRICK SPENS (from the singing of Ewan MacColl)

The loss of the Maid of Norway left Scotland open to Edward I's claims, and in 1303–4 when he was wintering in Scotland, we read of a number of Scottish musicians in his employ – amongst them John of Kinghorn, *'fistulari regis'*. This could mean he played the shawm, the recorder or the bagpipes. Nigel Beymer, Andrew of Clydesdale and Gilbert Bride all played trumpets for him, and he restored Elyas the Harper's lands to him in 1296. Harpers were held in esteem and were regularly given lands. The Galbraith family in Galloway and the MacO'Sennag family in Kintyre are early examples.[6]

Barbour, in his epic poem on Robert the Bruce, gives a splendid picture of the king using his horn to gather his men in a wooded glen near Carrick.

The king then blew his horne in hy,
And gart the men that wer him by,
Hald them still and all priwe,
And syne agane his horne blew he.
James of Douglas herd him blaw,
And at last, assone, gan knaw,
And said, 'sothly, yon is the king,
I knaw lang quhill his blawing.'
The thrid tym, thar withall, he blew,
And then Schir Robert Boid it knew,
And said, 'Yone is the king but dreid,
Ga we furth till him, bettir speid.

Not long after that, Robert the Bruce was able to meet his enemy full face to determine the survival of Scotland as an independent state. Horns almost certainly played an important role at the Battle of Bannockburn. The Bruce presented an ivory horn to the Burnetts after the battle (see Plate IX) and both the French historian – Froissart – and the Scottish poet/historian – John Barbour – show that the Scots army regularly used large numbers of horns. Barbour describes their use in 1327 to cover a strategic retreat in the middle of the night:

For we to morne her, all the day
Sall mak als mery as we may:
And mak ws boune agayn the nycht;
And then ger mak our fyris lycht;
And blaw our hornys, and mak far,
As all the warld our awyne war,
Quhill that the nycht weill fallin be.
The Scottis folk, that liand war
In till the park, maid fest and far;
And blew hornys, and fyris maid . . .

Froissart (in his late fourteenth-century *Chronicle*) confirms this description both for this ruse and later at the Battle of Otterburn: '. . . The Scots have a custom, when assembled in arms, for those who are on foot to be well dressed, each having a large horn slung round his neck, in the manner of hunters, and when they blow all together, the horns being of different sizes, the noise is so great it may be heard four miles off, to the great dismay of their enemies . . .'

We have seen that one such horn – the *duthach mor* – still survives on the island of Skye. We may imagine, then, an English sentry at his outpost, hearing, from where the Scots were camped, the uncanny sound of hundreds of horns at different pitches wailing and resonating across the hillside in the night.

There is a tradition that *Hey Tutti Tatti*, the tune Robert Burns made famous as *Scots Wha Hae Wi' Wallace Bled*, was heard at Bannockburn. It is highly likely. We know from French records that the Scottish archers brought this tune to France and that it was heard when Joan of Arc entered Orleans and probably also Rheims for the coronation of the French king whose body-guard was Scottish. That was only a century after Bannockburn, and the tune is still played in France.[7] A mere eleven years after Bannockburn, Robert the Bruce married his four-year-old son David to the seven-year-old Joan of Towers – sister of King Edward. Neither monarch attended and the historian Caxton writes:

At that time the Englishmen were clothed all in cotes and hodes, peynted with lettres and with flours, full semely, with long beardes; and therefor the Scottes made a bile, that was fastened upon the chirch dores of Seinte Petre, toward Stangate in the City of York, and thus said the Scripture in despite of Englishmen:

Long berdes hertheles,
Peynted hodes wytles,
Gay cote graceles,
Makes England thriftyles.

Which ryme, as saieth Guydo, was made by the Scottes princypally for the deformyte of clothying that at those days was used by Englishmenne.

The likelihood is that these words were also sung – and sung to the tune traditionally associated with the victory at Bannockburn – as part of a satirical entertainment, later to be known as a jig, but not necessarily associated with the dance of that name.

Example 5. HEY TUTTI TATTI (Traditional)

That such a mocking jig was sung and danced after Bannockburn is also known:[8]

Maydens of Englande, sore may ye morne,
For your lemmans ye have lost at Bannockysborne,
With heve alowe.
What! weneth the King of England
So soon to have wone Scotlande?
Wyth rumbelowe.

This songe was, after many daies, song in daunces in the carols of the maidens and mynstrelles of Scotland, to the reproofe and disdayne of Englyshemen, with dyvers others, whych I overpasse.

Scots Wha' Hae Wi' Wallace Bled might have been one of those 'dyvers others'.

The Gowans are Gay is a Scottish example of a kindlier popular song, a delightful conversation piece, redolent of spring. It was first written down in 1662 and the text is mostly in the language of that time. But the tune could be as old as you please, and the character of the text and tune together is surely mediaeval. So I have no qualms about placing this song any time from the late thirteenth century onwards. It tells of a mysterious encounter in a magical garden, of longing and unattainable love. The song also shows that aristocrats were not the only ones with ideals. It is the lady's maid who goes out to gather dew on May morning for her lady to wash her face in: but the maid herself is not for easy gathering and she leaves her lover with dreams only. The tune consists of nothing but thirds and is so simple it ought to be beneath comment. But once in one's head, it will never leave it, and its innocence and joy make it welcome there. Gowans are daisies and 'my jo' means 'my sweetheart'.

Example 6. THE GOWANS ARE GAY (*Forbes Partbook*)

Sometimes the dreams became realities, at least for a spell. James I (*b.* 1394, *r.* 1406–1437) (see Plate XIII) had been held captive in England for eighteen years of his youth, but he wrote his great poem – *The King's Quair* – after his marriage and coronation,[9] recalling his captivity and his first sight of the beautiful woman he had made his queen. James was a composer as well as a poet, and in *The King's Quair* he displays subtle control, delicate imagery and deep symbolism with a deceptive lightness of touch which, if duplicated in music, would have made him a composer of the utmost importance. He was said to be expert on harp, psaltery, organ, shawm, recorder, bagpipe, trumpet and drum. He touched the harp like Orpheus and was 'richt crafty in playing baith of lute and harp'.[10] But nothing of this remains, unless obscurely echoed in the works of Gesualdo, as Tassoni (a reliable witness)

reports: '. . . we can relate of James, King of Scots, that not only did he compose sacred vocal music, but discovered on his own a new kind of music, plaintive and sad, different from all others. In this he was imitated by don Carlo Gesualdo, Prince of Venosa.'[11]

James was a contemporary of the great and influential English composer, John Dunstable; and it may be worth some scholar's while to search the manuscripts for evidence of the Scottish king's compositions which were still considered seminal by one of the leading Italian poets nearly two centuries later. Meanwhile we shall have to content ourselves with his description of the beauty of birdsong:

And on the small green twistis sate
The little sweet nightingale, and sung
So loud and clear, the hympnis consecrate
of lufis use, now soft now loud among,
That all the gardens and the wallis rung
Right of their song, and on the copill next
Of their sweet harmony, and lo the text.

Worship ye that lovers bene this May,
For of your bliss the kalenid are begun,
And sing with us, away winter, away,
Come summer, come, the sweet season and sun:
Awake for shame! that have your hevynis won,
And amorously lift up your hedis all,
Thank love that list you to his mercy call.

It is worth quoting also from a version of the Orpheus story from later in the same century, as James I was regarded as a latter-day Orpheus. It is by that greatest of Scottish poets, Robert Henrysson. Henrysson refers to styles of music quite different from those of a ballad tune and, while basing his text on the theories of proportion which related music to the orbits of the planets, disarmingly confesses that he couldn't sing a note himself.

In his passage amang the planeitis all,
he hard a hevinly melody and sound,
passing all instrumentis musicall,
causit be rollyn of the speiris round;
Quhilk armony of all this mappamound,
Quhilk moving seiss unyt perpetuall,
Quhilk of this warld pluto, the saule can call.

Thair leirt he tonis proportionat,
as duplare, triplare, and emetricus,
enolius, and eik the quadruplait,
Epoddeus rycht hard and curious;
off all thir sex, sueit and delicius,
rycht consonant fyfe hevinly symphonyss
componyt ar, as clerkis can devyse.

Plate 18. DEDICATORY STONE FOR THE HOUSE FOR GLASGOW CATHEDRAL'S VICARS CHORAL, FIFTEENTH CENTURY

ffirst diatesserone, full sweit, I wiss
And dyapasone, semple and dowplait,
And dyapenty, componyt with the dyss;
Thir makis fyve of thre multiplicat:
this mirry musik and mellefluat,
Compleit and full of nummeris od and evin,
Is causit be the moving of the hevin.

James I 'brocht oute of Ingland and Flanderis ingenious men of sindry craftis to instruct his pepill', and musicians will have been among the crafts. Of their influence nothing survives from his reign, which ended after only thirteen years with his murder. James II had a Flemish wife, Marie of Gueldres, who encouraged music and founded the collegiate church of Trinity College, Edinburgh. Collegiate churches were independently financed and Trinity College had a choir of ten. The superb panels, commissioned from Hugo van der Goes for the new building, depict an angel playing an organ gifted to the collegiate church by Sir Edward Bonkill, first Provost of the College. He kneels in the foreground, his prayer conveyed by the heavenly art of music and the two angels, one behind the organ operating the bellows, the other at the keyboard (see Plate XII).

There was of course the basic court establishment of permanent musicians. In the Household Accounts for James III in 1474, the king's 'litill lutare, the page' was one. John Broune was another, and it is clear that the Flemish connection was kept going. 'Item, gevin at the kingis command the third of September to John Broun, lutare, at his passage our sey to lere his craft — five pounds.'

The musicians were not forgotten while they were away on their studies: '. . . a barrell of salmond that was send to a lutare to Bruges, at the kingis command.' They were also sent money to buy instruments and for an increase in travel expenses: 'to foure scolaris menstralis, be

the kingis command, to by them instrumentis in Flandris, eight pounds gret, answerand in Scottis money to twenty-one pounds, and help thair expensis and fraucht, fifty-six shillings; and therefter, becaus thai plenyeit thai gat our litill expens and fraucht, deliverit uther fifty-six . . . total thirty-six pounds twelve shillings.'

James III's interest in music was such that 'He delightit mair in singing and in playing upon instrumentis than he did in defense of the Bourderis and in the ministration of justice.'

His chief musical import was an Englishman, William Rogers, who is believed to have had a major effect on the quality of Scottish music. If so, it was not appreciated at the time for he was hanged from Lauder brig in the famous 'bell-the-cat' episode, which got rid of James's leading favourites. They were all dolled up in the highest fashion at the time, for though James fined the populace if they wore expensive imported silk, he made the fines payable to the heralds and minstrels, who were always exempted from such restrictions as they played in uniform. The favour shown to musicians continued with James IV who paid substantial fines for his musicians when they broke the law, the trumpeters being spared by him a payment of ten pounds in the Justice ayre, in the town of Ayr in 1489.

That singers at least were not overpaid is shown by the fact that Glasgow Cathedral had to double the salaries of some vicars choral in 1480. Perhaps that was the price of maintaining the standards set by the previous Bishop Andrew who had built a special house for them with a stone inset proudly announcing: 'These buildings Bishop Andrew caused to be erected for the priests who serve the flourishing choir of Glasgow' (see Plate 18).

The treble parts were taken by boys, some of whom would be training to be priests, and it seems that the king was expected to support and encourage them for in 1506 James IV authorised 'To the childir of the queir of Glasgo, in spur-silvir, nine shillings.'

The monarch's musical needs for personal worship, which would also represent the Christian ideals of the Scottish monarchy to the court and nation as well as to ambassadors, were met by the Chapel Royal. The Chapel Royal was founded in Stirling by Alexander I in 1120 – not long after the Norman invasions. It was funded by tithes from the king's domains around Stirling – so often the focal point of Scotland in her wars of independence. Perhaps that is why in 1384 the Chapel doors required two thousand large nails with pointed heads for their reinforcement. It was merely a chaplain who was in charge in those days – receiving five pounds a year – raised later to seven pounds ten shillings. The buildings were upgraded from time to time and in 1412 the chapel was renovated. In the 1470s James III rebuilt it and decked it out, also establishing it as a music school, and James IV reorganised the Chapel Royal on a grander scale – one that might have seemed bound to last, as he was as popular as his father was despised. There were sixteen canons and six boy clerics all trained in song. There was a dean, a sub-dean, sacristour, chanter, thesaurer, a maister of the bairns, and the chancellor.[12]

By the end of the fifteenth century there were 'sang schools' from Kirkwall to Melrose, in cathedrals, monasteries, collegiate churches and parish churches. The Aberdeen and St Andrews sang schools were always strong and Dunkeld claimed they were the best in the land (see Chapter VII). Scotland now had universities in St Andrews, Glasgow and a new one in Aberdeen. They were well dispersed, while the English only had two, close to each other, but music does not survive from the Scottish universities, though they almost certainly will have commissioned pieces for solemn occasions. Likewise nothing of the music that might be associated with Rogers and his entourage is known. Only at the end of the fifteenth century is there manuscript material and substantial records of musicians at court and, occasionally, what they performed. For instance, we know that in 1497 *Greysteil* was sung for James IV by two fiddlers who must have had fine memories since it is nearly three thousand lines

long. They were given nine shillings for it. *Greysteil* is one of the great mediaeval epics, remarkable as a poem and all the more remarkable for the survival of the tune that it was sung to. When Andy Hunter performed it for the first time in centuries for BBC Radio 3, he had no idea how well it would sustain the text. The whole romance, if sung, will last perhaps two hours, and not much less if simply recited. It turned out that this declamatory tune, hypnotic, strange, and repeated over and over, acted superbly as a secure but flexible vehicle for a tale both out-landish and deeply symbolic.[13]

The tune only survives in a nineteenth-century transcription of Robert Gordon of Straloch's lute book of 1627 – now lost. But its wide range, primitive structure and ambiguous tonality suit the text so well that it is natural to assume they were made for each other, giving us a unique insight into the courtly performance of a late mediaeval metrical romance. The example includes the lute harmonies which may well reflect how the epic could have been accompanied on clarsach rather than fiddle, for the lute derived some of its repertoire from the travelling harpists. The second half of the tune is poised high in the voice on a declamatory note. It calls for good singing, but is commanding in effect, and the repeated phrase has a powerful insistence.

Example 7. GREYSTEIL (from *Gordon of Straloch's Lute Book*, 1627)

The harpists were of some standing in the community. They were certainly regularly at court, receiving payments for performing. On 2 January 1491, James IV authorised payment as follows: 'To Martyn MacBhreatnaich Clareschaw ten shillings and til ane oder ersche clareschaw five shillings'.

Martyn MacBhreatnaich came from Galloway and the other player, though described as 'ersche' would as likely be Scottish as Irish, for the term was used to cover Gaelic speakers generally. It was not uncommon for harpers to be blind: 'Item, to the blind harpair, be the Kingis command, seven shillings.'

But variations in payment are not explained. Was it for seniority, quality or quantity that in the same month in 1505 fourteen shillings was paid 'to the Countess of Craufurdis harpar be command'?

Performers were not always men. There is a record as early as 1398 of a harpist with the name 'Meg of Abernethy', so there were female clarsairs around from early days, and there are entries for female singers: 'Item, to tua wemen that sang to the king, eighteen shillings.' Five shillings more than two women received for singing in the king's chamber the year before (1505). James IV's records also show many payments to musicians from England, France and Italy, as well as to jugglers, dancers and others who will have used music.

There will also have been performers who were not paid in cash, but given employment instead. Such a troupe may be imitated in *The Pleugh Sang*, for this is a splendid, but not too complex part song for ploughmen to sing.

The troupe might enter the courtyard of a castle, dragging with them a plough hauled about by two men costumed as a decrepit old ox. They would then enact an ancient ritual as ploughmen, offering their services to the lord of the house — telling him his old ox is useless and recommending themselves by name, including False-lips Fergus, and by naming all the many parts of the plough to show their knowledge. Some of the names hark back to Pictish times, suggesting a very ancient origin for the words. One of the troupe could play the repeating bass part on a tenor shawm (a sort of fierce oboe), two others would sing the imitative upper parts. The whole thing is known to musicologists as a 'fricassee' — literally a stew, but it ends with a splendidly assertive 'amen', and is the sole musical relic of an old folk custom, once known throughout Europe.

In the evening there would be minstrels in the Minstrels' Gallery, of which several survive

(see Plate 19A and B). Other musicians would be squeezed in elsewhere, for during and after the evening meal there would have been much music and dancing. At the court the poets would be there too, wrangling with each other for fun in a satirical and earthy style known as a 'flyting'. Dunbar was particularly good at this and it was possibly from the Gaelic culture that this form of bardic rivalry was derived, for the flyting survived in Gaelic into the eighteenth century. But Dunbar makes sport of Highlanders and their music, referring particularly to the coronach (chorus) sung for the dead in part of his *Dance of the Seven Deadly Sins*, implying that the lament was a kind of hallmark of Gaelic culture.

Than cryd Mahoun for a heleand payane;
Syne ran a fynd to feche MakFadyane
Far northwest in a nuke:
be he the corronach had done showt,
In hell grit rowme thay tuke.
Thae tarmegantis, with tag and tatter,
Full lown in Ersche begowth to clatter
The Devill sa devit wes with thair yell,
He smourit thame with smuke.

Example 8. THE PLEUGH SANG (conclusion, from the *Wode partbooks*)

Plate 19A. MINSTRELS GALLERY, THE MAIN HALL, DOUNE

James IV, at whose court that will have been heard, was a native Gaelic speaker so Dunbar was taking a liberty, but the bardic orders in Scotland have usually been granted that liberty, satire having been a traditional part of the training of Gaelic poets whose position in society had been enshrined in the Celtic law for hundreds of years. *The Dance of the Seven Deadly Sins* would probably have been intoned or sung as well as danced to in a wild kind of morris dance.[14] Morris dancers with bells were common at court as this entry in the *Accounts* for 1507 shows. 'Item; to thirty dozen of bellis for dansaris delyverit to Thomas Boswell, four pounds, twelve shillings'.

We have tantalising glimpses from the poetry of the period of a wealth of popular song, as in *Peblis to the Play*:

> [He] cleikit up ane hie ruf sang,
> Thair fure ane man to the holt,
>
> He quhissilit and he pypit bayth,
> To mak hir blyth that meiting;
> My hony hart, how sayis the sang,
> Thair sall be mirth at our meeting,
>   Yit,
> Of Peblis to the Play.

Even more tantalising is the brilliant medley for three voices, *Trip and Go Hey*. Written down in the late sixteenth century, it preserves fragments of many songs all mixed up in a wonderful patter of words – lovers chasing in and out of the greenwood; moments of joy, moments of regret pacing out the dance with perfect timing and subtlety. It was probably performed by revellers, perhaps masked, who would draw the onlookers into the dance. Many of the scraps of song which appear in it are to do with love, the most extended one being the story of the seduction of a girl by a young friar. Although it has been suggested it was a Twelfth Night revel dating from the 1520s,[15] the atmosphere is redolent of spring; and the fact that so much of it obviously consists of quotations from popular songs suggests that it embedded a lot of material from the fifteenth century, and occasionally even from earlier centuries. *The Gowans are Gay*, though not quoted, is typical of the style. Sometimes all voices sing together, at other times there is a conversation in song. It is a treasure of a piece. A few extracts from the as yet unpublished text and music will have to suffice:

> *I saw three mariners sing row rumbelow*
> *Upon yon sea strand a.*
> *As they began their notes to tune*
> *The piper's drone was out of tune*
> *Sing jolly Robin, sing young Tobin*

Plate 19B. MINSTRELS GALLERY, THE RETAINERS' HALL, DOUNE

Example 9. TRIP AND GO, HEY (*Wode* and *Forbes Partbooks*)

Burnie boy. What will you my jo?
Where hast thou been?
On the green at the dancing.
What saw thou there?
Gay ladies fair.

Hey doun a doun a doun a hey
the ring of the rash of the gowan
In the cool of the night came my lady home a
Ever alas for every shame

The jolly young frier has raisit my wame
That ever I did it, ever I did it, did it, did it.
Alas for shame, betrayed am I
Uncourteously alone alone alone.

Trip and Go Hey provides this chapter with its *Envoi*. A farewell to the dance, to the day, and to the middle ages, a period in Scottish music thin in source material and yet, in the writings of the makars and what does survive musically, providing us with some of its most evocative memorials.

The dancing is done;
Sisters adew.
So hie we now home; sisters adew.
The heav'n is full of mirth and jo;
Adew, farewell, now will we go.

CHAPTER VI

GAELIC BARDS, BAGPIPES AND HARPS
1100–1600

The mediaeval French distinguished between troubadour, minstrel and *jongleur* and, in the Gaelic-speaking world, similar social and professional divisions at one time existed between 'fili', 'bard' and 'druth'. Cattle were the basic unit by which the many strata of Celtic society were valued, and unjust injury to a bard would cost less in milk cows than for a fili; but bards were given land and entitled to hospitality and protection, whereas the druth, like the *jongleur,* had little status as a popular performer. Nowadays we use 'bard' to cover both bard and fili, but it seems that the bards were the musicians, whereas the functions of the fili were much more than artistic. They were historians, genealogists and even prophets.[1] A fili might well be an aristocrat, as was St Columba, who defended their order. Their poetry developed an arcane syllabic style, with complex systems of rhyme, assonance, and alliteration, which has come in for ill-placed criticism in that the delivery of this poetry was musical. Since the music is either lost or has been substantially ignored, attention has focused largely on poetic technique, and the overall artistic effect in the context of its function has yet to be fairly assessed.

One of the earliest reliable accounts of the survival of the bardic orders into modern times comes from Martin Martin in the 1690s during his travels in the west of Scotland. It gives a picture of a decaying order, no longer understood, but still divided between Orator (fili) and Poet or Bard with their main functions retained and their remarkable method of composition and memorising related. Martin Martin spoke Gaelic and his report is valuable for, though he comments often, he does not appear to censor information.

The Orators, in their Language call'd *Is-Dane*, were in high esteem both in these Islands and the Continent; until within these forty Years, they sat always among the Nobles and Chiefs of Families in the *Streah* or Circle. Their Houses and little Villages were Sanctuaries, as well as Churches, and they took place before Doctors of Physick. The Orators, after the *Druids* were extinct, were brought in to preserve the Genealogy of Families, and to repeat the same at every Succession of a Chief; and upon the occasion of Marriages and Births, they made *Epithalamiums* and *Panegyricks*, which the Poet or Bard pronounc'd. The Orators by the force of their Eloquence had a powerful Ascendant over the greatest Men in their time; for if any Orator did but ask the Habit, Arms, Horse, or any other thing belonging to the greatest Man in these Islands, it was readily granted them, sometimes out of respect, and sometimes for fear of being exclaim'd against by a Satire, which in those days was reckon'd a great dishonour: but these Gentlemen becoming insolent, lost ever since both the Profit and Esteem which was formerly due to their Character; for neither their Panegyricks nor Satires are regarded to what they have been, and they are now allow'd but a small Salary. I must not omit to relate their way of Study, which is very singular: They shut their Doors and Windows for a day's time, and lie on their backs, with a Stone upon their Belly, and Plads about their Heads, and their Eyes being cover'd, they pump their Brains for Rhetorical Encomium or Panegyrick; and indeed they furnish such a Stile from this dark Cell, as is understood by very few: and if they purchase a couple of Horses as the Reward of their Meditation, they think they have done a great matter. The Poet, or Bard, had a Title to the Bridegroom's upper Garb, that is, the Plad and Bonnet; but now he is satisfy'd with what the Bridegroom pleases to give him on such occasions.[2]

Something of the style of the fili, as rendered by the bards, still exists in the Gaelic tradition, virtually exclusively in the west of Scotland. There are only two examples in the oral tradition in Ireland – an instance of the indebtedness of Ireland to Scotland for the survival of the common cultural legacy. Many of the great Gaelic manuscripts were written in the twelfth to sixteenth centuries and contain poems and tales of pre-Christian heroes and heroines and, though they have undergone modification, the oral versions of their texts, which Scottish tradition has preserved, are remarkably true to them in quality, spirit and even on occasions in fine detail.[3]

When it comes to their sung performance, however, things are less straightforward; and since these works did not really exist until performed and their performance was a musical one, the music becomes crucial. Their survival, possibly from much earlier than the twelfth century when the texts were first written down, is one of the most remarkable examples of the strength of the oral tradition in Europe. It has, therefore, special musical significance, and deserves fairly detailed treatment, though some of this has been placed in the chapter notes.

The whole question has been confused by references to the influence of Latin plainsong on Gaelic heroic chant, for which no musical examples have been produced. The only obvious connection is that of intoning on one note and since this is a fundamental technique throughout the world, whether Christian, Buddhist or Aboriginal, there is no need to assume the Christian religion introduced it. It is just as likely that Christian chant grew out of earlier singing practices, and commentators from Augustine on seem to acknowledge this.[4] We have seen (Chapter II) that the Fianna were credited by the monkish historians with a wide variety of vocal techniques. Chant is one of these and it could as easily be the source for Gaelic vocal styles as Latin plainchant. To what extent Latin metre influenced Gaelic poetry is also much debated. Early Gaelic poems are mostly syllabic and are stated to be without metrical stress. But surviving performance styles, including those of the waulking songs which preserve many ancient features, find no difficulty in rendering texts which are analysed as unstressed with as heavy a stress as can be imagined.[5] Any oratorical presentation tends to use stress, as politicians do with even the crassest of prose, and it is a natural instinct to perform syllabic verse with a regular rhythmic stress. On the other hand, Patrick MacDonald, writing in the late eighteenth century has this to say: '. . . in a few of the slow plaintive tunes . . . sung by the natives, in a wild, artless, and irregular manner, . . . they themselves, while singing them, seem to have little or no impression of measure.'[6] This, however, may not refer to the ancient Ossianic ballads which are usually described as being sung rather quickly.[7]

Rhyme has also been said to be imported from continental Latin. But rhyme, along with assonance and alliteration, is handled in the Gaelic-speaking world from an early stage with such distinctive abandon and virtuosity, that it is hard to believe that it arose out of imported Latin poetry, without the stimulus of existing practices in the native Gaelic of the poets.[8]

What this means for the music is that we should not reject performances with a regular metre, and nor should we impose them. Just as with plainchant some are all for freedom, others have a more metrical approach. Some divide the material into two classes of heroic ballad – the 'duan' which is more chant-like and may relate to the *chanson de geste*, and the 'laoidh' (English 'lay') which is more song-like. Others say there is no such division.[9] Given that two forms of singing a laoidh survive in the tradition, the distinction may still prove to be useful. Examples are given here of various approaches.

The first is from the earliest published notation of a laoidh, made by Patrick MacDonald in 1784.[10] The text comes from the MacNicol collection of 1755[11] and is simply placed underneath without any attempt to reconcile the stress of the verse with the stress of the music as Patrick MacDonald has notated it. The story relates the defeat of Magnus Barelegs in the late eleventh century or early twelfth century. Magnus was King of Norway and had annexed the Western Isles, even Iona, and amongst his galley-slaves was St Magnus of Orkney. In the laoidh, King Magnus's defeat is attributed to the Fianna and is told as though by Ossian to Patrick. Historically, therefore, it links the defence of Gaeldom from pseudo-historical to early Christian, to Viking times; and no doubt was sung with similar feelings on subsequent occasions, including after the 1745 Rising when the Gaelic world seemed doomed, and new efforts to preserve its culture were made.

Example 1. MANUS (Patrick MacDonald, 1784)

(Psalm-singing cleric, I think you mad not to listen to a tale of the Fenians of whom you know nothing)

This tune is in two balanced parts, each rising and falling within the range of a fifth, but a tone apart – the double-tonic effect. Whatever distortions MacDonald's rhythmic notation may have introduced, each line of poetry is matched by a line of music and the number of notes is almost identical with the number of syllables. With a little adjustment the words and the tune fit readily together, remembering that Patrick MacDonald suffers from the same difficulty as all transcribers – that he has not space to show the variants for every verse, so has given an average.

The same laoidh was recorded two hundred years later from Donald Sinclair.[12] The text is similar and, after the first verse, the tune shows similarities also, though its rise and fall is concentrated into one dramatic leap of a seventh. The double-tonic contrast is retained with a move to the lower pitch in the middle. Between the two versions there is a clear identity of character and a partial one of substance. The differences may reflect varying performing styles which could themselves be as old as the subject-matter. We have no reason to suppose that the bards of the past were any less idiosyncratic or geographically distinct than those of today, when it comes to performance.

Example 2. LAOIDH MHANUIS (School of Scottish Studies, SA 1968/26 B9)

(Virtuous cleric, if you were on the shore at the battle by the waterfall, you would think well of the Fenians.)

The chief champion of the unmetred approach of singing this repertoire is William Matheson, particularly in his performance of *Laoidh Fraoch*. Fraoch loved and was loved by the daughter of Queen Maeve and King Aillil. They disapproved of the match and Maeve tried to get rid of Fraoch by sending him to fetch rowan berries across a loch in which there was a monster. When he succeeded, she claimed she needed a whole branch, and on this second attempt Fraoch was caught. Maeve's daughter threw him a sword with which he killed the beast, but in most versions Fraoch dies. In others, Maeve and Aillil regret their cruelty, the wounded Fraoch is led by horn players into Aillil's fort – the occasion when thirty of Aillil's finest men die of rapture – and Fraoch is put in a bath of raw pig and calf flesh and his wounds are cured. He recovers to

take part in the great cattle raid of Cooley. (Echoes there of the bronze age horns and of the bull cult that was at least two thousand years old [see Chapter I].)

The tune for *Laoidh Fraoch* has many of the characteristics of the traditional tunes for the oldest ballads in Scots – the wide range, including the characteristic octave leap; the basically pentatonic character of the scale; the suitability of the tune for declamation and repetition.[13]

Example 3. LAOIDH FRAOCH (from the singing of William Matheson)

(A sore sickness fell on Maighre's daughter of the generous drinking horns; that was when she sent for Fraoch and he asked what was her wish.)

By contrast, here is a reconstruction of *Deirdre's Farewell to Scotland*. The text is syllabic and mediaeval in origin. The tune was collected by Edward Bunting from the ninety-year-old harper Hempson, at the end of the eighteenth century. It was traditionally associated with this text and came from both Northern Ireland and the Highlands. It was played on the wire-strung harp with the finger-nails, with a regular pulse, and Bunting noted down the style of accompaniment which is a drone with the tune shadowed

Example 4. DEIRDRE'S FAREWELL (music from *Bunting 1840*, text from *Glen Massan Manuscript*, fifteenth century)

in parallel thirds and sixths.[14] We have seen how parallel thirds were a British and Scandinavian preference from early mediaeval times. The tune is very simple and uses only six notes of the scale, so we have no good reason to object to this beautiful music on grounds of authenticity.

This is just a fragment of the poem,[15] which tells movingly of Deirdre's sorrow at leaving Glen Etive and Glen Massan and Glendaruel (in south-west Scotland) where she had spent a happy exile with her lover Naisi, and from which they returned to their tragic betrayal and death.

Another of the great tales of love and betrayal is that of Dhiarmad and Grainne. It ends with the death of Dhiarmad, poisoned by the bristles of a magical wild boar he has killed. His jealous rival, Fionn, three times lets slip from his cupped hands the spring water which would save Dhiarmad's life. This version of *Laoidh Dhiarmad* was collected on the island of Skye in 1870 by Francis Tolmie and is marked to be sung 'Rather slow' and can be sung with a regular pulse.[16] Like *Deirdre's Farewell*, it makes brief but telling escapes from a basic reciting note; the first half with a dramatic drop of a seventh, the second half breaking away from the pentatonic scale by introducing an extra note (A) which adds greatly to the expressive effect.

Example 5. LAOIDH DHIARMAD (from the singing of Margaret MacLeod, 1870)

(Last night the hill-top was green, today it is red with the blood of Diarmad;
Had it not been what Fionn had sought, it would have been grievous to the Fianna.)

These tunes may seem simple, but they have not lasted perhaps a thousand years in a community never short of great tunes, without good reason. They serve the same functions as the ballad tunes for the mediaeval literature in Scots with the same quality and distinction. Like water from a good spring, they deserve to be treasured. The simplest things are the hardest to make perfect and we are luckier than we know in having such pure melodic sources that can reflect the images of our remotest past with clarity, and still retain their own flavour.

The Battle of Harlaw (1411) is one of the earliest events in Gaelic history to which there are clear musical references. A 'brosnachadh' or incitement to battle was composed by Lachlann Mor MacMhuirich before the battle. Lachlann Mor was one of a long line of bards in his family, for bardic skills were passed from father to son. The MacMhuirichs were descended from Muireadhach O'Dalaigh, a bard and teacher who fled Ireland in 1213 after killing a tax-collector with an axe.[17] His descendant's poem retains the characteristics of Columba's *Altus Prosator* for it is syllabic, abecedarian (see Chapter II) and at its conclusion returns to its opening. It is metrical as well as syllabic and was probably sung to a harp accompaniment, for harps were brought to battle.[18]

It is just possible that music for this remarkable poem survives in an English manuscript of 1624 or 1625, largely devoted to music for masques.[19] In it there is a tune called *The Batell of Harloe*. It was an epic battle which might have been re-enacted with music for James VI and I, just as Shakespeare dramatised Macbeth in his honour. The tune has been written down by somebody unfamiliar with the style of performance from which I assume it has been taken. Bar-lines were mainly used as a guide to the eye at this period, and the bar-lines in the manuscript so completely negate the musical sense, that rearranging them is essential. What emerges is a 6/8 March with a single variation in bagpipe style. That this is a Highland, even Norse-influenced tune, is clear from the repeated phrases, wide intervals and contrasting tonalities, with the second and fourth phrases a tone apart. We shall see in a later chapter that bagpipe music is often related to Gaelic song, and since this tune does not fit the traditional ballad in Scots (see below) it seems natural to try it with the brosnachadh composed for the same battle. This is pure speculation, but it fits the words well in both rhythm and character. It is forceful, repetitive, and demands just the right speed of performance to give the words urgency.[20]

The Battle of Harlaw established the limits of the ambitions of the Lords of the Isles. Though the Highlanders still regard it as a victory, the Lowland ballad claims their defeat on account of the death of Red Hector. The tune is closely related to one in the piping tradition, a

Example 6. HARLAW BROSNACHADH (original barring above the music, original note values are halved)

A Chlan-na Cuinn, cuimh-nich-ibh Cruas an am na h-ior ghail-e: Gu h-àirneach, gu h-arr-an-ta, Gu h-ath-lamh, gu h-all-an-ta, Gu beò-dha, gu barr-a-mhail, gu brìoghmhor, gu buan-fhear-gach, Gu cal-ma, gu cur-an-ta, Gu crò-dha gu cath-bhua-dhach

(Children of Conn, remember hardihood in time of battle: Be watchful, daring, be dextrous, winning renown, Be vigorous, pre-eminent, Be strong, nursing your wrath, Be stout, brave, Be valiant, triumphant . . .)

Lament for Red Hector of the Battles which recalls with power and dignity the death of one of the leading Highlanders at the Battle of Harlaw. Even Red Hector's opponents, the Irvines, honoured his memory. It is a primitive example of a kind nowadays known as piobaireachd, which consists of a long tune and then variations on it, but this has only one simple variation. Here are the two tunes set one above the other, showing clearly that they share the same pentatonic mode, basic shape, rhythm and character. The ballad, however, has a refrain that does not fit the pipe tune, which is not surprising as pipe tunes do not have refrains. We have no proof that this tune dates from 1411, but its close association with the words make it at least a possibility. The Lowland ballad has later Jacobite accretions, but has been shown to preserve the order of battle more accurately than other sources, with the Lowland armies divided to cover two passes from the mountains until they knew which one the Highlanders would emerge from. This suggests that it is rooted in direct experience of the battle itself.[21]

Example 7. BATTLE O' THE HARLAW (*Lady John Scott's manuscript*, c. 1830 [above] transposed up a tone) LAMENT FOR RED HECTOR OF THE BATTLES (Thomason, *Ceol Mor* 211 [below] with the abbreviations written out in full)

As I cam in by Gari-och's land An down by Neth-er-ha There was fif-ty thous-and hiel-and men A march-ing to Har-law. wi a drie arie dred-ie drum dree drie

It is just possible that the Highlanders were led into battle by the bagpipes in 1411, and that the tune has been borrowed from them for the ballad; but we should be cautious, as the early history of bagpipes in Scotland is bedevilled with inaccuracies. It may be that the Scots were long familiar with instruments with more than one thin drone, for three Pictish stones show sets of triple pipes (see Chapter II), but the air was not fed to them through a bag as Farmer imagined.[22] The earliest Gaelic reference I have found to bagpipes is in the fifteenth-century Irish manuscript of the *Second Battle of Moytura*, much of which is clearly a great deal older:

Come Daurdabla!
Come Coir-cethar-chuir!
Come summer, Come winter!
Mouths of harps and bags and pipes!

This seems obscure enough to satisfy most tastes! 'Daurdabla' is not satisfactorily glossed or translated, 'Coir-cethar-chuir' means 'four-angled-music'. The words are those of a charm used by a god to call his quadrangular lyre to come to him from its peg, which it obligingly did, killing nine men en route. Of the bags and pipes we hear no more, but the god – the Dagda – played 'the three things whereby cruit-players are distinguished, sleep-strain and smile-strain and wail-strain. He played wail-strain to them so that their tearful women wept. He played smile-strain to them so that their women and children laughed. He played sleep-strain to them, and the hosts fell asleep.'[23]

The three strains of music (see also Chapter V) we might nowadays interpret as lament, dance-tune and lullaby still have exactly the same powers (over men too) – at least for those of us who do not choose to stiffen our necks. The first two of these functions have been adopted also by the bagpipes.

Sadly, claims for the presence of bagpipes in Scotland before the fifteenth century do not hold water. The Gaelic word 'cuisle' means a flute or pipe and implies no reference to a bag. The word 'chorus' used by Giraldus and repeated by Brompton in the twelfth century probably refers to the cruit, not the bagpipe as Collinson suggests,[24] and the two poems with a mention of bagpipes (*Colkelbie Sow* and *Peblis to the Play*) are early sixteenth-century. A poem attributed to

Plate 20. ANGEL BAGPIPER AT ROSSLYN CHAPEL, FIFTEENTH CENTURY

one of the MacVurich bards describes the pipes scornfully as 'piob gleadhair' – rowdy – and goes on to say they are 'the two sweethearts of the black fiend – a noise fit to rouse the imps of hell' but this poem is much later than has been suggested.[25]

Pictures and carvings give little help. There are two carved stone bagpipers on Melrose Abbey, one of them a pig; but they are well after 1385 when Melrose was razed to the ground, and much of the subsequent work is regarded as having been done by imported masons.[26] There is an angel playing bagpipes carved in Rosslyn Chapel, and that is all we have to go on for the fifteenth century (see Plate 20).

The earliest reference to bagpipes in English is in Chaucer's *Prologue* (1386). In Scots it is in

Dunbar's *Testament of Mr Andrew Kennedy* printed in 1508:

I will na preistis for me sing
Dies illa, dies ire,
Na yit na bellis for me ring
Sicut semper solet fieri:
Bot a bag pipe to play a spryng,

By the sixteenth century they were well established as military instruments. There is an English reference to shrill Scots pipes at Flodden in the 'Percy Folio' (see Chapter VII), and a French officer, describing battles near Edinburgh in 1549, writes: 'the wild Scots incite themselves to battle by the sounds of their bagpipes!'[27]

The Scottish historian, George Buchanan, in a 1582 Preface for Monro's *Description of the Western Isles of Scotland*, writes of the Highlanders:

Instead of a trumpet, they use a bagpipe. They are exceedingly fond of music, and employ harps of a peculiar kind, some of which are strung with brass, and some with catgut. In playing they strike the wires either with a quill, or with their nails, suffered to grow long for the purpose; but their grand ambition is to adorn their harps with great quantities of silver and gems, those who are too poor to afford jewels substituting crystals in their stead. Their songs are not inelegant, and, in general, celebrate the praises of brave men; their bards seldom choosing any other subject. They speak the ancient Gaelic language a little altered.

Although *The Battel of Harloe* has been conjecturally married to a Gaelic text (see above), the variation which goes with it seems to be for bagpipes. The tune itself fits the pipes with little change and it would be natural for the brosnachadh tune to have been taken into the repertoire, especially as the power of the bagpipes (with the three drones possibly already in use) would suit an incitement to battle.[28] If this is so, then it is the earliest written evidence of bagpipe music.

Example 8. THE BATTEL OF HARLOE (BM 10444, 1624–5, transposed up a tone, note values halved)

We will return to the bagpipe in later chapters, but it is time to look at the clarsach. What kind of instrument was it and how did the clarsairs operate? Some clarsairs spent most of their time travelling round the country playing in the big houses to earn their keep, just as Scottish musicians do today. Others would be basically attached to one household, possibly, in the case of those in the pay of bishops, accompanying plainchant or performing in mystery plays. We know from the Treasurer's Accounts for 1506–7 that the bishops of Ross and Caithness and the prior of Whithorn, each had clarsairs in his employ. As for the instruments themselves, we have three similar clarsachs, two in Scotland, one in Dublin, to give us a clear picture of the Highland harp in the fourteenth and fifteenth centuries (see PlateX and XI). There is a slight hump in the shape where the highest strings are secured; this is to give strength. The left hand played the higher notes and the instrument would rest on the left shoulder. The sound box was often made from a single piece of willow, but the two Scottish instruments, the Lamont harp and the Queen Mary harp as they are known, were made from hornbeam, specially imported from England. The Lowland harp had gut strings and was plucked with the flesh.

To this day, tuning a clarsach is a slow and important business. In former times it was considered so important that penalties for stealing a tuning key were laid down in the ancient Brehon laws. The same applied to the tiompan – the Celtic lyre also known as the cruit. The death of St Columba is described as leaving the country like a cruit without a tuning key. You could put a clarsair out of work for a while by cutting his fingernails, and pay the penalty in plectrums if you were in the wrong. In any event, the music they tuned-up with was dignified, and though it was taken down from an Irish player, there was regular traffic between Ireland and Scotland among the harpists, so such basic music as a tuning prelude may well have been common to both countries (we will see in a later chapter how the harp key took on a different meaning in the hand of Ruaridh Dall Morrison). This *Tuning Prelude* for clarsach could date from the late middle ages on grounds of style and because it is peculiarly suited to its task which is the oldest task in harp playing (see p.80). It was

collected by Edward Bunting (in his 1840 publication *The Ancient Music of Ireland*) who himself describes the occasion:

> This extremely curious piece was taken down from Hempson's performance in the year 1792, and is given as he played it. It was with great reluctance that the old harper was prevailed on to play even the fragment of it here preserved . . . he would rather, he asserted, have played any other air, as this awakened recollections of the days of his youth, of friends whom he had outlived, and of times long past when the harpers were accustomed to play the ancient caoinans or lamentations, with their corresponding preludes. When pressed to play, notwithstanding, his peevish answer uniformly was, 'What's the use of doing so? no one can understand it now, not even any of the harpers.'

Although Hempson was in his nineties, he was still a good player. Edward Bunting wrote that the arpeggios were played downwards. This was not the usual practice in classical music – both his manuscripts and the printer have shown them in the conventional way, starting at the bottom – but Bunting would not have stated the opposite unless he meant it.

Example 9. TUNING PRELUDE FOR CLARSACH (from the 1840 publication; Bunting's manuscript version is clearly a hurried partial transcription)

It is possible that *The Battel of Harloe* was also played on the clarsach, for musicians are always borrowing from each other's repertoires. We have seen in *Greysteil* (Chapter V) how the clarsach may have accompanied the voice, by transferring the music from the lute; but the truth is that not one single piece of music for the Celtic harp was written down until the late eighteenth century. This may not merely be by accident. The clarsairs worked closely with the fili, accompanying recitations of genealogies, and songs in praise of heroes and chieftains. But the fili who composed these were inclined to develop secret codes to maintain their own exclusivity, and these codes used the Celtic Ogham alphabet and are still teasing scholars.

Ogham is strange. It is an alphabet which nobody needed because the Roman alphabet was available already. Even if it had its origins before the arrival of the Roman alphabet, not one verb and therefore not one sentence survives anywhere. But what if it was not used for writing in the ordinary way? Its letters were grouped phonetically, the vowels in one group, the consonants part of the arrangement too. There were five groups of five letters and they took their names from trees – harking back to Druidic tree worship. The Gaelic alphabet still takes the names of its letters from trees. Trees house birds and their wood makes harps. Birds make music, harps make music – a bird is frequently carved at the top corner of a harp. Could there be a connection between ogham and harp music?[29] (See Plate 1.)

The arrangement of ogham letters suggests their sound value was crucial. Individual symbols use from one to five lines, straight or angled and related to a central dividing line, and would be easily represented by hand signs, or could stand for harp fingering, or the notes or strings the fingers played.

Example 10. OGHAM ALPHABET

It is likely that harpists used all five fingers rather than the modern practice of using four per hand only. In other words ogham may have

been a notation. This idea is over a hundred years old now and no direct evidence has been produced to prove it. But as ogham – particularly Pictish ogham – remains obscure and was designed to be so, we should not give up trying to verify a theory for which there is much circumstantial evidence. It may have assisted memory or have been used like sol-fa, or the pipers' more ancient equivalent – canntaireachd, or have defined rhythms or patterns rather than individual notes. The meaningless syllables in many Gaelic choruses, by which songs are often identified, demonstrate that spoken sounds have long been used to represent notes or rhythms.[30]

The Armenians had a secret notation and we know the Celts deliberately made some of their work hard to understand by using obscure or outdated vocabulary or by inserting redundant letters or words or even altering word order, or mis-spelling words. A long poem in praise of St Columba prides itself on just that. None of this can be directly illustrated in music, but we may have an echo of it in the Welsh Ap Hyw manuscript.

Although Ap Hyw was harpist to James VI and I, the material in the manuscript he wrote is unquestionably mediaeval. It was also extremely difficult to decipher, though its alphabetic notation is probably obscured more by Ap Hyw's ignorance of the old bardic ways, than out of a desire to confuse the unworthy. What it contains is relevant to Scotland, not only because Giraldus had said that everyone looked to the Scots as the best musicians, but because the music itself consists of systematic variation techniques that also apply to bagpipe music. Ap Hyw calls one of his metres 'the Scottish metre' and its broken chord pattern

Example 11. AP HYW: SCOTTISH METRE (above)
PIOBAIREACHD: THE MEN WENT TO DRINK (below)

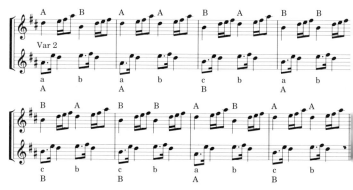

is a mirror image of the formal pattern of a number of piobaireachd. There is also a striking similarity between the repetitions and returnings to one note in the Welshman's harp variations and some of the variations in piobaireachd and, seemingly, a more recent transcription of Ap Hyw's manuscript points to further similarities in the use of grace-notes.[31]

It would be nice to be able to believe that this is evidence of shared instrumental music structures in the Celtic community during the mediaeval period. The best work on the structure of piobaireachd was undertaken by Major General C.S. Thomason in 1900. He maintained that it was fundamentally that of poetry. We have seen how the structure of poetry revealed the musical structure in the *Inchcolm Antiphoner* and it may be that one day the structures of poetry, music and visual design in Celtic art will be shown to be intimately related, and ogham may have a role in this: but it will take more than the cursory glance this book has been able to give it, before possibilities can be claimed as realities.

As for clarsach repertoire, we will return to it later via the lute manuscripts of the early seventeenth century, but will fill the gap meanwhile with a borrowing from a different instrument now extinct, the 'gue'. This final example is of a Shetland tune, probably originally performed on the gue. 'Before violins were introduced, the musicians performed on an instrument called a gue, which appears to have had some similarity to the violin, but had only two strings of horse-hair, and was played upon in the same manner as a violoncello.'[32] The piece is called *Da Day Dawis* – the day dawns. It was associated with the winter solstice and the dawn of lengthening days.

'Long before daylight, the fiddlers present themselves at the doors of the houses, playing a tune called the Day-Dawn, the interesting association of which thrills every soul with delight. . . . This tune has long been consecrated to Yule day, and is never played on any other occasion.' *Da Day Dawis* was collected in Shetland some time before 1822 when it was first published.[33] It demonstrates well the economical use of musical motifs in the Shetlands[34] and is still in the repertoire of Shetland fiddlers. The tune itself could well be fifteenth century. William Dunbar, writing at the end of that century protested:

Your commone menstralis has no tone,
Bot Now The Day Dawis and Into Joun.

If this was the *Now the Day Dawis* they were playing in Dunbar's time to announce a new day to the populace, it would serve us a lot better of a morning than the National Anthem and the groaning mechanism of Big Ben. *Da Day Dawis*'s gentle curlings round one note, followed by the octave leap so characteristic of early ballads, and the mysterious unwinding and return, make it a tune of outstanding beauty and serve also as a reminder that the culture of Gaelic-speaking Scotland was intimately bound up with that of the speakers of Norn in the Northern Isles. Time and again one is halted by the astonishing variety of our melodic inheritance and grateful that so many of our people have honoured it in the remembrance.

Example 12. DA DAY DAWIS (Hibbert, *Description of the Shetland Isles*, 1822)

SCALE OF THE IRISH HARP OF THIRTY STRINGS, TUNED IN THE NATURAL KEY, TERMED,

" ᏞᎬᎪᏟᏆ ᎶᏞᎬᎪᏚ," *or half note.*

METHOD OF TUNING USED BY THE OLD HARPERS.

Tuned for high bass key.

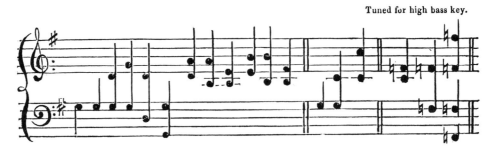

Tuned in octaves to the top.   Tuned in octaves to the bottom.‡

C sharp,§  occasionally tuned to F sharp, (a fifth.)

* The Irish harp had no string for F sharp, between E and G in the bass, probably because it had no concord in their scale for that tone, either major or minor; but this E in the bass, called " Teadlecthae," or *fallen* string, in the natural key termed " Leath Glass," being altered to F natural, a semitone higher when the melody required it, and the sharp F's, through the instrument being previously lowered a semitone, the key was then called " Teadleaguidhe," the *falling* string, or high bass key.

† This is the number of strings indicated by the string holes on the sound board of the ancient Irish harp, now in Trinity College, Dublin, erroneously called " Brian Boiromhe's Harp," and was the usual number of strings found on all the harps at the Belfast meeting, in 1792.

‡ It will be observed by the musical critic, that only two major keys, viz., G one sharp, and C natural, were perfect in their diatonic intervals on the Irish harp; but the harpers also made use of two ancient diatonic minor keys, (neither of them perfect according to the modern scale,) viz., E one sharp, and A natural. They sometimes made use of D natural minor, which was still more imperfect, though some of their airs were performed in that key, and were thought extremely agreeable by many persons.

§ The harpers said that this single note, C sharp, was sometimes made use of, but the Editor seldom met with an instance of it.

CHAPTER VII

THE GOLDEN AGE
1490–1550

The Renaissance in Scotland is primarily associated with the courts of James IV (r.1488–1513) and James V (r.1513–1542), and this is supported by the musical evidence. But it should not be thought of as a time of sweeping away the old mediaeval practices, for these were tenacious. On the Island of Inchcolm the monks held to their chants in praise of Columba, in the court *Greysteil* was still sung (see Chapter V) and we shall see that in the music of Robert Carver the mediaeval survived alongside newer influences. This mixture of continuity and innovation was supported by James IV who was to license Walter Chapman and Andrew Millar to bring in the first printing presses to Scotland, but they were to use them to restore Scottish customs where those of the great cathedral of Salisbury had more recently prevailed:

> And als it is divisit and thocht expedient be us and our counsall that in tyme cuming mess bukis, manualis, matyne bukis and portuus bukis efter our awin Scottis use and with legendis of Scottis sanctis as is now gaderit and ekit be ane reverend fader in God and our traist counsalour Williame, bischop of Abirdene, and utheris, be usit generaly within al our realme als sone as the sammyn may be imprentit and providit; and that na maner of sic bukis of Salusbery use be brocht to be sauld within our realme in tym cuming . . . under pane of escheting of the bukis and punising of thair persons, bringaris thairof within our realme in contrar this our statut, with al rigour as efferis.[1]

James IV was one of the most remarkable men in Europe. Don Pedro de Ayala, a lingering emissary from Spain, wrote of him: 'He is of noble stature, neither tall nor short, and as handsome in complexion and shape as a man can be . . . his knowledge of language is wonderful . . . before transacting any business he hears two masses. After mass he has a cantata sung, during which he sometimes despatches very urgent business . . .'[2] (see Plate XIV).

James IV was also interested in architecture. Fine palaces were built at Falkland and Holyrood, and Linlithgow Palace was extended

to include a new chapel with carvings of angels playing musical instruments. We read in the Household Accounts that William the Frenchman installed a new organ in Linlithgow. 'Item to Gilleam, organist, makar of the Kingis organis, for expensis maid be him on the said organis in goat skynnis, and parchment for the belloes, in naillis and sprentis of irne, in glew, papir, candill, coill, etcetra . . . eight pounds, four shillings.'

The new chapel had a gallery with easy access to the royal apartments, and the Chapel Royal Choir used to wake the king with music. We can imagine them on a Christmas morning doing so with the medley known as *All Sons of Adam*. Snatches of popular carols are featured in it and they include the first known version of *I Saw Three Ships*. Near the end, there is some old-fashioned *fauxbourdon* for the part the angels sing, because angels would naturally stick to the old ways, singing in Latin and in parallel intervals. *Fauxbourdon* means 'false bass' and is an attempt to explain that only one part was given, the others being improvised according to a variety of rules. It was a technique which persisted in Scotland until quite late.[3]

Example 1. ALL SONS OF ADAM (*Wode and Forbes partbooks*)

At Christmas, the court would be alive with people, many in hope of favours traditionally dispensed at Yule and New Year. On one occasion the treasurer, whose business it was to keep the king's frequently ruinous finances in some sort of order, abandoned his usual practice of naming the recipients, as hopeless:

'January the First 1506. Item, that day giffin to divers menstrales, schawmeris, trumpetis, taubroneris, fithelaris, lutaris, harparis, clarscharis, piparis, extending to sixty-nine persons, ten pounds and eleven shillings.'

This is a huge number of musicians by the standards of any European court of the period, and although it is exceptional, it is clear from the records that the Scottish court was musically very busy. James IV set himself up as a leading renaissance prince. He built the world's biggest ship – the *Great Michael* – possessed some of the finest artillery and armour in Europe, imported the latest in Italian trumpeters from Mantua, was a musician himself and entertained his young English bride – Margaret Tudor – by playing on clarychordes (a simple keyboard instrument) and lute, which pleased her 'verrey much'.[4]

Perhaps he played her *I Long for the Wedding*. This tune was first written down in the early seventeenth century, but is much older than that in character. The first half grows out of the darkness of the lute's lower strings and is strictly pentatonic. The second half uses the same mode as the bagpipe scale and also the characteristic Scottish shift down one degree of the scale. The harmonies could not be simpler, and the whole tune has clearly smelled the wind from a western ocean.

It was a hopeful time in 1503. The marriage was intended to bring a permanent peace between Scotland and England, so the Scots put on a tremendous show to impress the English who accompanied Margaret on her way. The leading court poet – William Dunbar – wrote a splendid poem, *The Thistle and The Rose*, to symbolise this ideal union. He also wrote the text of a marriage song of which, sadly, only the tenor part of the music survives. It describes her as 'fayre, fayrest of everye fayre, princess most pleasant and preclare, the lustyest one alyve that byne welcum of Scotland to be Quene, young tender plant of pulcritude.'[5]

This was all too true. She was only thirteen, was homesick within a few weeks; and when her husband was killed at Flodden fighting the English (so much for the hopes of peace) she proved herself lusty indeed. Her liaisons caused many troubles, and a song of that time – *Woe worth the Time and eke the Place that she was to me Known* may well have been sung with her in mind. The tune is very curious. The first few bars could almost be a psalm or hymn tune; but as it moves on, it includes a phrase that comes straight out of folk-song, and then suddenly, and very artfully it slows up the rhythm with a sensitive use of the wistful effect of echo. Despite its variety, simplicity and sophistication side by side in such a tiny space, it all hangs together, a little masterpiece:

Example 3. WOE WORTH THE TIME (*Wode, Stirling, Edwards Partbooks*)

Example 2. I LONG FOR THE WEDDING (*Straloch Lute Book*, 1627)

Music was not confined to the court, though its passage throughout the realm undoubtedly stimulated it. The 'monocordis' and 'organis' travelled around with the king as the household accounts tell us. In 1497, John Hert carried the monocordis from Aberdeen to Stirling and, on 15 October 1504, eighteen shillings was paid 'that samyn nycht in Dunnottir to the chield playit on the monocordis be the kingis command.'

Dunnottar Castle, perched on a crag and almost surrounded by the sea, must be one of the wildest situations in which the monocordis has ever been heard. Nowadays it is called the clavichord – a keyboard instrument of delicate tone in which the strings are struck by metal tangents. The organis was a small portative organ which could be carried strapped to the back, and one's heart goes out to the 'ii childer that bure the organis and their bellysis ouir the Month and again.'

The Cairn o' Mount, a 500-metre pass on the route to Aberdeen, is not a hospitable part of the world for the transportation of organs and their bellows, and the two youths no doubt often earned their twenty-eight shillings battling into the teeth of the bitter north-east gales. Once arrived, however, they might well have joined in the music and general rejoicings on Queen Margaret's entry into Aberdeen, described here by William Dunbar:

> Ane fair processioun mett hir at the port
> In a cap of gold and silk full pleasantlie,
> Syne at hir entrie, with many fair disport,
> Ressaveit hir on streittis lustilie;
> Quhair first the salutatioun honorabilly
> Of the sweitt Virgin guidlie mycht be seine,
> The sound of menstrallis blawing to the sky;
> Be blyth and blissfull, burgh of Aberdein.
>
> Syne come thair four and tuentie madinis ying
> All claid in greine of mervelous bewtie,
> With hair detressit as threidis of gold did hing,
> With quhyt hattis all browderit rycht bravelie,
> Playand on timberallis and syngand rycht sweitlie;
> That seimlie sort, in ordour weill besein,
> Did meit the quein, her saluand reverentlie;
> Be blyth and blissful, burcht of Aberdein.'

We do not know what the four and twenty maidens sang, or how good were the minstrels who were 'blawing to the sky' but a piece such as *Into a Mirthful May Morning* is the sort of music that might have been used to entertain the queen. The simple chordal style and bold rhythms suggest that it could have been a dance as well as a

song, a combination of pleasures very common at the time:[6]

Example 4. INTO A MIRTHFUL MAY MORNING (*Forbes and Squyer Partbooks*)

All the above examples are anonymous, but it is with the Renaissance and its more personalised and humanistic approach that we begin to feel contact with individual composers. Among them was a young man writing music of maturity and sensitivity – Robert Carver. For a composer of such genius it is remarkable that not one single comment upon his music has come to us from his contemporaries. Nor are his dates of birth and death known, though recent research, as yet unpublished, suggests he was born as early as 1484–5 and was still alive in 1568.[7]

Carver was trained as an Augustinian canon at Scone – of whose abbey no trace remains. There were sang schools from Kirkwall to Melrose, in cathedrals, monasteries, collegiate churches and parish churches, some of them three hundred years old, near enough. Aberdeen and St Andrews were always strong. From Dunkeld, however, we can get an idea of what life was like in a choir-school such as will have obtained at Scone; for Alexander Myln, writing in 1517 in his *Vitae Episcoporum Dunkeldensium*, declared it had the best choir in Scotland, and has left us delightful portraits of the members, of their characters, talents and their duties, from which one can tell that anyone trained in such surroundings was expected to do a good deal more than sing. Myln was later to become Abbot of Cambuskenneth, but was at Dunkeld long enough to record the arguments over the appointment to the bishopric of another great renaissance figure, Gavin Douglas, remembered for his brilliant and vivid translation of the *Aeneid,* at his own declaration into 'the language of the Scottish natioun – kepand na sudroun [English] bot our awin language.'

That nationalistic pride, also evident in the quotation from James IV (above), seems to have been as much a spur to creativity as was the renewed interest in classical learning to which the word Renaissance ultimately refers, and of which Douglas's translation is one of the greatest examples. On a tiny and homely scale, that pride finds expression in the affectionate intimacy of Myln's description of the choristers. It is worth reproducing the passage in full.

Sir Stephen Yong is naturally the most cheery of men, and looks it. He is an advocate in the consistorial court, a chorister steady in the chant, and very expert in the ordinary. Master John Pennicuke has studied grammar, logic, philosophy, music and canon law. He is the pillar of the choristers and a sedulous observer of canonical hours. He is chaplain of Tullepowry, and in the home which he keeps his mother has an honoured place. Sir Alexander Richardson is a faithful man who presides honourably over a household where he has brought up promising boys of his kin. Some of them have been fitted to enter religious houses, some to be priests, others for the choral service. He is the most conscientious member of the choir at divine service, and at Mass his devoutness is most exemplary. Sir William Lacock, chaplain of St. Peter and vicar of Retray, is a good figure of a man, who works very hard out of doors, especially at repairs to the houses of the founders of his chaplaincy. But for his efforts the chaplaincy would be reduced practically to extinction. Sir James Lawder, one of the chaplains of Abernyde, is a modest and honourable young man, a good musician, honouring his mother. He is an advocate of the consistorial court, kind and trustworthy, and highly beloved for his gentle ways and his deference to his seniors. Sir William Martyne, chaplain of St. Katherine, is respected and has musical gifts. His brother John, a young priest, simple and devout, with a mastery of music, has supplemented his grammatical training with a good character and diligence in divine service. Sir Patrick Gardner, another of the four chaplains of Abernyde, presides over his own house and is distinguished by care in matters of clothing, furniture, and food for the poor. Devout and simple, he always speaks at the dictates of his heart. His knowledge of the Irish tongue and his serious and estimable character qualified him to become vice-penitentiary. Sir Thomas Bettoun, chaplain of Muklere, is a quiet man, highly trained in the theory of music as well as the art of singing. He is steady and correct in all manner of chanting, and a pillar of the choir. He honours his mother, whom he maintains. He hates inactivity, is careful in the matter of his household furniture, and is an industrious gardener. Sir Alexander Fairefoule, who is well trained in grammar, has studied cases of conscience, and is therefore considered a suitable confessor. He is also a trustworthy and sound notary. He maintains his house from the goods of the chaplaincies of Abernyde. Sir John Martyne, rector of Loyd, John Leslie, chaplain of All Saints, and William Scherar, chaplain, are priests born in the city of Dunkeld, all thorough musicians and accustomed from their youth to take their part in service and rule the choir. Sir Finlay Simsoun, clerk of the consistorial court, writes in a very good style and is most faithful in the discharge of his office. Entreaty, bribe, hate or love could not lead him from the straight path of duty. Without thought of personal profit he keeps strictly on the way of obedience.

One of the main records of the kind of music such a choir will have sung, apart from plainsong, is the *Carver Choirbook.*[8] It contains what the Scots called 'Musick Fyne' – music in several parts. Nowadays we would call it 'art' music. The manuscript is named after Carver because much of it is given over to his compositions written in his own hand. His signature appears more than once. Carver is probably Scotland's greatest composer, yet the study of his work is still in its infancy, most of it is unpublished and only in 1991 were his works recorded (see Discography). The collection starts with pieces by composers represented in the famous *Eton Choirbook,* which means that the Scots were familiar with the splendid florid style of their southern counterparts. But from the rest of the manuscript it is clear that Scotland had its own traditions and was closely in touch with the Flemish masters, who are represented by a *Missa L'Homme Armé* by one of the finest continental composers of his time, Guillaume Dufay (*d.* 1474). There are some anonymous works, including an incomplete one which develops a florid complexity of unsurpassed brilliance and beauty and which seems to have been performed at various centres in Scotland (see below).

But the chief glory of the manuscript (*c.*1500 – *c.*1560) is Carver's own music, five polyphonic settings of the Mass and two motets from this source only (see Plate XVI). By Carver's day 'motet' meant any kind of religious vocal composition that did not set the text of the Mass itself. His two motets are one in honour of Christ – *O Bone Jesu* – for nineteen voice parts, and the other in five voice parts in honour of the Virgin Mary. This latter work – *Gaude Flore Virginali* – symbolises her seven joys in its seven verses: the Annunciation, the Visitation, the Nativity, the Adoration of the Magi, the Presentation in the Temple, Christ Disputing Among the Doctors, and the Assumption.

It is a subtle, well-balanced piece of great purity. Feminine in principle, its restrained modesty uses the full five parts only in the outer verses. In the fifth verse which speaks of the suffering of Mary, Carver employs three and then two voices only, while exploring dark harmonies that few, if any, of his contemporaries had tried. But within this smaller ensemble Carver uses much variety – the higher voices, plaintive for the Mother of Sorrows and, in a beautiful and joyful passage with the parts weaving in and out, he depicts the blissful throne of heaven.

Example 5. CARVER: GAUDE FLORE (*Carver Choirbook*)

The final section uses all the voices to the end – '*durabunt et florescent per aeterna saecula*' – lasting and flourishing for ever. This music achieves a high degree of refinement, but with scope for the great gestures which will have appealed to the king whose *Book of Hours* contained a copy of the text of *Gaude Flore*.

It is possible that Robert Carver was the natural son of Bishop Arnot whose surname he occasionally used. Why then was he called Carver? The name was not a common one. Perhaps he was adopted by David Carver who built the gallery, lofts and ceiling of the Chapel Royal at Stirling, with which town Carver was almost certainly closely associated.[9] Some of his music was written for this building, and it is possible that he himself was master of works when the choir of Stirling Parish Church was built. It is interesting that while the main body of the choir is roofed in timber, the east end, the impressive apse which commands the road ascending the castle hill, is roofed in stone (see Plate 21). Carver might have used this area to blend and focus the sound of a semi-circle of singers, given that he may have been involved in the making of the spaces in which music was to be heard. This may partly account for his mastery of vocal sonority and texture.

The most obvious example is the famous opening to his motet in honour of the name of Jesus, *O Bone Jesu*. It is a nineteen-part motet.

With sixteen adult male voices and six boys doubling two to a part, nineteen real parts was the maximum available. A less subtle composer might have been tempted to lift us from our seats by starting with the full range and riches of such a texture. Instead Carver starts with two voices only. But within the space of a few bars he shows his hand, building to a vast ensemble on the name of Jesus. Almost immediately this is set in relief by three and four-part textures; and in the great block chords he shifts the voices, delaying one or two, altering the harmonic emphasis by changing the layout. This is vocal writing of immense sophistication, in which a sound which might become too monolithic is kept alive by contrasted and varied scoring, so that our ears never become dulled by something too rich and homogeneous. Moreover, we can tell from Carver's own corrections in the score that he made changes to improve the texture. The parallel with great architecture is irresistible.

The possible occasion for the composition of this astonishing work is itself remarkable. James IV, as a very young man, allowed himself to be manipulated into a position as a leader of

Plate 21. CHOIR OF THE CHURCH OF THE HOLY RUDE, STIRLING, SIXTEENTH CENTURY

Example 6. CARVER: O BONE JESU (*Carver Choirbook*)

a faction against his deeply unpopular and artistically engrossed father, James III. His father was murdered in cold blood while escaping after defeat by the rebels. The new young king was profoundly affected and sought absolution from the Dean of the Chapel Royal who

> pat him in goode hope of forgiveness thairfor be godis mercie in Jesus Christ. Sa the king continewid in the said castell ane sessone bot he was ever sade and dollorous in his mynd for the deid of his father that he was constranit be his conscience to use ane signe of repentance, and for this same cause gart mak ane belt of irone and wore it daillie about him and eikit it everie zeir during his lyftyme certane unce wyght as he thocht goode.[10]

In the young king's *Book of Hours*, mentioned above, is a beautiful miniature depicting a royal funeral service in St Andrews Cathedral, decorated for the occasion with special heraldic banners and a vast number of candles and with the choir, with shocked expressions, singing a *Requiem Mass* for

James III (see Plate XVII).] If James IV wanted to honour his father's memory with a more personal artistic gesture, then he could have found no better way than in commissioning a great work of art in penitential mood. *O Bone Jesu* is just such a work: a personal prayer, invoking the name of Jesus over and over with a ritual repetition in the text that harks back to ancient times.

James IV may have started his reign in sorrow, but his was a vigorous court, full of music. Apart from payments to musicians mentioned above (see also Chapter V), he authorised many payments to many individual singers. But the most constant expenditure of all went on the brilliant sound of the new trumpets, complete with trumpeters from Italy. There were four or five players, with the very latest thing in trumpet design from Mantua. In the royal colours of red and gold they looked magnificent, adorned with banners and special badges with a little golden trumpet sewn on to their tunics to distinguish them. Alongside the four Scottish 'trumpeters of war' and any visiting trumpeters attached to some of the nobility, they must have been able to make a tremendous impression. Clearly they were valued, for they got top pay and, in 1515, ten pounds was given to Bestiane Drummonth 'to help his expens by his wages abiff written, because he past with licence to visy his frendes in Itale'.

Perhaps a case of home-sickness. But what did the trumpeters play? Though no music survives, the instruments themselves give us an idea, and the musicians must have been highly skilled. After all they came from Italy for one reason only – to play their brilliant trumpets. They will almost certainly have developed a technique on natural trumpets hard to imitate today.

Trumpets announced the Heralds, the beginnings of tournaments, and generally anything that required announcing, war included. They were heard when Mons Meg, the great cannon specially cast for the king, was rolled out and fired. Trumpets were also used to provide a drone for dancing to, and they were possibly used in church for special celebratory Masses.

Voices were certainly trained to imitate trumpets. Conrad von Zabern, writing in 1474 says that 'anyone wanting to sing well must use his voice in three ways: resonantly and trumpet-like on the low notes, moderately in the middle range and more gently for the high notes.'[11]

But that was just his notion. Others liked to sing out on the high notes too, and von Zabern protests: 'Another more obvious fault is singing high notes with an unrestrained, full and powerful voice . . . in a well-known college I once heard singers with these trumpet-like voices singing as loud as they could on the highest register as though they wanted to break the windows of the choir.'

On 14 October 1511, James IV's flagship, the *Great Michael*, was launched. She was named after the avenging archangel Michael and her purpose was to lead a pan-European crusade against the infidel. The trumpeters were there for the launch – it is possible that the music for such an occasion was a *Six Part Mass* by Robert Carver.[12] The Mass is a cyclic one. That is, each section starts with the same music, more or less.

It has the sound of trumpets lurking behind it, even in the *Dona Nobis Pacem*. They were just as good at claiming peace at the point of a sword, then as now.

Example 7. CARVER: SIX PART MASS – DONA NOBIS PACEM
(*Carver Choirbook*)

This work too is full of contrasts, here expressing the mystery of prayer in a very brief, but strangely incantatory moment, almost pagan in effect.

Example 8. CARVER: SIX PART MASS – SUSCIPE
DEPRECATIONEM NOSTRAM (*Carver Choirbook*)

Only a few bars later the mood is jubilant, expressing the glory of the Holy Trinity by imitative entries and perfect chording, creating a bright and brilliant sound, although the range of the voices is actually quite restricted.

There is another Mass of Carver's with clear military connotations, his Mass based on the ribald crusading song – *L'Homme Armé* (beware the armed man!). It is the only British Mass to use this tune, so popular on the continent – but Carver, being a Scot, had better access to continental developments than his English contemporaries who were so often at war with the French. It is possible that Carver was educated in Louvain, as the matriculation roll for 1504 mentions a Robert from St Johnstone (that is to say Perth) which would be the natural place-name for a student from neighbouring Scone to give. At Louvain he would have encountered the works of Ockeghem, Dufay and Josquin, and we have seen that he had copied Dufay's Mass on *L'Homme Armé*, as well as works by English contemporaries whose elaborate decorative style he had already absorbed. The use of the tune may identify Carver's Mass as the one dedicated to Pope Julius II by the bishop, chapter and canons of the Chapel Royal '*cum armorum insigniis*' ('with insignia of arms') in 1509. Julius II also proposed a crusade, but he later excommunicated James IV. Here is a section of Carver's *L'Homme Armé* Mass, in which the last phrase of the tune appears first in the tenor, but then yields to a passage of complex decoration in which all the parts actually develop their embellishments from the tune itself, the '*Cantus Firmus*' as it was known, which underlies the entire Mass. These decorative turns are very characteristic of Carver.

Example 9. CARVER: MISSA L'HOMME ARMÉ – PLENI SUNT CAELI ET TERRA GLORIATUA (*Carver Choirbook*)

Embellishing *Canti Firmi* (usually in the tenor part) was not unique to Scotland – Morley later complained about it in England – but in Carver's music it may well reflect a native predilection. James IV was the last Gaelic-speaking king, a fact not to be overlooked in considering the overall cultural climate in Lowland Scotland.

Robert Carver's life was passed on the very edge of the Highland line at a time when Gaelic was commonplace and Gaelic singing was well known. Quite probably some of his singers will have started off singing in that tradition and it will have been Carver's business to train them into his own ways and the ways of Europe in general. We have seen above that there was a Gaelic-speaker in the choir at Dunkeld. Gaelic singing would also have done nothing but encourage Carver in his love of highly decorative solo lines (see Chapter II). What seems extremely difficult for modern voices to perform in terms of vocal flexibility is native to the Gaelic tradition and may well have had a place in the Scots tradition also.

Gabor Darvas, introducing his edition of *L'Homme Armé Mass*, was one of the first to recognise Carver's individuality:

> This long and ambitious composition splendidly asserts the individual stylistic features. . . . Carver was a sure-handed master and a true virtuoso of the art of counterpoint and its relevant possibilities . . . richness of imitation . . . versatile application of metrical proportion, augmentation and diminution. The texture of the movements and smaller sections of the mass shows extraordinary variety. . . . It is typical of Carver's imaginative form-building that the melody of 'L'Homme arme' does not remain simply a *cantus firmus*, but becomes in places the starting point for chains of musical ideas, the melody itself becoming modified, developed or assuming a hidden form . . ..[13]

A variety of vocal production was and still is a vital part of Scottish musical life and gives an idea of the breadth of vocal context in which Carver operated. We shall see in a later chapter that embellishing the *Cantus Firmus* may even have survived as late as the eighteenth century in Scotland, for Robert Bremner makes critical comment on something which sounds very like it.[14]

Variety itself is not uniformly applied in Carver's music. One can admire the use of contrast in *O Bone Jesu*, but in a related work, the *Ten Part Mass*, he sustains a rich and convoluted ten-part texture which is almost overwhelming and hypnotic. There is a special reason for this. Carver himself tells us in the manuscript that this Mass was written '*ad honorem dei et sancti michaelis*'. The Mass would then be performed on the feast day of St Michael, and the proper sung texts for the day would include the one on which this Mass is based and from which it gets its name – *Dum Sacrum Mysterium*: 'While John beheld the sacred mystery, Michael the archangel sounded the trumpet. Forgive, oh Lord our

God – Thou who openest the book and loosest the seals thereof.'

This apocalyptic vision is supported by the text of the sequence usually sung in this connection, which names the nine orders of angels and states: 'The angels are the work of Thy primeval hand, we the latest fashioned in Thine image.'

Carver has made use of the mediaeval symbolism of this text. The ten parts of his Mass represent the voices of the nine orders of angels, and the tenth lost order replaced by the voices of men. This has not only a wonderful suggestion that man can share in the heavenly chorus, but actually supposes that what we are listening to *is* the heavenly chorus. This helps to explain the extraordinary character of some of the music in which we are invited to step outside our ordinary time and partake imaginatively of eternity, so the pace of contrast is not that of the hurried desire for change of humanity. So remarkable are these passages that they were at one time completely misunderstood. After the Reformation Carver's work was not looked at again until the twentieth century, so no one knew what to expect and he was at first ignorantly accused of technical incompetence because in such passages he employed dissonance, false relation and held on to mediaeval traits which allowed parallel fifths and octaves.[15] These were essential features of organum, but were rejected by theorists and many composers from the sixteenth to the nineteenth century because they were thought to sound too bare and open, and to undermine the real movement of parts. Carver, like Bach and Haydn, did not always stick to such artificial rules.[16] Instead he used these effects as part of a technique for which there exists a unique Scottish term – cant organe. The term appears in Gavin Douglas's description of the court of Venus in his *Palice of Honour*, written around 1501.

Accompanyit lustie zonkeirs [youths] with all
Fresche ladyis sang in voice virgineall
Concordis sweit, divers entoned reportis,
Proportionis fine with sound celestiall,
Duplet, triplet, diatesserial,
Sesqui altera and decupla resortis,
Diapason of many sindrie sortis,
War soung and playit be seir cunning menstrall
On lufe ballatis with mony fair disportis.

In modulatioun hard I play and sing
Faburdoun, pricksang, discant, countering,
Cant organe, figuratioun, and gemell,
On croud, lute, harp, with monie gudlie spring,

Schalmes, clariounis, portatives, hard I ring,
Monycord, organe, tympane, and cymbell.
Sytholl, psalterie, and voices sweit as bell,
Soft releschingis in dulce delivering,
Fractionis divide, at rest, or clois compell.

It has been shown that 'decupla resortis' and 'cant organe' refer to a semi-improvised polyphony based on very simple slow-moving chord sequences.[17] So this uniquely Scottish technique is no casual error, but a deliberate and sophisticated device. Over and over, the voices oscillate between G minor and F major chords, the parts flowing so freely and yet coherently that it gives the effect of a complex rose with all its petals in motion. Like Dante's image of the rose, we have here an aural image of eternal life, permanent and assured, but beautiful and alive, formalising an improvisatory technique which would allow all present to feel that they had a potential part in it.

Example 10. CARVER: TEN PART MASS – QUI SEDES
(*Carver Choirbook*)

Perhaps the most compelling occasion on which that Mass has been heard was when it was used to provide music for the coronation of the infant James V only twelve days after the death of his father James IV in the catastrophic defeat by the English at Flodden. Fortunately the hurried coronation took place on or close to the feast of St Michael, so the Mass suited the occasion and Carver even changed the date on the manuscript to make it seem as though the work were newly composed. If ever the assistance of the heavenly chorus was required in Scotland it was on that coronation day. But it must have been listened to with heavy hearts. So great was the loss to the Scottish nobility, including several bishops, that they could scarcely muster enough dignity for the event – all because of the king's impulsiveness in battle, as Don Pedro de Ayala had prophetically pointed out. 'He is courageous, even more so than a King should be. I have seen him often undertake most dangerous things in the last wars. I sometimes clung to his skirts and succeeded in pulling him back.'[18]

A contemporary English description of the battle notes the confidence of the Scots, displayed in music as well as armour and artillery.

They trumpetts full trewly: they tryden together,
Many shames in that showe: with their shrill pipes:
Heauenly was their Melody: their Mirth to heare,
How the songen with a showte: all the shawes over![19]

Flodden was a catastrophic loss, remembered to this day throughout Scotland in the song made famous by Jean Elliot. In fact her poem was based on a traditional fragment of verse:

I've heard them lilting at the ewes milking,
The flowers of the forest are a' wede away.
I ride single on my saddle,
For the flowers of the forest are a' wede away.[20]

The tune, commonly played by pipers on Commemoration Day and other occasions of communal mourning, was first committed to paper in the Skene manuscript in the 1620s.

Example 11. THE FLOWERS OF THE FOREST (*Skene manuscript,*
1620)

Whether words and music came into the world together some time shortly after Flodden we do not know. But the tenacity of the associations that Jean Elliot tapped into in 1756 has lasted for two and a half centuries since, so why not two and a half centuries before?

Robert Carver lived through all of this and was still composing in 1546. But there is a huge unexplained gap in his output, confused by scholarly disagreements over the dates of his compositions. A possible reason for that gap will be given in the next chapter, where his Mass, *Pater Creator Omnium,* is considered. But it does not account for his great *Five Part Mass* which may precede or follow the gap. This work is based on a setting of the obscure text – *fere pessima* – 'a wild beast has devoured my son Joseph', which tells of Jacob's grief on discovering Joseph's blood-stained coat. Various ingenious explanations have been given for Carver's use of this tune as a *cantus firmus.* They range from grief at a son's death from plague, to implied criticisms of Pope Julius, or Henry VIII, or other candidates.[21]

Only one thing stands out clearly, that the conclusion of this Mass is one of the most deeply felt and perfectly structured pieces of music of the Renaissance. Its prayer for peace is set, as is the whole Mass, in the Phrygian mode, a mode which emphasises the interval of the semitone and which Carver uses over and over with intensely sad effect.

Example 12. CARVER: FIVE PART MASS – AGNUS DEI (*Carver Choirbook*)

Carver's use of imitation at the end of this work begins to control the structure in a way that was becoming the norm on the continent. It is never done slavishly by Carver, however, though it is certainly smooth and eloquent, and he can use his harmonic sense to deeply moving effect in a structural way quite different from the ancient mediaevalism of the *Ten Part Mass.* Here, at the end of the *Five Part Mass,* for the first time in the entire work, he allows the music briefly to breathe in a warmer key, introducing E flats and B flats to give a more kindly turn to the sad Phrygian semi-tones. It is a moment of heart-rending tenderness in the midst of the world of bleak sorrows with which this great work ends.

Example 13. CARVER: FIVE PART MASS – DONA NOBIS PACEM
(*Carver Choirbook*)

Carver's music is only just becoming available for study,[22] and there remains much to be explained. Often there are things which seem to have a very particular meaning, but which are puzzling, as in an extraordinarily beautiful passage from the *Five Part Mass*. It follows on the rich sound for 'Lord God of Hosts', and is a setting of the words '*pleni sunt caeli gloria tua*' – the heavens are full of thy glory. One might expect a grandiose gesture. Instead the tenor sustains a single note for seventeen measures round which an aetherial web is woven by three other solo voices; but what does this striking section symbolise?

It is easy enough to pass off this sort of inventiveness as just that. A purely musical contrivance popped into the texture because that is how Carver felt at the time, but this seems unlikely. The Renaissance mind, only a little less than the mediaeval one, was well aware of significances (straightforward and mystical) in music, numbers, words, images, nature and man – and used them. The Mass itself was and is a supremely symbolic service, a symbolism which was still in use two hundred years later in the works of protestant Bach. It may well be that in many situations we only recognise half of what is going on. For instance, the same section of text is singled out for special treatment in the

Ten Part Mass. Carver sustains a canon at the ninth (one part imitating the other almost exactly at a pitch nine notes lower), round which the entire '*pleni sunt caeli*' is built. Nowhere else does he use a canon as sustained as this, but to what end we do not know.

Another factor which can only be partially taken into account is that of the influence of Carver's own Scottish contemporaries. So little survives that not much can be made of it, and yet what there is is so full of character and energy that one should be very careful not to fall into the notion that Carver was an isolated genius looking to models from outside Scotland.

Salva Festa Dies, for instance, is marvellously virile music. Powerful syncopated rhythms celebrate the descent of the Holy Spirit at Whitsun, radiating over the whole earth. It is in old-fashioned *fauxbourdon* style, the parts moving mostly in parallel intervals, but no less striking for that.

Example 14. SALVA FESTA DIES (*The Art of Music*, 1580)

Salva Festa Dies comes from an anonymous Scottish treatise called *The Art of Music* (see Chapters VIII and X) which contains, among other things, a complete Mass waiting to be revived. The same holds true of the *Carver Choirbook* in which several anonymous pieces, including a Mass, *Deus Creator Omnium*, have yet to see the light of day. Some of these may be Scottish[23] and one of them, though incomplete, is an astonishing piece in praise of the Virgin Mary. It is a setting of the *Ave Gloriosa*, combining the simple beauty of a carol-like tune with contrapuntal sophistication.

In each new section of the piece, the music becomes more elaborate, the tune is presented at different speeds in different parts and, in the final section that survives, the altos and tenors are sent off on a florid line of such joyous virtuosity, dancing and weaving through the texture (brilliantly reconstructed by Isobel Woods),[24] that hearing it makes one gasp with admiration – and this was not the end of the piece. Perhaps it is as well the rest was lost, for we would be hard put to perform it nowadays if it had any more complications! But it shows that the musical Renaissance in Scotland reached to as high flights of fancy as anywhere else, producing works which

could combine dignity, simplicity and joyous complexity while commanding with technical skill the exuberance of their expressive freedom.

Example 16. AVE GLORIOSA (*Carver Choirbook*, realised by Isobel Woods)

Example 15. AVE GLORIOSA (*Carver Choirbook*, realised by Isobel Woods)

CHAPTER VIII

REFORM
1513–1580

The Battle of Flodden in 1513 could very well have spelt the end of Scotland as an independent nation, but the English either did not have the resources or did not choose to follow up their victory. It says much for the Scottish nation that it held together under a king only one year old, and recovered its status in Europe within a few years, but there was change on the way everywhere. The first rumblings of the Reformation were being heard, and even a vast and powerful nation such as France staggered under its impact. In 1525 King Francis I was captured fighting a papal alliance at Pavia, and only returned after payment of a crippling ransom. Later we will look more closely at this battle in which the Scots were deeply involved, as it was chosen as the name and subject-matter for a very remarkable piece of Scottish music.

The court of James V being at that time a regency, the child king was looked after by the courtier, poet, dramatist and Lord Lyon King of Arms to be, Sir David Lindsay. Years later, in *The Complaynt of Schir David Lindesay*, addressed to the king, he describes their times together and the little boy's love of music, his first words being to ask Daddy Lindsay to play the lute:

Auld Willie Dile, were he on live,
My life full weill he could descrive:
How as ane chapman bearis his pack,
I bore thy grace upon my back,
And sometimes stridlingis on my neck,
Dansand with mony bend and beck.
The first syllabis that thou did mute
Was Pa, da Lyn: upon the lute
Then playit I twenty springis, perqueir,
Whilk was great piete for to hear.

But with the intrigues of his father's widow, Margaret Tudor, and her vicious brother, Henry VIII and, above all, the intrigues of the Scottish nobles, there was a period when the court was essentially a prison for the king, under the control of Douglas. The young king nicknamed him

Greysteel. Perhaps he saw old Douglas as a menacing presence from the other world, or perhaps old Douglas taught him the epic tale (see Chapter V). When James finally broke from his captivity in 1528 he proved himself an unforgiving man. He slaughtered Douglases ruthlessly and the ballad of *Johnny Armstrong* records with bitterness his capture and summary execution by James. The Armstrongs were powerful border reivers and peace with England depended upon James's ability to control them. Johnny Armstrong on the other hand, saw himself as defending Scotland's rights and, as a true friend of the king, treated treachorously.

All the tunes for this border ballad belong to one group and it may even be that they derive from a lost tune called *Johnnie Armstrong's Dance*, mentioned as early as 1549, only twenty years after the execution of Armstrong. The tune was first printed in the mid-eighteenth century in instrumental guise, but was later picked up from the singing of the former town-piper of Jedburgh, which is in Armstrong's Border country.[1] It is wide-ranging, dramatic and mostly pentatonic and though the story itself is four hundred and fifty years old, it is still a lively part of our musical heritage.

Example 1. JOHNNIE ARMSTRONG (Stenhouse, *Illustrations*, 1853)

Some speiks of lords, some speiks of lairds, And sick - like men of hie de - grie; Of a gen - tle - man I sing a sang, Some - tyme call'd laird of Gil - nock - ie.

The years from the 1520s to the 1560s were dangerous times even for apparently innocuous people such as composers. The court had been deprived of one composer, Patrick Hamilton, burnt at the stake, and another, Robert Johnston, who had fled to England. The martyrdom of Patrick Hamilton, for his preaching of the new Lutheran doctrine of reform, probably deprived us of much fine music, for we are told that 'he composed a Mass for nine voices for the office of the missal which begins, *Benedicant Dominum omnes angeli eius*, and superintended its execution in the cathedral as precentor of the choir.'[2]

One skilled composer of whose works just enough survives to give us an inkling of his quality is Sir John Fethy. The title 'Sir' simply meant that you were an ordained priest, but Fethy was also a distinguished musician, as Thomas Wode (see below) tells us: 'This sang of repentance was composit be sir Jhone Fethy bayth letter and not. This man wes the first organeist that ever brought in Scotland the curius new fingering and playing on organs, and yet it is mair nor threescore yeiris since he com hame – this is wreatin in fifteen ninety two . . . I call this man Shir Jhone, that he myght be knawin for he wes a papeist preist, and the first trim organeist that ever wes in Scotland.'[3]

In 1498 Fethy went abroad to university by leave of his abbot at Arbroath and thirty years later we know that he was 'Master of The Sang Schule' in Dundee and later at the St Nicholas Sang Schule in Aberdeen where the council records record his appointment: 'The said day, the 18th September fifteen forty four, the hale consale being covenit togidder, hes feit Sir Jhone Fethy to be one of the prebendaris of their Quier and to haif thair organes and sang schole for the instructioun of the men and the guid barnis and keeping of them in gude ordour . . . forr the quhilk thai haf gifin him twenty pounds yeirlie of fee . . . '

He later moved to the Edinburgh Sang Schule where, amongst his other duties, he tuned the organis. When Wode describes his fingering as curious he does not mean odd, but clever, sophisticated. It is possible that he was one of the first to introduce the use of the thumb in keyboard playing, most players in those days using only the three central fingers.

O God Abufe is indeed a song of repentance, a sober offering ending with the words 'Ask grace of him who givis grace to all and he will help in thy necessity'. It is sombre and dignified, blending imitation with straight chordal passages in a powerfully devout piece of writing which, though by a papist priest, conveys much of the mood of self-examination that came with the ensuing great reform.

Example 2. JOHN FETHY: O GOD ABUFE (*Thomas Wode Partbooks*)

One of those caught in the midst of the mood for reform was Sir David Lindsay of the Mount – James V's tutor. Lindsay's *Ane Satyre of the Thrie Estatis* was entertainment for a mature man, able to eat strong meat. It was a play first produced in 1540 and avowedly attacking 'the noughtines in Religion, the presumpcion of Busshops and mysusing of preists' – by which Lindsay means their misbehaviour. This play was performed for the king and queen, and the kings of Scotland were in the habit of making bishops of their own bastards, so Lindsay was sailing close to the wind. At the same time he knew the power of love and sensuality and could express them with beauty in the words of Dame Sensualitie, no doubt aware that they exercised considerable power over the King himself.

Behauld my heid, behauld my gay attire,
Behauld my hals, luvesome and lily-white;
Behauld my visage flammand as the fire,
Behauld my paps, of portrature perfite!
To look on me luvers has great delight;
Richt sa has all the kings of Christendom –
To them I have done pleasure infinite
And specially unto the Court of Rome . . .

I hauld it best now, or we farther gang,
To Dame Venus let us go sing a sang.

It is typical of the post-Reformation that the words for the song to Venus may survive only in a religious parody of them by the Wedderburn brothers, who themselves had been writing religious plays in the 1540s. But the music for the parody also appears in an early manuscript with the title *O Ladie Venus Heire Complaine*, so with a small adjustment of the words, we can restore the original song.[4]

Example 3. SONG TO VENUS (*Thomas Wode, R. Edwards, Forbes Partbooks*, text reconstructed)

and the slightest imperfection or dullness shows up instantly. Johnston passes the test brilliantly, first one voice, then the other leading, like two ripples of sound overlapping in the air, with subtle use of dissonance.

Example 4. ROBERT JOHNSTON: DICANT NUNC JUDEI (Ms BM Roy. 24.d.2)

A composer of that period who certainly had a desire for reform was Robert Johnston (*c.* 1500 – *c.* 1560), a priest from Duns in the Scottish Borders. He fled to England, accused of some unknown heresy,[5] probably around the same time that another Borders Johnstone moved south from Annandale, and in his grandson bequeathed to England one of her greatest dramatists and poets – rare Ben Jonson. Maybe his grandfather knew or was even related to Robert Johnston.

Ave Dei Patris is a work of Johnston's (probably written while he was still in Scotland)[6] in honour of the virgin – a cult on which the Reformation was to turn its back. Johnston gives each invocation a different vocal scoring, (as Carver did for his *Gaude Flore*) starting with the upper voices, contrasting them with the lower ones and then bringing all five parts together in smooth-flowing counterpoint of great purity.

By comparison, *Dicant Nunc Judei* is for two voices only and announces the resurrection, challenging the Jews not to blame the soldiers who guarded the tomb, but to worship the risen Christ singing 'Alleluia'. It would have been sung in procession round the aisles of the church. Being in two parts, it is easy to hear the voices imitating each other. Technically, two-part writing is perhaps the most testing of all, for the composer's ideas are completely exposed

Benedicam Domino, an anthem in praise of Queen Elizabeth, was probably written for the court of Henry VIII and the words changed to fit her reign, from which later period the first copies survive. The mixture of Latin and English shows that the Reformation was beginning to oust Latin in favour of the vernacular; and although this is sophisticated music, full of points of imitation, it

Example 5. ROBERT JOHNSTON: BENEDICAM DOMINO (Ms BM Add. 4900, 30513)

sets the words more or less a note for a syllable, ensuring clarity and directness of expression.

The piece as a whole is bold and lively and ends with a dance-like passage for the words 'Let us give laud to God most high and for our Queen now let us pray that she may reign to God's glory'.

Example 6. ROBERT JOHNSTON: BENEDICAM DOMINO
(Ms BM Add. 4900, 30513)

Life in the court of Henry VIII was not necessarily all that secure, whether you were Lutheran or no. It has been suggested that Johnston was personal chaplain to Anne Boleyn whom Henry had beheaded when he wearied of her. Kenneth Elliott thinks this very unlikely,[7] but it is true that Johnston set a poem said to have been written by Anne Boleyn on the eve of her execution in 1536:

Defiled is my name full sore
Through cruel spite and false report,
That I may say for evermore
Farewell my joy, adieu comfort.
Full wrongfully you judge of me
Unto my fame a mortal wound,
Say what you list, it will not be;
You seek for that cannot be found.

Johnston uses sorrowful descending phrases for the first half and more assertive phrases for the accusatory second half. Perhaps he was canny enough to wait the ten years or so until the death of Henry VIII before making this piece public, or contented himself with playing *Defiled Is My Name* on the organ as was commonly done with vocal music.[8] Johnston lived into the reign of Queen Elizabeth and it is a curious phenomenon of English history that with the falling away of the cult of the Virgin Mary, they took up the cult of the virgin queen, and innumerable poems were written raising her to the status of a goddess. But

there was still scope for performances of works such as *Gaude Maria Virgo* in praise of the true virgin. This is Johnston at his best – smooth and refined. There is not one chromaticism in the whole piece (as though it used the white notes of the keyboard only). In the hands of a lesser composer such a restriction of resources would sound bland, but Johnston's handling is masterly. The piece has something of the quality of a carol – the one form in which the cult of Mary has survived in the protestant world – and at the end he introduces just a hint of tension and dissonance for the word 'inviolate' to express the secret mystery of that concept. One could not travel much further away from the great early extravagances of Carver, but one is not thereby left without images of great beauty. This simple music speaks straight to the heart; joyous, refined, worthy of its subject, the imitations turning what could sometimes be a mechanical exercise into a beautiful folding and refolding of a kindly paean of praise.

Even in psalm settings (which became the central texts for sung worship as they had been in the early days of the Celtic Church) Johnston shows that there was still life after Reformation. His setting of *Psalm 67* has a delightful change of rhythm for the words 'May God, even our own God, bless us; may God bless us, and let all the ends of the world fear him'. What he does is to dispel all fear in a kind of a dance. Johnston was influenced by the new continental style of more immediate expressive word setting, so when he wrote this he knew his setting of the words was dispelling the very fear of which they spoke.

EXAMPLE 7. ROBERT JOHNSTON: PSALM 67, DEUS
MISEREATUR NOSTRI (*Wode Partbooks*)

It is clear from this that religious music was not intended to come to a lifeless standstill, though the *Scottish Psalter* of 1564 was to prove to be the first of many that did little more than diminish the role of music which, in its high art form, was seen as insufficiently functional. Too elaborate; too many notes to a syllable; God

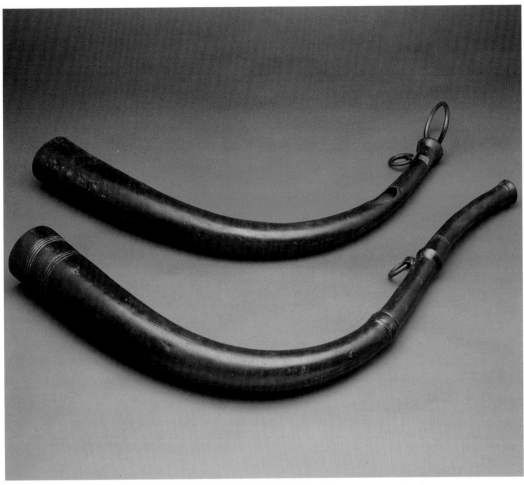

PLATE I. LATE BRONZE AGE HORNS, EIGHTH CENTURY BC, FROM DRUMBEST, CO. ANTRIM

PLATE II. THREE CARNYX PLAYERS ON THE GUNDESTRUP BOWL, FIRST CENTURY BC

PLATE III. DAVID PLAYING A TIOMPAN? FROM THE HIBERNO-SAXON CANTERBURY PSALTER, EIGHTH CENTURY AD

PLATE IV. FORTINGALL IRON BELL, EIGHTH CENTURY

PLATE V. LITTLE DUNKELD BRONZE BELL, NINTH CENTURY

PLATE VI. BRECHIN BELL TOWER, ELEVENTH CENTURY

PLATE VII. PICTISH STONE CARVING AT NIGG,
EIGHTH CENTURY

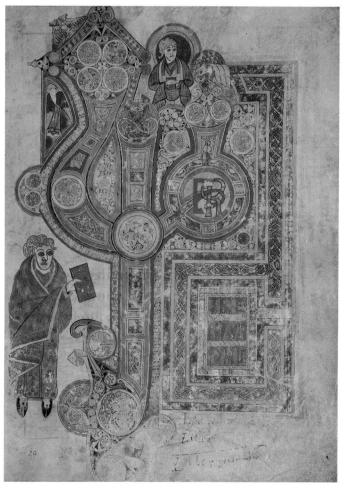

PLATE VIII. ILLUMINATED PAGE FROM *The Book of Kells*,
NINTH CENTURY

PLATE IX. THE IVORY HORN OF LEYS, FOURTEENTH CENTURY

PLATE X. QUEEN MARY CLARSACH, FIFTEENTH CENTURY

PLATE XI. LAMONT CLARSACH, FIFTEENTH CENTURY

PLATE XII. *Sir Edward Bonkill* BY HUGO VAN DER GOES, FIFTEENTH CENTURY

PLATE XIII. *James I*, BY UNKNOWN ARTIST

PLATE XIV. JAMES IV AND QUEEN MARGARET,
Seton Armorial, c.1580

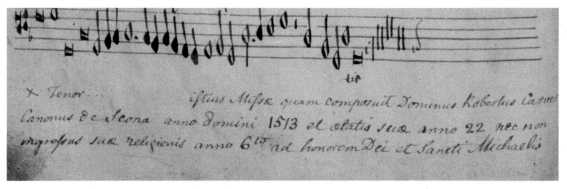

PLATE XV. Eighteenth-Century Gloss of Carver's Signature in the *Carver Choirbook*, sixteenth century.

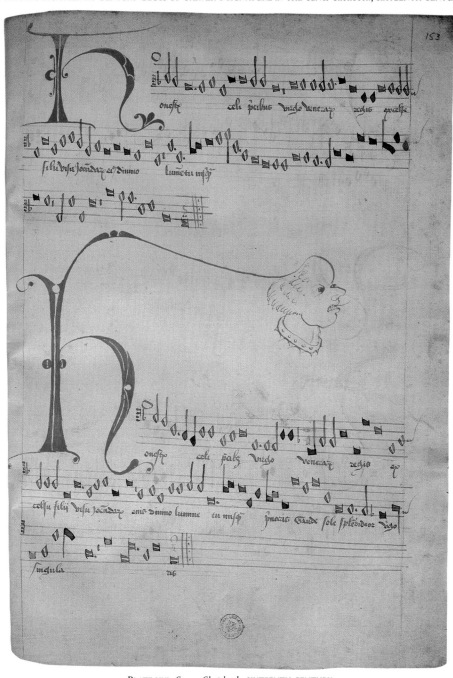

PLATE XVI. *Carver Choirbook*, sixteenth century

should be praised in the languages people spoke: all these were the popular cries of the day, and only recently did the Roman Catholic church finally bow to the vernacular. But even in the sixteenth century the changes were gradual and gentle. A work such as *Descendi In Hortuum Meum* – a lovely setting of part of the *Song of Solomon* – uses Latin, but the words are more clearly set and the parts are more obviously organised into some pattern, with none of the extravagant decoration that Robert Carver was writing at that very time. It dates from 1520 when James V was still a boy. But this is not mere sober restraint. It has been well described as presenting 'smooth refined vocal lines . . . there is a new subtlety about the harmonic progressions . . . a new indulgence in refined sensuousness . . . a piece of . . . perfect narcotic beauty.'[9]

'Perfect narcotic beauty' is appropriate for music which sets the *Song of Solomon*: 'I went down into the garden of nuts to see the fruits of the valley, and to see whether the vine flourished and the pomegranates budded . . . Return, return, O Sunamite; return, return, that we may look upon thee.'

Particularly lovely is the expressive setting of '*revertere revertere*' – return return – the voices responding to each other in pursuasive invitation,

reflecting the influence of the great Flemish composer, Josquin, who was the leader of this new style.

Of course that languorous music and text were given an allegorical interpretation in the sixteenth century – the longing of Christ for the true church – and they may even have contained some expression of desire for reform. Carver too was probably troubled by the turbulent religious climate. In 1531 his fellow Scot and namesake – Robert Richardson – published in Paris a criticism of the Augustinian order to which they both belonged:

> At vespers, when they enter the choir, they are noisy, get in each other's way, disturb the singing, and make an exhibition of themselves to all men, like dumb dogs that cannot bark . . . one man, with the service already begun, asks his neighbour what has been prepared in the kitchen? what kinds of fish, cooked in what manner? He says the wine has been heavily watered and the ale is too frothy . . . Others, driven by bursts of levity, pray to God saying 'miserere mei Deus, Tibi soli peccavi', while they and their fellows mingle this with jokes and laughter.[10]

Richardson goes on to object to:

> ' . . . those who introduce new masses of their own, formed after their own fancies. It is so prevalent that some would wish a different mass to be sung: and so confusions and arguments arise in the service of the Lord, when one reviles the work of another, always finding fault either with the mass, or the sound, the voices or the notes . . . Good God! how much valuable time is inanely wasted in sung masses in England and Scotland!'

Carver was probably one of those criticised and in 1546 he composed a setting of the Mass far simpler than anything he had done before. There were compelling reasons for conforming. That same year Cardinal Beaton was murdered in St Andrews in revenge for the burning of the protestant George Wishart for heresy. The Council of Trent, at which the reform of music was much discussed, was also set up that year. It was a sensible time to compromise. Carver left out a lot of the text so it could be sung more simply and rapidly as plainsong, and in many sections he set words a note to a syllable in a style he must have thought of as one of puerile simplicity, and he also used the *fauxbourdon* style (see Chapter VII). Carver may have written this work for Stirling Parish Church when it became a collegiate church, in 1546. The choir there was probably small and less accomplished and without choirboys, so Carver's Mass has no treble voices.[11]

Although the *Carver Choirbook* is the most important source for Scottish renaissance poly-

Example 8. ANON: DESCENDI IN HORTUUM MEUM
(*Wode partbooks*)

phony, there are others. The *Douglas-Fisher Part Books*, perhaps from the collegiate church of Lincluden in Kirkcudbrightshire, contain two Masses, one of which is related to Carver's *Five Part Mass*, while the Mass, *Felix Namque*, has been likened to the work of Peebles.[12]

David Peebles is another who might well have felt aggrieved by Richardson. He too wrote in a high renaissance style, and were it not for Thomas Wode we would know nothing of him. Wode, a priest from Lindores Abbey, was personally responsible for saving a huge body of Scottish music which would otherwise be lost to us. He had a justified notion of the importance of his work: 'I have said in ane of their bukis that musik will pereishe, and this buke will shaw you sum resons quhy, we se be experiance, that craft nor syence is not learnit bot to the end he may leive be it quhen he hes the craft or science.'[13] 'To ane great man that has bot ane resonable gripe of musike; thir fyve bukis wer worthy thair wayght of gould.'[14]

He wrote the music out in part-books, but they are neat, and almost all of the double-set he made are preserved, so the music can be reconstructed easily (see Plate XVIII). One of the delights of Wode's part books is the number of marginal comments he squeezed in. Here he is writing some time after 1562 describing David Peebles and his setting of *Si Quis Diliget Me*.

> David Pables sumtyme ane channone in the abbay of Sanctandrous – ane of the principall musitians in all this land in his tyme. This sang was set about the yeir of God 1530 and presentit to Kyng Iamis the fyft . . and being a musitian, he did lyke It verray weill . . . the King had ane singular guid eir and culd sing that he had never seine before, bot his voyce wes rawky and harske. Ane lytill before pinky Francy Heagy sumtyme ane nouice in the abbay of Sanctandrous a trim playar upon the organs and also ane disseiple to David Pables, maid this fyft pairt to this, si quis diliget me, quhilk I knaw not bot I sall mak it knawin god willing. It is sa lang since I notit this that I have forget.[15]

In fact he did remember and wrote it down in one of the other part-books. 'Ane lytill before pinky' refers to the battle of that name in 1547. David Peebles' offering to King James V – *Si Quis Diliget Me* – sets the words 'if anyone loves me, he will keep my word, and my father will love him; and we will come to him and make our home with him'.

This is music of peaceful and moving reassurance, with smooth flowing lines that are never without interest. One hopes its kindliness gave Thomas Wode some consolation in copying it down next to the page where, despairingly, he wrote, 'I cannot understand bot musike sall pereische in this land alutterlye. . .'[16]

Example 9. DAVID PEEBLES: SI QUIS DILIGET ME (with extra alto part by Heagy; *Wode partbooks*)

There also survives a Scottish book of musical theory which contains a number of works which may be Scottish, though several of the examples are by foreign masters such as Josquin, and the theoretical material is, as the book's title declares, gathered from earlier continental theorists. It is called *The Art of Music Collectit out of All Ancient Doctouris of Music* and includes music by Robert Johnston and possibly by John Black and Andrew Blackhall, Scottish composers of the mid-sixteenth century.[17] The choice of examples is a broad one, and the treatise shows preoccupations with canon and fauxbourdon that probably reflect Scottish interests. We know from another source, *The Inverness Fragments*, that *fauxbourdon* continued in use at Inverness Parish Church much later than might be expected.[18] But these sources are last gatherings that cannot disguise the end of a great era.

In leaving that era we are saying farewell to centuries of productive days at the Chapel Royal, though they were briefly revived later. We are also saying farewell to a style of music that was expansive, free and imaginative, and yet rooted in mediaeval mysteries. Alongside that music grew a new, more tightly constructed, more perfectly controlled style. David Peebles' *Si Quis Diliget Me* illustrates it. Carver himself was influenced by it. It came from the continent

Plate 22. Cappella Nova singing a Carver Mass in front of the fifteenth-century Choir Screen of Glasgow Cathedral

early in the sixteenth century and it was taken up by Scots at home – and abroad in England – and was better suited to compromising with Reformation ideals. Nonetheless, Peebles did not find it easy to restrict himself to simple part-settings of psalms 'in reports', as it was known when some small independence was permitted in the part movement with a little imitation at the beginnings of lines. Thomas Wode gives us an insight into Peebles' reluctance:

> . . . my lord James (wha efter was Erle of Murray and Regent) being at the reformation, pryour of Sanctandrous, causis ane of his channons, to name, David Pables, being ane of the chieff musitians into this land to set three pairtis to the tenor, and my lord commandit the said David to leave the curiosity of the musike; and sa to make plaine and dulce, and sa he hes done; bot the said David he wes not earnest; bot I being cum to this toune to remaine, I wes ever requesting and solisting till they war all set . . .[19]

Peebles, however much under protest at the new simple style and Wode's requestings and solicitings, must have composed this particular setting with feeling, for the words are from Psalm 3: 'Lord how are they increased that trouble me!' His *Quam Multi Domine* was written 'at the command of ane venerable Father in God, Robert Commendatour of Sanctandrous, 1576' and Wode added 'and his setting verray grave and dulce'.

But of the great and mystical musical celebrations of High Mass, there was scarcely a note to be heard, unless unrecorded in small private chapels with restricted forces, or on a few defiant occasions such as those at Kirkoswald, Maybole and Paisley which led to the trial of the sub-cantor of Glasgow in 1563, for assisting at Mass along with forty-seven others.[20] It was not necessarily ignorant mobs who prompted this sort of vengefulness. We have none other than the Regent of Scotland, the Earl of Moray to thank for burning books which had belonged to the Chapel Royal: 'Item tayne be my Lordis Grace and brint vi Mass Buikis.'[21]

Whole churches were destroyed, partly because of economies and a reduction in clergy, but also out of intolerance: 'it was found reasonable and expedient that the parochiners of Restalrig should repaire to the kirk of Leith, and that the kirk of Restalrig be razed, and utterlie destroyed as a monument of idolatrie.'[22]

This probably means that it was finely embellished and furnished, but the loss was not only of services, books and buildings, it also entailed loss of work for musicians for whom the church was a major source of employment. But there can be no more pathetic description of the failure to sustain that centuries-old tradition than in this quotation from Thomas Randolph, describing what happened on 14 December 1561 in the Chapel Royal. It is possible that Carver, by then an old man, was present to witness it, the end of all he must have worked for. He will have certainly heard of it: 'Her grace's devout chaplains would, by the good device of Arthur Erskine, have sung a high mass: The Earl of Argyle, and the Lord James, so disturbed the quire, that some both priests and clerks, left their places, with broken heads, and bloody ears: it was a sport alone, for some that were there to behold it; others there were that shed a tear or two, and made no more of the matter'.[23]

CHAPTER IX

THE TWO MARIES
1540–1590

The bleak, but true picture of the end of serious musical activity in the Chapel Royal in the 1560s with which we ended the last chapter, does not mark the end of art music in Scotland as a whole. But it was a turning point, one which faces us in the direction of a major development in Europe: the growth of purely instrumental music. Of course there had always been instrumental music, but little was written down as it was secular and most of the people who could write music were employed as priests. When the church made music it sang it. Without the human voice and the religious text there was little excuse for music in religion, or so they appear to have thought. Dancing and dance music were peripheral to the holy repertoire.

At the same time there was undoubtedly a growing bad conscience about indulgence in the arts. James Melville, recalling his student days at Saint Andrews in the early 1570s, displays the typical equivocation of a man who loves music and feels a protestant guilt about it.

> I learnit my music, quhairin I tuik greitar delyt than in law, of Alexander Smithe, servant to the Primarius of our College, quha had bein treinit up amangis the monkis in the Abbay. I lernit of him the gam, plein sang, and monie of the treblis of the Psalmis, quhairof sum I could weil sing in the Kirk; bot my naturalitie and eisie lerning be the eir maid me the mair unsolid and unredie to use the form of the art. I luvit singing and playing on instrumentis passing well, and wald gladlie spend tyme quhair the exercise thairof wes within the College; for two or thrie of our condiscipulis playit feloun weil on the virginalis, and ane uthir on the lute and githorn. Our Regent had also the pinaldis in his chalmer, and lernit sumthing, and I eftir him; bot perceiving me ower mekil carryit eftir that, he dishanit and left off. It wes the greit mercie of my God that keipit me from anie greit progres in singing and playing on instrumentis, for gif I had atteinit to anie resonabil messour thairin, I had nevir done guid uthirwayis, in respect of my amorous dispositioun.[1]

The various instruments which so seduced Melville were at the height of their popularity. The 'githorn' (cittern) was a kind of guitar. The 'virginalis' was a responsive keyboard instrument with quills to pluck the strings, calling for lively finger-work and strong rhythms to make up for the fact that the volume cannot be graded. The 'pinaldis' was possibly another name for the spinet – a small keyboard instrument also with plucked strings. The lute's soft expressive powers made it popular as an accompaniment for the voice, but it came in various sizes and with varying numbers of strings which made for considerable range and variety. The little mandora lute could be bright and lively as well as plaintive, whereas the larger lutes had considerable power and resonance. These were solo instruments as well, and some of the music for them involved rich chording and complicated part-writing (see Plate XIX).

The Scottish lute repertoire, however, is notable for the sparse style of writing, and it has been rightly suggested that this is derived from the clarsach,[2] Scottish performers taking their own distinctive repertoire from their oldest and most favoured instrument. The lowland clarsach, gut-strung and plucked with the flesh of the fingers, sounds not dissimilar to the lute and, interestingly, the Highland clarsach with metal strings plucked with the nails, is quite close in sound to the virginals, though it has more resonance and sweetness of tone. Several examples of the Scottish lute repertoire from early seventeenth-century manuscripts are given in this book and all support the statement that 'they are all the more touching for their lack of sophistication. They have the gift of saying much with very little.'[3]

Most of our early instrumental music is based on dance and continued so, well into the eighteenth century. With James V's marriages to Frenchwomen, French music and dance had an even greater influence on Scottish music than before; the long-standing alliance between Scotland and France had already established

Plate 23. CARVING OF A SIXTEENTH-CENTURY FIDDLER

the most flexible and resonant of a number of bowed stringed instruments which included the fithel and rebec. These latter two were smaller and more strident in tone and the style of music and playing which they probably employed may have survived in part in the striking and energetic playing that can still be heard from traditional Scottish fiddlers (see Plate 23). A tune recently discovered in the binding of a sixteenth-century book perhaps gives us a clue to their lost repertoire, its repeated notes strongly suggesting vigorous bow action.[5]

Example 1. UNTITLED

© Kenneth Elliott

many cultural links and was such that Scotland allowed herself to be ruled for several years by James V's French widow, the remarkable Marie de Guise, even though she fought against the Scottish tide of reform. A song that may have been sung by her to her baby Mary while in hiding from the English at the Priory of Inchmahome on the Lake of Menteith was Alexander Scott's *Lament of The Master of Erskine* (MB42 – *Musica Britannica* XV). Scott was a composer and poet and it is thought this song was addressed to Marie de Guise herself. She was rumoured to have loved and been loved by Robert, Master of Erskine. Hence the words: 'Departe, departe, allace, I must departe From hir that hes my hart, with hart full soir.' Well might he thus address the widowed queen for he was off to fight the English at the Battle of Pinkie (1547), and there his departure was for eternity.[4]

At Inchmahome her mother might have heard another song of Scott's which reflects with deep sorrow on the loss of his wife, not through death, but simply because she ran off with someone else. He ends every verse with the thought that she should be his, the music repeating each rueful variation of the idea.

With the French queens came French musicians – violers and others. The viols were

The household accounts suggest that the viols gradually overtook the fithel in the Scottish court, but John Bellenden, writing in the mid-sixteenth century seems to have thought they were all inappropriate for the high-born:

Show now what kinds of sounds musical
Is most seemly to valiant cavaliers.
As thund'ring blast of trumpet bellical
The spirits of men to hardy courage stirs
So singing, fiddling, and piping not ever is
For men of honour or of high estate.
Because it spouts sweet venom in their ears
And makes their minds all effeminate.[6]

Bellenden means the lowland pipes, or similar, for Buchanan writes not much later that 'the bagpipe was substituted for the trumpet by the West highlanders' and that can only mean the great Highland pipes: none of the others could possibly act as a substitute for a trumpet, and the Highland bagpipes could never be described as making the mind effeminate.

As for fiddling being sweet, it all depended on your point of view. De Brantome, in his account of Mary Queen of Scots' arrival in Edinburgh in 1561, writes disdainfully of the musicians amongst the crowd, criticising their violins, rebecs, and out-of tune psalm singing: '*vindrent soubs sa fenestre cinq ou six cens marauts de la ville luy donner l'aubade de meschants violons et . . . petits rebecz, dontil n'y en a faute en ce pays la; et se mirent a chanter des psaumes, tant mal chantez et si mal accordez, que rien plus. He, quelle musique et quel repos pour sa nuict!*'[7]

But this popular serenade of psalm singing and out-of-tune fiddle playing was said by John Knox to have been well received by the queen: 'a cumpanie of most honest men who, with instruments of musick, and with musicians, gave their salutatiouns at her chalmer windo. The melodie, as sche alledged, lyked her weill, and sche willed the sam to be continewed sum nychts efter with grit diligence.'[8]

Let us assume the best. Probably nothing would have pleased the French historian Seigneur de Brantome, who admired her beyond measure. Mary could have been serenaded by the ex-students of the Edinburgh Sang Schule (the Reformation had closed it only the year before). The sort of music they might have played is *Ane Exempill of Tripla* which was copied into their theory book, *The Art of Music*, only a few years later when their school was reopened (see Chapters VIII and X). The *Cantus Firmus* round which the parts play is probably a popular tune of the time (MB74).

As for the psalm singing, it probably was raw enough with five or six hundred people singing psalms which, after all, they could only have been learning to sing very recently as the first Scottish psalter came out three years later. No doubt Knox had been pushing psalms already along with John Craig, minister in Edinburgh's Canongate who had recently escaped from the Inquisition after spending nine months with the high tides of the river Tiber coming up to his waist. He was happier preaching in Latin than in Scots, but he contributed to the new Scottish psalter which was in the vernacular.

Scots will have been a problem for Mary too. French was her native tongue and she was fond of reading, and was a good writer in French as we can see from part of a touching poem composed by her on the death of her first husband, the little Dauphin of France. It reads with genuine feeling even in translation and was almost certainly intended to be sung, though no music has been identified for it.

If to repose my limbs apply,
And slumbering on my couch I lie;
I hear his voice to me rejoin,
I feel his body touching mine;
Engaged at work, to rest applied,
I have him still for ever at my side.

But here my song, do thou refrain
From thy most melancholy strain,
Of which shall this the burden prove:
'My honest heart full lively love,
Howe'er I am, by death disjoin'd,
Shall never, never diminution find.'[9]

Mary had been brought up in the company of the great French poet, Ronsard, to whom she dedicated more than one poem of her own. Ronsard was familiar with Scotland which he had visited as a boy.

There was a thick haar in August 1561 when Mary Stewart arrived on the coast of Scotland, bewailing her beloved France. As her ship lay at anchor, the trumpeters perhaps acting as fog-horns, we may imagine her passing the time with both her own music and verse. De Brantome was with her on the ship waiting for the fog to lift so they could land at Leith. He says of her that 'She had yet more, that perfection to fire the world, a voice very sweet and good, for she sang very well, blending her voice with the lute, which she touched so daintily with that fair white hand.'

She may even have composed the Galliards which bear her name,[10] the *Queen of Scots Galliard* and the *Galliarda la Royne d'Ecosse*, both courtly dances, well-mannered, unpretentious, but lively.

Example 2. GALLYARD QUEEN SCOTTE (*Marsh Lute Book, c.*1595)

Mary's supposed affair with David Riccio, whose charms (notwithstanding the doubtful portrait of him [see Plate 24]) were apparently more musical than physical, suggests that music was one of her main consolations. He was certainly highly paid and Melville describes him providing a bass voice for vocal ensembles: 'David Ricio . . . was a merry fallow, and a good

Plate 24. POSTHUMOUS PORTRAYAL OF DAVID RICCIO, SEVENTEENTH CENTURY

mucitien; and hir Maieste had thre varletis of hir chamber that sang thre partis, and wanted a beiss to sing the fourt part; therfor they tald hir Maieste of this man to be ther fourt marrow, in sort that he was drawen in to sing somtymes with the rest.'[11]

The sort of music Riccio might have taken part in would have included *Support Your Servant Peirles Paramour*. This is a typical song addressed to the poet's mistress who has all virtues except pity for her lover. It is a version by the Scottish poet James Steill of a poem by Marot, whose original will have been known to the queen from her youth in France, but it is the music which truly distinguishes it. The parts are expertly written, each with its own beauty and coherence but with the voices as a whole rising and falling away from expressive lover's sighs which bring together both longing and unease. No doubt, when sung with the queen as the object of desire, it will have been easy enough to think of Riccio as a potential seducer (MB39).

Riccio's murder must have seemed to Mary as the ultimate in negative brutality. Knox thought it a fine deed, no doubt seeing the hand of heaven in each of the fifty dagger-strokes with which this probably innocent foreigner was put to death by some of the leading men of the realm.

Dancing was another of Mary's pleasures of which Knox disapproved. With the French came several dance forms, especially the Galliard and Pavan. They followed on the Basse-Danse which had pervaded Europe, as had the Branle. Thoinot Arbeau describes it entertainingly in his *Orchesographie* of 1588:

> The branle is danced sideways and not forward. When you commence a branle several others will join you, as many young men as do damsels, and sometimes the damsel who is the last to arrive will take your left hand and it will thus become a round dance. . . . Many branles take their name from the countries where they are customarily danced. The Poitevins dance their branles de Poitou, the Scots their Branles of Scotland and the Bretons branles which they call the Trihory or papsy. . . . Some ignoramuses have corrupted the movements of the branle of Poitou but I will not be a party to this and I shall give you a tabulation of the manner in which I danced it of yore with the maidens of Poitiers. . . . The Scottish branles were in fashion about twenty years ago. The musicians have a suite comprising a number of these branles, all differing in their movements, which you can learn from the said musicians or from your companions. They are danced in quick duple time as you see in the tabulation of the two following branles, which are the first and second in the suite.[12]

The Scots also originated their own dances. The word 'jig' used for a dance first occurs in the work of the poet and composer Alexander Scott:

> *Sum luvis, new cum to town,*
> *With jeigis to make thame jolly;*
> *Sum luvis dance up and doun,*
> *To maiss their melancholy.*[13]

Of course many dances were very simple and did not need to be written down. They were part of the oral tradition, passed from voice to voice and player to player. One which found itself committed to paper at the relatively early date of 1615 was *The Scottish Huntsupe*. This was an 'aubade' – a dawn tune probably known to the Stewart monarchs, who all loved hunting. It relieved them of what was known as the Stewart disease – a kind of melancholy – whenever they were inactive. They would have heard *The Huntsupe* with pleasure as they mounted early in the morning, the mists clearing off the meadows or lingering among the trees of their great deer parks and forests.

The Scottish Huntsupe had secular words, but the Reformation led to much criticism of secular song and dance and, knowing that the people would not easily abandon these, the reformers gave the songs new texts with a religious purpose. So it is that we find words for *The Scottish Huntsupe* in *The Good and Godlie Ballads* put together by the two Dundee brothers Wedderburn in 1576. Their publication contained psalms, hymns, biblical passages and 'sundrye uther Ballatis changeit out of prophaine sangis'.

We will have to guess at the original text behind the religious paint. In the first verse it is easy – for 'Jesus our King' we simply read 'James our King'.

> *With huntis up, with huntis up,*
> *It is now perfite day,*
> *Jesus our King is gaine in hunting,*
> *Quha lykis to speid thay may.*

Example 3. TWO SCOTTISH BRANLES (Thoinot Arbeau, *Orchesographie*, 1588)

But by the fourth verse it seems to have been completely overtaken by the new doctrine:

The hunter is Christ, that huntis in haist,
The hundis ar Peter and Paull,
The Paip is the Fox, Rome is the Rox,
That rubbis us on the gall.[14]

The tune is determinedly repetitive, suggestive of simple horn calls but the bass notes on which it all depends form the harmonic progression known as the double tonic – moving up and down a tone. We can hear from this piece that at least one of the essential characteristics of Scottish traditional music is very old indeed. The rhythm canters along as though on horseback and later changes to 2/4, speeding up to a virtuoso conclusion.

Example 4. THE SCOTTISH HUNTSUPE (*Jane Pickering Lute Book*, c.1616)

Quite apart from music with the immediate practical purpose of waking people up, there was a huge variety of secular music to disturb the conscience of a Melville. He could, for instance, have been seduced by a love dittie such as *O Lusty May* – a month that has never lost its popularity and, in this case, with a summons to all lovers expressed in sprightly dance rhythm but with cadences that have echoes of the songs of Maytime of long ago (MB35).

Another source of attraction for Melville from his proper concerns might have been the lute which could have lulled him into an amorous melancholy with the hazy lazy wanderings of a tune that is all Scottish, pentatonic, and rejoices in the wonderful title of *Wo Betyde Thy Wearie Bodie*, seemingly too weary itself to escape from its own repetitions, and yet so seductive one could forgive it twice the length.

Example 5. WO BETYDE THY WEARIE BODIE (*Straloch Lute Book*)

After such dreamy stuff one can imagine Melville at least permitting himself a dance tune to wake up with. The standard dance coupling of the day was a Pavan and Galliard, both dance forms imported from France. In fact the Pavan was possibly Spanish in origin – slow, stately, perhaps in imitation of the parading of the 'pavo' – the peacock. It replaced the French Basse Danse and moved in a measured two beats to the bar.

'The next in gravity and goodness is called a Pavan, a kind of staid music ordained for grave dancing and most commonly made of three strains, whereof every strain is played or sung twice.'[15] Thus writes the English composer and music teacher, Thomas Morley. William Kinloch (see below) wrote a particularly fine *Pavan*. It is a dance of measured confidence, to which Kinloch has added chromatic colour and lively rhythm – vigorous and dignified all at once. He quotes from his fellow virginalist, William Byrd, the great English composer who was still wedded to the catholic cause which we shall see Kinloch shared with him also.

The Galliard that belongs with this Pavan is a livelier dance, three beats to the bar, only this kind of writing is more for listening to than dancing – for in the latter quarter of the sixteenth century we are at the beginnings of solo keyboard music – 'after every Pavan we usually set a Galliard (that is a kind of music made out of the other), causing it to go by a measure which the learned call 'trochaim rationem', consisting of a long and short stroke successively. This is a lighter and more stirring kind of dancing than the Pavan, consisting of the same number of strains.'[16]

It seems as though Kinloch was regularly crossing the border, for he made his own setting of *Johnstounis Delyt* – a tune by the English composer Edward Johnstone. Most of the secular music from this period is anonymous, but just as composers become named in Renaissance religious music, so do they begin to step out of their anonymity in secular compositions. In the world of the ballad, however, anonymity remained the norm.

Two particularly fine and famous ballads give us an insight into society in Mary's reign. In 1562 not long after her arrival she made a progress through Scotland, staying at Fetternear House in Aberdeenshire where Jean Meldrum made herself a favourite of the queen. She must have been a remarkable girl. She fell in love at first sight with Sir George Gordon of Glenlogie and told him she would have him or die. He joked about it at first, but she fell sick and her chaplain wrote a letter so movingly expressing her plight, that Glenlogie came and promised her his hand. Happily, she recovered rapidly. The many versions of this ballad are remarkably consistent melodically, as though this story and this tune were inseparable companions. How old? Who can say? Like many of our finest Scottish tunes it has a wide range and requires a good singer – but you can be sure that whoever first dreamt it up would be proud to hear it sung as it was by Lizzie Higgins in our own century, with clarity, steady rhythm, perfectly pitched; and expressed with a direct integrity full of the nobility of love, which is the theme of this ballad.[17] The tune is pentatonic, except for one descending phrase, but one could never mistake the great sweep of this melody for any other tune using only a five-note scale, though it does seem to have a relationship with *Port Jean Lindsay* which comes from the early seventeenth-century Straloch lute book.

The other ballad is that of *The Four Maries* – ladies in waiting to the queen. Doubt has been cast on its origins, but it seems clear enough from none other than John Knox that there were ballads on this very topic. Notice Knox's associating lewd behaviour with dancing, which Mary loved:

In the very time of the General Assembly, there comes to public knowledge a haynous murder, committed in the court; yea, not far from the Queen's lap: for a French woman, that served in the Queen's chamber, had played the whore with the Queen's own apothecary. The woman conceived and bare a childe, whom, with common consent the father and mother murthered; yet were the cries of a new-born child hearde, searche was made, the childe and the mother were both apprehended, and so were the man and woman condemned to be hanged in the publicke street of Edinburgh. . . . But yet was not the court purged of whores and whoredoms . . . for it was well known that shame hasted marriage between John Sempill, called the Dancer, and Mary Levingston, sirnamed the Lusty. What bruit the Maries, and the rest of the dancers of the court had, the ballads of that age do witnesse, which we, for modestie's sake, omit.[18]

It seems that these stories have been compressed into each other to form the ballad we know. Some say it is an eighteenth-century composition, since neither words nor tune have been traced any earlier, and because there was a Mary Hamilton in Russia who killed her own illegitimate baby. But that was a remote event and does not account for the other three Maries always featured in the ballad, so we may accept that it is what it says it is – one of the ballads referred to by Knox.

An interesting side-light on that ballad is contained in one of the versions which reads:

The King has gane to the Abbey garden
And pu'd the savin tree,
To scale the babe from Marie's heart
But the thing it wadna be.

Savin was used virtually exclusively to procure abortions and in the 1560s we know of a Mark Jameson, a 'vicar-choral' – that is, a

Example 6. GLENLOGIE (Christie, 1876)

Example 7. PORT JEAN LINDSAY (*Straloch Lute Book*)

member of the choir — at Glasgow Cathedral,
who included it in a list of plants intended for a
physic garden. He would have had just such a
garden behind his cottage opposite the cathedral
and the list of plants suggests that he was a
gynaecologist and an abortionist.[19] There are
several tunes, but the first half of the most
popular one (which was also picked up in the
USA) is wholly pentatonic. Whether it could be
the original tune or no remains undecided.[20]

Example 8. THE FOUR MARIES (Traditional)

More tender associations can be made with
Mary Beaton, another of the Four Maries. This
is her 'Row' — a dance form like the well known
Keel Row. It appears only in *The Rowallan Lute
Book* and is in the section that got soaked with
water, so not every note can be guaranteed. It
has a gentleness about it that goes well with a
lady in waiting. In one or two places it sounds as
though it imitates the French bagpipes, the
musette, which were the forerunners of our
Lowland pipes.

Example 9. MARY BEATON'S ROW (*Rowallan Lute Book, c.1620*)

Though heavily restricted by the cultural
limitations and religious intolerance of the
reformers, Mary herself still celebrated Mass,
and in 1566 her son, the future King James VI,
was baptised according to the rites of the church

of Rome, with the protestant earls waiting
patiently outside the chapel for the celebrations
to be resumed. Indeed the christening was the
occasion for one of the biggest triumphs Europe
had ever seen. It involved a mock assault on
Stirling Castle ending with a huge firework
display, the whole symbolic of Mary's role as a
peace-maker between catholic and protestant.
There was dancing and playing in abundance and
men dressed as hobby-horses singing Italian
songs; and food was served at the symbolically
round table on a moving stage pulled into place
by twelve satyrs accompanied by musicians
'dressed lyk maidens playing upon all sortis of
instrumentis'.[21]

Life at court, whether happy or unhappy, was
soon at an end for the queen who spent her last
years in prison with few consolations apart from
music and sewing and writing letters, perhaps
when she was lucky, to the accompaniment of
viols if so many were allowed in her chamber.
However, she was by no means forgotten and
conspiracies centred round her with musicians
closely involved. The brilliant keyboard player,
William Kinloch, was a secret emissary to Mary
in captivity in England, acting for a fellow-
composer and conspirator, James Lauder, who
here writes to his son John.

And as for your daggers and knives they are ready to be sent to
you, but I only wait for Mr William Kinlowgch's coming to
London, who is in this country at present and ready to pass to
London, and by whom I shall write more at length . . . praying
daily the eternal God to preserve the Queen's majesty. Edinburgh
the second of October fifteen eighty-two. Signed James Lauder.[22]

Lauder was employed in the court of the
young James VI , perhaps educating him further

Example 10. LAUDER: THE GOLDEN PAVAN (*Thomas Wode
and other Partbooks*)

in music, composing for him, and running an errand to London in 1579 to buy the king 'twa pair of virginells'. Only one piece of Lauder's survives complete – a Pavan written in 1584 for the murdered Darnley's uncle, Robert Stewart, Lord of March. It is very fine indeed – *The Golden Pavan* it was called, and rightly so. It is a little sombre as well as stately, and is full of subtle imitation.

Lauder, whom the French knew to be 'very affectionate to the Queen' went to France in 1586, the year before Mary's execution, perhaps allowed by James VI in the hope that he would compromise himself as the poet Montgomerie was later to do. Montgomerie, perhaps a leading light in the pro-Mary conspiracies, wrote a poem for Lauder called *James Lauder I wald see Mare*. 'I wald see Mare' is an anagram of James Lauder. It is also a coded way of saying 'I wish to see Maria Regina' – Mare – Mary.

> *James Lauder, I wald see Mare*
> *I wald see mare nor anything I sie.*
> *I sie not yit the thing that I desyre*
> *Desyre it is that does content the ee*
> *The ee it is whilk settis the hairt in fyre*
>
> *Aspyre I sall in esperance to speid*
> *To speed I hope thoght danger still I dreid* [23]

It is in this context that the Battle of Pavie becomes relevant. It took place in 1525 in northern Italy between the French and an imperial coalition of Spanish and Papal armies. Why should the Scot William Kinloch write a piece of music about it? The battle was not merely a power struggle between temporal monarchs: it represented a confrontation between the French King Francis I, who was interested in religious reform and an alliance supporting the Roman Catholic orthodoxy. The Scots were closely involved. Scotland's King Regent – the Duke of Albany – was partly responsible for the overall strategy on behalf of the French. The people of Pescara admitted allegiance to three kings in Italy: the King of France, the King of Navarre and the King of Scots. A young Scottish prince was killed in the battle (possibly Armand Claude Gordon) [24] '. . . then a ruffian came who had traitorously killed the Prince of Scotland. The King, recognising a gold chain, wept for the Prince's death. He was only eighteen years of age and the most beautiful creature I have ever seen.

It was great pity seeing him dead surrounded by hundreds of candles in the Monastery of Pavia where he lay.' [25]

Fifty years after the Battle of Pavie there was still a chance that France would turn protestant and that James VI would own up to his catholicism and join forces with his imprisoned mother to turn Scotland catholic again. So Kinloch's *Battel of Pavie* would have meant a lot to its audience. The battle was thought of as the last great chivalric encounter complete with puissant knights in armour on noble steeds. The story was told all over Europe, romanticised and exaggerated. In fact it started when the manoeuvring armies bumped into each other in thick dawn mists and was all over in a couple of hours. 'All is lost except honour' was the French king's comment.

Kinloch's *Battel of Pavie*, among the large genre of instrumental Battle Pieces, is by far the most extensive and carefully thought-out work, and shows that he could master what was for those days a very large-scale form. It is a single movement and it starts with a growling brooding theme of severe nobility.

Example 11. WILLIAM KINLOCH: BATTEL OF PAVIE
(*Duncan Burnett Music Book, c.1610*)

William Byrd wrote a piece not dissimilar in intent, but it consists of separate movements and lacks the structural coherence of the Kinloch which is also melodically more inventive, as well as exploiting the various textures of the virginals while keeping the insistent sounds of drums and trumpets in mind. Kinloch's piece ends with a splendid celebratory dance imitating fife and drum and with echoes of an early sixteenth-century Catalan piece called *La Guerra*.

Example 12. WILLIAM KINLOCH: BATTEL OF PAVIE (*Duncan Burnett Music Book*)

Mary Queen of Scots was a good player on the virginals. Sir James Melville merely says she played very well for a queen, but being jealously quizzed by Queen Elizabeth at the time, probably did not dare give Mary her full due. This music was almost certainly played to and possibly played by her. We have seen how Kinloch acted as secret agent to her during her captivity. He may have given her copies of his own music, though it is unlikely she would have been able to match

his brilliant keyboard playing, of which we can be confident since his music requires great dexterity in both hands. Perhaps he relieved her sorrows with his crazily good-humoured *Fantasie*. The hapless Melville at St Andrews would have known it too, as Kinloch probably hailed from nearby Dundee. The *Fantasie* is full of harmonic colouring and hilarious sequences and certainly not conducive to a proper study of the law, which was Melville's chosen lot.

If, as is possible, Kinloch had wealthy connections in the Low Countries[26] he might have acquired a really up-to-date set of virginals to play the piece on – one known as '*mutter und kind*' because tucked away in its side was a second baby keyboard which you could take out and operate separately from or in conjunction with the keyboard below (its 'mother') – rather like an octave doubling stop on a harpsichord. Perhaps it had the special buzz bar too, that pressed against the strings to give them a different tone colour. It is not unlikely. Scots regularly studied in the Netherlands and Kinloch's *Fantasie* seems to be written for such an instrument, for the parts are written as though the left hand were above the right hand which only makes sense with two keyboards. Thomas Morley, writing in delightful style in the 1590s, describes the virtues of a Fantasie: 'The most principal and chiefest kind of music which is made without a ditty is the Fantasy, that is when a musician taketh a point at his pleasure and wresteth and turneth it as he list, making either much or little of it as shall seem best in his own conceit. In this may more art be shown than in any other music because the composer is tied to nothing, but that he may add, diminish, and alter at his pleasure.'[27]

Another favourite type of composition of the period was called a 'ground'. A modern equivalent is the twelve-bar blues – that is to say a bass line or sequence of chords above which a tune can be improvised and varied while the bass or chords repeat. Many of these basses were the common property of composers throughout Europe and have names. The *Passamezzo antico*, the *Passamezzo moderno*, the *romanesca*, the *basso di Firenze*, etc.

One of the things a ground made easier was composing large-scale pieces. After all you could just repeat the bass and twiddle about for a bit longer and still the whole thing was guaranteed some kind of coherence.

The tune Kinloch puts above his ground bass is full of distinction and nobility, the variations tremendously inventive rhythmically. The fingering is always lively and there is a gradual and carefully structured increase of activity culminating in rapid passage-work for the left hand with the ground bass transferred temporarily to the top part. Then the piece is ready to return to the more solid chordal style of the opening.

Example 13. WILLIAM KINLOCH: GROUND (*Duncan Burnett Music Book*)

more than he received, and he had a large family to support. A part-song such as *Absent I Am Rycht Soir Agains My Will* would have had a double meaning for him with loyalties divided between the exiled queen in England, and his own family and the small but dependable sum he got from her son in Scotland. This is a rare song for those days — a song of true and faithful love surviving absence. It seems very straightforward, but a small change of metre and an unexpected chord betray a lot of underlying feeling (MB45).

A captive at Fotheringay, Mary had only limited opportunity to express her feelings to others. She scratched her only rhyme in English onto the window glass:

From the top of all my trust
Mishap has laid me in the dust.

Her appeal in Latin strikes deeper:

O Domine Deus! Speravi in Te;
O care mi Jesu! nunc libera me.
In dura catena, in misera poena, desidero te;
Languendo, gemendo, et genu flectendo,
Adoro, imploro, ut libera me![29]

Even music must have been a source of sad reflection as well as consolation. The music for *The Time of Youth* was entered into *The Art of Music* at about the time she was in prison. We may think of her listening to this sad rejection of the pride of youth, no doubt taking its words deep into the confusion of regrets and bitternesses that must have occupied her heart.

Example 14. FETHY: THE TIME OF YOUTH (*The Art of Music*)

We have seen how Kinloch's fellow composer James Lauder was involved both with the deposed Queen Mary and her son King James. But in James's court he was poorly paid and lived outwith the court, unlike the Hudson family of violers whom James had imported from England and appears to have favoured at the expense of others.[28] Lauder wrote to his son John asking him to persuade Mary Queen of Scots to help him out financially. The last time he had gone to London to gather his salary in, it had cost him

To serve the flesh I thought it best
As long as youth did with me last,
But to my God now I protest
Before I die
My soul with him in heav'n to rest
Eternally.

Great thanks be to his Majestie
That time and space hath lent to me
Of all my youth and fantasie
For to deplor,
Wherefore I think his face to see
Into his Glore.

CHAPTER X

AT THE COURTS OF THE
LAST KING
1570–1630

Mary was executed in 1587. By comparison with her own restricted pleasures, the court of James VI succeeded in re-establishing Scotland as a cultural centre of importance. James had finally assumed power in 1579 and made his entry into Edinburgh where he was greeted by the magistrates, four violers and a group of sangsters. They each received thirty shillings and it cannot be said that such a greeting could have amounted to very much. But we do have an entertaining part-song which was probably sung on that occasion – *Nou let us sing to our yong king* (MB48 – *Musica Britannica XV*). The words continue 'Lord save our King sing alltogither That he may do some princelie thing That we may live lyk faithfull brether.'[1] It doubled as a drinking song, featuring a request from each of the four voices in turn for drink as a necessary adjunct to good singing: treble, counter, tenor and bass join together declaring that 'This art of music is richt dry'. No doubt they found an easy and acceptable remedy. It could also be sung as a somewhat imperfect round, which is how it is presented here – the places for the other three parts to enter are marked with a star.

Example 1. NOU LET US SING (Thomas Wode, *Quintus Partbook*)

James VI was keen on music and set about repairing much of the damage done to it by the Reformation. Most of the song schools had been closed in 1560 but as soon as he took over from the Regency, Parliament passed the following statute:

> For instruction of the youth in the art of musik and singing, quhilk is almost decayit, and sall shortly decay, without tymous remeid be providit, our Soverane Lord James VI with avise of his thrie estatis of this present parliament, requeistis the provest, baillies, counsale, and communitie of the maist speciall burrowis of this realme, and of the patronis and provestis of the collegis, quhair sang sculis are foundat, to erect and set up ane sang scuill, with ane maister sufficient and able for instruction of the yowth in the said science of musik, as they will answer to his hienes upon the perrel of their foundationis, and in performing of his hienes requeist do unto his Majestie acceptable and gude plesure.[2]

Interestingly the Scottish Parliament called music a science, though the treatise that has been referred to previously and which was probably written for the Edinburgh sang school in 1580, calls itself *The Art of Music*. Art or Science, it certainly contains recondite matter. In *The Fifteenth Canon* the two parts have the same music, only the lower part plays it backwards against the upper part. In *The Nyntene Canon* one part is the same as the other but played twice as slowly.

Example 2. THE NYNTENE CANON (*The Art of Music*)

The word 'canon' also meant a simple rule or technique and some of these are more inspiring to read about than to play:

The Saxt Canon. 'The modulator of the example consequent moist follow the lark quhilk with his song fro the earth to the meid spoir dois ascend, fro hyvene furth schew, revertent with the samyn canticle resonant to the prestyne place dois descend.'[3]

Example 3. THE SAXT CANON (*The Art of Music*)

Other canons had a religious symbolism:

The Sevint Canon. 'In the beginning of this exempill fyve pausis of brevis ar to memorie commendit, quhilkis to similitud of the silenc of Zachary ar figurat, as be this mandat of the auctor is demonstrat . . . In the beginning the tenor Zacharizes five times.'

Old Zaccharias was struck dumb by the news that his elderly wife was pregnant. She was the mother of John the Baptist. So this obscure musical curiosity, hidden away in a treatise, had its sense of fun. A hundred and fifty years later, Bach was still delighting in this sort of musical game.

Thomas Wode, meanwhile, was steadily continuing his great compilation of music, the bulk of which consisted of skilful settings of the psalms. Not all of these were originally intended for the church. One classic example is Blackhall's version of *Judge and Revenge my Cause* (MB11).

'The forty-third psalm set be Maister Andro Blackhall at the earnest suit of Lord Morton who presentit the samin to kyng Jamis the saxt at Stirling in the moneth of February . . yeir of God 1578.'[4]

The words of the psalm – 'Judge and Revenge My Cause' – had been displayed on a banner at the Battle of Carberry with beside them a portrayal of the murdered Darnley and his son, the infant James VI (see Plate 25). Morton, at a time when he was in danger from rivals, presented the psalm setting to the king as a reminder of his past services and in the hope of understanding in the present. Blackhall's music did Lord Morton no good. He was executed a year or two later in 1581 on the pretext that he had assisted in the murder of Darnley rather than deplored it.

However, the king did enjoy music and was surrounded by poets, many of whose works –

Plate 25. DARNLEY, THE CARBERRY BANNER

even extended ones – would have been sung rather than declaimed. James was a scholar and was visited and admired by the French poet du Bartas, and much courted by the great Scottish poet Alexander Montgomerie. Montgomerie was part and parcel of the catholic plots and was eventually banished from the court, but the settings of his fine poems no doubt lived on in his absence, for James wrote a touching verse epitaph for him.

Montgomerie often refers to music with clear and accurate knowledge and there are several settings of his work which give an insight into the musical and poetic beauties of James VI's court in Scotland, such as *Evin Dead Behold I Breathe* (MB55) and *What Mightie Motion* (MB56). Another poem which would have been sung and for which it would be pleasing to find the music on account of the subject-matter, is his echo poem *To The, echo, and thou to me agane*. Blackhall set a particularly lovely poem of Montgomerie's – *Adieu O Daisie of Delight* to music, using a popular court air (MB49). This air was used for other poems including Montgomerie's greatest achievement, *The Cherrie And The Slae*, which symbolised his preferred Roman Catholicism as the sweet cherry and Presbyterianism as the bitter sloe.[5] The shapeliness of the tune with its repeated phrases is perfectly matched by the words in graceful assonance.

Mary's execution seems chiefly to have been noted in Scotland by various counter-plottings which finally led to James VI setting up a convention and dinner at Holyrood House followed by a destruction of gibbets, a release of debtors and a public pledge of friendship among nobles, accompanied by trumpets, singing and cannon from the castle. But the divisions were not so easily overcome that they could be dispelled with a few blasts on a trumpet and a well-meaning psalm or two and even in a cheerful roundel there could be concealed bitter and dangerous experiences. One such is *As I Me Walked* from David Melvill's collection. The words were by his brother James Melvill, who saw his lack of technical progress in music as a deliverance from his too great love of it (see Chapter IX). But he could find a place for it in a divine context for he has parodied the original love poem that goes with this round by writing a Christian allegory – Christ guiding the ship of the soul through stormy waters. James Melvill

Example 4. ANDRO BLACKHALL: ADIEU O DAISIE OF DELIGHT
(*Wode partbooks*; words from *The Cherry and the Slae*)

knew all about stormy waters. He was a thorough presbyterian and his king, James VI, was an episcopalian. In 1584 this antagonistic situation became serious and Melville had to escape an arrest warrant by disguising himself as a shipwrecked mariner and making for Berwick in an open boat. Maybe that is the experience he put into his poem, with Christ his guide and pilot, and the cheerful anonymous music of the round, the vessel to carry his hopes.[6]

Example 5. AS I ME WALKED (Melvill, *Book of Roundels* XCV, 1612)

That sort of music was very much for domestic consumption and was popular, as one can gather from Melvill's title page:

Ane buik off roundells
Whairin thair is contained songs and
roundells that may be sung with
thrie, four, fyve, or mo voices
haifing prettie and plesantt
letters sum in Latin and
sum in Inglish quhilks
ar an hundreth in number.
     Collected and notted by david melvill. 1612.

One can imagine *As I Me Walked* sung in the parlour of some gentle divine, but there were other rounds more suited to the drunken midnight revelries of Sir Toby Belch and Sir Andrew Aguecheek in Shakespeare's *Twelfth Night*. Sir Andrew, it has been said, was modelled on the eccentric character of the Scottish composer and retired mercenary, Tobias Hume.[7]

The most memorable of the struggles between the king and his courtiers was that which involved the Bonny Earl o' Murray. He was described as 'a comely personage of great stature, and strong of body like a kemp' – that is to say a prize fighter. There are various versions of the ballad *The Bonnie Earl o' Murray*, some of which accuse James VI's queen of adultery with the earl, but there is no basis for this. He was killed by the treachery of his great rival Huntly, who had been sent to apprehend him and set fire to Donibristle House where he was staying. Eventually he was flushed out and forced his way through Huntly's men, only to be discovered by the glow of his smouldering hat and basely slaughtered rather than captured. The king never punished Huntly.[8] The tune for this ballad emerges in print in 1733 and is a remarkable example of the wide vocal range which the ballads expect of their singers. This one, at an octave and a sixth, is a spectacular instance. The use of the flattened seventh note of the scale (the

F natural) is another hallmark of the Scottish idiom, as are the trills and grace-notes; but what strikes one most is that it also achieves such dramatic nobility within a shape that still retains a satisfying formal balance (see Plate 26).

Example 6. THE BONNY EARL OF MURRAY (Thomson, *Orpheus Caledonius II*, 1733)

Whether there had been anything between Anne of Denmark and Moray or no, there was real celebration for the birth and baptism of an heir to the throne of Scotland – Prince Henry – and it was turned into a major international event, just as James VI's own baptism had been. During the service the twenty-first psalm was sung 'according to the art of music' – which means sung in reports. Singing psalms in reports was a musical device peculiar to the French and Scots, it being a way of allowing imitation and some sense of musical subtlety into the otherwise bland presentation of psalms in four-square harmonies. It would not have been accompanied on the organ on this occasion, because the Earl of Mar had stripped the three organs and everything else deemed papistical from the Chapel Royal not long after the king's baptism – for which he was exonerated by an Act of Parliament. He had made such a good job of ruining it that it had to be

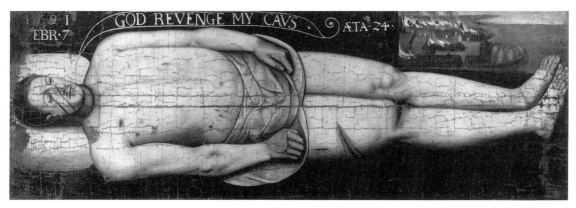

Plate 26. THE MEMORIAL OF JAMES STEWART, EARL OF MORAY, 1591

rebuilt hurriedly in time for this next royal baptism in 1594.[9]

The event was as splendid as the new religion would allow. It had originally been intended that a live lion should draw in a chariot bearing food at the end of the celebratory dinner (there had long been a lion kept in Stirling Castle as symbol of the Scottish monarchy). In the end it was decided the lion would be too terrifying, though of course he would have been as heavily drugged as were the performing bears of the day. Instead they used a black man – who on other occasions would quite probably have been employed as a bass drummer, or playing the cymbals, instruments imported (as was the idea of bowing stringed instruments) from the Middle East by the crusaders.

> They being refreshed, a certane space, came in a black More drawing a chariot, wherein was the desert, presented by ladies Ceres, Facundia, Faith, Concord, Liberalitie and perseverance. The chariot returning, entered an artificiall and weill proportionned shippe, the lenth of her keell eighteene foote, and her breadth eight foote, from the bottom to the high flag foure foote; the sea made counterfooted. On her fore sterne was Neptunus, the Thetis and Triton; about the shippe, mariners and steirsmen. The mast was reid, her taikling and cords of silke, with threttie-five peece of brazen ordinance; all the sailes of double white taffetie. The pylot in cloth of gold moved the shippe, wherin were musicians, and Arion with his harpe;[10]

In fact Arion was sitting upon the ship's nose, which resembled the form of a dolphin, and he might have played a tune such as *Rory Dall's Port*. Blind Rory Dall O'Cahan or O'Kane, as his name would be spoken in English, was an Irish harper and composer who came to live in Scotland. He visited the court of James VI,[11] and his music was popular enough to be copied into more than one early lute manuscript only a decade or two later (see also Chapter XI). This tune appears in both the Skene manuscript as *Port Ballangowne* and the lute book of Robert Gordon of Straloch attributed to Rory Dall, and is clear evidence of tunes by clarsairs being played by lutenists.

Next in the entertainment came 'musick in greene holyne howboyes, in fine parts' [part-music for oboes made of holly wood]. And . . . after thanks being given, there was sung with most delicate dulce voices, and sweet harmonie, in seven partes, the 128th psalm, with fourteen voyces, and musical instruments playing.'

We do not have this psalm in seven parts, but Andro Blackhall set it in five parts, for a

Example 7. RORY DALL'S PORT (*Straloch Lute Book*)

similar celebration, it being originally composed in 1575 for the first marriage of the Earl of Mar. The psalm was accompanied by viols and oboes and other instruments. Music and text are full of kindly prospects of the promised Jerusalem and visions of the king's offspring and grandchildren to come, standing symbolically like olive trees around the table on which his food was served.

After that followed viols, with voices in 'plaine counterpoint'. These latter delivered themselves

Example 8. JOHN BLACK: REPORT on PSALM 50 and WHEN SHALL MY SORROWFUL SIGHING SLACK? (*Duncan Burnett Music Book*)

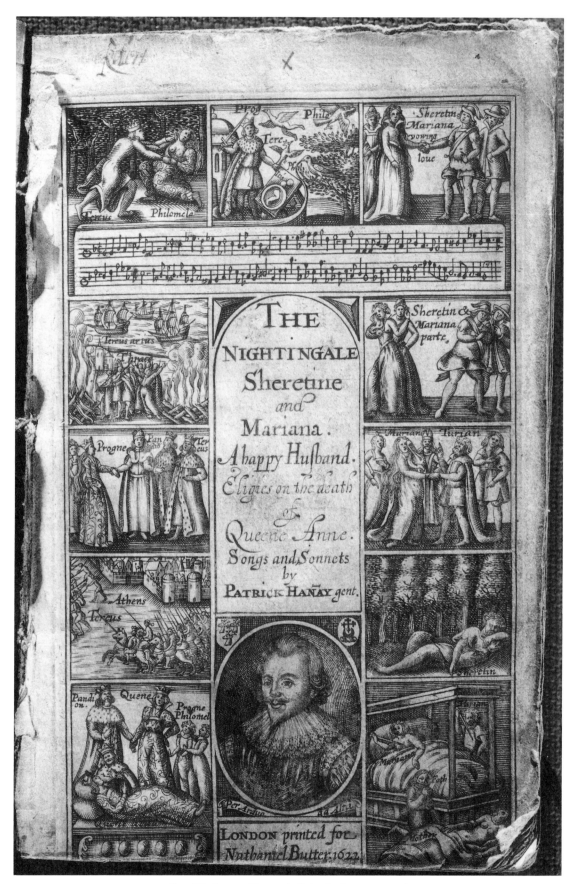

Plate 27. PATRICK HANNAY'S *Philomela* (LONDON, 1622)

of Latin hexameters specially composed for the occasion, then followed 'A still noise of recorders and flutes'. It might have been music such as John Black's *Report* on *When Shall My Sorrowful Sighing Slack?*, played on recorders. The tune of the title was a popular one by the English composer Tallis. Black, with great skill, has taken snatches from it and woven them round the tune used for Psalm 50. Psalm 50 inveighs against idolatry and ceremony without due reverence, so it would have been highly appropriate for the ceremony of baptising a protestant prince. (Example 8.)

This royal baptism was probably one of the last extravagant cultural gestures made by any monarch in Scotland. When James moved to England in 1603 he returned only once to his native land, and subsequent monarchs have done little to make good the loss. From the moment James became king of England, Scotland lost a centre of gravity with the consequence that many of its most talented people were drawn to London.

Amongst poets who went south was one Patrick Hannay, swapping Galloway for London and the kudos of publication there. His best poem is *Philomela* (see Plate 27) and, seeing that Philomela is the Nightingale, it is right and proper that it was understood to be sung. What makes it interesting historically is that the poetic metre, and therefore the music that goes with it, have been loosened up. The rhythms and rhymes are delivered more freely and with less accentuation, and the vocal line sounds quite close to what we now know as recitative – the reciting style which was developed primarily in Italy for dramatic declamation in the then new art form of opera. The music is anonymous. (Example 9.)

Another export to England, by a circuitous route, was the mercenary soldier and amateur composer and performer on the viola-da-gamba, Tobias Hume. Hume is usually credited with being English, though nothing is known of his early years, but his name and profession, at that period, link him firmly with Scotland. His connections with Poland further underline this, as there was a huge contingent of Scots in that country and very few English at the time.[12] Hume's appearance in London, established by publication of his music there in 1605 and 1607, strongly suggests that he had gone there to seek favour at court from the king and his wife, Anne of Denmark. He was quite possibly acquainted with yet another emigré

Scot, the poet Robert Aytoun, secretary to the queen, whose good offices may have secured him permission to dedicate his second publication, *Captaine Hume's Poeticall Musicke*, to her. There are a number of settings of Aytoun's poetry, one or two of which may be Scottish.[13]

Nothing is known of Hume's early days. We can guess he was born around 1569, because he entered the Charterhouse almshouse in 1629, and to do that you had to be sixty years old. But prior to 1605 the best place to find him was on the battlefields of Europe, in Russia or Poland, for Europe was full of Scots mercenaries, soldiers of fortune escaping the poverty and unemployment at home which characterised the latter end of the sixteenth century. There were Scots regiments everywhere.[14] Religion may also have been a factor for the name Tobias comes from the Apocryphal books of the Bible, which were not accepted by the protestants: Tobias Hume may be presumed, then, to have come from a catholic family, and this may have disadvantaged him.

When Hume finally made his way to London in his thirties, no doubt hoping for peace and

Example 9. WALKING I CHANC'D (Patrick Hannay, *Philomela*, 1622)

preferment, there were various ways he might try to endear himself in the Stewart entourage. His first publication, *The First Part of Ayres . . .* of 1605, was dedicated to the Earl of Pembroke, but reflects his continental experiences, with pieces such as *The Duke of Holstones Almaine*, and *Beecus an Hungarian Lord his Delight*, as well as several Polish airs. There are over a hundred pieces in this remarkable collection, which includes works for solo viola-da-gamba, songs and consort music in five parts (to be performed on two bass viols), and other works for viols or lute. With or without dedications, there is always a sense of individuality in Hume's work. Partly it is because he was a great innovator. His is the first book devoted virtually exclusively to the viola-da-gamba which was a bowed six-stringed instrument which came in different sizes and pitches, and was rested on the leg, rather than the viola-da-braccia which was rested on the arm. Hume writes for the viola-da-gamba with an astonishingly advanced understanding of its potential. In *Harke Harke* the melancholy slightly husky sound of a bow on a bass viol is contrasted with plucked chords, and the music ends with the instruction that the final chords should be drummed with the back of the bow, the very first use of this technique. The effect overall is sad and ruminative, with suggestions of a distant throbbing on the repeated low note that is slightly menacing.

Example 10. TOBIAS HUME: HARKE HARKE (Viola-da-gamba; from *The First Part of Ayres*, 1605)

The throbbing may suggest drums, for neighbouring pieces in the book are often connected by title or key and the piece following *Harke Harke* is called *A Souldiers Resolution* and is full of military sounds which he points out in the score '. . . counter march . . . the second part, the Cettill drum . . . March away'. Perhaps he already knew of Kinloch's *Battel of Pavie* (see Chapter IX) for Hume's music is a continuous composition unlike

Example 11. TOBIAS HUME: A SOULDIERS RESOLUTION (Viola-da-gamba; from *The First Part of Ayres*)

Byrd's *Battel* which is a collection of separate pieces.

In Hume's first collection there is also a delightful sequence with titles which suggest a different sort of soldierly pursuit and connecting thread than that of battle. The titles are highly suggestive although some of them pun on viol playing.[15] They appear in the book in this order: *My Mistress hath A Pretty Thing*; *She Loves it Well*; *Hit It In The Middle*; *Tickle Tickle*; *Rosamund*; *I am Falling*; *Tickle Me Quickly*; *Touch Me Lightly*.

There is a disarming directness about Hume, and it comes through in his prose style also, for his prefaces to his publications are vigorous and blunt. In *The First Part of Ayres*, which has the alternative title *Musicall Humors*, he determines to make a virtue of it.

> Alwaies thus to the Reader. I do not studie Eloquence, or professe Musicke, although I doe love Sence, and affect Harmony. My profession beeing, as my Education hath beene, Armes, the onely effeminate part of mee, hath beene Musicke; which in me hath beene alwaies Generous, because never Merecenarie. To praise Musicke, were to say, the Sunne is bright. To extoll my selfe, would name my labours vaine-glorious. Onely this, my studies are farre from servile imitations, I rob no others inventions, I take no Italian Note to an English Dittie, or filch fragments of Songs to stuffe out my volumes. These are mine owne Phansies expressed by my proper Genius, which if thou doest dislike, let me see thine, *Capere vel noli nostra, vel ede tua.* Now to use a modest shrtnes, and a briefe expression of my selfe to all noble spirits, thus, My Title expresseth my bookes Contents, which (if my hopes faile me not) shall not deceive their expectation, in whole approvement, the crowne of my labours resteth. And from henceforth, the statefull instrument Gambo Violl, shall with ease yield full various and devicefull Musicke as any other instrument. For here I protest the Trinitie of Musicke, parts, Passion and Division, to be as gracefully united in the Gambo Violl, as in the most received Instrument that is, which here with a Souldiers Resolution, I give up to the acceptance of all noble dispositions. The friend of his friend, Tobias Hume.
> Your Viols must be tuned as the Lute, beeing the best Set that ever was invented, for these kind of Musickes, which may bee compared with the highest and curious musicke in the world.[16]

Indeed they can be so compared. Thurston Dart went so far as to declare that 'Here, indeed, are all the technical features of Bach's music for unaccompanied violin and cello, in works composed eighty years before Bach was born.'[17] Dart is talking about *Captain Hume's*

Lamentations. He describes it as eloquent, but one could also claim for these *Lamentations* a combination of philosophy, dignity and deep feeling that has much more than a technical right to be mentioned in the company of Bach, and the same can be said of Hume's Pavans, which include the sad and lovely piece called *The Passion of Music*. Its stately progress starts, characteristically, with a yielding descending scale.

Example 12. TOBIAS HUME: THE PASSION OF MUSIC (for four viols; from *Poeticall Musicke*, 1607)

Dart claims for *Captaine Humes Galliard* that it is 'one of the earliest sets of divisions on a ground: each section of the galliard is repeated with variations of increasing brilliance, to an extemporized accompaniment.'[17]

The brilliant use of the viola-da-gamba was not only ahead of its time, it was controversial. Hume's frequent use of chords undercuts one of the most important roles of the lute as an accompanying instrument, as well as in solos, and that was to provide harmonies. The great lutenist composer, John Dowland, criticised Hume's claims for the instrument. In his *A Pilgrim's Solace* Dowland laments that the upstart cocksure younger generation of lutenists have not counter-attacked. As for himself, poor fellow, he says: 'Perhaps you will ask me why I do not under goe this business myself? I answere that I want abilitie, being I am now entered into the fiftieth year of mine age: secondly because I want both meanes, leasure, and encouragement'.

Hume probably had none of those either, but it was he who was proved right. Where is the lute now? Or indeed where was it even half a century after Dowland? Whereas the viola-da-gamba and its successor, the cello, have held sway in their turn, ever since. But Hume was not confined to it, for he wrote for various ensembles and offered

alternative instrumentations. *A Spanish Humour* is also described as *The Lord Hayes' Favourite*. Here we see Hume bringing his continental goods home, for Lord Hayes was James Hay of Kingask, a Scot who had moved south, and a favourite of the king's. Thomas Campion wrote a famous masque in honour of Lord Hayes' first marriage in 1607. Masques were semi-dramatised entertainments with leading parts taken by the aristocracy and with a strong element of music and song. Perhaps Hume's music was heard on the same occasion. One of Hume's pieces is called *Maske* and may have been played at a Masque. Hume claims it as *The Earl of Sussex's Delight*. Getting permission to attach the name of a leading individual to a piece of music was an obvious way of currying favour for it. But Hume was clearly down on his luck. He appealed to James's queen. She was Danish, and he may well have met her during his war services on the continent. This is the dedication of his *Poeticall Music* of 1607, as engaging in its prose style as in its sentiments.

To the sacred Majestie of Queene Anne . . . I will only presume in most devoted zeale, to offer up this last hope of my labours, to your most princely acceptance, humbly imploring, that it would please your thrice-royall spirit, not to esteeme my Songs unmusicall, because my Fortune is out of tune; or to grant me little grace, because my deserts may be valued nothing: but be once pleasd (Right excellent Princes) as the onely and last refuge of my long expecting hopes, to patronize and second the modest ends of the Author of these uncommon Musiques, not for anything he yet can claime of just merit, but for what ample gracings of the King and my excited affection to do your Majesty service, may happily expect.[18]

The first piece in the book is *The Queenes New Yeeres Gift* — a languid song accompanied by two lutes and viola-da-gamba. The poetry is as beautiful as the music and is also by Hume — who in this role should not be confused with his contemporary, fellow Scot and famous poet, Alexander Hume. It starts 'Cease Leaden Slumber dreaming, my Genius presents the cause of sweet musickes meaning' and begins the New Year like an awakening from bad dreams to the delights of 'musicks harmony'. It is among the finest of all Jacobean songs and, on the strength of it alone, Hume will never be forgotten. (Example 13.)

Another piece, *The King of Denmark's Health* was surely intended to appeal to the queen. 'I cease to offend your delicate eare with my harsh style, and therefore kissing the ground that sustaineth your Sacred person, I ever rest The humblest of your subjects, Tobias Hume.'[18]

Example 13. TOBIAS HUME: CEASE LEADEN SLUMBERS
(two lutes and viola-da-gamba; from *Poeticall Musicke*)

Hume's is a sad appeal in ways. It implies he was low in funds and little thought of, but he is right to say that these are 'Uncommon Musiques', for Tobias Hume was not only ahead of most of his contemporaries in his understanding of the viola-da-gamba, but also in his call for expressive variety in performance.

Not all was sorrow for Tobias Hume. He produced an extraordinarily frivolous hunting song with dramatic effects on his favourite viola-da-gamba, proudly subscribing: 'Here endeth the hunting Song, which was sung before two Kings, to the admiring of all brave Huntsmen.'

One other consolation for Tobias Hume, apart from his viola-da-gamba, was his pipe. Tobacco was a recently imported commodity which James VI and I thoroughly disapproved of: 'It is a custom loathesome to the eye, hateful to the nose, harmful to the brain, dangerous to the lungs',[19] but Hume appears to have written the text as well as the music of a song in its praise – a song of dry wit and good soldierly sense.

> . . . *Love makes men scorn all coward fears,*
> *So doth tobacco.*
> *Love often sets men by the ears,*
> *So doth tobacco.*
> *Tobacco, tobacco,*
> *Sing sweetly for tobacco!*
> *Tobacco is like love, o love it.*
> *For you see I have proved it.*

James was one of the last kings to keep a fool – that class of entertainer immortalised by Shakespeare. James's fool was Archie Armstrong and the king loved him enough to grant him a patent for the manufacture of the tobacco pipes of which he so much disapproved. Here is a tune – *Aderneis Lilt* – sufficiently odd in character to suit a fool. It comes from the *Skene Mandora Book* of 1615, a Mandora being a kind of small high-pitched and plaintive lute with five strings. The music is splendidly eccentric with quirky rhythm and melody, fit for a caper from Archie Armstrong or with Toby Hume himself.

Example 14. ADERNEIS LILT (*Skene Mandora Book*, 1615)

We cannot long comfort ourselves with tobacco and capers as far as Hume is concerned. His petition written in 1642 in old age and weakness of mind, is confused with the echoes of old battles and unrighted wrongs. It is one of the most touching and remarkable documents to come from the pen of any composer:

> Right Honourable and Noble Lords,
> I doe humbly intreat to know why your Lordships doe slight me, as if I were a foole or an Asse: I tell you truely I have been abused to your Lordships by some base fellows; but if I did know them, I would make them repent it, were they never so great men in your sight. . .
> I am an old and experienced Souldier, and have done great service in other forraine Countries as when I was in Russia, I did put thirty thousand to flight, and killed six or seven thousand Polonians by the art of my instruments of warre when I first invented them, and did that great service for the Emperor of Russia . . . And therefore I humbly beseach you all Noble Lords, that you will not suffer me to perish for want of food, for I have not one penny to helpe me at this time to buy me bread, so that I am like to be starved for want of meat and drinke, and did walke into the fields very lately to gather snailes in the nettles, and brought a bagge of them home to eat, and doe now feed on them for want of other meate, to the great shame of this land . . . .[20]

Although the removal of the court and attendant musicians left a space in Scottish musical life that has yet to be filled, there was still music in the land. Quite apart from the flourishing of music in the Gaelic-speaking west, whether on bagpipes, clarsach or the human voice (see Chapter XI), in castle and town house there were lutenists, virginalists, viol players and singers compiling manuscript collections which are still yielding treasures. The important role of music in a large household in Scotland is well illustrated at Crathes Castle, for it was enshrined on the ceiling of one of the rooms in 1599 in a series of texts and paintings of the nine muses, seven playing instruments (see Plates XX and XXI). Clavichord, fiddle, bass viol, lute, flute, harp and cittern. Probably they made up a consort – a little orchestra. The flute is curious, for it swells out at the end, though it is blown sideways like the modern flute. The family at Crathes were the Burnetts of Leys, the owners of the ivory horn presented to them by Robert the Bruce and that dare not be blown. One of their number was Duncan Burnett.

Example 15. DUNCAN BURNETT: PAVAN (*Duncan Burnett Music Book*)

5 May 1638 . . . [the council] . . . seeing that the musik school is altogether dekayit within this burgh to the great discredit of this citie . . . and that Duncane Birnett, who sumtyme of befoir teatchit musik within this burgh is desyrous to tak up the said school againe and teitche musik thairin, hes granted licence to the said Duncane Birnett to tak up ane musik school within this burgh.[21]

It is thanks to Burnett that most of the keyboard music of the period has survived. He was obviously a fan of William Kinloch's, whose lively music features prominently and almost exclusively in his book. But his own music contrasts strongly with Kinloch's exuberant style. Where Kinloch uniquely doubles the length of one dance form by immediate elaboration (hence its title *The Galliard of the Lang Pavan*), Burnett, who copied the piece out, wrote music of a more sober character, but perhaps with more inherent depth of feeling. Though technically less demanding than Kinloch, who exploits an ability to articulate repeated notes, Burnett's music also makes free use of bravura passages for the left hand in his setting of *The Queine Of Inglands Lessoune*; and his magnificent *Pavan* has solemnity and vigour. (Example 15.)

Outside the organised music of song schools and music masters there was always the huge body of traditional dance tunes and ballads, and some of these found outlets that were not liked by the authorities. For instance, one of James VI's interests was witchcraft, and music had its place in that activity. At the famous North Berwick witch trial of 1590, Agnes Thompson was accused with others that they 'took hands on the land, and daunced this reill or short dance. . . ' playing *Cummer* (that is, woman) *Gae Ye Afore* 'upon a small

trumpe called a Jewes trumpe.'[22] This is the first mention of the reel as a dance, anywhere in the world, and it was poor Agnes's last dance for she was strangled and burnt for her part in the meeting.

Cummer gae ye afore, cummer gae ye,
Gin ye winna gae, cummer let me,
Ring-a-ring-a-widdershins,
Linkin lithely widdershins,
Cummers carlin crone and queyn
Roun gae we.

The trump, or jew's harp, was an ancient instrument from the Middle East and being so small could be taken anywhere. The twanging metal tongue which vibrates between the teeth produces a single note, but by skilful shaping of the mouth the harmonics are so modified that tunes can be played – even fast reels. The tune of *Cummer Gae Ye Afore* has not been discovered. Bagpipes were also used at covens and we do have *Kilt Thy Coat Maggie* from the Skene manuscript of 1620, which was one of the tunes played by John Douglas on the pipes at a later coven at Tranent.[23] (See Example 16.)

Witches were not the only people, usually innocent, to whom irrational fears were attached. The gypsies and the travelling people were often

Example 16. KILT THY COAT, MAGGIE (*Skene*, 1620)

regarded with alarm. The leading gypsy family took the name of Faw. In 1540 James V granted privileges to his 'beloved John Faw, Lord and Earl of Little Egypt'. When gypsies were later ordered to leave Scotland or be hanged, most of them moved to remoter parts of the country. They were again formally expelled in 1609 and in 1611 Willia Faa and three others were hung for 'abiding within the kingdom, they being Egyptians'. In 1624, Captain Johnnie Faa and seven others were hanged for the same reason.[24]

The ballad of *Johnnie Faa* is one of the most widely known in Scotland and most versions tell the story of Lady Cassilis running off with this same man. The tale has travelled like the gypsies. It has been picked up in America and Ireland, and in Norfolk it is sung also with the mention of Lady Cassilis. Some time before 1630 a tune called *Lady Cassilis Lilt* was noted down in the *Skene Mandora Book*. It is the progenitor of the vast majority of the tunes that go with the ballad, so right from the start there is a connection between the story and the music. The original river mentioned in the story – the Doon in Ayrshire – still has a crossing place known as The Gypsies' Steps. The refrain was borrowed and made famous by Byron – Nae mare I'll gang a-rovin, a-rovin in the nicht.

Example 17. LADY CASSILIS LILT (*Skene*, 1620)

The magic of the gypsies' music is of crucial importance in the story. In some versions Lady Cassilis' husband forgives her because she has been seduced by magic. The phrase used is that they 'cast the glamour o'er her'. By good luck there also survives a tune in the *Rowallan Lute Book* of the 1620s. The tune is called *The Gypsies' Lilt* and it is so strange that it can only be explained as

deliberately casting of the glamour over us. Over and over it repeats the same weird chord.

Example 18. THE GYPSIES' LILT (*Rowallan Lute Book*)

❋   The tablature is clear for the many appearances of this chord which is clearly intended as the main feature of the pie

There is no precedent for this music. It has a gypsy magic all on its own, and is now at least three hundred and seventy years old.

Although Tobias Hume had announced the dawn of the new age of the viola-da-gamba, the lute still held its own for a while, one of the last great collections being made in Scotland at the end of the seventeenth century – *The Balcarres Lute Book*. It remained the standard instrument of poetic suffering for love. Here to close the chapter on James VI is a beautiful sonnet which puts the lute to that use. It was written by one of the few who was not sucked south – William Drummond of Hawthornden – and he withholds, with great artistry, to the very last words, the cause of all the sorrow.

Sound hoarse sad Lute, true Witnesse of my Woe,
And strive no more to ease selfe-chosen Paine
With Soule-enchanting Sounds, your Accents straine
Unto these Teares uncessantly which flow.
Shrill Treeble weepe, and you dull Basses show
Your Masters Sorrow in a deadly Vaine,
Let never joyfull Hand upon you goe,
Nor Consort keepe but when you doe complaine.
Flie Phoebus Rayes, nay, hate the irkesome Light,
Woods solitarie Shades for thee are best,
Or the blacke Horrours of the blackest Night,
When all the World (save Thou and I) doth rest:
Then sound sad Lute, and beare a mourning Part,
Thou Hell may'st moove, though not a Womans Heart.[25]

CHAPTER XI

MUSIC OF THE WEST
1530–1760

It has been said that there was a gap in the creation of new songs in the Gaelic tradition during the fifteenth and sixteenth centuries, perhaps attributable to the break-up of the Lordship of the Isles.[1] The West of Scotland had been virtually under separate rule, achieving its high-water mark at Harlaw in 1411 (see Chapter VI). But the power of the chieftains was partly broken by James IV, and a period of instability followed, marked by particularly bitter and cruel rivalries between the MacDonalds and the MacLeods.

That stated, the usual vision of wild chieftains in remote glens living on porridge and whisky is a nonsense. They used their birlinns (swift galleys which could be rowed or sailed and were versatile and manoeuvrable) to import wines and silks (the standard drink in the Highlands at the time was claret),[2] educated their sons in universities on the continent and in Scotland (which by 1600 had four universities to England's two); were often familiar with Latin as well as being bilingual in Gaelic and Scots;[3] preserved both orally and in manuscript a vernacular literature older than any in Europe (see Chapter III) much of which was fitted to music; retained in part one of the earliest codified legal systems in Europe[4]; and were able to do all this in spectacularly beautiful country, abundant in fish and game and, in summer, blessed with rapid communications by sea.

In these circumstances, a picture of musical sterility seems an unlikely one. In any case, the Gaelic culture has produced music under every kind of disruption and oppression, and the picture is made the more incredible when one remembers that half the landmass and half the population of Scotland was still Gaelic-speaking at the end of the sixteenth century. From the early sixteenth century we have *The Book of the Dean of Lismore*, a vital repository of Gaelic poetry, alas without any music, though much of it will have been sung or recited with musical accompaniment and was written in many cases by poets contemporary with the manuscript.[5] However, such music as survives in the oral tradition demonstrates that there was vigour in most genres, whether work-song, lament, laconic chant, or lullaby.

Some material has been transmitted in forms other than the presumed original, and one of these forms is the waulking song in which sections of ballads, love-songs and eulogies have been preserved.[6] Though we shall begin with a waulking song which does just that, it is worth keeping in mind the proviso of the great Gaelic poet, Sorley Maclean, with respect to poems and songs (one of which is noted below) relating the sufferings of the MacGregors: 'They are obviously poems of power, intensity and a bare economy of detail and language. Perhaps they owe much of their spare intensity to their never having become waulking songs, for the waulking songs were almost certainly in many cases coarsened in rhythm and cluttered with irrelevant details, lessening their intensity.'[7]

The rhythm of a waulking song is obviously paced to go with the work, which involves the rhythmic thumping of cloth soaked in human urine on some kind of a board. Over most of Scotland this was done with hammers driven by water mills from as early as the sixteenth century. But in the Highlands it seems to have been done mostly by hands and feet.[8] Shrinking a length of tweed sufficiently to make it waterproof could take many hours and involve several songs, for it was thought unlucky to repeat a song at the one piece of work. To help make each song last, the chorus is sung after every line and in many cases each line itself is repeated, which has the advantage that it can be reflected upon by singer and listener.

Songs for waulking were sung almost exclusively by women, whose work it was (see Plate XXX). They belong to a class of song used to accompany other kinds of repetitive work, and occasionally sharing a repertoire – rowing (almost exclusively male work, see Chapter II), grinding, milking, and waulking itself. They often have a chorus of meaningless vocables and this is thought to be a very ancient feature.[9] The words were sometimes improvised for the verses and sometimes borrowed from a variety of older songs, but many have remained unchanged in their confused form for well over a hundred years, suggesting an innate conservatism. The music is repeated over and over, but in its context it is absolutely compelling.

One of the oldest of these songs, *Rinn Mi Mocheirigh – I Rose Early*, dates in part from 1539 when the MacDonalds of Sleat, a district on the Isle of Skye, were left with only a child as a chieftain. His father, Donald Gorm, was killed in the siege of Eileann Donan Castle and this seems to have given the MacLeods of Raasay the upper hand.[10] Whether the love song which forms the first stanzas was in praise of Donald Gorm or is a later interpolation is not known. As for the music, while each solo verse goes two steps down the scale, the beginning of the chorus reverses that and goes back up, so they balance each other. The rest of the chorus does the same thing but expands the tune both upwards and downwards – again balanced, creating a simple but effective piece of miniature organisation. To achieve this it uses only five notes, so it is strictly pentatonic. The tune may be simple, but its rhythms have a great swing to them – partly through use of the Scotch snap (see the Introduction) – and its outline is as full of character as a finely shaped hillside over which one can travel many times with pleasure. A rough précis of the words is given below, but in all cases the superiority of the original Gaelic must always be understood.

Example 1. RINN MI MOCHEIRIGH – I ROSE EARLY (from the singing of Mrs Archie MacDonald)

I rose early to meet my beloved . . . do not be jealous, Ni Mhic Ailein: I am deeply in love with your first love and I will praise him even if you find it hateful. I would travel with you, even across the rough Irish sea where ships fire at each other: I would accompany you where there was dancing – many a reel going to the little graceful-sounding pipes; to the great pipes with the deep drone; and the sweet well-tuned clarsach.

That ships firing at one another are considered noteworthy may also date the verse. The only battle James IV's flagship, *The Great Michael*, ever fought was an easy ransacking of the English stronghold at Carrickfergus in Northern Ireland. She made herself known in the Hebrides on the way, her fourteen gunners no doubt impressing the locals with her firepower as the birlinns did not carry cannon. The little pipes, the great pipes and the clarsach were all to be heard in the first half of the sixteenth century, and the reel as a dance was possibly established by then too, though its first mention in English or Scots is in 1590 (see Chapter X). *Rinn Mi Mocheirigh* ends with fine clannish feeling, looking backwards to the semi-mythological Celtic hero Cuchullain and the loss of a great chieftain; and forwards to the hoped-for dominance of Clan Donald.

In the confusion of the cattle-raid, women are weeping, cattle lowing, and I cannot pick out my own among them. Our country is without a chief, depending on a handful of a boy; but as birds flock together so the MacDonalds will rise with us, the MacLeans, never known to panic, the Camerons from Ghalbhainn of the great trees: and the MacLeods will be defeated and the Campbells driven into the pool. If I were strong and manly, I would not follow MacLeod of Raasay, but Donald the Grim, dark-skinned Donald who is no more. If I were strong and skillful as Cuchulainn, the day would be Clan Donald's.

The words and tunes of waulking songs do not necessarily belong together, though the antiquity of the tunes is probably less in doubt than that of the words, the general trend having been to find new words for old tunes, rather than the reverse. But in less eclectic types of song there is a greater likelihood that they were conceived together, and this may apply to the famous Gaelic lullaby, *Grigor Criodhal*, which brings timeless elements to a specific event. *Beloved Gregor* dates from 1570 and tells of the execution of Gregor of Glenstrae. James VI was particularly hard on this notorious clan, whose adherents owned little land and survived on raiding others, though the Dean of Lismore and his two sons, who produced *The Book of the Dean of Lismore*, were MacGregors. The song is traditionally held to have been composed by the daughter of Duncan Campbell of Glenlyon, Grigor's widow. Her father did not think he was good enough for her and with his kinsman, Sir Colin Campbell of Glenurchy, had him beheaded at Kenmore on Loch Tay in 1570, apparently in his wife's presence.[11]

As with many Gaelic songs, the refrain comes before the verses. It repeats the old protective formulae.

Ba, ba mo leanabh – Ba ba my baby, ba hu ho my baby. Many a night in the wildest weather, Gregor would find me a cranny and we would sleep together in its shelter. I searched for you through the house but I will not find you at my table. Greatest treasure in all the world, they spilled your blood yesterday, and put your head upon an oaken stob, separate from your body. Tonight, when the young women of the township are quietly asleep, I shall be beside your grave beating my two hands.

Clapping hands was an integral part of performance of the caoine or lament. The tune is pentatonic and in its tiny compass evokes gentleness, love and deep sorrow. Set against the brutality that lies behind it, it produces a complex mix of intense feeling with faultless economy.

Example 2. GRIGOR CRIODHAL – BELOVED GREGOR
(from the singing of Anne Lorne Gillies)

The retention of ancient practice is found in many areas of Gaelic life. The three basic strains of Celtic music, laughter, sorrow and sleep music, have been referred to already (see Chapters V and VI). The latter might seem a mere phantasy drawn out of magical Celtic mists, but some, such as the old and the bereaved, find sleep hard to come by, and as late as the nineteenth century the ancient Fenian lays were used for this purpose – a woman in South Uist was kept in the household of the Reverend George Munro's widow primarily to sing her to sleep at night. The lullabies serve the same function for a baby. Sleep music may also have been used on active campaign. Did Shakespeare have this in mind when he had Brutus's boy soothe him with the lyre? And when a clarsach player accompanied the clan in battle – as we know they did at this time in the late sixteenth century – might he not also have

soothed his Highland chieftain, only to stir him into action in the morning by singing a brosnachadh (see Chapter VI)?

A strange – indeed chilling – use for a song in battle was at the Battle of Carinish which was one of the last great clan battles between the MacLeods and the MacDonalds. It started with the rejection of a one-eyed MacLeod bride, who was returned without compliments by Donald Gorm of Sleat on the Island of Skye (after a spell of usage). She was sent back accompanied, it is said, by a one-eyed servant and a one-eyed dog. The insult led to the desperate Battle of the Cuillin as well as that at Carinish, which took place in 1601. The refrain of the song was originally sung as a chorus by the attendant women at the battle who raised their voices so their own men would not be discouraged by hearing MacDonald's cries of pain as his foster-mother pulled the arrows out of his body.[12]

'The blood of your fragrant body was seeping through your clothing. I myself was sucking it until my breath was smothered.'

Women drinking the blood of wounded or dead relations is not a rare motif and is at least as old as the Deirdre story. The tune is as strange as the occasion, with phrases of uneven length, and it has an unforgettable shape, rising to its top note with an effort that seems to parallel the effort of pulling out the arrows, though it is basically a song of praise and encouragement.[13]

Example 3. A MHIC IAIN 'IC SHEUMAIS – JOHN SON OF JAMES
(from the singing of Mrs Kate MacMillan)

Peace between the MacLeods and MacDonalds was restored only when James VI intervened. He had a low opinion of Highlanders, perhaps motivated by the Highlanders' reluctance to pay taxes and give up feuding: 'As for the Highlands, I shortly comprehend them all in two sorts of people: the one, that dwelleth in our mainland, that are barbarous for the most part, and yet mixed with some show of civility: the other, that dwelleth in the Isles, and are utterly barbarians, without any sort or show of civility.'[14]

Gaelic music was not all harps and laments, and though lullabies and laments are linked by shared features in the refrains, *Taladh Choinnich Oig* is a lullaby that is full of confidence – so much so that one wonders if it ever put little Kenneth MacKenzie of Kintail to sleep. Which Kenneth was actually enraptured by this panegyric on the whole race of MacKenzies is not clear. But it seems likely that he was one of several Kenneths whose cradles were rocked in Eilean Donan Castle any time between the fifteenth and early seventeenth century.[15] Seemingly his father shod his horses with gold and gave them wine to drink; but if the baby MacKenzie had had the wit to understand them, he would have taken all these compliments and vauntings as little short of the truth and the very least that was due to him.

Another song from this period which demonstrates the variety of character in Gaelic music is *Oran Na Comhachaig – The Song of the Owl* – said to have been composed by Donald MacDonald of Lochaber in his old age. He was also known as Donald son of Finlay of the poems which may account for the fact that this long song is a conflation of several on different topics. The old man protests that when he had two legs to walk on, the mountains were nothing to him to climb, but now fitted out with three – hobbling with a stick – he trails slowly along. One tradition said that, when Donald put a large section of hollow tree-trunk on the fire, the owl itself emerged and took its place on the hearth beside him to watch the conflagration of its former home. The old man feels pity for the owl he hears in the night. They are birds of a feather. If the owl was as old as Clan Donald, he would have reason enough for being gloomy. *Oran Na Comhachaig* was probably put together in the early seventeenth century and was collected from the singing of Angus MacLellan at the entirely suitable age of ninety-six.[16] The style of the poem, the tune and its delivery are old too, for the poem is syllabic, the tune is narrow in range, pentatonic in mode, and its rhythms are unstressed. It has a sense of wry comedy, but it is a thin humour, starving physically and spiritually on the edge of the grave. A melancholy owl of a song. (Example 4.)

There are other songs whose dating is not certain but which may come from this supposedly lean period in vocal music, and of these *Cairistiona* is probably the best known. The

system of fostering children was still prevalent in the Highlands and this is another song sung by a foster-mother, this time a lament for a young woman of noble birth. It may be as old as the fifteenth century, for it refers to their having spent a year at the court of the king – meaning a MacDonald Lord of the Isles on Islay before the Lordship was abolished.

'Of course, the ineffable magic of the melody to which *Cairistiona* is sung is so difficult to separate from the haunting poetry of the words themselves'.[17] To this judgment by Sorley Maclean there need be no addition.

Other aspects of the old repertoire persisted. *The Charm Against a Hail Shower* (see Chapter II) which undoubtedly retains pre-Christian elements, though invoking God, was still being sung and even influenced the tune for a newly composed song. *Is Fhada Tha Mi An Cul – I am Far from the Ridge of Ben Edra* is sung by a headless body driven out of Morar by Iain Garbh of Raasay, who lived in the seventeenth century when witch-hunting was at its height. Basically the same tune is the vehicle for driving off the evil spirit as for keeping back the threatening hail shower.[18]

Iain Garbh MacLeod, to whom that song is attributed, was drowned at Easter in 1671. He must have been a remarkable man for his death was lamented many times over and the cause is usually given as witchcraft. His sister is said to have composed a lament for him on every ensuing Friday for a year. One version attributed to his former wet-nurse derives from the belief that she was the witch and was bribed by the chief of the MacDonalds to drown this leading MacLeod.[19] She repented and composed this exquisitely beautiful lament with its tragic sweep up and down suggesting the waves that overcame his boat and that break on the sea-shore where she sits lamenting the tragedy she herself created.

The power of art is great, for it can find beauty where there was perhaps mere commonplace. The truth of the drowning of Iain Garbh

Example 4. ORAN NA COMHACHAIG – THE SONG OF THE OWL
(from the singing of Angus MacLellan)

has little to do with witches, unless alcohol be a witch or the Reverend James Fraser be a liar, for the following year he gave his account:

> This April the Earle of seaforth duelling in the Lewes, a dreadful accident happened. His lady being brought to bed there, the Earl sent for John Garve MacLeod of Raasay, to witness the christening; and, after the treat and solemnity of the feast, Raasay takes leave to goe home, and, after a rant of drinking upon the shoare, went aboord off his birling and sailed away with a strong north gale of wind; and whither by giving too much saile and no ballast, or the unskillfulness of the seamen, or that they could not manage the strong Dutch canvas saile, the boat whelmed, and all the men dround in view of the coast. The Laird and 16 of his kinsmen, the prime, perished; non of them ever found; a greyhound or two cast ashoare dead; and pieces of the birling. One Alexander Macleod of Lewes the night before had voice warning him thrice not to goe at all with Raasay, for all would drown in their return; yet he went with him, being infatuat, and dround with the rest. This account I had from Alexander his brother the summer after, Drunkness did the Mischeife.[20]

Example 5. CUMHA DO IAIN GARBH – LAMENT FOR IAN GARBH (from the singing of Finlay MacNeill)

The truth does not, however, diminish the tragedy in fact or in memory, and here is another lament for him, stressing the sorrow of the Earl of Kintail.[21] Once again the tune spreads itself widely – a characteristic of Scottish song compared with the traditional music of many other nations. It suggests that vocal accomplishment was an expected thing in this country and in the performances of the best Gaelic singers we can certainly hear it.

Example 6. CUMHA DO IAIN GARBH – LAMENT FOR IAN GARBH (from the singing of James Campbell)

(The verse follows a similar outline)

The examples given here are all necessarily short. In song and ballad, duan or laoidh, the cumulative effect is lost; but the music of all of these relies entirely on repetition, albeit flexible, in order to support the more substantial formal structures of the verse. However, we know that Gaelic musicians were capable of creating large-scale musical structures in the form of piobaireachd (see below), and it is possible that something similar was done on the clarsach, perhaps in its role partnering the recitation of a genealogy or a eulogy. None of this clarsach music has come down to us. It was taught orally (many clarsairs were blind, so notation would not have served them) and it can perhaps be guessed at only in primitive exercise-book form from the *Ap Hyw* manuscript (see Chapter VI). Though lute and fiddle were available in Highland households,[22] the clarsach was the main vehicle for such music and, since it had at least a four-octave range, was capable of complex effects and rich chords and textures such as those described by Giraldus (see Chapter IV). Some of the harps may have been capable of chromatic notes: a fragment of a harp with 52 strings, known as the Dalway harp, has been convincingly interpreted in this way[23] and this would allow it to be used in consort music even when the harmonies were adventurous.[24]

In the household of a Highland chieftain at this time, with filidh, bard, clarsair, piper, fool, all part of a considerable retinue of intensively trained and highly skilled people and including a personal bodyguard of the finest young men in the clan, an evening's entertainment recounting the deeds of the chieftain and his ancestors could have been of epic proportions. A Highland chieftain would have been flattered at a level not far short of that of an Italian prince whose society was no less factious or bloody.

At that time, in the late sixteenth century, in northern Italy they were creating a new art form, initially intended for the aristocracy and now known as opera. First thoughts would set opera and Gaelic eulogy as far apart as western culture would permit, but it may not have been so.

When Vicenzo Galilei (father of Galileo) quoted Dante as the authority for the Irish having introduced the harp into Italy, he was writing of one of the instruments used to accompany Italian recitative – one whose repertoire was partly shared with Scotland and whose manner of performance may have influenced the whole idea of dramatic musical presentation which was at the heart of opera. Recitative was the technique which made opera possible, allowing for rapid delivery of texts describing the deeds of the heroes of antiquity, using a simple chordal accompaniment and rhythmically free but pitched declamation. Writing in 1581 of the Irish harp (with which we may identify the Highland clarsach on the evidence that the Queen Mary and Lude harps and the Trinity College Dublin harp are very similar in design)[25] Galilei has this to say:

> The harps used by these people are greater than ordinary. They generally have strings of brass, with a few of steel for the highest notes, as in the harpsichord. The musicians keep the fingernails long, carefully shaping them in the manner of the quills with which the strings of the spinet are struck. The number of these is 54, 56 and even 60. . .
>
> A few months ago I carefully examined the distribution of the strings of this harp (with the assistance of a gentleman of Ireland) and I found it to be the same as that which a few years ago, with double the strings, was introduced in Italy, though some people (against every good reason) claim that they have newly invented it, and try to persuade the ignorant that only they know how to play and tune it.[26]

Vicenzo Galilei was one of the Camerata – the associates who met at Count Bardi's house and invented opera – and it has been claimed that Monteverdi used an Irish 'double harp' for the chorus of nymphs in his opera *Orfeo*.[27] James VI and I and his queen each kept an Irish harper, and Irish harpers were known in Denmark and Germany as well as Italy.[28] Scottish Gaelic and Irish were beginning to separate at this time, but the clarsairs came and went between the two countries with the habitual freedom of wandering minstrels, the Scottish clarsairs usually being sent to study in Ireland and Irish players frequently coming to Scotland (see below).

Of course, opera in the hands of a Monteverdi extended its dramatic situations over an ambitious structure. It was supported by vast concentrated wealth, and nothing comparable emerged from northern Europe for several decades, partly because of religious objections stemming from protestant suspicion of the theatre. The Reformation spread only a little less rapidly in Gaeldom than elsewhere[29] but it did not suppress the love and practice of music – always valued in the West of Scotland, as George Buchanan's history published in 1582, admits (see Chapter VI). He is echoed by John Monipennie, but with emendations: 'In place of a drum, they use a bagpipe. They delight much in music, but chiefly in Harps and Clairschoes of their own fashion. The strings of the Clairschoes are made of brass wire, and the strings of the Harps, of sinews . . . They sing verses prettily compound,

contayning (for the most part) prayses of valiant men.'[30]

The close similarities with Irish bardic practice are underlined in the above and find their Irish equivalent in the memoirs of the Marquis of Clanricarde. The continuing musical connections find expression in other ways. A Scottish waulking song enshrines one of the oldest known Irish songs – *Callen Og A Stiura Mi – I am a Girl from the River Suir*. Shakespeare's Pistol refers to it, but neither he nor the Hebridean Scots understood that it referred to the river Suir in Ireland, so it has been misrepresented for centuries.[31] The original is sung by a young man wishing for more musical skill on the harp to attract the girls.

Another Irish connection from the days of James VI and I relates to the status of musicians. The English, aware of the importance of the poet/musician in Celtic society, did their best to ridicule him,[32] but in Scotland a visiting Irish musician had a right to expect better. Such a one was Rory Dall O'Cahan. The word 'Dall' means that he was blind – a loss not without advantages for clarsairs, partly because the instrument has to be played by feel as you cannot clearly see your fingers on the strings without poking your head round the side very awkwardly.

O'Cahan came from Ireland and lived and worked mostly in Scotland but was affronted by Lady Eglintoun when she demanded a tune somewhat peremptorily. O'Cahan refused and left Eglintoun Castle, and it took some fine wheedling to recall him. In reconciliation he wrote *Give Me Your Hand*.[33] It is addressed directly to the countess, but has been a favourite with folk musicians for many years now. It is found in a Scottish lute manuscript from the early seventeenth century and it is a lovely flowing tune that has retained its essential outlines in Scotland and Ireland through the centuries, the version notated by Bunting in the late eighteenth century being quite close to that in the Margaret Wemyss manuscript from the 1640s. It is basically pentatonic, but makes a feature of a single expressive flat seventh (asterisked) just before the end, as though graciously bowing its way out.

It is said that O'Cahan made such an impression at the Scottish court that James called him over and rested his hand on his shoulder, to

Example 7. DA MIHI MANUM – GIVE ME YOUR HAND
(*Lady Margaret Wemyss Manuscript*, 1644)

which O'Cahan declared that 'a greater than King James has laid his hand on my shoulder?'[34] It says a lot for James VI that he did not rebuke the man when it turned out that the person supposed to be greater than James was The O'Neill, a man far from sympathetic to the cause of unionism which James set in motion and worked for with such care. Another tune attributed to Rory Dall O'Cahan, appears as an example in Chapter X and it shares with *Give Me Your Hand* an extended second half.

O'Cahan was only one of many Irish clarsairs to visit Scotland. An Echlin O'Cathain (1729– *c.* 1790) was not only a regular visitor but is represented in the Scottish *Maclean-Clephane* manuscript which contains 36 harp tunes, possibly collected before Bunting's work at the 1792 Belfast harp festival.[35] Hempson, who played at that festival (see Chapter VI), also visited Scotland, and Scottish clarsairs studying in Ireland include Murdoch MacDonald[36] and Ruairidh Dall Morrison (see below).

Scotland itself still had many professional clarsairs in the seventeenth century. The Earl of Sutherland, the Laird of Grant, the Campbells, the house of Argyll, the MacLeans of Duart, Mull, Brolas and Coll, the MacLeods of Dunvegan, the Hamiltons of Arran and several others all employed them.[37] But there were antagonisms between them and the fiddlers, who were an ever-increasing tribe. In 1594 Ogilby, a fiddler, was executed for the murder of Caldell, a harper;[38] and in 1638 the Laird of Grant's agent explained the failure of his clarsair to return from the Lowlands, saying that there had been a drunken fight with a violer and the clarsair was 'hurt in the hand; quhair he is or hou he wilbe, I can nochte learne, for I haif nocht bein werie curious to speir that questioun.'

As for the violer, John Hay, he was 'werie euill hurt in the heid, quhair out of thair is two boneis cum, and it is in dout gif ever he wilbe weil.'[39]

If he had first injured the clarsair's hand, the violence to him is more readily understood. But the world of the clarsair could also be one of dignity and refined beauty, as expressed a decade later in *The Royal Lament*. The Highlands generally remained more loyal to the crown and *The Royal Lament* is said to have been composed by the Laird of the Island of Coll, John Garve MacLean, when the English executed Charles I in 1649. MacLean of Coll was a fine clarsach player and his music survives in more than one source.[40] This beautiful tune, given here as recorded by James Oswald in the eighteenth century, has much in common with the Irish harp tunes noted by Bunting,[41] further emphasising our closely connected cultures. In the first half its shapely phrases echo each other, but move each to a different note, poised for the next phrase. The second half expands the range and comments expressively on the basic ideas, adding new rhythms but retaining

Example 8. THE ROYAL LAMENT (Oswald, *Caledonian Pocket Companion*, 1740s)

the same structural feature of ending phrases on a different note. This is melodic writing of a quality that few monarchs have had the fortune to evoke in their passing.

Although the clarsach held on for a while into the eighteenth century, Gaelic music as a whole was learning to live with a newly dominant instrument, the bagpipes, and a serious challenger (yet to be seen off) in the violin. So, the status of bard and clarsair declined, as evidenced by the decreasing value and diminution of their traditionally held lands.[42] In the sphere of vocal music too, new verse forms were coming in, with a whole succession of bards and bardesses producing superb poetry, most of it intended to be sung, on every sort of subject and with many varieties of poetic style.[43] As late as the end of the seventeenth century, Martin Martin describes the bards working up inspiration in a darkened room with a stone on their chests, but declares they are on the decline (see Chapter VI). Such practices may well have been very ancient, perhaps akin to the experiences of priests in the darkened and sound-proofed passage cairns of the Stone and Bronze Ages. We do not know whether this technique was also used by the female bards, but the bardesss Mary MacLeod (c. 1615–c. 1706) chose to be buried under a weight of stones. It is common in Gaelic song for the writer to be a woman and a number of female bards are well known. Needless to say there were rivalries, none more entertainingly expressed than in *A Bhradag Dhubh* – black besom – a flyting or improvised satirical contest between a poetess from Barra and one from Uist.[44]

However, the magical powers that were always associated with music, its ability to put you to sleep, to make you laugh or cry, whether you wished to or no, and its power as a vehicle for devastating satire, were all forces which could also be laid at the door of witchcraft. Perhaps that is why Mary MacLeod was banished from the MacLeod household, though she had nursed many a chieftain.[45] This is a lullaby attributed to her. Kate MacDonald explained the background in these words: 'This is the song that Mary MacLeod made, when she had composed some song or other for someone and there must have been something wrong with it, and they put a ban on her. She was not to sing a song outdoors or indoors – but it was on the threshold . . . the piece of wood at the bottom of the doorway, that was where she would stand, and so she was neither out nor in and she made that little song.'[46]

Hilliu-an, Hilleo-an,
There was a time when I could sing a song:
I could sing a croon just as well;
Today I can just croak to myself.
You are my plovers and my chicks,
My plovers and my chicks and my eggs,
And the soft rushes where I would sit,
My little child who has not yet spoken.
With my bow and my little quiver
Hiri my love Fionaghala,
I would not give you bread
Without butter on top of it.

The tune could hardly be simpler. Its protective refrain and repetitive phrases, based on the major third interval, put it musically in the same class as the charms and lullabies referred to in Chapter II.

Example 9. HILLIU-AN, HILLEO-AN (from the singing of Kate MacDonald)

It is not clear whether Mary MacLeod was a musician as well as a poet, but there is no question that her poems were meant to be sung and that she loved music, praising harp and pipes and fiddle. *MacLeod's Wonted Hall* refers to the sound of chessmen rattling and of the harp playing. It would have been an elegy for Norman MacLeod, only it was written when he was merely ill and idly enquired what sort of a panegyric she would write if he were to die. She produced a fine poem full of praise of him as warrior, hunter, host and patron, set to a tune that arches over two stanzas at a time. Each stanza is repeated so that it is heard sung to both halves of the tune – a kind of interlacing of melody and poetry peculiar to Gaelic song and creating a sense of formality and unhurried dignity.

A similar song – *Gur Muladach* – is set on the island of Jura where Mary MacLeod is said to have stayed during her banishment, and another variant takes the form of a waulking song – like the Barra boasting song. The singer protests that she is falsely accused of being pregnant and hurls abuse at her accuser in whose household they only serve fish, whereas in her own it is venison they get. It is spirited in rhythm and active in outline.[47] When Mary MacLeod died she asked not only to be covered with stones but to be laid face down. Whether or no this relates to accusations of witchcraft, she was certainly remembered with affection by Patrick Og MacCrimmon, a piper whose playing she herself had praised saying the pipes surpassed all other music when Patrick's fingers stirred them. It is quite possible then that he composed the piobaireachd *Lament for Mary MacLeod*, described below.

The death of Mary MacLeod, significant as she was, did not leave the Highlands short of bards. Two of the best known were Iain Luim MacDonald (1625–post 1707) and Sileas MacDonald (*c.* 1660 – *c.* 1730). Iain Luim was a poet with a superb but cruel turn of imagery, a Royalist, a sharp-tongued political satirist, and prompter of the avenging of the infamous murder of the young chief of the Keppoch MacDonalds when he returned from his education abroad, determined to improve the behaviour of his clan.[48] Iain Luim personally knotted together the heads of the seven murderers and presented them to the avenger-in-chief. His invective was so savage that one can understand why bardic satire was truly feared. The best idea of the character of his poetry that is recorded in music (for, as usual, this poetry was intended to be sung) is the magnificent tune to which his poem on the battle of Inverlochy is sung. The battle in 1645 was one of Montrose's great victories in defence of Charles I, but Iain Luim himself is credited with the strategic foresight which won the day, though he had the sense not to fight himself on this occasion, telling his chieftain, MacColla, that if he died there would be no poet to sing his praises. MacColla appreciated this canny excuse.[49] The triumphant song, with two confident octave leaps – the second higher in pitch – and a variety of rhythmic units in its short space that gives

it tremendous vigour, sends out a musical challenge as magnificent as the belling of a stag in autumn.

Of the same blood was Sileas MacDonald of Keppoch who may have herself played the clarsach[50] and whose lament for a clarsair, *Cumha Lachlainn Daill – Lament for Blind Lachlan*, is followed by another poem of hers stating that the clarsach is: 'Dearer to me than the fiddle and bass, I will not mention the organ, my favourite music was the ringing of your strings through your hard wooden boards.'

She has been associated with the female equivalent of the bardic practices noted by Martin Martin (see above), having possibly used trance-like states created by starvation as a source of inspiration.[51] *Cumha Lachlainn Daill* is, however, a straight-forward poem of personal regret which is interesting also for the fact that it names a number of her favourite tunes as well as naming different song types. Lachlainn Daill may have been a MacKinnon from Skye. The tune to which this song apparently belongs,[52] appears in a fine version in Simon Fraser's *The Airs and Melodies Peculiar to the Highlands of Scotland and the Isles* published in 1816. The poem is syllabic rather than stressed, but that does not prevent it from fitting this extended metrical air which, like *MacLeod's Wonted Hall* covers two stanzas at a time. The tune seems to have been popular for it is used for two other poems by Sileas, and also by Duncan Ban MacIntyre (see below) who is doubtfully credited with its composition by Fraser. Recently, William Matheson and Fanny MacIsaac have recorded this tune (*Alasdair a Gleanna Garadh*) in much freer rhythmic style. Fraser may well have regularised his material for publication and seems to have introduced chromaticisms (bracketed in the example) to fit in with classical harmonies, but the date of publication and his own pedigree make his a vital source. We must also accept the possibility that by the early eighteenth century Gaelic poets and musicians were themselves willing to accept influences from the classical tradition, with which they will certainly have had at least occasional contact in the big houses and castles where there would be keyboard instruments. This influence is particularly marked in Ireland, where O'Carolan blended native and classical styles with popular success, and we know from

Example 10. Latha Inbhir Lochaidh – The Day of Inverlochy (from the singing of James Campbell)

the *MacLean-Clephane* manuscript[53] that his music was circulating in Scotland. The Reverend Patrick MacDonald, writing in 1784, complains of this classical influence: '*The Lady in the Desert* as played by an old harper, and as played according to the sets now in fashion, can hardly be known to be the same tune.'

But he also writes in a passage immediately following and not usually chosen for quotation, 'those, which have been preserved by tradition, may naturally be supposed to have been gradually degenerating. To render these airs therefore more regular, especially in their measure, is, in fact, bringing them nearer to their original form.'[54]

There is therefore good evidence from a source committed to the tradition, not long after the composition of *Cumha Lachlainn Daill* in the 1720s, that music associated with the clarsach and clarsairs should have a degree of metrical regularity.[55] Since the song laments a clarsair, we may take it that on metrical grounds at least there is no need to reject Simon Fraser's version.

Contemporary with Mary MacLeod and also employed at Dunvegan (see Plate 28) by the MacLeods was Ruairidh Dall Morrison (c. 1656–

c. 1714). He was blind from smallpox, but this was almost a qualification for a clarsair, and he was duly sent to study in Ireland, before returning to his harper's lands and to perform at the castle.

Perhaps his most richly entertaining work is his *Lament for the Lost Harp Key* (*Faill nan Crann*). The loss of his tuning key to a clarsach player is a matter for great sorrow, but in this song the harp key is a phallic symbol and Ruairidh's loss is both tragic and hilarious. He has given this superb piece of ribaldry a tune of considerable beauty, which serves only to heighten the humour.[56]

Example 12. RUAIRIDH MORRISON: FAILL NAN CRANN – HARP-KEY FAIR (from the singing of Anne Lorne Gillies)

A righ, gur cruaidh mo sgeul, mo chràdh geur, mo chreach, mo chall o laigh air m'inn-tinn sac
(Alas, my tale is distressing, for me a pain and a loss, since a weight came

's a laigh air m'ac-fhainn mall; on dh'im-ich uam an crann, 's nach fhaigh mi sham-hla 's tir,
on my mind and my equipment failed; Since I lost my harp key I cannot fin

gur adh - bhar mul-aid leam mo chrann a bhith d'am dhith.
one like it anywhere, to be without it causes me much grief.)

But Ruairidh Dall Morrison was to be just about the last clarsach player in Scotland. The clan system which supported clarsairs was beginning to fail as chieftains moved their attentions south; and in Ruairidh Dall's case his overt loyalist leanings after 1688 and criticism of his patron's son for letting the standards of patronage of his forbears slip, probably did not help:[57] 'Echo is dejected in the hall where music once sounded, where the poets resorted is now without mirth, pleasure drinking, merriment or entertainment . . . without dalliance or voice raised in tuneful song.'

He had in fact been dismissed and there is a tune called *The Harper's Dismissal* which relates to one he used for a song in honour of Iain Breac MacLeod.[58]

But the crushing consequences of the failure of Bonnie Prince Charlie in 1745 destroyed the whole economy and social structure which could support musicians in the Highlands. The bagpipes and fiddle were gaining ground too so when Ruairidh Dall heard a fiddler playing harp tunes he said, 'If fiddling is music that's enough of it.' A tune he wrote is called *Contempt for Fiddlers*.

Example 11. CUMHA LACHLAINN DAILL – DEOCH SLAINT' AN RIGH – LAMENT FOR BLIND LACHLAN (Fraser, *Airs and Melodies*, 1816)

Slàn a chaoidh le ceòl na clàr - saich On a ghlac am bàs thu, Lach - lainn;
(Farewell to harp music   Since death took you, Lachlan;

Cha bhi mi tuille gat iar-gain, Ni mò dh'iar-ras mi chaoidh t'fhaic-inn; Fhuair mi mo chleadadh
I need not hope to see you ever again.   I have known your

ri - d'cheòl - sa Nuair a bha mi òg 's mi 'm phais - dean, 'S ged a thàinig m i'n tao-bh tuath uat
music since I was little,   and though I lived to the North of you,

Thigeadh tu air chuairt do m'fhàr - daich. Nuair a chi - thinn thu a' tigh-inn Dh'éir - eadh mo
you visited my house.   My heart rose when I saw you coming to the house

chridhe san uair sin; Gheibh - inn uat sgeula gun mhear - achd Air na dh'fharr - aid - inn de dh'uais - libh;
I would get news about you from everyone.

Nuair a thàr - la - maid le chéil - e B'e Sléibhte tois - each ar - sean - chais:
When we met we would talk about Sleat first

Gheibh - inn - se uat sgeul - a còmh - nard Air Dòmh - nall ag - us air Mair - ghread.
and you would tell me the latest news about Donald and Margaret.)

Plate 28. DUNVEGAN CASTLE FROM THOMAS PENNANT'S *A Tour in Scotland*, 1774

Martin Martin however, saw fiddles as a sign of musicality, and he observed of the people of Lewis in the 1690s: ' . . . several of both sexes have a Gift of Poesy, and are able to form a Satire or Panegyrick ex tempore, without the Assistance of any stronger Liquor than Water to raise their Fancy. They are great lovers of Musick; and when I was there they gave an account of eighteen men who could play on the Violin pretty well, without being taught.'[59]

The growing ascendancy of the fiddle was such that our first written examples of the variation form for Highland pipes known as piobaireachd comes from fiddle manuscripts in the first half of the eighteenth century.[60]

It was round about the turn of the seventeenth century that one of the most remarkable art forms emerged from the Highlands – the bagpipe piobaireachd. The origins of piobaireachd are obscure and not always discussed in a spirit of scholarly detachment.[61] Some say it grew from the repertoire of the clarsach, others think it was vocal in origin. We have already looked at these possibilities (see Chapter VI) but might try a different approach by considering what the instrument itself is fitted for. What makes the Highland bagpipes unique is the power of their sound. We know that in the sixteenth century they were used by Highland armies instead of trumpets. Even though they may only have had two drones, one of them was certainly a large drone.[62] Because the sound travels over a long distance and can be heard above the noise of a crowd, it is a good instrument to march to, or to act as the centre of a gathering. To gather a clan the piper might initially sound the rhythm and tune of the clan's signature-tune, such as *Piobaireachd Dhonuil Dubh – Black Donald's March to Inverlochy*, which was their traditional gathering place as well as the site of a famous battle (see Plate 29).[63]

Another such tune is *The End of the Little Bridge* which fits the battle cry 'Chlanna nan coin', and *The MacGregors' Gathering* is also a clan cry.

Plate 29. PIOBAIREACHD DHONUIL DUBH, IN ALEXANDER CAMPBELL'S *Albyn's Anthology*, 1816

at Inver_locky; come ev'_ry hill plaid, and true heart that wears one;

come e_very steel blade, and strong hand that bares one.

1st. Variation.

Doubling of 1st. Variation.

Example 13. THE MACGREGORS' GATHERING (Campbell, *Albyn's Anthology*, 1816)

Thàin' na Griog-al-aich! thàin' na Griog-al-aich! thàin - ig, thàin - ig, thàin' na Griog-al-aich!

Having started with such a tune, if you are to keep going while people gather, you will have to find ways of extending it without merely repeating yourself. Since the Highland bagpipes are at their worst when stopping and starting there is a strong incentive to keep going – more so than on almost any other instrument. The natural thing is to find a way of varying your first ideas without having to think up something completely new. All over Europe they were doing the same thing at that time – inventing variations ('divisions' was the word in use) on popular tunes. Kinloch composed divisions on a ground bass (see Chapter IX) and the initial tune of a piobaireachd is also called a 'ground' – 'urlar' in Gaelic. But there the resemblance ends. You cannot play harmonies on bagpipes. All you have is a drone, not a bass line. Nor can you play any tune you choose, because all you have is nine notes. These are tuned so that they can be divided into three pentatonic scales, and many piobaireachd grounds are based on those scales, with a full appreciation of the different effects each one has against the unaltering drone.[64]

There are other good reasons for the instrument demanding its own techniques and forms. The sweeping arpeggios possible on the clarsach are impossible on the pipes, you cannot get louder and softer, and notes cannot be repeated

Example 14. PENTATONIC SCALES AVAILABLE ON THE HIGHLAND BAGPIPES

without a different note in between, because the sound of the chanter cannot be stopped once the bag is under pressure. To counteract these limitations, simple grace-notes and elaborate 'cuttings' have evolved, some played so rapidly they are scarcely detectable, and these can be used to give the impression of repeated notes (see Example 19).

As an example of a piobaireachd that seems to have grown out of the fingering as well as the

function of a piper we have *MacLeod's Salute*. It is supposed to have been written by Donald Mor McCrimmon in 1603 after James VI had patched up the MacLeod-MacDonald feud, and there was indeed a piper of that name and at that time.[65] The tunes associated with Donald Mor tend to share a feature which makes one believe they may be by the same man, for it is a trick of fingering with the left hand – a run down on to the lowest, loudest and most discordant note on the bagpipes, the low G, powerful in effect against the constant A of the drones.[66] It is known as the note of Gathering and Donald Mor's piobaireachd fits in with that perception.

This *Salute* is also known as a rowing piobaireachd. Bagpipes were used to encourage rowers, for which they would require a good steady pulse, and this tune certainly has an obsessive melody and rhythm to it. It is a strong, almost harsh piobaireachd which accumulates tremendous energy as the variations gather in complexity – the usual procedure in piobaireachd. A new, higher note is added in the first two variations, and later on the usual form of cutting is rearranged so that certain melody notes seem to get pushed aside with a sort of rough gesture. It is a thrilling effect, especially in this piece where there are sometimes three of these cuttings (known as *Crunluath-a-mach*) in a row. At the end of this crowning variation the music returns to the ground or urlar, though the urlar was certainly repeated at other points in the composition.

Example 15. CRUNLUATH-A-MACH (*above*); MACLEOD'S SALUTE OR ROWING PIOBAIREACHD (*below*)

Another piobaireachd, and a well-attested one, inspired by a purely piping occasion, was *I Got a Kiss of the King's Hand*, composed before the Battle of Worcester in 1651 in which Cromwell defeated Charles II and his largely Scottish army. It is the first clear indication that there was a McCrimmon who was a highly thought of piper and whose music for the occasion is documented. The story is told by the

Reverend James Fraser, writing in the late seventeenth century.

There was great competition betwixt the trumpets in the army: one Axell, the Earl of Hoomes trumpeter, carried it by the King's own decision! The next was anent the pipers; but the Earl of Sutherland's domestick carried it of all the camp, for non contended with him. All the pipers in the army gave John McGurmen the van, and acknowledged him for their patron in chiefe. It was pretty in a morning in parade viewing the regiments and bragads. He saw no less than 80 pipers in a croud bare-headed, and John McGyurmen in the middle covered. He asked what a society that was? It was told his Majesty: Sir, yow are our King, and yonder old man in the midle is the Prince of Pipers. He cals him by name, and, coming to the King, kneeling, his Majesty reacht him his hand to kiss; and instantly played an extemporanian port I Got A Kiss Of The King's Hand; of which they were all vain.[67]

This is an insistently boastful and proudful piobaireachd which nevertheless failed to prevent the decimation of the Scots in the ensuing battle.

Pipers were not bards, but they were and are associated with ancient musical legend. *The Cave of Gold* is a piobaireachd with closely allied songs, all related to the Celtic legend of the Lughnasa musician who, at the time of the harvest, vanishes into a cave or a fairy mound in search of a treasure – a search from which he never returns. I have heard this story told of a sea-cave in Skye, the belief being that the piper can still be heard playing far inside. In another version he does battle with a monster and cries out, 'Oh that I had three hands, two for the pipes and one for the sword.'[68] This story has parallels with the Orpheus story (see Chapter V) as well as with tales in which the art of music is learnt underground from the fairies. There is a clear connection between these and the bardic practice of working in the dark (see above). Another ancient function which the pipes seem naturally to have inherited is that of the lament, through its relationship with the caoine (see Chapter I).

Some bards regarded the pipes as upstarts.[69] But it was bards primarily – and other 'idlers of this class' – who came in for James VI's criticism and it may be that his views had real influence, for the bardic tradition begins to weaken at this time and the piper becomes more important – and none more important than he who played *The Piper's Warning to His Master*. The story goes that the owner of Duntroon was returning by sea with reinforcements in about 1615, not knowing that his enemies had taken his castle. To warn him of the trap laid for him his piper got permission to play a welcoming piobaireachd but

included such obvious alterations that his chieftain realised from the mutilated tune drifting across the water to him that there was something wrong.

The tune has two names, *Duntroon's Warning* and *The Sound of the Waves Against the Castle of Duntroon*. Here is the urlar, unmutilated. It goes well with the rhythm of the slow surge of waves and can also be sung to appropriate words first recorded in the nineteenth century – 'Greetings to you, health to you, greetings to you at Duntroon'. Then the warning is inserted – 'They are coming on you, here they are upon you, be on your guard at Duntroon' and finally it returns to its original subject-matter – the words that the waves are speaking: 'The piobaireachd of the room in the roof of the house, the sound of the waves against the castle of Duntroon.'

Example 16. DUNTROON'S WARNING

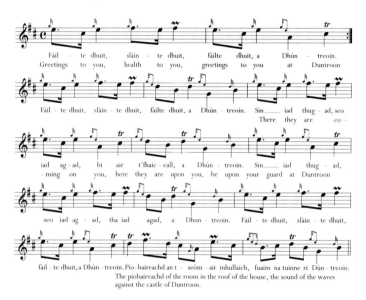

The words were perhaps based on the original words for the Salute to the owner of the Castle, but reworked later just as the piper mutilated the tune to save his master. He is said to have been mutilated himself by his enemies cutting off his hands so he could never play again. A handless skeleton was found at Duntrune at the beginning of this century.[70]

The importance of the piper is well reflected in the fact that they, like the bards and clarsairs, held hereditary lands. The splendour of their full dress (compared with a town piper such as Geordie Sime with his border pipes) is seen in the portrait of the Laird of Grant's Piper (see

Plate 30. *Geordie Syme*, PIPER AT DALKEITH, BY JOHN KAY,
LATE EIGHTEENTH CENTURY

Plates 30 and XXII), and the skill was passed down through families such as the MacArthur piping family who ran a small teaching establishment on Skye, as did another of the famous piping families, the McCrimmons, pipers to the MacLeods. Other outstanding piping families were those of the MacKays (one of whom was blind), pipers to the Mackenzies of Gairloch, and the Rankins, pipers to the MacLeans of Duart.[71]

As with the clarsairs, the method of teaching was essentially oral, but there was a system of notation used by pipers, which was vocalised as well as written down. The system is known as canntaireachd. Broadly speaking, the vowels indicate the notes and the consonants the finger movements or grips that ornament them:

Example 17. CANNTAIREACHD

Hiarod - in - tra hiho - droro - din

This system, which is unique to Scotland, has regional and individual variants without a centralised norm. In this it ressembles the Gaelic language, but is none the less effective for having no standard form. Canntaireachd is sung with remarkable truth to the subtle idiosyncracy of the bagpipe scale, but there is a saying in Sassenach Scotland, 'That's all hidorum hodorum', meaning it is all nonsense. But 'hidorum hodorum', is none other than canntaireachd and to accuse it of being nonsense is to make as big a fool of oneself as the Highland Society did when they sent a man away with a whole book of it at the turn of the nineteenth century, telling him it was useless to them.[72]

However, there is also pseudo-canntaireachd in which the syllables do not stand for notes but imitate the general effect, sometimes done with a clarity of diction and vocal gymnastics which would put many a classically trained singer to shame.[73]

The earliest manuscript (and published) source of music specifically for the bagpipes is that of Joseph MacDonald, who prepared his book on his way out to India in 1760, where he died young, long before it was published in a very inaccurate form in 1803, reprinted in 1927. No properly edited version of *A Compleat Theory of the Highland Bagpipe* has yet become available and what is truly the single most significant work in the history of piobaireachd has been given scant attention, when it should be in the hands of every pupil of the pipes. The book takes the form of a tutor and gives many examples of cuttings, of which several are no longer in use, though they are extremely effective.

It is scarcely possible to hear a complete piobaireachd performed in anything like the manner in which it would have been in the eighteenth century with, in many cases, the urlar repeated in the middle or just before the final variation, just as it was in the violin piobaireachd (see below) and as Joseph MacDonald and others indicate it should have been.[74] Worse still, many of the expressive cadences which embellish the main melody notes have become so exaggerated that the melody is obscured by them. The general attitude of pipers to Joseph MacDonald has been such that the most complicated cutting was thought to be impossible to execute and was simply the result of ignorance. But this cutting was performed, probably for the first time since Joseph MacDonald's days, by Alan MacDonald for *Scotland's Music* (the BBC Radio series), so pipers will have to think again and learn to include twenty-note cuttings where appropriate, one after another, as though they'd been there in their fingers all along. It is an impressive sound and makes a great climax to a piobaireachd (see Chapter I, Example 4).

Example 18. LAMENT FOR MARY MACLEOD

Urlar. 1st line

The study of the structure of piobaireachd is equally open to revision. Many of the urlars are built up out of small recurring units and various patterns have been detected in these, all of which involve large numbers of exceptions or manipulation of the analysis and none of which leaves one with much sense of its purpose.[75] It may be that the *Ap Hyw* manuscript will offer some clues and that closer study of other sources[76] will produce worthwhile results, but it is kinder to look at piobaireachd at this stage with two examples of the variety that can be found within what might seem the very limited resources available. The first is the *Lament for Mary MacLeod* (see above) which has a gentle rocking motion to the tune and in which the usually showy variations are smoothed down. It is entirely suitable for the death of a woman who had nursed seven chieftains.

The second example is the urlar of *Lament for the Children*. Highland pipes are crudely described as warlike and raucous, but in music such as this they can convey both anguish and tenderness, with a power and intensity that few could match. This extended melody is revered by all lovers of piobaireachd, and justly so. Based on the third pentatonic scale shown above, it is poised high in the range of the instrument, the weak top A being here used with an effect of pathos in the central section.

Example 19. PATRICK MOR MACCRIMMON: LAMENT FOR THE CHILDREN

Another source of information on early piobaireachd comes from arrangements for violin.[77] The effects the violinists achieved in imitating the pipes made for some remarkable innovations in unaccompanied fiddle writing, considering they were doing this at the same time as Bach was trying to work out what could be done in the same medium. The Scots sometimes retuned the instrument to make it resonate better and to provide a drone effect that would ring out well: they experimented with double stoppings (playing more than one note at a time) and all sorts of different bowings producing a well-balanced, sometimes moving, sometimes exciting composition.

While fiddle piobaireachd tell us a lot about the actual shape of bagpipe piobaireachd, the same is true of the great piobaireachd songs, one

Example 20. MCINTOSH'S LAMENT (Patrick MacDonald, 1781)

of the finest being for *McIntosh's Lament* which occurs in versions for pipes and for fiddle. It tells of a McIntosh whose black horse was destined to kill him and was composed by his widow. In one version, though, the tragedy takes place on the eve of their wedding and recounts how she beat the time of her lament on the coffin lid – a practice which was a normal part of caoining – and in a traditional fiddle performance Donald MacDonnel plucks on the low G string to indicate the sound of her hands on her bridegroom's coffin.[78]

McIntosh's Lament is still well known and it also seems to many to have inspired the famous theme in Dvořák's *New World Symphony*. Dvořák used tunes he had heard in America and this most famous of Scottish laments will have been sung and played regularly in the States by the many Scottish émigrés. The pitch Dvořák thought of as its own was probably the actual pitch of the bagpipes in his day. The very similar structure of the tune, and the fact that Dvořák largely sticks to its pentatonic outline, makes the identification highly likely.

A tune which relates both the fiddle and the clarsach to the pipes is the *Lament for the Bishop of Argyll*, possibly composed to commemorate the death of Bishop MacLean in 1687 and found in two eighteenth-century sources, the first being the beautifully penned *MacFarlane* manuscript of 1740, the second a loosely related version in Daniel Dow's *A Collection of Ancient Scots Music* of 1776. The overall shapes are similar and though neither fits the bagpipes, they can readily be made to do so. The Piobaireachd Society has published the MacFarlane version as a bagpipe lament. There is no question that the MacFarlane manuscript is intended for violin, the Dow collection for violin

(or flute) and harpsichord, but these are clearly arrangements and the question is were they arranged from the bagpipes or from the clarsach? Bishops commonly kept a clarsair and Hector MacLean's home island was Mull – a strong centre of clarsach playing. Whatever the answer, these two sources show that Highland music was in the melting pot, and are important because they represent some of the earliest attempts to note down what may have been piobaireachd.

Song and piobaireachd remain, however, the closest natural companions. The range of the pipes is similar to that of the voice, whereas fiddle and clarsach have always been able to move well beyond it; and pipers sometimes used words to help them memorise tunes, supposing they did not find canntaireachd convenient. One piobaireachd song which has become well known among non-Gaelic singers is *McCrimmon's Lament*. The history of the McCrimmons is obscure. That there were McCrimmon pipers associated with the MacLeod's of Dunvegan, and that they held land at Boreraig across the water from Dunvegan Castle on the island of Skye is undisputed. *MacLeod's Salute* is not unreasonably attributed to Donald Mor McCrimmon and *I Got a Kiss of the King's Hand* was composed in 1651 by a piper with a name very like McCrimmon. But we have no definite birth or death dates for either, and there is a great deal of bogus history and poetry, Gaelic and English, mixed up with *McCrimmon's Lament*. But there is also truth to be had from it.[79] The basic story is that Domhnall Ban McCrimmon composed the piece when leaving Skye, the chorus of the song predicting that he will never return. In fact he was the only person killed at the rout of Moy in 1745, travelling with the MacLeods and Lord Loudon in the hope of capturing the prince. The MacLeods did not support the Jacobite cause. McCrimmon's death was foreseen by Patrick MacAskill whose account was recorded in 1763. He had had a sudden vision of the six-foot-tall piper as he left for his last march as no bigger than a boy of five years of age.

Many will recollect the song as one traditionally sung at the quayside when people are emigrating. Just about this time – 1745 – Rob Donn Mackay must have written his piobaireachd song for Ishbel MacKay. The piobaireachd it matches is called *The Prince's Salute* and is doubtfully associated with the landing of the Old Pretender in 1715. But the words belong to it absolutely and represent a new and interesting type of poetry introduced by Alasdair MacMaster Alasdair, written to fit the bagpipe form rather than the piobaireachd growing from the song.[80] Rob Donn pictures Ishbel all alone tending the cows with their calves: ' . . . look at her, sad this day and every day all alone at the foot of the hills – God and Mary! You who have no wife, if you go to seek one, now is your time.'

Poor girl, she died in 1747, within a year of her marriage, having given her husband a daughter to remember her by. But for her remembrance for the rest of the world there is this:

Example 21. ISEABAIL NIC AOIDH – ISABEL MACKAY
(transposed to bagpipe pitch from the singing of James Campbell)

There is one other particularly fine piobaire-achd song – *Moladh Ben Doran*. It was composed by Duncan Ban MacIntyre in the 1750s and is a poem of over 500 lines, intended to be sung in its entirety as a piobaireachd with variations, the ground returning regularly in between.[81] The ambitious scale of this conception is quite astonishing, particularly when one realises that Duncan Ban could neither read nor write Gaelic and had to compose the entire work in his mind and get it transcribed later. He worked mostly as a forester in Glen Orchy, his surroundings dominated by Ben Doran; and his love for the mountain and everything that lived on it, bird animal and plant, shines through his poetry and finds vivid expression in the traditional piobaireachd form, first of all praising the

mountain, then, in the first variation, the little hind with its tapered head, short-tailed, slender-limbed, exploring the wind with her keen sharp nostrils. The urlar returns more than once between the variations and the last variation des-cribes the hunting of the hind, before repeating part of the opening of the poem as one does in a bagpipe piobaireachd, which, as we have seen, was done long ago in some of the oldest of Celtic poetry and design.

That such a work should come from an illiterate forester in a glen does not surprise people who are aware of the history and oral tradition behind it; but to a visiting Italian – and there were several in Scotland – it would have seemed strange and marvellous had they come across it. Not that the vocal style was anything like as curious as that of the great Tenducci who had been castrated to keep his vocal chords in the heavens, nor the scale so unusual in a world getting used to opera and oratorio; but the whole approach was much more patient and, in certain respects, more serious, for the middle of the eighteenth century was the period of the *style galant* – the gentle, cultivated simplicity of a J.C. Bach who had turned his back upon the vast and profound structures that his father, Johann Sebastian, had been evolving. But these are matters for another chapter.

We shall leave this chapter with mention of another unique and fascinating aspect of Gaelic music – *port-a-beul*. It means 'mouth-music' and refers to the ingenuity of the people when under the brutal suppression of their culture following the failure of the '45 rising. The bagpipes were not actually banned, but a man was hanged for being in possession of a set in York in 1746, so they were essentially silenced.[82] But their role as the providers of music for dancing was already imitated by the human voice which, with a virtuosity that is breathtaking, can patter its way through reels and strathspeys to keep some sense of joy alive at a dark time. It has to be heard to be appreciated[83] and its musical defiance is still enjoyed though no longer required.

THE
PSALMES
of DAVID
in Profe and Meeter.

With their whole Tunes in
foure or mo parts, and
fome Pfalmes in Reports.

Whereunto is added
many godly Prayers, and
an exact Kalendar for
XXV. yeeres to come.

Printed at EDINBURGH by the
Heires of ANDREVV HART,
ANNO DOM. 1635.

CHAPTER XII

FROM COVENANTERS TO CULLODEN

1630–1750

As the Scottish church struggled to establish its presbyterian identity against episcopalian pressures from its own ruling monarchs, narrowing itself for self-protection, so did its music narrow down. Psalm 124 arranged in four simple parts by Andrew Kemp in the late sixteenth century is typical. It has its own proper tune and there is still a little rhythmic life in it, but its basic purpose is to be sober and direct and not to confuse the words (MB26 – *Musica Britannica* XV).

It was not easy for people who had been denied any chance of singing in church suddenly to learn how to do it, so instead of every one of the hundred and fifty psalms being associated with its own tune and no other, a group of tunes known as Common Tunes became popular because you could sing any psalm to them. By the time Edward Millar brought out his great psalter in 1635 (see opposite), there were thirty-one common tunes. Charles I made him Master of the Music in the Chapel Royal. The tunes were drawn from all over Europe, but some were definitely Scottish – such as *Dunfermline,* possibly written by the 'good and meike' John Angus of Dunfermline Abbey.[1] It is still sung today. Millar's *Psalter* even included some tunes in reports – that is with imitating parts, such as the version he published of Psalm 6 (MB 24).

One might, from this, have reasonably hoped for a revival of sorts, but by the end of the century only fourteen tunes were published with the psalter, so one can guess that the process of learning a wide repertoire of tunes made little headway. People everywhere relied on a precentor to set them off on the right tune at the right pitch and with the right words, seeing many could not read letters, never mind music – so if the precentor was poor, the repertoire was bound to narrow down. There was also a lengthy period of civil war and a lack of the kind of patronage and stability that organised music requires and which the execution of Charles I by the English did not help (for MacLean's *Royal Lament* see Chapter XI).

The Psalms of David – 'the three fifties' as the Celtic monks used to call them – were, and remain, central to the worship of God in the Scottish church. The Scots always loved David because he was the chief bard in the Bible. He appears on ancient cross after ancient cross with his Celtic harp, sometimes sitting on his bardic chair (see Chapter II), and, if he was singing, you can be sure it was one of his own psalms. But David's singing will have been much closer to that of the Gaelic psalm singing. Nothing like it is to be heard anywhere else in Western Europe – in Chapter II it was suggested it has its roots in the Middle East, where it is still paralleled in singing styles believed to be unchanged from the days of the apostles. But if we try to transcribe *Coleshill* as sung by Effie and Murdina MacDonald, we will be faced with an insoluble conundrum. The tune is plain and is not especially old, but they have woven it into a wonderful Celtic knot, embellishing and intertwining, transforming it into something rich and strange in which each verse takes over two minutes to perform, so that the words are stretched out and become living, singing things.[2] The two sisters bring to their worship a shared commitment which, apart from its religious significance, is beautifully sustained, intense but flexible singing in which they pass musical phrases from one to the other in a subtle rope of sound.

The MacDonald sisters sing 'of the opening of the gates of righteousness, of the stone which the builders refused becoming the head stone of the corner, of the Lord's doing, marvellous in their eyes', in the surroundings of their own stone-built home in Lewis where the embellishment of vocal lines is particularly marked.[3] It was in Lewis in the 1880s that a young man travelling through a township said he had heard a mile of singing, 'for the family worship was so general and continuous that it seemed unbroken from one end of the township to the other'.[4]

The tune *Martyrs* was a true product of the Reformation in the sixteenth century, first published in Scotland in 1615. Again, transcription of a Gaelic rendition is scarcely possible. This is especially true of congregational singing where each individual has a certain freedom of tempo and embellishment so that the tune is heard slightly out of phase with itself and, as it were, in different colours simultaneously.[5] This too is part of a tradition as old as Christianity, with its nearest parallels in the Middle East. Even a small congregation singing thus sounds like a large body of people. The technique is called 'free heterophony', but the phrase gives no idea of the uncanny emotional charge which such singing produces, not least when sung fervently in the tiny and remote churches in the Hebrides, though from the seventeenth century to the mid-twentieth century, congregations will have been crowded in and sometimes were a thousand-strong.

The Gaelic translation of the metrical psalms only became available in the late seventeenth century.[6] But of the metrical rhythm nothing really survives in performance, and to most ears neither does the tune, though it is still present. Decoration of the psalm tunes was more marked in Gaelic psalm singing, but at first was not confined to it. Embellishment was natural to people unable to read music and singing very slowly, and precentors were essential throughout the country to help congregations remember the words and the tune, and to set a pitch. This they did by 'lining-out' the psalms: that is to say introducing each line of the psalm in advance of the congregation.

Sir John Clerk was one of many classically trained musicians who took a dim view of the practice of embellishment: 'This custom of breaking notes into smaller as the voice ascends or descends or makes cadences, is very frequent amongst the skilful performers, for these knowing nothing of the laws of Harmony fall into gross irregularities. The best of all graces is to sett them in notes and consider them with the counterpoint, whereby the faults will plainly appear. Some very short breakings and lesser faults, may be allowed, but those long Graces used by some are intollerable and especially in the worship of God.'[7]

Attempts were made to reduce these practices by the Englishman Channon and by the disgraceful, and successful court action in 1755 against the Aberdeen weaver, Gideon Duncan, who quit the choir at St Machar's to support the congregation in the old and slower style, thereby causing chaos. He was imprisoned and fined.[8] Another precentor confronted the composer/publisher Robert Bremner who was also trying to get rid of 'Graces and Quavers' (see Plate 31). Bremner describes the encounter:

Plate 31. *Mr John Campbell, Precentor*, BY JOHN KAY, LATE EIGHTEENTH CENTURY

Endeavouring once to convince an old Man, who was Precentor in a Country church, how absurd he rendered the Music, by allowing so many different sounds to one Syllable, when there was only one intended; he replied, with a good deal of briskness, that he did not value what any Man intended, and that he believed the People of the present Generation knew nothing of the Matter; for his Master was allowed to understand that Affair thoroughly, and he told him, there ought to be eight quavers in the first Note of Elgin Tune.[9]

The reformers of psalm singing had less effect in the Gaelic-speaking community where organs were virtually non-existent, where the diatonic scale was unfamiliar (some of the psalm tunes are altered in the Highlands to make them purely pentatonic),[10] and where the Gaelic language sounded awkward in the straight-jacket of an unfamiliar metrical ballad form in unrelieved quatrains. The freedom to decorate the melody so that each member of the congregation makes an individual act of worship out of his or her own singing fulfils the highest ideals of the Reformation by processes the reformers probably never envisaged.

It is as well that something of spiritual value emerged from the period, for most of the music associated with the bitter struggles of the times, however tragic or comical, reveals humanity at its worst. A mild and hilarious example is found in the practice texts used for rehearsing psalms outwith an act of worship. It being considered a sacrilege to perform the holy writ with one's mind focused on the music, substitute texts were encouraged in the eighteenth century, when church choirs were formed and sung worship began to be re-appropriated by choirmasters. The extent of the spirituality of the words and of the value attached to the many noble psalm tunes to which they were sung, is best judged by the following example:

> The high high notes o' Bangor's tune
> Are unco sair to raise;
> An' trying hard to reach them gars
> The lassies burst their stays.

Almost as musically edifying is

> All people that Old Hundredth sing,
> With cheerful voice this measure take;
> Gar ilka line wi' grandeur ring,
> Put on the seventh note a shake.[11]

Clerk and Bremner were no doubt suitably appalled by the shake on the seventh note. But mostly the laughter was not harmless. Typical of the seventeenth century was what went on between Lady Rothiemay and her neighbour Frendraught who had been responsible for the slaughter of her husband and son. Sweet was her revenge when the Highlanders had looted and burnt Frendraught's house to the ground in 1634, and such was her glee that she 'dancit with the licht horsemen in the place of Rothiemay, the cushion dance'. The cushion dance is a

kissing dance better known as *Babbity Bowster*, (bowster being a bolster) so no doubt the light horsemen got their share of kisses that day.[12] If ever there was a tune with the word fiddle written all over it, this is the one. The rhythms seem designed for the kind of articulation that a violin bow is best at: the tune jumps cheerfully across the strings, the bottom one probably tuned up to an A to give the whole instrument more of resonance, and all-in-all it seems to be totally without decorum. Great sport among the smoking ruins of your neighbours.

Example 1. BABBITY BOWSTER or WHO LEARNED YOU TO DANCE AND A TOWDLE? (*Skene Lute Book, c.1625*)

Dance was very much a part of social life and comment. We first encounter the old form of the mocking jigge at and after Bannockburn and the tune to which that jigge was sung – *Scots Wha Hae* – was of course still current. But a different mocking jigge appears in a satire of 1641 called *The Northern Discovery* in which the Governor of Edinburgh Castle keeps a fiddler and a fool who

> goe to singing Scots jigges in a jearing manner at the Covenanters, for surrendering up their Castles as followeth, The fiddler hee flings out his heeles And dances and sings: Put up thy dagor, Jamie, the parliament is ended . . . Then the Foole hee flirts out his folie, And whilst the Fidler playes hee sings.[13]

Just a year earlier in 1640, the Covenanters showed that putting up daggers was not their style. A brutal example is kept bitterly alive in the ballad of *The Bonnie Hoose o' Airlie*. The Earl of Airlie was away from home, fighting at York for

Example 2. Put Up Thy Dagor Jamie (*Blaikie Manuscript*, 1692)

King Charles I. The Earl of Argyll took the opportunity to burn the house to the ground and his lieutenant did the same thing to its neighbour, Forther Castle. Both of these houses were owned by the Ogilvies, and Argyll's savage and personal malice was such that he had to get official retrospective approval for it from the Covenanters. They gave it. Lady Margaret and her children were in the one house, Lady Airlie in the other. They escaped with their lives, but whether the pregnant Lady Margaret was indeed raped by Argyll in full view of his troops because she would not save her castle by yielding to him, cannot be proved. Accusations in the ballads of the bitter covenanting years are sometimes almost as wild as those of today's popular press. Some versions have an anachronistic mention of Prince Charlie – but ballads are often slightly updated to keep them relevant. The tune was first noted in the nineteenth century.[14] Its narrow six-note range and bland repetitions, combined with the stark matter-of-fact words, match the almost childish viciousness of the subject-matter.

During these years there were no theatres, dancing was frowned on and even after the

Example 3. The Bonnie Hoose o' Airlie (*The Scottish Minstrel*, 1820–24)

Restoration a town piper was tried for 'reviling a parson'. He innocently maintained he had only played 'ane spring' – a lively dance tune: if its title happened to be *Deil Stick the Minister*, well what did that signify?[15]

The Restoration did indeed restore some sense of jollity and was the direct occasion for the first publication of secular music in Scotland. It came out with only one of the intended four parts and contained largely imported music, or music dating back to the sixteenth century. It had an Introduction by the Master of the Aberdeen Sang School and the words of songs were carfully chosen, one of them suggesting that the Restoration was like Christmas and Charles II like Christ. That it took two hundred years to happen after the arrival of printing in Scotland gives some idea of the power of the Reformation to stifle any recognition in print that life was occasionally a pleasurable thing. But in private they had few inhibitions and the Reverend Robert Edwards could, in 1630, happily enter the text of a fearful ballad of brother-sister incest (*Sheath and Knife*) in his commonplace book;[16] and the precentor at Lauder Kirk in 1677 (a man by the name of Taitt)[17] was quite ready to tuck an indelicate round into his manuscript book, cheek-by-jowl with the psalms. It is still unfit to print.

In the same manuscript there is a fascinating round for seven voices consisting entirely of Scottish street cries without any added parts or embellishments, and it gives us a unique insight

Example 4. Old Pots and Pans – Street Cries (*Taitt Manuscript*, 1677)

Plate 32. The Riding of the Scottish Parliament, late seventeenth century

into social life on the streets of a Scottish city. The vendors are selling chandlery, salt, fresh oysters, country curds and fresh whey, white sand for cleaning the plates and, lastly, telling a tinker to stick his tongue up the cat's arse.

The Restoration of Charles II to the English throne (he was already crowned King of Scotland) was greeted at least in Edinburgh with undisguised delight and with an illumination showing Cromwell being chased by the devil into hell, in the form of an explosion of fireworks. At the Mercat Cross six violers celebrated by 'playing there continually', though they and the other musicians standing by were rendered inaudible by the noise of the crowds and had a rival attraction in the form of a puncheon of wine set 'upon the foot of the cross' and running from a waterspout. Mons Meg was blasted off, bells were rung and there were trumpets and a drum march.[18]

In England too, the Restoration brought benefits for Scottish music in the 1686 edition of Playford's *The English Dancing Master*, which contains several Scottish tunes. The Restoration helped to make Scottish music popular down south. Among the Playford family's many publications there is *A Collection of Original Scotch-Tunes (Full of the Highland Humours) for the Violin*. It was published in 1700. *The Scotch Trumpet Tune* appears in an English publication of 1697 but could have

been the one heard in Edinburgh. Trumpets and kettle drums were played on horseback for solemn processions such as the opening of the Scottish Parliament (see Plate 32) and though this tune is scored for harpsichord, it seems clear that it is an arrangement with the rhythm of the bass line representing the drums, the upper parts the trumpets.

Example 5. The Scotch Trumpet Tune (adapted from *The Harpsichord Master*, 1697)

Charles II was keen on music. He could sight-sing reasonably and he retained a liking in particular for Scottish tunes.[19] Although Scottish music began to enjoy a vogue in England, it was also criticised – a character in a Shadwell play speaks of a Scotch song 'more hideous and barbarous than an Irish cronan'[20], and we have quoted Pepys's puzzled reaction in the Introduction, finding what the Scots enjoyed to be altogether strange.

However, on one occasion in London a down-at-heel Scottish laird, unable to get an audience, attracted the king's attention by slipping onto the organ bench after a service in the Chapel Royal and playing *Brose and Butter* – a favourite tune of Charles II.[21]

One thinks of the Royalists as the cheerful sensualists, but the Covenanters were not all prayers and miseries, and there is no better proof of that than in the song *Dainty Davie*. Dainty Davie was the Reverend David Williamson, a Covenanter who took refuge in the house of Cherrytrees from the Royalist troops. Lady Cherrytrees concealed him in her sixteen-year-old daughter's bed, her daughter being unwell and in it at the time. Williamson seems to have cured her of one ill with another for he made her pregnant while her mother regaled the troops downstairs with strong drink. He married the girl (he was married six times in all) and if the song is anything to go by she seems not to have regretted one instant of it. Charles II, hearing of Williamson's behaviour, 'wished to see the man that discovered so much vigour, while his troopers were in Search of him: And, in a merry way, declared, that when he was hiding in the Royal oak, he could not have kissed the bonnyest lass in Christendom.'

Williamson justified himself by a disarming choice of text from Paul's Epistle to the Romans: 'For that which I do I allow not: for what I would, that do I not; but what I hate, that do I.

Now then it is no more I that do it, but sin that dwelleth in me. For I know that in me (that is, in my flesh) dwelleth no good thing . . .'[22]

'Dainty' in Scots means 'pleasant, good-looking, good-natured' and can apply to things as well as people. 'Leese-me-on' is an expression of pleasure with no equivalent in English. The tune given here is as sung by Jean Redpath but its source seems to be a mystery.[23] It is a good example of what was happening to Scottish tunes as the seventeenth century progressed, for it has a second strain which changes it from a modal hexatonic tune into one that uses the whole scale and implies more obvious harmonies.

At about the same time as the Reverend David Williamson was spreading his seed there was unfolding a love story as unhappily different as it is possible to imagine. On top of one of the turrets of Fyvie Castle in Aberdeenshire there is a little stone trumpeter. Most castles had their professional trumpeters and so did the military. In 1672 the Scottish Parliament passed an Act 'that the heritors of everie Shire allow yeirlie fourtie eight pounds Scotes to the Trumpiter who serves their Troup, and twelve pounds Scotes to every Drummer who serves their Companies'. But, despite their better pay, the status of trumpeters cannot have been high, for when Annie Smith, the miller of Tiftie's daughter, fell in love with the Trumpeter of Fyvie, her father, mother and brother beat her so unmercifully that she died of a broken back. They felt she had picked a man beneath the notice of a miller's daughter. In one version her sisters taunt her when she listens out for her lover's trumpet call from the battlements, saying 'your cow is lowin' on ye'.

Even the support of Lord Fyvie for the match was of no avail. Annie was buried in Fyvie churchyard in 1673. No more moving document to her tragedy could be conceived than Jane Turriff's and Sheila MacGregor's singing of the

Example 6. DAINTY DAVIE (from the singing of Jean Redpath)

Example 7. MILL O' TIFTIE'S ANNIE (from the singing of Jane Turriff)

ballad three centuries later, with feeling as natural and undiminished as must have given rise to it in the first place.[24] The tune's two phrases are perfectly balanced, but the ambiguity between major and minor modes carries it beyond balance and wistfulness into the direct appeal of utter sorrow. (See Example 7.)

It is one of the most touching aspects of our musical history that a ballad such as that, describing an individual tragedy among people who might be thought of as having no historical consequence, has held its own alongside the wider doings of the world, recognising the universal in the particular without fear or favour. One of those wider doings was the Battle of Bothwell Bridge, which took place in 1679, just six years after the death of Mill o' Tiftie's Annie.

The Covenanters were gathered on the south side of the River Clyde, camped indecisively for days. We can imagine them being woken by fife and drum with a *Reveille*.

Example 8. THE REVEILLE (*Compleat Tutor for the Fife*, 1759–60)

The calls given here come from a mid-eighteenth century tutor for the fife and drum, but were probably of long standing.[25] They are remarkable for their distinctiveness – and have to be, so that there is no confusion about the order. After breakfast *The General* would have been played to call everyone to parade. With the arrival of Monmouth's forces on a hill overlooking the Covenanters' positions from across the river, *The Gathering* would have been sounded to call the men to their alarm posts and to gather to their

Example 9. THE GATHERING (*Compleat Tutor for the Fife*, 1759–60)

colours. This command seems to have been associated exclusively with Scotland, all the military references to gatherings having been made by Scots – Thomas Simes and Sir James Turner. The English called their equivalent command *The Assembly*.[26] *The Gathering* may well relate to the Highland piper's gathering.

The Covenanters remained indecisive. Everything was discussed by committees of ministers and, driven by deep religious convictions, no doubt many felt that the Lord would uphold them. They may well have sung psalms. Monmouth asked them to lay down their arms within the hour, but the discussions went on, so his men crossed the bridge and the battle began. That will have been the cue for the *To Arms*. The battle was a farce. The Covenanters ran out of ammunition and their cavalry panicked at the first shots and retreated into their own foot soldiers. One man remained defiant – a covenanting piper who, according to James Hogg, stood in full view of the Royalists, derisively playing *Awa Whigs Awa*. When he was hit by a bullet he continued trying to play as he rolled down the bank, his pipes grunting under his arm, until he fell into the river and his body 'was carried peaceably down the stream among a great number of floating Whigs'.[27]

If the Covenanters were lucky there might just have been a couple of musicians with enough self-command to play *The Retreat* before everyone had completely disappeared, but this is a tune clearly designed for a strategic retreat carried out in good order and spirit, so it seems unlikely.

Example 10. THE RETREAT (*Compleat Tutor for the Fife*, 1759–60)

The Royalists will probably have marched off in good order to the good old *Scots March*. All over Europe the lads who fifed and drummed for the Scottish regiments will have frequently played *The Scots March*. The drum rhythms recall the old words 'Ding Doun Tantallon, Ding

Doun Tantallon'. They are supposed to relate back to James V's siege of Tantallon Castle in 1527 when he was routing out Archibald Douglas; and the rhythm of that drum beating certainly fits *The Scots March* which appears in *Elizabeth Rogers' Virginal Book* of the 1650s.[28]

Example 11. THE SCOTS MARCH (adapted from Elizabeth Rogers' *Virginal Book*, c.1650)

The Scots March had such a reputation that the Dutch played it instead of their own music in 1632, 'Thinking thereby to affright the enemy' but, 'being charged they made a base retreat'.[29]

Defeated or victorious, when it was time for lights out *The Taptoo* was played. Taptoo is the original of tattoo. It was the signal for the regimental sutler to turn off all the taps on the beer barrels, a device certain to send everyone to their beds.

The music and the spirit of those days is still to be heard on fife and drum at Orange parades, but no longer against the background of such tremendous political change – the defeat of James VII at the Battle of the Boyne in 1690, the Treaty of Union amalgamating the parliaments of Scotland and England in 1707, and the two failed Jacobite Risings of 1715 and 1745.

There was a less fervent musician at Bothwell Bridge, the fiddler Pate Birnie, who, on being asked to take part in the battle, turned tail and is said to have run all the way to Edinburgh without stopping.[30] There was a native tradition of fiddle playing stretching back many centuries

and Birnie will have been one of its exemplars (see Plate 33). His normal place of residence was on the Kinghorn ferry where he used to regale the passengers with fiddle music and song, and he is credited by Alan Ramsay with both words and music of the deathless masterpiece *The Auld Man's Mare's Deid*. It is a tremendous piece of vivid Scots, describing a decrepit old horse, and the music is one of the oldest examples we have of the strathspey with its heavily dotted rhythms that suit the violin so well.

Example 12. PATE BIRNIE: THE AULD MAN'S MARE'S DEID (Johnson, *Scots Musical Museum*, 1771)

The strathspey is first referred to by Boyd in 1653: 'To please the King the Morris dance I will; Stravetspy, and after, last of all, The Drunken Dance I'll Dance within that hall.'[31]

Pate Birnie's companion used to dance on a table-top to add to the amusement and Allan Ramsay, that gentle purveyor of the pastoral image of Scotland in his ballad opera, *The Gentle Shepherd*, recollected Pate's ways with superior amusement:

> . . . he wad gang,
> *And crave their pardon that sae lang*
> *He'd been a-coming;*
> *Syne his bread-winner out he'd bang*
> *And fa' to bumming.*[32]

Bumming – not a kindly word to use for a man who probably had to lower his standards for his audience as much as the other way about, as 'bumming' means to make a humming or droning noise. Two centuries earlier Birnie and his like might have been singing and playing a romance epic like *Greysteil* to James IV instead of resenting King William. Then there was the new more suave Italian style which threatened to reduce the status of Scots fiddlers and Pate Birnie did not like it, as Ramsay's poem tells us.

Another fiddler who has left us an early example of the strathspey style was James

Plate 33. Pate Birnie, EIGHTEENTH-CENTURY ENGRAVING

MacPherson. His one surviving piece is known as a *Rant,* which means exactly what it implies. MacPherson was a gipsy freebooter who was rescued from prison by two fellow fiddlers, Peter and Donald Broun, but was recaptured in the Grampians and hanged at the cross at Banff on 16 November 1700, at the age of twenty-five. It was still a crime to be a gipsy in 1700. It has been said that many of his actions (which frequently involved theft) were characterised by kindness and brotherly love towards the poor and oppressed: sadly, when the poor and oppressed gathered round to watch him die and heard him play his *Rant,* or *Testament* as it is also known, no

X.
For our lang biding here.

WHEN we came to *London* Town,
We dream'd of Gowd in Gowpings here,
And rantinly ran up and down,
In rifing Stocks to buy a Skair :

We daftly thought to row in Rowth,
But for our Daffine pay'd right dear ;
The Lave will fare the war in trouth,
For our lang biding here.

But when we fand our Purfes toom,
And dainty Stocks began to fa',
We hang our Lugs, and wi' a Gloom,
Girn'd at Stock-jobbing ane and a'.

If we gang near the *South-Sea* Houfe,
The Whilly-Wha's will grip ye'r gear,
Syne a' the Lave will fare the war,
For our lang biding here.

XI.

Plate 34. *For Our Lang Biding Here*, FROM THOMSON'S *Orpheus Caledonius*, 1733

one would take the proferred fiddle when he was done, so he smashed it defiantly across his knee. A broken violin, said to be his, is lovingly preserved by the MacPherson clan but I do not believe anyone has had the indecency to date it.

It is unlikely that MacPherson composed the *Rant* the night before his execution and no contemporary evidence suggests that he was even a fiddler. But his trial and death are genuine, the tune was written into a manuscript book by Margaret Sinclair in 1710 as *MacFarsance's Testament*, and the words date from 1705, though they make no mention of fiddle-playing or smashing; so all-in-all we may take it that the tune and the man somehow belong together in an act of last defiance.[33]

Satire and invective were not confined to gipsies, as can be heard in *The Soo's Tail Tae Geordie*. Geordie was George I and the sow was one of his mistresses, either the Duchess of Kendal or more probably the Countess of Darlington, who was so vast she was called 'the elephant' in England. In Scotland she was just a sow ('soo')

and her song must have originated in the 1720s; a different tune with the same title and satire against the fat mistress was played on violin with deliberately piggish squeals at the end, to be made by scraping the bow behind the bridge.[34]

George I and his mistress were partly resented for being neither of the House of Orange nor the House of Stewart as Queen Anne had been. But it was during her reign that the Treaty of Union was signed. On the very day of the signing, the carillon player of St Giles mounted into his loft to give his daily hour-long recital. His was a splendid new carillon made by John Meikle in 1698–99. There were twenty-one bells and the carilloner (a violinist called Francis Toward) had himself supervised their tuning and hanging.[35] The bells were removed in the early twentieth century, but right through the eighteenth century they gave pleasure. Edward Burt, visiting from England in 1726 commented that the recital included 'Scots, English, Irish and Italian tunes to great perfection, and is heard all over the city'.[36] People used to stop and listen in the High Street, and later that century Alexander Kincaid wrote: 'In the tower of St Giles' Church is a set of bells which are rung out or played upon by the hand with keys, like a harpsichord, the person having leather covers to his fists, by which he is able to strike with more force. They play all manner of tunes very musically; and a yearly salary is paid for playing upon them. . . .'[37]

Perhaps one day some public-minded Edinburgh citizen will restore the carillon. But on that day in 1707 what tune did the carilloner choose to beat out on the keys with his leather-covered fists? He was no fool. He knew the whole city was listening and he also knew his audience understood what he meant when with the most ironic musical gesture Scotland has ever known he chose to play *Why Should I be Sad on My Wedding Day?*[38]

As the Chancellor, the Earl of Seafield said, as he descended for the last time from his official chair in the Scottish Parliament, trying to conceal his emotion: 'Thus endeth an auld sang.' Yes, in Scotland even our parliament was thought of as a national song.

Not long after the treaty was signed James Oswald published a tune in his Caledonian Pocket Companion called *A Parcel of Rogues in a Nation*. Burns worked up the words for it and it could hardly express any greater contempt for what was done. The tune itself is sad and wistful rather than bitter, but it points a finger of accusation that is pointing to this day. For the people of Scotland who had no votes in the matter the Treaty of Union – though it rescued many investors from the financial ruin of the Darien Scheme (see Chapter XIII) – was a betrayal of the nation. But it was not the sole source of ruin, for the Scots were setting themselves up as bankers and Money was beginning to grow tusks. The song of two Scots who have lost their all on speculative investments in London tells us sharply enough that nothing has changed in the morality of that notional commodity. The text was first published by Allan Ramsay in his *Tea-Table Miscellany* of 1724. William Thomson republished it in London with its tune in 1733. His *Orpheus Caledonius* was the first published collection of Scottish folk-song made by a Scot which included the music. The song is *For Our Lang Biding Here* and the money was lost in the famous South Sea Bubble scandal of 1720 (see Plate 34).

The years following the Union were the years of the Jacobite Risings. Books have been filled with the songs and music associated with them, and quite a few are genuine. It may be that all we have left of Bonnie Prince Charlie is locks of hair, bits of clothing, pieces of silver and a portrait or two, but what really keeps him alive is song. Sadly, of the most famous songs associated with the period, one is a concoction of James Hogg's (see Chapter XVI), and another a Victorian fake.

The Skye Boat Song – 'Speed Bonnie Boat' – has joined the tradition with the help of Lady Wilson (who added the inferior, repetitive second half of the tune in 1879), and Sir Harold Boulton who provided the words in 1884. Like many a fake *The Skye Boat Song* has earned a great success, but nothing much like it was heard by the Young Pretender. What, in reality, might have been sung as the young prince was carried over the sea to Skye? An unnecessarily romanticised version of *Kishmul's Galley* was made by Marjory Kennedy-Fraser, but the original is close to the truth of the times. It is a waulking song, but it shares its rhythm with rowing songs and it describes MacNeil of Barra's galley. There is a tradition that Noah offered the MacNeil a place in the Ark but was politely turned down as MacNeil had a boat already. *Kishmul's Galley* was composed in the seventeenth century by the bardess Nic Iain Fhinn from the neighbouring island of Mingulay who featured earlier in the Barra boasting – a satirical battle between two poetesses (see Chapter XI).[39]

Example 13. KISHMUL'S GALLEY (from the singing of Janet McKinnon)

An Fhideah Airgid – 'The Silver Whistle' – is also a proud song. It is one of many that provides an impressive use of the Scotch snap. The refrain is beautifully shaped, a rising welcome balanced by a more modest and tender phrase. It was composed just at the time Prince Charles landed on the island of Eriskay on 18 July 1745.

Who will sound the silver chanter
Now that my King's son has come to Scotland?
On a great ship across the waves
On a stately ship with silver rigging?

Young Charles of the beguiling blue eyes –
Welcome, welcome, love and renown to you!
Playing of fiddles and the choicest of music for you!
Who will sound the silver chanter?
Who is to say that I will not sound it myself?[40]

The great Gaelic poet, Alasdair MacMaster Alasdair, also took up the cry of welcome with *Moch sa Mhadainn is mi dusgadh* – 'Early in the morning as I awaken Great is my joy and hearty laughter – you are the choicest of rulers – in that modest cheek runs blood that is pure and undefiled. And if the crown were placed upon you Joyful would be your friends And Locheil, as he ought, Would be drawing up the Gaels for battle.'[41]

The tune below is the only one used for this poem and it has everything you could ask of it. It starts – as do most Gaelic songs – with the refrain, a broad-gestured swinging one that works in powerfully with the high declamatory verses. The whole thing is full of assertion and confidence and many a complex aria pales into insignificance beside such musical and poetic authority.

Example 14. ALASDAIR MACMASTER ALASDAIR: MOCH SA MHADAINN – EARLY IN THE MORNING (from the singing of James Campbell)

Naturally the bagpipes will have been heard by the prince as the clans gathered at the summons of Locheil. *My King Has Landed in Moidart*, composed by John MacIntyre, has an urlar that claims to have its roots in the eighteenth-century MacCrimmon tradition. The prince was not only familiar with the sound of the pipes but actually played them. He may have been taught by a piper of the Black Watch regiment who had been on the continent since 1743 and fought at Fontenoy in 1745. The Black Watch did not have official pipers, but there will certainly have been pipers among them.[42]

The Jacobites had scarcely taken Edinburgh before they had to defend it from Sir John Cope's army at Prestonpans in 1745. With local help they were able to sneak up through the dawn mists and score a notable victory. A local farmer, Adam Skirving, wrote the song which has since become so famous, *Hey Johnnie Cope are ye waukin yet* (that is, awake yet). It was written immediately after the battle, according to tradition, and there is another song attributed to him full of interesting circumstantial detail which refers to the local coalmines and is in the same derisive style as the old mocking jigge of Bannockburn days.[43]

It is after the Battle of Prestonpans that Bonnie Prince Charlie might first have come across the composer John Reid, then just twenty-four years old. Having gathered enough men, Reid had been commissioned as a lieutenant in Loudon's Highlanders and was taken prisoner by the Jacobites. But he was back with his regiment the following spring, and disobeyed orders, risking court-martial to capture £12,000 sterling from the Jacobite army – a severe blow to their stretched finances.[44] He emerges in a later chapter as a member of the Temple of Apollo. In the meantime we shall follow the Jacobites south from Prestonpans, for which no better description can be found than Andy Hunter's singing of *King Fareweel*. Derived from a broadside ballad dating from the period, Hunter's version amalgamates various sources of words and music to produce – as Hamish Henderson has so rightly described it – 'a seamless garment'.[45] It is eloquent testimony to the creative continuity of the oral tradition, in this case the very fact that it is not a replica of an eighteenth-century original arguing for its greater authenticity. The tune is a kind of clarion call, proud and arresting, and its truthfulness and clarity bring us within earshot of the campaign itself.

The return of the Jacobite army from Derby via Carlisle is commemorated in the internationally famous song – *Loch Lomond*. The tune is a variant of *The Bonnie Hoose o' Airlie*, the words relatively modern.[46] It certainly has no place in the mid-eighteenth century and in any case scarcely anybody knows how to sing it. It has had heaped upon its head more appalling and ignorant performances than any song has a right to bear. Its subject-matter is one of bitter and ironic tragedy. The Jacobite soldier awaiting execution claims he will reach Scotland before his companion as his spirit will get there first by the low road. This is usually rendered by singers and arrangers with an inane chirpiness more suited to selling washing-up liquid. One day perhaps it will be restored to its proper dignity, but a more accurate reflection of what would have been heard at such an execution is to be found in *The Celebrated Trumpet Tune*.

'Upon the Circuits in Scotland this Air is played by his Majesty's Household Trumpets attending the Lords of Justiciary, when that high (Solemn) Court has occasion to Exercise its most painful Duty.'[47] In other words, it was played at executions. Nathaniel Gow published it in the early nineteenth century but marked it as being 'very old'. One should not dismiss this as mere wishful thinking on his part, either on factual or stylistic grounds. Nathaniel Gow had received a classical training in music from the Reinagle family, the father having been employed as a state trumpeter on the advice of the Earl of Kelly, whose Mannheim training ensured he knew a good trumpeter when he heard one. We may assume then that when Nathaniel Gow was appointed a state trumpeter in 1782 he had been well trained and knew that the repertoire he was performing had not been composed yesterday.

Example 15. THE CELEBRATED TRUMPET TUNE (Niel Gow, *Book V*, late eighteenth century)

No doubt that tune was played frequently in the years following Culloden which, on 16 April 1746, saw the whole extraordinary story brought to an end. There is no popular ballad commemorating Culloden. It was too horrific. The scale of the tragedy and terrible ensuing brutality of the English was beyond reckoning. But the individual tragedies were not lost because of that. This most desolate of songs – *Mo Run Geal Og – My Fair Young Love –* was probably composed by Christiana Fergusson, widow of William Chisholm.

> Alas young Charles Stewart, it is your cause that has left me desolate. You took from me everything that I had, in war for your sake. It is not sheep or cattle that I mourn but my husband, from that day when I was left alone with nothing in the world but a shirt – My fair young love.
>
> Alas and alas! What a wretch I am, ceaselessly sighing. I lost hope of your return, my heart sank into despair. Neither fiddle nor harp will raise it, neither pipe nor gaming nor any music; since the day they laid you to rest, young men's advances do not rouse me – my fair young love.[48]

Example 16. MO RUN GEAL OG (approximation from the singing of Flora MacNeil)

A majority of the poetry and music in the English-speaking world comes from men, but there can be few cultures in Western Europe to which women have contributed on such equal terms and so movingly as in Gaelic song, bringing one face to face with direct realism and uncompromising intensity.

This period was most terrible for the Gaelic community, resulting as it did in the complete collapse of their social system and the beginnings of the Clearances. It is not surprising then, that the evangelical movement should have made great strides in the west. This was partly because of the positive fact that bibles were now available in Gaelic, but there was, and there remains more than vestigially, a quality of religious feeling rarely matched in the Lowlands. Eloquent expression is given to that continuity of feeling by Murdina MacDonald's singing of the evangelical hymn *Tha do Rioghachd Lan do Ghloir –* 'Thy Kingdom is full of glory' – whose words seem particularly apposite to the period following Culloden. As with the psalms, the embellishment of the basic melody turns the four-square cut-outs of regular music into a personal creative act that grows as the words grow and as human nature still grows in those parts, from the beauties and sorrows and joys of the natural world about them.

Many are the troubles and hardships that thy people undergo in the wilderness, each one calling out for relief in his own extremity. But all these troubles and sorrows will work to gain them unending joy; there will be no memory of the glen of tears and they will have the crown of glory as their reward. . . . not small is the suffering of thy people; the hard heart and the worldly mind. In their thoughts they would seek to be above, removed from the cold husks of this world; but their desire is not being fulfilled – to live for Christ, in his love; many a time it seems to them that the ocean has ebbed away. How dejected thy people will be in this glen when thou hidest thy countenance from them, how oppressive will be their nights. No human comfort can bring consolation to their minds; they will be like the little sparrow left alone when they cannot find their Beloved.'[49]

Example 17. THA DO RIOGHACHD LAN DO GHLOIR
(approximation from the singing of Murdina MacDonald)

CHAPTER XIII

FROM ROME TO HOME
1660–1720

There are perhaps three universal languages that convey feeling as well as information: music, dance and fine art. Often they receive scant respect in the curriculum and to take up music as a profession is still regarded as a maverick thing to do. In seventeenth-century Scotland it certainly was, for there were few openings for employment, there being scarcely any provision for music at all. There were song schools attached to churches, but organs were banned from them and the music was simple four-part settings of metrical psalms. Nothing to stretch either the technique or imagination of even the dullest. Aberdeen had the best of these schools and from it emerged the *Forbes Cantus Partbook* – Scotland's first published secular music. But the music in it was mostly a century old or else imported and, though it was all meant to be sung in parts, only the melody line (the cantus part) was printed, presumably for lack of demand. In the big houses and castles the ballads were still sung, or played, just as they were among the people in general; but to these were added the lute and the violin, and the children in the household were taught to write music as well, and this has bequeathed us manuscripts, several written by young women – Lady Margaret Wemyss, Margaret Ker, Lady Ann Ker, Lady Jean Campbell and Lady Montgomerie.[1] Their repertoire often included Scottish tunes. The harpsichord was studied too, though in those days the virginals and spinet, smaller, less ambitious instruments, were still much in use. We have an odd little suite of keyboard pieces in a manuscript that belonged to young Lady Montgomerie, and each one is given a nationality. *The Duch Man* sounds cheerful enough, as they all do and there is no mistaking the *Scotts Man* (see Introduction).

This is pleasant schoolroom stuff, but simple in the extreme. Singing was taught in the home

too, especially psalm-singing, but there was nothing demanding in the 'classical' repertoire being sung in Scotland, so it too was of the simplest. The best-known teacher was imported, as his name – Louis de France – tells us. He taught at the Aberdeen Song School from 1675, but after five years he moved to wealthier pastures, teaching privately in Edinburgh. We have his song-book[2] and, like the Forbes cantus, it is mostly old-fashioned or foreign – and where were the composers and musicians to take Lady Montgomerie any further? Nowhere.

A young musician with talent had to go south. John Abell of Aberdeen certainly did have talent, for he was born with one of the most remarkable voices Europe was ever to hear. He probably studied under Thomas Davidson who wrote the Preface to the *Forbes Cantus Partbook* and was Louis de France's predecessor as Master of the Aberdeen Sang Schule. But to find a proper outlet for his voice, John Abell went to London and in 1679 joined the Chapel Royal in London as a musician 'in ordinary' on £40 a year.

Soon Abell was appointed as a lutenist and violinist as well, performing music of the kind included in the great Scottish lute collection from Balcarres. As well as Scottish airs skilfully adapted, it contains French and English pieces.

Example 1. THE DUCH MAN (*Companion to Lady Margaret Wemyss manuscript, c.1670*)

Many were arranged by Mr Beck, a German music tutor at Balcarres, remembered for his battle with Scotland's Master of the Revels in 1694. Beck merely wanted to hold a concert without paying a licence fee and fortunately he won. The collection was made a decade after Abell moved south, but he will have been familiar with the style of treatment and will have known in London that Scottish music was enjoying a vogue. Charles II was still king and so admired Abell's singing that he sent him abroad to show the Italians what good voices were produced in Britain. Being a catholic and a Scot may well have helped him in a Stewart court, though Abell is one of those Scots who is frequently referred to as English. In 1684 he returned to Scotland, perhaps with some political work to do – musicians were commonly used for spying – and in the same year he also went to Italy, returning in good voice as that splendid English diarist, John Evelyn tells us: 'After the supper came in the famous treble, Mr. Abel, newly returned from Italy. I never heard a more excellent voice, and would have sworn it had been a woman's, it was so high and so well and skilfully managed, being accompanied by Signor Francisco on the harpsichord.'[3]

Abell seems to have been that rarest of creatures, a true male soprano. The Italians had a way of obtaining male sopranos: they castrated them. But Abell was no castrato and indeed he scandalised London society by marrying the sister of Lord Banbury, one Lady Frances, who had set her heart on him. It was alright for a singer to earn money – lots of it. But marrying into the aristocracy was quite another thing:

> Lord Banbury's sister, Lady Francis, is married to Abell, the singing master; her brother is extremely concerned at it. As soon as Lord Banbury knew of it, he put her out of the house. She was married that night that the company was there, which was a Tuesday, and on Wednesday night my Lady Exeter and my Lord Exeter and my brothers and sister and Lord Banbury and Lady Frances and Sir Mortan and his Lady supped at Mr King's in the Great Room where the musick plays of public days, and I could not perceive anything of love between them for she courted my brothers as much as ever she used to.[4]

John Abell was not just a singer, lutenist and violinist, he was also a composer. There is a lovely echo song of his, in the sentimental Italian pastoral style, a love song full of pantings and pleasure, set in Italian. It has been criticised for being Italianate,[5] which seems a little unfair on an Italian song.

Despite the vindictive snobs, Abell's marriage lasted and twenty-three years later could still provoke a satirical attack from Thomas Brown of 'facetious memory' who exclaimed: 'Who would not bring up their children in a quire? or who would not learn to sing. . .it was a pity so many gallant men should want for their loyalty, while a jackanapes cou'd get an estate for a song.'[6]

For a while all went well for Abell. He was one of two musicians who accompanied James VII and II wherever he went,[7] and he became wealthy enough to mount a musical entertainment to celebrate the birth of a royal son. It could have been a model for Handel's *Water Music* thirty years later:

> Mr. Abell, the celebrated musician, and one of the Royal band, entertained the publick, and demonstrated his loyalty on the evening of the 18th June 1688, by the performance of an aquatic concert. The barge prepared for this purpose was richly decorated, and illuminated by numerous torches. The musick was composed expressly for the occasion by Signor Fede, Master of the Chapel Royal, and the performers, vocal and instrumental, amounted to one hundred and thirty, selected as the greatest proficients in the science. . . . The first performance took place facing Whitehall, and the second opposite Somerset House where the Queen Dowager then resided. Great numbers of barges and boats were assembled, and each having flambeaux on board, the scene was extremely brilliant and pleasing. The music being ended, all the nobility and company that were upon the water gave three shouts to express their joy and satisfaction; and all the gentlemen of the musick went to Mr. Abell's house, which was nobly illuminated and honoured with the presence of a great many of the nobility; out of whose windows hung a fine machine full of lights which drew thither a vast concourse of people. The entertainment lasted till three of the clock the next morning, the musick playing and the trumpets sounding all the while, the whole concluding with the health of their Majesties, The Prince of Wales, and all the Royal Family.[8]

It was the Old Pretender, albeit in swaddling clothes, whose arrival was celebrated, and not long after the bloodless revolution of 1688, Abell 'was discharged as being a papist' from the Chapel Royal, lost his patronage, had probably spent all his money on the water music, and had

Example 2. JOHN ABELL: THE FIFTH SONG (*Songs in Several Languages*, 1701)

to leave his wife behind and grub a living in Europe. We get glimpses of his progress: 'Abel the Musician who is very poor, and comes to sing and beg in these courts, is gone to Hanover to offer his services.'. . .'Abell is now with me and his catholicity does not hinder him from singing Victoria for us' [this was when the Protestants recaptured Namur]. . . 'That harmonious vagabond Abell is now here'.[9]

We also hear from Sir John Hawkins's account of a most extraordinary story which goes to show that the profession of musician can be a desperately hazardous one:

Abell distinguished himself by singing in public in Holland, at Hamburg and other places, where, acquiring considerable sums of money, he lived profusely, and affected the expense of a man of quality, moving about in an equipage of his own, though at intervals he was so reduced as to be obliged to travel, with his lute slung at his back, through whole provinces. In rambling he got as far as Poland; and upon his arrival at Warsaw, the king having notice of it, sent for him to his court. Abell made some slight excuse to evade going, but upon being told that he had everything to fear from the king's resentment, he made an apology, and received a command to attend the king next day.

Upon his arrival at the palace, he was seated in a chair in the middle of a spacious hall, and immediately drawn up to a great height; presently the king with his attendants appeared in a gallery opposite to him, and at the same instant a number of wild bears were turned in; the king bade him chose whether he would sing or be let down among the bears: Abell chose the former, and declared afterwards that he never sung so well in his life.[10]

Eventually Abell met up with King Billy and wormed his way back into some sort of favour. His chief means was the composition of a splendid and grovelling piece hailing the victory of the protestants over his own catholic faith at the Battle of the Boyne. The obsequious dedication he wrote when it was published as one of his *Songs in Several Languages* in 1701 no doubt continued to oil the wheels (see Plate 35).[11]

Abell calls his cantata *The Third Song*, but it is an extended piece, though it exists only as a vocal part and a scantily figured bass. The figured bass was a recent idea, and a clever one. The idea was that any intelligent musician given the melody line and the bass line, would be able, with a little guidance, to invent the rest to suit himself and the occasion and the other performers. The guidance consisted of figures next to the bass notes which indicated what chords to use in cases of doubt. It gave opportunities for freedom and flexibility, particularly when accompanying soloists, and applied to instruments which could play chords, such as harpsichord, harp, organ, etc. To help reinforce the bass, cellos, basses or bassoons would be added. This accompanying group is known as the 'continuo section', because it keeps the music going, sometimes through thick and thin.

The Third Song calls for violins, trumpets and a chorus. (Abell may have had access to the slide trumpet of the day which could play a complete chromatic scale.) It is a substantial and varied composition. There are no da capo arias (that is, arias which repeat their opening section at the end, often with the soloist adding flourishes to show off) but it is basically a cantata with a mixture of arioso and recitative. It leans on the blunt rhythmic style of Henry Purcell, but what really distinguishes this piece is the splendid vocal line, full of brilliance and show. Sung by a male soprano it must have had an electrifying effect.

Example 3. JOHN ABELL: THE THIRD SONG (*Songs in Several Languages*, 1701)

Abell next wormed his way back into London Society by advertising his return and saying he was English in a poem addressed *To All Lovers of Music*:

After a twelve years' industry and toil,
Abell, at last, has reach'd his native soil,
And hopes so long an absence may prepare
This audience to be kind as it is fair.
Not that he vainly boasts of bringing home
The spoils of France, of Italy, and Rome,
Or thinks to please the judges of the town,
From any other climate than his own;
But humbly begs, since foreigners could raise
Your admiration, and receive your praise,
Since soft Fideli could your passions move,
And fortunate Clemente gain your love,
That he with some advantage may appear,
And, being English, please an English ear.

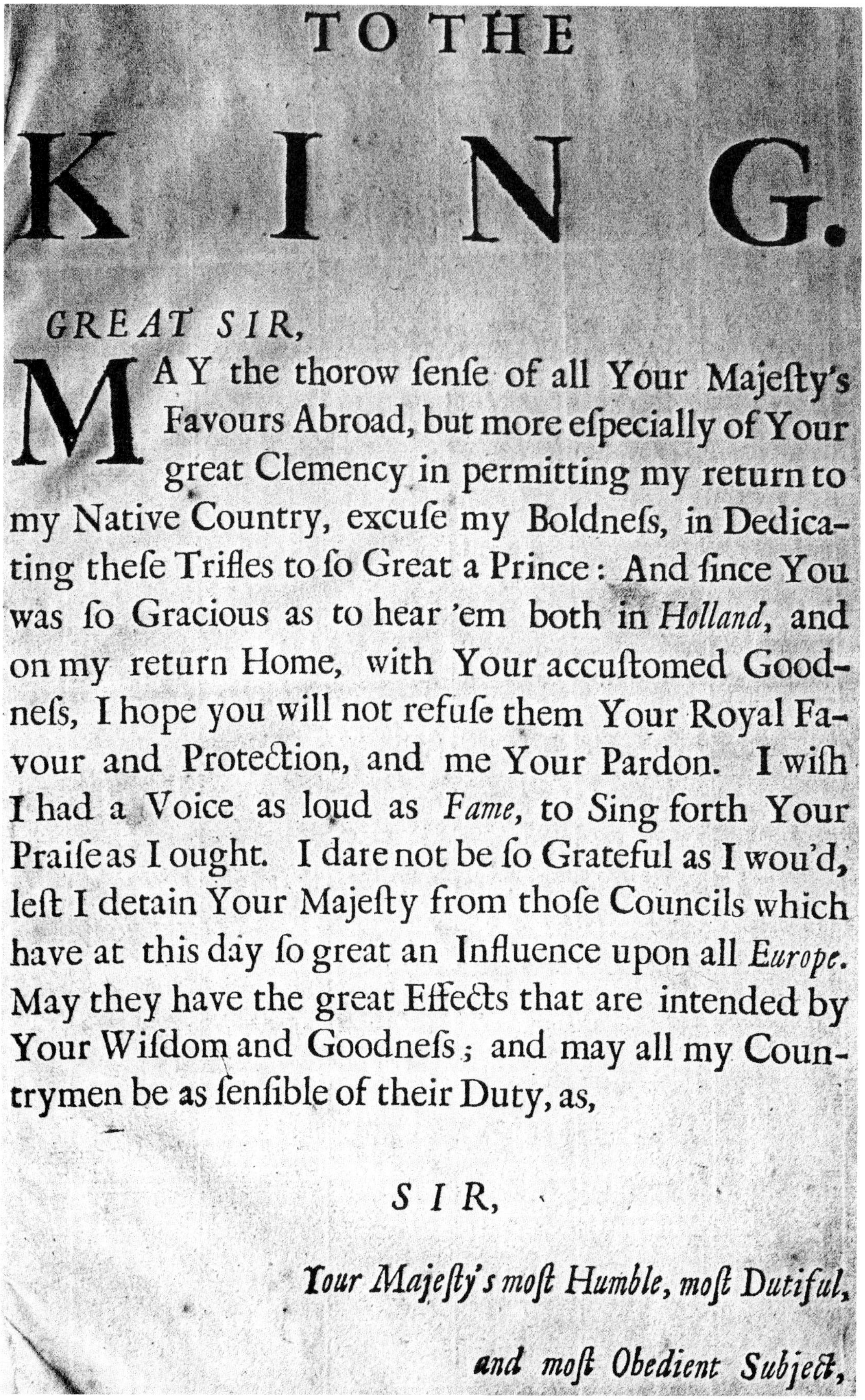

TO THE

KING.

GREAT SIR,

MAY the thorow fenfe of all Your Majefty's Favours Abroad, but more efpecially of Your great Clemency in permitting my return to my Native Country, excufe my Boldnefs, in Dedicating thefe Trifles to fo Great a Prince : And fince You was fo Gracious as to hear 'em both in *Holland*, and on my return Home, with Your accuftomed Goodnefs, I hope you will not refufe them Your Royal Favour and Protection, and me Your Pardon. I wifh I had a Voice as loud as *Fame*, to Sing forth Your Praife as I ought. I dare not be fo Grateful as I wou'd, left I detain Your Majefty from thofe Councils which have at this day fo great an Influence upon all *Europe*. May they have the great Effects that are intended by Your Wifdom and Goodnefs ; and may all my Countrymen be as fenfible of their Duty, as,

SIR,

Your Majefty's moft Humble, moft Dutiful,

and moft Obedient Subject,

Plate 35. DEDICATORY PAGE FROM ABELL'S *Songs in Several Languages*, 1701

Perhaps he had laundered his accent as well, though it would not have been noticed when he sang. But he was not at everyone's beck and call, as we hear from the great Irish dramatist, Congreve: 'Abell is here: has a cold at present, and is always whimsical, so that when he will sing or not upon the stage are things very disputable, but he certainly sings beyond all creatures upon earth, and I have heard him very often both abroad and since he came over.'[12]

He was always careful about his voice and the eighteenth-century German musicologist, Mattheson, recalled: 'Some years ago there was also a . . . singer by the name of Abel who was held in very high esteem and who was heard in Holland as well as in Hamburg, etc, with great applause. He possessed several secrets for keeping his tender and natural alto voice perfect until a late age. An uncommon moderation and selection in eating and drinking helped this very much.'[13]

Abell appears to have kept in court circles, for his *A Song on Queen Anne's Coronation* was performed in the Stationer's Hall on 1 May 1702. It demands a high tessitura clearly designed for his own extraordinary voice. Nahum Tate's text is not up to much: loud proclamations and dutiful rejoicings replace the seas of tears shed over the dead King Billy – fearful stuff; but somehow Abell makes it stick with the melodic clarity and brilliance of the vocal line, and there would probably have been a trumpet part, if the band parts had survived.

Abell also wrote a birthday ode for Queen Anne during a brief spell of employment in Dublin as 'Master of the State Musick' for the Viceroy, the Duke of Ormonde.[14] It is a lengthy and appealing musical entertainment using recitatives and arias and with John Abell himself as Apollo. The nine Muses and the daughters of Jupiter and Mnemosyne were possibly sung by the boy sopranos of St Patrick's Cathedral, who were usually employed on such occasions. If so, their presence may explain the modest vocal requirements, including the part for Apollo which is more difficult, but not so as to make the contrast grotesque.[15] They all sang panegyrics of the queen and the whole was interspersed with instrumental music, which includes dance movements. It is scored for flute, two recorders in D, two oboes, two violins, viola, two cellos, and continuo, plus the voices who also sing in duet and chorus. Abell imported the Italian notion of dividing his musical forces to create spatial effects and he still kept the lute, which he played so well, as an accompanying instrument. The piece has yet to be revived and thoroughly deserves it, not only for its melodic charms, but for its variety of presentation.[16]

Example 5. John Abell: Birthday Ode to Queen Anne (*Tenbury manuscript*, early 1700s)

Example 4. John Abell: A Song on Queen Anne's Coronation, 1702

Abell ended up unhappily in obscure poverty, as the English music historian, Sir John Hawkins tells us: 'About the latter end of Queen Anne's reign Abell was at Cambridge with his lute, but he met there poor encouragement. How long he lived afterwards is not known, but the account of his death was communicated to the gentleman who furnished many of the above particulars by one, who, having known him in his prosperity, assisted him in his old age, and was at the expense of his funeral.'[17]

While Abell was re-establishing himself in London, John Clerk, a brilliantly talented and exceptionally musical young aristocrat from Penicuik, south of Edinburgh, was wresting himself away from the affectionate but too close concerns of his father. The Clerk family crest is 'a demi-man, winding a horn, proper' and their motto is 'free for a blast'. They hold their lands on condition that they blow three blasts on a horn when the sovereign comes to hunt on the Burgh Muir, so there were ancient musical rites to be inherited when John Clerk was born on 8 February 1676.

Young Clerk's education was not a success either at Penicuik or Glasgow University, and he eventually made his way to Leyden, as did many Scots, to study law. We can follow his progress through his own memoirs and correspondence. His comments on music-making in Europe are of great interest and have not received much attention, so it is worth reporting them extensively.[18]

We can imagine this young, handsome and earnest Scot (see Plate 36) settling in well enough, but law gets small mention:

> I boarded in the house of a learned german, who taught privately Mathematicks, Phyilosophy, and Musick, one Sarnbuchius. Here I spent my time both profitably and agreeably, for I applied myself very closely to all three studies. In the last I was a kind of proficient even before I came to Leyden, for I play'd tollerably well on the Harpsecord, and since I was 7 years of age I touched the Violin a little.[19] . . .
>
> As I found there was no keeping of good and vertuous company in either Holand, France, or Italy, and far less in Germany, without as much of the practice of musick as to enable one to bear a part in a Concert, I bestowed a great deal of pains on the Harpsecord, and in a year after was as well qualified to perform my part on that instrument as any Gentleman in Holand. I found that this piece of skill was indeed of very great use to me afterwards in the course of my Travels through Germany, Italy, and France.[20] . . .
>
> As for companions, I had no particular one but the famous Herman Bouerhave, he was then a young physitian, and, as he was a mathematician and phyloposher, I hapned to contract a very great friendship for him. He was likeways a Musitian, so

> that by a propensity to the same studies we not only lived like Brothers together while I staid at Leyden, but continued a correspondence together while he lived. . . . What I admired most of Dr. Booerhaven's genius was, that tho' he was a big clumsey man, with fingers proportionable, yet from the time I had left him in Holland, he had acquired a dexterity in playing on the French Lute above all men I had ever heard.[21]

Clerk's father was not pleased with these artistic leanings, though he himself enjoyed buying paintings, for he writes: 'You were sent by me to Holland to studie not architecture, nor policie nor fidling nor to see curiosities for that is no dutie, but to studie law.'[22]

In the end the wiser counsels of youth prevailed, prompted perhaps by this letter from an enthusiastic young Scot in Rome, recommending Clerk to come and visit. The call was irresistible and Clerk started on the long trip by stage coaches, no doubt reading the alluring letter from his friend on the way:

> From John Paterson. Rome, May the sixth 1697.
>
> The musique here is divine, but it's impossible to get any, but that which is printed, I have used all the means in the world but can have nothing. I have got my self acquaint with Signor Bernard Pasquino, the greatest master of the world for the organ, and so by consequence he composes incomparably fine, and I will assure you observes all Mr Zumbach's rules, not that he's acquaint with these rules but only because he has found by a million of experiences, that such a note in such a case, sounds best and makes the best harmony, in such and such consonants. That way which you speak of in your letter is the true free French way of playing, which is no base – but the thro[ugh] . . . bass which the Italians play, is always played with a full hand, and the left hand as full of consonants as the right, they never let the fifth nor the octave be twice successively in the same voice, for it's a monstrous fault in composition. . . . I have heard Corelli play several times, but I was strongly baulked of my fancy when I saw him, for I thought to have seen a handsome gentill fellow, whereas he made, for all the world, just such a figure, as one of our Dutch fiddlers, but indeed he plays like an angell. I'm glad at all my heart that you design to come here. I'm confident you will think it worth your while.[23]

Clerk did not go straight to Rome, but took in Vienna on the way, where the music was also Italian. Here, for the first time, we encounter his oddly mixed feelings about the propriety of an aristocrat indulging a taste for music.

> While I staid at Vienne . . . Lord Lexington introduced me to the Emperor. When the Emperor understood from him that I was a great lover of Music, he invited me to his private opera kept in the Imperial Garden of the Favretti, where the Emperor always resided, about 3 quarters of a mile from Vienna. . . . The Music was very grand, viz. two Herpsecords, one on each side, 4 great Bass violins, as many Lutes and Theorbos, and above 30 violins and other instruments. The actors or singers were mostly Italians, for as his Imperial Majesty was himself not only fond of Musick to distraction, but a performer himself on the Herpsecord, he took care to entertain all the best Musitians that Italy cou'd produce, and they were all provided with the best salaries. . . . His Capelmasters were Italian, and all his operas and comedies were in this Language. . . . He not only sings and

Plate 36. *John Clerk of Penicuik aged 19*, BY MIERIS, LATE SEVENTEENTH-CENTURY ENGRAVING

plays on the herpsecord, but he composes very well both for the Chapel and chamber. . . . At his court it was an ordinary thing for him to sit down and entertain the company with his Musick, singing and playing very finely; but I confess this sight was so shocking to me that it had like to have spoiled all my inclination to performing myself, if it had not been that I foresaw I was not rich enough to purchase Musick any other way than what I made myself, especially in my own country, where at this time there is no such thing,. Nothing could be more ridiculous than the odd figure the poor old Emperor made on such occasions.[24]

> If it happen that a stranger know nothing of music, he will do well at least to dissemble a great deall of pleasure to hear them play, for they love to be admired for their skill which for the most part is verie ordinarie.[25]

Not surprisingly, then, he moved on, but his beginnings in Rome were not auspicious. He had little money and fell ill:

> I was not in Rome above three days when I again fell into the distemper of the small-pox, which Doctor Booerhaven thought he had cured me of. . . . It came upon me with the same symptoms, but with greater violence than before . . . after the violence of the distemper was over I broke out in Boils, and had successively three Feavers, each of them very severe . . . the Ladies of the Society of the Tour di Spechio were my chief Benefactors . . . I went after my recovery to wait on them. . . . How these acts of charity and civility were done to a young stranger I know not, but I supposed they heard that I was a young man in distress near their Monasteries, which was enough for charitable Italian Ladies.[26]

Perhaps it was as Clerk recovered that he set to work on composing a cantata using a text provided for him by the same Doctor Booerhaven.

Example 6. JOHN CLERK: CANTATA – EHEU, EHEU!
(Clerk papers, 1697?)

It was in Latin, but that was natural enough as Clerk and Booerhaven used Latin as their common language, for among educated people it was still a *lingua franca* across Europe. The text of this cantata was certainly appropriate: '*Eheu, Eheu!* Alas, alas, how the life of mankind laments with awful sufferings . . . man is born amidst tears . . . the mind has no peace, there are no peaceful rejoicings, but illnesses attack the body.'

For a young man in his twenties this is a remarkable composition. He chose the dark colour of the bassoon instead of the usual cello to provide the bass part, and he may have used organ rather than harpsichord to match this. The opening adagio makes bold use of dissonant suspensions between the violin parts and the bass line, and the effect of the sighing repeated notes drooping down the chromatic scale convey the feeling of world-weariness that so often accompanies a serious illness. Above this the voice declaims in beautifully shaped phrases, philosophical in character rather than protesting or agonised. (Example 6.)

The adagio is followed by a more flowing aria but, when the opening tune is repeated – as it almost always was in the arias of those days – Clerk cuts the voice short on the words *saeva mors* (savage death) leaving the instruments significantly alone to conclude this first half of the cantata.

The second half is no less remarkable, for though the text tells us that a time will come that will bring better things, it turns out that the better things are not in this life but the next. Clerk changes the key to the relative major and the bass line becomes cheerfully active, the vocal line gently florid, but it is dancing on the edge of the grave. The final allegro is a dark little jig in the minor key advising us to leave the earth with joyful singing, but with expressive harmonic colourings. There is nothing macabre about this

Example 7. JOHN CLERK: CANTATA – EHEU, EHEU!

music, just an extraordinary maturity of outlook and a poise all the more remarkable for being maintained on the cliff-edge between life and death that Clerk himself had experienced.

But let us follow Clerk out of his sick bed and into what was then the musical capital of Europe.

> My two great diversions at Rome were Musick and Antiquities. I excelled to a fault in the first, but the practise of musick gave me easier access to the best company in Rome than other strangers had. My masters were Bernardo Pasquini, a most skillful performer and composer on the Organ and Harpse, and Archangelo Correlli, whom I believe no man ever equalled for the violin. However, as I bestowed most of my time on the Harpsecord and the knowledge of musical compositions, I profited but little on the violin. . . . He gains a great deal of monie, and loves it for the sake of laying it all out on pictures. . . . He seldom teaches any body; yet, because he was pleased to observe me so much taken with him , he allowed me 3 lessons a week during all the time I stay'd at Rome. He was a good well-natured man, and on many accounts deserved the Epithet which all Italians gave him of the divine Arc Angelo.[27]

This was a great honour for Clerk and suggests that Corelli must have thought highly of him. But everyone thought highly of this personable young Scot, as Father James Forbes recounted: 'Young Pennycook has enjoyed all the honours and satisfaction which only noblemen of the best quality could have expected. It is truly his sweet and obledging humor has made him deserve all these favours, even of strangers.'[28]

Clerk also had the support of a cousin, about whom he wrote to his father: 'You may perhaps think I have a dangerous person beside me when my Cousin is not only a catholic but a Fryer of the order of St Francis, for after the battle of Kilecrankie he came to Italy.'[29]

No doubt it was this cousin's influence which persuaded him to attend the Mass on the festival of St Peter at which he exclaimed: 'the musick was exceedingly divine, being the compositions of the famous Palestrina.'[30]

The atmosphere of such music all around him clearly inspired Clerk, and another exceptionally fine work, probably from this period, is his cantata *Dic Mihi Saeve Puer*. Like *Eheu, Eheu!*, it is in the minor key, the culprit this time not being disease and death, but the boy Cupid. Clerk later admitted to his father: 'Dear father I have considered what you write about my old amours . . . the old magott is perfectly out of my head . . . this was the chief motive of my going to Italy . . . I thought going further from home might give the young lady time to marry.'[31]

This may have been a specious excuse – a way of pursuading his father, who had always opposed the Italian trip, that it had been undertaken in a spirit of filial duty, but it is also possible that Clerk genuinely missed the girl.

Dic Mihi starts with an expressive introduction to the opening recitative and arioso protesting at the cruel beauty of Cupid, a boy with the limbs of a young girl who inflicts '*mille mille vulnerae*' – a thousand thousand wounds. The vocal writing is magnificent: intense, sensuous, varied. Clerk seems to have a complete command of the whole range from dry recitative delivering words efficiently, through more melodic declamation, to full cantabile style suitable for an aria. This variety of presentation, and mood was part of the technique of Corelli which was so highly admired. But Clerk has made it his own.

Example 8. JOHN CLERK: CANTATA – DIC MIHI SAEVE PUER (Clerk Papers)

There follows a languishing arioso section which blends protest and submission to the fires and chains of love, and this leads into a prayer to Venus to have pity, which Clerk sets in the form of an old-fashioned triple-time galliard. The choice is deliberate. The Italians, according to Morley, writing a century earlier: 'make their Galliards plain, and frame ditties to them which in their masquerades they sing and dance, and many times without any instruments at all, but instead of instruments they have courtesans disguised in men's apparel who sing and dance to their own songs.'[32]

Clerk's galliard has a spare instrumental accompaniment and re-enacts that ancient love ritual, the confused sexuality of the courtesans matched by the confused sexuality of Cupid; the whole dedicated to Venus.

Example 9. JOHN CLERK: CANTATA – DIC MIHI SAEVE PUER

Clerk ends with the singer's heart aflame with the tortures of love, longing for release in death from the bow of dread desire, the lustful bands of young tender girls. The music is in places distracted, in others despairing, and ends in desperate but clearly hopeless determination. It is a little masterpiece of emotional drama and deserves international recognition. So too does *Odo Di Mesto Intorno* – a fine full-scale cantata for his friend Wriothesley Russell, Second Duke of Bedford. The words of the cantata were written for the duke's departure for Naples from one of the great Roman villas at Frascati. Thus, proudly, young John Clerk inscribed the score: 'This Cantata was made by me at the Duke of Bedford's desire. The Poesie was made by one of his servants, an Italian, and performed by Corelli, and other musicians before his grace and many of the Roman nobility. . . .'

The Duke of Bedford was only eighteen and was on the Grand Tour. But he was possibly the wealthiest Englishman of his day, holding also the title Lord Tavistock and, by his marriage, the title Baron Howland. Clerk was bound to miss such a patron and friend, so it is not too surprising

that he should write a farewell cantata. Nor need he have felt any diffidence. His music was admired by Zumbach and Kremberg in Holland, by Bottoni in Italy,[33] and almost certainly by Corelli too, otherwise it is scarcely likely Corelli would have been prepared to perform in the work of his own pupil before such an august company on such a significant occasion.

The occasion was almost certainly significant in another way. The duke had, it is true, been married for three years; but at the drawing up of that agreement he and his wife's combined ages was a mere 28.[34] The consummation of the marriage is therefore likely to have been delayed, and since Clerk's cantata refers to absence making the heart grow fonder and anticipates delicious amatory prospects, it seems likely that the duke was on his way to making his young wife his own in the flesh as well as on paper.

Two pieces of music form the opening sinfonia of Clerk's cantata and reflect its two basic moods: sad leave-taking and anticipation of nuptial joy. In all Clerk's music the mood is perfectly judged and deeply sensitive to the texts. First the soprano recitative expresses the sorrows of Nature and of Man, and the following plaintive aria and recitative explain the cause – the departure of the young English hero.

Example 10. JOHN CLERK: CANTATA – ODO DI MESTO INTORNO (Clerk Papers)

The next aria is more cheerful. Exhorted by the previous recitative it banishes sorrows claiming, in its central section, that a feeble heart is no good in such a case. Here is the turning point, for exactly the same must apply to the restraint the young couple presumably underwent for three years. The active bass line encourages and the outer sections of the aria make lovely play with the words '*lontananza d'amor*' in which distant love becomes seductively yielding.

Example 11. JOHN CLERK: CANTATA – ODO DI MESTO INTORNO

Ma - io - reaccresse il fo - co lon - ta - nan - za d'a - mor lon - ta
nan - za d'a - mor lon - ta nan - za d'a - mor

There follows a magnificent section sending the young hero forth in virgin white to meet his beloved in the battle of love prepared by Cupid. But love *only* is to conquer and its victory is to be peace. The aria is full of excitement and echoes of military fervour, but it never steps outside the gentility proper to the occasion. The vocal line is brilliant but not excessive, and the writing for the two violins is marvellously active, amorous fanfares answering each other, but always coherent.

Example 12. JOHN CLERK: CANTATA – ODO DI MESTO INTORNO

al - la bat - tag - lia   fer - ro non va - glia   d'ar - cier - i ar - di - ti

ma più gra - di - ti   ve - dan - si i cor

Now that the battle of love is joined at close quarters, little Cupids frolic around the couple. They are delicately expressed by the violins and the vocal line. The cantata ends with a piece of lingering and deliberate sensuality. The violins intertwine amorously and the gentle but determined rise and fall of the vocal line is its

own explanation. It brings to an end a work of great charm and variety which deserves a regular place in the repertoire.

All the above works have been only recently resuscitated. There is another substantial vocal work of Clerk's awaiting revival, and this is his five-part cantata, a work in the contrapuntal religious style of the time.[35] It is deeply serious in intent, but, until it is heard, its full significance cannot be judged.

Clerk eventually had to bring his travels to an end, returning via Livorno where he may have stayed to enjoy the opera, and then Genoa: 'At Genoa I staid about a week … I was entertain'd with great Civility at one of the Assemblies, where there was Musik and gameing. I participated a little in the first, tho' I found that it was not the best place in Italy for Musick.'[36]

He did well to stay so briefly, if his cousin Cosimo's warning is to be believed: '… att Genoa you are in a place off a great deal of moral danger and therfor must arme more against it and shun all occasions. Remember your uncle James his faite and lett that scare you. Pardon me my dearest Jack I write so freely. . .'[37]

Clerk pressed on homeward towards Edinburgh where the recently formed Edinburgh Musical Society eagerly awaited his return from Italy with a hoped-for shipload of music, and musical thoughts of home came to him by surprise in France: 'In our way, as I lay at Orange, I happened to be agreeably surprised about midnight with singing of Psalms, for it seems my Landlord was a Protestant, and had ventured to live there, tho' most part of all the Protestants of that country hapned to be banished out of France some years before.'[38]

Clerk had been advised to visit Couperin in Paris, but it seems unlikely that he did: 'Paris was agreeable to me only for the conversation I found there. . . . Operas and comedies here, Musick, and all entertainments except Dancing, displeased me exceedingly.'[39]

At about the same time as Clerk was thinking of leaving Rome, another Penicuik man was in foreign parts. Captain Robert Penicuik was helping to establish Scotland's only and ill-fated colony on the Panama isthmus at Darien. His chief action was to save a drunken French captain at peril of his own life, but he was dismissed in 1699 for disobeying orders of the Council.[40]

By the time Clerk had reached Paris, news of the troubles of the Darien Scheme was reaching Europe. The colony was ill-conceived and the Scots had been harassed and obstructed by an unwonted co-operation between the English and the Spanish. With the former there followed a trade war and eventual compromise in the form of the Treaty of Union. Clerk was one of the architects and signatories of that Treaty which enabled the vast losses to be repaid; but he was also a patriot and before the final collapse of the colony, composed a fascinating cantata with the splendid title *Leo Scotiae Irritatus* – 'The Scottish Lion Angered'. The Latin words were by his old friend Dr Booerhaven and the last pages of the score are missing, though we have the complete text. It is just possible that Clerk abandoned the work with its triumphant concluding vision, if he was beginning to learn of the final capitulation of the colony. In any event it is a great pity *Leo Scotiae Irritatus* is not complete as it is full of invention and dramatic word-setting.

Five movements survive. The first is a clarion call to arms with the enemy scattered and destroyed. The second is a calmer reflection on God's support for the Scots, and the third renews the battle. Compared with the battle of love in his Italian cantata, the writing here is much more martial.

Example 13. John Clerk: Cantata – Leo Scotiae Irritatus
(Clerk Papers)

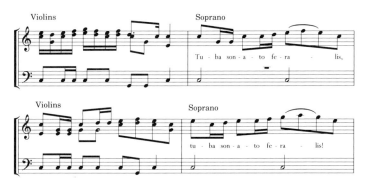

The next movement is the most interesting: acknowledging that Fortune's wheel is turning against the Scots, it asks for it to be reversed. Clerk uses a ground bass specially shaped to imitate the endlessly repeating rise and fall as one rises and falls on each turn of the wheel.[41] Against this the voice sings in broken phrases,

vainly enumerating Scotland's virtues – praise, righteousness, law and religion, justice and equity.

Example 14. John Clerk: Cantata – Leo Scotiae Irritatus

The last surviving movement looks forward to the gentle peacefulness of a Scottish pastoral idyll in the new colony.

When Clerk finally came home he assessed his situation.

Musick had always great charms with me, but this was so far from hindering my application to Books that on the contrary it was thereby the more promoted, as it kept me often at home when I had sought for relaxation abroad. My favourite instrument was as formerly the Herpsecord, because it furnished me at pleasure all the parts of an entire concert of Musick . . .[42]

I understood pictures better than became my Purse, and as to Musick, I rather performed better, particularly on the Harpescord, than became a Gentleman.[43]

Sadly it seems he either wrote no solo keyboard works, or they have not survived, but he did continue composing for a while and an appealing violin sonata of his survives which shows that by 1705, when this sonata was probably written, Clerk was introducing Scottish elements into his style. The opening Preludium is wholly Italiante with its flourishes of scales, but the brief Andante Variations which follow have some Scottish touches and following a slow air there is a final Scottish jig which romps away with the piece. This work is also of structural interest, embodying the idea of Platonic ideal forms of which the thematic ideas of the whole sonata are the material manifestations. Clerk's study of the classics is here put to use as part of an aesthetic which is remarkably ahead of its time, creating unity by thematic cross-references, the ideas derived from each other while allowing for contrast – a technique he also used in *Dic Mihi Saeve Puer*.[44]

Things did not always go happily for Clerk. He lost his wife in childbirth and appears to have been profoundly depressed for a while. Music also probably had to take a back seat to the law and politics, though his interest in it was partly channelled into architecture which he probably saw as a pursuit more appropriate to a man of his station if we remember his shock at the Emperor in Vienna singing and playing.

> Being now oblidged to live up to the strict character of a judge, my Father insisted with me that I should again enter into a married life. . . . I to comply with their wishes, led my thoughts in an overly way upon two ladies, one was a young Lady of great Quality, The other was a lightheaded Beauty, and consequently as improper for me as the other . . .but their names I here bury in silence.[45]

The name of one of the girls was not, however, buried in silence. She was Susanna Kennedy, to whom Ramsay's *The Gentle Shepherd* was dedicated. Clerk sent her a flute but when she tried to play it, it would not sound and on taking it apart she found inside a love poem attributed to Clerk himself. Susanna chose to become the Countess of Eglintoun rather than Lady Clerk, but no doubt she played the flute just the same. The poem deserves a special place in the musician's heart.

> *Harmonious pipe, how I envye thy bliss,*
> *When press'd to Sylphia's lips with gentle kiss!*
> *And when her tender fingers round thee move*
> *In soft embrace, I listen and approve*
> *Those melting notes, which soothe my soul to love*
> *Embalm'd with odours from her breath that flow,*
> *You yield your music when she's pleased to blow;*
> *And thus at once the charming lovely fair*
> *Delights with sounds, with sweets perfumes the air.*
> *Go, happy pipe, and ever mindful be*
> *To court the charming Sylphia for me;*
> *Tell all I feel — you cannot tell too much —*
> *Repeat my love at each soft melting touch;*
> *Since I to her my liberty resign,*
> *Take thou the care to tune her heart to mine.*[46]

Clerk's longest poem is an interesting essay on architecture and landscape gardening which concludes with the practical intention of building a house that would realise his ideals. Behind those ideals always was music and a love of nature. The poem is a song. The thrush is the first inhabitant: its love-song the ideal artistic expression of domestic joy. The house was duly built and called Mavisbank – to enshrine the idea of the thrush in the very name of the property. The same ideal of return to nature is carved on the portico, the original being in Latin: 'This house in the lap of the surrounding woods, smiling on all sides with waters and gardens and the singing of birds, is neither proud nor pretentious, but as you see it: comfortable, attractive and pleasant. It was designed by Sir John Clerk, Baron of Exchequer, in 1724, joining Nature and Art in equal union, for himself and his family to live in, in peace and tranquility.'[47]

Mavisbank is now in a ruinous condition, but its ideals of proportion should appeal equally to musicians as to architects for its restoration, for Clerk saw the two disciplines as sisters.

> Architectory is what a great many pretend to judge of tho this is certain that nature has qualified few, very few, for this part of knowledge. Let not this assertion seem strange, for there is such an affinity between Musick and Architectory, that as one cannot be said to be a good musician who cannot discover an imperfection in a note, tho' it be only in a 4th 5th or 6th part thereof, so one cannot be said to be a good Architect, who cannot discover a defect in the proportion of a stone to the 4th 5th or 6th part of an inch.[48]

If we could also restore his secret Arcadian valley with its extraordinary and allegorical approach expressed in terms of music, we would be rich indeed:

> No-one can get across to it but by the mouth of a frightful cave. To those who enter, therefore, first occurs the memory of the Cuman Sibyl, for the ruinous aperture, blocked up with stones and briars, strikes the eye. Then comes upon the wayfarer a shudder, as they stand in doubt whether they are among the living or the dead. As indeed certain discords set off and give finish to musical cadences in such a way as to render the subsequent harmony more grateful to the ear, so does the mouth of this mournful cave with its long and shady path followed by the light and prospect, make the exit more delightful. For suddenly the darkness disappears, and as it were at the creation of a new world.[49]

Abell and Clerk were lone figures in this relatively lean period for Scottish classical music, but it is sad that, while both made a considerable musical impression outside Scotland, they have had little or no honour in their own country for nigh on three hundred years. Clerk in particular establishes himself as a composer well able to handle the musical *lingua franca* of Europe, not just with precocious competence but with a personal conviction and feeling which raises him far above the ordinary and which is rich enough to merit much closer study.

CHAPTER XIV

THE TEMPLE OF APOLLO
1740–1770

The feeling for nature that is so inescapable in Scottish music and song and that has kept our faith with our musical traditions, was a feeling we were to export later in the eighteenth century to the whole of Europe through the writings of Thomson, Burns, Scott and Byron. Our music has been less influential, but scarcely less significant, being both a symbol and a reality of the rural joys and sorrows which were cultivated in the eighteenth century by such as Allan Ramsay, who used native airs and colloquial speech in *The Gentle Shepherd*. He directed his pastoral drama at the middle and upper classes, who in Scotland were beginning to lose touch with their roots, since the Houses of Parliament in London required of them that they drop the Scots tongue and intonation, to which end they took elocution lessons as though suffering from some kind of vocal error. This was a kind of cultural imperialism which, more than anything, affected the sounds that Scots made and, through both speech and song, it was bound to have a particular meaning to musicians. The response among Scotland's composers was immediate, unique and delightful. They took their own native idioms and blended them with classical ideals and Italian forms, thereby creating an aesthetic environment which bypassed ignorant mockery, erecting their own Temple of Apollo, but by no means confining themselves to the Scottish genres they developed.

The Temple of Apollo was the title of a music society in London that was essentially Scottish, but the choice of name has a wide significance. Apollo was the aristocrat of Greek music, wielding the lyre as opposed to the rural pipes of Pan. The relationship between the cruit and the clarsach on the one hand, and the pipe and later bagpipes on the other, was not dissimilar. But though the eighteenth century developed a huge divergence in life and musical style between aristocrat and peasant, the desire to bridge the gap was, in the Scottish arts, rather more than a sentimental hankering after lost innocence. As far as the Scottish composers and poets were concerned, the Temple of Apollo was a place where Scottish traditional music had a right to be heard; and in a different but highly influential movement of Scottish origin, the Freemasons spread throughout Europe an ideal of social equality and brotherhood which eventually included the Austrian Emperor (whose Lodge was raided by his Empress's secret police) and found its profoundest expression in Mozart's *The Magic Flute*, where popular music also has a place in the Temple of Sarastro.[1]

The Temple of Apollo also evokes the classical world in general and, as emerges in the work of James Oswald, a blend of naturalism and classic form associated with Horace. Whether one can truly cultivate the natural as opposed to alter it beyond reasonable recognition is still debated in Scotland. Cultivating folk music naturally leads to a confusion of genres, and Scottish musicians still become distressed over where the traditional ends and the classical begins. A pleasant emblem of the significance and influence of the movement is the confusion that persists over the tune first published in 1746 as *The House of Glamis*. Is it traditional, or was it composed by a classically trained musician, for it is also known as *Roslin Castle* and is attributed to James Oswald?[2] It was rightly popular in the eighteenth century among the pastoral pipe players, themselves thought of as a charming part of the rural idyll. The pastoral pipes are a kind of ancestor of the Irish uilleann pipes, soft-toned and with a style of gracing which produces an effect of pleasant burbling that can also be plaintive. The air is supplied by a bellows operated by the elbow, not fed by the mouth. As for the tune, what need its beauty care for unanswerable aesthetic conundrums?

Example 1. JAMES OSWALD(?): ROSLIN CASTLE (*The Caledonian Pocket Companion*, 1740s)

There was, however, a definite prejudice against the dominance of the Italian style in music, perhaps initiated by the presence of the composer and flautist Barsanti, in Edinburgh from 1735 to 1743; the composer and violinist Pasquali, who died in Edinburgh in 1757 after five years' residence; and later in the century, Domenico Corri and his brother, and Girolamo Stabilini. The chief protestors, however, are the poets Ramsay and Fergusson (see Chapter XV). The Italians happily adapted themselves to Scottish music (not so the German composer Schetky, in Edinburgh from 1772 until his death in 1824) and the Scottish composers did not so much protest at the Italianate as adapt it, and the same holds true for the instrument which was its chief purveyor, the violin. The new instrument, a vast improvement in resonance and tone quality on its predecessors, obviously stimulated all types of musicians. One gets a sense of adventure and fun in the Scots fiddle writing of the time – for instance left-hand pizzicatto (plucking the string while still playing with the bow) is used to illustrate the title of a tune called *Hit Her on the Bum*, and the sound of hens clucking is imitated in *The Hen's March* – probably composed by James Oswald for the pantomime of *Fortunatus* which opened in Drury Lane in 1753.[3]

The extraordinary exuberance with which the Scots took up the violin is well displayed in a set of variations on *The Reel of Tulloch* – a pipe tune in the early eighteenth century and a pipe tune today, but transferred to the violin with superb rhythmic pointing and syncopations, mostly composed by David Young in 1740 (see Plate 37 and Example 2).[4]

But if Apollo and Pan were to cease to be rivals then more concessions were going to have to be made to the Apollonians. That this division was widely understod musically is indi-

cated by J.S. Bach's secular cantata *Phoebus and Pan* (Phoebus being another name for Apollo). In old Bach's work, Phoebus wins the competition and the whole thing is a pleasant by-way from the vast and profound structures he evolved in the *B Minor Mass* and the two *Passions*. In the music of his son, J.C. Bach, cultivated simplicity (including arranging Scotch songs and using Scottish tunes in two of his piano concertos) was the order of the day. The *style galant* – the gentle, tuneful and intellectually undemanding manner of the mid-eighteenth century – held the floor.

Insofar as the *style galant* implied a tolerance of folk music, the Scots could be claimed to be among its chief initiators, one of the first having done so furth of Scotland, for Alexander Munro published his set of twelve violin sonatas in Paris in 1732. Each sonata was based entirely on one Scots tune, but worked into foreign forms – an opening allegro stating the theme, followed by the equivalent to the minuet, corrente, and gavotte and only coming home with the jig which was by then common to the whole of Europe. Surprisingly, the adaptation works beautifully, as though the standard practice of improvising variations on Scots tunes required only a nudge to be turned into what was then the relatively simple form of the 'Sonata da Camera' or 'Chamber Sonata' (hence 'chamber music') and was at that time less serious, and more influenced by dance forms, than the Sonata da Chiesa – literally 'Church Sonata'.

Munro's 'da Camera' sonatas, though not uniformly successful, are unique in their formal adventure and should have gone down well amongst the exiled Stewarts in France, and should also have appealed to the nation that was soon to

Example 2. THE REEL OF TULLOCH (*David Young manuscript*, 1740)

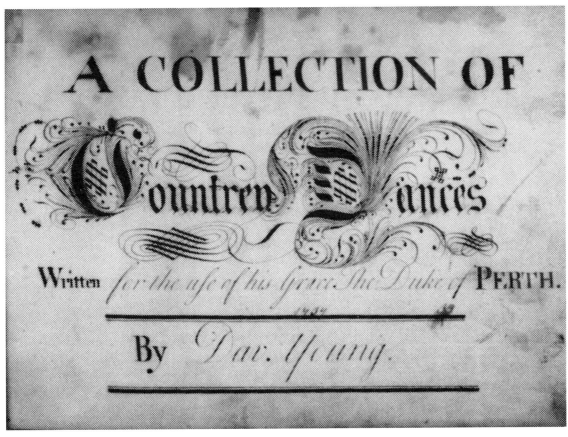

Plate 37. David Young's superb calligraphy from the *Drummond Manuscript*, 1734 – Title Page and Gilliecalum

harbour the rustic ideals of Rousseau. But of their composer and his reputation we know nothing. His sonata based on *Bonnie Jean of Aberdeen* shows how a Scots song can, with a little rhythmic ingenuity and melodic gift, become as lovely a minuet or as lively a gavotte as any thoroughbred classic:

Example 3. ALEXANDER MUNRO: SONATA ON BONNIE JEAN OF ABERDEEN, 1732

Charles MacLean (*fl.* 1737) also composed in a Scottish style. He published sonatas based on the tunes *Pinkie House*, *The Birks of Invermay* and others, some of them later reworked by Robert MacKintosh (*c.* 1745–1807)) who updated the genre in the 1770s with new bowing styles and occasional harmonic experiments, one of them parallel to a Haydn composition composed the year before.[5] But MacLean was also ready to work in other styles, which he does with liveliness and, in the slow movements, feeling. His *Sonata in A* – after a brief introduction – is in the form of a lively toccata which has some vigorous moments for the cello as well. He could also observe the more thoughtful requirements of the Sonata da Chiesa, picking up the solemnities of the Handelian manner which prevailed in London, starting his *G Minor Sonata* with typical baroque bass line and not afraid to use double stopping on the violin to give the effect of two different parts on the one instrument, or to end with a minuet in which the decidedly dark characteristics of G minor prevail.

One of the best known musicians of his day, and one who lived and worked in Scotland, was

William McGibbon (*c.* 1690–1756), violinist and composer and good at both. He published a number of arrangements of Scots tunes, but the *C Minor Sonata* from the *Six Sonatas or Solos* of 1740 and the *G Major Sonata* for two German flutes (transverse flutes as opposed to recorders) or violins, with a thorough bass, published in 1734 (one of twenty-four trio sonatas published in four sets), are entirely Italian in character.

Example 4. WILLIAM McGIBBON: SONATA IN C MINOR (Edinburgh, 1740)

He himself claims the trio sonatas as being in 'imitation of Corelli' whose music will have been well known to him and with whom he could have felt a direct link through Corelli's pupil, Sir John Clerk. The *G Major Sonata* is a Sonata da Chiesa with four movements, slow-fast-slow-fast, and is elegantly written and more spacious in character than the work of MacLean.

McGibbon's style is fluent rather than characteristic, but several of his works could be as easily played by a small orchestra as by a chamber group and have been performed successfully in that garb. Haydn was just two years old when the *G Major Sonata* was written, but when he started composing, he too drew no clear boundaries between orchestral and chamber music. Composers used what came to hand, though the Earl of Kelly (see below) produced works unequivocally orchestral in character. McGibbon appears to have been an outstanding violinist, expecting a higher level of technique than had ever been looked for in Britain[6] and from which we may take it that performances at the concerts of the Edinburgh Musical Society (formed in 1728) were of a high standard.

This sort of music was known to Bonnie Prince Charlie, for, on the eve of Culloden in Kilravock House, where chamber music was much cultivated, he joined in the music-making, playing the cello and helping pass what must have been a tense evening. Perhaps someone with a sense of humour might have set before the musicians the parts of McGibbon's sonata based on the old mad Portuguese dance called *La Folia*. Folly has always had space to manoeuvre: Bach used the tune in his *Peasant Cantata* of 1742; Lully, Vivaldi and Pergolesi had all had a go at it; Corelli had taken it up and McGibbon has provided its framework with his own variations starting soberly enough and keeping to the slow-fast-slow-fast formula contrasting sobriety with mild dementia only, but it is lively and well made and does not outstay its welcome.

A subscriber to McGibbon's publications and performer beside him at the Music Society concerts was the physician David Foulis. Foulis's only known works are *Six Solos for the Violin . . . Composed by a Gentleman*, and a minuet and march. The solos (Foulis originally named them 'sonatas') are reliably ascribed to him. They are varied, lovely and beautifully written for the instrument. Judging from the variety of style and form, their composition was probably spread over a number of years.[7] Sonata I is in the baroque form that McGibbon was using. Its first movement has the characteristic dotted rhythms and pomp and circumstance of the French Overture, and the third movement shows a lively interest in texture, the violin part coloured by trills and double-stopping, and the bass line rising high into the treble stave in an expressive passage of imitation.

Sonatas V and VI are cast in three movements, the first slow, the second fast and the last dance-like in character, while the remaining three sonatas follow the Neapolitan pattern (fast, slow, fast) which was to form the basis of the classical sonata. This variety is also reflected in the internal structures of the music. Simple binary form is used for the siciliano-style Largo of Sonata III, but its first movement, bright and energetic, is in 'sonata form' with two contrasting themes in tonic and dominant keys, developed in the central section and recapitulated with alterations. This use of contrasting ideas with a key structure to support it was eventually shown to be capable of enormous expansion, but we see it here in its early days, even at this stage unsympathetic to the Scottish idiom, which makes no appearance in Foulis's work.

The fourth sonata starts with a complex Allegro Ma Non Troppo which already treats sonata form with great freedom of development, avoiding the usual division into sections with repeat marks and recapitulating the opening ideas in a coherent but thoroughly irregular manner. There are similar signs of adventure in the opening movement of Sonata II, which ends with a sonata-rondo and has for its Adagio movement a melody which simply goes on evolving until a brief echo of its opening brings it to a close. It shows that Foulis also had a poetic gift lingering sadly over a sustained pedal note in a half-forgotten Arcadia.

Example 5. DAVID FOULIS: SONATA NO. II (Edinburgh, 1770)

Foulis was a doctor by profession, but he must have been a very competent player, and his compositional skills suggest that had he applied himself to more ambitious things he would have been a composer to reckon with. Though he came from a wealthy family, he died in poverty, apparently rejected by them, either on account of a marriage they disapproved of or of his having continued his medical studies in Leyden rather than return home to take up the family estates which seem in any case to have followed an odd line of succession. His position in Scottish music is similar, the record of his activities scanty, his undeserved obscurity only recently corrected.[8]

Foulis, Munro, MacLean and McGibbon are all figures of importance, but the most prolific and significant of the Scottish composers, and one who consciously developed a native style within a classical framework was James Oswald. Oswald is one of the most remarkable and unsung heroes of Scottish music. He is remembered as a leading publisher, is given some acknowledgment as a collector, but as a composer he has been unjustly forgotten. Though he is a miniaturist rather than working on the grand scale, he built up one or two major structures out of his tiny masterpieces, and his contribution in terms of the development of a new musical aesthetic was both vital and influential, one of his chief devotees being Robert Burns.

Oswald was born in 1710, the second son of John Oswald and Elspit Horn of Crail in Fife and was buried at Knebworth in 1769. In 1715 the Jacobite rebels were billeted in Crail and, at five years old, Oswald may have been impressed enough to remember their presence. Music, however, seems to have been the most important influence in his upbringing, for two of his brothers were also musicians[9] and a notebook of his, dated 1731, has recently been discovered in Dunfermline where we know he was a dancing master in 1734. It contains copies of Italian music and workings of Scots song arrangements,[10] suggesting that from his early twenties he had a clear notion of what seems almost to have been a mission – to show the music-loving and music-purchasing public that the Scots had their own musical genius and that it could demand an honoured place alongside the Italian style which had swamped Europe.

Although his great achievement was to blend them successfully, he was conscious of potential antagonisms between Italian and Scottish styles, as is made clear in more than one of his works. As a composer and dancer knowledgeable in Scottish as well as continental dance forms, he probably got thoroughly fed up with the capers of visiting continentals, knowing there was no need for such artificial airs and graces. His song *The Dancing Master* satirises them, starting with pseudo-Italian recitative and continuing with a high-stepping tune with mannerisms just verging on the silly. He published it in *The Gentleman's Magazine* in 1754 where its sentiments no doubt went down well. Two other works with similar satirical intention, *The Dustcart Cantata* and *The Wheelbarrow Cantata*, are described below.

James Oswald was Scotland's chief representative of the *style galant*, and his own *Sonata*

on Scots Tunes has been described by scholars as lightweight and naïve.[11] This judgment of it not only assumes that such characteristics are artistic vices, but fails to appreciate that Oswald might have composed the work with a clear and sophisticated understanding of its aesthetic purpose, a thing made all the more probable by the evidence of his notebook and by all his subsequent work, but ultimately justified by the loveliness of the music itself. The sonata was published in 1740, with each movement based on a different Scots tune, and if its melodic purity and shapeliness are lightweight, then much of Handel's *Water Music* will have to be similarly dismissed. The tunes are *O Mother What Shall I Do?* making a beautifully shaped opening largo, then an adagio based on *Ettrick Banks*, touching and thoughtful. Next comes an andante based on *She Rose and Let Me In*, and *Cromlet's Lilt* is a largo both dignified and lyrical. The whole is rounded off with variations on *Polwart on the Green* with the tune returning as it might in a miniature concerto grosso, witty, stylish and making one regret all the more that his other contributions to this genre appear to be lost.[12]

Example 6. JAMES OSWALD: SONATA ON SCOTS TUNES
(*Collection of Scots Tunes*, 1742)

Although Oswald's career in Scotland as a publisher and professional musician was probably reasonably assured, he was drawn, as were many Scots, to London, where aristocratic patronage centred round the court was likely to prove far more lucrative. He made the move in 1741, at first working for the publisher John Simpson in St Martin's Lane. When Simpson died, Oswald took over the business. He was forty years old and ten years married to another Scottish exile, Mary Ann Melville, with whom he had eloped.[13]

He must have missed Scotland. He could scarcely keep it out of his music. He published no less than fifteen volumes of Scottish folk music while in London, having already produced two in Edinburgh: a labour of love as well as profit. Did Scotland miss him? Yes, if we are to believe *The Scots Magazine* from October 1741. In it Allan Ramsay lamented Oswald's going south.

> *Dear Oswald, could my verse as sweetly flow,*
> *As notes thou softly touchest with the bow,*
> *While all the circling fair attentive hing,*
> *On ilk vibration of thy trembling string,*
> *I'd sing how thou woulds't melt our sawls away*
> *By solemn notes, or cheer us wi' the gay,*
> *In verse as lasting as thy tunes shall be,*
> *As soft as the new polish'd Danton me.*

Danton Me was an old tune – Mitchell used it in his opera *The Highland Fair or Union of the Clans* performed at Drury Lane in London in 1731, but Oswald polished up many tunes with new variations. Ramsay continues:

> *But wha can sing that feels wi' sae great pain*
> *The loss for which Edina sighs in vain?*
> *Our concert now nae mair the ladies mind;*
> *They've a' forgot the gait to Niddery's wynd.*
> *Nae mair the Braes of Ballandyne can charm,*
> *Nae mair can Fortha's Bank our bosoms warm,*
> *Nae mair the Northern Lass attention draw,*
> *Nor Pinky-House gi' place to Alloa.*

Alloway House was definitely one of Oswald's – one of his best, perhaps inspired by the fact that it was near his old home in Dunfermline. Niddery's wynd was where the Edinburgh Musical Society held its concerts, in St Mary's Chapel. Later they were to build their own St Cecilia's Hall (see below).

> *O Jamie! when may we expect again*
> *To hear from thee, the soft the melting strain,*
> *And, what's the loveliest, think it hard to guess,*
> *Miss St — - t, or thy Lass of Inverness?*
> *When shall we sigh at thy soft Cypress-grove,*
> *So well adapted to the tale of love?*
> *When wilt thou teach our soft Aeidian fair,*
> *To languish at a false Sicilian air;*
> *Or when some tender tune compose again,*
> *And cheat the town wi' David Rizzio's name?*

Here Ramsay indicates that Oswald was already imitating the Italian style well enough to deceive audiences; but Oswald was not the first to use David Riccio's name as a selling point.

William Thomson had done the same thing in his *Orpheus Caledonius* in 1725 and the pair of them seem to have fooled Geminiani with that ploy. But it did not fool many Scots; they knew no Italian could have written such tunes, no matter how much Geminiani liked to believe it. Geminiani, in his *Treatise* of 1749, wrote that two composers had appeared in the world whom he admired: David Riccio and Giovanni Baptista Lulli. Of the two, Riccio got the greatest credit for civilising melody with all the 'Native Gallantry of the SCOTISH Nation'. In fact the greatest civiliser of melody in the whole world – the great David Riccio, was simply Mr Anonymous Scot when he was not Mr James Oswald, across whose shop counter Geminiani probably checked the proofs of his own duets which Oswald published for him.[14] Geminiani also worked with Scots tunes, but he perhaps tries to do too much, and Oswald's own treatment of Scottish melody seems more sensitive.

Oswald was not the first Scot to collect and present Scottish music and song. Allan Ramsay had already published texts with indications of the tunes they were to be sung to, and William Thomson pirated them and published them with the tunes, and the pair of them kept business going, pirating words and music from each other's successive editions. William Thomson was not just a publisher, but one of George I's favourite singers. His father was Daniel Thomson, the Scottish State trumpeter who played at the inaugural concert of the St Cecilia Society in Edinburgh in 1695. One of those whose work was batted about by Ramsay and Thomson was Lady Grisell Baillie, an orderly woman whose account book gives us an insight into aristocratic expenditure on music. Here are some typical entries from the first decade of the century, with costs in pounds, shillings and pence sterling (she kept a track of several currency values):

> For tickets to Steals consurt 7.2.0:
> For copiing music at 1C. the 4 lines 1.12.5 St:
> For tuning spinet a month 0.4.10 St:
> To S. Carmany Playing master 0.18.0 St:
> To Carmany for singing 2.14.0 St:
> hire of spinet 0.8.10 St:
> copiing music 0.1.7 St.[15]

The orderly image is softened by the knowledge that this same woman had written the humorous but sad words for *Werena' My Hearts Light I Wad Die* (published by Ramsay) to a tune they matched perfectly (published with the words by Thomson). Oswald, however, published only the tunes, frequently in arrangements for violin or flute, and was not ashamed to add to their number with several of his own. But Ramsay was going to miss Oswald as a performer as well as a composer of the kind of music he approved of:

Alas! no more shall thy gay tunes delight,
No more thy notes sadness or joy excite,
No more thy solemn bass's awful sound,
Shall from the chapel's vaulted roof rebound.

This last remark may refer to Oswald as a cellist or bassist (the chapel being St Mary's) or to his voice. Whether he sang in chapel or no, he probably sang at the Masonic Lodge, perhaps alongside Sir John Clerk of Penicuik, also a freemason. Oswald set two masonic songs in his Edinburgh days. The first one is full of appropriate symbolism – the special properties of the number three were reflected by using three parts and three beats in the bar – and parallel thirds and linked notes to indicate friendship. But where the words speak of freedom and sweet innocence enlarging the mind, Oswald introduces the more mind-enlarging effect of counterpoint and octave leaps in the parts. But always the phrases come to an end on an octave or a unison – the perfect symbols of unity in diversity. There was dissonance too, for there were always fears and discordant elements to be overcome. His masonic anthem *Grant Me Kind Heaven* is deliberately cast in ancient mould like a sixteenth-century galliard, but one of the graver sort. Published in 1740, it sets a standard of subtlety and symbolism that would take thirty years to be matched by another freemason composer, Wolfgang Amadeus Mozart. It is quite possible that Oswald's music or its influence filtered through to the Viennese masonic lodges, for the continental lodges all looked to Scotland as the parent of their ideals.[16]

Oswald composed another masonic anthem. It spoke of the great mason kings of old, of secrets, and of solemn notes and flowing wine. It too is for three voices, with three beats in the bar except in the chorus – but whether that also is significant remains a secret itself.

In 1740 Oswald advertised in the papers that he was off to Italy, perhaps encouraged by Clerk, but we do not know whether he made the trip. In any event he was in London in 1741. London

was full of Scots. Among them were the authors Mallett and Smollett. In 1746 Smollett and Oswald had probably collaborated when Oswald put music to Smollett's *Tears of Scotland*, protesting at the brutality of the Duke of Cumberland after the defeat of Prince Charles at Culloden, while in the ballrooms down the Strand they were cheering the butcher whenever he appeared. When someone told Smollett to be careful what he wrote for fear of offending the English, he just added one more damning verse. Other Scots in London were the Earl of Stair and the Duke

Example 7. JAMES OSWALD: THE FREEMASON'S ANTHEM
(Collection of Scots Tunes, 1742)

of Queensberry, who (according to Farmer)[17] had helped to sponsor the Royal Academy of Music (1719), and the Earl of Abercorn, who was involved in the setting up of the Academy of Ancient Music (*c.* 1710). The Reverend and Honourable Alexander Hume, who helped young Charles Burney (see below) get his first proper job, was a music lover too, as was Dr John Armstrong, another Scot, who had saved Burney's life by sending him into the country.[18]

The Scottish contingent in London also included the young Earl of Kelly who had just come into his inheritance and was scattering his new-fangled music from Mannheim without any thought for getting it properly published; George Drummond with his fourth wife and the £20,000 that came along with her; and Clerk turned up occasionally rooting out architects, builders and landscape gardeners like Sir William Chambers and John Abercrombie and John Stuart, Earl of Bute – all of them Scots and some of them hanging round the Dowager Princess of Wales, waiting for her son to become king. Oswald was waiting for that too. He had probably been promised the post of Chamber Composer to His Majesty King George III to be, on the strength of his relationship with his father Frederick, the Prince of Wales[19] – and it was a promise to be fulfilled. The brotherhood of free-masonry may also have helped in these matters.

Yet another Scot in London was the lie-a-bed poet, John Thomson, whose fine poem, *The Seasons*, had raised people to a new and more profound understanding of Nature, though it seems unlikely that it had much influence on Oswald's work, for Thomson's poem has only a few relatively conventional references to plants. But who in the world could match Oswald's own achievement on that front?

Oswald composed no less than ninety-six violin sonatas with figured basses, each named after a different flower or shrub, classified by its season – two complete sets and not one plant, and not one tune repeated. For twelve of them at least he issued second violin parts thus turning them into trio sonatas. This is an astonishing venture to have undertaken, a rational ordering of Nature, an Aristotelian list based not on scientific classification but on the natural flowering time of the plants, with the exception that the second set for winter is classified as trees

and shrubs. The full significance of Oswald's *Airs for the Seasons* is not remotely appreciated and requires much work, but a good example of the subtlety and refinement of conception which underlies it is *The Narcissus*. There are just two movements for the brief dancing life of the flower. The first one is in the style of a Scottish air, but with reflections and echoes added because Narcissus fell in love with his own reflection and was beloved of Echo. This is a perfect example of the native and the classical in each other's arms.

Example 8. JAMES OSWALD: THE NARCISSUS (*Airs for the Seasons*, 1747)

The second movement reflects the fact that the Narcissus was a dancer's plant. The medicine from it was good for strained sinews and stiff joints; and the Narcissus bending in the breeze leads the first dance of spring. Oswald had quoted Horace on the cover 'Now Cytherea leads the dance' – and this dance is a Scottish jig full of the cheerfulness of the spring. In fact the quotation from Horace appears on the cover of each of the eight sets, irrespective of the season (see Plate 38). It is an explicit claim for the Scottish dancing-master to make, and Cytherea – Venus – the Goddess of Love, is the source of his inspiration.

Abercrombie was a leading gardener employed in the royal gardens in London from 1744, and it could have been from him that Oswald got the notion of including *The Sneezwort* in his *Airs for the Seasons*, a plant supposed to help you sneeze. The first movement is pathetic and lugubrious, streaming with the cold in miserable D minor chromaticisms, and the second is a

Iam Cytherea Choros ducit Venus, imminente Luna:
Iunctæque Nymphis Gratiæ decentes,
Alterno Terram quatiunt Pede. —— Hor:

Airs
for the SPRING,
By
James Oswald,
Printed for the Author, and sold at his Musick Shop,
St Martins Church Yard.

Plate 38. TITLE PAGE OF OSWALD'S *Airs for the Seasons*, 1747

Plate 39. *The Sneezwort*, FROM JAMES OSWALD'S *Airs for the Seasons*, 1747

pastorelle – a chilly autumn hunting scene but again in the minor key and with a desperate urge to sneeze, which is not gratified until the trills near the end (see Plate 39).

Another sonata which might relate to a *Materia Medica* is *The Lilac* which has a languid sinuous first movement, and then two dance movements with the cello part tugging at the rhythms of the violin, the last one a 9/8 jig in the major key. Perhaps Oswald smiled to himself at having raised the Lilac's use as a vermifuge to a higher plane. On the other hand *The Heliotrope* is not interpreted medically, but for its name and supposed attributes. That is why the sonata ends with a slow movement, a largo amoroso; because the flower loves the sun, it is supposed to follow it, and at evening gaze fondly upon it.

The sonata for *The Marvel of Peru* – an extraordinary flower imported from the new world that miraculously produces flowers of three different colours from the one stem – is a particularly imaginative response to the nature of the plant. The music comes in three movements, each one as colourful and different from its neighbour as could be, but all on the one stem. The first movement is called *Scortese* – the Italian for rustic. But it is Scottish rustic, not Italian – as well-shaped a tune as anyone could produce and showing its hand at the end with pure pentatonic melody. Being Scottish we may assume that it is blue.

The colour of the second flower is a cheerful comedian's red. Its title is *Comic,* and it might serve for some light entr'acte on the stage with everybody chasing everybody else, the sort of thing Oswald probably helped Burney with in *Queen Mab* for the Drury Lane Theatre.[20] But there was another reason for the comedy. The Marvel of Peru produced jalap – one of the best purgatives to be had from an apothecary. It would certainly keep you on the run, in much the same spirit of comedy as in Molière's *Le Malade Imaginaire*. Given its title in English it may also be that Oswald thought of this movement as being in an English theatre style. The colour red is then appropriate for the rose of England or for the red of St George's cross.

The last movement is a French musette: related to the first, but different, for the French bagpipes, which a musette imitates, are rustic but not Scottish. The bass line imitates the upper

part almost canonically. The colour of the flower of France is the white of the lily. We have then a tri-national, tri-coloured, tri-charactered marvel, and quite apart from the wit with which the idea has been worked out, the music is a delight from start to finish. Many of the sonatas would go well on flute or oboe and the formal structures which Oswald employs in *The Seasons* are full of variety. He uses anything from one to five movements, some of them tiny, others expansive. He

Example 9. JAMES OSWALD: THE MARVEL OF PERU (*Airs for the Seasons*, 1747)

employs, naturally enough, a wide variety of dance forms. *The Thistle* as the emblem of Scotland has a splendid reel in it, and a deeply nostalgic Scottish air, marked amoroso and played entirely in double-stopping, beautifully laid out for the left hand and thoroughly affecting. *The Nightshade* ends with a hornpipe, having started with an aria, perhaps because Nightshade is also called Belladonna as Italian prostitutes used it to make their eyes sparkle. It is certainly a bright-eyed movement. The Italian ports (as we gathered from the warnings to Clerk in Chapter XIII) were notorious for prostitution and the central sostenuto in B minor may be suggestive of nightshade in more than one meaning. The concluding sailor's hornpipe, in triple time and with lively syncopations, is thoroughly English in character, from which we may guess that the visiting sailors have had a good time of it.

How many of the *Airs for the Seasons* are susceptible to this kind of analysis has yet to be discovered, nor will it be a straightforward business, for it seems that Oswald has combined different approaches, symbolic, by verbal association, mythological, medical, and botanical. The names, significances and varieties of plants have also changed since his day, and patient research has yet to find a flora, herbal, materia medica, horticultural calendar or even a vast dictionary from the seventeenth century or first half of the eighteenth century that matches Oswald's usage. Perhaps he worked from several sources, some not published, or had the habit of walking in fine gardens with knowledgeable people.

The Seasons was not Oswald's only grand compendium, his greatest publishing success being perhaps his compendium of kisses – *Colin's Kisses* – to poems by Dodsley. Robert Dodsley, the English butler who had risen to be poet, playwright and major literary publisher, has inspired Oswald to some of his best songs in this group of twelve. It has a reasonable claim to be considered as the first song cycle. Composers had grouped songs together in the past, but these were different. They were by the one poet, the music by the one composer, all on the one subject – kissing. They belonged together – a round dozen of them, almost like a season of kissing, a kiss to a month – and Oswald allowed

the tune for one song to influence the tune for another. The poems clearly appealed to him. The first is called *The Tutor* and Oswald had been a dancing master and music tutor – and those humbler origins ending up with his being a major publisher may have given him a fellow feeling for Dodsley as a man. The second and third songs are *The Secret Kiss* and *The Borrow'd Kiss*. Given his and Mary Ann Melville's elopement, these too may have had special meaning for Oswald. Then there were *The Rapture, The Stolen Kiss* and *The Kiss Repaid*, the first two related musically – a pair of Scottish lovers, like themselves.

The Kiss Repaid is a cheerful minuet, and of course there is a *Parting Kiss* – 'One Kind Kiss before we Part'. Dodsley was not to know that Burns would one day take those words and remould them into *Ae Fond Kiss* and Oswald was not to know they would be set to a different tune that he claimed was by Rory Dall (see Chapter X) but others say is Oswald's own. After the parting there was naturally an *Imaginary Kiss* – a fleeting fantasy this one, but followed by *The Feast* which is real enough, one of his loveliest Scottish tunes, personal and private, but ending with a spirited acceptance that is more public and therefore more conventional. Next comes *The Meeting Kiss* – a reunion after absence which Oswald composed in the grand Handelian manner with his tongue firmly in his cheek.

Example 10A. JAMES OSWALD: THE RAPTURE (*Colin's Kisses*, 1742)

Example 10B. JAMES OSWALD: THE STOLEN KISS (*Colin's Kisses*, 1742)

Example 11. JAMES OSWALD: THE MEETING KISS (*Colin's Kisses*, 1742)

The last two songs are the best of all. *The Reconciling Kiss* goes beyond tenderness and suggests behind it all something of pain too, of a quarrel that has left a hurt. And *The Mutual Kiss* which brings it all to a happy end is a generous-hearted wide-ranging tune, warm, content and loving. But that was natural enough. He composed these songs in 1742, just as he was getting to know Mary Anne Melville, not long after he had moved to London. They may even have been a kind of pledge that kept love alive in a foreign land.

LONDON, alas! which aye has been our bane,
To which our very loss is certain gain,
Where our daft Lords and lairds spend all their rents,
In following ilka fashion she invents.

Example 12. JAMES OSWALD: THE MUTUAL KISS (*Colin's Kisses*, 1742)

Still envious of the little we had left,
Of JAMIE OSWALD last our town bereft.

Meanwhile, to keep our heavy hearts aboon,
O publish a' your works and send them soon;
We'll a' subscribe, as we did for the past,
And play while bows may wag or strings can last.
Farewell – perhaps, if you oblige us soon,
I'll sing again to a new fav'rite tune.

Ramsay's complaint is still relevant, but Oswald was no mere craven in moving south. He knew how to make use of the London life around him, satirising it wickedly in two entr'actes called *The Wheelbarrow Cantata* and *The Dustcart Cantata*. The first features Porter Will and Cerissa, who sells cherries. They are doubly satirical, for the music would pass for a simple Italianate aria, with all the mannerisms of that genre but done well, whereas the sentiments are ridiculous. The mismatch is hilarious. The apparent charms of a well-wrought arioso are exposed as merely conventional, but the petty arrogances of the aristocratic world are mimicked and made fun of when they are seen to operate just as selfishly among porters and sales girls.

The Dustcart Cantata was sung as an entr'acte in *The Old Woman's Oratory*. Oswald composed it 'In the manner of the moderns' and here too he

Example 13. JAMES OSWALD: THE DUSTCART CANTATA, *c.* 1753

exploits the combination of ridiculous words and absolutely straight-faced Italianate music. He has not cheated or exaggerated at all. Sung in Italian everybody would have said how charming, how expressive, how pretty. But in English the proud primadonna was filthy and mounted on a dust-cart and the hero who adored her was a tinkering Tom – a stage worse than a peeping Tom. It and *The Wheelbarrow Cantata* were heard in the public gardens too. Oswald published a lot of songs for performance there and dedicated a book of them to his friend, John Robinson Lytton, to whom he lent money. In fact Oswald when himself a widower was to end up living with and eventually marrying Lytton's widow, Leonora, in Knebworth House, where he died.[21]

Lytton leads us to the controversial Society of the Temple of Apollo, a musical venture which Oswald founded, and really did exist. Charles Burney claimed that it consisted solely of himself, and recent commentators have swallowed his testimony whole, but it is not to be trusted.[22] To begin with, Oswald himself founded it, on Burney's own admission. A number of works by different composers were published under its aegis, and it held concerts at Robinson Lytton's house.

Oswald hid Burney's name behind that of the Temple of Apollo, which was really a kindness to Burney who was licking his wounds after months of use and abuse by the odious Thomas Arne. The other composers published under the Society's name were much more accomplished – St Martini, John Reid, and one of Oswald's star pupils, Benjamin Hallett. McArdle produced a mezzotint of the boy when he was just starting out, with a caption: 'Benjamin Hallett, a child not five years old, who, under the tuition of Mr Oswald, performed on the flute at Drury lane theatre, Ano 1748 for 50 nights with extraordinary skill and applause, and in the following year was able to play his part in any concert on the Violincello.'

Oswald published his sonatas under the name Dottel Figlio – talented child – worthy of the Society's umbrella.

Burney should really be called MacBurney. But the MacBurneys, apparently ashamed of their past, which they suppressed, dropped the Mac. Young Burney came to Oswald looking for work and Oswald gave him a helping hand allowing him to contribute a few bass parts. But Burney's bass parts are terrible compared with Oswald's, being derived largely from conventional formulae, patternings made out of broken chords, whereas Oswald, perhaps because he was a cellist as well as a better composer, wrote bass parts that had some independence and life to them. Frederick Prince of Wales had been a cellist and Oswald had been able to dedicate publications to him. The prince had been all for the British style of music and Oswald was probably a kindred spirit – a man more of the people, as was the prince himself, than of the vicious, almost insanely petty world of his parents, George II and consort. In the light of these shared musical proclivities, Frank Kidson's suggestion that the Society of the Temple of Apollo may also have involved a political element related to the position of the Prince of Wales (who was also a keen gardener) is more than plausible.

Oswald's output was prodigious, and though everything was small scale, he compensated for this to a certain degree by publishing groups of works: *Twelve Serenatas for two violins and a violincello with a thorough bass for the harpsichord; Ten favourite songs sung by Miss Formantel at Ranelagh; Six pastoral Solos for a Violin and Violoncello with a thorough bass for the organ or harpsichord.* At the end of the second Solo where there was some blank paper to fill, Oswald finished off the lines of the stave into the shape of feathered quill pens with the head of a bird in the middle. There were *Twelve Divertimenti* for the guitar, which were bound to sell well among the ladies of leisure whose latest instrumental craze was the English Guitar – a sort of cittern more like a lute in appearance than the traditional guitar (see Plate XXIII). These pieces are indeed diverting, and now and again turn up little harmonic touches of great beauty, though they cast the book of rules aside. The parallel fifths or the exposed second inversions of these two are touching in their deliberate naïveté; judged perfectly for scale, they show that even the *style galant* can catch your breath with feeling.

Example 14. JAMES OSWALD: DIVERTIMENTO VII
(*Twelve Divertimenti for English Guitar*, 1758)

Robert Bremner (*c.* 1713–1789), who was an enterprising Scottish publisher based in Edinburgh and London, produced the first really serious tutor for the English guitar which explored more than the most elementary technique (see Plate 40).[23] The music in it consists of arrangements of

Plate 40. FRONTISPIECE FOR BREMNER'S *Instructions for the Guitar*

popular Scottish songs and also of military music such as *The Highland March* and two Moorish tunes. In many military bands there would be a Moorish drummer or cymbal player, and they often used a Moorish instrument known as a crescent or a Jinglin' Geordie – an instrument with little bells or tambourine-like discs attached which jingled away merrily. The sparkle of military music was, of course, an important attraction in recruiting.

Oswald had an eye for potentially profitable ventures, publishing his *Fifty-Five Marches for the Militia* for the fifty-five new militias to go with the fifty-five counties where they were to be raised. He went to a lot of trouble to make the marches as different from each other as he could and, considering the limitations of the trumpets of the day, he managed pretty well: *The Cambridgeshire March* is cheerfully strutting; *The Cardiganshire March* is bold and spirited; and *The Buckinghamshire March* features trills and one sharp little taste of dissonance.

It seems unreasonable to attempt to make a judgment of James Oswald's significance in European music history. He would be lost in it beside Bach and Handel, Haydn and Mozart. And yet his contribution to it, though so little known

nowadays, is marked by a consistency of aesthetic (and it is an interesting aesthetic), a skilful handling of his ideas with a particularly well-crafted and refreshing approach to bass lines, a quick wit and, above all, by a spontaneous and inexhaustible gift for beautiful melody. Many of Oswald's tunes, if transferred to orchestra and attached to a more famous name, would end up among the best-loved and most admired products of his part of the eighteenth century. His achievement is one for which we should be grateful, for he brought freshness, beauty and humour to a world of music too often wrapped up in an anonymous and fashionable prettiness. Oswald can be pretty too, but there is a deep poetic inspiration behind the best of his work, drawing on the great well of the Scottish tradition. There is, after all, genius in the construction of a bee's wing as well as in that of the eagle.

In the light of these remarks, there is a delicious irony in the fact that Oswald probably presided over the birth of *God Save The King*. He was almost certainly the first to harmonise it in the form known today, for Simpson published it after Oswald had joined him, and Simpson was no arranger.[24] It was always a wretched tune, rhythmically unimaginative, as square as a box and accompanied by words insulting to half of the land mass to which it is supposed to apply. Played on a musical clock made by John Smith of Pittenweem to a late eighteenth-century design, it finds its true métier. Like the ideals of those days, the clock's sense of control over its own destiny has been disrupted by the passage of the very thing it was supposed to have the measure of – namely time. There had been respectable philosophers who believed that God ran the universe like a clock, others who believed that language could be clearly analysed and defined, and there were many of the opinion that nature was there to be tamed. Mountains could not be tamed so they were coarse and vulgar, and nobody climbed them except Highlanders. As for *God Save The King* – was it not the very symbol of order, national unity, and loyalty to the established hierarchies, keeping the wild in check?

The Scots, however, were not uniformly wooed by such opinions. They loved nature, and that included mountains. A large proportion of them were of the opinion that the man born to be king was a Stewart not a Hanoverian; and many were not, and still are not in sympathy with the philosophy of time as enunciated by clockwork. As for music, most Scots remained loyal to the native air so it is only poetic justice that the Pittenweem clock has failed to retain a single coherent version of the Scots tunes in its original repertoire. *The Last Time I Cam o'er The Moor*, *Roslin Castle* and *The Waulking of the Fauld* have abandoned the little bells and hammers, leaving behind them only *God Save The King*, itself tottering on the edge of chaos.

John Smith of Pittenweem will pobably have been familiar with Lord Pittenweem – otherwise known as Thomas Alexander Erskine, Viscount Fenton, Sixth Earl of Kelly, who was born at Kellie Castle in Fife in 1732. The clockmaker would have known him by the local nickname, Fiddler Tam, for the Sixth Earl played the fiddle. There is a *Strathspey and Reel* attributed to him which show that he too started his musical life in the locally approved manner. In Scotland traditional and classical music and dance could exist cheek-by-jowl, like Jacobites and Hanoverians, so it was the same young man who wrote a classical minuet for his sister, Lady Ann Erskine, the minuet being the well-ordered and elegant court dance of the day. Kelly's contri-

bution to the form is particularly distinguished.[25] One other work of Kelly's is Scottish, a *Largo* based on the well-known ballad *The Lowlands of Holland*.

When Kelly's father, the Fifth Earl, was imprisoned for fighting on Bonnie Prince Charlie's side (with the three retainers he persuaded to join him) this ferocious parental act of rebellion left the heir with reduced prospects. But instead of looking for gainful employment, young Kelly went to Mannheim, studied composition and thereafter displayed few Scotticisms in his style, though his speech remained broad Fife. He then proceeded to live off the sale of the lands he inherited. All this was, in its own way, an act of rebellion. The aristocracy were expected to build up their lands and, as we saw with Sir John Clerk, they did not regard music as anything other than a dilettante occupation for a gentleman. Many years later Charles Burney, established as a leading music historian, wrote of fiddler Tam:

> The late Earl of Kelly, who was possessed of more musical science than any dilettanti with whom I was ever acquainted, and who, according to Pinto, before he travelled into Germany, could scarcely tune his fiddle, shut himself up at Mannheim with the elder Stamitz, and studied composition, and practised the violin with such serious application, that, at his return . . there was no part of theoretical or practical music, in which he was not equally versed with the greatest professors of his time. Indeed, he had a strength of hand on the violin, and a genius for composition, with which few professors are gifted.[26]

When Kelly came back from Mannheim he became a central figure in musical life and in June 1774 he provided a substantial part of the music for the first *fête-champêtre* held in Britain. This was a five-day entertainment at Lord Stanley's country estate – the Oaks at Epsom – to celebrate his marriage. Modelled on French rural festivals, it cost £5,000. There was an orchestra in the orangery and indeed London and its environs had been cleaned out of orange trees to prettify the place, so the concept of rural naturalness must have seemed a little stretched. Kelly's *Minuet for Lord Stanley* was played on clarinets, horns, violins and continuo. This is an extremely lively piece, suitable for a twenty-two-year-old aristocrat given to horse-racing and cock-fighting and, like Kelly, fond of his pleasures. The *Minuet* for his wife is suitably soothing by comparison. (See Example 15.)

Another Scottish musician who was to become a central figure in London musical life was John Broadwood, harpsichord and fortepiano

Plate 41. *The Lover's Message*, BY THOMAS ERSKINE, SIXTH EARL OF KELLY, edition of 1836

maker, who had recently moved down from Scotland, at first working in partnership with Shudi, but soon in charge of his own family business which was to become one of the leading creative forces in the development of the piano. Broadwood no doubt would have sought to attract Kelly's patronage in London, and Kelly may well have played a Broadwood instrument, though how proficient he was at the keyboard is not known. Unlike Oswald, who will have

been tied to his business, Kelly probably moved between England and Scotland freely and his gifts were equally appreciated in his home country.

'It has only to be added, that, to that same period at which other great men of Scotland have appeared, it has been reserved to produce the greatest secular musician in his line, in the British islands, the late Earl of Kelly.' Thus Thomas Robertson, writing in 1784 in his *Inquiry into the Fine Arts*.

> In his works the fervidum ingenium of his country bursts forth; and elegance is mingled with fire. From the singular ardour and impetuosity of his temperament, joined to his German education under the celebrated Stamitz, and at a time when the German overture or symphony, consisting of a grand chorus of violins and wind-instruments, was in its highest vogue, this great composer has employed himself chiefly upon symphonies, but in a style peculiar to himself. While others please and amuse, it is his province to rouse, and almost to overset his hearer. Loudness, rapidity, enthusiasm, announce the Earl of Kelly.[27]

Robertson is careful to temper his admiration of Kelly's liveliness with at least a nod in the direction of eighteenth-century propriety: 'His harmonies are acknowledged to be accurate and ingenious; admirably calculated for the effect in view, and discovering a thorough knowledge in music. From some specimens which he has given, it appears that his talents were not limited to a single style; and which has made his admirers regret that he did not apply himself to a greater variety of subjects. He is

Example 15A. KELLY: MINUET FOR LORD STANLEY, 1774

Example 15B. LADY BETTY STANLEY'S MINUET, 1774

said to have composed only one song; but that an excellent one – It is called the Lover's Message.'[28] (See plate 41.)

It is indeed excellent, though there is also a concert aria (see below). Love was a subject close to Kelly's heart: 'We had a splendid ball at the Abbey of Holyroodhouse . . . Lord Kelly danced with Miss C . . . ; by the fire of whose eyes, his melodious lordship's heart is at present in a state of combustion. Such is the declaration which he makes in loud whispers many a time and oft.'[29]

> What appears to have been singularly peculiar to this musician, is what may be called the velocity of his talents; by which he composed whole pieces of the most excellent music, in one night's time. Part of his work is still unpublished; and not a little probably lost. Being always remarkably fond of a concert of wind instruments, whenever he met with a good band of them, he was seized with a fit of composition, and wrote pieces in the moment, which he gave away to the performers, and never saw again: and these, in his own judgment, were the best he ever composed.[30]

We have lost much of Kelly's music as a result of this cavalier approach which was part of his whole convivial life-style. He is credited with having founded the Capillaire Club which 'was composed of all those who were inclined to be witty or joyous'. Naturally, he wrote a piece of music specially for them to dance to – perhaps at their annual ball which, in 1774, was attended by nearly two hundred ladies and gentlemen. Capillaire was a kind of eighteenth-century cocktail which the members drank exclusively from small liqueur glasses engraved with the name. Here the Scottish poetess, Alison Cockburn, mentions the club in a letter to the great Edinburgh philosopher, David Hume:

> Goodness! How little you know of our world. Dear man, you can be member of the Capilaire, and then have Sunday set apart for that and topeing, besides parties all the week long. I confess the ladies are still backward in that article, which is owing either to that jade Fortune, or these days' husbands, I can't tell which. But no fear, come along; bring you vices we shall find objects for them. As for the Godly, there is not one here. They are all gone to England to Whitefield and Wesley. Even Peggy Kyle is now a candle-maker and not a preacher. All, all are worshippers of Mammon.[31]

Kelly would have been happy in such company, for religion was not his strong suit and it was said of him that his nose was so red it would ripen cucumbers (see Plate 42). We can picture the members of the Capillaire Club, perhaps David Hume included, dancing to Kelly's *Capillaire Minuet*, one trusts without a trace of sobriety, religion or care for the safety of empty glasses.

It would be thoroughly unfair to overstress Kelly's conviviality, for there must have been a serious and disciplined side to him, first of all in achieving a high degree of proficiency as violinist and composer, secondly in the fact that he became Grand Master of the English and Scottish masonic lodges simultaneously, an honour which has never fallen upon any other man. We have noticed the significance of masonic music in connection with Oswald and it seems likely that Kelly had a hand in the design of St Cecilia's Hall – that beautiful oval concert room, completed in 1762, which still serves Edinburgh so well (see Plate XXIV). Aristocratic masons were not stone cutters and builders, but some, like Sir John Clerk, were amateur architects, and there was a general agreement that music and architecture were closely allied. Kelly had been a school-mate of Robert Mylne, a freemason and the architect of St Cecilia's Hall. He and Kelly could have met in a masonic lodge in London and Kelly may have brought Mylne to Edinburgh and advised on the acoustics – which are very fine.

It may well be that as we get to know Kelly's music better, connections between it and freemasonry will emerge, but one thing is clear; a symphony such as his one in C major was not merely a piece of chamber music transferred to orchestra, but composed with a concert hall and concert audience in mind. This symphony is typical of the neglect which Scottish music has suffered. The eighteenth-century parts required little editing, the scoring does not call for a large orchestra, so it is cheap to put on, and (above all) the music is excellent and thoroughly appealing; yet it only received its first modern performance in 1991 for the radio series *Scotland's Music* and might otherwise be languishing still. It is a work of historical interest also, being an early part of that process which led to the large-scale structures that we associate with the symphony nowadays. It is bold and thoroughly public. There are three movements, the first one bursting into the eighteenth-century concert hall with that great novelty from Mannheim – the crescendo – and continuing to surprise with lots of work for the horns and oboes, and contrasts of loud and soft. Some years later, young Mozart was to be equally excited by the quality of the orchestral playing in Mannheim where techniques we now take for granted were first evolved. Simple things such as training the players to come in together with the same kind of attack, loud or

Example 16. KELLY: SYMPHONY IN C MAJOR, BEFORE 1761

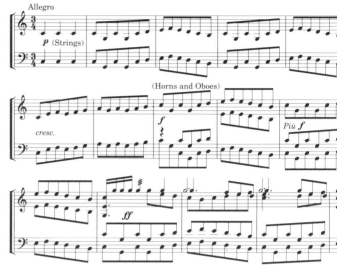

Plate 42. *Thomas Erskine, Sixth Earl of Kelly*, BY ROBERT HUME,
MID-EIGHTEENTH CENTURY

he must have been one of the first to train British musicians to imitate it. Equally fine is his Overture *The Maid of The Mill* (Overture number 28). This is also a symphony, the terms being almost interchangeable, though it was composed as a curtain-raiser for the highly successful comedy of that name, first given at Covent Garden in 1765.[33] It is an ebullient piece with thrilling rhythmic energy, and deploys his

Example 17. KELLY: SYMPHONY IN C MAJOR, BEFORE 1761

soft, or getting louder as an ensemble, not just as individuals, were thrilling novelties and Kelly was the first to exploit them in Britain. Bremner published his six symphonies, opus 1 in 1761 and soon afterwards, Collet, Hook and Norris (all in England) followed Kelly's lead.

The slow movement is in the dark key of C minor and it too has crescendos. As for the last movement it is an exhilarating presto full of sportive trills and a much more lively bass part than many composers were managing to produce.

It was told of Kelly that 'In the midst of a turbulent and tumultuous movement of a symphony in twelve or fourteen parts, if any instrument failed either in time or tune, though playing a different and difficult part himself, he instantly prompted the erroneous performer with his voice, by singing his part without abandoning his own',[32] and we may also assume that as the introducer of the Mannheim style

PLATE XVII. REQUIEM MASS FOR JAMES III FROM JAMES IV's *Book of Hours*, 1503

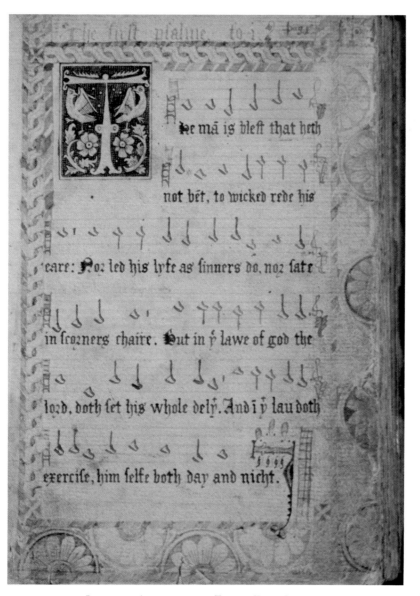

PLATE XVIII. A PAGE FROM THE THOMAS WODE PARTBOOKS,
*c.*1580

PLATE XIX. INSTRUMENTS IN THE MARGIN OF THE
THOMAS WODE PARTBOOKS, *c.*1580

PLATE XX. CALIOPE WITH A HARP, CRATHES CASTLE CEILING, EARLY SEVENTEENTH CENTURY

PLATE XXI. CRATHES CASTLE – NINE MUSES CEILING, EARLY SEVENTEENTH CENTURY

PLATE XXII. *Piper to the Laird of Grant*, BY RICHARD WAITT, *c.*1714

PLATE XXIII. AN ENGLISH GUITAR

PLATE XXIV. ST CECILIA'S HALL, EDINBURGH

PLATE XXV. *Niel Gow* BY HENRY RAEBURN, *c.*1793

PLATE XXVI. MUSICIANS IN ORGAN GALLERY WITH ROBERT BURNS IN FOREGROUND BEING INDUCTED INTO THE FREEMASONS,
DETAIL FROM *Meeting of Kilwinning Number 1 Lodge*, BY STEWART WATSON

PLATE XXVII. *General John Reid*

PLATE XXVIII. HAMISH MACCUNN AS A DANDY IN *Two Strings To Her Bow* BY JOHN PETTIE, 1887

PLATE XXIX. *Marjory Kennedy-Fraser* BY JOHN DUNCAN

PLATE XXX. *Wool Waulking*, BY KEITH HENDERSON, 1927–28

most exciting crescendos, and expressive use of the oboes, horns and bassoon which constitute the wind section. The mixture of wit and lyricism in the central adagio and the elegant anticipation of the concluding rondo-minuet, make this a classic of its kind.

Example 18. KELLY: SYMPHONY IN B FLAT MAJOR (*The Maid of the Mill, c.* 1764)

The recent discovery of the Kilravock partbooks, now in the possession of the leading authority on eighteenth-century Scottish music, David Johnson (to whose commentary I am indebted), will provide us with nineteen works of Kelly's of which sixteen were previously unknown.[34] They include some of his best music, along with student work, experiments, and an abandoned fugue. There are nine string quartets, nine trio sonatas (three already known), and a duet sonata for two violins. The *Trio Number 8 in C* from the 1760s incorporates a complete fugal movement by Fritz, but Kelly has corrected Fritz's mistakes and then added the elegant outer movements, the first being particularly expressive and gracious.

The *Quartet Number 9 in A* is especially fine and David Johnson has pointed out that Haydn (who was born in the same year as Kelly) had at that stage produced nothing so rich as this work. The allegro molto is one of his most vivid examples of his liveliness of temperament. The adagio is based on the first four bars of a Barsanti

concerto grosso which Kelly might have picked up when he was eighteen and was playing in the Edinburgh Musical Society orchestra. Each half of the movement starts with Barsanti but is soon worked into new combinations, turning Barsanti's contrapuntal figures to deeply expressive use. This movement is in F sharp minor, the exquisite sadness of the ending only being emphasised by its final F sharp major chords. Kelly, however, still supplies these quartets with a figured bass for the harpsichordist to play from, though Foulis in his later sonatas abandoned doing so. By the end of the century the figured bass was dying out, for composers increasingly took more care over the inner parts, making them more interesting and allowing them to contribute to the overall argument of the music as well as the texture. The harpsichordist's improvised harmonic fillings-in then became not merely redundant, but likely to clash with the other parts.

There are other works of Kelly's worthy of attention. The *Symphony in E Flat* (Overture number 17) with its three times three opening raps on the door (possibly masonic as are the raps at the start of *The Magic Flute*) and its skittish Presto finale; and the lovely *Trio Sonata in C*, number 4, with its elegant sighs exchanged between the two violins at the end of the first movement.

Example 19. KELLY: TRIO SONATA IN C, 1769

Death is no respecter of good humour and good living, and the latter caught up with the Sixth Earl of Kelly in 1781. A trip to a spa on the continent came too late. He died in Brussels on his way home. Let us hope that he was able to face his end with true masonic equanimity as *Death is Now My Only Treasure* seems to indicate. It is a short, but very lovely concert aria in the key of three flats, in three-four time, full of passages in parallel thirds. Three is an important number in freemasonry and these instances may be taken as symbolic; whether or no, it is certain that the character of the piece, which cheerfully accepts death as a true friend, is best explained in a masonic context. It was originally sung by the brilliant castrato – Tenducci.

Example 20. Kelly: Concert Aria – Death is Now My Only Treasure

Caleb Whiteford's lines on Kelly's death match the mood:

To thee John Warre! I Caleb Whiteford send
The honour'd bust of a departed friend;

Me too the bonds of firmest Friendship tied,
And half my soul took flight when Kelly died!

Whose Sense refin'd, whose wit devoid of Gall,
Ne'er wounded any, but delighted all.
Where shall we seek such Pleasantry to find
That cheerful constant sunshine of the Mind?
How vain the Labour, and the Search how vain,
Unless himself should visit Earth again!

But though no longer we behold him here,
Kelly still shines in a superior Sphere:
That Soul of Melody, that feeling Heart,
In Heaven's high Concerts surely bears a part;
And, though alas! from former Friends remov'd,
He still enjoys that Harmony he loved![35]

From the Reformation to the late eighteenth century, the history of Scottish music can only boast of two composers who made truly distinguished contributions to the larger scale forms of classical music – Sir John Clerk and the Earl of Kelly. They were both aristocrats, both took themselves abroad to study, both treated their brilliant compositional talents in a cavalier manner. Abell (whose works are significant rather than distinguished), Oswald, McGibbon and others, were professional performers or publishers, often from less advantaged backgrounds and probably with little leisure for study in between teaching, performing, currying favour and running businesses. Oswald never attempted a symphony, though his contribution to the theatre music of his day may have been greater than is supposed,[36] and he may have composed a number of anonymous items, including some attributed to Burney.

Why this lack of major works from a country capable of producing so many great writers and thinkers such as Thomson, Smollett, Ramsay and Hume, and great painters such as Ramsay the younger and Raeburn? The answer is simple enough. To be a painter or a writer was respectable. To be a musician was to be a servant. Mozart virtually destroyed himself breaking out of that servitude. It was one of the greatest acts of artistic and social rebellion and it was highly dangerous even to the most gifted musician the world has ever known, and familiar from childhood with most of the courts of Europe. What chance was there then for a budding composer in Scotland, which had no court and whose wealth had fled south to be spent, as Ramsay bitterly comments, on foreign fashions? There was no chance.

But there was change in the air. The idea that music was faintly respectable and might be worthy of academic study (though it was one of the few subjects Plato permitted to be taught in his Academy) had already dawned in England and Ireland. The chair of music at Oxford was established in 1626, in Cambridge in 1684, and Dublin followed a century later in 1764. But Scotland had to wait until 1839 for the munificence of a retired general to fund a chair of music. He was John Reid, whom we last heard of fighting the Jacobites (see Chapter XII). After their defeat, he served in France but in 1755 was in North America with the Black Watch,[37] probably waiting eagerly for a ship to bring a copy of his first set of flute sonatas published by Oswald in London in 1756 under the auspices of the Society of the Temple of Apollo.

The German flute was introduced to Scotland by Sir Gilbert Elliot in 1725 and became immensely popular.[38] It was a simpler version of our modern flute and was called the German or transverse flute to distinguish it from the recorder which in those days was also called a flute. Its popularity, particularly in the hands of a sensitive player like John Reid, is disarmingly evoked in this letter from Alison Cockburn to Miss Cumming:

> Of all the sounds I ever heard (and my soul has soared to heaven before now), of all the sounds I ever heard, Colonel Reed's flute well, it is amazing the powers of it. It thrills to your very heart. He plays in any taste you please and composes what he plays. You know my taste is the *penseroso*, and so it is his. He played me five acts of a tragedy that went to my heart, and I spoke in to myself all the words of it. I would not let him speak the epilogue. You must hear him, Sylph. O how I regretted your absence tonight, but here is a letter will bring harmony enough to you. My niece Clerk was so good as entertain me with Colonel Reed tonight. He is a gentle, melancholy, tall, well-bred, lean man; and, for his flute, it speaks all languages. But those sounds that come from the heart to the heart – I never could have conceived it. It had a dying fall – I was afraid I could not bear it when I heard it perfectly. I can think of nothing but that flute, so good-night, good Sylph.[39]

Reid composed twelve sonatas which are still popular with flautists. *Solo V* in the first set uses the same descending figure to initiate each movement, *Solo VI* of the second set is more showy, ending with a minuet and variations, and another with many attractions is *Solo II* of the second set, which is clearly Scottish in the third movement.

Example 21. REID: SOLO II, 2ND SET, 1762

Reid will have had the thought of James Oswald, its publisher, kept well in mind by the fact that one of Oswald's own compositions – *Lovely Nancy* – was used by the British military in America as a signal for retreat. We have already mentioned Oswald's own trumpet marches for the English and Welsh militia, but Reid, as a military man himself, wrote marches, some of which remain popular to this day. His march for the Third Regiment of Foot, *Lord Amherst's,* was published by Robert Bremner in 1778, complete with German flutes (or oboes), two clarinets, two horns and a bassoon, and in America in 1807. Reid's sojourn in the New World was no mere formal affair of land acquisition, parade-ground marches and military balls. He took part in the capture of Montreal from the French in 1760, was wounded in two places in the capture of Martinique, suffering 'a violent contusion on one thigh which for several days threatened mortification' and saw his young brother, Alexander, killed in Cuba in the same year – 1762. It was from Montreal that he returned to make an excellent marriage to Susannah Alexander, whose father, ironically enough, had had to emigrate because of his support for the Old Pretender. But James Alexander left his daughter a wealthy and well-connected woman and between them Susannah and John Reid at one time owned at least thirty-five thousand acres of prime land on Lake Champlain, land Reid had fought over during the revolution. Perhaps they danced at their wedding to Lady Harriet Hope's reel, one of many which crossed the Atlantic, appeared in several American fife manuals and was mentioned in a collection of the *Most Fashionable Country Dances*, published in New Haven in 1799.[40] But the story of Scottish music in North America is beyond the scope of this book.

Reid eventually came back to Scotland, unable to keep proper control over his American estates. He was promoted to general and, having no heir to leave his fortune to, he decided instead to found a chair of music at Edinburgh University, where he had spent the happiest days of his life, studying law, for which he had no use. It was his erection of a Temple of Apollo in the Scottish instead of the English capital. On receiving the money, the University Senate proceeded to disperse it so unwillingly that they were finally challenged successfully in the courts and reluctantly accepted their responsibilities.[41] Just to show that we have not forsaken our old idiocies, we have recently reduced the number of university music departments in Scotland from five to two, a series of acts of breathtaking irresponsibility with potentially profoundly damaging effects to our culture and to the prospects for training and employment for our best musicians.

The first occupant of the Reid chair of music was John Thomson (see Chapter XVI); but let us salute the old General as he is best remembered to this day – as composer of the famous march, *The Garb of Old Gaul*, which still serves as the slow march of all Scottish battalions. Someone once carped about it being too full of sequences, but whoever it was has long since been trodden underfoot by its devotees.

Example 22. REID: THE GARB OF OLD GAUL

Reid died a true soldier. When the great assault upon the old social order came in the form of the French revolution and the Napoleonic wars, and Britain was threatened by invasion in 1803, General Reid received notice of it and the old fellow responded by writing that though in his eighty-second year and very deaf and infirm, he was willing to raise his feeble arm in the defence of his country (see Plate XXVII).[42]

The Napoleonic threat had its own roots in the French Revolution, and it was that revolution which had partly inspired Robert Burns to revive the old Scots march known as *Hey Tutti Tatti* and give it words – *Scots Wha Hae Wi' Wallace Bled*, maybe in the hope that it would inspire his fellow-countrymen to action. It is sung today, largely by people who would not offer their nation so much as a nose-bleed, never mind their feeble arm in the eighty-second year of their age. One is reminded of old Tobias Hume (see Chapter X) who, if he had had a fortune, might well have spent it on funding a chair of music. Perhaps we should call in the military.

CHAPTER XV

THE SCOTS MUSICAL MUSEUM
1760–1850

We ended the last chapter with the Napoleonic threat. But in many parts of Britain it was seen as a potential source of deliverance from a domineering, wealth-appropriating aristocracy. Musically speaking this led, in Scotland, to a rejection of styles associated with the upper classes, and to an emphasis (fully in accord with the new romantic movement) on traditional music and instruments. Perhaps this is one reason for old General Reid's bequest having been treated so shamefully.

The role of the military in music is not one to be sniffed at. The Highland bagpipes may have been temporarily suppressed as an instrument of war, but for the same reason they were later adopted, and the army still provides one of the main training centres for pipers in Edinburgh Castle, encouraging the playing of piobaireachd as well as regimental marches, reels and strathspeys. The Black Watch regiment was host to General Reid and it was from another member of the Black Watch, Mackay of Bighouse, that Captain Simon Fraser acquired much of the music for his *Airs and Melodies Peculiar to the Highlands of Scotland*, which is the second most important early collection of Highland music, and was first published in 1816 (see Plate 43). It is clear from the frontispiece and Fraser's introduction that the ideals of the Temple of Apollo were still very much alive. Niel Gow on the left and a member of the extinct bardic class on the right are crowned with laurels by a muse. In the background, the rural idyll continues untouched by Culloden, or laws against poaching, famine or emigration; and the obedient natives are pictured on the right rowing the tourists of Europe to Fingal's Cave. Unfortunately Fraser included no words, added bass lines to the airs, and probably regularised their ryhthms, though he was critical of Oswald and McGibbon for adding variations.

The most important collection of Gaelic music (also without song texts) is the Reverend Patrick MacDonald's *A Collection of Highland Vocal Airs*, the first part of which was gathered in by his brother Joseph (see Chapter XI), who wrote home from India with all the nostalgia of the Scot abroad. His letter is reproduced in the Preface: 'What would I give now, far from the theatre of those delightful scenes, for one night of my old beloved society, to sing those favourite, simple, primitive airs along with me? It would bring me back to the golden age anew.'

Planning the publication so that 'those sweet, noble, and expressive sentiments of nature, may not be allowed to sink and die away', he proposes a dedication to 'some chieftain of rank'. But he is sadly uncertain of their understanding of their own culture: 'If Sir James McDonald is not prejudiced, and rendered cold to the Highlands, by his corrupt English education, I hope he will duly prize it.'

In the end it was dedicated to The Highland Society in London, a body which did much to preserve Gaelic material, though its editorial and scholarly standards are a source of frustration to modern scholars, and not all of the vital material which passed through the hands of its members has been recovered.

The pastoral idyll which Joseph's letter evokes was, however, threatened with extinction. The industrialisation of agriculture, the alienation of land-owners from their tenants, the growth of industry and the first birth-pangs of a notion of social equality (in all of which Scotland took a leading part) changed the whole order of life,

Plate 43. TITLE PAGE OF SIMON FRASER'S *Airs and Melodies . . .*, 1816

producing social and environmental tensions yet to be resolved. Well aware of these rapid changes, people such as the MacDonald brothers, Simon Fraser and James Johnson set about preserving what they could of the past. In order to do so they had to fit it for publication, and the tastes of the time required the addition or alteration of words and of musical accompaniments. James Johnson produced his with figured basses by Stephen Clarke, which was not a good idea as they were going out of fashion, and George Thomson persuaded Beethoven, Haydn and others to give them fully written-out accompaniments with opening and closing 'symphonies' in beautifully produced but costly editions. In both these major projects one man was central – Robert Burns.

Burns participated fully in the romanticisation of Scotland and her sorrows and joys. That said, he also contributed more profoundly to the preservation of its true culture than anyone before him except perhaps James Oswald, whom he clearly greatly admired, for he used several of Oswald's tunes. He was doubly indebted for *Ae Fond Kiss* – to Oswald for the tune which may be by him or may be by Ruairidh Dall, we shall never know – and to Robert Dodsley for the starting point of the words which were in *Colin's Kisses* in *One Kind Kiss Before We Part*. But Burns's own text transcends all to create one of the great lyrics, worthy indeed of a place in the Temple of Apollo and surely undisputed by the traditionalists, however suspect its pedigree (see Plate 44).

Until I am complete master of a tune, in my own singing, (such as it is) I never can compose for it. – My way is: I consider the poetic Sentiment, correspondent to my idea of the musical expression; then chuse my theme; begin one Stanza; when that is composed, which is generally the most difficult part of the business, I walk out, sit down now and then, look out for objects in Nature around me that are in unison or harmony with the cogitations of my fancy and working of my bosom; humming every now and then the air with the verses I have framed; when I feel my Muse beginning to jade, I retire to the solitary fireside of my study, and there commit my effusions to paper; swinging, at intervals, on the hind legs of my elbow-chair, by way of calling forth my own critical strictures, as my pen goes on.[1]

Thus Robert Burns, explaining his method of composing lyrics for Scottish airs. One of his finest is *Ay Waukin' O* – the sad complaint of a girl who cannot sleep for thinking of her love. Burns wrote the words, basing them on an old fragment: 'I invariably hold it sacrilege to add any thing of my own to help out with the shatter'd wrecks of these venerable old compositions; but they have many various readings.'[2]

Plate 44. *Ae Fond Kiss*, FROM JOHNSON'S *Scots Musical Museum IV*, 1793

Well, a poet is allowed his poetic licence. In fact Burns added and altered a great deal – not always for the good, but in the case of *Ay waukin O* he produced a masterpiece of song in which it scarcely seems possible that words and music could have been conceived separately.

Burns was one of the very first poets to get to the heart of melody with words, and for that alone he is a poet of international stature, for it was a new thing to enter so deeply into the feeling and inner mood of a tune and realise it in language. Thomas Moore did the same thing for Irish melody, though perhaps with less distinction, and Schubert was the composer who more than any other created melody to match existing words with a similar act of artistic insight and

Example 1. AY WAUKIN' O (Johnson, *Scots Musical Museum III*, 1790)

Sim - mer's a pleas - ant time, Flowers of ev' - ry col - our; The wat - er rins o'er the heugh, And
I long for my true lov - er! Ay wauk - in, O, Wauk - in still and wear - y:
Sleep I can get nane, For__ think - ing on my Dear - ie.

2. When I sleep I dream.
When I wauk I'm irie;
Sleep I can get nane
For thinking on my Dearie.
Ay waukin &c.

3. Lanely night comes on,
A' the lave are sleepin':
I think on my bonny lad
And I bleer my een wi' greetin.
Ay waukin &c.

depth of response. Scotland never had a Schubert. She had her own body of incomparably lovely and lively melodies, so there was less of a gap to be filled than in the salons of Vienna.

On the other hand, in the salons of Vienna you could hear Beethoven sonatas, and nobody in Scotland was coming anywhere near that achievement. It seems we were deliberately turning our backs on anything that might seem to lead to it. The Earl of Kelly's symphonies and quartets and trios led nowhere. MacLean, Munro, Oswald, McGibbon — they might just as well not have bothered as far as their successors were concerned. Their beautiful music, their unique skill in adapting the native and continental styles to each other, left no grandchildren to learn from them in their old age. The arrival of that most revolutionary of instruments, the piano-forte, seems unmarked by even one sonata worth remembering, though one of its most famous manufacturers was a Scot – John Broadwood. At least a century was to pass before a Scot was to write a symphony or a string quartet to follow Kelly's. These are astonishing facts from a country so full of music and so gifted in song. One could parade the usual geographic, economic and political arguments and they would carry much truth with them. But there was little or no will to counteract them, with one fine exception in John Thomson (see Chapter XVI). Quite simply, the Scots turned their backs on the new musical architecture of Haydn, Mozart and Beethoven

and on anything that seemed to be leading towards it, in order to defend a musical environment which they believed was too beautiful and too vulnerable to risk.

> On Scotia's plains, in days of yore,
> When lads and lasses tartan wore,
> Saft Music rang on ilka shore,
> In hamely weed:
> But Harmony is now no more,
> And music is dead. . . .
>
> Now foreign sonnets bear the gree
> And crabbit queer variety
> Of sound fresh sprung frae Italy
> A bastard breed!
> Unlike that saft-tongu'd melody
> Which now lies dead. . . .
>
> MacGibbon's *gane: Ah! waes my heart!*
> The man in music maist expert
> Wha cou'd sweet melody impart,
> And tune the reed
> Wi' sic a slee and pawky art;
> But now he's dead. [3]

Why should Robert Fergusson, who wrote his *Elegy on the Death of Scots Music* in the 1770s have felt Scottish music was so threatened? The man whose death he laments (McGibbon) could be as Italianate as the next man. Among a few immigrant continental musicians, Domenico Corri, whose technique did not stretch to any great complications of style, was ready enough to publish Scottish airs, and Fergusson was him-self an opera-goer, a good singer, and very young for such doomsday views – he died at the age of twenty-four. So do we take this poem as anything more than a *jeu d'esprit*? The answer has to be 'yes'. Fergusson had a profound influence on Robert Burns and may well have partly inspired Burns's great work as a folk-song collector.

Nor was Fergusson alone in his unjustified paranoia. Unjustified because not only was this a period of tremendous collecting and preserving of Scottish poetry and song, it was also a period through which it survived in all its forms, whereas its supposed rival very nearly died altogether in Scotland. [4] *An Essay Towards the Improvement of the Musical Art* shows Alexander Mollison introducing a serious analysis of musical structures and their moral virtues (which harks back to Plato, the most restrictive of the Greeks) as justification for what seems to have been a bad case of inverted snobbery. It was published in Glasgow in 1798.

The writer of the following essay had, from early youth, felt the delightful effects of simple and pathetic melody. He frequently noticed, what many others no doubt have experienced, that different strains made different impressions on his mind – that some highly exhilarated the spirits, while some gently soothed the mind, inclining it to tenderness and pleasing melancholy; and others inspired it with a kind of mental courage and elevation, easier to be felt than expressed. He eagerly sought the enjoyment of those pleasant sensations: and, in the Scottish airs, he frequently found that simple and pathetic expression which suited his taste. After having long admired and enjoyed these, he bestowed some attention on that refined harmonic music which is in such general use at present. In this 'mingled world of sounds,' however, he found his expectations disappointed, and his feelings not a little tantalized. The intricate modulations of the melody, and the perplexing combinations of the harmony, seemed, with regard to expression, to be a mere chaos; ill suited to gratify the mind which had felt the strong influence of the music that moves the passions.[5]

Robert Burns defended his own tastes in similar fashion:

I am sensible that my taste in music must be inelegant and vulgar, because people of undisputed and cultivated taste can find no merit in many of my favourite tunes. – Still, because I am cheaply pleased, is that any reason why I should deny myself that pleasure?. – Many of our strathspeys, ancient and modern, give me most exquisite enjoyment, where you and other judges would probably be shewing signs of disgust. – For instance, I am just now making verses for Rothemurche's Rant, an air which puts me in raptures: and in fact, unless I be pleased with the tune, I never can make verses to it.[6]

In this opinion he had the support of Stephen Clarke who arranged the tunes for Johnson's *Scots Musical Museum*. Burns set to it the words *Lassie wi the Lint White Locks*. Johnson has been overshadowed by Burns, who became the driving force behind what grew to be a six-volume collection, but he had this to say to Johnson, and we should respect it: 'I can easily see, my dear Friend, that you will probably have four Volumes. Perhaps you may not find your account, lucratively, in this business; but you are a Patriot for the Music of your Country; and I am certain Posterity will look on themselves as highly indebted to your Publick spirit. – Be not in a hurry; let us go on correctly; and your name shall be immortal.'[7]

As soon as Burns had realised there was genuine interest in the project, he took his collecting very seriously: 'Inclosed I have sent you a sample of one of the old pieces that are still to be found among the peasantry in the West. I once had a great many of these fragments and some of these here entire; but as I had no idea then that any body cared for them, I have forgot them.'[8]

In a way he became a Scottish musical and poetic antiquarian, putting a high value on anything that could be declared ancient: 'the old song of the olden times, and which has never

been in print, nor even in manuscript, untill I took it down from an old man's singing.'[9]

The greatest success of all antiquarian efforts has, however, to be yielded to James MacPherson's *Ossian*. MacPherson gathered genuine and pseudo-Gaelic material, reworked it, added to it and published it in a kind of free verse which influenced many of the great writers in Europe and inspired many composers.[10] He was not a sham – no more so than Burns. Like Burns he mixed his own ideas with traditional material and it is not always easy to say where the one stops and the other begins. Like Burns, his influence was enormous, but it has not lasted except where he has been set to music by composers such as Schubert. Appropriately, one of the first in the field with settings of *Ossian* was James Oswald. Oswald was not a fake either. He collected, he altered, he added. Why should he not? As far as they were concerned the tradition was living and they were a part of it.

The sort of thing Mollison would have approved of by way of simple and pathetic melody that was at the same time a genuinely new invention might have been Oswald's *Songs of Selma*. They are definitely not traditional in either words or music, though imitating aspects

Example 2. OSWALD: SONGS OF SELMA (Johnson, *Scots Musical Museum II*, 1788)

of the tradition. The idiom is undoubtedly Scottish, but to match the looseness of the words the whole shape of it is much looser than Oswald's usual style, yet Burns was happy to see this kind of music and verse published in *The Scots Musical Museum,* whose title implies that the exhibits are of a certain age, not the products of yesterday. But we should not protest. It was not even an error for Burns and Johnson to call their collection a Museum. In their day the word still had something to do with the Muses and had not collected too much dust.

It was Oswald who was Burns's great predecessor as a collector, and one particularly fine tune which Oswald had gathered in, inspired Burns to his best. Burns knew it as 'a beautiful Jacobite air' and writing in 1791, just after the French Revolution and in the year of Mozart's death, he declared that 'When Political combustion ceases to be the object of Princes and Patriots, it then, you know, becomes the lawful prey of Historians and Poets.' It is *There'll Never Be Peace Til Jamie Comes Hame*, and in it he was looking to his own time and to Scotland's future as much as to her past.[11]

Example 3. THERE'LL NEVER BE PEACE 'TIL JAMIE COMES HAME (Johnson, *Scots Musical Museum IV*, 1793)

It would have been performed in the drawing-rooms of Edinburgh in Burns's day, harmonised by Stephen Clarke and accompanied by forte-piano, the smaller ancestor of our modern grand pianos. Fortepianos were becoming increasingly common and, since the bulk of those made in Britain were made by a Scot – John Broadwood – working in London, it is not surprising that these

instruments still predominate wherever forte-pianos survive. Niel Gow's son, Nathaniel, sold them along with almost every instrument you can think of, as well as sheet music, in his Edinburgh shop.

Burns was not a musician. He played the fiddle but, according to his sister: 'His playing was like his singing – rude and rough; But crooning to a bodies' sel' does weel enough.'[12]

Among Burns's many qualities, his ability to change register and be at home in different social milieus was important to his survival as a writer. But in his *The Jolly Beggars – A Cantata*, one senses he felt himself closest to home, and yet it attempts to do something that essentially cannot be done – reproduce a jolly evening in a pub. Reading it or singing it to oneself it is a marvellous and biting comedy; in performance it is arch, artificial, almost kitsch. The use of the words 'canatata' and 'recitativo' imply an eighteenth-century Italianate presentation with harpsichord, in imitation of *The Beggar's Opera* but in a situation where it is less appropriate and where the clash between the vigour of the Scots and the inevitable watering-down of the appropriate music by the use of any keyboard instrument grinds on the nerves. So too do the singers, always with inappropriate voice-production and accent and embarrassing inability to recreate low life in their acting. Some of Scotland's most terrible evenings have been dedicated to musical performances of this work. Nonetheless, it is in his work in Scots, in his native idiom, that Burns finds his true vigour, and he appreciated the same in others, not least among musicians. *Whistle O'er the Lave O't* is included in *The Jolly Beggars*: rendered with the true style of a James Dickie on fiddle, or a Jimmy MacBeath singing it, there is nothing to beat it for devil-may-care panache. But neither of these inimitable performers would ever have been able to work alongside a recitativo.

I am a fiddler to my trade,
And a' the tunes that e'er I play'd,
The sweetest still to wife or maid,
Was whistle o'er the lave o't.
At kirns and weddings we'se be there,
And Oh! sae nicely's we will fare;
We'll bouse about, till Daddie Care
Sings whistle o'er the lave o't.

Whistle O'er the Lave O't is one of many Scots songs with indelicate suggestions: 'fiddling' has

Example 4. JOHN BRUCE: WHISTLE O'ER THE LAVE O'T
(Oswald, *Caledonian Pocket Companion*, 1757)

always been a double-entendre and whistling a way of avoiding the overexplicit (see Plate 45).

Burns may not have been much of a fiddler, but he knew good fiddling when he heard it and was duly impressed by Niel Gow both as man and musician. Gow raised the social status of professional musician, which in those days was not very high. Even for a Haydn, a Mozart or a Beethoven, living by music was both financially and socially hazardous and they were working in one of the wealthiest environments in the world. For a man like Gow to hold his own amongst the aristocracy on whom he depended took, as Burns no doubt knew also, a good deal of moral courage.

One of Burns's greatest lyrics to a tune that has never really won our hearts as it deserves, but has all the honest dignity and simplicity that is looked for by so many and belongs to so few, is *A Man's a Man for a' That*.

Example 5. A MAN'S A MAN FOR A' THAT (originally 'Tho' Women's Minds'; Johnson, *Scots Musical Museum III*, 1790)

Plate 45. *The Fiddler of Glen Birnie*, BY JOHN KAY

That dignity and simplicity was one of the ideals of the masonic order which Burns was to join. There is a retrospective painting of the occasion which has gathered in the background a group of musicians who were also members (see Plate XXVI). Gow was one who would have truly qualified for membership in Burns's eyes at least: ' – Breakfast with Dr. Stewart – Niel Gow plays – a short, stout-built, honest Highland figure, with his greyish hair shed on his honest social brow – an interesting face, marking strong sense, kind open-heartedness, mixed with unmistrusting simplicity (see Plate XXV).'[13]

On one occasion when the ladies would not stop dancing although supper had been announced, Gow, who often had to play for over twelve hours at a stretch, cried out in exasperation: 'Gang down to your suppers, ye daft limmers, and dinna haud me reelin' here, as if hunger and drouth were unkent in the land – a body can get naething dune for you.'[14]

Niel Gow's strathspey *Miss Stewart of Grantully* is the sort of music he was best at and that was in such demand from the young ladies. It uses only the notes of the bagpipe scale, has as a structural feature the Scottish love of the double tonic, and with its Scotch snaps and dotted strathspey rhythms for which Scots fiddlers have developed their own bowing techniques, it can be said to represent the quintessence of Scottish dance melodies.

Dance was at last coming into its own. The kirk had so frowned upon it that even the

Example 6. NIEL GOW: MISS STEWART OF GRANTULLY
STRATHSPEY (*First Book of Niel Gow's Reels*, second edition, 1801)

instrument of dance, the fiddle, was denounced from pulpits. Harps were played in heaven, fiddles and bagpipes in hell: by such means do people who imagine themselves superior in morals, taste or culture attempt to do down the creative impulses of those with whom they cannot share, or whose music they do not understand. But at the end of the eighteenth century they had lost the struggle and the violin was triumphant on the dance floors of the big houses and the workers' cottages and the public assembly rooms, and the musicians migrated without difficulty from one to the other, playing as readily at a penny wedding as a society ball, often with an added bass line on the cello (see Plate 46).[15]

Native music was being cultivated alongside the native landscape, and there is a delightful account of the impression that music and nature could make on a young lady's mind, written as though they were almost interchangeable. It is a perfect expression of the genuine attractions of the Scottish aesthetic of the time.

Plate 46. *A Highland Wedding*, BY DAVID ALLAN, UNDATED

On this journey I first remember old Niel Gow being sent for to play for us at the inn at Inver – not Dunkeld – that little village we passed through, and went on to the ferry at Inver, which we crossed the following morning in a large boat. It was a beautiful ferry, the stream full and deep and dark, the banks overhung by fine timber trees, a glimpse of a newly-planted conical hill up the stream, only thick wooding the other way. I don't know whether this did not make more impression upon me than Niel Gow's delightful violin, though it had so over-excited me the night before that my father had had to take me a little walk by the river-side in the moonlight before I was rational enough to be left to sleep.[16]

There was often a topicality to the titles of the dance tunes that were composed profusely at this time. Gow's strathspey, *Highland Whisky*, his slow air *Farewell to Whisky*, and the strathspey *Whisky Welcome Back Again* were composed when in 1799 whisky distilling was forbidden, fortunately not for long. But Gow's musicianship had no need of topicality to take effect.

There is perhaps no species whatever of music executed on the violin, in which the characteristic expression depends more on the power of the *bow*, particularly in what is called the *upward* or returning *stroke*, than the Highland reel. Here accordingly was Gow's forte. His bow-hand, as a suitable instrument of his genius, was uncommonly powerful; and when the note produced by the up-bow was often feeble and indistinct in other hands, it was struck in his playing with a strength and certainty, which never failed to surprise and delight the skilful hearer. As an example may be mentioned his manner of striking the tenor C in 'Athol House'. To this extraordinary power of the bow, in the hand of great original genius, must be ascribed the singular felicity of expression which he gave to all his music, and the native Highland *gout* of certain tunes, such as 'Tullochgorum', in which his taste and style of bowing could never be exactly reached by any other performer.[17]

That was how *The Scots Magazine* recalled Gow in its obituary. *Tullochgorum* had been a favourite with Robert Fergusson too:

Fidlers, *your pins in temper fix,*
And roset weel your fiddle-sticks,
And banish vile Italian tricks
From out your quorum,
Nor fortes wi' *pianos mix,*
Gie's Tulloch Gorum'[18]

Gow was very much a family man and all his surviving sons were musical. We get a glimpse of his tenderness when Andrew was ill: 'If the spring were a little advanced and warmer, I would have Andrew come down by sea, and I will come to Edinburgh or Dundee to conduct him home. We will have milk which he can get warm from the cow, or fresh butter, or whey, or chickens. He shall not want for anything.'[19]

Andrew died before his father, and so too did William, whose reel, *Mrs Dundas of Arniston*, is still popular. But the deepest expression of family feeling from Gow reveals another side to his musicianship: 'He excels most in the strathspeys,

which are jigs played with a peculiar life and spirit, but he executes the laments or funeral music with a great deal of pathos.'[20]

Niel Gow's Lament for the Death of his Second Wife shows that he had depth of feeling as a composer as well as a performer. In the *Fifth Book* which his son published, was printed underneath the lament: 'They lived together upwards of thirty years, she died two years before him. She had no Issue.' It is one of the loveliest tunes ever written. It makes use of the rich tone of the violin's lowest string, which suited Gow's style, especially as he held the violin resting on his chest rather than his left shoulder. The tune's second half is unusual. Normally second strains are played twice. But Gow writes his out three times, each time with a slightly different way of ending it, the last one overflowing sorrowfully into the repeat of part of the first half as though reluctant to relinquish her memory. It is full of tenderness, and grace, and beauty.

Example 7. NIEL GOW: NEIL GOW'S LAMENT FOR THE DEATH OF HIS SECOND WIFE (*Fifth collection of Strathspeys . . .*)

Niel Gow's epitaph is as delightfully homely as he seems to have been. It reads:

Gow and time are even now,
Gow beat time, now time's beat Gow.[21]

It would be a mistake to think of Gow as a virtuoso fiddler. The music he played and composed required little in the way of shifting position for the left hand, and he was not a good sight-reader, though he could pick things up by ear reasonably quickly. He also played in a reasonably limited number of keys, though some, like William Marshall and Jamie Duncan were venturing further afield. Here a fiddling tailor complains: 'I've keepit dacent company a' my days and I'm nae gaun to change my ways noo. At this moment Jamie Duncan's playing 'Mony Musk' in four flats, and I say that the man that wad do that is fit for ony kin' o' rascality.'[22]

Despite such revisionism amongst some fiddlers, others pressed forward with a nod to the new ways. John Gow, for instance, tries his hand at introducing chromaticisms into a Scottish air. He called it *John Gow's Compliments to the Minstrels of Scotland* – and this extract from it works not badly at all:

Example 8. JOHN GOW: JOHN GOW'S COMPLIMENTS TO THE
MINSTRELS OF SCOTLAND (*Sixth Collection of Strathspeys . . .*)

William Marshall also explored more difficult keys and composed continental minuets as well as the strathspeys for which he was famous. Like Gow, he was dependent on the aristocracy and achieved a considerable status, though unprompted by revolutionary fervour. Marshall was a Tory and a clock-maker among other things and frequently put away his violin for months on end.[23] *Craigellachie Bridge* expresses his admiration for Telford's bridge and is one of his very best strathspeys.

The most famous of Niel Gow's sons was Nathaniel. We have heard of him as a State trumpeter and a publisher and music seller. He was also a composer, best remembered for his *Caller Herrin'*, which he says was 'Composed from the original cry of the Newhaven fishwives selling their fresh herrings in the streets of Edinburgh'.

Example 9. WILLIAM MARSHALL: CRAIGELLACHIE BRIDGE
(*Marshall's Scottish Airs*, 1822)

It comes complete with the street cry – 'Buy My Caller Herrin'', followed by the George Street bells at practice.

The Gows were not the only fiddlers. There were Daniel Dow, Alexander McGlashan, Simon Fraser of Gilnockie who made one of the first collections of Gaelic airs, giving their Gaelic titles, and there was Reid Rob MacIntosh, who taught Nathaniel. Like the Gows, they all composed, just as many fiddlers do today; and they survived in much the same manner, by playing

Example 10. NATHANIEL GOW: CALLER HERRIN'

for dances. Reels, strathspeys, jigs, hornpipes – we are still getting the same fun out of the music as Burns recorded two hundred years back.

A pigmy scraper wi' his fiddle,
Wha us'd at trysts and fairs to driddle,
Her strappin' limb and gaucy middle
(He reach'd nae higher,)
Hae hol'd his heartie like a riddle,
and blawn't on fire.

Wi' hand on hainch, and upward e'e,
He croon'd his gamut, ane, twa, three,
Then, in a Arioso key,
The wee Apollo
Set aff, wi' allegretto glee,
His giga solo.[24]

So Burns, like Oswald, also saw Scottish music as worthy of Apollonian status, though what he describes is decidedly Dionysiac. The dichotomy was never resolved. In the late Georgian withdrawing room, talk of the soil was welcome but the smell of it was not. Burns wrecked the words of *Dainty Davie* (see Chapter XII) with successive revisions,[25] cleaning it up for George Thomson's publications with their mostly unhappy arrangements of Scottish songs by Beethoven, Haydn, Pleyel, Kozeluth and Weber. These were the greatest composers of the day, but Scottish music largely defeated them. The basic structures of their music, the movement from one key to another, the reconciling of ideas that seem opposed to each other, were utterly at odds with the modal nature of Scottish song and its structural and melodic integrity. To many it seems that they gild lillies with great skill, intrusive harmonies, and foolishly fussy harpsichord accompaniment. Haydn's arrangement of *The Birks o' Abergeldie* has all these, though spirited claims have been made for some of their arrangements.[26] As for the Scots, few worked in any kind of European style. One exception was Alexander Campbell, whose setting of Goldsmith's *When Lovely Woman Stoops to Folly* was published around 1790.

Questions of authenticity have always had their embalmers on the one hand and their grave robbers on the other, and poor Alexander Campbell, who died in miserable poverty, is, one hopes, now spared their attentions. He came from Callander, was an organist in Edinburgh and taught Sir Walter Scott music for a spell in about 1783. He was also a composer, poet and arranger, and published a useful collection of Scots Song called *Albyn's Anthology*.

Campbell was born in 1764 – five years younger than Burns, six years older than James Hogg and ten years older than Robert Tannahill. But it was Tannahill who ensured that he would have a place in the hearts of all musical Scots by writing words for one of his tunes. The resulting song is *Gloomy Winter's Now Awa'*. Doubts surrounded it. The tune was first published by the Gows as *Lord Balgonie's Favourite* and described as 'a very old Highland tune'. But that means little. It is not that the Gows claimed melodies as their own that were not; but they were as slack as everybody was then about naming composers. As for the title, well, everything was somebody's favourite – it was a way of getting sponsorship or a small recompense for a new tune, and as for its being very old and Highland, it is possible that the first strain grew out of that background of musical thought, but the rest of the tune (which seems to be all of a piece anyway) does not fit that billing. Campbell claimed it as his own (see Plate 47).[27] Let him hold on to it, for it is a fine tune and well served by the equally sad figure of Tannahill whose songs were sung on the Braes of Gleniffer by many hundreds of people in Renfrewshire for years after he tragically drowned himself.

Example 11. ALEXANDER CAMPBELL: GLOOMY WINTER'S NOW AWA' (late eighteenth century)

Yet another famous literary figure closely involved with music was James Hogg. He was a good singer and not a bad violinist, though he claimed that he was 'so little a musician that I can scarcely be said to understand the first principles of the art'. He is remembered by musicians for his *Border Garland* and *Jacobite Reliques of Scotland*. Half of the Jacobite reliques are Hanoverian and the one that is most remembered and frequently rendered as the genuine

PLATE 47. ALEXANDER CAMPBELL'S ORIGINAL OF *Gloomy Winter's Now Awa'* FROM *Albyn's Anthology*, 1816

thing is *Donald MacGillivray* which Hogg admitted to be 'no other than a trifle of my own which I put in to fill up a page'. The fact remains that it is exceptionally good, making use of the characteristic double tonic effect with proud insistence.[28]

Example 12. JAMES HOGG: DONALD MACGILLIVRAY
(*Jacobite Relics*, 1819)

One of Hogg's best songs comes from the *Border Garland*. It is called *The Mermaid's Song* and is definitely intended for the Edinburgh ladies. Hogg wrote the words and the tune has been claimed for him also, though most of the tunes in that collection were traditional. The beautiful setting is by James Dewar and shows that sensitive adornment is perfectly possible.

Example 13. HOGG/DEWAR: THE MERMAID'S SONG
(*The Harmonicon*, 1829–31)

Sir Walter Scott was also profoundly involved in song. Alexander Campbell 'would never allow that I had a bad ear; but contended, that if I did not understand music, it was because I did not choose to learn it.'[29] Campbell was not a patient teacher, and he may have run into the same prejudice in Scott as in Alexander Mollison, for Scott aligned himself with Jeremy in Congreve's *Love for Love*, saying, 'I have a reasonable good ear for a Jigg but your solos and sonatas give me the spleen'.[30] And he wrote in his diary of his daughter: 'Anne is practising Scots songs, which I take as a kind of compliment to my own taste, as hers leads her chiefly to foreign music. I think the girl sees that I want and must miss her sister's peculiar talent in singing the airs of our native country. . .'[31]

Scott's other daughter Sophia was equally musical and copied ballad airs into her music book, amongst them *Jock o' Hazeldean*. Scott loved to hear her sing it, preferring her rendition to Madame Caradori's, and James Hogg reported that: 'She loved her father so . . . I shall never forget the looks of affection that she would throw up to him as he stood leaning on his crutch and hanging over her harp as she chaunted to him his favourite old Border Ballads or his own wild Highland Gatherings. . . .'[32]

Example 14. JOCK O' HAZELDEAN (*The Songs of Scotland*, 1854)

The words for *Jock o' Hazeldean* were substantially reworked by Scott himself and it was first published by his old teacher, Alexander Campbell. Its earliest known version is *My Lady Binnis Lilt*, from Lady Margaret Wemyss' lute manuscript of the 1640s. The tune is much altered but recognisable, and Scott has responded to it with understanding to produce a very beautiful song.

It is only at this period in the early nineteenth century that the term 'Border Ballad' became current, largely because Scott focused his attention on the narrative ballads of the Scottish border country with which he was so familiar.

With the transition from Burns to Scott we finally step over the threshold of the withdrawing room and firmly into the nineteenth-century approach to the setting of folk-songs. The piano-lid is opened, the handsome edition with rural scenes, vignettes of Burns and Highland Mary and other favourites is before us, lovingly edited by a George Farquhar Graham, or a John Thomson, a Finlay Dun or a J.T. Surenne. Their work does no more injury to the original tunes than did Stephen Clarke or any of the other publishers and arrangers. They continued to research the background of the tunes and words and, far

Example 15. MY LADY BINNIS LILT (*Margaret Wemyss Manuscript, 1648*)

from representing a Victorian insensitivity, they are direct descendants and inheritors of the ideals and productions of Ramsay and Burns. They adapted the native air with as much truth as society would allow them and, in cleaning up some of the lyrics, they echoed Burns himself. We do exactly the same today.

CHAPTER XVI

THE WITHDRAWING ROOM AND THE CONCERT HALL 1820–1920

The late eighteenth century saw the beginnings of the period known as the Romantic. The belief in fixed discoverable laws of nature and of art gave way to a new faith which held more sacred the free and unique growth of individuals. Nature no longer required taming; instead she was worshipped in her wildest moods. Scotland, being particularly experienced in the wildness of nature, became a tourist attraction as well as a major stimulus to the movement, its writers from McPherson to Byron being in many ways its pioneers, and its painters eagerly taking up the new awareness. Of our composers, only John Thomson can be said to have contributed significantly to the new movement. Much later in the nineteenth century he was followed by Mackenzie, MacCunn and Wallace, none of them far behind their continental models and deserving far more attention than they get, but not one of them as brilliantly talented or stylistically versatile as Thomson.

For composers, this was the period in which the tonal system, based on varying material by repeating it in different keys or by using new keys to introduce new ideas, began to expand into large structures of which the symphony became the symbol, though everything from sonatas to whole operas was planned on tonal schemes, journeying from key to key by a process known as modulation. The schemes became increasingly complex, the keys far more remote than the A flat major complained of by a Scots fiddler (see Chapter XV). We have seen that the Earl of Kelly used F sharp major which was positively outlandish in his day. The harmonies also became more and more enriched. Key changes were sometimes made without any preparation, which, in the hands of a Schubert, is a technical equivalent to changing gear smoothly without using the clutch. In the nineteenth century the orchestra also became very much larger and this increase in scale affected all types of music.

Scottish composers did little or nothing to initiate this process. The higher degree of modalism in their melodic inheritance already partly satisfied the need to vary the certainties of one key by reaching out towards others, for the harmonic implications of many Scottish melodies are ambiguous. The continued vigour of her traditional music also partly supplied a musical response to the interest in romantic landscape and subject-matter, for it was thought of as 'wild' and therefore natural. The response of the few classically trained musicians in Scotland to the vast upheaval of style and increase of scale which romanticism brought, was largely to continue arranging the native airs, but for the drawing-room voice with pianoforte accompaniment. John Thomson (1805–1841), Finlay Dun (1795–1853), James Dewar, J.T. Surenne, and many others, kept that faith with tradition. Alone amongst them, John Thomson worked towards handling grander forms calling for the large-scale planning which traditional music could not provide, save in piobaireachd, though Finlay Dun may have composed two symphonies, now lost.

The development of the pianoforte was in itself a major revolution in music. By the 1830s this relatively new instrument was common property and many people were able to study not just piano music but all sorts of works arranged for piano which required its extended range. It had opened up a new world in which a huge and subtly graded variety of pitch, volume and colour could be drawn out of one instrument in a way never dreamt of before, and its popularity was deserved. Not even on the organ could such subtle gradation be achieved. In any case it was only in the nineteenth century that organs of any size became widely available in Scotland as they had often been frowned on by the presbyterian churches. Some of the new arrangements for pianoforte appeared in a London music journal, *The Harmonicon* and, in Glasgow, William Hamilton published the first Scottish music journal, the *British Minstrel*, pioneering cheap music supplements in penny and twopenny numbers in 1842.

A charming insight into that new world of pianoforte sound is provided by the letters of the precocious nine-year-old, Catherine Paton Jameson. We can imagine her in 1830, practising a bagatelle in the withdrawing room of the Jameson household in Royal Crescent, Edinburgh. The *Bagatelle* is by young John Thomson. The title

Example 1. JOHN THOMSON: BAGATELLE (unidentified printed source)

means that it is a mere trifle – a tiny possession not to be taken too seriously. Three years earlier Ludwig van Beethoven had died and among his late works he included some of these so-called trifles – mere bagatelles – but they are profound and subtle in their simplicity and are certainly not to be trifled with. Nor is John Thomson's. It owes something to Beethoven. A trusting simplicity, breathing easily and speaking kindly with just one small show of temperament.

Catherine Jameson knew John Thomson well:

> Edinburgh November the 5th 1830. My dear Tom, I am very busy with my lessons. I go on much in the same style as when you was here. John Thomson sent me a present of a Rondo of his composition it is very difficult he told me he saw you in Paris. I wish it had been me, how I should love to see you. Mr. Hargitt has given me a present of two pieces of his composing they are very pretty. I have played a beautiful duet with Mr. Hargitt won't it be delightful when you come back to play it with you. Rachel was telling me you are to take lessons on the Piano Forte. I hope you have not forgot . . . I send a kiss to you with my kindest love . . . your affectionate cousin Catherine Paton Jameson.[1]

Thomson wrote the *Rondo* that Catherine Jameson (not surprisingly) found so hard to play, when he was only twenty-three, and it says much for his own keyboard and composition abilities. The *Rondo* is typical of the neglect which Thomson's music has suffered. It had to be transcribed by myself from his manuscript copy, once owned by Mendelssohn, and was composed for a Miss Bannerman, who remains unidentified; but she too must have been a good player. Clearly influenced by Beethoven, especially in the lovely use of the crystalline textures of the upper notes of the piano, it has its own poise, power and freshness; and it confidently blends display with the beautiful and expressive simplicity of the recurring rondo theme.

In a letter to Catherine Jameson, Thomson reveals himself as a man of modesty and self-criticism:

> My dear Miss Catherine, I have been equally astonished, delighted and gratified with your gift – astonished at the early development of your musical fancy – delighted with the manner in which you have expressed it – and gratified that I should be considered worthy of a copy of The Fantasia. The composition, though it may exhibit signs of inexperience, is very good, and gives promise of much greater things. But while I say thus much allow one who takes and trusts to take, a lively interest in your future career, one, who, however undeservedly, has been somewhat schooled in the applause of indulgent and partial friendship, to warn you against admitting the influence of such approbation to too great an intimacy with your feelings . . . I tell you that had not my first attempts at composition been thoroughly laughed at I should have been a miserable scribbler . . . To

Example 2. John Thomson: Rondo (*Reid Library manuscript*)

Allegro Moderato
(Rondo theme)

part of first episode

the hearty laughing which my maiden efforts raised, do I owe, therefore, any accuracy in composition which I may now possess. Observe I do not mean to place myself in parallel with you by any means; I was 14 before I began to write, you are now but 9 . . . I am merely anxious to make you avoid little inaccuracies in your harmonies: the defects in the design of your Fantasia I must leave to abler hands. I shall call on you when you please: and believe me With every good wish Your sincere friend John Thomson. 29 Melville Place 7th July 1830.[2]

John Thomson was one of the greatest hopes in Scottish music and his early death was one of our greatest losses. Born at Sprouston in Roxburghshire in 1805, he was just twenty-five when he wrote that letter. His father was Minister of St George's in Edinburgh and, with the aid of R.A. Smith, was responsible for a high standard of singing in church and composed several psalm tunes, so young Thomson was brought up in musical surroundings. With a recommendation from Mendelssohn he studied composition in Germany and eventually became Scotland's first Professor of Music, occupying the Chair at Edinburgh University which was endowed by General Reid and whose portraits still adorn the Reid School (see Chapter XIV).

Thomson died before completing even one year in his post, leaving a widow and a quantity of music largely forgotten.

His early works demonstrate his ability to absorb many styles: a Polish *Mazurka,* full of fire and stiff military rhythms; a *Waltz* marked 'con fuoco' and wildly excited; two Italian concert arias which would sound well in the best Italian company, and songs of all sorts. All these are works for the withdrawing room, which was probably Thomson's main outlet in his early days when Scotland still had no chair of music, no academy of music, no court to commission music, no ambassadors to carry it abroad. The stable institutions necessary for the production of compositions on an ambitious scale were almost wholly absent, and music education was largely confined to the middle and upper classes in the privacy of their own homes where singing and pianoforte were favoured. But the drawing-room studies should not be underestimated, when a ten-year-old Catherine Jameson, as well as composing and playing the piano, was getting singing lessons: 'I often dream you are here when I awake I am vexed to find it is but a dream. I have composed several songs and Waltzes, some of them are thought rather pretty. I have only had five or six lessons of singing since you went away. My voice is much as it was.'[3]

She also reveals that her standard at the piano was much higher than one might expect. Weber's *Concertstuck* is extremely difficult and if she was able to play it in public she must have been a prodigy in the making: 'I am fonder of music than ever. Oh! had I a pair of ten league boots to carry me to Berlin to see yourself and hear the delightful music . . . Professor gave a grand concert on Thursday last . . . I played two pieces on the Piano Forte, the first was a Concertstuck by Weber with orchestral accompaniments . . . I am very partial to Signor Rumpini as a master, my Italian singing is much easier now from understanding the language.'[4]

Singing in Italian was still common – as was composing settings of it, though Thomson never composed an Italian opera. Neither did Beethoven, though he had lessons in setting Italian. Thomson's own background in singing will have largely been formed by the church where choral singing was in a bad way until reformed by R.A. Smith. Smith, born in England, was the son of a Paisley weaver.

The boy returned to Paisley as a weaver too, but became precentor and music teacher at the abbey where he improved the choir at the cost of silencing the congregation, save for one old woman. 'Na, na,' she said. 'She would not be silent, but would praise the Lord wi' a' her micht, whether she kent the tune or no.'[5] Perhaps she prompted Smith's move to St George's where he died six years later aged forty-nine. The Thomson family were deeply distressed and John Thomson composed a funeral anthem, untraced. He wrote to the famous ballad collector, James Motherwell: 'As for music, I would not allow myself to put down a note until it came without compulsion. I hope I have in some measure succeeded.'[6]

Such was the loss felt at the death of Smith that no less than 35 people helped to watch over his grave. It being January 1829, they watched from four in the afternoon until dawn to preserve his body from grave-robbers such as Burke and Hare.

'I and Mrs Smith are quite overwhelmed with the behaviour of the Paisley band, which I think has done honor to itself . . . When they heard on Sunday that Mr Smith's two eldest boys were nightly watching the body, they insisted on relieving them at 12 and continued at their sacred post during the rest of the night!'[7]

But 1829 brought a new and more important musician into Thomson's life – and Catherine Jameson's: 'I have got several pieces composed by Mr Felix Mendelssohn, they are highly thought of by all the scientific people here, I think they are quite beautiful.'[8]

The Scottish tour by Mendelssohn and his companion, the poet Klingemann, was one of several prompted by the enormous success of Scottish literature in which a visit to Sir Walter Scott was obligatory. Mendelssohn wrote home from Edinburgh in July 1829. 'Beloved Ones, – It is late at night, and this is my last day in the town of Edinburgh. To-morrow morning we go to Abbotsford to see Sir Walter Scott; the day after to-morrow, into the Highlands. The windows are open, for the weather is beautiful and the sky full of stars. Klingemann, in shirt sleeves, sits by my side writing. So much for scenery.'[9]

The pair got little out of Sir Walter, whose household had become a tourist office. Whether Thomson made the pilgrimage to the man to whom all European literature and many composers looked for their material is not known; but his setting of Scott's *Yes Thou May'st Sigh* (sung by Louise in *The Fair Maid of Perth*) is a fine one, capturing the strange mood of false reassurance, with its uncanny staccato arpeggios on the piano, the uncompromising low note for the voice, and the strange evanescent ghostly cadence at the end – a superb little miniature.

The song could have been heard by Mendelssohn, for he met Thomson and they formed a friendship which led to Thomson's travelling to Germany to study.

The bearer of this letter is a young man, Thompson, who has shown me much kindness here, and whom I have often had the pleasure of meeting at a mutual friend's. I earnestly beg of you to smooth down for him as much as possible any difficulties he may encounter in Berlin. I regret to say that he speaks neither German nor French, so you will have to do as you were in Edinburgh, and talk English through thick and thin. He is very fond of music; I know a pretty trio of his composition and some vocal pieces, that please me very well. I beg you the more to be kind to him, and believe the more that you will fulfil my request, as I now know by experience how comforting it is to be kindly received in a strange land.[10]

The trio that Mendelssohn admired was probably the *C Major Trio*, an excellent work whose revival is long overdue. Thomson made a piano arrangement of the adagio which was published in *The Harmonicon* in 1832. It is deeply serious and beautifully sustained, with a fine central section generous in its nobility. On the other hand, Mendelssohn might also have had a look at Thomson's *Trio Number 2 in G Minor*, written in 1826, by which year Thomson had already had some instruction from Cramer and Moscheles, for he notes on the title page that they had made revisions in pencil, though the revisions are minor ones. Cramer and Moscheles were then based in London, the latter having known Beethoven. There were several Scottish contacts with Beethoven. John Smith from Glasgow visited him, Donaldson from Edinburgh attempted to commission a trio for three pianofortes from him, and George Thomson (no relation of John Thomson) had already received and published a number of arrangements of Scottish, Irish and Welsh songs as well as attempting to commission an overture, violin sonatas and so on. Of the Scots songs, Beethoven declared that two of them had pleased him very much and that he had composed them 'con amore'.[11] We need not be surprised, then, at John Thomson's knowledge of the latest developments in musical style, to which the *Trio Number 2* bears witness. The first movement has an impressive slow introduction and the allegro moderato contrasts nervous urgency with a second subject of Schubertian warmth.

Example 3. JOHN THOMSON: TRIO IN G MINOR (*Reid Library manuscript*, 1826)

The second movement is a minuet, fierce and delicate by turns, and the warm melodic conversation of the andantino grazioso features the cello. The last movement is an allegro molto appassionato full of hectic and fearful energy followed by a glowing first episode.

It would be easy to claim that Mendelssohn has had a say in this, but it was written in 1826, when Mendelssohn (the younger of the two men) was seventeen. Mendelssohn was undoubtedly fully fledged at seventeen but his style at that time can simply not have been known to Thomson, himself at twenty-one a remarkable musical

prodigy. It is easy for commentators to seek refuge in parallels with the best-known composers and cry 'derivative'. But in this instance one may legitimately assert that it could just as well have been the other way round and young Mendelssohn have picked up a bit from the brilliant but extraordinarily modest and unassuming young Scot whose works he perused in Edinburgh.

As befits a composer writing at a time when romanticism was at its height, much of Thomson's music is dark and tempestuous, or gloomy and brooding. But he was perfectly capable of good fun. His *Cheerful Glee* for three voices makes it its business to dispel the darkness and if it will not go away it will be drowned in wine. He composed it on 10 March 1833, presumably with the intention of putting winter thoroughly behind him.

If Thomson was a pleasant young man, so too was Mendelssohn. Unspoilt by the silver spoon in his mouth, like Thomson of course, he burnt himself out, always helping others, ready to oblige, and Thomson was one of those whom he assisted:

> Show him what will interest him; Fanny should play a good deal to him, he must hear her songs performed by Rebecca; give him a good notion of music abroad. Father once blamed me at Paris for not being kind enough to strangers, and justly so, I believe. But I have got over that fault now that I am far away from you; I have learnt to appreciate it. In such a spirit I offered him the letters to Berlin, for which he did not ask; now you must continue to befriend him.[12]

No doubt they did, but Thomson's stay in Europe is scarcely documented. We are told in early music dictionaries (but never with any supporting material) that Thomson met Schumann.[13] In 1837, Schumann was regularly in the company of a beautiful eighteen-year-old Scottish pianist – Robena Laidlaw – and here again we come to a remarkable musical coincidence. Thomson, apparently in Leipzig in 1838, dedicated a copy of his *Drei Lieder* – three songs – to Mendelssohn, and they are not only in the style of Schumann but are as fine as any song Schumann wrote, the trouble here being that practically every one of Schumann's songs was composed in or after 1840 – two years after Thomson's songs had been published in Frankfurt. Of course Schumann's piano style could have influenced Thomson, but the feeling for the voice, the evocative use of postludes for the piano, the relationship between voice and piano – these are all Thomson's. The first song is a setting of a German translation of Byron's *There Be*

None of Beauty's Daughters. The way the voice floats onto the surface of the piano prelude and is supported by it throughout, hanging longingly onto the word *'traumen'* – lulled by the winds that seem dreaming – is one of the most beautiful things in all song. Byron gave his poem the title *Stanzas for Music*. It could not have been more perfectly set.

Example 4. JOHN THOMSON: DREI LIEDER (Leipzig, 1838)

The second song is a setting of Schiller's *Canadian Death Song* – a wild burial scene of a hunter whose possessions are to be interred with him in the frozen wastes. The music is virile, dramatic and goes past us like a hurricane. It is all that Schiller could have asked for.

The final *Serenade* sets a poem by von Uhland; a conversation between a sick child and her mother. The child wakes hearing distant sweet sounds. The mother says there is nothing to hear. The child replies that the music is not of this earth and that the angels call her 'So, Mother Dear, Goodnight'. Thomson suggests

the distant call of the music simply and effectively with a broken chord that is allowed to die away to nothing each time. The melody is a beauty and the end perfectly judged.

It is not the place of this book to explore the extraordinary influence of Scottish history, literature and landscape on continental composers. It is, however, a measure of that influence that Thomson, a Scot, should set a poem written in English by Byron, a Scot, in a German translation. But it was Mendelssohn, above all, whose tour of Scotland has remained a kind of touchstone for us, who caught something of the mood of the country, though none of the continental composers shows any serious understanding of a Scottish musical idiom (nor for that matter does Thomson outside his folksong settings). Mendelssohn at least visited the country and reacted sensitively to it and the *Hebrides Overture* is as great a musical compliment as we could ask for, but there was the *Scotch Symphony* as well:

In the evening twilight we went today to the palace where Queen Mary lived and loved; a little room is shown there with a winding staircase leading up to the door; up this way they came and found Rizzio in that little room, pulled him out, and three rooms off there is a dark corner, where they murdered him. The chapel close to it is now roofless, grass and ivy grow there, and at that broken altar Mary was crowned Queen of Scotland. Everything around is broken and mouldering, and the bright sky shines in. I believe I found to-day in that old chapel the beginning of my Scotch symphony. Now farewell![14]

Thomson did not live to write a Scotch Symphony; or maybe he felt, sensibly enough, that Mendelssohn had done the job for him. Instead he took a hero from the first century BC Germanic wars against the Romans – Hermann – and made a highly successful opera (*Hermann* or *The Broken Spear*) which was performed at the English Opera House in October 1834. Only the Overture is performed these days, but if any of the rest of the music comes up to its quality, then we should be hearing it too, for this overture is worthy of a regular place in the repertoire. Dark, sombre, in the style of Weber's high German romanticism, it shows yet again that Thomson could absorb a style with consummate ease and produce fine music in the process. The orchestration is outstanding – confident, sonorous and colourful. But what this music chiefly demonstrates is that Thomson's ideas are themselves orchestral – broad gestures, powerful unanimous statements, shaped and paced to allow the great beast that an orchestra really is, to breathe deep and true. Its lyricism is as expansive as its energy and high drama which releases itself at the last minute into a brilliant D major.

We should make more of this young man who could pick up, and in some cases seems to have anticipated, any style he chose – Italian aria, Mendelssohnian geniality and delicacy, Weberesque dark romance, Schumannesque sensitivity; who arranged Scots songs; who wrote the world's first programme notes; who first sat in our first chair of music. He was also loved in his day, for his affectionate nature and good temper.[15] That warm relationship with his colleagues is enshrined in the part-song *When Whispering Winds*. On 28 October 1836, the Edinburgh Professional Society of Musicians held its first annual dinner. John Thomson wrote a glee for five voices to celebrate the occasion. *When Whispering Winds* is essentially an ode to music. The vocal writing is luscious and Thomson has lavished attention on it. The glee was a kind of part-song immensely popular throughout the nineteenth century but kept alive nowadays only

by devotees. Thomson's is a beautiful example of the genre, and it is a pleasure to think of the musicians gathered together with their glasses ready, their bellies filled, their eyes moist as they indulged in this gorgeous composition, the composer himself no doubt guiding them through its many subtle beauties.

Thomson left a widow – the daughter of the principal of Edinburgh University – but they had only enjoyed a few months of married life. Many of his works are waiting to be resurrected: several songs; three operas including an overture; a string quartet; a Benedictus and Osanna for solo voices, chorus, semi-chorus and orchestra; a flute quartet; a flute concerto and a piano trio.[16] He must have been a prodigious worker; and he had taken his university duties so seriously one suspects he drove himself into the ground.[17] I hope those who stood by his grave to guard his young corpse from the body-snatchers did their duty by him more faithfully than we in the music profession have done; but I suppose we are all fragile.

Not fragile was the composer Alexander Campbell Mackenzie, born in 1847 of a musical family and living into his late eighties, though he did have to spend a year in Italy in middle life to recuperate from over-work. At fifteen years of age he actually saw Hare, then old and blind, selling bootlaces and matches in Trafalgar Square.[18]

Mackenzie was one of the most important, and is one of the most inexcusably neglected, British composers of his age. He met Liszt, who admired his compositions;[19] was a close friend of Sarasate, who played his *Violin Concerto* and *Pibroch Suite* world-wide;[20] was intimate with Paderewski, for whom his *Scottish Concerto* was commissioned and who played it widely;[21] and knew Grieg who, well aware of his own Scottish Greig ancestry, expatiated on the similarity between Norwegian and Scottish traditional music after hearing Mackenzie's *Burns Rhapsody*.[22] Hans von Bulow so admired Mackenzie's *Piano Quartet* that he sought out the composer in Edinburgh to congratulate him, and took part in a performance in Germany shortly after, as well as conducting, as did Richter, a number of Mackenzie's works.[23]

Mackenzie's memoirs, *A Musician's Narrative*, are among the most entertainingly informative of their kind. His self-knowledge and self-criticism are endearing, and his intellectual,

Example 5. JOHN THOMSON: GLEE – WHEN WHISPERING WINDS (*Reid Library manuscript*, 1836)

Plate 48. SIR ALEXANDER CAMPBELL MACKENZIE, OCTOBER 1890

composed popular Scots tunes.[27] The Scottish aesthetic in favour of traditional melody remained as strong as ever. When Mackenzie's father died in 1857, the publisher, James Ballantyne, ended his memorial poem thus:

While Scotland mourns her minstrel gone,
And all our breasts with sorrow thrill,
Let's pray that his young orphan son
In time his father's place may fill:
And thus our country still shall be
The home of simple melody.

He added a note: 'Mr Mackenzie's eldest son, a boy of ten years of age, inherits his father's musical talent, and is being educated in Germany.'[28] The place of study was Sondershausen, which had a superb ducal orchestra and in its choice of repertoire was far in advance of most of Europe.[29] Mackenzie was appointed as a second violinist in this orchestra at the age of eleven, so he was clearly an outstanding young musician, also gaining invaluable experience in the art of writing for orchestra, in which he was a master though rarely an adventurer. He was fifteen before he returned to continue his studies at the Royal Academy of Music in London, having to re-learn English, and earning a living improvising piano accompaniments in music hall. As a student he passed off one of his piano improvisations at an exam as a Schubert *Impromptu,* deceiving the RAM principal, George Macfarren.[30] Years later Mackenzie was to reign as principal himself for no less than thirty-six years; he set the institution back on its feet and set up the Associated Board whose examinations are still the standard test of young musicians in Britain (see Plate 48).

One of his first published works was the 1873 *Piano Quartet.* It should stand proud in the repertoire, not only as a beautifully crafted work, but one of depth and character. The great-hearted striding generosity of the first movement with its exalting preparation for the recapitulation (Ex6) is followed by a scherzo worthy of the best of Schumann, with whose style it has much in common without any hindrance to its blend of delicacy and warmth. The fine variations, derived from a subtle canzonetta theme, are full of temperament and instrumental character; and the Finale has the same joyous spread of feeling one gets from the finest works of the Romantics.

moral, and human awareness are manifest also in his music, to which may be added sensuality and vigour. At his best he can achieve great things. We can take Liszt at face value when, after hearing him conduct Liszt's own *St Elizabeth,* he declared to Mackenzie, 'Well, perhaps after all you would have written it better yourself.'[24]

Liszt also admired Mackenzie as a conductor.[25] Even Bernard Shaw (often very critical of Mackenzie) melted once or twice – and Shaw was prepared to sacrifice everything except a well-turned sentence or a flippant remark for the sake of journalistic effect.[26]

Mackenzie, like Thomson, came from a musical family and studied in Germany; but unlike Thomson he incorporated Scottish idioms into his large-scale works, being one of the pioneers of the musical nationalism of the latter half of the nineteenth century, which was to release such creative energy all over Europe. His father was a Scots fiddler, and father and son both

Example 6. MACKENZIE: PIANO QUARTET – FIRST
MOVEMENT (Allegro, ma moderato e tranquillo; Leipzig, 1873)

The *Benedictus* from his *Six Violin Pieces Opus 37* is an expressively extended melodic line which does indeed bestow a blessing, its rich textures varied by passages of clarity, its warm harmonies never allowed to cloy. It is not difficult to play and should be a favourite for

Example 7. MACKENZIE: BENEDICTUS, 1888

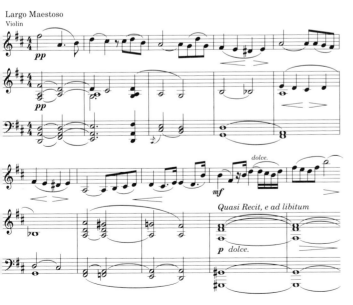

amateurs and professionals in its arrangement for small orchestra.

The *Larghetto and Allegro* for cello and orchestra was arranged in the reverse direction for cello and piano. The cello writing is outstanding, tender and melting but with a suggestion of underlying sadness. It was composed in Edinburgh in 1874 for the cellist Daubert, at a time when Mackenzie was exhausting himself teaching well over a hundred pupils a week; in the Ladies College he had eight of them seated at eight pianos simultaneously, which shows that they were well ahead of us in resources, if not teacher/pupil ratios.

Wanting to become a full-time composer, exhausted and ill, and with a wife and child, Mackenzie quit Edinburgh for Florence, with orders from his doctor and recommendations from von Bulow. It was in Italy that he wrote his one relatively successful opera, *Columba*, celebrating the life of St Columbanus of rowing-song fame (see Chapter II). The Overture is imposing, but only a revival will tell us if the opera itself is strong enough. Also from the Italy years came his finest oratorio, *The Rose of Sharon*, a setting of parts of *The Song of Solomon*. The form had been developed in particular by Handel as a way of providing a semi-dramatised musical evening when the theatres were shut, but it became one of the best ways for a composer to gain a reputation in the later nineteenth century, there being many huge choral societies eager for new works (see Plate 49). Chorus, soloists and orchestra were employed to outline some grand series of events with passages of reflection and comment, the large majority of oratorios being on religious subjects. Mackenzie was pelted with roses at the first performance of *The Rose of Sharon*, the audience clearly understanding that the Prologue and Epilogue explaining the religious allegory were not to the point. Mackenzie himself knew what the work was about:

. . . its much-disputed spiritual significance attracted me in a lesser degree than the glowing imagery of the Eastern love story . . . When Bache once spoke of the musical settings of these passages as 'sugary', I replied that I meant them to be as sweet as I could possibly make them . . . in a completely revised edition [published in 1910] with the omission of Prologue and Epilogue, some of the words rewritten and a new Part IV, any suggestion of a religious basis disappeared.[31]

Plate 49. Berlioz's Messe des Morts, being performed in Glasgow in 1885 by 'Twym'

In many ways it shows us that the Victorians were well aware of the joys of making love, for it is full of delicious yieldings which compare favourably with our own tendency to aggressive posturing. The awakening of the Sulamite which opens Part III creates an atmosphere of ravishing sensuality with the simplest of musical means and not a hint of Wagner, and in more innocent mood, the setting of 'The Lord is my shepherd' is as fresh and beautiful and trusting as the words deserve. (See Examples 8 and 9.)

Fun, grandeur and warmth are the guiding characteristics of his concert overture *Britannia*. Mackenzie describes it as nautical. It has references to *The Sailor's Hornpipe* and *Rule Britannia*, and an opening of naval gunfire on the timpani which bursts into a splendidly rhythmical allegro contrasted with calmer lyrical seas. It should be regular fare on the last night of the Proms, having the best characteristics of Britannic works without the bombastic chauvinism of most of them.

Mackenzie also made distinguished contributions to works for soloist and orchestra. *The Scottish Concerto* for the great pianist, Paderewski, is powerfully energetic, as well as infused with Scottish lyricism. The piano writing is brilliant and colourful and there are also moments of beauty and wit (Example 10). The *Pibroch Suite* for violin and orchestra (which has no real connections with piobaireachd) opens with an extended melodic line of inspired loveliness which Sarasate must have revelled in. Mackenzie's understanding of the orchestra and of works for soloist and orchestra will have partly derived from his training as an instrumentalist rather than a chorister or organist like his contemporaries in England. The *Violin Concerto* has also many beauties, though it could do with being shorter.

Mackenzie admired Wagner immensely, but there is always a lightness and dash about him on the one hand, or a kindly sentiment on the other, which he wisely left uncoloured by Wagner's powerful and more adventurous style. Mackenzie's main defect is that he lacks a cutting edge (a failing shared by Mendelssohn's more pedestrian works) and this leaves in the end an impression too comfortable to really stir us from our seats.

Mackenzie's was not a searching style. He allowed himself to become an establishment figure not just as Principal of the RAM, but as

Example 8. Mackenzie: The Rose of Sharon – Part III, The Sulamite's Dream, 1884

a composer too. His memoirs reveal not only that he thoroughly enjoyed being part of the establishment, but that he saw it as his business to perpetuate it. *A Musician's Narrative* concludes

Example 9. Mackenzie: The Rose of Sharon – Part II, The Lord is My Shepherd

Example 10. MACKENZIE: SCOTTISH PIANO CONCERTO, 1879

with an envoi that exposes a fundamental flaw in his intellectual grasp; an inability to realise that today's dissonance is often tomorrow's garden party music; and a failure to understand that the creative world is not a comfortable one. Beethoven and Wagner had both shocked the world in just the same way as Mackenzie seems to be shocked. He knew of Debussy, Stravinsky and Bartók. Not one of them is named. Instead he indulges in grumblings of a kind unworthy of his own great gifts and occasional great achievements. It is a pity, but it should not take away from our appreciation of his best works. There is much more to him than the honest and workmanlike, and in his most inspired moments he gives voice to the best qualities of an age and an ethos of Dickensian delights, which he himself realised in

his splendid overture for Dickens's *The Cricket on the Hearth*, which he made into an opera with spoken dialogue that might well prove to be a worthwhile revival.

Hamish MacCunn (1868–1916) was the son of a Greenock shipowner. Both his parents were musical and their son composed his first piece at the age of five. An oratorio, commenced at the age of twelve, was left incomplete for the very good reason that he got more fun out of fishing and sailing. At fifteen he won a scholarship to the Royal College of Music in London and there he stayed. He was a dashing young man who married the daughter of a Scottish painter, Pettie, who has immortalised him both as Bonnie Prince Charlie and as the preferred escort for the family governess strolling simpering between MacCunn with the sword-stick and some honest loser. The painting is called *Two Strings to Her Bow* (see Plate XXVIII), a costume piece in which the young lady looks insufferably smug.

MacCunn saw himself very much as the musician of the future, eschewing abstract music in favour of the new poetic and descriptive approach of Liszt, but with a delightful streak of plain thinking. Shaw interviewed him and got some splendidly dusty answers to questions such as who was his favourite composer: 'You might as well ask me which I like best, my arms or my legs.'

Or did he (as was Wagner's practice) write his own words for setting to music?: 'I have not the vocabulary. I can find music but not words. Besides, if I write the book, you will be expecting me to paint the scenery too, on the same principle.'

Finally, Shaw, aware he was meeting his match, said he 'had the hardihood to ask Mr MacCunn for his notions of press criticism'. '"I think," said the composer, fixing his eye on me to indicate that he felt confident of my approval, "that criticism, above all things, should not be flippant, because if it is, nobody respects it."'[32]

Game, set and match to Mr MacCunn.

Hamish MacCunn is cursed with the 'one work' syndrome. *The Land of the Mountain and the Flood* is an excellent piece repeated and re-recorded by lazy promoters and conductors. They should try *The Dowie Dens o' Yarrow*. It is scored with an exciting variety from the darkest to the most brilliant, and is unerringly and economically developed from a theme with a strong Scottish flavour. The ballad on which the piece is based tells of the murder of a knight by the seven brothers of the girl who loves, and dies of sorrow, for him. Shaw protested that being cast in sonata form it could not properly tell a story, but he ignores the sudden effect of the ending which comes as a powerful and unexpected check to the youthful confidence of the knight.

MacCunn has the ability to outline large melodic landscapes with great sweeping phrases which can turn a commonplace poem, such as *A Song of the South* into a great song, or open up a whole new vista by a simple change of harmony in *I Will Think of Thee My Love*. He wrote over one hundred and fifty songs during his short life as well as a major opera, *Diarmid*, which anticipates Debussy; but his masterpiece is *Jeanie Deans*, an opera which should have been a part of Scottish Opera's repertoire from the start. This, one of the finest of British operas, was revived by Opera West in 1986. It is based on Scott's *Heart Of Midlothian* which tells of Jeanie Dean's successful pleading for a pardon for her sister,

Example 11. MacCunn: I Will Think of Thee My Love
(*Album of Six Songs*)

Example 12. MacCunn: Jeanie Deans, Act IV Scene I, 1894

accused of child murder, and it moved one critic to say that 'the music is frankly astonishing . . . The Act One duet between Effie and Staunton is not far short in its style and effect of the great Siegmunde and Sieglinde duet from Valkyrie.'[33]

MacCunn can be at least as harmonically adventurous as Wagner, and his writing for voices certainly bears comparison, as does his ability to pace or vary the drama musically, as in the scene where Jeannie's impassioned pleading with Queen Anne in Richmond Park is contrasted with the charm of the madrigal sung by the queen's attendants. The crowd scenes are splendidly handled and there are moments of humour and also of great tenderness, as in the moving and nostalgic aria for Effie thinking of happier days. (See Examples 13.)

William Wallace (1860–1940), another son of Greenock, graduated MB and MCh in 1885 at Glasgow University and went on to study ophthalmology in Vienna, Paris and Moorfields; but the ear proved stronger than the eye and he finally settled on music, studying at the RAM where he continued as a teacher for many years.[34] As a composer his main contribution was as the

Example 13. MACCUNN: JEANIE DEANS, ACT II SCENE II

first British exponent of the symphonic poem, of which he wrote at least six; but there are other works including a hilariously satirical cantata, *The Massacre of the MacPhersons*, an impressive but overinflated *Creation Symphony*, a lovely suite for Maeterlinck's *Pelléas et Mélisande* and a number of fine songs (including the *Freebooter Songs*), as well as four books on music.

The symphonic poem was a new form established by Franz Liszt, in which the structure of the music is as much motivated by poetic and literary conceptions as musical ones. The great Scottish pianist, Frederick Lamond (see below), studied with Liszt and reports him as saying to a pupil working on the Chopin *Polonaise in A Flat*: 'I don't want to listen to how fast you can play octaves; what I wish to hear is the canter of the horses of the Polish cavalry before they gather force and destroy the enemy.'[35]

Programme music (of which the symphonic poem is a prime example) is still regarded as structurally loose and unorthodox, but is more

positively understood as a return to some of the declamatory roots of music in which its role in relation to story-telling (as in the complementary roles of bard and filidh) is expressed in orchestral terms. Wallace wrote his first symphonic poem, *The Passing of Beatrice*, clearly under the influence of Liszt, whose *Dante Symphony* it could be considered as completing by taking us from Purgatory to Paradise. The score is headed by the following note:

> This Symphonic Poem is based upon an episode which Dante does not describe. He and Beatrice are taken up into the Empyrean. Paradise opens before them, -
>
> *In fashion then as of a snow-white rose*
> *Displayed itself to me the saintly host,*
> *Whom Christ in his own blood had made his bride.*
>
> Dante is lost in wonderment at the vision, and in turning to question Beatrice, finds that she is no longer by his side, but has passed away from him to take her place within the rose of Paradise. The music is designed to illustrate the passing, or transition, of Beatrice from earthly to immortal form.[36]

The music itself is intensely romantic in idiom, combining the purity and sensual imagery of the Dante in which the angels are likened to bees bearing the honey (symbolic of Christ) from a white rose made up of the souls of the blessed. It is to the third circle of petals of this rose that Beatrice is translated. With its lush harmonies and rich orchestration, Wallace's music is something more than sweet. The strings, with violins divided and half of them muted, set a tone of hushed reverence, and their opening ascending motif provides the rhythmic basis of most of the work. This motif goes through a process of transformation: a hymn, an intense chromatic passage for woodwind of deep personal feeling, which rises to a passionate and ecstatic expression of love, and finally a calm and ethereal peace.

The six-hundredth anniversary of the death of Wallace's namesake, William Wallace, was an opportunity of national importance not to be missed. Wallace rose to the occasion with a work of powerful celebration. It is derived from the old marching tune of the Scottish soldiers, *Hey Tutti Tatti*, made famous by Burns as *Scots Wha' Hae wi' Wallace bled*; but the tune only emerges overtly at the end. Perhaps his best work is *Villon,* an ingenious and adventurous depiction of the life of the infamous mediaeval French poet, reprieved from the hangman's noose in 1463. Compassion, ironic detachment and volatility mark the piece, which has one of the most daring and imaginative endings of any, being a low note sustained on the bass clarinet, and a single stroke on a gong, dissipating all the brilliance, the pious penitence of the hymn to the Virgin, and the pipe and tabor dance which has preceded it.

Example 14. WILLIAM WALLACE: VILLON (Symphonic Poem Number 6, 1910)

Plate 50. *Frederick Lamond*, BY 'TWYM'

Frederick Lamond (see Plate 50), who has been mentioned as a pianist and was particularly renowned for the depth and power of his Beethoven performances, was also born in the 1860s. He is almost forgotten as a composer, but produced a successful *Symphony in A*, a *Cello Sonata*, an orchestral overture *Aus Dem Schottischen Hochlande* in the Scottish-Germanic vein, a *Piano Trio* which, though lacking melodic distinction, has

tremendous energy and a command of texture, and a set of *Clavierstucke Opus 1* which are subtle and beautiful studies in keyboard writing.[37]

Not one of these composers lived for any great length of time in Scotland. A lone figure from the period, Learmond Drysdale, returned from London in 1904 at the age of thirty-eight, initially to teach in the recently established Athenaeum – the precursor of the Royal Scottish Academy of Music and Drama – but he died in 1909 at the age of forty-three, and with him died great hopes. His dramatic cantata *The Kelpie* is bursting with exuberance and the ecstatic love duet between the disguised and dangerous lover and the too-eager girl, combines unflagging pace with variety and passion, supported by a rich harmonic vocabulary and an unselfconscious romanticism which sweeps all before it.

The galloping motif for the water-horse is similarly energetic but is used with great flexibility. The work is driven by the total emotional conviction of Drysdale's music. There is no subtle intellectuality about it; no deeply considered psychology; simply the power of a composer who knows exactly what he is doing and why. If a work like this could be as easily displayed as a painting is hung, it would be permanently on view. But this applies to so much of the music referred to in this chapter. It is costly to resurrect it and entrepreneurs, ignorant and doubtful of the quality, are reluctant to take the risk, and it comes from a period and a culture of High Victorianism which we are only just beginning to accept once more as a valid part of musical experience.

Example 15. LAMOND: ROMANZA ED INTERMEZZO
(Klavierstucke, Leipzig, 1890)

Beautiful music was also supplied by Drysdale for *Fionn and Tera*, a short opera on a poor libretto by the Duke of Argyll which Drysdale, in a long and tactful letter, proposed tightening up for a promised production in London.[38] Death interrupted its orchestration which was completed by his fellow-Scot, David Stephen. Farmer speaks in the highest terms of Drysdale's music for *Hippolytus,* and there is a considerable list of works including an opera, *The Red Spider*, which received over a hundred performances.

Tam o' Shanter is Drysdale's best-known work. First heard at the Crystal Palace, conducted by August Manns (who was an outstanding champion of British music and premièred many works) it raises Tam's feelings to Wagnerian levels of expansiveness and contrasts them with a brilliantly scored fleeting journey on horse-back. It has been unjustly eclipsed by Malcolm Arnold's equally brilliant orchestral essay on the same subject. Arnold is closer to the character and incident of the poem, Drysdale more in the grand theatrical manner, but sharp-witted as well as broad-gestured.

The *Short Trio*, for piano, violin and cello, shows a more French side to Drysdale's vocabulary. This is a supremely lovely single movement work that compares well with similar movements in the Fauré piano trios, upon which it improves by virtue of its greater concision. Here again one is struck by the absolute assurance of Drysdale's technique and intentions: but his work is almost entirely in manuscript and this points to one of the major institutional shortcomings in Scotland, that there has been no major music publisher to make the larger-scale works of our best composers available. The English publishers, particularly Patersons and Novellos, have occasionally done their bit, but Mackenzie had to turn to Germany for publication of his *Scottish Concerto,* Lamond's works were published in Germany, Thomson's songs in Leipzig, and Novello have disposed of all the Mackenzie material from their cellars. Yet, in their day, these composers filled concert halls throughout Britain and many of their works travelled abroad and were well received.

All the assessments above have to be themselves judged in the knowledge that only a fraction of the composers' works was available on recording or has been heard at all recently in performance. Now that recording makes it possible to secure a permanent record of music

Example 16. DRYSDALE: I HAVE LOVED THEE LONG (*The Kelpie*, 1891)

in performance, it should be a national musical priority to do so with a substantial part of this repertoire, for it is an inheritance of which we have been cheated, and whose full riches can only be tantalisingly guessed at until it once more plays upon the ear.

CHAPTER XVII

SEA, FIELD AND MUSIC HALL

1820–1910

Farewell tae Tarwathie, adieu Mormond Hill
Dear land of my fathers I bid you farewell
I'm bound for Greenland and ready to sail
In hope to find riches in hunting the whale.

Example 1. FAREWELL TAE TARWATHIE (from the playing of
Lindsay Porteous)

T his was the tune used by the whalers, sung, fiddled or played on the trump – the jew's harp. The jew's (jaws) harp is an old and widespread instrument. It was played at the witches' coven in 1590 (see Chapter X) and is a grand instrument for a sailor. It fits in the pocket, is durable, and does not require too much breath or activity. It is twanged between the teeth and the notes are made by changing the shape of the mouth. Huddled up against a bulk-head in a freshening wind watching Mormond Hill and the coast of north-east Aberdeenshire slipping away, it was as comforting a musical instrument as could be hoped for.

The cold land of Greenland is barren and bare
No seed time or harvest is ever known there
The birds here sing sweetly on mountain and dale
But there's nae a birdie to sing to the whale.

Tarwathie is just inland from Fraserburgh and the poem was written by George Scroggie in the 1850s, to an older and well-travelled tune that has had many other uses, but that was its use then.[1]

The fiddle is also a reasonably portable instrument for a sailor and the Shetland whaling reel *Da Mirrie Boys o' Greenland* uses simple finger

patterns that may have helped dictate the shape of the tune. Traditional fiddlers do not articulate their fingers as much as classical ones, and they tend not to use the pinkie at all. But a man on a whaling ship, gripping frozen ropes, cold chains, and fighting frostbite would be doing well to play with even three fingers when he had the leisure. The reel as a dance, and with a tune similar to this one, seems to have spread from Shetland to the Netherlands.[2]

Example 2. DA MIRRIE BOYS O' GREENLAND (from the fiddle
playing of Gilbert Gray)

Other thoroughly portable instruments, though mere striplings compared with the antiquity of the trump and the fiddle, were the concertina and the mouth-organ or 'moothie', known in genteel circles as the harmonica. The concertina was invented in England in the early nineteenth century at about the same time as the mouth-organ emerged from Germany and the accordion from Austria and France, and was another favourite sailors' instrument, small, expressive and flexible. All three novelties achieved rapid international popularity. They had the great advantage of being able to provide harmonies on portable instruments a lot cheaper than a piano. The concertina and accordion became particularly associated with the growing Sunday school and Temperance movements whose repertoires often included religious parodies of popular songs, just as had been done in the late

Plate 51. A SHETLAND WEDDING, AUGUST 1963

sixteenth century in *The Good and Godlie Ballads*. Later, gospel, mission hall and Salvation Army all joined the craze and some of the repertoire was adapted from Scottish music, or newly composed. In the fishing communities of the North-east the mission hall style of singing still survives.[3]

One result of the fiddle's portability has been the cross-fertilisation between the Shetland and the Norwegian hardanger fiddle style. The Harding fiddle uses sympathetic strings and lots of drone effects, and these latter may well have travelled to Norway via Scotland, perhaps influenced en route by the old Shetland stringed instrument, the gue, which may have been an ancient bowed lyre or a two-stringed Icelandic fiddle – we shall probably never know – but may also have relied on drone effects.

The fiddle and accordion are commonly used at Shetland weddings to lead the march to the church (which could be a six-mile trek in every kind of weather) with a gunner at the rear (see Plate 51). It is a Shetland custom still kept alive, as is the fiddle playing. *Du's Bon Lang Awa'* was played to accompany the groom's march to the bride's house. The melodic outline could as easily be from the mainland as from Shetland, but the rhythm and phrase lengths are much less regular in effect than the bar-lines suggest and it could as well be notated with two as opposed to three beats in the bar. The effect is one of an odd jauntiness.[4]

Example 3. DU'S BON LANG AWA' (from the fiddle playing of P. Fraser)

The most portable of instruments is the voice and it is a useful one too for regulating the rhythm of work such as hauling on ropes or turning the capstan that pulls up the massive anchors. The songs for this work were known as rope shanties or capstan shanties, though a shanty could serve for more than one job. *Haul Away Your Bowline* was sung when pulling the foresheet, the pull being made on the underlined '*haul*'. It is unequivocally a Scottish shanty, for its tune is none other than Nathaniel Gow's *Caller Herrin'*.

Before electric light there was gaslight and before gaslight there was oil-light – whale-oil light. Whale oil had many uses and, to give an idea of its

Example 4. HAUL AWAY YOUR BOWLINE (from the singing of George Innes Junior)

importance, 18,383 tons of it were landed in Britain in the year 1862 alone. But not every year was a good one: 'Mr Nimmo has been here this morning measuring the house, we are to get in gas immediately. The Whale fishing has been so very bad the oil will be very expensive this winter.'[5]

Thus nine-year-old Catherine Jameson (see Chapter XVI), writing to her cousin in Paris. It was all very comfortable for her with such ready alternatives in cosy Edinburgh, but we know what sufferings lay behind that shortage of whale oil. The year was 1830 and in that year nearly every ship mentioned in the song *The Bonny Ship The Diamond*, all of them from the north-east coast Scottish whaling fleet, were lost in the Greenland ice in a storm. The only way to outface that sort of memory when you start out on the next year's trip is to sing it into history. *The Bonny Ship The Diamond* was recorded by A.L. Lloyd who learnt it on the whalers himself.[6]

It is not surprising that some of the best tunes associated with the sea come from the Northern Isles, and of these *Da Auld Swarra Jupie* is one of the most interesting. Its uneven phrases and rough-hewn shape are dignified at the same time, and have echoes of the Norwegian style too. The title refers to the woollen vest the fishermen wore next to the skin. The tune must be played 'in deep sorrow' because it is a lament for a fisherman drowned along with many others in the old sixtereen days, the sixteereens being six-oared open fishing-boats. It was bad luck to name the man, so his clothing was lamented – probably the only thing he could have been identified by anyway.[7]

Example 5. DA AULD SWARRA JUPIE (from the playing of John Stickle)

Throughout the fishing community in Scotland the seals (or selchies) were both hunted

and held in a kind of strange veneration for they are so like humans. Their calls can sound uncannily human: after all they come to land to breed and originally evolved from four-legged land creatures which reverted to the sea. They were often clubbed to death for their skins, but not all would be dead and the miserable sight of a living skinned creature may partly have given rise to the belief that some seals were people in disguise, that if you took their skins from them you would trap them on land, but once they got their skins back they would always revert to the sea. The most famous of the ballads associated with this legendary idea is *The Grey Selchie of Sule Skerrie*. Sule Skerrie is a rock so wild and small and remote that few will even have heard of it. But the fishermen know of it and in such places one can conceive of strange creatures which can interbreed with humans as well as their own kind. The tune is basically pentatonic and rises and falls like a short swell on an uneven sea. Like so many of the great ballad tunes, its simplicity never palls, but acts as a perfect support for the story in which the selchie lover and son are killed by the woman's gunner husband after the selchie has escaped to his own wife under the waves.

Example 6. THE GREY SELCHIE OF SULE SKERRIE (from the singing of John Sinclair)

The idea of a life at the bottom of the sea is not so strange an imagining when one remembers how many have found their final resting place there. For the widows who have no graves to tend, the ocean is the element they must address themselves to. There is no more poignant expression of that sense of loss and of new-found identity than in the Gaelic lament *Ho Roinn Eile*. It was collected by Francis Tolmie from whom Marjorie Kennedy-Fraser obtained much of her material. How old it is we cannot say. Sorley Maclean has considered the possibility that at heart it is at least as old as the early seventeenth century[8] – but there are occasions when it is not improper for an historian to use the word 'timeless' and this is surely one of them. The rise and fall of the music and the wonderful range of the imagery drawing the two together, are oceanic in character and are not to be measured. The refrain is pentatonic, but each verse ends with a 'flattened seventh' (the E flat) which darkens the colour of the tune and changes the modal effect. The term 'flattened seventh' is commonly used in this context, for want of a better one, but it is derived from the ordinary major scale and tells us more about that than it does about tunes with similar modal effects.

> O Alan of the brown hair, mouth of tender tones, of mirth and of melodious laughter! Noblest among men, great was my devotion to you. I could recognise the movement of your boat, and you, beloved, at the stroke oar. How it grieves me that your bed is the sea-weed; that those who wake you are the seals; your tall candles the shining stars; and your violin music the murmur of the sea. O little gull! O white gull! Come and give me your tidings. Where have you left the dead men? I left them on an island of the sea, back-to-back, and without breath.

Example 7. HO RIONN EILE (from the singing of Mary Ross)

The evocative use of the imagery of the sea was matched by a similar feeling for the land. Nor was the repertoire merely one stimulated by work, historical events, or drawn from the past. The lovely song, *An Nighean Donn Na Buaile – Brown-haired Girl of the Cattle-fold* – was composed in the nineteenth century by Donald Fraser of Fannich. It is a song of unrequited love, picturing the girl going out to the cattle. It uses standard imagery, though the closeness of sea and land in the west is pointed by likening the colour of her skin to the seagull. The tune has been described as nineteenth-century Irish in character because of the prominence of the fourth and sixth degrees of the scale.[9] This kind of tune was and is popular throughout Scotland and may reflect a parallel development, perhaps stimulated by Irish immigrants. (Example 8.)

A highly respected musician who, like Marjory Kennedy-Fraser, sometimes misunderstood and distorted the material he came across was Joseph

Example 8. AN NIGHEAN DONN NA BUAILE (from the singing of James Campbell)

Mainzer. Mainzer was a left-winger who had been evicted from two European countries, probably for writing seditious operas. He was trying both to popularise and to improve choral singing among the masses, like R.A. Smith (see Chapter XVI) and like Bremner in the mid-eighteenth century. He made a big impression and was very disappointed not to get the Reid chair of music after John Thomson's death, but he is now remembered chiefly for his work on the Gaelic psalm tunes. Confronted with an unprecedented style of singing as copied down by Robert Brown, Mainzer tried to respect it, recognising that the elaborate decorations disguised tunes well known elsewhere; but he also regularised it, harmonised it and distorted it, through ignorance, one might say, but it turns out he was quite deliberate about it.

Example 9. FRENCH (Psalm tune realised by Mainzer, 1844)

If we wish them to be understood and appreciated in all their natural beauty, we must of necessity make a concession to the lovers of Music . . . who would follow the musical thought but very imperfectly, were it not for the addition of fundamental harmonies . . . . As the people, however, in clothing their thoughts in musical forms, care little for rules, there sometimes appear harsh, or at least to our ears, unusual turns and cadences, which compel us . . . to enter boldly on hitherto untrodden ground.[10]

Mainzer saw himself as some kind of musical missionary to the working classes, but his resultant unsatisfactory compromise is now so much a part of Gaelic cultural self-awareness that it is sung every year at the end of the National Mod and it would be a brave man who would recommend that they forget about it.

What Mainzer was trying to convey to the so-called 'lovers of Music' should not have required either harmony or rhythmic direction. Its musical dignity was and is based on practices so ancient and alien to harmonisation, practices in which the individual has room for expression but in which the corporate identity is strong, that it is hard to understand how Mainzer's versions have found any acceptance.

No matter how solid the faith of congregations, the effects of the clearances and of starvation during the 1840s were devastating and it is from this period that the many songs of exile have their origins. Even the brother of a chieftain, Norman Nicholson, was not exempt, for the factor for the MacDonald estates pursued him relentlessly for his hunting activities and he had to exchange the slopes of Blaven for Canada and Australia, where he was drowned. Although this song must date from around 1825, the events are still alive in people's minds for the present writer once received a letter from a descendant of the factor, saying the man was just doing his duty. Nonetheless she loved the sadness of the song with its magnificent swinging refrain: 'I can scarcely ever climb to the high moors. My slender gun is rusted and I'll not go to hunting with it again. It was hung up on the nails, and

that's not where I'd like things to stay. To be on my elbow on Blaven, on a hillock with a loaded gun. Big Patrick from the head of Loch Onich wronged me though he didn't gain by it. But if the law were not so strong I would be safe from every danger.'[11]

For a privileged few, shooting was not for the pot but for diversion, and it had its equivalent for young ladies, even musical ones like Catherine Jameson: 'Helen and I were at the Archer's Hall today with Mr MacDougal an English gentleman . . . he taught me to shoot when you come back don't you think it will be nice for you and I to go out and shoot together. The Professor says it is quite common on the continent for Ladies to use the bow.'[12]

But for many, the use of bow or gun was to keep a starving family alive and doing that was called poaching, and if caught you were sent to Botany Bay or Van Diemen's Land. On the Forth and Clyde Canal in Glasgow there is a dock at Maryhill still known as The Botany, because men to be transported to Botany Bay were put on barges there to join ship at Bowling. Many of these were sold as white slaves. *The Braemar Poacher* is a splendidly defiant song in praise of poachers, representing one half of a genre; the other half of which were, for obvious reasons, laments. This tune (which is a version of *'Twas in the Month of August*) makes bold use of octave leaps to underline its defiance.

Example 11. THE BRAEMAR POACHER (from the singing of Ewen MacColl)

The evolution of traditional tunes by small alterations in oral transmission, or by their being assembled from fragments of others, is a vast study in itself. The nineteenth century was rich in the production of such songs, in Gaelic, Scots and English, and the history of their evolution would also require extensive study of the influence of music imported from other countries, as well as

Example 10. 'S GANN GUN DIRICH (from a performance by Ossian)

KELVIN GROVE.

ARRANGED BY J. T. SURENNE.

Let us wander by the mill, bonnie lassie, O,
To the cove beside the rill, bonnie lassie, O,
    Where the glens rebound the call,
    Of the roaring waters' fall,
Through the mountain's rocky hall, bonnie lassie, O.

O Kelvin banks are fair, bonnie lassie, O,
When in summer we are there, bonnie lassie, O,
    There, the May-pink's crimson plume,
    Throws a soft, but sweet perfume,
Round the yellow banks of broom, bonnie lassie, O.

Though I dare not call thee mine, bonnie lassie, O,
As the smile of fortune's thine, bonnie lassie, O,
    Yet with fortune on my side,
    I could stay thy father's pride,
And win thee for my bride, bonnie lassie, O.

But the frowns of fortune lower, bonnie lassie, O,
On thy lover at this hour, bonnie lassie, O,
    Ere yon golden orb of day
    Wake the warblers on the spray,
From this land I must away, bonnie lassie, O.

Then farewell to Kelvin grove, bonnie lassie, O
And adieu to all I love, bonnie lassie, O,
    To the river winding clear,
    To the fragrant scented brier,
Even to thee of all most dear, bonnie lassie, O.

When upon a foreign shore, bonnie lassie, O,
Should I fall midst battle's roar, bonnie lassie, O,
    Then, Helen! shouldst thou hear
    Of thy lover on his bier,
To his memory shed a tear, bonnie lassie, O.

Plate 52. *Kelvingrove,* FROM *The Songs of Scotland,* 1854

of the impact of increasing musical literacy encouraged in church choirs, choral unions, and by cheap publishing and the use of the tonic-solfa system. This latter form of syllabic notation became extremely popular and, being based entirely on the key system, may well have assisted its influence on Scottish song. But the other side of the coin retained old tunes with remarkable faithfulness to versions which can be found in early manuscripts.

The divisions between rich and poor were not so great that they could not be crossed. Catherine Jameson as a singer would have had Scots folk-song as part of her repertoire – and, had she been in Glasgow, then *Kelvingrove,* arranged skilfully and pleasantly by Surenne, would have surely been in her repertoire. The words were by Thomas Lyle and are sung by a young man off to foreign wars, the original words being deemed unfit for performance:

> Kelvingrove, a picturesque and richly wooded dell, through which the river Kelvin flows, lies at a very short distance to the north-west of Glasgow, and will in all probability soon be comprehended within the wide-spreading boundaries of the city itself. At one part of it is an old well called the Pear Tree well . . . it is a favourite place of resort for young parties from the city on summer afternoons. The original name was, 'O the shearin's no for you', which was the first line of a song now deservedly forgotten.[13]

This is a nice example of nineteenth-century propriety. The tune is exactly the same and the words of the *Shearin's No for You* are delightful and were not forgotten; it is just that in a drawing-room it was scarcely seemly to refer to expecting a baby at all, never mind in words so objectively practical as these: 'O the shearin's no for you my bonny lassie o, o the shearin's no for you, for your belly's round and fu' and your back it winna boo, my bonny lassie o.' The girl cannot bend to shear the corn, because she is so far on in her pregnancy (see Plate 52).

Kelvingrove is an example of the many songs taken from the tradition into the middle classes; but there were songs written by the middle classes which found their way happily into the repertoire of the labouring classes and travelling folk. One such is *The Echo Mocks the Corncrake.* The words are clearly of the 'art' variety and were published in the mid-nineteenth century. In folk songs echoes do not mock and constancy is not likened to a pendulum and joys are not described as rural. The corncrake makes a most unmusical rasp, but on summer evenings like the one in the song, in the

days when corn was still sheared and corncrakes and lovers survived the process, it will have had its own charms and pleasant associations.

Ploughing, unlike the shearing of corn, was strictly a male preserve and was rooted deep in our culture. In the nineteenth century it was not that much changed. Horses drew the plough instead of oxen, and it took three men to guide it – one to lead the horses, one to hold the plough, and the third to lean with a stick on the ploughshare to keep it in the ground. This man would keep his eye open for dinner, which was brought out to the fields, and the song passed the time by alternately abusing and encouraging the horses and in anticipation of the food – it is being reaped, threshed, winnowed, dried, ground, sifted, kneaded, baked – until at last it arrives. The tune is none other than that of the caoine or lament of ancient provenance – the same tune referred to in Chapters I and II, and though it was noted down in Ireland, may well have been heard in Scotland where there were many immigrant Irish farm-workers.

The ploughboy in this next song is not so much at the mercy of others, for this is a song in praise of *The Plooman Laddies* in which even the miller and the merchant have to yield to the charms and sexual innuendos of the work of the ploughboy. The tune is descended from *The Rigs o' Rye* and comes from the singing of Lucy Stewart.[14] Its cheerful stride and uncompromising assertion of the major key, with a strong 'leading note' (the D), give it an air of happy certainty.

Example 12. THE PLOOMAN LADDIES (from the singing of Isla St Clair)

Another song of happy certainty is *Lovely Molly*. It was popular in Perthshire at country social meetings in the mid-nineteenth century and has been quoted in the Introduction to this book as an example of one of many Scottish tunes using the leap of an octave. It is interesting also for its expressive refrain which seems to echo the shepherdess's voice calling her sheep to the

Plate 53. A BOTHY BAND

hills, as well as the old phrase 'ca' the yowes to the knowes' itself. The refrain is an integral part of a tune which makes pleasant and unusual play out of the contrast between F major and minor, but still retains a native modality with the flattened seventh. The decorative end of the third phrase is also unusual and the story a delight. A young man buys a ewe lamb from an old shepherd. Since it is to start a new flock, he asks for the best and the best is promised. When the old shepherd is told that the ewe lamb is his own daughter, lovely Molly, he accepts the cheating words as binding and, Molly being privy to the ploy, all ends happily (see Introduction Ex 4).

The sense of pride and pleasure in that song presents the cheerful side of agricultural life of those days when many of the bothy ballads were composed. Agricultural workers, living for six-month spells together in cramped bothies before having a chance to hire themselves out to someone else, often entertained themselves and others making music on fiddles, pipes, whistles, mouth-

organs, jew's harps, accordions, melodeons, concertinas, and, of course, voices ready for non-sense and ribaldry parodying words and using the music of popular tunes to get the feet stamping (see Plate 53).[15] A favourite was *The Stool of Repentance* – a famous jig tune recalling the stool in the kirk on which miscreants, usually adulterers, had to sit on consecutive Sundays to their sup-posed disgrace: but the tune's cheerful character suggests it must have been such a common punishment nobody was much bothered by it.

The nineteenth century saw great movements of people not only emigrating to North America and Australasia where their music still survives, but within the British Isles with migrant workers, particularly from Ireland, bringing new tunes across national boundaries, not only to farms but mills and mines. Farming was hard but reason-ably healthy, but mill work and mining were dangerous. Modern songs like *The Wark o' the Weavers* paint a picture of near slavery, but the men and women who swept the floors of the

Plate 54. THE REEL OF TULLOCH, NINETEENTH CENTURY

jute mills appear to have had no songs, and they were truly at the bottom of the heap, their lungs destroyed with dust and their pay and status so low they seem to have been beneath notice. Mining, being more dramatic an activity, has at least gathered some mystique around it.

In the last chapter we were in the company of the High Victorians: big orchestras, vast halls, huge audiences, but in the galleries of the High Blantyre mine the music was that of pick and shovel and the pit canary whose cheerful singing was a guarantee that the air was still safe and whose silence was an ominous warning. No doubt the canaries fell silent at High Blantyre, just south of Glasgow, in 1877, but not soon enough. An accumulation of fire-damp – that is to say methane – exploded with little warning and a vast volume of smoke, coal and wood shot up from the mine shaft shattering the cage and throwing the hoisting gear high into the air and scattering men around like ninepins. Of the 233 men and boys who had gone down the mine early that morning only twenty or so survived.

It took days to recover the bodies and the work was hindered by choke-damp (carbon dioxide) laden with coal dust which clung to the bodies of the rescuers for whom the cure was evidently to cover them with earth. *The Blantyre Explosion* was collected from an old Blantyre miner and is thoroughly Irish in character.

The Blantyre Explosion is but one of many examples enshrined in popular ballads, of the price that was paid by many for the benefit of few. But the fabulous wealth of the leading industrialists and the aristocracy, which fed

Example 13. THE BLANTYRE EXPLOSION (from the singing of Robin Morton)

upon such suffering and poverty, did not prevent traditional musicians from taking pleasure in aristocratic patronage.

Queen Victoria's piper, Angus MacKay, helped to feed a continuing demand for Scottish traditional music at all levels of society and was followed in that office by William Ross, both publishing important collections of pipe music. Nor were fiddlers left out of royal patronage, Willie Blair being dubbed 'the Queen's fiddler' and, later, James Scott Skinner was to become violin teacher to Queen Victoria's tenants and composer of *Our Highland Queen* in her honour.[16] Queen Victoria herself arranged for the publication of some of Blair's compositions, after his death in 1884.[17] Dance, as always, was a mainstay of the tradition, and the photograph of *The Reel Of Tulloch* being danced in the midst of moorland by Victorian kilties, is no more posed than were the many occasions on which dances were performed for the Queen on remote and romantic spots dear to her sensibilities (see Plate 54). This kind of patronage merely continued a tradition which had supported Gow and Marshall in their day and, though it diminished, it did not wholly disappear before other opportunities for employment, over and above the traditional one of dancing-master, offered themselves.

Example 14. SCOTT SKINNER: THE PRESIDENT (second variation, 1904)

One of the main new outlets came in the form of concert appearances which included public performance in theatrical and musical entertainment, now provided for on a large scale, music hall being one of the major outlets. Here the influence of the piano as an accompanying instrument may have taken ever more solid a hold on the popular fancy, and the harmonic style, driven by the classical key system, began increasingly to impose itself on existing as well as new melodies. The result was that tunes underwent even more chromatic alteration than they had already suffered in the eighteenth century, in particular the seventh note of the scale being sharpened to provide the sense of finality that classical musicians sought in the perfect cadence – a musical equivalent to the full stop.

Typical products of this development, which had plenty of tartan wrapped round it in Scotland, were Scott Skinner and Harry Lauder, both of whom were able to move from performing for local audiences to international tours. At one time they joined forces, forming (with two others) a group called The Caledonian Four and filling the London Palladium and the Albert Hall, and it was Lauder who unveiled Skinner's memorial headstone in 1931 a few years after one of the most remarkable funerals for any musician. When old Skinner died, aged eighty-four, he was long past his best and had suffered a humiliating and ill-advised final American tour. But the people remembered him with love and pride, and the streets of Aberdeen were lined by thousands to watch his coffin pass by, his fiddle lying on top in its open case.[18]

Example 15. SCOTT SKINNER: FORBES MORRISON STRATHSPEY

Skinner was a traditional Scots fiddler, trained by his elder brother and his father who, having lost three fingers of his left hand, simply changed hands – an old dancing-master's trick. At the age of ten, Skinner went to Manchester and studied with Charles Rougier of the Halle Orchestra, returning to Scotland to take up his father's trade of dancing-master, as well as teaching fiddle and performing a mixed repertoire of classical and traditional music.[19] To some the two sit ill together, but in his lifetime he was an international success, several of his compositions are learnt by every Scots fiddler worth the name, and he has still many devotees. Nor are all his compositions tinged with the appealing Victorian sentiment of the famous *Cradle Song*, or the showy classical techniques of *The President* with its arpeggios and chromaticisms drawn, no doubt, from his studies as a classical fiddler. To the purist, *The President* has only a peripheral place in the tradition, but it is still played in country pubs in Aberdeenshire by fiddlers who would make short work of purists if given the chance.

One of Scott Skinner's most famous tunes is *The Bonny Lass o' Bon Accord*, inspired by Wilhelmina Bell, daughter of a cellist and herself a good dancer, but working as a waitress in a hotel to help pay off the debts of her father's friend. Skinner was touched and responded: '"Never mind, my lassie," said I, cheerfully . . . "I'll ma' a tune that'll maybe keep ye in min' when we're baith deid."'[20]

The promise was kept and seems likely to hold true for at least another century, for it has been popular ever since its publication in 1888. It follows the same formal pattern as Niel Gow's *Lament for the Death of His Second Wife*, repeating its second strain three times in slightly different versions.

But as a composer Skinner is at his best in the old traditional forms of reel and strathspey, which require that special fire and energy in bowing so peculiar to Scotland, but which depends, not upon allowing the bow to rise from the string as in classical music, but on maintaining close contact with it. It is from this brilliantly controlled contact that the rich quality of sound in good Scots fiddle-playing is derived, and Skinner knew it and insisted upon it in his incomparable prose: 'The Writer's Experience Of Bows – The fishing-rod bow is of no avail for a veteran. Too too eel and sliddery or smack. A strong and fairly light bow seems best for Scotch music. One you can't staccato with; a stick which bends like a cane. . . Here you need the rigidness to prevent the bow from leaving the string.'[21]

The strathspey *Forbes Morrison* gives a good idea of the rhythmic vigour characteristic of the Scotch fiddle style he so loved, and which was carried on by fiddlers such as James Dickie and John Murdoch Henderson who, with William

Honeyman, did much to record on paper the style and compositions of Skinner and others.

Skinner's professional companion and admirer, Harry Lauder (1870–1950), has been the butt of Scots fury for too long. This brilliant comedian made a living out of an entertainingly kenspeckle approach to his own culture, full of wry observation as well as sentiment, and delivered with typical music-hall aplomb to melodies of varied distinction and authenticity. So powerful was his success and influence that the image he purveyed, with blackthorn stick and yards of tartan, Glengarry bonnet, bow-tie, pipe and massive sporran, became the overriding image of Scotland. Scots loved it as much as foreigners, and even as an old man, long past his singing best, he broadcast regularly during the Second World War, to the great solace and comfort of many, such old war-horses as *Keep Right On to the End of the Road*. He was knighted for his services and the more recent critics of his image misunderstand his roots in comedy, which has the right to do what it pleases, and dies if it is obliged to kowtow to cultural sensitivities. In their day, Lauder, Melba (also Scottish) and Caruso were the three biggest record sellers in the world; and at one time Lauder was earning $4,500 a week at the New York Theatre in Times Square.

It is ironic that just as regulated versions of classical harmonies became entrenched in the presentation of traditional music, the whole key system was being led away from harmonic certainties by Wagner, Brahms and Debussy. Debussy's closest Scottish connection was with Mary Garden (1874–1967), the Aberdeenshire soprano who created the part of Mélisande in *Pelléas et Mélisande*, his only opera and a role in which he regarded her as unsurpassed. She starred and directed at the Chicago Grand Opera, being responsible for the creation of Prokofiev's *The Love of Three Oranges*. Her first recording was of Debussy songs, with the composer at the piano. Debussy's influence was first felt in Scotland in the arrangements of Marjory Kennedy-Fraser and the compositions of J.B. McEwen and F.G. Scott, both of whose work is discussed in the next chapter.

Like Harry Lauder, Kennedy-Fraser (see Plate XXIX) is another upon whom much opprobrium is heaped, perhaps with more justification, for she, in her own way, commercialised the traditional

THE SEAL-WOMAN'S CROON.

(An Cadal trom.)

From the traditional singing of
Kenneth Macleod.

Noted and arranged for voice and pianoforte by
MARJORY KENNEDY-FRASER.

Plate 55. THE SEAL-WOMAN'S CROON, BY MARJORY KENNEDY-FRASER, 1910

Gaelic music she collected (much of it at second-hand from Francis Tolmie),[22] aware of its significance but unprepared to bring to it the scholarly disciplines it called for, though she did make some field recordings now in Edinburgh University Library. But is it fair to blame her for failing to be a scholar and a folklorist, and instead choosing to present the material she found in a form suited to her own gifts? And what were those gifts?

To consider her contribution fairly it has to be understood in the cultural climate of the day and given the same courtesy that is finally being shown to MacPherson (whose handling of his raw material is not dissimilar) of acknowledging that a new interest in Gaelic material was fostered by her efforts.

Example 16. KENNEDY-FRASER: SPINNING SONG (*Songs of the Hebrides*, 1909)

well for voice, and as a musical arranger her work is excellent. She avoids the stilted harmonic language of the academics of her day, using harmonies derived much more closely from the melodic lines, and she has a command of piano texture which fully realises her somewhat romanticised (and frequently sanitised) approach to her originals. She knew exactly what she was doing, understanding that her harmonisations were merely reflections of her own taste and that the very scales, never mind the melodies, were unreproducible in notation. She states clearly the difficulty that still faces the most conscientious of folklorists:

> Unfortunately, all these scales, as sung by the people, differ slightly from anything we can convey by any system of notation as yet in use. If in noting them down and thus trying to preserve them by other than the traditional aural method we sacrifice something of their character in this respect, it is imperative we go further and compensate for this loss by furnishing them with an instrumental accompaniment . . . the modern art of harmonic accompaniment . . . helps to reveal . . . the salient points and characteristic features of a tune.[23]

Many may disagree with her solution to the problem, but it has had deep musical meaning for many more, including the famous music critic Ernest Newman on the one hand, and native Gaelic singers proud to sing Kennedy-Fraser's versions at the Mod, on the other.[24] Taking her songs as art songs, without any pretensions to authenticity, then she can be claimed to have produced some very fine work. The floating chords and arabesques of the accompaniment for *The Seal-Woman's Croon* are very similar to passages in Debussy whose work was just becoming established by 1910 when this was published. The influence is a natural one. Debussy was as much affected by the remote celticisms of Brittany and the sea he so loved   as was Kennedy-Fraser in the Hebrides (see Plate 55).

Kennedy-Fraser's adventurousness extends to a free use of dissonance in *The Spinning Song*, very similar to the kind of treatment Bartók was to give to the traditional music of central Europe.

On the other hand, her alterations are often hard to justify and she is certainly not blameless on the musical front. *Ho Rionn Eile* (see Example 7) was turned by Kennedy-Fraser into *The Seagull of the Land Under Waves*, its rhythms altered to no advantage, and its mode unnecessarily distorted.

As for the sanitisation of texts, it is sometimes downright comical. A seduction in a shieling

Daughter of the internationally successful Scottish singer, David Kennedy, she places things

interrupted at its most delicate moment by the girl's mother, is turned into arrant nonsense about cows 'dripping milk of lulling' in the middle of the night as a kind of benison on the inhabitants. Quite apart from the silliness of the conception, a cow dripping milk in the night would be in an acute state of discomfort, and what it would have been doing indoors in a tiny shieling when it ought to be outside grazing is not explained. But the complaint here should be as much against Kennedy-Fraser's collaborator, Kenneth Macleod, who was a perfectly respectable native Gaelic-speaker from Eigg who obviously thought this sort of stuff was entirely acceptable. Similar licence is taken by today's folk/rock groups who make use of Gaelic song, such as Runrig, who also have an international following and who are part of as conscious a revival as was the Gaelic Mod – the equivalent of the Welsh Eisteddfod – or the birth of the clarsach society (see Chapter XIX).

What emerges from this brief survey of traditional music in the nineteenth century is a picture not far different from that of the eighteenth century. Some musicians exploited their talents commercially, frequently flirting with classical music and still sometimes dependent on aristocratic patronage; others continued as they had always done, playing and singing at ceilidhs, dances and weddings, sometimes for pay and sometimes for the fun of it and a meal and a drink; yet others had little thought for any kind of regular performance, but their songs and ballads found favour and have been preserved by others like them and subsequently collected. So rich was the tradition in the north-east in particular, that to show on a map all the places and persons referred to in the bothy ballads would probably require a scale of six inches to the mile.[25]

As far as publication was concerned there was a similar continuity. The more elaborate piano accompaniments or the thicker chords of the accordion, were no more nor less traditional than their predecessors, the figured and unfigured basses of the eighteenth century, which they replaced. The niceties of society were respected with texts that could not raise a maiden's blush from Ramsay, through Burns, to the many effusions of nineteenth-century lyricists, with Kennedy-Fraser in the same tradition. The word is an awkward one. The tradition itself can never be defined. Is it proper to describe the long strand of sanitised texts as traditional? If not, what are we to make of most of Burns, or Temperance songs? To some the concept of an urban tradition is almost a contradiction in terms; to others tradition is what their teacher taught them; to others again, it is established by the earliest documentary evidence; to another group it must be orally transmitted – a stance which leads researchers into quagmires of literacy, chance contacts, publication dates and routes of transmission. Perhaps it is best to leave it with the thought that the vigour of the tradition lies in the fact that there are so many different notions of what it is and, as we shall see, that vigour and freedom of approach remain as strong as ever.

What does gradually emerge as a new element, more in the texts than in the music, is an increasing social awareness and readiness to protest at social injustice. In the eighteenth century such songs are primarily directed at Whigs or Jacobites. In the nineteenth century industrialists, land-owners and the laws which supported them are the chief targets. Cheap publishing and increased literacy, as well as increased suffering, gave impetus to song as a form of radical social protest, and it was a ground-swell which was to find more than an echo in our own century.

CHAPTER XVIII

THE CLASSICAL TAKES ROOT
1910–1970

The Scottish Renascence is a term applied to the period between the wars. It will not do as far as music is concerned, however. It would be more appropriate fifty years later when the necessary institutions were finally in place and a number of excellent composers were working on home soil; or fifty years earlier, to take account of the work of Mackenzie, MacCunn, McEwen and Wallace, though McEwen does take us into the interwar period. All four lived and worked in London, and with good reason.

Scotland was, in classical music terms, marginal. Its Academy of Music (descendant of the Athenaeum) was not to become a really significant institution until the second half of this century. The Scottish National Orchestra was part-time from its founding in 1891 until 1951, the first Scottish conductor in sixty-eight years (Alexander Gibson) being appointed in 1959. The first full-time orchestra was only formed in 1935 against much opposition, and was a small BBC studio orchestra of thirty-five players, reaching symphonic size only in 1967.[1] The first full-time professional opera company was not formed until 1962, spearheaded by the composer Robin Orr, and Alexander Gibson. Ballet came later still. For a long period Scotland had only one university music department and, even into the 1950s, the occupant of the Chair of Music at Glasgow University (founded as late as 1929) was also principal of the Royal Scottish Academy of Music, a piece of organisational cheese-paring which put far too much power, work and responsibility in one person's hands.

Almost all of these developments took place in Glasgow, though the BBC orchestra spent its first five years in Edinburgh. Glasgow, being the larger of the two cities, was a natural centre; but it is a sad indication of the lack of political and cultural direction from the nation's great capital city, where some of the world's largest financial institutions have their head offices and where a Secretary of State is ensconced and a Royal Palace is maintained for the reigning monarch. These could have commanded much of worth, instead of presiding over a city which has, musically, had to struggle against the indifference of those who should be its leaders. Striking symbol of this sad situation is the outstanding venture of the Edinburgh International Festival (founded in 1947), which still has no proper opera house, whose main concert hall is run down, and which, year after year, battles for cash, though in 1974 it was estimated to be earning over £15 million annually for a community who refused to match a government grant offer for the opera house. The grant was withdrawn five years later.[2] The Festival still maintains its position as one of the great international festivals, though its initial lead in supporting Scottish music has badly fallen away, just when that music was most worthy of inclusion, though 1992 promises better things.

Between the wars, and before these institutions came into being, the main employment opportunites for musicians were in the teaching profession, which was strictly regulated by the Teacher Training Colleges and the Music Inspectors, or as church organist and choirmaster where the music was rigidly controlled by the enduring effects of the Reformation which limited church music to psalms, hymns and a desultory anthem or two. There was little to compare with the great traditions of the English choir schools which fostered so many musicians, with only the occasional exception such as the song school at the episcopal cathedral of St Mary's in Edinburgh. No wonder then, that the great Scottish tenor, Joseph Hislop, was largely based in Scandinavia and appeared in opera in Scotland only once. A delightful story is told of him and two other Scottish singers while performing in Puccini's *La Bohème* at

Plate 56. SIR JOHN BLACKWOOD MCEWEN

Covent Garden. Hislop was partnering the famous Nellie Melba (Helen Porter Mitchell, whose father was a Forfarshire farmer). The ageing Melba had been particularly unpleasant to the rest of the cast and, as she sank back to her death as Mimi, Hislop whispered to William Anderson (a Scottish bass playing Colline) 'We'll no hae grannie lang noo!'[3]

For composers, the situation with respect to commercial outlets was no better than it had been for the previous generation. Music publishers and record companies of any size and reputation were not to be found in Scotland, the exceptions of Bayley and Ferguson, Mozart Allen and William MacLellan's brave ventures being unequal to the needs of the country.

Into this barren institutional landscape the Scottish composer was born shivering so violently that the first necessity of life should have been to find the strength to leave. Even Erik Chisholm, who devoted tremendous energy to the promotion of classical music in Scotland, eventually deserted for a Chair of Music in Cape Town, to be joined

briefly by Ronald Stevenson. Not long after, Iain Hamilton and Thea Musgrave both left for the USA and when they returned it was to London. They cannot be blamed. The necessary cultural confidence to encourage new work and support composers was lacking because little was done to foster composition in the institutions responsible for it. As late as 1960 the Royal Scottish Academy of Music and Drama was telling prospective composition students that the subject was not taught. Nor was there any syllabus in place for a diploma in that unheard-of activity, and as for Scottish music or culture in general, they did not feature in any of the courses – a situation recently remedied.[4]

Despite all this, the composers themselves showed a remarkable resourcefulness and it says much for their qualities that Scottish composers dominated the Royal Academy of Music in London for half a century, from 1888 to 1936, not only through the principalship being in the hands of Mackenzie and McEwen, but with MacCunn and Wallace as teachers, Wallace being part of a group in rebellion against the academicism of Mackenzie, who seems to have found space for him nonetheless.

John Blackwood McEwen (1868–1948) (see Plate 56), though mostly resident in London, was one of that small, but immensely talented band of composers who began the re-establishment of Scotland as a significant force in classical music. Both he and Mackenzie were knighted for their services and McEwen left an important bequest to Glasgow University to commission and promote Scottish chamber music, to which he had himself contributed with great distinction.

McEwen was born in the Borders, and his native Galloway inspired him to an expression of the moods of the Scottish landscape as an integral part of his composition rather than only colouring it, as it tends to do in the work of Mackenzie and MacCunn. One of his best pieces is *Under Northern Skies*, a wind quintet composed in 1939. McEwen had a particularly imaginative ear for texture, and the blend of texture and colour in the opening weave of *Under Northern Skies* is magically done. The mystery of the music is enhanced by the use of whole tone scales in which all the notes are a tone apart, resulting in a deliberate lack of direction or clear sense of start and finish. The whole-tone scale helps to form part of an impressionistic harmonic language which McEwen developed early in his career. The title of *Under Northern Skies* is a reliable signpost to the character of the piece, which spreads a pellucid light, fresh and chilly, but with more shades of colour than the hot haze of the Mediterranean can often afford.

The superb Quartet No 8 composed at Cap Feret in 1913 and which he entitled *Biscay,* also creates a wonderful sense of light, this time associated with the sea, which infuses so much of McEwen's work and links him directly to the French impressionists as well as to his own country. Impressionism had produced a fine response among Scottish painters such as Peploe who, like McEwen, were able to draw upon the qualities of their own environment, both natural and artistic. The first movement of *Biscay,* 'Le Phare', sends out its cheerful and brilliant flashes

Example 1. McEwen: Quartet for Strings, 'Biscay', First Movement, 'Le Phare' (1913)

across a seascape occasionally obscured with mists. It is a superb realisation of atmosphere, demanding great sensitivity and refinement in performance.

The lazy and veiled colouring of 'Les Dunes', tinged with melancholy, is a masterpiece of impressionism, and the final vivace, 'La Recleuse' is a jaunty rondo and 'trio', stylishly French and

Example 2. McEwen: Quartet for Strings, 'Biscay', Third Movement, 'La Recleuse' (1913)

beautifully textured, full of the melodic and harmonic wit which Poulenc (then a teenager) was later to pursue with such verve.

France features also in his fine settings of Verlaine's poetry, in translation as well as the original, and it would be interesting to know what contacts he made there in the early 1900s.

McEwen's feeling for Scotland finds overt expression in *Hills o' Heather* for cello and piano, though with a subtlety as well as a power that its Lauderesque title does not evoke. Here is an example where that amiable image of Scotland does indeed intrude on reality in a negative way. There should be nothing whatever wrong with such a title. The image it should evoke is one of undisputed beauty. McEwen sadly subtitled it *A Retrospect*, having completed it in far-away London in March 1918 as the First World War ground to a close. Its defiant, wild and uninhibited rhetoric is not technically too demanding and it should have a place in the repertoire of all Scottish cellists.

The same splendid rhetoric is taken up in the first movement of the *Sonata Fantasia* for

28

Avison Ed.

Plate 57. *Grey Galloway*, BY SIR JOHN BLACKWOOD MCEWEN

29

Avison Ed.

violin and piano, completed in 1921, and whose last movement is a vivacious extension of the

Example 3. McEwen: Sonata Fantasia for Violin and Piano, 1921

spirit of the reel, but with uneven bar lengths and sophisticated harmonies, supported by a piano part bubbling with fun.

McEwen's orchestral works are also impressive, though the *Solway Symphony* (one of five) and the *Viola Concerto* (composed for the leading viola player, Lionel Tertis) could both do with cutting – something a modern editor might one day undertake, for both works contain fine music. *Grey Galloway*, one of three 'border ballads' for full orchestra, is one of his best large-scale works. It was completed in September 1908 and matches the powerful and dark rhetoric of the opening ideas with a second subject of haunting loveliness which grows out of a Scottish as well as an impressionistic background. McEwen lavishes attention on the orchestration to ensure just the right texture and atmosphere (see Plate 57).

In these and other such works, McEwen realises, more completely than any previous Scottish composer, a synthesis between native and contemporary classical idioms. His formal procedures may sometimes be of a more classical character than Scotland's landscape would suggest and the large-scale works might have benefited from a more organic approach, but his refinement and sophistication in the best of the chamber music and songs are not sufficiently appreciated. His music scarcely features in public concerts, nor is it understood to what an extent his was a major stylistic achievement. His output was

substantial and only a small proportion of it is known. He continued to compose well into his old age, and one of the most impressive of all McEwen's works is the *Fantasy Trio* of 1943, written when he was seventy-five. It is scored for violin, viola and cello in the sharp-edged key for stringed instruments of C sharp minor. It seems at times to be a dark and anguished response to war. A brooding andante with stabbing rhythms and sour harmonies introduces an allegro of nervous vivacity with a strange meno mosso like a blank-faced stare with its bare fifths and mechanically repeated oscillating chords. The string trio medium is not an easy one, for composer and performers are thoroughly

Example 4. McEwen: Trio (no. IV) 'Fantasy' for Violin, Viola and Cello, 1943

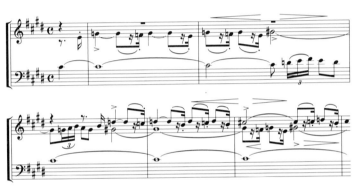

exposed. McEwen touches this raw nerve, but with a sure hand, conveying profound unease with mastery of the material.

By contrast, F.G. Scott's talents did not lie in large-scale forms, but his claim to a distinguished place in the history of Scottish music and, indeed, in the history of song, should be undisputed. If the reputation of Henri Duparc can survive on a mere dozen or so songs, then Scott is assured of permanence on the basis of many more of equal beauty and mastery.

Scott (1880–1958) was, like McEwen, a son of the Borders. He had all the necessary qualifications for a great song-writer: he understood the human voice; he was a great melodist; he was able to realise the inner essence of the poetry he set; and he had a respect for the rhythmic and tonal values of language, especially Scots. Such sensitivity has not bothered many composers, even great song-writers being prepared to override poetic rhythm and intonation for their own inner sympathies with the verse. Choice of text is less crucial. The requirements of a lyric are very different from those of other forms of poetry, and the lyrics of Muller evoked as great songs from Schubert as did the poetry of Goethe. Scott, however, had a uniquely privileged position in this respect, for he had been the teacher of Hugh MacDiarmid, and remained friend, stern (even savage) critic and delighted collaborator with him for many years. MacDiarmid, as one of the greatest lyric poets in a country which has produced many great lyrics before and after Robert Burns, gave Scott material so vivid and sharp in its imagery, and yet so suggestive and haunted by inner mysteries as well as outer certainties, that it is not surprising that the composer should have set so many of his verses, and done so supremely well (see Plate 58).

Milkwort and Bog-Cotton (1932), a masterpiece which makes of this astonishing lyric an even more deeply moving and understanding statement of love for the whole creation, is one of the greatest songs of any age. The integrity of the vocal line is still flexible enough to accommodate the rhythmic

Plate 58. Hugh MacDiarmid and F.G. Scott

nuances of the verse; the harmonies are no mere colourist's trick, but with subtle feeling follow and expand upon the shifting moods of the poetry; the shape of the whole, perfect.

Such songs are not fortunate accidents in Scott's output. There are many of similar quality, and varied in idiom according to the nature of the

Example 5. Scott: Milkwort and Bog-Cotton, 1932

Example 6. Scott: The Eemis Stane, 1924

poem. *The Eemis Stane*, composed in 1924, the year after Scott began to attend the Salzburg International Contemporary Music Festivals, shows him extending impressionistic harmonies towards greater dissonance while maintaining a vocal line entirely grateful to the voice, but with a sense of the mysterious view of the world and its destiny expressed through subtle chromaticism and disturbance of the underlying tonality.

Wheesht, Wheesht and *Crowdieknowe* each extend the harmonic language in similar ways and Scott has been proclaimed as the first composer of classical music in Scotland to confront the twentieth century.[5] This fails to do justice to McEwen and also narrows our view of the twentieth century to that of the Second Viennese School. This movement, led by Schoenberg, attempted to embody techniques designed to avoid a sense of tonality, into a system in which the twelve semi-tones of the chromatic scale were to be used without any audible effect of favour for any one as a key note or even vague tonal centre. It was necessarily antipathetic to a Scottish idiom which, though not conventionally tonal, is disinclined even to mild chromaticism. Scott's skill in blending the two is remarkable, but his debt to the Second Viennese School relates more closely to the expressive work of Alban Berg than the expressionistic work of Schoenberg.

This expansion of Scott's vocabulary did not affect his attachment to tradition. *The Old Fisherman* rests firmly, appropriately and beautifully within older conventions; and *Babie-Clouts*, a setting of Burns's famous poem of a young mother longing for the man who made her pregnant to make love to her again, evoked from Scott a song so utterly imbued with the tradition that it is now occasionally sung without its accompaniment. Perhaps one day it will become such an entrenched part of the tradition that objections will be raised if the accompaniment its composer intended were restored!

St Brendan's Graveyard approaches the tradition from another angle. Jean Lang's poem evokes the windswept atmosphere of a cemetery, named after one of the early Celtic saints, on the remote western island of Barra. Scott reproduces the sense of timelessness with a vocal line floating in disembodied beauty and simplicity over a piano part which subtly varies the drone effect which is part of the overall intention of imitating

piobaireachd. The score is marked 'Like a pibroch – impersonal and without nuance'. This attitude to piobaireachd is wholly misplaced, but that does not harm the extraordinary quality of

Example 7. SCOTT: ST BRENDAN'S GRAVEYARD, 1931

this song, which requires, and has found, a performance of great refinement and controlled expression for it to succeed.[6]

It is typical, not just of F.G. Scott, but of that tradition which he studied, extended and loved, that the words he chose for his own gravestone were: 'Nature I loved and next to Nature, Art.'

St Brendan's Graveyard has benefited from the impressionistic evocations of Marjorie Kennedy-Fraser, whose work Scott studied as part of his investigation of his native musical roots. She, in turn, was one of the first admirers of his songs, another being the remarkable, almost cult-figure of Kaikhosru Shapurji Sorabji.[7] Sorabji's own works have remained obscure, partly because he put a ban on their performance for some years, but his *Opus Clavicembalisticum* (which he premièred in Glasgow in 1930) set down a marker of monumental pianistic and contrapuntal virtuosity which was undoubtedly a goad to the muse that inspired Stevenson's *Passacaglia* (see below).[7]

F.G. Scott excepted, the period between the wars might have been one of musical gloom had it not been for the great energies of Erik Chisholm, whose eventual removal to Cape Town (there was no apartheid in Chisholm's department) deprived Scotland of one of its most significant composers, promoters and conductors. Twice he brought Bartók to Scotland, discussing piobaireachd with him and developing ideas related to the absorption of traditional idioms into contemporary music; and others who came in connection with the Active Music Society (founded by Chisholm in 1929) to introduce and perform their own music were Casella, Hindemith, Medtner, Schmitt and Szymanowski. Chisholm was also the first in the world to mount a complete performance of Berlioz's *The Trojans*, with the Glasgow Grand Opera Society in 1935 — an incredible achievement, consistently ignored by professional opera companies throughout the world, who like to imagine themselves first in the field. He also gave the British première of Mozart's *Idomeneo,* which had waited from the 1780s until 1934 for the privilege of a hearing in these islands, and (on tour from South Africa in 1956–57) the British première of Bartók's *Bluebeard's Castle*.[8]

As a composer he is acknowledged as a powerful innovator, though more than one critic has pointed to a certain uneasiness in his idiom.[9] His ballet *The Forsaken Mermaid* (one of four for Margaret Morris's Celtic Ballet Company), carried the Celtic mist school of thought over a new threshold, embedding it in the structure of the music, as in the piobaireachd which forms the Second Interlude (see Example 8).

The publication of *The Forsaken Mermaid* (composed for two pianos) used up all the funds of William MacLellan at the Dunedin Society, thus ensuring that Scott's songs remained unpublished for a while. Scott, disappointed by this outcome, wrote of Chisholm: 'He is a real snake in the grass, is Erik, and I get on guard whenever he makes a move in my direction.'[10]

This, however, did not prevent Scott's daughter, Lillias, from becoming Chisholm's second wife, thereby inspiring him to produce a group of settings of her own verse, as fine as many of her

father's songs. What is sad about the situation is that there should have been any need for scrabbling for funds in the first place. Publication is of great importance to a composer, the appearance of a score with the approval of a publisher and properly type-set immediately raises its status, irrespective of its true qualities, and makes it readily and legibly available to performers. One of Chisholm's few works available in print was *The Celtic Songbook* published in Russia on the recommendation of Shostakovich. *Oisean's Song* (with a text in English and Russian translated from the sixteenth-century *Book of the Dean of Lismore*) uses deep piano sonorities to suggest the Celtic hero dragging stones for St Patrick's Church. Although the song is strophic, the piano part changes for each stanza, sustaining the interest of the vocal line in much the same way as Kennedy-Fraser had done.

Among Chisholm's major works are three concertos. The *Violin Concerto* was premièred at the Edinburgh Festival, he himself performed his *Piano Concerto 'Pibroch'* with the Scottish Orchestra and, with great success, at the Amsterdam Festival of 1933 and his *Piano Concerto No 2* (the 'Indian'), based on Hindustani themes, was performed by Agnes Walker in Sweden, London, Moscow and Poland, its complexity approaching that of one of his major orchestral works, *Pictures from Dante*.[11]

Example 8. Chisholm: The Forsaken Mermaid, Second Interlude, 1940

Chisholm's main output, including his highly acclaimed operas produced in South Africa, is virtually unknown in his home country. One hopes there will be opportunites to improve on this situation so that a man who was clearly a major force in music-making in Scotland and South Africa can be given his due. He was a difficult person. In the seventeenth century he might have been described with more anatomical dispassion as 'choleric', but he was a great patriot and doughty champion of new music when others remained entrenched and kept their heads well below the parapet.

'In his last years in South Africa his schedule of work was incredibly heavy and contributed to his untimely death at the age of sixty-one. Perhaps his diet of fried mushrooms, whisky and love didn't help to prolong his always restless life.'[12]

Similarly neglected is Ronald Center (1913–1973) whose major cantata, *Dona Nobis Pacem* and impressive post-Bartókian *Piano Sonata* have only recently been recorded. The cantata is a work of arresting spiritual uncertainty – a kind of harbinger of Britten's *War Requiem* in its mixture of texts and dramatic musical insistences. But perhaps his most consistent music is to be found in the refined beauty and wit of the *Bagatelles* or the piano suite, *Children at Play*.[13]

The Scottish idiom featured also in the works of David Stephen (1869–1946), whose *Coronach* for orchestra was frequently performed and should not have slipped out of hearing, and in the prolific output of Ian Whyte. Whyte (1901–1960), conductor, arranger and composer is remembered in that latter capacity only for the suite from his ballet *Donald of the Burthens*. The ballet was performed at Covent Garden with considerable success and should be considered by Scottish Ballet for revival. The finale blends bagpipes and orchestra in a lively version of the *Reei of Tulloch*. A number of his works were heard at the Edinburgh Festival, including a *Symphony,* a *Piano Concerto* and his *Violin Concerto* which was much admired by Max Rostal. Whyte, the accuracy of whose ear was legendary, built up the BBC Scottish Orchestra, evoking an unsolicited tribute from Sibelius for his conducting of the Finnish master's music.

Contemporary with Whyte was Hugh Roberton (1874–1952), later Sir Hugh, an arranger and conductor rather than a composer.

He is remembered as one of those peculiarly gifted choirmasters who have the mixture of charm and absolute savagery necessary to take a choir to the top. The Glasgow Orpheus Choir (1901–1951) was the body which he founded, presided over as ring master and brought to an international standing, which died with him. It had its own very distinctive style: incredibly disciplined, full of sentiment, and somehow managing to sound like glycerine. Ian Whyte would not let Roberton near his new BBC orchestra, declaring that Roberton would ruin it.[14] The Phoenix Choir, which rose from the ashes of the Orpheus, also achieved much distinction; but there were in the first half of the century over a hundred choirs in the Glasgow area alone, and many more throughout the country, often putting on major works under leading conductors such as Barbirolli. The decline in choral singing since those days is one of the few major musical and institutional losses of this century.

The Second World War led to a certain amount of musical retrenchment. The BBC at first broadcast mild pap in the curious belief that this would keep the populace confident and happy;[15] more seriously, it had a profound effect upon the progress of contemporary music, for Hitler's régime had a retrogressive effect and many avant-garde composers and Jewish musicians fled to America and elsewhere. Scotland benefited from this by the arrival of the distinguished Austrian composer and musicologist, Hans Gal (1890–1987), who was invited to join the staff of Edinburgh University Music Department by Donald Tovey. Gal taught a number of Scottish composers, as well as bringing to students (in nearly forty years of teaching) an experience and musicality second to none, and which had direct links with the great classical traditions. His compositions, subtle, humane and finely wrought, deserve greater notice. The eloquent wit and poetry of his *Three Marionettes* (piano, four hands), the gentle beauty of the *Three Songs to R.M. Rilke* (for three female voices and piano) are qualities to be found in numerous works. His important contributions to opera are sadly not known in this country. Gal was a musician of profound integrity and legendary skills, whose approach is best summed up in his own words: 'The only true way for anyone with a genuine artistic urge and imagination is truth . . . if one speaks the truth, it may be irrelevant; but if one speaks untruth, it is always a damned lie.'[16]

Tovey (1875–1940), composer and musicologist, is particularly remembered for his analytical programme notes, perhaps picking up some echoes of the first occupant of the Reid Chair, John Thomson, who had originated the idea and was one of only two Scots ever appointed as Professor in the one hundred and fifty-year history of that music department. The other, John Donaldson (*c*. 1790–1865), was troubled for most of his tenure with a (finally) victorious battle to get the university to honour Reid's will in full.[17] Tovey founded the Reid Orchestra which was semi-professional and which, among some notable Scottish premières, gave his *Cello Concerto* with Casals as soloist in 1934, who should have been knighted alongside Tovey in 1935 for braving its difficulties which, in a concerto lasting a full hour, would benefit from heavy pruning.

One of the very few Scots to be appointed to a chair of music in Scotland was Professor Robin Orr (1909–), a distinguished composer whose *Symphony in One Movement* is well wrought and who, as a founder and chairman of Scottish Opera had several operas performed by them, the most recent – *On the Razzle* – demonstrating that in his late seventies his is still a lively musical mind, though any potential forcefulness is usually kept well within disciplined bounds. He is more at home in the subtle delicacies of the *Three Chinese Songs*, than the social realism of Clydeside which provides the plot of *Full Circle*.

One of the consequences of the war was that the new continental music did not impinge upon British composers as soon as it might have done; and when it did, it became a cult. Scotland was in the forefront of the assimilation of the latest music. The Musica Viva series of concerts put on by the Scottish National Orchestra under Alexander Gibson in the 1960s, was one of the most adventurous projects ever undertaken. The more recent Musica Nova concerts, having been put into the siding of a special festival, do not quite match that daring. The first British performances of Schoenberg's *Violin Concerto* and Stockhausen's *Gruppen* were given in Glasgow, and alongside them the works of Iain Hamilton, Thea Musgrave and Thomas Wilson were also heard.

All three composers were profoundly influenced by twelve-tone technique, and the possibilites of extending its ordered atonal democracy to rhythm, pulse and other basic aspects of music were explored. Melody and lyricism did not find a ready home in this style and the explosive effect of the confrontation was best exemplified by the outraged reception given at the 1959 Edinburgh Festival to Iain Hamilton's *Sinfonia for Two Orchestras*, commissioned for the Burns bicentenary. Hamilton, knowing well enough that most of Scotland would be hoping for something more akin to the splendid and cheerfully tonal work of a Cedric Thorpe-Davie (1913–1983) (whose distinguished music for *Ane Satyr of the Thrie Estatis* and for *The Gentle Shepherd* is still played), produced a powerful and uncompromising essay in which he honoured Burns, not in the remembrance, but by producing the most adventurous Scottish score of his day.

Hamilton's was a courageous act. His own earlier *Violin Concerto* displayed an amiable style and his move to adopt a thoroughly contemporary and European style was a clear break with the entire tradition of Scottish music, including most of its classical music. He has recently returned, as have many others, to a more tonal manner, but many of his major works such as *Alastor* and *Aurora* were written using serial techniqes to such an extent that when he returned to tonality and key-signatures he confessed: 'I was at first afraid I might have forgotten how to use them.'[18]

Hamilton (1922–) was just beginning to put serial technique behind him when he was offered a commission by Scottish Opera and responded with *The Catiline Conspiracy*. This highly concentrated work, classical in subject-matter, tightly structured both dramatically and musically, did not endear Hamilton to his Scottish audiences any more than did the *Sinfonia*. There is a starkness about the action, much of which is plotting rather than events, and the characters are not a loveable lot, on which point Hamilton maintained: 'I take no sides but stand behind each character in whatever situation they may find themselves. This does not mean that I have no point of view regarding some of the deep issues at stake in Catiline, it is simply that I refuse to condemn or condone; that is for the characters and the audience to settle as best they may. At the most one can warn.'[19]

The Catiline Conspiracy is a score marked by its clarity, assisted by careful motivic characterisation. *Anna Karenina*, premièred by the English

National Opera in 1981 is, however, a work in which characterisation is supported by assigning different tonal centres rather than using tiny motifs and points towards a re-emerging lyricism.

Example 9. HAMILTON: THE CATILINE CONSPIRACY, ACT II SCENE III

One of Hamilton's most powerful works is the *Epitaph for this World and Time,* for three choruses and three organs, composed in 1970 and in places overwhelming in its effect.

The Edinburgh-born composer, Thea Musgrave (1928–) writes music more overtly dramatic in style, though she too was much influenced by the structural controls of serialism. Her early *Bairnsangs* are relatively traditional and are distinguished additions to the centuries-old repertoire of fine Scots songs, but her main works are in the orchestral and concerto forms. The *Horn Concerto* is an outstanding example of her ability to dramatise contemporary techniques to great effect. Extending the ideas of her *Clarinet Concerto*

in which the soloist moved from group to group within the orchestra, she placed members of the horn and trumpet sections of the orchestra around the hall, setting up a conversation between them and the solo horn, with thrilling results. This spatial development – originated by the Venetian composers centuries earlier, pursued by a Scottish predecessor, John Abell (see Chapter XIII), given its most famous post-war exposition in *Gruppen,* taken up by Hamilton's *Sinfonia* and reflected even in the development of stereo sound – has never found a more appropriate

Example 10. MUSGRAVE: MARY QUEEN OF SCOTS

Plate 59. A SCENE FROM THOMAS WILSON'S *Confessions of a Justified Sinner*

outlet. The horn was traditionally an outdoor instrument associated with the hunt and with answering horn calls through the woods, and Musgrave evokes all the poetry and excitement of that past without conceding to mere prettiness, but exploring new sonorities and textures with imagination.

Her opera, *Mary Queen of Scots*, first produced and recorded in America where, like Hamilton, she worked for several years, is less adventurous but has many finely imagined scenes ranging from the atmospheric fog-bound arrival of the young queen, to the exciting evocation of the court dances into which she introduces Bothwell and his troops singing a ribald Dunbar poem. The contrast and overlap of genteel French and vigorous Scots is managed with musical and dramatic skill (see Example 10).

Thomas Wilson, though born in America in 1928, has lived and worked in Scotland for almost all his life. His work is deeply serious and is often motivated by a strong moral sense which has found expression in a number of impressive religious works, particularly the *Missa Pro Mundo Conturbato* of 1970 where doubt and faith confront each other in an increasingly rich harmonic language, which developed into something approaching liturgical drama a year later in the *Sequentiae Passionis*. Wilson's moral sense found an even more intense outlet in his opera *The Confessions of a Justified Sinner*. This outstanding work, showing profound insight into one of Scotland's greatest novels (it was James Hogg's masterpiece) went too deep for the critics from the south, but was more fully appreciated in Scotland and should be taken to other European countries where the psychological drama it so movingly unfolds is more likely to be understood. André Gide was one of the first continentals to appreciate the full stature of the novel; Wilson, in insight and technique, was the ideal composer to give voice to its disturbing exploration of the borderlines between good and evil, rationality and insanity. This work was a landmark in Scottish music, and should be honoured as such (see Plate 59).

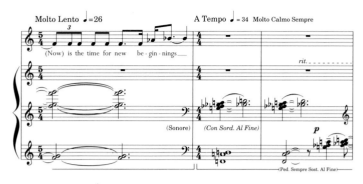

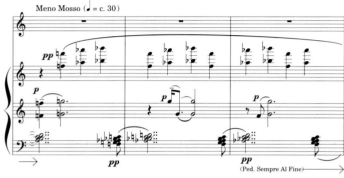

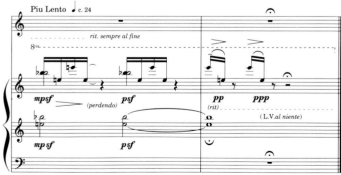

Example 11. WILSON: THE WILLOW BRANCHES – VII SPRING SONG, 1983

Wilson's *Piano Concerto* is one of his most impressive achievements to date though, interestingly, it is substantially built out of quite disparate earlier works – the *Piano Trio* and the exquisite group of songs *The Willow Branches*. It is from a moment of intense longing and searching for love in the songs that the melody for the concerto's central slow section is taken.

The *Piano Trio* provides the final section of the concerto with an angular rhythmic vitality which was at one time a compositional mannerism but, in its new setting, proves effective, especially given the gradually emerging role he has devised for the piano:

> What eventually emerged from all this preliminary thinking was the idea of standing the priorities of the 'heroic' concerto on their heads – letting the orchestra rather than the piano dominate in the early stages, sweeping all before it by sheer impetus and aggression, while the soloist took on a quieter and more persuasive role, moderating and gradually transforming the orchestra's energies a little bit at a time. In other words, the soloist would take on an Apollonian role, standing for poetry, order, restraint, humour, intelligence and so on, while the orchestra would be cast in the more disruptive and turbulent Dionysian aspect.[20]

Wilson was aware that this scheme was partly modelled on Beethoven's *Fourth Piano Concerto*, but he has allowed the idea to permeate the structure of the music, even the note 'sets' which contrast with and complement each other and form the basis of the whole work. The *Piano Concerto* has recently been recorded with David Wilde as the soloist; but one of Wilson's most successful works internationally has been the *St Kentigern Suite*, toured by the Scottish Chamber Orchestra. It evokes the spirituality which underlies the legends associated with the seal of the city of Glasgow, whose patron saint is Kentigern.

Wilson's manner is earnest, even in lighter works such as his orchestral portrait of Shakespeare's *Touchstone*. His style involves an intensity of expression which relies heavily on chromatically enriched harmonies and melodic motion making much use of semi-tones and the interval of the tri-tone, though more recently gilded with sensuous instrumentation. He is not a composer in whose musical company one can often relax, but the technical assurance and expressive integrity of his music have earned him the proper respect of his contemporaries and successors, for whom he has now become an elder statesman.

Parallel to Wilson's influence on the west of Scotland has been that of Ronald Stevenson on the east. Stevenson (1928–) was born in England, but his ancestral Scotland called him home, where he became a friend of MacDiarmid and brief colleague of Chisholm, pianist extraordinaire, and a man of immensely wide cultural sympathies. He represents more than any a continuity in Scottish classical music, which has not prevented him from evolving a highly exploratory technique, influenced in particular by Busoni. One of his major works, *The Keening Sang for a Makar*, was composed in memory of F.G. Scott, and his recent vocal work, *In Memoriam Robert Carver*, is a fine tribute with passages of irridescent vocal beauty. But his most widely admired composition (like *The Keening Sang for a Makar*, composed for solo piano) is the vast *Passacaglia on DSCH*. The letters stand for Dmitri Shostakovich, whom Stevenson greatly admires and whose initials, like the name BACH, can be represented in notes by using the German musical alphabet. The passacaglia as a form is similar to that of the ground bass, referred to in relation to William Kinloch (see Chapter IX), in which a bass-line is repeated over and over with a series of variations above it. Stevenson became so absorbed with this theme that he wrote: 'I went on piling up variations over that ground bass until they grew into hundreds. I don't know how many hundred: I've never counted them. I felt the nature of the work was "aqueous" – it should flow. For that reason it should be in one movement. And in the flow should be other forms, similar to what geologists call "aqueous rocks".'[21]

The *Passacaglia on DSCH*, taking eighty minutes to perform, is the longest single-movement work for piano ever written and, needless to

say, makes extraordinary demands on the pianist – namely, Stevenson himself, or John Ogdon, who recorded it for EMI. It is a fascinating work, a magnificently ambitious omnium-gatherum in the manner of MacDiarmid's *In Memoriam James Joyce*, in places drawing together themes from widely varying sources of classical music, as in this passage where DSCH, BACH and the Dies Irae are combined (see Example 12).

Its virtuosity lies not only in the pianistic inventiveness of the work (itself a compendium of piano technique) but in the astonishing fertility with which Stevenson has treated the motif (it is too short even to be a theme) which forms the basis of every bar. Sir William Walton wrote of it:

> It is really tremendous – magnificent. I cannot remember having been so excited by a new work for a very long time. It is in the line of such great works as Busoni's Fantasia Contrappuntistica, and he, I am certain, would have been among the first to acclaim it. I enjoy its uninhibited exuberance and originality, and the absence of fashionable 'isms' appeals to me. Though it is long in actual duration, it does not seem a bar too long in performance.[22]

Stevenson's fanatical search for a synthesis of his experience has not, however, blinded him to the small perfections that can be achieved with a simple lyric. It is with one of these that the final chapter of this book is concluded. The MacDiarmid parallel is again apt, and attitudes to Stevenson's work follow that parallel, his many devotees as utterly convinced by his large-scale achievements as F.G. Scott was unconvinced by MacDiarmid's. One of those achievements, though built from smaller units, is his setting of his namesake, R.L. Stevenson's *A Child's Garden of Verses* in response to an inspired commission from the BBC to celebrate the centenary of their publication. This song-cycle is one of those rare artistic meetings of child and man in which there is no condescension, but all the clear-sightedness of youth, yet confused by the touching ambiguities of the encounter. Stevenson's own strange blend of tonal gestures from different periods of European music here defies being categorised and bypasses the accusation of eclecticism by the perfect wholeness of the conception (see Example 13).

It was a sign of growing confidence in the musical community that this post-war period saw the arrival of composers from England for whom Scotland was beginning to have sufficient attractions and outlets. Distinguished visitors included the brilliant and witty Frank Spedding,

Example 12. STEVENSON: PASSACAGLIA ON DCSH

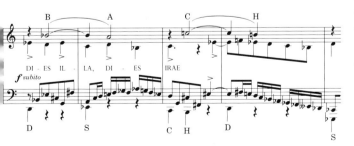

Example 13. STEVENSON: A CHILD'S GARDEN OF VERSES,
Dedication

whose *Bellini Studies* show that he has a poetic side to him which explores the Bellini theme he has chosen with skill, beauty and a superb feeling for the two-piano texture employed in the work. Spedding was an influential composition teacher at the Royal Scottish Academy of Music and Drama.

William Wordsworth, by comparison, spent the best part of his creative career in the heart of the Grampians, composing works with a matching spaciousness that draws him out of English pastoralism into music of power, grandeur and integrity. The *Fifth Symphony* and several of the string quartets provide fine examples. Likewise Kenneth Leighton brought an earnestness of purpose which is evident in almost everything he wrote. His music is overtly intense and crafted with a strong sense of line as well as a powerful command of counterpoint; his broad harmonic and rhythmic vocabularies, however, are used insistently and his textures are often heavy. His opera *Columba* contains many lovely passages, but it is a pity that it was composed in ignorance of the existence of Columban chant in the library of the university of which he was Professor of Music for many years.

The renaissance of Scottish music is now in the hands of native Scots of younger generations who have benefited from the skills and example of their predecessors, establishing themselves in their own right, no longer obliged to fight for credibility, but confident of their deserved position in the world of music beyond Scotland, where many of them have received their greatest recognition. That that situation is showing signs of being remedied is thanks, in substantial part, to the courageous tenacity and unquestioned stature of composers such as Wilson and Stevenson who have kept faith with their country by living in it.

CHAPTER XIX

A NEW ACCOMMODATION
1950–

This final chapter, being concerned with Scottish music in the last half of the second millenium AD has more than contemporaneity and a millenial date to justify its being the concluding one. It is only since the Second World War, as we saw in the previous chapter, that classical music has firmly taken root in Scotland. The perceived divisions between classical, traditional and popular have been added to by innumerable sub-divisions, catered for by specialised groups, record labels, festivals and radio stations. Jazz, rock, light, country and western, and many other designations might seem to point to a fragmentation of taste and culture. Classical music itself has its afficionados in specialised domains. These have been reflected in the titles of festivals and groups, such as Musica Viva, Musica Nova, the Scottish Early Music Consort, the Scottish Baroque Ensemble, the Scottish Chamber Orchestra and the New Music Group of Scotland – by no means the only specialist ensembles, though all flexible enough to break out of any mould.

The cheap and universal access to all these kinds of music through mechanical reproduction might have been expected not only to encourage this apparent fragmentation but also to bring live music, traditional or classical, to an ignominious end, confined to recording studios. If anything, the reverse has been the case. Musicians and enthusiasts rarely confine their interests to one chosen type of music, and concert giving has never been more frequent than in the last decade. Festivals with a high music content, pioneered by the Edinburgh International Festival, but joined by Glasgow's Mayfest, the Perth Festival, the St Magnus Festival, the Glasgow and Edinburgh Jazz Festivals and Folk Festivals, the Aberdeen Youth Festival and many more of all kinds in smaller centres, are as often as not providing music for local appreciation as for the tourist. This multiplicity of choice, in which the occasional exclusive clique largely operates to its own disadvantage, justifies naming this chapter 'A New Accommodation'; for at long last Scotland is able to support a full range of musical facilities, available over most of its terrain through touring companies and local initiatives, and focused where need be in the larger centres and on major festivals. Above all, it has brought forth a group of composers of outstanding ability who themselves cross musical divides, and most of whom are able to practise their art in their own country, and the same is beginning to happen in the world of pop music also. This enormous increase in activity, still continuing, means that this chapter can only give a superficial account, but that in itself is necessary.

In such an environment, how does traditional music fare? That heritage which we have so long defended and reinterpreted, might seem vulnerable, faced with exposure to so much from within Scotland, never mind from practically every musical culture under the sun. Yet it has done more than survive; it has burgeoned. The songs and ballads have not only been preserved by recording; they have been passed on by these means and by live transmission, so that there are younger singers with a care for the repertoire and capable of sustaining it where, before, an outmoded snobbery was complaining of 'the cracked-voice recordings of authentic folk-crones, of interest to sociologists rather than musicians'.[1]

The story of the folk music revival in Scotland has been told elsewhere[2] but it is important at least to outline it here. Up until the 1940s, Scottish traditional music was collected haphazardly and made available usually in mutilated form, with a very few honourable exceptions such as the London publication, the *Journal of the Folk Song Society* under the aegis of Lucy Broadwood, descendant of the Scottish piano maker, John

Broadwood. In the north-east, the magnificent collecting work of Gavin Greig and the Reverend James Bruce Duncan had mostly to wait until the 1980s–1990s to appear in print – a fine publishing venture still in progress.[3] Francis Child had gathered together the texts of many of the 'Muckle Sangs' – the great ballads, but only in 1959 were they systematically provided with their tunes – a monumental work undertaken by the American, Bertrand Harris Bronson, and which took until 1972 to be completed. As far as traditional instruments were concerned, the clarsach, having died out, was relaunched on a wave of Celtic mystification at the first National Mod in 1892 – by Marjory Kennedy-Fraser's daughter, Patuffa, and by the Clarsach Society in 1931; the small pipes were a forgotten sweetness, and only the Highland bagpipes and the fiddle continued to hold their own.

As far as performance of rural traditional music was concerned, most of the material was still sung among the travelling people and the farm-workers. Urban folk-song also survived in its own birth-places. But in both cases the environments in which they were produced were under threat. Mechanisation was turning agriculture into industry, and industry itself was changing so that the camaraderie of the coal-mine, the noise of the jute-mill, or the clamour of the shipbuilding yard, were giving way to the clack of typewriters or the unrelenting self-satisfied purring of computers.

The chief public outlets for Gaelic music were the annual local Mods as well as the National Mod itself. But these continued to perpetuate the ideals of the late nineteenth century; also, the main public opportunities for the performance of piobaireachd were, like the Mods, competitive. The effect of this competitive atmosphere was to make performers adjust to the expectations of adjudicators, whose selection and judgment is often open to criticism. In defence of this continuing practice it can also be claimed that it is a stimulus to people (particularly to school-children and their teachers) who might never otherwise bother to work up their skills. In a culture where the traditional outlet of the ceilidh has been increasingly eroded, there is a case for the more artificial respiration of the Mod; and as far as piping is concerned, the competitive element is at least as old as the Battle of Worcester (see

Chapter XI). It is also easy enough to criticise the Kennedy-Fraser-influenced approach of the revivalists of the clarsach, but their society still functions and has broadened out into major teaching programmes in schools as well as involving a much higher degree of scholarship than was available at the beginning of the century, though they, along with the Mods and the world of piping, still hold on to competition.

Nonetheless, the earlier approach to traditional music, in which the orthodoxies of academic musicians were seen to be threatening to corrupt the pure source from which they drank by the addition of the musical equivalent of chlorine, was to be thoroughly shaken up by the folk music revival which started in the 1950s and is still active. This revival was, as much as anything, politically inspired. Scotland had provided Britain with much of its industrial and military power for well over a century, but industrial decline was on the way and an awareness that the sacrifices that had been made in two world wars had brought little improvement in social conditions or understanding of Scotland's distinctive cultural and economic needs, helped to foster a powerful socialist movement which used song as one of its chief forms of expression. That this movement had its roots in America in the first part of the century, and was fostered by collectors and broadcasters in America is no accident; for both the USA and Canada continued to be the generous recipients of thousands of Scottish immigrants, driven away by a variety of factors which it is not the place of this book to explore, but which created a climate in which old orthodoxies and snobberies were simply by-passed. One of the first serious collectors, Alan Lomax, came over from the USA on a recording mission for Columbia Records, and was joined by Hamish Henderson and Francis Collinson, two of the first researchers at the School of Scottish Studies.

The School of Scottish Studies was set up in Edinburgh in 1951 with a vast remit covering not just traditional music and song in Scotland's three languages, but the whole traditional culture, rural and urban. Amongst its chief progenitors was Sidney Newman, Reid Professor of Music. It coincided with a period of growing national awareness of which a powerful emblem was the *Lias Fail* – the Stone of Destiny. It is fitting that

Plate 60. CALUM JOHNSON, PIPER AND SINGER, PLAYING AT COMPTON MACKENZIE'S FUNERAL, 4 DECEMBER 1972

this book should refer to the potent social symbolism of ringing rocks in its first chapter and, without any forcing of the evidence, find itself doing so in its last. This stone (which was supposed to utter a cry when sat upon by the rightful successor to the Scottish throne) was stolen by Edward I and used subsequently as the legitimising seat upon which the monarchs of England and, later, those of the united crowns, were installed. It was taken back to Scotland on Christmas Day 1950 without the approval of the Dean and Chapter of Westminster Abbey (where it resided), in a gesture of nationalist defiance which gave rise to a song and which has become part of Scotland's folklore. Whether the original or a fake was returned seems likely to remain for ever obscure. No sound was heard from it at the coronation of Queen Elizabeth, but there was a lot of other noise going on at the time.

The founding of the School of Scottish Studies led to the uncovering of an incredible wealth of traditional material, without which this book would have been groping in the dark, and which lays heavy stress on the absolutely vital importance of Scotland's cultural institutions. It provided also a focus for the collecting and reviving undertaken by many others, from Pete Seeger to the late Ewan MacColl, and has been the source of material for folk groups and solo performers of every shape and description. In the world of the ballad, singers and performers such as Jeannie Robertson, Betsy Whyte, the Stewart family from Blair, Duncan Williamson, and many more were discovered, to everyone's

astonishment except their own, to be sustaining a repertoire centuries old. In the Gaelic-speaking world the same was true and Francis Collinson and J.L. Campbell, again among many others, recorded material from Calum and Annie Johnson and a whole host of singers, some of which can be reasonably assigned to a pre-Christian culture, but which was rich in song from the seventeenth century to the present day. Calum Johnson (source of some of the most important material in this book) was also a distinguished piper and a friend of the writer Compton MacKenzie, at whose funeral on their beloved island of Barra, he played and died (see Plate 60).

The songs and ballads which were collected were not merely of the past. Ewan MacColl, whose own roots were in the tradition, added many items to it and composed tunes such as *Sheath and Knife*, for Child ballads which lacked them,[4] or songs about social conditions such as *The Terror Time*. It gets its title from the words of Maggie Cameron living in the typical tinker's bow tent in Cookson's field at Alyth in 1964: 'Winter – that's the terror time – no place to go nor doesn't know where to go. Doesn't know any

Example 1. MACCOLL: SHEATH AND KNIFE (from the singing of Ewan MacColl)

place to go and sit. And it doesn't matter whether it's snowing or blowing. You've got to go.'

MacColl is also remembered for his outstanding series of radio ballads which brought the music of the tradition, particularly of Scotland, into the understanding of people all over Britain who had lost contact with such realities. MacColl is by no means the only one to have added to the traditional repertoire with distinction. Hamish Henderson's *Freedom Come-All-Ye* is in virtually every traditional musician's repertoire. It is a powerful ballad against war, and highlights a significant aspect of the folk revival, which was focused in the peace movement and particularly against the installation of nuclear weapons in Scotland. One of the leading members of the revival was the Labour politician, the late Norman Buchan.

Nor was the world of the Gael living only in the past. Calum Ruadh, the 'Bard of Skye', composed a splendid satire on the men of the Free Church who attempted to stop Sunday ferries, as well as a fairy song out of his own dreaming and a touching lament for his brother, murdered in Malaya. His method of composing songs in his head is revealing, as is the style of performance. When Thorkild Knudsen multi-tracked different versions by Calum Ruadh of the same composition so that one can hear how various strands of melody are sorted to make up the full tune, Calum Ruadh declared: 'That's it! That's just how it is!'[5]

He also makes a distinction between the musical delivery of a song when sung to himself and sung to an audience that goes deeper than the difference between formal and informal. To himself he chants at a lower pitch in most cases, but raises the pitch and brings out the tune more for public performance. Perhaps this offers a solution to the problem of distinguishing between duan and laoidh, outlined in Chapter VI; namely, that the same text could be delivered in two different forms according to the occasion, and that these forms were closely related.

Alongside all of this were traditions fully conscious of their own significance and supporting themselves commercially, to the extent that a few individuals could afford to be fully professional. A music hall singer such as Lauder was not alone. Will Fyfe and others contributed to the image, and it has its descendants in

pantomime, which is a still-thriving theatrical form in Scotland to all of which the Logan family have contributed much over the years. Something of that world is perpetuated in the ever-popular *Scots Magazine* (the longest-running magazine in the world) which has changed its image and contents only superficially in the last fifty years and manages to honour those days alongside contributions more scholarly and up-to-date. Indeed, the sentimental Scottish attachment to certain kinds of musical and social security are still catered for by fiddle and accordion bands, or request programmes on radio in which the songs of yesteryear refuse to bow to changing fashions; and the repertoire of dance bands is continually expanded by new compositions in a style that has scarcely changed in two hundred years. Reels, strathspeys, jigs, hornpipes, titled and composed just as the Gows and Marshall titled theirs, and some just as good, are only differentiated from their predecessors by the harmonic backing of the accordion whose style is itself a hundred years old, at the least. The foot-stirring rhythmic genius of the great dance-band leader, Jimmy Shand, has made him a legend in his own lifetime. Rhythm and dance are at the heart of these attractions, and the continuing pleasure that Scottish country dancing provides throughout the land, whether at the weddings of the young or the reunions of the old, is a measure both of the social appeal of set dances and of the vitality of the music, without which they are nothing. I have known people to sneer at this aspect of Scottish culture, but if they could experience the fun and emotional stimulus that people get out of it they would be fierce in its defence, whether in the more genteel form of the Scottish Country Dance Association, or its wilder manifestations in a village hall.

The fiddle, however, still rules over the accordion. It cannot be matched by the accordion in slow airs, nor can the vigour and subtlety of its bowing in the traditional style be reproduced; and the addition of harmony is no substitute. The quality and extent of Scots fiddle playing is a remarkable phenomenon. From the thriving fiddle playing of the Shetlands to the more elaborately decorated style of the west Highlands and the core of the tradition in the north-east, standards of playing put many more expensively trained musicians to shame. The dismissive reader is best dealt with in the words of Yehudi Menuhin:

> Their music knows no detour – it goes straight to our feet if dance we must, to our eyes if cry we must and always directly to our hearts evoking every shade of joy, sorrow or contentment. . . . The genuine Scottish fiddler has an infallible sense of rhythm, never plays out of tune and is master of his distinctive and inimitable style, which is more than can be said of most 'schooled' musicians. We classical violinists have too obviously paid a heavy price for being able to play with orchestras and follow a conductor.[6]

The continuing strength of the fiddle tradition was marked in particular by the superb playing of Hector MacAndrew, whose grandfather was taught by James McIntosh (a pupil of Niel Gow's) and who himself had classical training and whose pupil within the tradition, Douglas Lawrence, earns his living as an orchestral player. The links with classical music (going back to the early eighteenth century) were sustained by family traditions such as that of the Hardies who, in the present generation, still perform a mixed repertoire, their dynasty having commenced in the eighteenth century with the brilliant violin maker Matthew Hardie. This long line of fine violin and bow makers includes famous names such as Dodd in the eighteenth century, Mann in the nineteenth century and Smillie in the twentieth century.[7] The tradition is strong in all parts of the country. The late Andrew Poleson, Tom Anderson and Aly Bain in the Shetlands; Angus Grant in the Highlands and Islands tradition; Ron Gonella, Alasdair Hardie, Jo Miller, and many more representing different aspects of the mainland traditions, have sustained a wide variety of styles, and there have been a number of finely produced and well-anotated fiddle collections and recordings issued, preserving details of style and technique. However, it has been claimed that the oldest style of Scots fiddling is dying out, though something of it survives in the Cape Breton fiddle tradition.[8]

As for the pipers and drummers, they go from strength to strength. Younger players such as Robert Wallace, Allan MacDonald and Murray Henderson are worthy successors of great players such as John Burgess and John MacFadyen and, far from being slaves to tradition, are ready to compose music themselves as well as adopt new approaches to piobaireachd in particular, and piping in general. Their skill and musicality is second to none, and it is a measure of the international strength of the tradition that Murray Henderson comes from New Zealand and that, on the pipe-band front, the World Pipe Band Championship competition has been won by a Canadian band. Love of the bagpipes is shared with many nations, from Brittany to Oman, Egypt and India to China, where the pentatonic nature of Scottish music finds a natural partner. These connections are not merely in the mind. They occur on the ground, for Scottish traditional folk groups and individual pipers travel the world. The enduring appeal of the Scottish style of pipe music, however sentimentalised or embellished, remains a force to be reckoned with. *Amazing Grace* became an international hit, and (though it was a pop song) *Mull of Kintyre* drew most of its inspiration from that same idiom and was the first single in the world to sell more than two million copies, putting the Liverpudlian Paul McCartney in much the same record-selling league as Harry Lauder. Literally hundreds of new compositions have been published and have found a place in the repertoire and, though they may not break new ground beyond introducing occasional 'seconds' (harmonies) or more modern cross-rhythms, they are, many of them, worthy of their place. A good example is Robert Wallace's *The Barlinnie Highlander*, dedicated to the deputy governor of that famous prison and as rhythmically nippy as a prison governor no doubt has to be. It is a hornpipe, making use of the traditional double-tonic effect, but in the third section adding cross-rhythms (see Example 2).[9]

Perhaps most notable of all is the adoption of The Corries' *Flower of Scotland* as an unofficial national anthem. The last phrase of the tune is clearly based on the bagpipe scale and is sung correctly by vast crowds, though the flattened seventh might well be sharpened by the sports enthusiasts of other countries in order to make it conform to standard European practice. The committed singing of this tune at the famous rugby grand-slam victory for Scotland over England has been widely accepted as one of the prime causes of that win. It may not be one of our best tunes, but it is remarkable testimony to the deep-rooted appeal of nationalism in Scottish music in an age of thoroughly international idioms, in which the same crowds are eager participators.

Example 2. ROBERT WALLACE: THE BARLINNIE HIGHLANDER

The support of the army for the bagpipes has naturally led over the past two centuries to their close involvement with drums. With respect to drumming, the work of the late Alex Duthart, who incorporated Swiss styles into the already fine techniques of Scottish drumming,[10] has produced a standard of playing of tremendous virtuosity in which a musician such as Peter Anderson can hold an audience in thrall for several minutes with a single drum and two sticks, but in which the basic disciplines of ensemble required for pipe-band drumming are still maintained. Classical percussionists have been to Duthart for lessons, and his own drum compositions have been published.

In the ballad singing tradition there has been continuity also. Singers such as Lizzie Higgins, Jean Redpath, Norman Kennedy, Andy Hunter, Sheila Douglas, Gerda Stevenson, the singer and fiddler Jo Miller and many more, do not merely reproduce the performances of older generations: they honour their spirit and pass it on, giving and taking in the manner that is itself traditional. Others such as Alex Campbell and Archie Fisher moved from the tradition towards a more American-influenced style.

Parallel to these sustained traditions has been the flourishing of folk groups, some sticking largely to traditional instruments, others bringing in electric guitars, synthesizers, keyboards and exotic instruments. Among the first were Heritage, Clutha, The Whistlebinkies and The Boys of the Lough, whereas Ossian, Capercaillie, and The Battlefield Band could be more closely identified with the second, though the division is far from rigid. The bands who have stuck to the traditional instruments have, nonetheless, altered it by bringing them together; the clarsach, fiddle and bagpipes having apparently not been used in ensemble before. The same variety of approach is heard in the presentation of Gaelic traditional song. Flora MacNeil, Finlay MacNeill and Anne Lorne Gillies sing mostly unaccompanied or with traditional instruments, but other fine singers such as Christine Primrose and Catherine-Ann MacPhee sometimes work in less traditional ways, and groups such as Na h-Oganaich and Runrig have mixed Gaelic tradition with rock music with great success. Runrig are deeply indebted to Gaelic song, of which they perform many traditional items in modern dress (see Plate 61).

Plate 61. Runrig, 1988

Their rhythmic, harmonic and instrumental innovations are in many ways more violent intrusions upon the original material than Kennedy-Fraser's, but are approved (where Kennedy-Fraser is derided) because they are of their own time and fashion. They serve the same important function of demonstrating that the power and universality of Gaelic song can speak to all generations and wear the clothing of the day without loss of identity or dignity.

There has also been genuine revival of broken traditions. The number of fine clarsairs has doubled in recent years and there are now two or three who can play the metal-strung harp. Patsy Seddon and Mary McMaster of Sileas, Rhona MacKay and Judith Peacock who have played with The Whistlebinkies, and Alison Kinnaird, Marie-Louise Napier and Savourna Stevenson have explored and extended the repertoire with increasing skill and sensitivity. The small pipes and the border pipes have been resuscitated by Robert Wallace and by Gordon Mooney and Hamish Moore, the latter having also used them as a jazz instrument with the saxophonist Dick Lee. The overall picture is one of vigour and variety and is immensely encouraging.

Such vigour by no means absorbs all the musical talents of the nation. Pop music in Scotland has also flourished to such an extent that one can legitimately claim that few countries have been so prolific of musical talent per capita in recent years.

The roots of Scottish rock music lie in the ballrooms and folk clubs of the 1950s where American country, hill-billy and rhythm and blues styles began to replace traditional Scottish music. The influence of American roots music first crossed over into the mainstream via Glasgow-born Lonnie Donegan, whose skiffle group reached the British and American Top Ten in 1956 with *Rock Island Line*. Donegan had recorded the song when he was a member of Chris Barber's Jazz Band and he went on to become the leading Scottish light of the skiffle boom of the mid-1950s, though his career remained firmly based in London.

Scotland was at first slow to accept rock music. Interestingly it made its first real progress in rural centres, farmers in tackety boots enthusiastically invading the stage in Inverness in the 1960s and The Beatles making their first Scottish appearance in Elgin in 1963. Like The Beatles' native Liverpool, Glasgow was steeped in the transatlantic crossing of musical styles. It was common-place for merchant sailors to arrive in Glasgow with the latest blues, early Tamla Motown and rock'n'roll imports. Scottish beat groups like The Poets, The Beatstalkers, The Pathfinders and The Athenians specialised in covers of US rhythm and blues hits. Each group attracted its own screaming fans and a healthy regional scene developed throughout Scotland. Edinburgh had The Boston Dexters, Glasgow Dean Ford and The Gaylords, Aberdeen The Misfits, Dundee The Poor Souls and Buckie Johnny and The Copycats.

Lulu and The Luvvers were the first to hit the charts – their cover of The Isley Brothers' *Shout* was so raw that many fans thought they were an American band. The Poets from Glasgow scored a ground-breaking hit in the same year (1964) with *Now We're Thru*, an eerie self-penned ballad which paved the way for other Scottish groups to record their own material. The Poets' recordings are an early example of innovation in Scottish rock music, but the most legendary innovator of them all was Alex Harvey – he was among the first musicians to go to Hamburg in the late 1950s, his Big Soul Band became a top attraction in the 1960s and in the 1970s he formed The Sensational Alex Harvey Band. Their mix of mime, vaudeville, hard rock, interpretations of Jacques Brel songs and use of the Scottish vernacular was unique and distinctive and their shows at the Glasgow Apollo in 1975 are still regarded as a pinnacle of live performance.

Also from those days were Scottish-influenced groups which owed something to the folk scene such as The Incredible String Band and Jethro Tull. Jethro Tull (whose name is that of a Scottish agrarian reformer) have shown the influence of Scottish social and musical backgrounds, particularly in numbers such as *The Pine-Marten's Jig*; more recently The Proclaimers made a hit out of *Lochaber No More*, and Deacon Blue's album *Raintown* is particularly associated with Glasgow, not just by title, but by mood and by a melodic clarity which is reflected in the texture.

Returning to the 1970s, other notable bands include The Average White Band, The Bay City Rollers, Nazareth and Frankie Miller, all of whom have had international success; but in Scotland at the end of the decade there was a major shift away from traditional rock values. The London punk explosion was quick to spread north and Scotland was soon awash with punk, thrash and new wave groups. The Skids, The Scars, The Jolt, and Johnny and The Self Abusers all made rough, rowdy and sometimes witty records which swapped musical expertise for raw energy. Johnny and The Self Abusers immortalised the Glasgow venue Saints and Sinners in their first single, which was also the first recording by Jim Kerr and Charlie Burchill, who soon went on to form Simple Minds. Simple Minds are Scotland's most consistently successful rock band. They reached Number 1 in the USA in 1984 with *Don't You (Forget About Me)* and their 1989 album *Street Fighting Years* sold in excess of three million copies.

Simple Minds' success paved the way for other Glasgow bands to follow and by 1985 Glasgow was the record companies' first port of call in their search for new talent. Wet Wet Wet, Texas, The Big Dish, The Blue Nile, Horse, Deacon Blue, Love and Money, Hue and Cry and many others from the Greater Glasgow area signed major recording contracts, and for a time it seemed that a vibrant and self-sustaining Scottish rock industry could become a reality.

So far this has failed to happen. The lack of a suitable infrastructure, properly funded and integrated, is as serious a drawback for pop music as it is for classical. There are indeed good rock bands, recording studios and organisations such as MIST (the Music In Scotland Trust) the SRIA (Scottish Record Industry Association), and Scottish Enterprise, all of which have provided funding and support to the Scottish rock community; and in 1991 a Scottish chart was established in which the top twenty reflected the taste of the Scottish buying public rather than, essentially, that of England. This increasing sophistication of the Scottish market can do nothing but good for the future emergence of bands and of opportunites for them to develop musical styles which are not dictated by other markets. But there are no major Scottish-owned record labels and no Scottish-based distributors capable of handling both mainstream and specialist rock products, so all major profits from publishing and recording still flow south, just as they did twenty-five years ago. In their song *Letter from America* The Proclaimers mourned the demise of traditional Scottish industry. In the former industrial town of Bellshill a whole new generation of Scottish groups are building a national following. They include Teenage Fan Club and BMX Bandits, but they too have signed to labels furth of Scotland.

When it comes to classical music, much the same holds true; but it is important to realise that though this chapter has divided our music into three genres of traditional, popular and classical, the barriers between them exist only in the minds of minorities, and a number of significant composers work in more than one field, as will emerge. The creation of the Scottish Music Archive (under the guiding hand of Frederick Rimmer) to provide a resource centre for Scottish classical music, was an important step towards establishing the viability as well as the availability of many compositions. It remains the only library where Scottish music can be found in the form of performing material as well as for reference and in audio form. When the institution became the Scottish Music Information Centre it expanded its holdings to cover the whole history of Scottish music, including traditional music, adding a publishing venture to the existing hire and sale of works in manuscript.

To write of composers of one's own generation, thriving and active, when one belongs in their company, is an unwise procedure; but it is unavoidable in this history, if only because the extent of the response of composers to the arrival of the necessary institutions in classical music should be recorded from a contemporary perspective. The selections and judgments are dictated by space, current opinion and personal feeling, in that order. It is courteous to write of our visitors first.

As well as reaching out towards international audiences and exporting composers, Scotland has played host to a number of foreign composers. We have already mentioned Gal from Austria and Wordsworth, Leighton and Spedding from England (Chapter XVIII); and to these may be added two further English composers, Harper and Maxwell Davies, both of whom have had an important impact on Scottish music-making, as have the New Zealander Lyell Cresswell, the Welshman John Hearne, and the Icelander Haflidi Hallgrimsson.

Edward Harper, though often as earnest as his compatriot, Leighton, is not always so – his *Bartók Games* being especially clever. The opera *Fanny Robin* pursued Harper's interest in Thomas Hardy, but his most powerful work to date is *Hedda Gabler*. It was an act of daring to make an opera out of that great and terrifying play, but Harper has genuinely added to its theatrical effectiveness, at least in English translation to which he brings additional poetry and intensity with sufficient distinction to make one realise that, after all, *Hedda Gabler* is an obvious choice for operatic treatment. Harper is director of the New Music Group of Scotland which has commissioned and performed many works from Scots.

The works of Sir Peter Maxwell Davies are only considered here peripherally. Numerous publications and recordings are available and that fact alone demonstrates an imbalance of resources between the north and south of Britain, for many of the works he has composed in Scotland and demonstrating an interest in things Scottish are not exceptional when set alongside their Scottish contemporaries and predecessors. That he has used his considerable influence and skills so positively is something for which Scottish musicians should be grateful. In particular, he set up the St Magnus Festival in the Orkney Islands, which has commissioned many new works from Scottish composers; and he himself has responded to Scotland's musical heritage with something of the enthusiasm of a Max Bruch, working in almost Victorian mood with shades of local colour in the slow movement of his *Violin Concerto*, or the use of bagpipes in *An Orkney*

Example 3. DALBY: NOZZE DI PRIMAVERA

Wedding, with Sunrise in which he shares the same difficulty as did Ian Whyte with *Donald of the Burthens*, that you cannot successfully compose for bagpipes at the written pitch of A because they all play very nearly in B flat. Pipers have been patient with this (and much else) beyond the call of the sternest military duty.

A number of Maxwell Davies' works make use of Scottish legends in the modern equivalent of the nineteenth-century Ossian craze. *The Lighthouse* and *The Peat-Cutters* are good examples, or *Stone Litany,* which is based on a mis-reading of two runic stones,[11] which fact does not appear to affect the strength of the music in the slightest. But he has shown a deeper response in the *Second Symphony* in which the meeting of the Atlantic and the North Sea in the turbulent waters upon which his home looks out, has inspired the structure and mood of a work that

moves closer to the kind of understanding that has, so far, been brought to things Scottish by only one visitor – Mendelssohn – with whom the prolific Maxwell Davies has much in common.

Lyell Cresswell has the reputation of thinking up the most intriguing titles for his pieces – an entertaining poem could be constructed out of a mere list of them. But *White On White*, an 'a cappella' setting of Greek poems by Jannis Ritsos, depends on no titular gimmickry. Its virtuoso handling of the voices builds on fragmentary ideas with astonishing sureness of texture, suggesting in one setting a statue emerging from the naked marble as the range and density of the parts stretch and intensify; in another the growth of a sense of distance between man and star in isolated phrases to an intense cry of loneliness. *Salm* (one of several impressive orchestral works) builds an entire movement out of a gradual intensification and expansion of aspects of Gaelic psalm singing, the Scottish idiom having been influential more than once in his music.

John Hearne's recent *The Four Horsemen* for brass ensemble brings a new concentration and power to his writing, worthy of the terrific subject of the four horsemen of the Apocalypse which inspired its sometimes brutal energies. Hearne has done much to foster the Aberdeen International Youth Festival at which Hallgrimsson's *Daydreams in Numbers* was premièred by the Helsinki Junior Strings. The technical mastery of this piece reflects the composer's experience as a cellist, and its beauty of texture and breadth of expression are an inspired response to the astonishing abilities of the orchestra, as well as demonstrating a flexibility of idiom not always apparent in his more rigorous works.

Turning to the native composers of the generation following Musgrave, Hamilton, Orr and Wilson is to turn to a group who have founded their reputations abroad as well as at home, and the majority of whom choose to live in Scotland, exceptions being John Lunn and James Dillon.

Working for the BBC as Head of Music in Scotland for many years provided Martin Dalby with a base from which to promote the works of Scottish composers, as well as one from which he could support his own composing. Dalby studied in Italy with Petrassi and, despite some early flirtations with serial technique, his essentially gentle and lyrical nature has blossomed. A masterly orchestrator, Dalby has contributed with distinction to a wide variety of media, including the powerful and popular work *A Plain Man's Hammer* for wind band. His loveliest score is, appropriately, a wedding gift to his wife, ex-member of the orchestra over which Dalby presided and which his efforts, among those of many others, helped to save. *Nozze di Primavera* is a work of lush beauty that realises everything its title implies. Lurking subtly in its texture is the music for *Ex Te Lux Oritur* – the wedding hymn for Margaret of Scotland and Eric II of Norway (see Chapter V, and Example 3, opposite).

Most recently *The Mary Bean* was premièred at the London Proms by the Royal Scottish Orchestra (formerly the Scottish National Orchestra), being commissioned to celebrate their centenary. As with a number of Dalby's compositions there are references to older Scottish music – in this case Columban chant. But Dalby has never allowed these influences to become overt. They take more the form of private and personal stimuli and messages, and it is this combination of private and public that gives much of his music an intriguingly restrained communicativeness, as full of thought as much of Tippett's music, with which the rich complexity and evanescent textures of *The Mary Bean* have points of contact.

Dalby's colleague in the BBC, David Dorward, has also been a composer of thoughtful nature. Indeed this is an aspect of Scottish music of their generation and of their predecessors which has yet to be appreciated fully by the younger generation, whose proper self-confidence and panache occasionally lacks intellectual strength. Dorward is at his best in intimate works such as *Kithara* – 'Three Hellenic Dances' for guitar solo which are exquisitely conceived for the instrument. A similar refinement and skill is evident in the choral work, *The Weather Beasts*, though in a major work such as *The Golden Targe*, he is capable of magnificence. The chamber opera *Tonight Mrs Morrison* (one of a series commissioned by the BBC in the 1960s)[12] showed that Dorward has a sense of musical drama expressed in the taut neurotic energies of the dance that leads to the heroine's death, and contrasted with the expressive ballad which mourns her in music of beauty and simplicity.

The Edinburgh-based composer, John McLeod, has chosen a less disciplined control of his considerable compositional energies. This has resulted in works which have created an immediate appeal, notably the recent *Percussion Concerto* and *Piano Concerto* of which the *Glasgow Herald* wrote: 'McLeod has constructed a dramatic "tour de force". The stark juxtaposition of materials hurtles the music forward with an almost numbing force.'[13]

The Gokstad Ship, a symphonic poem commissioned by the often impressive National Youth Orchestra of Scotland, toured Scandinavia with great success. His style develops dramatic contrasts rather than integrated development, though the unusual chain-like structure of the *Clarinet Quintet* combines a novel kind of organisational coherence with occasional frolicsome touches.

Example 4. WEIR: THE ART OF TOUCHING THE KEYBOARD

But for the frolicsome there is no one to match Judith Weir. Weir's talents are of the oddest. Who else has been able to create a highly successful mini-opera out of a single voice? *King Harald's Journey to Byzantium*, outrageously silly in places, nonetheless gets away with it. And who would dare to name a sequence of keyboard miniatures *The Art of Touching the Keyboard* after the great Couperin, and produce such perfectly judged explorations of sonority and texture without any show and within the space of a few minutes? Set against the impressive but arrogant compendiums of Stockhausen's *Klavierstucke*, Weir's *The Art of Touching the Keyboard* comes as a breath of fresh air, having as much to say with a fraction of the time and effort.

One is reminded of Satie at his best. There is the same probing wit, and a delicacy and refinement that is very French and may indeed have its origins in shared cultural perceptions. The east-coast Scottish mind, which is undoubtedly a major factor in Weir's work, is historically an analytical one that has produced great engineers, philosophers, doctors and economists;

Example 5. McGuire: Calgacus

it is also one with a brand of humour to which the word 'pauky' supplies only a poor clue for tourist consumption. Of the stimulus of background she has said: '. . . perhaps it stems from the fact that my parents were from Aberdeen where a genuine folk-music tradition still exists – that music was something spontaneous and home-made, something you could knock together and to which everyone could contribute.'[14]

One of Judith Weir's chief successes has been in opera, *A Night at the Chinese Opera* being widely acclaimed. *The Vanishing Bridegroom*, commissioned for Glasgow's year as cultural capital of Europe (1990), received a mixed reception. Set in the Highlands – always a danger area because it is nearly always perceived superficially – the related story-lines attempt a cumulative structure more convincingly managed by Malipiero in his *Torneo Notturno*. The music, however, has moments of great beauty and imagination, but appears to have made too many concessions to melody for some current critical fashion. The recognition of the central role of melody has usually been a part of Scottish music and its gradual return to the forefront in the music of the composers mentioned here is a welcome development.

One who has set himself determinedly in that direction is Edward McGuire. Combining classical and folk musician in his own person (he plays flute and clarsach for The Whistlebinkies) and preserving an apparent innocence which should never be presumed upon, McGuire has made a place for himself in Scottish music which is a practical example of the ideals to which he subscribes. He is not sufficiently credited for his pioneering work and the boldness and originality of his composition. He is the composer of the only really outstanding orchestral work to involve bagpipes. Where Maxwell Davies's unpretentious but superficial *An Orkney Wedding, with Sunrise* gains the plaudits of the newspapers, McGuire makes a genuine and deeply understood exploration of the role of the bagpipes in vast terms. He has a proper technical understanding of the instrument and its idiom which results in the entry of the pipes on a tune of great beauty, power and

Plate 62. SCENE FROM EDWARD MCGUIRE'S *Peter Pan*

feeling, nobly paced and set against an ever-increasing battery of sounds from percussion and orchestra in one of the most dramatic pieces of orchestral writing from the pen of any Scot. The work is called *Calgacus* after the Pictish leader who was defeated at Mons Graupius by the Romans and whose speech before the battle is reported by Tacitus. The famous line 'You make a desert and call it peace' comes from it and has spoken powerfully to McGuire, who is not keen on imperialism (see Example 5).

Mention of McGuire's 'innocence' is not casual. His opera *The Loving of Etain* passes from myth to reality with calculated naïveté, Celtic echoes mingling with cocktail music in an uncanny combination which teases and disturbs. The transitions are handled with technical mastery. Such an approach takes great risks and McGuire sometimes stumbles over a text or a conception that loses credibility through lack of intellectual control. But the risks are worth taking and it was an inspired thought that commissioned from him a score for Scottish Ballet for *Peter Pan*. This is perhaps his loveliest and most impressive achievement to date; but this beautiful score and entrancing ballet was greeted with pathetic condescension by all the critics (save that of the *Glasgow Herald*) and adored by the audiences. Here we have the welcome inversion of many foolish prejudices, a modern piece (for McGuire's style is anything but conservative) which was an immediate and unqualified hit with the people who paid for entry, and sneered at by those who did not. One would not wish even to flirt with a populist approach, but it is gratifying to know that the so-called unbridgeable gap can be bridged. McGuire is the right person to do it. The fairy music, of exquisitely conceived hushed magic, stands easy comparison with Britten's for *A Midsummer Night's Dream*, and the wit of the Scottish dances which McGuire incorporates into the pirate scenes outshines Britten's somewhat arch treatment of the mechanicals in that same opera. *Peter Pan* has been toured as far as Hong Kong and has twice supplied Scottish Ballet with their Christmas show and will surely do so again (see Plate 62).

Another Glasgow-based composer who combines a subtle wit with a speculative turn of mind that draws lines between distant poles is John Geddes. The wit is evident in the delightful *Leo Dreaming* for solo trombone and tape. Leo is Geddes's cat and his wildest dreams are astonishingly realised for him within the framework of his whiffling breathings. Geddes is another relatively unsung pioneer. His early *Symphony* is a fine work, with a slow movement exploiting Gaelic idioms on low flutes, overlapping and weaving, in a manner that goes far deeper than most. Recently, his *Voyager* for orchestra has won deserved international acclaim, the more remarkable for the fact that this is an undemonstrative and thoughtful work with a mystical thread that links it both to the Voyager space probe and to Halley's comet which was passing at the time. Geddes's music is often characterised by brittle nervous rhythm and scoring, but he has lyrical gifts as well. The two are brought together in his *Callanish IV* for solo cello, the lyrical phrases are based on the nineteenth-century Gaelic psalm tune *Stornoway*, the dramatic contrast with the pizzicato phrases evoking the power of the famous Callanish stone circle on the island of Lewis, whose capital is Stornoway and where Gaelic psalm singing survives in its full vigour.

It is an astonishing fact that Gaelic had never been set or sung in any extended classical composition until William Sweeney's *Salm an Fhearainn* (Psalm of the Land). This historic work in essence reproduced and enlarged upon Gaelic psalm singing to produce sounds and textures for a cappella voices that had never been heard in a classical context. Sweeney has followed this with another extended setting of Gaelic by the poet Angus MacNicol, *An Seachnadh* (*The Avoiding*), both works being commissioned by Cappella Nova. Like McGuire, Sweeney crosses the musical divides, in this case between jazz and classical, for he is a clarinettist and devotee of jazz. The results have been some of his finest music, music that should earn him a wide audience. The Concerto *An Rathad Ur* (The New Road) for the brilliant Edinburgh saxophonist, Tommy Smith, was a *tour de force* for both composer and performer. First performed on BBC2, its concert-hall debut was one of the many St Magnus Festival scoops.

Sweeney uses a broad brush on a canvas occasionally too large for the material, but he also achieves a control over the passage of time that has much of the power of piobaireachd.

Example 6. GEDDES: CALLANISH IV (FOR SOLO CELLO)

Nine Days for clarinet and tape (or ideally three other clarinets sustaining a drone from different aural perspectives), explores the relationship between piobaireachd and its embellishments, and the characteristics of the clarinet.

Example 7. SWEENEY: NINE DAYS (FOR CLARINET)

Its haunting beauty epitomises Sweeney's style which is characterised by the building of large structures out of motifs of direct appeal, often influenced by modal or pentatonic outlines. Nowhere is this more movingly realised than in his major orchestral work, *Sunset Song*, in which he incorporates the tune for *The Flowers of the Forest* just as Lewis Grassic Gibbon did in the novel from which the piece takes its name. The expansion of the theme in orchestral terms is managed with a true insight that honours the inner essence of the melody (see Chapter VII) while setting it in the context of powerful rhythmic mechanisms appropriate to the industrial revolution which overtakes Grassic Gibbon's trilogy. *Sunset Song*, commissioned by the STUC in honour of its retiring president, Jimmy Milne, was for Sweeney a labour of love. Coming from a trade-union family and himself an ardent trade-unionist, Sweeney is as aware as his contemporary

Glaswegians, McGuire and MacMillan, of the social and moral responsibilities of the artist, without in any way compromising their aesthetic freedoms.

All three have been involved in educational work, some of it as part of the Strathclyde Concertos scheme in which Strathclyde Regional Council in conjunction with the Scottish Chamber Orchestra commissioned a number of concerti from Sir Peter Maxwell Davies which were tied to work in schools by Scottish composers who received a matching commission.

James MacMillan's is an outstanding talent, also motivated, but not circumscribed, by strong left-wing political convictions (see Plate 63). *Songs of a Just War* sets poems by Neruda, Soutar and Tsou ti-fan; and his concern with South American society is also expressed in *Busqueda*, an important music theatre piece commissioned by the Edinburgh Contemporary Arts Trust, and of which *The Independent* wrote: 'It is hard to think of another contemporary figure who is so lyrical and dramatic, and yet so thoroughly in command of his material.'[15]

The lyricism that finds noteworthy expression in *Study on Two Planes* for cello and piano seems related to his occasional participation in traditional music, and lyricism and drama are both at the heart of his recent commission for the London Proms, *The Confessions of Isobel Gowdie*. This orchestral work makes a powerful and emotional statement out of the brutalities and prejudices that were part and parcel of the witch-hunt, hammering out its central repeated chords with uncompromising musical assurance, and evoking an explosive response at its première. One of the most prolific of composers, his ability to work up a small number of ideas into convincing large-scale forms is something he shares with Maxwell Davies.

MacMillan, along with most of the composers living in Scotland, has made use of the electronic music studios available in Glasgow and Edinburgh and which are an important (and expensive) part of the musical infrastructure. But it is the live musicians who provide the most vital outlet. In the world of chamber music, composer-led ensembles such as the New Music Group of Scotland under Harper and the Paragon Ensemble under composer, conductor and flautist, David Davies, have been of vital importance in placing

Plate 63. JAMES MACMILLAN

contemporary Scottish music in the European context in which it is best understood. The John Currie Singers and Cappella Nova have performed a similar service in vocal music, and so too have the BBC Scottish Symphony Orchestra and the Scottish Chamber Orchestra in the sphere of orchestral music. Scottish Opera have also quite a good record of commissioning, but the Royal Scottish Orchestra has a long way to go before it can claim that it fulfils what should be one of its central roles. Its promotion of Musica Nova has not always been as whole-hearted as the quality of the event deserved and its centenary programmes do not include a single commission paid for out of their own coffers. There is therefore still a lurking suspicion that at the heart of Scotland's musical culture there are those whose knowledge, awareness and sense of direction lag well behind the society they are supposed to serve.

Based in London, but motivated by a compositional Calvinism that strikes one as Scottish in its rigour, is James Dillon, who became one of the featured composers at Musica Nova. Dillon's aesthetic has developed to a point where if he sees anything emerging in his musical explorations that looks familiar to him, he goes off at a tangent from it. This wiping clean of the slate as soon as it seems a recognisable word is squeak-ing its way into existence, produces an alienating effect on most audiences and per-formers, but is not without its moments. Recognition in this view is essentially a kind of observational laziness; but there is a problem of philosophy here. Continuously to reject the emergence of recognisable patterns or forms is itself a repetitive and formulaic approach, though it is presented as organic and relates to the philosophy of Heraclitus, who maintained you could never step into the same river twice (or even once say his critics, apparently unaware that this statement neither refines nor alters the position).

Put into compositional practice one has to say that the river is easily identified and that stepping into it is not a comfortable process. Nor would Dillon have it be a comfortable process. *Helle Nacht* is his first major orchestral work and draws its title from Hölderlin's translation of *Antigone*, describing the burial alive of Antigone herself. The obsessive avoidance of anything resembling pulse creates the kind of discomfort Dillon is looking for, and he achieves moments of elemental power that are clearly attributable to the philosophy that is questioned here, just as Iannis Xenakis (by uncompromising observation and adherence to the realities of forms, be they architectural or derived from human speech) produces aural images unlike the work of any other composer, while resting on a philosophy of mathematical precisions which he admitted, when pressed, are in truth mere approximations, and necessarily so.[16] It will take a fiery spirit to emerge tempered and fit for grinding from the furnace Dillon has created for himself, but he shows signs of being able to achieve it.

Another London-based Scot is John Lunn, who made a distinguished contribution to the popular music album, *Man Jumping*, with a subtle number called *Down the Locale*. His string quartet, *Strange Fruit*, with its demanding 'walking bass' part for the cellist and its jazzy rhythms made a strong impression; but his most startlingly impressive work to date is *Jazz Pointilliste* with its scat-style vocal line and its brilliant contrasts of frenetic jazz-oriented energy with moments of still beauty and reflection of great poignancy.

Ian McQueen, like Weir, has contributed with distinction to the operatic repertoire, *Judith Och Holofernes* having been premièred in Sweden with wide critical approval. His affection for the voice and his feel for melody, coupled with his interest in working with children, demonstrate an increasingly humanising style among younger Scottish composers – a desire to work with the community, not in splendid isolation from it.

The list of composers whose work is discussed above could have been extended, and the music in any case merits proper study rather than passing reference. The absence of that proper study for so much of the work referred to (throughout this book, not just in the twentieth century) is a matter for serious reflection on the part of our music graduates and those who train them. The classical may have taken root, but the roots are still shallow. We are lamentably unaware of much of our own musical heritage: our only orchestra with any real independence of box office pressures and Scottish Arts Council grants – the BBCSSO – has three times been threatened with extinction (the last time as recently as 1981) and was only saved by a huge effort and unremitting public protest;[17] the number of our university music departments has been cut from five to two in the last decade, with consequences yet to be felt but likely to be extremely serious for music in the future; the teaching of music in schools, more particularly the vital role of peripatetic instrumental teachers (be they training budding violinists, pipers, or pop stars) and the residential orchestral courses which act as the focus for these activities, are among the first to be cut when cuts are threatened, as they are; our national opera company teeters on the edge of financial impasses, as is the way with opera companies; disgracefully, we still do not have a national theatre company which, if it existed, would be potentially of great significance to composers and musicians, indeed to all the arts; our capital city has no opera house worthy of the name, and the new Glasgow concert hall, the only concert hall in Scotland that is built to international standards, was built without one penny from the Westminster government or the Scottish Office – a terrifying reflection of the political anomalies and cultural ignorance under which the country struggles to preserve its identity. The absence of any major recording and music publishing companies based in Scotland is also a severe handicap. All this should warn us against any complacency.

Likewise, the oral tradition, dependent on an environment that is itself fragile, is a vital part of our culture which requires a sensitive approach to the development of the nation's resources, be they in teaching, tourism, industry or crofting, or the long-overdue official recognition of Gaelic, if it is to continue to give us the riches we have been fortunate to inherit. It also requires an understanding that place is important in human life and that the usefulness of mobility of labour should not become a necessity, and that the language and customs of different parts of the country should not be starved of resources for the sake of centralised schemes. The teaching of fiddle or clarsach by people sensitive to the tradition is as important in Shetland or Lewis as it is in Aberdeen or Edinburgh.

These warnings may appear to some readers as unseemly in a history; but they are an important comment upon the history of Scotland's music. It is not fully understood just how dependent music is upon well funded institutions. A painter requires relatively cheap materials and a well-lit room and, so long as he has cakes and ale he can work, and his work can be seen. A writer requires no more than paper and pencil and a sheltered place to use them (though cakes and ale are helpful too) and her work is ready to be passed round. But a composer requires musicians and a place for them to be heard and a time organised for that activity. Sometimes the place itself has to be large – a church, an opera house, a hall capable of responding to the sound of a full symphony orchestra. Showing the score, even to trained musicians, is little better than presenting the reader with a poem in which several of the lines are illegible. The musicians have to be trained and employed in a sufficiently enlightened manner to allow them to study new music, not least from their own country, as well as the music of the dead from all over the world. Their training takes many years and involves the purchase of the highly sophisticated tools of the trade, instruments that cost thousands of pounds, be they new or old. It is an expensive and lengthy business, and a vulnerable one. Moreover the composer cannot even learn how to progress without public performance of his work.

These things understood, there has never been a more productive and promising period of music-making at every level than exists at the time of writing. There are now several composers of outstanding ability and international standing living and working in Scotland, and the quality of music-making over an immensely wide field of activity is, for the size and resources of the country, truly astonishing, and is reflected in the many prestigious tours abroad undertaken by pop groups, traditional musicians, folk groups, orchestras, ensembles and individuals. We have yet to produce another Robert Carver, but the conditions now exist in which it becomes possible, even likely, not least because the Scots have never lost touch with their traditions. Moreover, the native gift for melody is as alive as ever it was, and it is on that note that this book comes to an end, with Ronald Stevenson's setting of MacDiarmid's *Ae Gowden Lyric*.

Ae Gowden Lyric claims – and what musician worthy of drawing breath would claim anything other? – that one golden lyric is not only better than the castle's soaring wall, and all the achievements and history that that image implies; it is better than anything else at all. Stevenson's setting could never be mistaken as traditional, but it could not have been born without that tradition: it is both new and wholly Scottish. Its soaring vocal line demands from the singer a technical mastery and a deeply-informed expressive simplicity that has been at the heart of Scotland's lyric traditions for hundreds of years. It is a song so unaffectedly expressive of the enduring qualities of Scottish music that it feels as though we had all had a share in its making, as though it were our own private gift to ourselves.

Example 8. STEVENSON: AE GOWDEN LYRIC

Down by the burn, where scented birks
Wi' dew are hanging clear, my jo,
I'll meet thee on the lea-rig,
My ain kind dearie, O.

Plate 64. ILLUSTRATION FOR BURNS'S *The Lea Rig*, 1896

CHAPTER NOTES

INTRODUCTION

1. Adapted from Whitley Stokes (trans.), *Adamnan's Vision* in *Fraser's Magazine*, Feb 1871, Vol. III, No. XIV, p186.
2. Alessandro Tassoni, *Prose Politiche e Morali*, ed. Rossi, Laterza and Figli, Bari 1930, p340. Joseph Cooper Walker, *Memoirs of Alessandro Tassoni*, Longman, London 1815, pp99–107.
3. Richard Hoppin, *Medieval Music*, Norton 1978, p507. The ms. known as *Anonymous IV* refers to major and minor thirds as being thought 'the best concords' in 'the region which is called Westcuntre'.
4. Francis Collinson, *The Traditional and National Music of Scotland*, RKP 1970, Chapter I; and David Johnson, *Music and Society in Lowland Scotland in the Eighteenth Century*, OUP, London 1972, pp150–163.
5. Roger Fiske, *Scotland in Music*, Cambridge University Press, 1983, Chapter I, esp. pp14, 24.
6. For Branles, see Thoinot Arbeau, *Orchesographie*, trans. Mary Evans, Kamin Dance Publishers, New York 1948, pp146–149; and Estienne du Tertre *Danceries*, ed. M. Expert, Maurice Senart, Paris 1908, pp114–115. For the jig see C.R. Baskervill, *The Elizabethan Jig*, University of Chicago Press 1929, pp11, 12 and 40 et seq. Baskervill does not think the jig is peculiarly Scottish, though much of his evidence, including the earliest, is admitted to be Scottish. He does not mention that Sir William Keith and Robert Johnson were both Scottish (p46).
7. Alexander Scott, *Ballat maid to the Derisioun and Scorne of wantoun Wemen*.
8. As Note 4.
9. Alexander Mollison, *An Essay Towards the Improvement of the Musical Art*, Glasgow 1798, Preface.
10. William Tytler, *Dissertation on the Scottish Music*, Society of Antiquaries 1780.

CHAPTER I

1. Professor Eogan at a conference, *Ireland and Scotland*, Edinburgh University, 18 February 1989.
2. John M. Coles, *Irish Bronze Age Horns and Their Relations with Northern Europe* in *The Prehistoric Society*, No. 11, 1963, p339. Also J.V.S. Megaw, *Problems and non-problems in palaeo-organology: a musical miscellany* in *Studies in Ancient Europe*, eds. Coles and Simpson, 1968, Leicester University Press, p347.
3. *Reports of the Inverness and Dingwall Presbytery, 1643–1688*, the Scottish History Society Publications, Edinburgh 1896.
4. John McInnes, *Gaelic Poetry and Historical Tradition* in *The Middle Ages in the Highlands*, the Inverness Field Club, Inverness 1981, p143. Also W.M. MacKenzie, *The Book of Arran*, Vol. 2, The Arran Society of Glasgow, Hugh Hopkins, Glasgow 1914, pp289–290.
5. A.A.M. Duncan, *The Making of the Kingdom*, Oliver and Boyd, Edinburgh 1978, pp13–14.
6. School of Scottish Studies, 1951/10/A13.
7. Casa Lund, *The Sounds of Prehistoric Scandinavia*, in *Musica Sveciae*, Vol. 1, sleeve notes Items 11 and 10.
8. James H. Todd and A. Herbert, *Irish Version of Nennius*, Irish Archaeological Society, Dublin 1848, XXVIII, pp124–125 and lines 151–152, pp144–145.
9. Ms McKenzie of Islay and Sandy Buie of Jura in conversation with the author.
10. George Petrie, *The Complete Collection of Irish Music*, ed. Stanford, London, Boosey and Co., Vol. II, p261, No. 1027. There is an excellent article on the caoine, including a section on Scotland, by Brendan O'Madagain, *Irish Vocal Music of Lament and Syllabic Verse* in *The Celtic Consciousness*, ed. O'Driscoll, Toronto 1981, pp311–332.
11. Martin Martin, *A Description of the Western Islands of Scotland*, A. Bell, London 1716, pp71–72.
12. *The Ringing Stone* in *Tales of Argyll Lismore and Appin Edition*, Argyll Branch of the British Red Cross Society 1981.
13. Bernard Fagg, *The Discovery of Multiple Rock Gongs in Nigeria* in *African Music*, Vol. 1, No. 3, 1956, pp6–9.
14. Whitley Stokes (ed.), *Cath Maige Turedh* in *Revue Celtique XII*, p57.

15. Catherine Fagg in conversation with the author (see Note 13).
16. Stuart Piggott, *The Carnyx in Early Iron Age Britain*, in *The Antiquaries Journal* 39, OUP, 1959 pp29–30, and in conversation with the author.
17. Renato Meucci, *Roman Military Instruments and the Lituus*, in *The Galpin Society Journal*, August 1989, p90 and Plate XIII.

CHAPTER II

1. I am grateful to the leading Welsh folklorist, Phyllis Evans, for providing this and the wren song.
2. Brendan O'Madagain, *Gaelic Lullaby: A Charm to Protect the Baby?* in *Scottish Studies*, Vol. 29, 1989, pp29–38.
3. James Porter, *Harps, Pipes and Silent Stones: The Problem of Pictish Music*, in *Selected Reports in Ethnomusicology* 4, (1983) (Essays in Honour of Peter Crossley-Holland), pp259–260.
4. Ibid.
5. Anna Ritchie, *Picts*, HMSO 1989, p34.
6. Osian Ellis, *Hanes y Delyn yng Nghymru*, Gwasg Prifysgol Cymru, 1980, p16/17.
7. Eugene O'Curry, *On the Manners and Customs of the Ancient Irish*, ed. O'Sullivan, Williams and Norgate, London 1873, p363.
8. In Porter (Note 3) Ellis (Note 6) and Peter Crossley-Holland, *The Dagda's Magical Crot: Myth and Music in Ancient Ireland* in *The Mankind Quarterly*, No. 21, pp377–391. Also Ann Buckley, *What Was The Tiompan?* in *Jahrbuch fur Musikalische Volks und Volklorunde*, Musiverlag Hans Gerig, Cologne 1978, pp53–87.
9. Keith Sanger, *Clarsach and Cruit*, unpublished draft typescript kindly sent to the author.
10. Whitley Stokes, trans. *Amra Columcille* in *Revue Celtique*, Tome XX, Paris 1899, p409.
11. As 10, p181 and gloss.
12. Whitley Stokes, trans. *The Irish Prefaces to the Latin Hymns in the Liber Hymnorum* in *Goidelica*, Trubner, London 1872, p102.
13. Stuart Piggott, *Ancient Europe*, Edinburgh University Press 1965, p250.
14. The recording is in the School of Scottish Studies, 1966/93/B7.
15. *Ethiopia*, Vol. I S1T1&2 Tangent TGM 101, Scottish Tradition 6 Tangent TNGM120 S1T1&S2T1.
16. Michael Curran, *The Antiphonary of Bangor*, Irish Academic Press, Blackrock 1984, p193.

CHAPTER III

1. Winifred and John MacQueen, *Vita Merlini Silvestris*, in *Scottish Studies* Vol. 29, p84.
2. H.G. Farmer, *Miscellany A Lost Scottish Liturgical Fragment*, in *The Innes Review*, Vol. V, 1954.
3. John MacQueen, *Myth and Legends of Lowland Scottish Saints*, in *Scottish Studies*, 24, 1980, pp6 and 11, pp12–13.
4. Lady Gregory, *Gods and Fighting Men*, John Murray, 1904, p35, et seq.
5. Kuno Meyer, *Zeitschrift fur Celtische Philologie X*, Niemeyer, Halle 1915, pp346–347.
6. Cormac Bourke, *The Hand-Bells of the Early Scottish Church*, in *Proceedings of the Society of Antiquaries of Scotland*, 113 (1983), p464.
7. Standish O'Grady, *Colloquy of the Ancients* in *Silva Gadelica*, Williams and Norgate, London and Edinburgh 1892, p108
8. Recording made by Bernard Fagg. Also the author in conversation with Catherine Fagg. (See Notes for Chapter I).
9. Rev. H.T. Ellacombe, *Bells of the Church*, Exeter 1872, Ch. V.
10. Nancy Edwards, *The Archaeology of Early Mediaeval Ireland*, Batsford 1990.
11. Jane Stevenson, *Introduction*, in F.E. Warren, *The Liturgy and Ritual of the Celtic Churches*, The Boydell Press, Suffolk 1987, ppxliv–xlv.

12. Cormac Bourke, *The Hand-Bells of the Early Scottish Church* in *Proceedings of the Society of Antiquaries of Scotland*, 113 (1983), p466.
13. Ibid p467.
14. Bruno Stablein, *Zwei Melodien der Altirischen Liturgie* in *Musicae Scientiae Collectanea, Festschrift Karl Gustav Fellerer*, ed. Heinrich Huschen, Cologne 1973, pp592–596.
15. Jonas, *Heiligen Viten*, Book II.
16. Isobel Woods, *'Our Awin Scottis Use': Chant Usage in Medieval Scotland*, in *Journal of the Royal Musical Association* 112 (1987), pp27–28.
17. Michel Huglo, *Aaron Scotus* in *The New Grove*, p3.
18. Jane Stevenson in correspondence with the author. The relationship between early Celtic poetry in Latin and Gaelic is covered by many authors, especially James Carney in *Early Irish Poetry*, Mercier Press, Cork 1965. I am grateful to Jane Stevenson also for confirming the possible interpretation of 'casinum' in Sanctorum Piissime Columba as 'little house' in the sense of a monastery. Candida Casa at Whithorn is an early example of 'casa' being applied to a monastic settlement, and Dr Stevenson has found an early Hiberno-Latin concordance for 'casinum'. No sensible alternative interpretation for this section of the text has been suggested.
19. Eilidh M. MacKenzie, *Hebridean Weave: Textual and Melodic Relationships*, MA (Hons) Dissertation, University of Glasgow 1989, pp6,9,21,30.
20. For the distinctiveness of the Celtic church see James P. MacKey, *An Introduction to Celtic Christianity*, T & T Clark, Edinburgh 1989, especially the chapter by M. Forthomme Nicholson, *Celtic Theology: Pelagius*. Also F.E. Warren, *The Liturgy and Ritual of the Celtic Churches*, 2nd ed. with a new Introduction and Bibliography by Jane Stevenson, The Boydell Press, Suffolk 1987.
21. Richard L. Crocker, *Sequence* in *The New Grove*, p146, and Peter Dronke in *The Beginnings of the Sequence* in *Beitrage Zur Geschichte der Deutshen Sprache und Literatur*, Band 87 Max Niemeyer, Tubingen, 1965 pp58–65.
22. James F. Kenney, *The Sources for the Early History of Ireland*, Columbia University Press 1966; see under Loricae where provenances of continental manuscripts are given.
23. Alexander Carmichael, *Carmina Gadelica*, Vol. III, Scottish Academic Press, Edinburgh 1976, pp12–19.
24. Whitley Stokes, trans. *Fraser's Magazine*, Feb. 1871, Vol. III, No. XIV, p184 et seq. C.S. Boswell, *An Irish Precursor of Dante*, David Nutt, London 1908.
25. Peter Dronke, in *The Beginnings of the Sequence in Beitrage zur Geschichte der Deutshen Sprache und Literatur*, Band 87 Max Niemeyer, Tubingen 1965, pp58–65. and Hugh Williams, *Gildas, De Excidio Britanniae*, David Nutt, London 1899, Appendix C., p289 et seq.
26. Whitley Stokes, *The Bodleian Amra Columcille*, in *Revue Celtique XX*, 1899, p 419.
27. Aloys Fleischmann, *Celtic Rite, music of the* in *The New Grove*, pp52–53
28. Tomas O'Fiaich, *Irish Monks on the Continent*, in James P MacKey (ed.), *An Introduction to Celtic Christianity*, T & T Clark, Edinburgh 1989, p103.
29. As Note 27.
30. Calvin M. Bower (ed.), *Boethius, Fundamentals of Music*, Yale University Press, New Haven and London 1989, pxlii.
31. Richard L. Crocker, *The Early Medieval Sequence*, University of California Press, Berkeley 1977, p371.

CHAPTER IV

1. Richard Crocker, in *Sequence* in *The New Grove* p146 refers to the Irish influence on the West Franks; and Jacques Handschin in the *Deutsche Vierteljahrschrift fur Literaturwissenschaft*, Niemeyer, Halle 1927, p340; and pp399–400 asserts an Irish origin for *Musica Enchiriadis*; and Wolfram von dem Steinen says much the same in *Anfange* p194.
2. The use of thirds in the West country is referred to in the Manuscript, *Anonymous IV*, from the thirteenth century.

3. Edward Roesner, *The Manuscript Wolfenbuethal 628: A Study of its Origins and of its Eleventh Fascicle*, PhD Dissertation, New York University 1978, pp399–400.
4. Eilidh MacKenzie, *Hebridean Weave, Textual and Melodic Relationships,* MA (Honours) Dissertation, University of Glasgow 1989, pp6, 9, 14, 30.
5. Ernest H. Sanders, *Peripheral Polyphony of the 13th Century* in *Journal of the American Musicological Society,* Vol. XVII, No. 3, Fall 1964, pp264–265 and n.34. Sanders describes W1 as 'English'. Ingrid de Geer in *Earl, Saint, Bishop, Skald – and Music* Uppsala 1985, Section V, discusses the issue at length, demolishing far more than she constructs.
6. Giraldus Cambrensis, *Topographia Hibernica*, 94. The paragraph about the Scots is quoted in Chapter 2.
7. Mark Everist, *From Paris to St Andrews: The Origins of W1* in *Journal of the American Musicological Society*, Spring 1989. Most of the evidence cited above with respect to Bernham is suppressed in this article. The bulk of that evidence comes from David McRoberts, *The Medieval Church of St Andrews*, Burns, Glasgow 1976, especially the chapter on Bernham by Marinell Ash. Also useful are D.E.R. Watt, *A Biographical Dictionary of Scottish Graduates*, Clarendon, 1977, and John Dowden, *The Mediaeval Church in Scotland,*. Maclehose, Glasgow 1910; Edward Roesner, *The Manuscript Wolfenbuettel 628: A Study of its Origins and of its Eleventh Fascicle*, PhD Dissertation, New York University 1978.
8. The manuscript is *Bibliothèque Nationale,* Latin 12036. I am indebted for this information to David Chadd of the University of East Anglia. The transcription of the lament is my own and varies considerably from that of Alexander Blachley in *Music in Honour of St Thomas of Canterbury* ed. Denis Stevens, Novello and Company, London, p1. Blachley's transcription sets up a metrical basis and is very expressive in effect, though not always consistent in its interpretation of the manuscript. Rhythmic realisation of music of this period is a vexed question and probably the best guide in solo items such as this is the instinct of a performer who understands and has a feeling for Latin as well as music. See also Edward Roesner, *The Performance of Parisian Organum* in *Early Music,* 1979, p185. and *The New Grove* Notation, p359.
9. See Note 8.
10. *Bibliothèque Nationale*, Paris, Latin 12036.
11. Isobel Woods, *Our Awin Scottis Use* in *Journal of the Royal Musical Association* 112, 1987 p34.
12. As Note 11, p23
13. Edward Roesner, *The Origins of W1* in *Journal of the American Musicological Society* No. 29, 1976, pp337–380. Also Edward Roesner, *The Manuscript Wolfenbuettel 628: A Study of its Origins and of its Eleventh Fascicle*, PhD Dissertation, New York University, 1978.
14. 1C 165–99 925/26 EMI Electrola Deutsche Harmonia Mundi. Osterspiel Aus Notre Dame, Schola Cantorum Basiliensis, S4.

CHAPTER V

1. Bertrand Harris Bronson, *The Traditional Tunes of the Child Ballads*, Vol. I, Princeton University Press 1959. p275.
2. For other sources and discussion of the Orpheus story in Scotland see Marion Stewart, *King Orphius* in *Scottish Studies*,Vol. 17 Summer 1973, and Marion Stewart, *King Orphius* in *The Ninth of May*, Vol. 4, 1973, pp1–16.
3. See Duncan and Linda Williamson, *A Thorn in the King's Foot*, Penguin, 1987, pp252–257. The notation of the tune given above is my own: a kind of average derived from Williamson's recording of the ballad for BBC Radio Scotland. For a more precise rendering (but one which necessarily differs from verse to verse to reflect the flexible delivery), Linda Williamson's excellent transcription should be used.
4. *Ex Te Lux Oritur* is known as a Hymn. Dr Kenneth Elliott has suggested that it may be in embryonic mediaeval 'rondeau' form. Dr Warwick Edwards, whose transcription is given here, classes it as a trouvère song. I think it is a sequence. None of these views exclude each other.
5. Bertrand Harris Bronson, *The Traditional Tunes of the Child Ballads*, Vol. II, Princeton University Press, 1959. p29 et seq. Duncan Williamson has a different, very fine one.
6. H.G. Farmer, *A History of Music in Scotland*, Hinrichsen, London 1947, pp39–41.
7. L. Chomel Arr. *Vieilles Chansons, Vieux Airs et Vieilles Marches des Soldats de France*, C. Joubert, Paris 1911. The relevant march is stated to be taken from a manuscript in the Archives of the Chateau Royal de Blois. The library at Blois has since been moved to the Bibliothèque Nationale and the relevant manuscript is not listed as a music one which makes its re-discovery difficult.
8. C.R. Baskervill, *The Elizabethan Jig*, University of Chicago Press, 1929, pp40–41.
9. John MacQueen, *Poetry – James I To Henryson* in *The History of Scottish Literature* I, Aberdeen University Press, 1989, p56.
10. Bellenden, *Chronicles of Scotland*.
11. Alessandro Tassoni, *Prose Politiche e Morali,* ed., Bari, Laterza, 1930, p340. Joseph Walker, *Memoirs of Alessandro Tassoni*, Longman, London 1815, pp100–106.
12. Rev. Charles Rogers, *History of the Chapel Royal of Scotland*, The Grampian Club, Edinburgh 1882, ppxxxi–xxxii.
13. Purser, BBC Radio Scotland, *Scotland's Music Programme 5,* has an outline of the story with extracts from the original recording made for Radio 3. The source of the text is Laing, *Early Popular Poetry of Scotland*, Vol. II, Reeves and Turner, London 1895, pp119–210, which is preferred to the Percy version as being closer to the original Scots as well as bringing the tale to a more satisfying conclusion.
14. Annette Jung, *William Dunbar and the Morris Dancers*, in *Bryght Lanterns,* ed. McClure and Spiller, pp221–243.
15. Kenneth Elliott, PhD thesis, *Music of Scotland, 1500–1700*, University of Glasgow 1959, pp102–105. Music and text are to be found in the Thomas Wode part books for which see the bibliography.

CHAPTER VI

1. Eleanor Knott, *Irish Classical Poetry*, Three Candles Press, Dublin 1960, p7 et seq.
2. Martin Martin, *A Description of the Western Islands of Scotland*, London 1716, pp115–116.
3. Alan Bruford, *Gaelic Folk-Tales and Mediaeval Romances*, The Folklore of Ireland Society, Dublin 1969, pp248–249.
4. Francis Collinson, *The Traditional and National Music of Scotland*, RKP, London 1970, p44: and Alan Bruford, *Song and Recitation in Early Ireland* in *Celtica* Vol. XXI, Dublin 1990, p73. Both propose a plainchant influence. Collinson offers no analysis to support his suggestion of modal relationships. Such relationships could be asserted for any folk music throughout the world, never mind Latin plainchant, and would demonstrate nothing without precise analysis. Collinson admits the dangers of his comparisons (p48). Bruford has a perception of plainsong as being intoned on one note, as opposed to more melodic Anglican chant. This ignores thousands of highly melodic Latin plainchants and many monotonic Anglican chants, especially in psalm singing; it also ignores the fact that plainchant was composed over hundreds of years and did not arrive in one great influential lump among the Gaels, and it does not consider the possibly distinctive nature of Celtic plainsong in The *Inchcolm Antiphoner* (see Chapter III of this work). An interesting contribution to the sources of plainsong in which Augustine, Chrysostom and Cassiodorus are cited as evidence for folksong involvement is found in G.B. Chambers, *Folksong–Plainsong*, The Merlin Press, London 1956, which includes delighted and delightful support from Ralph Vaughan Williams's *Introduction*.
5. Alan Bruford, *Song and Recitation in Early Ireland* in *Celtica* Vol. XXI, Dublin 1990, p. 63. The flexibility which allows a good singer to fit irregularities to a regular pulse will meet most objections.
6. Patrick (and Joseph) MacDonald, *A Collection of Highland Vocal Airs*, 1784, p2.
7. Alan Bruford, in *The Singing of Fenian and Similar Lays in Scotland* in *Ballad Research*, Folk Music Society of Ireland, Dublin 1985, pp63–64. Also Francis Collinson in *The Traditional and National Music of Scotland*, RKP, London 1970, p49. Also Amy Murray, *Father Allan's Island*, New York 1920, p100.
8. Suggestions that stressed metres were imported seem to be weakening (see Note 4). Michael W. Herren (*Stress System of Hiberno-Latin Hendecasyllable* in *Celtica* Vol. XXI, pp223–230, especially p229) moves towards a position which accepts the importance of native speech stress in analysing early Hiberno-Latin poetry, without stating the most natural corollary of all, that the native Gaelic poetic tradition included the use of stress and adapted it for Latin poetry, but without the mechanical rigidities associated with continental Latin.
9. Anne M. Germain in *Scottish Gaelic Heroic Ballads,* PhD Dissertation, Boston University Graduate School 1973, supports the idea of two genres; so does Francis Collinson in *The Traditional and National Music of Scotland*, RKP, London 1970, p40 n.3. Alan Bruford, in *The Singing of Fenian and Similar Lays in Scotland* in *Ballad Research*, Folk Music Society of Ireland, Dublin 1985, p66, denies any separation of meaning between the two terms 'duan' and 'laoidh', but appears to be unaware of Germain's work. Bruford rejects evidence from Patrick MacDonald and Marjory Kennedy-Fraser on the grounds that their publications only give the rhythm for one verse, if that (op cit, p55 n.1). This seems unnecessarily radical. It assumes both have distorted the rhythmical evidence (which they may not always have done), ignores the preservation of melodic outline, and denies any possibility of reconstruction such as appears in Germain's work. That said, Bruford's article is excellent – both scholarly and open-minded.
10. Patrick (and Joseph) MacDonald, *A Collection of Highland Vocal Airs*, 1784, p16, No.122.
11. *Osshian Agus An Cleirich* in J.F. Campbell, *Leabhar Na Feinne*, ed. Thomson, Irish University Press, Shannon 1972, p72.
12. Alan Bruford, in *The Singing of Fenian and Similar Lays in Scotland* in *Ballad Research*, Folk Music Society of Ireland, Dublin 1985, pp68–69.
13. Hugh Shields (ed.) *Scealamhrain Cheilteacha*, An Clochomhar Tta, Dublin 1985, p34.
14. Edward Bunting, *The Ancient Music of Ireland*, Dublin 1840, facing p88 (music p1). Also Micheal O'Suilleabhain, *Bunting's Ancient Music of Ireland*, pp209–210. A version of the tune appears as No. 835 in George Petrie *The Complete Collection of Irish Music,* ed. C.V. Stanford, Vol. II, p208.
15. There are many sources for the words, including J.F. Campbell, *Leabhar Na Feinne*, ed. Thomson, Irish University Press, Shannon 1972, p29; Stokes and Windisch, *Irische Texte*, Leipzig, 1887, p127 from a fifteenth-century source.
16. Francis Tolmie, *Journal of the Folk-Song Society*, Vol. IV 1910–1913, p245.
17. Derick S. Thompson, *The MacMhuirich Bardic Family* in *Transactions of the Gaelic Society of Inverness,* Vol. XLIII, pp276–304 and Derick S. Thompson, *The Harlaw Brosnachadh* in *Celtic Studies, Essays in Memory of Angus Matheson*, ed. Carney and Greene RKP, London, pp147–169.
18. Francis Collinson, *The Bagpipe*, RKP, London 1975, p130.
19. The source is BM Add Ms 10444. It was written in part by Sir Nicholas Le Strange. See P.J. Willetts in *British Museum Quarterly* 29, 1965, pp79–81. Also John P. Cutts, *Jacobean Masque and Stage Music* in *Music and Letters* July 1954, Vol. XXXV, No. 3, pp185–200.
20. I am indebted to Professor Derick Thomson for assistance in determining the rhythm of the Gaelic. The repetition of phrases and melodic fragments in the music of the Shetlanders is noted by Patrick Shuldham-Shaw, *Folk Music and Dance in Shetalnd* in *Journal of the English Folk Dance and Song Society* V, No.2 December 1947, p76 and Peter Cooke, *The Fiddle Tradition of the Shetland Isles*, Cambridge University Press, London 1986, p104.
21. David Buchan, *History and Harlaw*, in *Journal of the Folklore Institute*, V, 1968, pp58–67; reprinted in E.B. Lyle, ed. *Ballad Studies*, Cambridge 1976, pp29–40.
22. H.G. Farmer *A History of Music in Scotland*, Hinrichsen, London 1947, p50.
23. Whitley Stokes, *The Second Battle of Moytura* in *Revue Celtique*, XII, p109.
24. Francis Collinson, *The Bagpipe*, RKP, London 1975, pp82, 88. The Brompton passage Collinson could not find is on p1075 of *Historiae Anglicanne Scriptorum*. The misinterpretation of 'chorus' see *Chorus (2)* in *Grove* 1954.
25. For dates see Gregory Kratzmann, *Colkelbie Sow and the Talis of the Fyve Bestes*, Garland, New York 1983, pp2–5. *Peblis to the Play* was dated by R. Lyall as early sixteenth-century in conversation with the author. It has been ascribed to James I and IV, but is not a play and James IV did not reign from 1424–1437 as Roderick Cannon states on p7 of his mostly useful book, *The Highland Bagpipe and its Music*, John Donald, Edinburgh 1988. Collinson in *The Bagpipe*, p138 and Note 20, claims the MacMhuirich quotation for Lachlan Mor, using for reference J.F. Campbell *Popular Tales of the West Highlands*, Edinburgh 1862, p56. But Campbell makes it clear that the MacMhurich he refers to wrote 'long after' Dunbar and is therefore over a century later than Lachlan Mor.

26. S. Cruden, *Scottish Abbeys*, HMSO, Edinburgh 1960, pp65–66.
27. Beague, *L'Histoire de la Guerre d'Ecosse*, Paris 1556, f.54.
28. Roderick Cannon, *The Highland Bagpipe and its Music*, John Donald, Edinburgh 1988, pp15–16.
29. For a fascinating speculative study of the idea see Sean O'Boyle, *Ogam the Poets' Secret*, Dalton, Blackrock 1980. An early and similar proposal, though less scholarly, was made by W. Williams in *Proceedings and Papers of the Kilkenny and South-east of Ireland Archaeological Society*, Vol. I, Part I, Dublin 1856, pp324–330. This is an area where angels fear to tread.
30. John MacInnes, *The Choral Tradition in Scottish Gaelic Songs*, published in *Transactions of the Gaelic Society of Inverness*, p47. Also Campbell and Collinson, *Hebridean Folksongs*, II, Clarendon Press 1977, pp267–268.
31. Ossian Ellis, *The Story of the Harp in Wales*, University of Wales Press, Cardiff 1980, pp19–49 – a brilliant piece of detective work where all before him were floundering. Alison Kinnaird tells me at the time of writing that Robert Evans in Wales has recently produced transcriptions which take traditional styles more into account, with good results. The forthcoming book by Keith Sanger and Alison Kinnaird – *The Tree of Strings* – will cover this among many other harp-related topics and is eagerly awaited. Thomason's book *Ceol Mor* (1900) was reprinted by EP Publishing in 1975 but is out of print again. It too is a brilliant piece of work where all after him are floundering.
32. Sir Arthur Edmondston, *A View of the Ancient and Present State of the Zetland Isles*, II, Edinburgh 1809, pp59–61 and 66–67.
33. Samuel Hibbert, *Description of the Shetland Isles*, Constable, Edinburgh 1822, pp555 and 607–8.
34. See Note 20.

CHAPTER VII

1. M.Livingstone, *Register of the Privy Seal of Scotland*, Edinburgh, 1908, No. 1546 pp223–224.
2. Ayala's report was originally in cipher. It appears in P. Hume Brown, *Early Travellers in Scotland*, 1891; and substantial sections are to be found in Agnes Mure MacKenzie, *Scottish Pageant*, Oliver and Boyd, Edinburgh 1946, pp95–104.
3. Stephen Allenson, *The Inverness Fragments: Music from a Pre-Reformation Scottish Parish Church and School* in *Music and Letters* Vol. 70, No.1 February 1989, pp1–45.
4. John Young, Somerset Herald, in Leland, *Collectanea* Vol. iv, pp284–285.
5. British Museum manuscript, Royal Appendix 58, ff 17v–18v.
6. See Helena Shire, *Song, Dance and Poetry of the Court of Scotland Under James VI*, Cambridge University Press, 1969. This is a most important and thoroughly recommended book.
7. Dr Kenneth Elliott, booklet notes for Cappella Nova, *Robert Carver* CD, Gaudeamus 124, 1991.
8. Isobel Woods, *The Carver Choirbook*, PhD dissertation, Princeton University 1984. Biographical and social information from this essential work appears in Isobel Woods, *Towards a Biography of Carver*, in *Music Review*, May 1989. James Ross's forthcoming *Musick Fyne: The Art of Music in Sixteenth-Century Scotland*, Toccata Press, will also be a most useful book and I am grateful to him for allowing me to study a draft typescript.
9. As 8, and see also Kenneth Elliott, *Music of Scotland*, PhD dissertation, Cambridge University, 1959 pp174–176 and Kenneth Elliott, *The Carver Choirbook*, in *Music and Letters*, Vol. 41, 1960.
10. Robert Lindsay of Pitscottie, *Historie and Cronicles of Scotland*, Edinburgh 1899, pp217–218.
11. Conrad von Zabern, *De Modo Bene Cantandi*, 1474.
12. James Ross has noted the militaristic elements in the work (see Note 8) and has speculated (in conversation with the author) that the mass might have been performed at St Mary's chapel at Newhaven where the ship was built. This might account for the contrast of relatively simple choral sections with complex writing for the soloists who could have been brought in to augment a local choir.
13. Gabor Darvas, Introduction to his edition of *Missa L'Homme Armé*, Editio Musica, Budapest 1975, distributed by Boosey and Hawkes.

14. Robert Bremmer, *The Rudiments of Music*, Edinburgh 1756, pxii, note.
15. Frank Harrison, *Music in Medieval Britain*, p344 describes *O Bone Jesu* as 'not free of technical errors' but 'not nearly so faulty as his modern editor would have us believe'. The editor in question is J.A. Fuller-Maitland (Year Book Press London 1926). Neither of these commentators will have been able to hear anything approaching a decent performance of the work, never mind any performances of his other works, with the possible exception of the *Ten Part Mass*.
16. Haydon criticised Albrechtsberger for laying down such rules. Haydon claimed the informed ear should be the only decider.
17. Isobel Woods, *'Cant Organe': A Lost Technique?* unpublished typescript of a paper delivered to the Royal Musical Association. I am most grateful to Dr Woods for a copy of the typescript.
18. As Note 2.
19. Percy Folio I p278.
20. Sir Walter Scott, *Minstrelsy of the Scottish Border*, Harrap 1931, p.493.
21. The wealth of possibilities is fed by the fact that the date of this Mass is still in dispute. According to Kenneth Elliott it belongs stylistically to the 1520s. According to Isobel Woods the copying order of the *Carver Choirbook* places it much later – in the 1540s. According to James Ross the apparent alteration of the underlay to create repetitions of words (thus enhancing word clarity) reflects the same reformation pressures that gave rise to Carver's much simpler four part Mass of 1546 – *Pater Creator Omnium*.
22. Most comment to date has been based on the reading of scores or on a very few performances, only some of them adequate. No matter how clever a commentator may be at reading scores, performance is the only true testing ground. Only in 1990 were Carver's complete works heard in good performances, followed by recordings in 1991 (see *Discography*). There is as yet no complete edition of the music in print. Study of Carver has therefore been confined to a tiny band of enthusiasts and can truly be said to be in its infancy.
23. Isobel Woods, *The Carver Choirbook*, PhD dissertation, Princeton University 1984 pp219–231.
24. This reconstruction was especially made for the BBC Radio Scotland series *Scotland's Music*. I am most grateful to Dr Woods for permission to quote from it.

CHAPTER VIII

1. *Johnnie Armstrong's Dance* is referred to as a popular tune in *The Complaynt of Scotland* (ed. Murray, p66) first published in Paris in 1550. See Bertrand H. Bronson, *The Traditional Tunes of the Child Ballads*, Princeton University Press, 1966, Vol. III, pp140–143 and William Stenhouse, *Illustrations of the Lyric Poetry and Music of Scotland*, Blackwood, Edinburgh 1853, pp327–336.
2. Alexander Alesius – see H.G. Farmer, *A History of Music in Scotland*, Hinrichsen, 1947, p113.
3. Thomas Wood, Cantus Partbook I, Edinburgh University Library.
4. The reconstruction was proposed by Helena Shire in *The Scotsman*, 12 September 1959, p10, though she did not make the substitution of the words used above.
5. As Note 3.
6. Kenneth Elliott, sleeve notes for *Ave Dei Patris Filia*, Alpha AC 558. Also in interview for *Scotland's Music*, BBC Radio Scotland, 1991–2.
7. As Note 6.
8. Three of Johnston's works appear in keyboard arrangements in the *Mulliner Book* which was compiled roughly between 1550 and 1575.
9. James Ross, *Musick Fyne*, Toccata Press (forthcoming).
10. Robertus Richardinus, *Commentary on the Rule of St Augustine*, G. Coulton (ed., Edinburgh, 1935 p87 and p80.
11. Isobel Woods, *The Carver Choirbook*, PhD dissertation, Princeton University 1984, pp34–35,141.
12. Kenneth Elliott, *'Church Musick at Dunkell'* in *Music and Letters*, July 1964, p231.
13. Thomas Wode Cantus Partbook I, pp176–177.
14. Thomas Wode Tenor Partbook pp166–167.
15. As Note 13.
16. As Note 14.

17. Judson Maynard, *An Anonymous Scottish Treatise . . BM Add Ms 4911*, PhD dissertation, Indiana University, 1961, Vol. I.
18. Stephen Allenson, 'The Inverness Fragments . . . ' in *Music And Letters*, Vol. 70, No. 1, February 1989, pp1–45.
19. As Note 14.
20. Pitcairn's *Criminal Trials*, Ii, pp427 and 430, referred to in John McQuaid, *Music and the Administration after 1560*, in *The Innes Review*, Vol. 3, 1952, p15.
21. *Inventaires de la Royne Descosse*, Robertson (ed.) Edinburgh, 1863, p187.
22. Quoted in John McQuaid, *Music and the Administration After 1560*, in *The Innes Review*, Vol. 3, 1952, p14.
23. G. Chalmers, *The Life Of Mary, Queen of Scots*, I, London 1818, p54.

CHAPTER IX

1. James Melville, *The Historie of the Lyff of James Melvill*, Bannatyne Club, 1829 (titled *The Diary of Mr James Melvill*).
2. Matthew Spring, sleeve notes for *Scottish Lute Music* BIS LP-201.
3. Ronn McFarlane, booklet notes for *The Scottish Lute*, CD Dorian DOR-90129.
4. Helena Shire, *Song, Dance and Poetry of the Court of Scotland under King James VI*, Cambridge University Press, 1969, pp47–48.
5. Kenneth Elliott, to whom I am most grateful, has supplied the following information: 'An anonymous instrumental composition possibly of Scottish authorship and related to the *basse-danse* is recorded in an early sixteenth-century source. It will be fully discussed in an article in the forthcoming volume of studies relating to the reign of King James V, edited by Janet Williams.' The music is written in the fly-leaves of a book which belonged to Hector Boece and was passed on to Theophilus Stewart, bursar of King's College, Aberdeen, and then to a student, James Douglas, who may be responsible for the notation which probably dates from between 1530 and 1570.
6. Quoted in Farmer, *A History of Music in Scotland*, Hinrichsen, 1947, p80.
7. Brantome, *Oeuvres Completes du seigneur de Brantome*, V, Foucault, Paris 1823, pp95–96. Also p86.
8. John Knox, *The History of the Reformation in Scotland*, ed. David Laing, Wodrow Society, Edinburgh 1848, Vol. 2, p270.
9. George Chalmers, *The Poetic Remains of some of the Scotish Kings* [sic], John Murray, London 1824, pp186 and 187.
10. Dr Warwick Edwards, sleeve notes for *Mary's Music*, Chandos, ABRD 1103.
11. Sir James Melville, *Memoirs of His Own Life*, Edinburgh 1827, pp131–132. See also Gordon Donaldson, *The Edinburgh History of Scotland*, Vol. 3, pp120–121.
12. Thoinot Arbeau, *Orchesographie*, trans. Mary Evans, Kamin Dance Publishers, New York 1948, pp128, 130, 146–147, 148.
13. Alexander Scott, *Ballat maid to the Derisioun and Scorne of wantoun Wemen*.
14. A.F. Mitchell (ed), *A Compendious Book of Godly and Spiritual Songs* (1567), 1897, pp174–175.
15. Thomas Morley, *A Plain and Easy Introduction to Practical Music*, ed. Harman, Dent, London 1952, p296.
16. Ibid.
17. Lizzie Higgins, *What A Voice*, Lismor LIFL 7004. See also Bertrand H. Bronson, *The Traditional Tunes of the Child Ballads*, Princeton University Press, 1972, Vol. III, pp414–421, and Vol. IV Addenda, pp507–508. The background story comes from William Motherwell, *The Ballad Minstrelsy of Scotland*, Gardner, Paisley 1893, pp506–507.
18. John Knox, *The History of the Reformation in Scotland*, ed. David Laing, Wodrow Society, Edinburgh 1848, Vol. 2, pp415–416.
19. J.H. Dickson and W.W. Gauld, *Mark Jameson's Physic Plants in Scottish Mediaeval Journal*, 1987:32, pp60–62.
20. Bertrand H. Bronson, *The Traditional Tunes of the Child Ballads*, Princeton University Press, 1972, Vol. III, pp150–155. Also Sir Walter Scott, *Minstrelsy of the Scottish Border*, Harrap, London 1931, pp476–477.
21. Michael Lynch, *Queen Mary's Triumph* in *The Scottish Historical Review*, Vol. LXIX, 1 No. 187: April 1990, pp1–21.

22. *Calendar of Scottish Papers*, 1582 No.187, p185.
23. Quoted in Helena Shire, *Song, Dance and Poetry of the Court of Scotland under King James VI*, Cambridge University Press, 1969, pp77–78 and p86.
24. William Forbes-Leith, *The Scots Men-At-Arms*, Vol. I, William Paterson, Edinburgh 1882, p95.
25. Fray Juan de Oznayo, *Batalla de Pavia* in *Coleccion de Documentos Ineditos para La Historia de Espana*, Tomo IX, Madrid 1846, pp478–479, trans. Carmen Billingshurst.
26. Thomas Riis, *Should Auld Acquaintance Be Forgot: Scottish-Danish relations, c.1450–1707;* see under William Kinloch, Burgess of Dundee who stayed at Elsinore in 1554, probably son of James Kinloch whose ship traded with Flanders. Information on *mutter und kind* instruments and arpichordum stop from John Raymond. See also, forthcoming, Grant O'Brien, *Ruckers, a Harpsichord and Virginal Making Tradition*, Cambridge University Press.
27. Thomas Morley, *A Plain and Easy Introduction to Practical Music*, ed. Harman, Dent, London 1952, p296.
28. John McQuaid, *Music and the Administration After 1560*, in *The Innes Review*, Vol. 3, 1952, p16.
29. Julian Sharman, (ed.), *The Poems of Mary Queen of Scots*, Pickering, London 1873, last two pages of the Introduction.

CHAPTER X

1. Kenneth Elliott (ed.) *Musica Britannica XV*, (MB in text) Stainer and Bell, London 1975, p214.
2. Act of Parliament, 1579, quoted in Millar Patrick, *Four Centuries of Scottish Psalmody*, OUP 1949, p109. The oft-quoted Charles Burney gives the impression that James VI and I was not musical and he is preceded in this opinion by Hawkins. William Dauney in his outstanding book, *Ancient Scotish Melodies*, Edinburgh 1838, pp108–111, and Henry Farmer, *A History of Music in Scotland*, Hinrichsen, London 1947, pp126–127, one trusts have put this calumny to sleep, for it seems to have had no basis save prejudice.
3. Anon., *The Art of Music Collectit Out of All Ancient Doctouris of Music*, BM Add Ms 4911. A commentary and edition was made by Judson Maynard, *An Anonymous Scottish Treatise . . .* PhD dissertation, Indiana University, 1961.
4. Thomas Wode Partbook, Bassus 1.
5. Helena Shire, *Song Dance and Poetry of the Court of Scotland Under King James VI*, Cambridge University Press, 1969, Chapter V.
6. *The Melvill Book of Roundels*, Bantock and Anderton (eds.), The Roxburghe Club, London 1916, pp37–39 and 188.
7. Thurston Dart, sleeve note for *Jacobean Consort Music*, Oiseau Lyre OLS155, and Jordi Savall, CD booklet note for *Captaine Tobias Hume* Astree E 7723.
8. Francis J. Child, *English and Scottish Popular Ballads*, Harrap, London 1904, p443.
9. Rev. C. Rogers, *History of the Chapel Royal of Scotland*, The Grampian Club, Edinburgh 1882, pplxxv et seq.
10. R. Waldegrave, *A true Reportarie of the most triumphant and royal Accomplishment of the Baptisme of Frederick-Henry, Prince of Scotland . . .'* Edinburgh 1594 and subsequent editions.
11. Bunting, *Ancient Music of Ireland*, Hodges and Smith, Dublin p68. The tune is in James Oswald, *Caledonian Pocket Companion*, Vol. II p58. (Edition printed for R. Bremner). For Clarsach variations see Bunting, *Ancient Music of Ireland,* variations by Lyons (late seventeenth century), pieces by Scott (early seventeenth century).
12. Information from Jerzy Pietrkiewicz whose *Loot and Loyalty*, Heinemann, London 1955, is an imaginary account of part of Hume's life.
13. See Kenneth Elliott, *Musa Jocosa Mihi*, Stainer and Bell, London, pp14–15. One of these is *Old Lang Syne* with words and music superior to those which have swept the world.
14. Ian G. Anderson, *Scotsmen in the Service of the Czars*, the Pentland Press, Edinburgh 1990, Chapter I.
15. I am grateful to Dr Warwick Edwards for pointing this out.
16. Tobias Hume, *The First Part of Ayres (Musicall Humours)*, John Windet, London 1605. Windet specialised in the delicate typography required.
17. Thurston Dart, sleeve note for *Jacobean Consort Music*, Oiseau Lyre OLS155.
18. Tobias Hume, *Poeticall Music*, John Windet, London 1607.
19. James VI, *A Counterblaste to Tobacco*, London 1604.
20. Tobias Hume, *The True Petition of Colonel Hume . . .*, John Giles, London 1642.
21. *Extracts From the Records of the Burgh of Glasgow 1573–1642*, The Scottish Burgh Records Society, 1876, p388.
22. *Newes From Scotland*, Wright, London 1591.
23. Mary Anne Alburger, *Scottish Fiddlers and Their Music*, Gollancz, London 1983, p15 and note.
24. Robert Graves, *English and Scottish Ballads*, Heinemann, London 1957, pp152–153.
25. *The Poems of William Drummond*, Wm. C. Ward (ed.), London, Routledge & Sons, I, p62.

CHAPTER XI

1. Francis Collinson, *The Traditional and National Music of Scotland*, RKP, London 1970, pp50–51.
2. Billy Kay, Cailean MacLean, *Knee-deep in Claret*, Mainstream, pp.127–140.
3. Donald Withrington, *Education in the 17th Century Highlands* in *The Seventeenth Century in the Highlands*, Inverness Field Club, Inverness, 1986. See also Note 17.
4. The Brehon laws were written down in early mediaeval times but are much older. In the West Highlands the administration of law remained largely in the hands of the chieftains who had their advisers specialising in law.
5. W.J. Watson, *Bardachd Albannach Scottish Verse from the Book of the Dean of Lismore*, The Scottish Gaelic Texts Society, 1978, pxviii.
6. Sleeve notes for *Scottish Tradition 3* Tangent TNGM 111.
7. Sorley Maclean, *Obscure and Anonymous Gaelic Poetry* in *The Seventeenth Century in the Highlands*, Inverness Field Club, Inverness, 1986.
8. MacCormick, Campbell and Collinson, *Hebridean Folk-songs I*, OUP, 1969, p3.
9. See Chapter VI, Note 30.
10. *Tocher 27*, School of Scottish Studies, Edinburgh, pp154–157.
11. Frances Tolmie, *Journal of the Folk-Song Society*, Vol. IV, 1910–1913, p197.
12. There are many sources for both tune and story. Most are listed in Campbell and Collinson, *Hebridean Folksongs*, Vol. III, pp250–256 and 366–369. See also *Tocher* 31–37, pp304–305.
13. The version given here is from the recording in the School of Scottish Studies, SA 1964/S2 A3 sung by Kate MacMillan.
14. James VI, *Basilikon Doron*.
15. Sleeve notes *Scottish Tradition 8 James Campbell of Kintail*, Side 2 Band 3.
16. Frances Collinson, *The Traditional and National Music of Scotland*, RKP, London 1970, pp60–62.
17. Sorley Maclean, *Obscure and Anonymous Gaelic Poetry* in *The Seventeenth Century in the Highlands*, Inverness Field Club, Inverness 1986, p95.
18. Frances Tolmie, *Journal of the Folk-Song Society*, Vol. IV, 1910–1913, pp186–187. See also *Tocher 34*, School of Scottish Studies, Edinburgh, pp226–227.
19. Sorley Maclean, *Obscure and Anonymous Gaelic Poetry* in *The Seventeenth Century in the Highlands*, Inverness Field Club, Inverness 1986, pp98–101.
20. James Fraser, *Polichronicon*, 1671, quoted in J. Carmichael Watson, *The Gaelic Songs of Mary Macleod*, The Scottish Gaelic Texts Society, Oliver and Boyd, Edinburgh 1982, pp114–115.
21. Sleeve notes *Scottish Tradition 8 James Campbell of Kintail*, Side 2, Band 1.
22. See the Accounts of the Lord High Treasurer.
23. Michael Billinge and Bonnie Shaljean, *The Dalway or Fitzgerald Harp (1621)* in *Early Music,* Vol. XV, No. 2, May 1987, pp175–187.
24. Peter Holman, *The Harp in Stewart England* in *Early Music*, Vol. XV, No. 2, May 1987, pp88–203.
25. Keith Sanger *Clarsach and Cruit*, unpublished typescript kindly made available – see also ChapterVI, Note 31.
26. Vincenzo Galilei, *Dialogo della Musica Antica*, Florence 1581, reprinted 1968, p143. The whole question may relate to the significance attached by Tassoni to the influence of Scottish music on Gesualdo. The regular traffic of musicians between Scotland and the continent, including Italy, makes these speculations much more than idle.
27. Grattan Flood, *The Story of the Harp*, Dublin 1905, p75.
28. See Note 23.
29. Dr James Kirk, *The Jacobean Church in the Highlands* in *The Seventeenth Century in the Highlands*, Inverness Field Club, Inverness 1986.
30. John Monipennie, *Certain Matters concerning the Realme of Scotland as they were A.D. 1597*, London 1603.
31. Campbell and Collinson, *Hebridean Folksongs II*, OUP 1977, pp200–209.
32. For instance John Derick, *Image of Ireland*, 1581, shows clearly in a woodcut the bard reciting to the accompaniment of a harper, but the scurrilous verses and crude draughtsmanship deliberately undercut the scene.
33. *Memoirs of Arthur O'Neill*, though his account is questioned in some of its details by Colm O'Baoill, *Some Irish Harpers in Scotland* in *Transactions of the Gaelic Society of Inverness*, Vol. XLVII, 1971–1972, pp148–150, who proposes the alternative that O'Cahan made the tune and met the king on his single return visit to Scotland in 1617 at the Eglintoun's Glasgow house.
34. As Note 33.
35. Keith Sanger, *Notes and Queries of the Society of West Highland and Island Research*, No. 15, May 1981, pp20–23. A photocopy of this ms is in the National Library of Scotland, MS 14949(b).
36. John Gunn, *An Historical Enquiry Respecting the Performance on The Harp in the Highlands of Scotland*, 1807, quoted in Sanger, as Note 25.
37. As Note 25.
38. Edinburgh Burgh Records, 27 September 1594, quoted in Alison Kinnaird, *The Harp Key*, Kinmor Music, p86.
39. W. Fraser, *The Chiefs of Grant*, Vol. II, 1888, p66.
40. Captain Williams describes him as 'a good player on the harp', National Library of Scotland Adv. Ms 28.3.12 f15r. *The Royal Lament* also appears in the MacFarlane and Fraser manuscripts.
41. Compare *I Am Asleep, And Don't Waken Me* in Edward Bunting, *The Ancient Music of Ireland*, Hodges and Smith, Dublin 1840, pp74–75, which Bunting indignantly notes is also claimed by the Scots.
42. Keith Sanger, *The McShannons of Kintyre: Harpers To Tacksmen* in *The Kintyre Antiquarian and Natural History Society Magazine* No. 28, 1990, pp9–15, plus correction in No. 29,1991, p20. This article also shows that harpers were given lands half the value of bardic families and that harpers and bards were on lands close to each other.
43. The whole question of the importance of new metrical forms is still an open one, too extensive to go into here. Annie M. MacKenzie, *Orain Iain Luim*, The Scottish Gaelic Texts Society, Edinburgh 1973, pxlii, points out that strophic metres were far from new. In the examples given above, *La Inbhir Lochaidh* is stressed but not regular, and Sileas' *Cumha Lachlainn Daill* is in one of the old syllabic metres. With what degree of stress these were sung is not known. When it comes to performance a skilful and sensitive singer can satisfy the demands of metre and natural stress even when they are antagonistic to each other.
44. Sleeve note to Flora MacNeil, *Craobh nan Ubhal*, Tangent TGS 124. Side 2 Track 1.
45. J. Carmichael Watson, *The Gaelic Songs of Mary MacLeod*, the Scottish Gaelic Texts Society, Edinburgh 1982, Introduction.
46. Kate MacDonald in *Tocher 25–30*, p150–151.
47. Sleeve note to Sileas, *Delighted With Harps*, Lapwing LAP 113C, Side 2 Track 3.
48. Franis Collinson, *The Traditional and National Music of Scotland*, RKP, London 1970, pp56–59 and Annie M. MacKenzie, *Orain Iain Luim*, the Scottish Gaelic Texts Society, Edinburgh 1973, pp238–240.
49. Ibid.
50. Kenneth MacDonald, *Unpublished verse by Silis Ni Mhic Raghnaill Na Ceapaich* in *Celtic Studies*, London 1968, p83.
51. Colm O'Baoill, *Bardachd Shilis na Ceapaich*, Scottish Gaelic Texts Society, Edinburgh 1972, plxiv.
52. As Note 41, p246.
53. See Note 35.
54. Patrick MacDonald, *A Collection of Highland Vocal Airs*, Edinburgh 1784, pp3–4.
55. William Matheson in *The Blind Harper*, Scottish Gaelic Texts Society, Edinburgh 1970, pp154–158, first proposed the metrical solution to fitting the traditional tunes to the poetry. Anne Lorne Gillies performed her own version for BBC Radio Scotland *Scotland's Music* and it is this version of *Lament for the Harp Key* and underlay which is used in the example.
56. Ibid.
57. As 55. pplvii–lviii and the end of *Creach Na Ciadaoin* as cited by Matheson.

58. Alison Kinnaird, *The Harp Key*, Kinmor Music, p87.
59. Martin Martin, *A Description of the Western Islands of Scotland*, London 1716, pp115–116.
60. For a useful treatment of this subject see David Johnson, *Scottish Fiddle Music in the Eighteenth Century*, John Donald, Edinburgh 1984, pp119–142.
61. I myself was taken to the Court of Session, the action was withdrawn, but this is not a unique experience. It is good to know that music can arouse such passions, sad that it fills lawyers' purses rather than musicians'.
62. Roderick Cannon, *The Highland Bagpipe and its Music*, John Donald, Edinburgh 1988, p5.
63. Note as 62, p97.
64. This fascinating theory was put forward by J.M.A. Lenihan and Seumas MacNeill in *An Acoustical Study of the Highland Bagpipe*, in *Acustica*, 4 (1954). MacNeill refers to this in his booklet *Piobaireachd*, BBC Publications 1968, pp26–29. It is true that this theory has not and probably cannot be backed up by an analysis of the tuning of bagpipe chanters in the past, because so few survive. But the circumstantial evidence is very strong for such a system to be adduced from more recent physical evidence, for piobaireachd certainly use the tonal contrasts possible. It is probably from the most frequent of these, the contrast between pentatonic in A and pentatonic in G that the Scottish 'double-tonic' effect is derived (see Introduction).
65. A remission granted under the Great Seal, 13 January 1614, refers to a piper called Donald MacCruimien. See *Book of MacKay*, pp126 and 414. Referred to in *Notices of Pipers* in *The Piping Times*. These notices are alphabetical and are spread over many issues.
66. Alan MacDonald (conversation with the author) attributes this characteristic to decorative vocal styles, especially from Lewis.
67. Rev. James Fraser, *Wardlaw Manuscript Chronicles of the Frasers*, ed. William MacKay, Scottish History Society, 1st Series, Vol. 47, Edinburgh 1905.
68. Daniel F. Melia, *The Lughnasa Musician in Ireland and Scotland*, in *Journal of American Folklore*, 80: pp365–373.
69. Niall MacVurich, *Seanachas Sloinnidh* in John Mackenzie, *Sar Obair nam bard Gaelach*, Glasgow 1841, p67.
70. A.J. Haddow, *The History and Structure of Ceol Mor,* 1982, p50.
71. Notices of Pipers. As Note 65.
72. Dalyell, *Musical Memoirs*, Thomas Stevenson, Edinburgh 1849, p9. The date given (1818) is probably a mistake for 1816.
73. A good example is on the Columbia World Library of Folk and Primitive Music, *Folk Songs From Scotland*, SL-209 Side 2 item 33.
74. Joseph MacDonald, *A Compleat Theory of the Scots Highland Bagpipe*, reprinted by Alexander MacDonald, Inverness 1927, p26. Also as Note 54, pp38–43. Also General C.S. Thomason, *Ceol Mor*, London 1900.
75. Seumas MacNeill, *Piobaireachd*, BBC Publications 1968, pp42–82: A.J. Haddow, *The History and Structure of Ceol Mor,* 1982, pp156–216: R.L.C. Lorimer sleeve notes and leaflet for *Pibroch 1* and *Pibroch 2*, Waverley records ZLP 2034 and 2035.
76. Well-authenticated and carefully edited piobaireachd from the earliest sources still need to be studied. It may be that canntaireachd versions will prove useful, though canntaireachd was partly kept secret, just as was ogham.
77. See Note 60.
78. Scottish Tradition 9, Tangent TNGM 141 Side 1 Band 2.
79. V.S. Blankenhorn, *Traditional and Bogus Elements in 'MacCrimmon's Lament'* in *Scottish Studies*, 22, 1978, pp45–67.
80. Sleeve and leaflet notes for Scottish Tradition 8, Tangent TNGM 140, Side 1 Track 1.
81. The poem appears in Angus MacLeod (ed.), *Orainn Dhonnchaidh Bhain*, the Scottish Gaelic Texts Society, Edinburgh 1952, pp.196–225 (see also the notes pp488–489). The music is printed in the Mod publications. No complete recording exists, but part was recorded unaccompanied by Angus MacLeod on a tape held at Cecil Sharpe House in London.
82. Francis Collinson, *The Bagpipe*, RKP 1975, pp170–171.
83. Good examples are on Catherine-Ann MacPhee, *Canan Nan Gaidheal* Trax 009 Side 2 Track 4 and Scottish Tradition 2, Tangent TNGM 110 Side 1 Track 6.

CHAPTER XII

1. Thomas Wode's description in his partbooks. See H.G. Farmer, *A History of Music in Scotland*, Hinrichsen 1947, p165.
2. Scottish Tradition 6, Tangent TNGM 120, Side 1, Track 2.
3. Scottish Tradition 6, Tangent TNGM 120 accompanying booklet.
4. From *The Oban Times*, October 1898, quoted on leaflet for Scottish Tradition 6 – see Note 2.
5. Scottish Tradition 6, Tangent TNGM 120 Side 2, Track 4.
6. The unsuitability of the metrical versions to Gaelic can be guessed at by the fact that the Synod of Argyll published the first fifty as late as 1659 and did not add the remaining one hundred until 1694.
7. Clerk Papers, GD18 4541, quoted by kind permission of Sir John Clerk of Penicuik.
8. Millar Patrick, *Four Centuries of Scottish Psalmody*, London 1949. Farmer understands this story rather differently. Patrick's version is preferred here. See pp156-159.
9. Robert Bremner, *The Rudiments of Music*, Edinburgh 1756, pxii, note.
10. For instance *Martyrdom* is altered in the third strain in Lewis to make it pentatonic.
11. Millar Patrick, *Four Centuries Of Scottish Psalmody*, London, 1949, pp171–174.
12. Robert Chambers, *Domestic Annals of Scotland*, I. See also William Dauney, *Ancient Scottish Melodies*, Edinburgh 1838, pp218, 237, 255-256, 278 and 308 and Mary Anne Alburger, *Scottish Fiddlers and their Music*, Gollancz, London 1983, pp16–17.
13. *Vox Borealis, or the Northern Discoverie*: a pamphlet printed in 1641, reprinted in *The Harleian Miscellany*, IV, 1809, pp422–441. See Charles Read Baskerville, *The Elizabethan Jig*, University of Chicago Press, 1929, pp56–57. This underlines further the close association of mocking jigs with Scotland.
14. Bertrand H. Bronson, *The Traditional Tunes of the Child Ballads*, III, Princeton University Press 1966, pp191–197. See also Rev. William Wilson, *The House of Airlie*, London 1924, pp211–223, and *The Greig-Duncan Folksong Collection,* Vol. 2, Aberdeen University Press 1983, pp170–175 and p541.
15. Sir John Lauder of Fountainhall, *Historical Notices of Scottish Affairs*, Edinburgh 1848. The tune is the last in Henry Playford's *A Collection of Original Scotch-Tunes*, London 1700, p16.
16. Ewan MacColl sang this ballad to a magnificent tune on *Blood and Red Roses*, Vol. 5, Blackthorne Records, ESB 83 Side 2 Track 4; but it was of his own making (letter from Peggy Seeger to the author). No traditional tune is known for it.
17. Walter H. Rubsamen, *Scottish and English Music of the Renaissance in a Newly-Discovered Manuscript*, in *Festschrift Heinrich Besseller*, Veb Deutscher Verlag fur Musik, Leipzig 1961, pp259–284. Rubsamen mis-reads Raitt for Taitt.
18. Robert Chambers, *Domestic Annals of Scotland,* II.
19. Thomas D'Urfey, *Pills To Purge Melancholy*: Sir John Hawkins, *A General History of the Science and Practice of Music*, Vol. IV, London 1776, p359, William Dauney, *Ancient Scottish Melodies*, Edinburgh 1838, p18.
20. Clara in Shadwell's *The Scowrers, c.* 1670, quoted in William Dauney, as above, p19.
21. Dauney, as above, pp18–19.
22. The full story is given in Purser, *Dainty Davie*, in *Stretto*, Vol.7, No.1, Spring 1987, pp32–36 which also gives the various tunes of that title.
23. The late Norman Buchan was unable to recall the source for the tune used by Jean Redpath and published by him in *The Scottish Folksinger*, nor does Jean Redpath recall where she got it from. The sources for the story are *Captain Creichton's Memoirs* (reprinted in the complete works of Swift who was the ghost-writer); and *Scotch Presbyterian Eloquence*. The best words are printed in Burns's *The Merry Muses*.
24. Scottish Tradition 5, Tangent TNGM 119, Side 4, Band 5a and 5b.
25. *The Compleat Tutor for the Fife*, London 1759?, pp12–15. See also Henry George Farmer, *The Scots Duty* in Reeves, *The Rise and Development of Military Music*, p34; also Farmer, unpublished typescript *Music from the Scottish Past – 18th Century Military Music,* for a BBC Scottish Home Service broadcast, 31 March 1936, in the Farmer papers, Glasgow University Library Farmer 205/3.
26. Thomas Simes, *Military Guide*, 1776.
27. James Hogg, *Jacobite Reliques*, Edinburgh 1819–21, p259.
28. Henry George Farmer, *The Scots March* in Reeves, *The Rise and Development of Military Music*, pp54–55.
29. Lewis Winstock, *Songs and Music of the Redcoats*, Cooper 1970, pp19–20 quoting Robert Monro's *Expedition* of 1637 Part II, p113.
30. Alan Ramsay, *Elegie To Patie Birnie*.
31. 1653, Z.Boyd in G.Neil, *Z.Boyd's Flowers Of Zion,* 1832, pxxx.
32. As Note 30.
33. Mary Anne Alburger, *Scottish Fiddlers and their Music*, Gollancz, London 1983, pp71–73.
34. *Greig-Duncan Folksong Collection*, I, pp121 and 530, also David Johnson, *Scottish Fiddle Music in the Eighteenth Century*, John Donald, Edinburgh 1984, pp239–243.
35. Helen Armet, (ed.) *Extracts from the records of the burgh of Edinburgh, 1689–1701*, Edinburgh 1962, for 13 September 1699.
36. Edward Burt, *Letters from a Gentleman in the north of Scotland*, I, London 1815, p189 (first published 1726).
37. Alexander Kincaid, *History of Edinburgh*, Edinburgh 1787, p159.
38. Francis Collinson, *The Traditional and National Music of Scotland*, RKP, London 1966, p118, n1.
39. John MacInnes, sleeve notes for Christine Primrose *'S tu nam chuimhne*, Temple TP024, Side A Track 4.
40. John MacInnes, sleeve notes for Flora MacNeil *Craobh nan Ubhal*, Tangent TGS 124, Side 1 Track 1.
41. Scottish Tradition 8, Tangent TNGM 140, Side 1 Band 6.
42. Francis Collinson, *The Bagpipe*, RKP, 1975, p170. and p166.
43. Stenhouse gives notes on Skirving in his *Illustrations*, pp105–107, and so does David Laing in his *Additional Illustrations* pp.*189–*198 for Johnson's *Scots Musical Museum*.
44. Thelma Reid Lower, *General John Reid* in *Nova Scotia Historical Quarterly*, 1979, Vol. 9 Jun–Dec, Part I, p117.
45. Hamish Henderson sleeve notes for Andy Hunter, *King Fareweel* Lismor LIFL 7002, Side 2 Track 5.
46. Interestingly, David Johnson pursuasively discovers *Loch Lomond* to be a derivative of *The Lowlands of Holland* in his *Music and Society in Lowland Scotland in the Eighteenth Century*, OUP, London 1972, pp103–104, But Bertrand H. Bronson, *The Traditional Tunes of the Child Ballads*, III, Princeton University Press 1966, pp191 and 194 makes as good a case for *The Bonnie Hoose O' Airlie* as the original.
47. Niel Gow and Sons, *Fifth Collection of Strathspeys and Reels*, Edinburgh, 3rd ed., p22.
48. John MacInnes, sleeve notes for Flora MacNeil, *Craobh nan Ubhal*, Tangent TGS 124, Side 1 Track 8
49. Scottish Tradition 2, Tangent TNGM 110, Side 2 Band 6.

CHAPTER XIII

1. Lady Montgomerie's signature is in the ms, known as *Companion to Lady Margaret Wemyss*.
2. James Maidment, *Analecta Scotica*, Vol. 2, Edinburgh 1834–1847, p263. David Johnson, programme notes for *The Songbook of Louis de France,* Scottish Early Music Consort, various dates and venues.
3. John Evelyn, *Diary*, 27 January 1682.
4. The Honourable Bridget Noel to the Countess of Rutland, quoted in Henry George Farmer, *A King's Musician for the Lute and Voice: John Abell (1662/3–1724)* in Hinrichsen's *The Musical Yearbook*, Vol. VII, London 1952, pp448–449.
5. Ian Spink, *English Song Dowland to Purcell*, Batsford, London, p258 in which the underlay of the English is declared to be faulty, although the original edition is in Italian (a point not mentioned), and its style is included in the criticism – 'There seems little point in continuing this catalogue of mediocrity' – a comment that should be made only by those wholly assured of their own superiority.
6. Thomas Brown, *Letters from the Dead to the Living* (Second Part), London 1708, pp34 and 36.
7. Highfill, Burnim and Langhans, *A Biographical Dictionary of Actors . . . Musicians . . .* Vol. I, Southern Illinois University Press, p7.
8. Quoted in Henry George Farmer, *A King's Musician for the Lute and Voice: John Abell (1562/3–1724)* in Hinrichsen's *The Musical Yearbook*, Vol. VII, London 1952, p449, source not given. A very similar report appeared in POTS on 26 June 1688.

9. Mr Cresset, writing from Zell to a friend in Holland, in D'Urfey, *Choice New Songs* BM K.2.g.15 in Glasgow University Library, Euing Px.22.

10. Sir John Hawkins, *General History of the Science and Practice of Music*, Vol. 2, London 1853, p725.

11. John Abell, *A Collection of Songs in Several Languages*, Pearson, London 1701.

12. William Congreve to Keally, 10 December 1700, *Literary Relics* 1792.

13. Ernest C. Harriss, *Johann Mattheson's der Vollkommene Capellmeister*, UMI Research Press, p241.

14. The libretto refers to Hibernia and to the queen as already crowned. Birthday odes were regularly performed in Dublin (information from Professor Brian Boydell and see Boydell, *A Dublin Musical Calendar 1600–1760*, Irish Academic Press, Dublin 1988, pp34–35 for Queen Anne). The appointment with the Duke of Ormonde, then Viceroy of Ireland, is confirmed in Henry George Farmer, *A King's Musician for the Lute and Voice: John Abell (1662/3–1724)* in Hinrichsen's *The Musical Yearbook*, Vol. VII, London 1952, p453; and Abell's presence in Ireland on other occasions is referred to in Highfill, Burnim and Langhans, *A Biographical Dictionary of Actors . . . Musicians . . .* Vol. I, Southern Illinois University Press, p8. Rosamond McGuinness in *An Eighteenth-Century Entertainment* in *Soundings*, 1973, pp66–84, identifies the work as most probably by Abell (the Bodleian and Tenbury Libraries accepted the ascription of the work to Eccles) with mostly pursuasive reasoning, but suggests it is a Coronation piece. Abell had written and published such a piece already. McGuinness does not explain the otherwise meaningless reference to Hibernia (the only country named in the text) or the fact that the dedicatee is clearly well established as monarch.

15. The probable use of the St Patrick's Cathedral choirboys was confirmed by Boydell and Nicholas Carolan. McGuinness (see Note 14) notes the slightly greater virtuosity of the part of Apollo; but it nowhere approaches the displays of his other works for the court.

16. The manuscript is in the Bodleian Library Music section, Tenbury Ms 765.

17. As Note 10.

18. I am grateful to Sir John Clerk of Penicuik for permission to quote from the Clerk papers in Register House, to which the ensuing notes prefixed by GD refer.

19. *Memoirs of the Life of Sir John Clerk of Penicuik 1676–1755*, Scottish History Society, Edinburgh 1892, pp14–15. Hereafter referred to as *Memoirs*.

20. *Memoirs*, p15.

21. *Memoirs*, pp17–18 and p35.

22. GD 18 5194/17, Sir John Clerk to John Clerk, 5 May 1696.

23. GD18 4536/2.

24. *Memoirs*, pp21–23 and note.

25. GD 18 2095, p2.

26. *Memoirs*, pp24–26.

27. *Memoirs*, p28 and note 3.

28. GD 18 5210.

29. GD 18 5207/3. Letter from John Clerk in Florence to Sir John Clerk, 1 March 1698.

30. *Memoirs*, p29 note 3.

31. GD 18 5207/11 letter from John Clerk in Rotterdam to Sir John Clerk, 19 September 1699.

32. Thomas Morley, *A Plain and Easy Introduction to Practical Music*, ed. Harman, Dent, London 1952, p297.

33. GD 18 5202/56, 24, 23, 27.

34. See *Dictionary of National Biography* under William Russell 1639–1683.

35. *Cantata a cinque voci reali*, GD 18 4538/2.

36. *Memoirs*, p31.

37. GD 5202/53.

38. *Memoirs*, p32.

39. *Memoirs*, p.34.

40. *Papers relating to the Ships and Voyages of the Company of Scotland Trading to Africa and the Indies 1696–1707*, ed. Insh, Scottish History Society, Edinburgh 1924, pp60, 79, 96,188–189.

41. I am indebted to Dr David Johnson for drawing my attention to this device.

42. *Memoirs*, pp73–74.

43. *Memoirs*, p36 n.1.

44. Dr David Johnson in a paper delivered to the Royal Musical Association, Edinburgh 11 May 1991 and in correspondence with the author. This line of research may well bear fruit with regard to others of Clerk's compositions.

45. *Memoirs*, pp74–75.

46. *The Poets and Poetry of Scotland* Vol. I, James Grant Wilson (ed.), Blackie, London 1876, pp100–101.

47. I am grateful for this translation of the Latin (for which see *Memoirs*, p249) to James Simpson, from his most interesting paper, *Sir John Clerk, A Judge of Architectory* (c. 1975).

48. *The Author to the Reader* (Introduction to *The Country Seat* by Clerk) GD 18 4404.

49. James Simpson, paper, *Sir John Clerk, A Judge of Architectory* (c. 1975).

CHAPTER XIV

1. For the Scottish origins of Freemasonry see David Stevenson, *The Origins of Freemasonry*, Cambridge University Press, Cambridge, 1988; and David Stevenson, *The First Freemasons*, Aberdeen University Press, Aberdeen, 1988. See also Note 16.

2. William Tytler ascribes the tune to Oswald in his *Dissertation on the Scottish Music*, first published in 1779 in Arnot's *History of Edinburgh*. Subsequent commentators, further from the events, have ridiculed the claim because of the earlier publication in McGibbon's *Second Collection* of 1746, but McGibbon could have had it from Oswald. Oswald published it under the title of words written for the tune by Hewit. He did not claim it as his own, but as Ramsay's poem indicates, he was prepared to own up to some melodies and pass others off without claiming them for himself.

3. Roger Fiske, *English Theatre Music in the Eighteenth Century*, Oxford University Press 1986, p231 and pp234–235.

4. David Johnson, *Scottish Fiddle Music in the Eighteenth Century*, pp102–103.

5. As Note 4, p166.

6. As Note 4, p193.

7. Muriel Brown, Supplement to *Six Sonatas for Violin and Keyboard by David Foulis*, Scottish Music Publishing, 1990, p11.

8. As Note 7, also Muriel Brown, *An Eighteenth Century Scottish Composer* in *Stretto* Vol. 6, No. 3, Autumn 1986, pp11–30.

9. I am indebted to Oswald's descendant, Heather Melvill, for much unpublished biographical information.

10. The ms. is being researched by Mathew Soutar; I am indebted to David Johnson for this preliminary outline of its contents.

11. Roger Fiske, *Scotland in Music*, Cambridge University Press, 1983, p20 and David Johnson, as Note 4, p164.

12. As Note 4, p197.

13. As Note 9.

14. Geminiani's *XII Duettos . . .* were published under the umbrella of *Apollo's Collection* (as were six sonatas of Tartini's) by Oswald, *circa* 1750. Geminiani's *A Treatise of Good Taste in the Art of Music* was published in 1749.

15. *The Household Book of Lady Grisell Baillie*, Scottish History Society, Edinburgh 1911.

16. H.C. Robbins Landon, *Mozart, The Golden Years,* Thames and Hudson, London 1989, p122 and Chapter XII, esp. pp228 and 236 and Appendix 6. *The Magic Flute* was re-interpreted after Mozart's death, with the Queen of the Night as an evil Jacobin, to appease the Austrian authorities who were fearful of the Freemasons. The Scottish connection, however distorted, was therefore still clearly recognised. Also, Katharine Thomson, *The Masonic Thread in Mozart*, Lawrence and Wishart, London 1977, esp. p12 and Chapter V in which the folk music element encouraged by Freemasonry is mentioned, as is the influence of *faux-bourdon*, which seems to have lingered in Scotland (see Chapter VII, Note 3).

17. H.G. Farmer, *A History of Music in Scotland*, Hinrichsen, London 1947, p241.

18. Klima, Bowers and Grant (eds) *Memoirs of Dr Charles Burney*, University of Nebraska Press, p87 and Roger Lonsdale, *Dr Charles Burney*, Clarendon Press, Oxford 1965, pp23 and 36–37.

19. Frank Kidson, *James Oswald, Dr Burney, and 'The Temple of Apollo'* in The Musical Antiquary, Vol. 11, pp40–41.

20. Roger Fiske, *English Theatre Music in the Eighteenth Century*, Oxford University Press, 1986, p231.

21. As Note 9.

22. As Note 19, pp39–41. The relationship between Oswald and Burney is discussed in the books referred to in Notes 18 and 20, mostly accepting Burney's own account. Burney makes no mention of Oswald in his *History* and credits him with nothing in his *Memoirs*, which, considering Oswald's official position if nothing else, is very odd. Perhaps there was some falling-out between the two men.

23. Philip Coggin, *This Easy and Agreeable Instrument: A History of the English Guitar* in Early Music, Vol XV, No. 2, May 1987, p210.

24. Frank Kidson, *Minstrelsy of England*, 1901, and Grove's 1954 under *God Save The Queen*.

25. See Philip Maund, *The Favourite Minuets . . . Composed by the Earl of Kellie*, Stirling 1990. I am most grateful to Philip Maund for sharing his research on these and others of Kellie's works. Also, *Minuets Etc* with an Introduction by Charles Kirkpatrick Sharpe, Thomas G. Stevenson, Edinburgh 1836, reprinted 1839.

26. Charles Burney, *A General History of Music*, London 1776–1789, Vol. IV, p677.

27. Quoted in *Minuets Etc* with an Introduction by Charles Kirkpatrick Sharpe, Thomas G. Stevenson, Edinburgh 1836, reprinted 1839, pvi.

28. As Note 27.

29. Andrew Erskine, Letters between the Hon. Alexander Erskine and James Boswell, Esq, London 1763, Erskine letter of 22 January 1762.

30. As Note 27. ppvi–vii.

31. Alison Cockburn to David Hume, 16 December 1768, *Letters and Memoir of Her Own Life by Mrs Alison Rutherford or Cockburn*, David Douglas, Edinburgh 1900, pp73–74.

32. Abraham Rees, *The New Cyclopedia*, London 1819, *Kelly*.

33. Roger Fiske, *English Theatre Music in the Eighteenth Century*, Oxford University Press, 1986, pp332–336.

34. The Kilravock ms. was discovered at Kilravock Castle in 1971 and subsequently bought by Dr David Johnson. Commentary on this manuscript and performances of it appear in the BBC series *Scotland's Music*.

35. National Library of Scotland Add. Ms. 36596, f.39, quoted in Appendix II of an unpublished thesis by Philip Maund, for whose assistance I am most grateful.

36. Roger Fiske, *English Theatre Music in the Eighteenth Century*, Oxford University Press, 1986, pp231–236.

37. An excellent account of Reid's years in America is given by Thelma Reid Lower, *General John Reid* and *General John Reid Part 2*, in *Nova Scotia Historical Quarterly*, Vol. 9, June and December 1979.

38. William Tytler, *On The Fashionable Amusements Etc . . .*, Society of Antiquaries, 1780, p509.

39. Alison Cockburn to Miss Cumming, 16 December 1768, *Letters and Memoir of Her Own Life by Mrs Alison Rutherford or Cockburn*, David Douglas, Edinburgh 1900, pp81–82.

40. Richard Crawford, sleeve notes for *The Birth of Liberty*, New World NW 276, Side 2 Track 1 (3).

41. Percy A. Scholes, *The Mirror of Music*, Vol. II, Novello and OUP, pp662–663.

42. Cannon, *Historical Record of the 88th or Connaught Rangers* quoted in Thelma Reid Lower, *General John Reid Part 2*, in *Nova Scotia Historical Quarterly*, Vol. 9, December 1979.

CHAPTER XV

1. Burns to Thomson, September 1793.

2. Burns to William Tytler, August 1787.

3. Robert Fergusson, from *Elegy on the Death of Scots Music* first printed in *The Weekly Magazine or Edinburgh Amusement*, 5 March 1772, pp13–18.

4. David Johnson, *Music and Society in Lowland Scotland . . .* OUP, 1972, pp199–200.

5. Alexander Mollison, *An Essay Towards the Improvement of the Musical Art*, Glasgow 1798, preface pp5–6.

6. Burns to Thomson, September 1794.

7. Burns to James Johnson, 15 November 1788.

8. As Note 2.

9. Burns to Thomson, September 1793.

10. Roger Fiske, *Scotland in Music*, Cambridge University Press, 1983, Chapter II chronicles the influence in literature as well as music, which was such that Goethe among others put MacPherson's work on a par with Homer. MacPherson's influence on Holderlin was significant, and *Ossian* was Napoleon's favourite reading. Operas based on MacPherson were composed by Lesueur, Mehul, Pavesi and others; and Loewe, Schubert and Brahms set the poems to music.

11. Burns to Alexander Cunningham, 12 March 1791.
12. Mrs Begg to Captain Charles Gray, quoted in Mary Anne Alburger, *Scottish Fiddlers and their Music*, Gollancz, London 1983, p137.
13. Burns, notes on his Highland tour of 1787, quoted in Alexander Murdoch, *The Fiddle in Scotland*, John Blockley London 1888, p45.
14. Joseph M'Gregor *Memoir of Niel Gow* in *A Collection of Reels and Strathspeys . . .* Edinburgh 1837.
15. The Gow family publications are supplied with cello parts and Gow is usually pictured playing with his brother Donald on cello.
16. Elizabeth Grant, author of *Memoirs of a Highland Lady* and *Guide Through Scotland* quoted in Mary Anne Alburger, *Scottish Fiddlers and their Music*, Gollancz, London 1983, pp98–99.
17. *A Brief Biographical Account of Niel Gow* in *The Scots Magazine*, January 1809.
18. Robert Fergusson, from *The Daft-Days*, first printed in *The Weekly Magazine or Edinburgh Amusement*, 2 January 1772.
19. As Note 14.
20. Dr Thomas Garnett, *Observations on a Tour through the Highlands of Scotland*, London 1811, Vol. II.
21. Quoted in Mary Anne Alburger, *Scottish Fiddlers and Their Music*, Gollancz, London 1983, p117.
22. William C. Honeyman, *Strathspey Players Past and Present*, Larg and Sons 1922, reprinted by The Hardie Press, 1984, p13.
23. *William Marshall, Letters*; National Library of Scotland ms., Acc 7035/11.
24. Burns, *The Jolly Beggars*.
25. Purser, *Dainty Davie*? in *Stretto*, Vol. 7, No. 1, Spring 1987, pp34–35.
26. Christopher Field, sleeve and song-sheet notes for *Robert Burns*, Chandos ABRD 1324.
27. Alexander Campbell, *Albyn's Anthology*, Oliver and Boyd, Edinburgh 1816, p66.
28. *Donald MacGillivray* is discussed comprehensively in William Donaldson, *The Jacobite Song*, Aberdeen University Press, 1988, pp100–103. Donaldson's Introduction puts forward the more than plausible theory that Burns and Hogg were part of an ancient mythologising tendency, prompted in their cases by the political events of the eighteenth century.
29. Quoted in Ailie Munro, 'Abbotsford Collection of Border Ballads': Sophia Scott's Manuscript Book with Airs in *Scottish Studies* 20, 1976, p92.
30. As Note 29.
31. As Note 29, p93.
32. As Note 29, p93.

CHAPTER XVI

1. Catherine Jameson to Thomas Jameson, Edinburgh University Library, ms. Gen 1996, 12/6.
2. John Thomson to Catherine Jameson, Edinburgh University Library, ms. Gen 1996, 12/18.
3. As Note 1.
4. Catherine Jameson to Thomas Jameson, 5 April 1833, Edinburgh University Library, ms. Gen 1966, 12/7.
5. Millar Patrick, *Four Centuries of Scottish Psalmody*, Oxford University Press, 1949, p194.
6. John Thomson to William Motherwell, 31 January 1829, Edinburgh University Library ms.
7. John Thomson to William Motherwell, 12 January 1829, Edinburgh University Library ms.
8. As Note 4.
9. Mendelssohn to his family, 30 July 1829, *The Mendelssohn Family* by Sebastian Hensel, Vol. I, third English edition, London 1882, p197.
10. As Note 9, pp197–198.
11. Elliot Forbes, *Thayer's Life of Beethoven*, Princeton University Press, 1967, p555.
12. As Note 10.
13. Early editions of Grove's and the *Dictionary of National Biography* state that he knew Schumann well, but they do not give their sources.
14. As Note 9.
15. Sir Alexander Grant, *The Story of the University of Edinburgh*, Longmans, London 1884, pp 458–459.
16. The manuscripts are housed in the Reid Library in Edinburgh.
17. Thomson communicated with William Horsley for assistance in planning his lectures (National Library of Scotland ms.3443 f.109), organised the first Reid concert on 12 February 1841, which involved over two hundred performers, and for which his programme notes were extensive, all this while suffering from the dropsy of which he died four months later.
18. Sir Alexander Campbell Mackenzie, *A Musician's Narrative*, Cassell, London 1927, p4 (note). This book is referred to in the ensuing notes as *Mackenzie*.
19. *Mackenzie*, pp126, 151 and 154.
20. *Mackenzie*, pp132–134.
21. Paderewski premiered the work at a Philharmonic Concert in 1897.
22. *Mackenzie*, p191.
23. *Mackenzie*, pp89–90. Von Bulow was impressed with and encouraged performances of *Cervantes* (Grove's 1928) in Glasgow and *Colomba* in Germany (*Mackenzie* pp112–113, 118–119) and Richter had premiéred the *Violin Concerto* (with Sarasate), promoted it in Vienna (with Rose) and conducted *Britannia* (*Mackenzie* pp132 and 238–239).
24. *Mackenzie*, p151.
25. *Mackenzie*, p152.
26. G.B. Shaw, *Music in London* ii, pp280, 324; iii, p240.
27. *Mackenzie*, pp11–12.
28. *Mackenzie*, p23.
29. *Mackenzie*, p19.
30. *Mackenzie*, pp47–48.
31. *Mackenzie*, pp122–124.
32. G.B. Shaw, *London Music in 1888–89*, pp110–13. According to A.M. Henderson's *Musical Memories*, Grant Educational Company, London and Glasgow 1938, pp59–72, McCunn was also a fine teacher and conductor and his apparent decline in composition was the consequence of overwork in trying to make a living.
33. Michael Tumelty, *Glasgow Herald*, 7 February 1986.
34. He taught harmony and composition, became professorial chief of the library and was a member of the committee of management and of the Associated Board of the Royal Schools of Music. (Letter from Walter H. Stock, 18 July 1985, to the author.)
35. Frederick Lamond on *Liszt as Teacher and Pianist*, BBC sound archive recording made in 1945.
36. Programme note heading the score published by Schott. Wallace's original scores are mostly housed in the Royal Academy of Music Library.
37. Lamond's *Clavierstucke* were published by Cranz in Leipzig.
38. The letter is kept at the front of the score in Glasgow University Library Cb10–x.2.

CHAPTER XVII

1. Shuldham-Shaw and Lyle (eds) *The Greig-Duncan Folk Song Collection* Vol. 1, pp33 and 501. It is played by Heritage on No Bad Records, NBLP–2.
2. Peter Cooke, *The Fiddle Tradition of the Shetland Isles*, Cambridge University Press, 1986, pp64–65.
3. Stuart Eydmann: *He'll Dry Awa' Yer Tears: 100 Years of Music and Song in the Gospel Hall and Mission*, paper delivered at a one-day conference on Scottish Traditional Music at Strathclyde University, 11 May 1991.
4. As Note 2, pp81–82.
5. Catherine Jameson to Thomas Jameson, 5 November 1830, Edinburgh University Library, ms. Gen 1996 12/7.
6. A.L. Lloyd on *A Sailor's Garland*, Transatlantic Records.
7. Tom Anderson, quoted on *Scottish Tradition 4*, Tangent TNGM leaflet notes for Side 1 Track 5.
8. Sorley Maclean, *Obscure and Anonymous Gaelic Poetry*, in *The Seventeenth Century in the Highlands*, The Inverness Field Club, 1986, pp89–90.
9. John MacInnes and Peter Cooke, *Scottish tradition 8*, leaflet notes for Side 1 Track 5.
10. Joseph Mainzer, *The Gaelic Psalm Tunes of Ross-shire*, John Johnstone, Edinburgh 1844, Introduction, pxi.
11. The song has been recorded by Ossian on *St Kilda Wedding*, Iona IR 001, Side 1 Track 6. The letter to the author was from Flora Dunlevy (Nicolson), 23 February 1987.
12. As Note 5.
13. G.F. Graham, *The Songs of Scotland* ii, Wood and Co, Edinburgh 1854, pp72–72.
14. Hamish Henderson, sleeve notes for *Isla St Clair* on Tangent TGS 112, Side 2 Track 3.
15. *Scottish Tradition 1*, Tangent TNGM 110, has a good selection of Bothy Ballads and excellent sleeve notes. Another good collection is Ewan MacColl and Peggy Seeger, *Bothy Ballads of Scotland*, Folkways FW 8758.
16. Hebbie Gray comments on J. Scott Skinner, Scotsoun, SBC 504.
17. David Duff (ed.), *Queen Victoria's Highland Journals*, Webb and Bower, Exeter 1980, pp84 and 230. Also Alexander G. Murdoch, *The Fiddle in Scotland*, John Blockley, London 1888, pp66–71. David Baptie, *Musical Scotland*, J. and R. Parlane, Paisley 1894, p15.
18. As Note 16.
19. Mary Anne Alburger, *Scottish Fiddlers and their Music*, Gollancz, London 1983, pp174–175 and p178.
20. The People's Journal, 21 April 1923.
21. J. Scott Skinner, *A Guide to Bowing*, first published *circa* 1900, reprinted by The Hardie Press, Edinburgh 1984, p20.
22. Ethel Bassin, *The Old Songs of Skye*, RKP, London 1977, Chapter XIII.
23. Marjory Kennedy-Fraser, *Songs of the Hebrides*, Boosey and Co, London 1909, pxxiii.
24. Newman is quoted in Maurice Lindsay, *Francis George Scott*, Paul Harris, Edinburgh 1980, p30.
25. Vocal items alone account for hundreds of places and names; if the reels, strathspeys, marches and jigs for fiddle or accordion are added, never mind the pipe tunes, including piobaireachd, the map becomes even more crowded. Much the same is true of the west coast in Gaelic song and instrumental music.

CHAPTER XVIII

1. John Purser, *Is the Red Light On?*, BBC Scotland, Glasgow 1987, pp1–2 and p34.
2. Noel Goodwin in *Edinburgh* in the New Grove's.
3. Michael Turnbull, *Joseph Hislop (1884–1977) Scotland's Golden Voice*, in *Stretto*, Vol. 7, No. 2, Summer 1987, pp7–8.
4. This was the present author's own experience, though a syllabus was put together in the end.
5. Maurice Lindsay in *Francis George Scott and the Scottish Renaissance*, Paul Harris, Edinburgh 1980, states on p32, 'There was thus no living tradition for Scott to base his style upon.' There was, of course, a vast living tradition among folk-singers, and an unbroken classical tradition of setting of Scots songs, to which most classical composers in Scotland had contributed, from Thomson through Mackenzie to MacCunn. Malcolm MacDonald in *Ronald Stevenson*, National Library of Scotland, Edinburgh 1989, p43, states that Scott's *Scottish Lyrics* Book III is where 'Scottish art-music had finally confronted the twentieth century'.
6. Isobel Buchanan and Lawrence Glover, on *Francis George Scott*, Scottish Records SRSS 5, Side 2 Track 11.
7. Maurice Lindsay in *Francis George Scott and the Scottish Renaissance*, Paul Harris, Edinburgh 1980, p99, records that Marjory Kennedy-Fraser 'though terminally ill . . . hoped she could be carried down to her music-room to hear Scott sing his own songs'. Sorabji wrote of Scott in wildly enthusiastic terms in *Scottish Art and Letters* No. 1, pp22–23. Malcolm MacDonald in *Ronald Stevenson*, National Library of Scotland, Edinburgh 1989, p42, refers to the influence of Sorabji on Stevenson.
8. Agnes Walker, *Erik Chisholm* in *Stretto* Vol. 6, No. 2, Summer 1986, p9.
9. Rimmer states 'Harmonic "distortions" in the basically traditional language he employed are inconsistently applied and as a result a viable idiom is not established' in *A History of Scottish Music*, BBC 1973, pp75–77. Agnes Walker in *Erik Chisholm* in *Stretto* Vol. 6, No. 2, Summer 1986, holds a similar view, pp7–8.
10. Quoted in Maurice Lindsay, *Francis George Scott and the Scottish Renaissance*, Paul Harris, Edinburgh 1980, p208.
11. Agnes Walker, *Erik Chisholm* in *Stretto*, Vol. 6, No. 2, Summer 1986.
12. As Note 11, p9.
13. *Ronald Center*, Altarus Records AIR–2–9100, and *Piano Music from Scotland*, Olympia OCD 264.
14. John Purser, *Is the Red Light On?*, BBC, Glasgow 1987, p13.
15. As Note 14, p9.
16. Quoted in John Purser, *Hans Gal – A Personal Appreciation* in *Stretto*, Vol. 7, No. 4, Winter 1987/88.
17. Percy A. Scholes, *The Mirror of Music*, Vol. II, Novello and OUP, pp662–663.

18. Quoted in Noel Goodwin, *Iain Hamilton At 65* in *Stretto,* Vol. 7, No. 4, Winter 1987/88, p5.
19. Quoted in Isobel Woods, *The Catiline Conspiracy Part II,* in *Stretto,* Vol. 6, No. 3, Autumn 1986, p36.
20. Thomas Wilson, *The Composer Speaks* in *Stretto,* Vol. 5, No. 1, Spring 1985, p13.
21. Quoted in Malcolm MacDonald, *Ronald Stevenson,* National Library of Scotland, Edinburgh 1989, pp45–46.
22. Sleeve notes for *Ronald Stevenson: Passacaglia on DSCH* played by John Ogdon on EMI ASD 2321.

CHAPTER XIX

1. Maurice Lindsay, *Francis George Scott and The Scottish Renaissance,* Paul Harris, Edinburgh 1980, p30.
2. Ailie Munro, *The Folk Music Revival in Scotland,* Kahn and Averill, London 1984.
3. The *Greig-Duncan Folk Song Collection,* (various editors) Aberdeen University Press 1981 – four volumes published so far.
4. Letter from Peggy Seeger to the author.
5. Sleeve notes for *Scottish Tradition 7,* Tangent TNGM 128.
6. Foreword to James Hunter, *The Fiddle Music of Scotland,* The Hardie Press, Edinburgh 1988.
7. Alexander G. Murdoch, *The Fiddle in Scotland,* John Blockley, London 1888. W.C. Honeyman, *Scottish Violin Makers,* Kohler, Edinburgh 1910.
8. Hugh Macdonald, *Scotch Myths and a Theory of Icebergs,* in *Stretto,* Vol. 6, No. 1, Spring 1986, pp6–10. The Cape Breton style has been recorded on more than one disc, e.g. *Cape Breton Scottish Fiddle,* Topic 12TS354.
9. Robert Wallace, *The Glasgow Collection of Bagpipe Music,* Scottish Music Publishing, Glasgow 1986, p35.
10. Alex Duthart, *The Maestro,* Alex Duthart Percussion Ltd, Wishaw 1987.
11. Letter to Peter Maxwell Davies, papers at the Scottish Music Information Centre.
12. John Purser, *Radio Operas, Opera Northern European Style,* in *Scottish International,* April 1969, No. 6, pp13-20
13. Michael Tumelty, *Glasgow Herald,* quoted in supplement to *John McLeod,* Griffin Music, 1987.
14. *Judith Weir,* Chester Music, London, undated brochure.
15. Quoted in *James MacMillan,* Universal Edition undated brochure.
16. Iannis Xenakis in public discussion at Xenakis Festival in Glasgow, Spring 1987.
17. John Purser, *Is the Red Light On?,* BBC Scotland, Glasgow 1987, Chapters VIII–IX.

SELECT BIBLIOGRAPHY FOR
GENERAL READERS

The Bibliography is divided into the following sections:

The National Library of Scotland is abbreviated as NLS.

Many of the books referred to are out of print but can be consulted at the Scottish Music Information Centre, 1 Bowmont Gardens, Glasgow G12. Telephone: 041 334 6393, or other major libraries.

For articles and more detailed references readers should use the Index and check the Chapter Notes. Record sleeves and booklets – especially those accompanying the *Scottish Tradition* series – often provide a lot of useful information, so the Discography should also be used. The music examples should also be referred to for information on sources.

I HISTORIES OF SCOTTISH MUSIC OR ASPECTS THEREOF

Alburger, Mary Anne, *Scottish Fiddlers and their Music*, Gollancz, London 1983. An easily used, straightforward and thoroughly informative book, primarily dealing with traditional fiddle music. Well indexed and illustrated.

Baptie, David, *Musical Scotland*, J. and R. Parlane, Paisley 1894. A dictionary of Scottish musicians which requires to be corrected and updated. Unreliable but an important source of information nonetheless.

Collinson, Francis, *The Traditional and National Music of Scotland*, Routledge Kegan Paul, London 1966 and 1970. An excellent book, not afraid of speculation but presented with more of the supporting scholarly apparatus than Farmer. Covers most aspects of traditional music. However, Collinson sticks to his definition and makes nothing of the relationship between traditional and classical.

Dalyell, Sir John Graham, *Musical Memoirs of Scotland*, Edinburgh 1849. Organised primarily by instrumental categories, this remarkable mixum-gatherum of source material and curiosities reflects the wide-ranging and fascinating mind of its author. Difficult to find one's way in, and there is no index, only a very thorough list of the contents.

Dauney, William, *Ancient Scottish Melodies*, The Edinburgh Printing and Publishing Company, Edinburgh 1838. Packed with interesting information and quotations from ancient sources, as well as transcribing the Skene manuscript. This book is not a history in the strict sense, and it is difficult to find one's way in, but the indexes are quite good.

Diem, Nelly, *Beitrage zur Geschichte der Schottischen Musik im XVII Jahrhundert*, Kommissions-Verlag von Hug & Co., Zurich and Leipzig 1919. In German. This is a useful booklet with discussion and transcription of many texts and some music. The Leyden and Agnes Hume manuscripts are considered in some detail.

Elliott, Kenneth, *Early Scottish Keyboard Music*, Stainer & Bell, 1958 and 1967. A useful collection, including cittern and violin music, but not including Kinloch's two most substantial pieces, *The Battel of Pavie* and *The Ground*, both of which have been edited by John Purser but are not published.

Elliott, Kenneth, *Fourteen Psalm Settings*, Oxford University Press, 1960. A representative selection of psalm-settings immediately following the Reformation.

Elliott, Kenneth, *Music of Scotland 1500–1700*, Doctoral Dissertation, University of Cambridge, 1959, Vol. 1. (Vol. 2 = MBXV, in part). A still useful source with contents lists and discussion of manuscripts, sometimes duplicating or improving on Willshire, for whom see below.

Elliott, Kenneth and Rimmer, Frederick, *A History of Scottish Music*, BBC, London 1973. Very small, but still the best concise guide to Scottish classical music, though also out of date. It has no index and few music illustrations, but is written with clarity and is in places a miracle of concision.

Elliott, Kenneth and Shire, H.M., *Music of Scotland* (Volume XV of *Musica Britannica*), Stainer and Bell, London 1957, 1964, 1975. A vital source book containing music from a two-hundred-year span (1500–1700) set out more or less chronologically. Companion volumes are urgently needed, but MBXV will always be a seminal work. The notes are a little thin.

Emmerson, George S., *Rantin' Pipe and Tremblin' String*, Dent, London 1971. An excellent book, packed with information, with good notes, bibliography and index.

Farmer, Henry George, *A History of Music in Scotland*, Hinrichsen, London 1947, is still the largest source of information on many aspects of Scottish Music History and represents a monumental achievement from a man with a vast spread of knowledge who also can write entertainingly. But it is out of date, unreliable and very poorly indexed, supplied with virtually no references and has no music illustrations. Even so it continues to be a most useful book.

Farmer, Henry George, *Music Making in the Olden Days*, Hinrichsen, London 1950. The story of the Aberdeen concerts from 1748–1801. Full of interesting titbits.

Fiske, Roger, *English Theatre Music in the Eighteenth Century*, OUP, Oxford 1986. A valuable collection of information with more than passing mention of several Scots, the title notwithstanding.

Fiske, Roger, *Scotland in Music*, Cambridge University Press, 1983. Thoroughly unreliable on Scottish musical idioms but otherwise an interesting and well-informed study of Scottish influences, especially literary, on mainland continental composers.

Glen, John, *Early Scottish Melodies*, J & R Glen, Edinburgh 1900. Full of excellent work, a useful (though now out of date) bibliography, and historical analyses of Scottish airs which are mostly very scholarly though occasionally argumentative. Only the tunes are indexed.

Harris, David Fraser, *Saint Cecilia's Hall in the Niddry Wind*, Oliphant Anderson and Ferrier, Edinburgh 1899. Excellent study. A chapter is given to St Cecilia's Hall in *Traditions of Edinburgh* by R. Chambers, Chambers, Edinburgh 1868.

Johnson, David, *Music and Society in Lowland Scotland in the Eighteenth Century*, Oxford University Press, London 1972. This seminal book is now best read in conjunction with David Johnson's *Scottish Fiddle Music in the Eighteenth Century*, John Donald, Edinburgh 1984, which not only adds a great deal, including a huge number of music examples with many complete works, but corrects occasional imbalances in the first book. Taken together these two books are vital contributions to the history of our culture, and deserve the highest praise. The indexing is adequate and the historical references stretch back into the seventeenth century and forward a little into the nineteenth century.

Munro, Ailie, *The Folk Music Revival in Scotland*, Kahn & Averill, London 1984. A useful account which has suffered much criticism. Currently being updated.

Oliver, Cordelia, *It is a Curious Story: The Tale of Scottish Opera 1962 to 1987*, Mainstream Publishing. Well-illustrated, journalistic account.

Patrick, Millar, *Four Centuries of Scottish Psalmody*, Oxford University Press, London 1949. Contains much useful information.

Purser, John, *Is the Red Light On?* BBC Scotland, 1987. The story of the BBC Scottish Symphony Orchestra. Well illustrated, anecdotal account with useful appendices but no index.

Shire, H.M., *Song, Dance and Poetry of the Court of Scotland Under King James VI*, Cambridge University Press, 1969. A fascinating account with a very few music examples, but much biographical and other information relating to musicians in the sixteenth century.

Willshire, Harry M., *Music in Scotland During Three Centuries*, unpublished work in University of St Andrews and at Scottish Music Information Centre. Still a remarkably useful thesis, not least for its lists and discussion of manuscript contents.

Wilson, Conrad, *Scottish Opera: The First Ten Years*, Collins, London and Glasgow. Well illustrated critic's look at Scottish Opera.

There is no history of Gaelic music, but *The Companion to Gaelic Scotland*, Derrick Thomson (ed.), Blackwell Reference, Oxford 1983, has some useful entries.

The general histories of Scotland make little or no mention of music.

Grove, whether new, old, older or very old editions, is thoroughly disappointing both for size and quality of entries on Scottish music and musicians, but does nonetheless contain information not to be had elsewhere, much of it under English headings, thereby revealing all too clearly the root cause of its inadequacies.

The Innes Review is mostly concerned with church history, especially Roman Catholic, but has occasional articles of specialist Scottish music interest.

The Scots Magazine has featured music on many occasions and some of the material and discussion in the letters pages is very well informed, but the quality of research is unreliable.

Scottish Studies is a scholarly publication with scattered articles of musical interest.

Stretto quarterly magazine and its successor, the monthly *Music Current*, both from the Scottish Music Information Centre, contain many articles of importance on all aspects of Scottish music and music-making.

Tocher, the occasional magazine of the School of Scottish Studies, contains much useful material on traditional music and tradition in general and many unique transcriptions of music and texts.

II SELECTED MANUSCRIPTS AND PUBLICATIONS UP TO 1700.

For a bibliography of manuscripts from 1680–1740 see David Johnson *Music and Society in Lowland Scotland . . .*, Oxford University Press, 1972. This is a selection in probable chronological order. The contents descriptions are only guides to the most significant material. The dates of many of these manuscripts are still under discussion, so those given here are approximate and refer only to the times of writing or compiling, not to the original date of the music or texts within them. There exists no adequate account of Scottish music manuscript sources. *Musica Britannica* XV has a list of manuscript sources and David Glen (see Section I) also has an important bibliography of manuscript and printed works.

c. 1250 *St Andrews Music Book,* known as *W1*. Early polyphony. Exists also in barely adequate facsimile edited by Baxter. Fascicle 11, which contains most of the material unique to the manuscript, has been transcribed by Edward Roesner – see Chapter IV, notes 7 and 13; transcriptions of other sections are scattered over a wide variety of publications. There is no definitive transcription. Wolfenbüttel Library.

c. 1300 *Sprouston Breviary* contains plainchant services for St Kentigern NLS.

c. 1300 *Inchcolm Antiphoner.* Celtic plainchant composed over a number of centuries, partly transcribed by Isobel Woods – see Chapter III, note 16. Edinburgh University Library.

c. 1500–1560 *Carver Choirbook.* Renaissance polyphony partly transcribed by Denis Stevens in *Corpus Mensurabilis Musicae 16*, Rome; American Institute of Musicology, 1959; by Isobel Woods – see Chapter VII, note 8; by Kenneth Elliott in *Musica Britannica* – see Section I; by Gabor Darvas in *Missa L'Homme Armé*, Editio Musica, Budapest 1975; and by Muriel Brown, published by Bardic Editions, commencing 1991. NLS.

c. 1550 *Inverness Fragments.* Plainsong and fauxbourdon from the Renaissance, transcribed in full by Stephen Allinson – see Chapter VIII, note 18. Fort Augustus Abbey.

c. 1560 *Douglas-Fisher Partbooks (Dunkeld Partbooks).* Renaissance polyphony, partly transcribed by Kenneth Elliott in *Musica Britannica* – See Section I. NLS.

c. 1580 *The Art of Music.* Scottish music treatise with several unique music examples, influenced by the Reformation but with older styles represented, transcribed in full by Judson Maynard – see Chapter VIII, note 17. British Library.

1562–*c.* 1592 *Thomas Wode Partbooks.* Mostly vocal part music from the Reformation, but with important earlier material, partly transcribed by Kenneth Elliott in *Musica Brittanica* – see Section I. Edinburgh University Library, British Library, Trinity College Dublin, and Georgetown University Library.

1605 and 1607 Tobias Hume, *The First Part of Airs*, John Windet, London 1605 (also known as *Musicall Humours*) and *Captaine Hume's Poeticall Musicke*, John Windet, London 1607. Facsimile reprints under the generic title *English Lute Songs 1597–1632,* Nos. 24 and 25, The Scolar Press, London 1977. Both publications have been transcribed into modern notation by Veronika Gutmann under the generic title *Prattica Musicale,* Vol. 2, Amadeus Verlag, Winterthur, Switzerland 1980.

c. 1610 *Duncan Burnett's Music Book.* Music for virginals mostly by William Kinloch and Duncan Burnett, partly transcribed by Kenneth Elliott in *Early Scottish Keyboard Music*, Stainer and Bell, London 1958 and 1967. NLS.

c. 1615 *William Mure of Rowallan Lute Book.* Major collection of lute music including many Scottish items, all in lute tablature. Edinburgh University Library.

c. 1620 *Robert Gordon of Straloch's Lute Book.* Music in lute tablature including many interesting Scottish items. The original manuscript is lost but an incomplete copy was made by G.F. Graham in 1847 and has manuscript status. NLS.

c. 1625 *Skene Lute Book.* Music for lute in lute tablature, including many Scottish items mostly transcribed in Dauney – see *Histories of Scottish Music* . . . , above. NLS.

c. 1627–1637 *William Mure of Rowallan Cantus Partbook.* Melody line of partsongs. Edinburgh University Library.

c. 1630–1665 *Robert Edward's Commonplace Book.* Vocal and instrumental part music with texts and including psalms, songs, ballads and motets with some French, Italian and English items included. NLS.

1643–1648 *Lady Margaret Wemyss Manuscript.* Songs, poems and lute music. NLS. A full account of the manuscript with a few transcriptions was published by Matthew Spring in *The Lute,* Vol. XXVII, 1987.

c. 1660 *Companion to Lady Margaret Wemyss Manuscript.* Lute and keyboard music. NLS.

1662, 1666 and 1682, John Forbes, *Cantus, Songs and Fancies*, Aberdeen, 1662,1666 and 1682. Copies in Aberdeen University Library. The 1682 edition was published in facsimile for the New Club Series, Paisley 1879. This is the first publication of secular music in Scotland. Only the cantus book was printed and only a small proportion of the music is Scottish. The introductory remarks are of interest.

c. 1680 *Robert Taitt's Music Book.* Part songs and psalms, including a few unique items, with texts, partly transcribed by W.H. Rubsamen – see Chapter XII, note 17. Clark Library, University of California, Los Angeles.

c. 1690 *John Leyden's Lyra-Viol Ms.* NLS.

c. 1690 *Balcarres Lute Book.* A substantial collection of lute music containing Scottish and French music. Matthew Spring's thesis *The Lute in England and Scotland after the Golden Age 1620–1750,* PhD thesis, Oxford University, 1986. This thesis is currently under consideration with OUP and it is very much hoped that it will be published. NLS.

1692 *Blaikie Manuscript.* Copy of a lost lyra-viol manuscript. Wighton Collection, Dundee.

III SELECTED EIGHTEENTH-CENTURY PUBLICATIONS

For a bibliography of general books related to eighteenth-century Scottish music see David Johnson *Music and Society in Lowland Scotland* . . . , Oxford University Press, 1972. For a bibliography of printed music in the eighteenth century, see David Johnson, *Scottish Fiddle Music in the Eighteenth Century*, John Donald, Edinburgh 1984. Entries are chronological, but grouped by publisher or composer, dated by their first publication.

Playford, Henry, *A Collection of Original Scotch-Tunes*, London 1700.

Munro, Alexander, *A Collection of the Best Scots Tunes*, Paris 1732.

Thomson, W., *Orpheus Caledonius*, London 1733, 2 volumes. The first Scottish publication of traditional songs with words and music.

Ramsay, Allan, *Musick for the Scots Songs in the Tea-table Miscellany*, Edinburgh, no date.

McGibbon, William, *Six sonatas for two german flutes or two violins* . . . Edinburgh 1729. *Six sonatas or solos* . . . Edinburgh 1740. *A Collection of Scots Tunes*, three volumes, Edinburgh 1742, 1746, 1755. *Six sonatas for two german flutes* . . . London 1745.

McLean, Charles, *Twelve Solos or Sonatas* . . ., Edinburgh 1737.

Oswald, James, *The Caledonian Pocket Companion.* There were many editions of this expanding collection of outstanding importance. The largest, though stating it was in ten volumes, extended to fifteen volumes and is dated 1760–1765. Most editions extend only to twelve volumes. *A Curious Collection of Scots Tunes* . . . Edinburgh *c.* 1739, in more than one edition and followed by *A Second Collection. Colin's Kisses*, London 1742. *Airs for the Four Seasons*, London, 1756. *Airs for the Four Seasons,* second set, London, no date. *Twelve Divertimenti for the Guitar*, London 1758. *The Dust Cart, A Favorite Cantata*, London 1753. *The Wheelbarrow, A Favorite Cantata*, London *c.* 1755. *Fifty-five Marches for the Militia*, London 1759. *Twelve Serenatas for Two Violins and a Violoncello*, London 1762. (This is a selection of the main items. Oswald published many songs and pieces of theatre music of his own as well as the works of others).

Reid, John, *Six Solos for a German Flute* . . . , London 1756. *A Second Sett of Six Solos* . . . , London 1762.

Bremner, Robert, *A Collection of Airs and Marches*, Edinburgh 1756–1761. *A Collection of Scots Tunes*, Edinburgh 1759. *A Collection of the Best Minuets*, London 1765. *A Collection of Scots Reels* . . . , London 1765. *Instructions for the Guitar*, London 1758/1765. *Twelve Scots Songs for Voice and Guitar*, London *c.* 1765.

Kelly, Earl of, *Six Overtures in Eight Parts,* op. 1, Edinburgh 1761. *The periodical Overture in eight parts*, London 1767. *Six Sonatas for Two Violins and a Bass*, London 1769. *The Favourite Minuets* . . . , London 1775.

McGlashan, Alexander, *A Collection of Strathspey Reels*, Edinburgh 1780. *A Collection of Reels* . . . , Edinburgh 1781.

Marshall, William, *A Collection of Strathspey Reels*, Edinburgh 1781. *Scottish Airs*, Edinburgh 1822. *Volume 2nd of a collection of Scottish melodies*, Edinburgh 1845.

MacKintosh, Robert, *Airs, Minuets* . . . , Edinburgh 1783. *Sixty-eight new reels*, Edinburgh 1792.

Gow, Niel and Nathaniel, *A Collection of Strathspey Reels*, Edinburgh 1784 onwards, extending to six books. The Gows produced other books and most came out in several editions.

IV MODERN SOURCES OF EIGHTEENTH-CENTURY MUSIC

Johnson, David, *Scottish Fiddle Music in the Eighteenth Century*, John Donald, Edinburgh 1984, contains several complete works by a variety of composers.

Johnson, David (ed.) *Twenty-one Scots Tunes for Solo Treble Recorder*, Forsyth Bros, London 1973.

Clerk, Sir John, of Penicuik, *Sir John Clerk of Penicuik Sonata in G*, David Johnson (ed.), David Johnson, Edinburgh 1990. Everything else of John Clerk's (later Sir John) is held in manuscript in the Clerk Papers in The Scottish Record Office.

Erskine, Thomas (see Kelly).

Foulis, *David, Six Sonatas for Violin and Keyboard by David Foulis* Muriel Brown (ed.) Scottish Music Publishing, Glasgow 1990.

Kelly, Thomas Erskine, Earl of, *Thomas Alexander Erskine Earl of Kelly Overture in C op. 1 no. 2*, David Johnson (ed.) David Johnson, Edinburgh 1990. *Trio Sonata in F*, David Johnson (ed.) David Johnson, Edinburgh 1991.

McGibbon, William, *Orpheus Caledonius Volume 1 William McGibbon Three Sonatas*, Peter Holtman (ed.) The Hardie Press, Edinburgh 1991.

Oswald, James, *Airs for the Seasons*, Jeremy Barlow (ed.) (4 volumes, one for each season, each with three sonatas) Chester Music, London 1983. Almost everything else Oswald wrote can only be obtained from eighteenth-century editions, for which see the British Union Catalogue of Early Music. This, however, only mentions the first set of *Airs for the Seasons*. The second set exists in a unique copy in the Wighton collection in Dundee Central Library. Photocopies of the second set and of most of Oswald's other works are held at the Scottish Music Information Centre.

Reid, John, *General John Reid Sonatas Nos 2 & 5 from Book II*, Paul M. Douglas (ed.) English Woodwind Edition 7, London 1984. *John Reid Three Solos*, Steve Rosenberg (ed.) Boosey & Hawkes, London 1985.

V FIDDLE

(Modern Commentaries and Editions. See Sections III and IV above for other sources.)

Alburger, Mary Anne, (see Section I above).

Cooke, Peter, *The Fiddle Tradition of the Shetland Isles*, Cambridge University Press, 1986 (with accompanying cassette).

Hardie, Alasdair, *The Caledonian Companion*, E.M.I. Music Publishing, 1981.

Hardie, Bill, *The Beauties of the North*, The Hardie Press, Edinburgh.

Honeyman, William, *Strathspey Players Past and Present*, The Hardie Press, Edinburgh 1984.

Hunter, James, *The Fiddle Music of Scotland*, The Hardie Press, Edinburgh 1988.

Johnson, David (see Section I above). Also *Scots on the Fiddle, 1 and 2*, David Johnson, Edinburgh 1991; and *Stepping Northward*, David Johnson, Edinburgh 1990.

Neil, J. Murray, *The Scots Fiddle*, Lochar Publishing, Moffat 1991.

Skinner, J. Scott, *A Guide to Bowing*, The Hardie Press, Edinburgh 1984.

VI BAGPIPES

Campsie, Alasdair, *The MacCrimmon Legend*, Edinburgh 1980. Highly contentious book but containing some useful and necessary correctives. It has itself become part of piping history.

Cannon, Roderick D., *A Bibliography of Bagpipe Music*, John Donald, Edinburgh 1980. Covers the main sources in chronological order. The specialist reader is referred to this book and his later volume (see below), and only a few selected volumes are mentioned here. See also under Section VIII.

Cannon, Roderick D., *The Highland Bagpipe and its Music*, John Donald, Edinburgh 1988. A straightforward and sensible book marred by one or two strange inaccuracies, but basically recommended. The bibliography is very helpful.

Collinson, Francis, *The Bagpipe*, RKP, London, 1975. An account of bagpipes in general which remains a standard book on the subject.

Dow, Daniel, *A Collection* . . ., Edinburgh 1776.

Glen, David, *David Glen's Collection* . . . In seventeen parts with a tutor and also published in various combined volumes, the last being issued in Edinburgh *c.* 1902–1907. A major source of pipe tunes of many kinds.

Glen, J & R, *Glen's Collection* . . . in three parts but later bound together, Edinburgh ?1870. An important and large collection of marches, dances and slow airs.

Haddow, Alexander John, *The History and Structure of Ceol Mor*, privately printed, Glasgow 1982. A remarkable gathering

of historical research into piobaireachd and its origins, with some interesting musical analysis. Haddow did not live to complete the book, but it is still of great importance and interest.
MacDonald, Allan, *The Moidart Collection*, Clo-Ciuil 1991. A collection by one of the finest pipers living, reflecting freer styles of playing and choice of repertoire.
MacDonald, Donald, *A Collection of the Ancient Martial Music of Caledonia, c.* 1822, reprinted by EP Publishing, Wakefield 1974. A fundamental source book for pipers.
MacDonald, Joseph, *A Compleat Theory of the Scots Highland Bagpipe*, first published 1803, reprinted by Alexander MacDonald, Glasgow 1927. The most important and oldest publication, sadly full of printer's errors and other inaccuracies. A properly corrected edition based on the original manuscript is in preparation.
MacKay, Angus, *A Collection of Ancient Piobaireachd or Highland Pipe Music*, Edinburgh 1838. A vital source book providing the basis of many of the Piobaireachd Society Publications, but much criticised by Alasdair Campsie.
MacNeill, Seumas, *Piobaireachd*, BBC Publications, Glasgow 1968, reprinted 1976. A most useful booklet, easily followed and well presented, though historically in need of updating and expansion.
MacNeill, Seumas and Richardson, Frank, *Piobaireachd and its Interpretation*, John Donald, Edinburgh 1987. A rather small and cosy book which makes up in pleasantries and piping familiarities what it lacks in scholarship.
Malcolm, C.A., *The Piper in Peace and War*, John Murray, London 1927. An interesting book full of information and anecdote.
Mooney, Gordon, *A Collection of the Choicest Scots Tunes*, The Lowland Pipers Society, Scotland 1982, and *A Tutor for the Cauld Wind Pipes*, Lowland and Borders Pipers Society, Scotland 1985. Both cheaply produced but indispensible.
O'Connor/Clarke, *From the Stone Age to the Forty-Five*, John Donald, Edinburgh. Bagpipes are the subject-matter of the final chapter.
The Piobaireachd Society Collections of piobaireachd have reached fourteen volumes and are still continuing. These are the standard texts, though there are mixed opinions about the editorial policy.
The Piping Times contains many useful studies and, over a series of issues, published a dictionary of pipers and piping.
Ross, G.F., *Some Piobaireachd Studies*, Peter Henderson, Glasgow 1926, and *A Collection of MacCrimmon and other Piobaireachd*, Peter Henderson, Glasgow 1929. Both are important publications.
Thomason, General, *Ceol Mor*. Published privately in 1893, reprinted in facsimile EP Publishing, Wakefield 1975. The most comprehensive collection of piobaireachd with the first good analysis of the form. Thomason's system of abbreviations, once learnt, is easy to follow, but not popular.
Wallace, Robert, *The Glasgow Collection of Bagpipe Music*, Scottish Music Publishing, Glasgow 1986. An excellent selection of recent bagpipe compositions as well as arrangements of traditional tunes by one of the world's leading pipers.

VII CLARSACH

Armstrong, R.B., *The Highland Harp*, Edinburgh 1904. Includes a detailed study of the Lamond and Queen Mary harps.
Bunting, *The Ancient Music of Ireland*, Hodges and Smith, Dublin 1840. Bunting's scholarship gets more criticism than it deserves. The opening dissertation on the Irish harp and harpers remains extremely useful and some of his transcriptions, especially those not in the main body of the music, are probably as faithful to the original performances as we have a right to expect. Bunting's publications have been reprinted in facsimile.
Kinnaird, Alison, *The Harp Key*, Kinmor Music. An excellent collection with well researched notes. Arrangements are designed to satisfy the performer rather than the historian.
Matheson, William (ed.), *The Blind Harper*, The Scottish Gaelic Texts Society, Edinburgh 1970. A most important book which also contains music and useful notes on it.
McLean-Clephane Manuscript (early nineteenth-century). A most important collection of harp airs, though mostly Irish.
O'Baoill, Colm, *Some Irish Harpers in Scotland* in *The Transactions of the Gaelic Society of Inverness*, Vol. 47. An important study.
Sanger, Keith – has published many excellent articles, including the following: *The McShannons of Kintyre* in *The Kintyre Antiquarian and Natural History Society Magazine*, No. 28, 1990. *Replies: The Maclean-Clephane Harp Music* in *Notes and Queries of the Society of West Highland and Island Historical Research*, No. 15, May 1981. *Auchinbreck's Harper*, ibid, No. XXX, February 1987. *Some Unruly Scottish Harpers* in *Folk Harp Journal*, No. 47, December 1984. *Portraits of an Irish Harper*, ibid., No. 45, June 1984. *Patrick O'Byrne and John Bell*, ibid., No. 53, June 1986. *Harperlands*, ibid, No. 49, June 1985. *Aspects of Harping in Lowland Scotland*, ibid., No. 58, Fall 1987. *Balvaird* in *The Kilt and Harp, Journal of the Scottish Harp Society of America*, No. 8, Spring 1986. *The Kilchoan Grave Slab*, ibid., No. 10, Fall 1986.

VIII GAELIC VOCAL AND INSTRUMENTAL

(See also Sections VI and VII above.)

Bassin, Ethel, *The Old Songs of Skye*, RKP, London 1977. An affectionate and often useful study of Frances Tolmie and her connections with Kennedy-Fraser.
Campbell, Alexander, *Albyn's Anthology*, Oliver and Boyd, Edinburgh, Vols I and II, 1816 and 1818. An important early collection with Gaelic texts. Campbell's arrangements are not of the best.
Campbell, J.L., and Collinson, Francis, *Hebridean Folksongs*, Oxford at the Clarendon Press, Vol. I 1969, Vol. II 1977, Vol. III 1981. A scholarly and important source for waulking songs, but with material of far wider relevance – a major achievement with music, texts, translations and analysis.
Coisir a Mhoid, Gairm Publications – several volumes and dates, available in staff and solfa notations. Gaelic songs harmonised as part songs with texts supplied in Gaelic only.
Dow, Daniel, *A Collection of Ancient Scots Music* (see Section III above).
Fraser, Simon, *The Airs and Melodies . . .*, Edinburgh 1816. A most important collection, sadly without texts, but with an interesting introduction and informative anecdotal notes.
Kennedy-Fraser, Marjory, *Songs of the Hebrides*, Vol. I, 1909, Vol. II 1917, Vol. III 1923, *From The Hebrides*, 1925, *More Songs of the Hebrides*, 1929, are heavily criticised for the style of their arrangements and their lack of scholarly discipline. The sources and alternatives for much of her material are listed in Campbell and Collinson Vol. III (see this section). There is, however, a danger of throwing out the baby with the bath-water. Her purpose was not scholarly, and her books remain the sole source for a few items.
MacDonald, Donald, see Section VI above.
MacDonald, Keith Norman, *The Gesto Collection of Highland Music*, 1895. Piano arrangements, including piobaireachd and songs with Gaelic texts. This is a substantial and important collection.
MacDonald, Patrick, *A Collection of Highland Vocal Airs*, Corri and Sutherland, Edinburgh 1784.
Matheson, William, see Section VII above.
O'Baoill, Colm, *Bardachd Shilis Na Ceapaich*, Scottish Gaelic Texts Society, Edinburgh 1972. Has useful notes on metres and tunes.
Shaw, Margaret Fay, *Folksongs and Folklore of South Uist*, Aberdeen University Press, 1986. A loving and scholarly study with music, texts and translations.
Tolmie, Frances, *Notes and Reminiscences* and a major collection of 105 songs was published in the *Journal of the Folk-song Society*, Vol. IV 1910–1913. A vital source with music, text and translations. See Bassin, Ethel.
Watson, J. Carmichael, *Gaelic Songs of Mary MacLeod*, The Scottish Gaelic Texts Society, Edinburgh, 1982.

IX JACOBITE SONG

Campbell, J.L., *Highland Songs of the '45*, John Grant, Edinburgh 1933.
Donaldson, William, *The Jacobite Song*, Aberdeen University Press, 1988. An excellent book which clears away many myths and has good notes and bibliography.
Hogg, James, *The Jacobite Relics of Scotland*, Edinburgh 1819–1821 (2 Vols).

X SCOTS SONG AND BALLAD

(See also Sections III and IX above.)

There are literally hundreds of collections. A few salient publications are mentioned here on account of their scholarly value.

Bronson, Bertrand Harris, *The Traditional Tunes of the Child Ballads*, Princeton University Press, Vol. I 1959, Vol. II 1962, Vol. III 1966, Vol. IV 1972. A monumental work of scholarship of outstanding importance. Recent criticism of his transcriptions as being too ready to conform to the tyranny of the bar-line are made by people who, if they lived a thousand years, would not remotely approach Bronson's achievement. The criticism has some limited validity, but the pedantry of transcriptions which attempt to reproduce every nuance and inflection serves only to distance the reader from the music.
Cameron, John, *The Lyric Gems of Scotland*, John Cameron, Glasgow, no date (late nineteenth or early twentieth century) first and second series. A huge collection of songs (vocal line only) with texts and notes in a robust and handsome pocket-sized publication. Though not particularly scholarly, the portability of this book makes it worth hunting for a copy.
Dick, James C. (ed.), *The Songs of Robert Burns*, Henry Frowde, London 1903, and *Notes on Scottish Song . . .* Henry Frowde, London 1908. A *fons et origo* of Burns studies.
Ford, Robert, *Vagabond Songs and Ballads*, Alexander Gardner, Paisley 1899. Only a few are given with music, but this is an excellent publication.
Graham, G.F., *The Songs of Scotland . . .*, Wood and Co., Edinburgh 1848–1849 in three volumes, also published as a single volume. Copious notes and a high standard of piano accompaniments make this an important collection.
Greig-Duncan Folk Song Collection Vols 1–4, ed. P. Shuldham-Shaw, E. Lyle & P.A. Hall, Aberdeen University Press, 1981,'83,'87,'89. A monumental work still in progress and of the first importance.
Greig, John, *Scots Minstrelsie*, T.C. Jack, Edinburgh 1983, in six volumes. Copious notes and illustrations and reasonable piano accompaniments.
Groves, David, *James Hogg Selected Poems and Songs*, Scottish Academic Press, Edinburgh 1986. A useful selection.
Low, Donald A. (ed.), *The Scots Musical Museum*, Scolar Press, 1991. A vital resource, though the editorial input is minimal and the various notes published in the nineteenth century to go with it have been sadly omitted. Readers are therefore advised to seek out editions with Stenhouse's Notes and the Additional Notes, in particular the edition of 1839 prefaced by David Laing. The Stenhouse Notes and Additional Notes by Charles Kirkpatrick Sharpe were also published separately in 1853 by Blackwood and Sons of Edinburgh.
Ord, John, *Bothy Songs and Ballads*, reprinted with a new Introduction by Alexander Fenton, John Donald, Edinburgh 1990 (first published 1930). A fundamental source book.
Simpson, Claude M., *The British Broadside Ballad and its Music*, Rutgers University Press, New Brunswick 1966. A vital book of major scholarly importance. It is best read alongside John Ward's article *Apropos 'The British Broadside Ballad and its Music'*, printed in the *Journal of the American Musicological Society*, Vol. XX, Number I, Spring 1967, pp28–86, which is an important source of addenda and corrigenda for Simpson's book.

XI MILITARY MUSIC

(See also Section VI above.)

Acheson, James *The Military Garden*, 1629.
Boag, William, *The Tenor Drum, Drums On Parade, The Rise of the Scottish Style of Side Drumming, Pipers in the Scottish Regiments*, Military Historical Society, August 1975.
Brander, Michael, *Scottish and Border Battles and Ballads*, Seeley Service & Co. Ltd, London 1975. Informative on the historical side, though the music is somewhat peripheral to the main interest of the book.
Farmer, Henry George, *Handel's Kettledrums*, Hinrichsen, 1950. Also *The Rise and Development of Military Music*.
Reeves, *Military Music and its Story*.
Winstock, Lewis, *Songs and Music of the Redcoats*, Cooper 1970.

XII STUDIES OF INDIVIDUAL MUSICIANS AND AUTOBIOGRAPHY

There are remarkably few of these. They are listed chronologically by musician rather than by author or publication.

Loot and Loyalty, by Jerzy Pietrkiewicz, Heinemann, London 1955. A splendid but entirely imaginary account of

Hume's adventures in Poland and Russia. It includes most of Hume's *True Petition . . .* in an appendix.

George Thomson – a man of his time, by Kirsten McCue, MA dissertation for the University of Glasgow, May 1989.

David Kennedy, by Marjory Kennedy and David Kennedy, Jun., Alexander Gardner, Paisley 1887. Portrait of the famous Scottish singer and father of Marjory Kennedy-Fraser.

A Musician's Narrative, by Sir Alexander Campbell MacKenzie, Cassell, London 1927. A very entertaining autobiography.

Scottish Composers, John B. McEwen, The Dunedin Magazine, Vol III, No. 3, December 1915.

Scottish Composers, Learmont Drysdale, The Dunedin Magazine, Vol III, No. 1, War Number 1916.

Francis George Scott and the Scottish Renaissance, by Maurice Lindsay, Paul Harris, Edinburgh 1980. A lively and opinionated account, more biographical than musicological.

Orpheus With His Lute, by Hugh and Kenneth Roberton, Pergamon Press, Curwen and Sons, Oxford 1963. Primarily concerned with Sir Hugh Roberton and the Glasgow Orpheus Choir.

Hans Gal, by Wilhelm Waldstein, Verlag Elisabeth Lafite Wien, Vienna. In German. A useful study.

Ronald Stevenson, by Malcolm MacDonald, National Library of Scotland, Edinburgh 1989. An excellent little musical biography.

Thea Musgrave, by Donald A. Hixon, Greenwood Press, Westport Connecticut. Described as a bio-bibliography.

SELECTED DISCOGRAPHY

CLASSICAL DISCOGRAPHY

The method of entry is chronological. Since this cannot be an exact system readers should glance up and down the line in the period that interests them: they should also check with dealers whether items are available in other formats than those mentioned. Many items exist only in recordings specially made for the BBC Radio Scotland series *Scotland's Music* and since these are in many cases of primary importance they feature here with the tag **SM**. They are NOT commercially available to the public but it will be possible to consult them at the Scottish Music Information Centre (SMIC). Educational and other suitable institutions may be able to purchase complete sets of the programmes from the BBC for study purposes.

For ballads, clarsach, fiddle, bagpipe and Gaelic music, see the *Traditional Discography* in the relevant sections.

There has been one set of five records/cassettes of a history of Scottish classical music, still available but very hard to obtain. All are produced by Scottish Records under the generic title *A History of Scottish Music*. Performance styles have changed since the first four were issued, but they all contain important material unavailable elsewhere and are still a vital source. They cover, respectively, the following centuries: 1. thirteenth-sixteenth century (*The King's Music* SRSS 1); 2. sixteenth century (*Songs and Dances of The Scottish Court* 33 SR 133); 3. seventeenth century (*Music of Castle, Burgh and Country-side* SRSS 3); 4. eighteenth century (*Baroque and Classical Scotland* SRSS 4); 5. nineteenth century (*The Nineteenth Century Rebirth* SRCM 116). This series is referred to below as **HSM**, followed by the relevant number.

1000 BC–0 AD

SM has the only Scottish material. Musica Sveciae MS 101/EMI 1361031 has relevant recordings.

0–500

SM has the only Scottish material. Musica Sveciae and Music From Archaeology 2 *Sounds of the Roman World* Archaic APX 862 have related material.

500–1000

SM again has the only Scottish material, but see *Inchcolm Antiphoner*. Music From Archaeology 1 *Sounds of the Viking Age* Archaic APX 851 have related items.

1000–1500

Music from Archaeology 3 *Sounds from Norman Times* Archaic APX 873 has a little relevant material and **SM** has some otherwise unrecorded items.

Inchcolm Antiphoner. **SM** A cassette and CD of a substantial portion of the *Inchcolm Antiphoner* is planned by Cappella Nova to be issued in September 1992 on the Gaudeamus label.

Ex Te Lux Oritur sung by Paul Hillier on *Troubadour Songs and Medieval Lyrics* Hyperion CDA66094.

Pleugh Sang on **HSM**1, also The Hilliard Ensemble on *Henry VIII* Saga 5444, and on *Coronach Scottish Renaissance Music*.

St Andrews Music Book. None of the material in this manuscript, unique or otherwise, has ever been recorded from the perspective of the manuscript's Scottish provenance, except for two items on **HSM**1. Various Scottish items are scattered under French and English headings. Pieces apparently unique to Scotland are incorporated into reconstructions of a mass in Notre Dame, and so on. The following are none the less recommended. Landini Consort *Nowell, Nowell,* Hill and Dale HD001 contains *In Rama Sonat Gemitus*. There are several items sung by Schola Cantorum Basiliensis on *Osterspiel Aus Notre Dame* on EMI Electrola Deutsche Harmonia Mundi 165–99 925/26. Also Capella Antiqua *Ars Antiqua* Das Alte Werk SAWT 9530/31–B. Also Schola Cantorum De Londres on *Adam De La Halle et le XIIIeme Siecle* Harmonia Mundi HMU 443. The Hilliard Ensemble on *Sumer Is Icumen In* Harmonia Mundi 901154 contains three items, described as 'probably English'. There is no evidence to support this whatever.

1500–1600

Mixed programmes **HSM**2 and 3 (see above).

Coronach O Lustie May, CMF 003, *Coronach: Scottish Renaissance Music*, CMF 001 and *Coronach Celtic Heritage*

are all mixed vocal and instrumental. Performances are folk influenced, lively and committed but not always to professional standards. Recommended none the less.

In A Garden So Green Saltire Vocal Quartet on Da Camera Magna SM 94035. Performance styles of this repertoire have changed, but still recommended and has some items not recorded elsewhere.

Early Scottish Music, The Kincorth Waits. Not a good quality recording, but has its moments.

Carver Choirbook anonymous Ave Gloriosa and Psalm 1 **SM** only.

Carver, Robert. Complete works on 3 cassettes or CDs, sung by Cappella Nova on *Robert Carver* Gaudeamus GAU 124, 126, 127. Recommended.

The two motets are also on CD sung by the Taverner Choir on *Taverner, Browne, Carver* Reflexe, EMI, CDC 7 49661 2. Recommended.

Anon., attributed to Carver. A Mass and some Reformation psalms are sung by Paisley Abbey Choir on *Cantate Domino* Abbey records Alpha ACA 532. Recommended.

Johnston, Robert. A record devoted to Johnston, sung by Paisley Abbey Choir on *Ave Dei Patris Filia* Abbey Records, Alpha ACA 558. Recommended.

Scottish Anonymous Manuscript **SM** Ane exempill of Tripla is on Mary's Music (see below).

Kinloch, Lauder, Burnett (see Keyboard Music below).

Keyboard Music mostly **SM**, but a few items on **HSM**2, *Mary's Music*, and several played by Alan Cuckston on EMI *Baroque Library (No. 32) Early Scottish Keyboard Music and Dances from the Dublin Virginal Manuscript*, HQS 1150. Style of performance has changed since this record was made, but it has character and items not recorded elsewhere. Recommended.

Mary's Music. A mixed programme related to Mary Queen of Scots, performed by The Scottish Early Music Consort, on *Mary's Music* record Chandos ABRD 1103 and on CD. Recommended.

Black, John. Report on When Shall My Sorrowful Sighing Slack is on *Virtuoso Recorder Music* Oiseau Lyre 414 277–1. His Lytill Black is on **HSM**1.

A mixed programme from The Baltimore Consort of Early Scottish Music on *On the Banks of Helicon*, Dorian DOR–90139 (CD and cassette) covers 1550–1700. Recommended. Arrangements and performance styles blend classical and folk with convincing results.

1600–1700

Hume, Tobias. A complete programme of viola-da-gamba solos is played by Jordi Savall on *Captaine Tobias Hume Musicall Humors* Astree E 7723. Recommended.

Consort items and songs are performed by Alain Zaepffel and others on *Dramatic Laments Elegies and Lullabies* ADDA 581033 CD: by Tragicomedia with David Cordier on *My mind to me a Kingdom is* Hyperion CDA66307 and on *A Musicall Dreame* Hyperion CDA66335. All recommended.

Lute. Pickering, Straloch, Skene mandora, and Rowallan lute books are featured by Ronn MacFarlane on *The Scottish Lute* Dorian DOR 90129. Recommended.

The Pickering, Straloch, Rowallen, Panmure 5, Lady Margaret Wemyss and Balcarres lute books are all featured by Jakob Lindberg on *Scottish Lute Music* BIS LP–201. Recommended.

Playford. Scottish items from his publications feature on The Broadside Band's *John Playford's Popular Tunes* Amon Ra Recordings CSAR 28.

Abell, John. Songs and cantatas **SM**. Nothing of Abell's is commercially available.

Clerk cantatas are all only available on **SM**. A scandal. A fragment of one is on **HSM**4. The violin sonata is on *Music of Classical Edinburgh*.

1700–1800

McGibbon, William. One item on *Scottish Baroque Ensemble at Hopetoun* CRD 1028. Recommended. Others on *Fiddle Pibroch and other Fancies* and *Music of Classical Edinburgh*.

Oswald, James. Nearly all the Oswald items referred to in Chapter XIV are **SM** items, including the Masonic Anthems, Guitar music, Collin's Kisses, Dustcart Cantata, Wheelbarrow Cantata, Trumpet pieces and songs. This is a scandal. The Narcissus, The Lily, The Nightshade and The Snowdrop from the *Airs For The Seasons* are on *Scots Fiddle High Style* and folk-song variations or arrangements on *Music of Classical Edinburgh*. The Marvel of Peru from the Airs For The Seasons is played by Evelyn Nallen on *The Nightingale In Love* ASV CD DCA 606. The Narcissus, The Nightshade, The Lilac, The Lily and The Sneezwort from the *Airs For The Seasons* are due out in Spring 1992 on Springthyme SPR CD 1033 and C 1033, performed by the Leda Ensemble.

Kelly, Earl of. As scandalously neglected as Oswald. **SM** only for the orchestral music and the aria, song and capillaire minuet as well as a quartet and trio from the Kilravock manuscript. The Trio Sonata in C and the Strathspey and Reel are on *Music of Classical Edinburgh*. The Trio Sonata in C is also on **HSM**4. Two minuets played by Gerald Gifford on *Georgian Harpsichord Music* Libra LRCD 156.

Foulis, David. Sonata in B flat on *Scots Fiddle High Style*. Sonatas in E major, F major and A major due out in Spring 1992 on Springthyme SPR CD 1033 and C 1033, performed by the Leda Ensemble.

Fiddle Pibroch and Other Fancies. Scotland's Cultural Heritage SCH 002. Eighteenth-century music including McLean sonata on 'Twas Within a Mile of Edinburgh Town', McGibbon's Sonata 'La Folia', Reid's Sonata No. 2 in G (but played on violin, not flute) and two piobaireachd on violin. Recommended.

Music of Classical Edinburgh. Scotland's Cultural Heritage SCH 001. Recommended. Includes Clerk's Violin Sonata, McGibbon's Sonata in C minor, Kelly's Trio Sonata in C, his Strathspey and Reel, and two minuets, and arrangements by Oswald and Bremner.

Scots Fiddle High Style. Scottish Records 33 SR 117. Uneven performances, but some good. Contains many works otherwise unavailable including Oswald's Airs For The Seasons, McLean's Sonata in G minor and Sonata in A, Foulis' Sonata in B flat, and five sets of variations on traditional tunes. Recommended.

Reid, John. The March for the 3rd regiment and the March for the eighteenth-century regiment are both on *The Birth of Liberty*, New World NW 276. His Sonata No. 2 in G (played on violin, not flute) is on *Fiddle Pibroch and Other Fancies*.

Burns, Robert. An interesting mixed programme, mostly vocal, from The Scottish Early Music Consort on *Robert Burns*, Chandos ABRD 1324 (CD: CHAN 8636). Recommended. Also *Classically Scottish* <BE> Records. See also Traditional Discography.

Music of Castle Fraser on Alpha ACA 509 contains three anonymous Polonaises which may be Scottish.

1800–1900

HSM5 contains MacKenzie's Piano Quartet, a McEwen trio and songs by MacKenzie and MacCunn. Recommended.

Thomson Entirely **SM** – which includes an overture, extracts from a trio, songs, part songs and piano pieces.

MacKenzie. Apart from **HSM**5 his works are only available on **SM** and Victorian Concert Overtures, Hyperion CDA 66515, which includes Britannia.

1900–1950

MacCunn, Hamish. Land of the Mountain and the Flood is on *Music of the Four Countries* EMI ASD 2400. Songs on **HSM**5.

McEwen, John B. One chamber work on **HSM**5 and the Solway Symphony on an impossibly bad archive recording held by the SMIC. Otherwise **SM**, in particular Grey Galloway and the Biscay quartet.

Wallace, William. Only on **SM**.

Drysdale, Learmond. Only on **SM**.

Scott, Francis George. Isobel Buchanan, Malcolm Donnelly and Lawrence Glover on *A Centenary Song Recital* Scottish records SRSS 5. Recommended. See *Piano Music from Scotland* in the 1950– section.

1950–

Music by Scottish Composers, Volume 1 SSC 001, contains Wilma Paterson's Casida del Llanto and John McLeod's the Song of Icarus (both for violin and piano); Thomas Wilson's Cancion for solo guitar; John Geddes's Callanish IV for solo cello and Janet Beat's electronic fantasy, Dancing on Moonbeams.

Music by Scottish Composers, Volume 2 SSC 002 is a piano duo recital and contains Frank Spedding's Bellini Studies; Hans Gal's Three Marionettes; Edward McGuire's Reflections and John Purser's Circus Suite for Mick.

Piano Music From Scotland has F.G. Scott Eight Songs (transcribed by Ronald Stevenson); Ronald Center's Piano Sonata, Six Bagatelles and Children At Play; and Ronald Stevenson's Beltane Bonfire and two Scottish Ballads. Olympia OCD 264.

Center, Ronald. Dona Nobis Pacem, the Piano Sonata and Three Nativity Carols are all on Altarus ASIR–2–9100. The Piano Sonata, Six Bagatelles and Children At Play are on *Piano Music from Scotland*.

Dalby, Martin. Two liturgical canticles. Benedictus Es is on RRC–400 1370–B RIAA, and Jubilate Deo is on Abbey LPB 789. Mater Salutaris is on Alpha ACA 532 and ACA 557.

Davies, Peter Maxwell. Most works are on disc and the list would be too substantial to include here. Details from Scottish Music Information Centre, British Music Information Centre and from publishers.

Dillon, James. Sgothan is on ICONS Antidogma AM – 1861 – 862.

Forbes, Sebastian. String Quartet No. 1 is on Argo ZRG 672.

Gal, Hans. See *Music by Scottish Composers* Volume 2.

Geddes, John. See *Music by Scottish Composers* Volume 1.

Hamilton, Iain. The Piano Sonata is on the Lyrita label; the Sonata Notturna is on Argo RG 475; the Cello Sonata and the Three Pieces for Piano are on Argo RG 425. Aubade and Paraphrase are on RCA VICS 1663. Epitaph for this World and Time and Voyage are on CRI SD 280; Sinfonia for Two Orchestras is on EMI ALP 2279.

Hallgrimsson, Haflidi. Daydreams in Numbers; Tristia; Strond; Verse 1 and Jacob's Ladder are all on Merlin MRFD 88101.

McGuire, Edward. See *Music by Scottish Composers* Volume 2; and in the Traditional Music discography under the Whistlebinkies.

McLeod, John. See *Music by Scottish Composers* Volume 1.

Musgrave, Thea. Night Music is on Argo ZRG 702; Monologue for Piano and Excursions are on Argo ZRG 704; Soliloquy for Guitar and Tape is on Deutsche Grammophon 2530 079; Colloquy for Violin is on Argo RG 328; Triptych is on EMI ALP 2279; Mary Queen of Scots is on Vox MMG 301; A Christmas Carol is on Vox MMG 302; Rorate Coeli is on Abbey LPB 798.

Orr, Robin. Symphony in One Movement is on EMI ALP 2279.

Paterson, Wilma. See *Music by Scottish Composers* Volume 1.

Purser, John. See *Music by Scottish Composers* Volume 2.

Spedding, Frank. See *Music by Scottish Composers* Volume 2.

Stevenson, Ronald. Passacaglia on DSCH is on EMI ASD 2321. Beltane Bonfire, two Scottish ballads and eight transcriptions of F.G. Scott songs are on *Piano Music from Scotland*.

Weir, Judith. An Mein Klavier and Michael's Strathspey are on NMCD002 (SPNM); The Art of Touching the keyboard is on Merlin MRFD 891706; King Harald's Saga and the Consolations of Scholarship are on Novello records NVLCD 109 and NVLC109; Scotsh Minstrelsy is on Abacus ABA 109–2 and Illuminare Jerusalem is on Hyperion CDH88031 and AFKA SK516.

Wilson, Thomas. See *Music by Scottish Composers* Volume 1. The Piano Concerto is on Chandos ABRD 1315.

Wordsworth, William. Four Lyrics on String Quartet No. 3 Discurio 001; String Quartets 5 and 6 were recorded by the Alberni Quartet and Three Wordsworth Songs are on CRD 1097 or CRDC 4097 (cassette).

SELECT DISCOGRAPHY OF SCOTTISH TRADITIONAL MUSIC

Discography Index

Sections

I   Gaelic Alphabetically by Artist/Group/Title.
II Scots Compilations Alphabetically by Generic and/or Individual Title.
III Scots Alphabetically by Artist/Group/Title.

IV Instrumental Alphabetically by Instrument, then by Artist/Group/Title.
    Subsections are IVB Bagpipes. IVBB Bellows Bagpipes. IVA Accordion IVC Clarsach IVF Fiddle IVFC Fiddle Classical IVT Trump
V   Scots Chronologically by Subject Matter (Codes To Other Sections Only)
VI Geographical Alphabetically by Place (Codes To Other Sections Only)

Method of Entry of Items

Alphabetically by performer or group by the initial letter only, followed by a number indicating order of entry in these lists only. Each entry is coded by the Roman Section Number, followed by the Initial Letter followed by the Arabic Number.

The list represents work in progress and has many omissions, some of which will be glaringly obvious to the initiated. There are code numbers with no entries to them, awaiting detail on known items or for likely additional material: they have been retained so that readers can fill them in for themselves. A full discography would be a book on its own.

The BBC Library has a song-title and an artists' index. The NSA does not. SMIC's index is occasionally by song title, rarely by artist, partly by record title, and mostly unindexed. Only some items are commercially available.

By far the best introduction to Scottish traditional music of all kinds is the outstanding series of recordings issued by the School of Scottish Studies, which are still available but very slow in delivery. (See II S1–S9). The Columbia World Library record is also excellent, but the NSA may be the only source of a copy. (See IIC1). The Topic label has issued a large number of fine recordings of authentic traditional performances. From a historical point of view it is difficult to divide the authentic from the spurious: individual performers and groups frequently mix both and scholars are not, and never will be, agreed on these matters.

I GAELIC (AND KENNEDY-FRASER)

I C1. Cairistiona, (Jackson G. and MacInnes M.) Iona IR006
I C2. Ceol na Gaidhlig. Scotsoun SSC GMP 014
I C3. Cormack, Arthur. Nuair Bha Mi Og Temple TP016

I G1. Gillies, A.L. The Songs of the Gael Lochshore LOCLP 1014

I K1. Songs of the Hebrides. Hyperion A66024
I K2. Songs of the Hebrides. Land of Heart's Desire. Meridian E77008

I M1. MacNeill, Finlay. Fonn is Furan Temple TP009
I M2. MacNeil, Flora. Craobh nan Ubhal Tangent TGS 124
I M3. MacPhee, Catherine-Ann. Canan nan Gaidheal Greentrax TRAX 009

I N1. Na h-Oganaich. Gael Force 3. Beltona SBE 160

I P1. Primrose, Christine. 'S tu nam Chuimhne Temple TP024
I P2. Primrose, Christine. Aite Mo Ghaoil Temple TP006

I R1. Runrig. The Highland Connection. Ridge RR001
I R2. Runrig. Recovery. Ridge RR002

See Also II 2, II 3, II 6, II 7, II 8. III H1. IV BB3. IV C4.

II SCOTS COMPILATIONS

II C1. Columbia World Library Folk Songs from Scotland. Columbia SL–209
II C2. Coarse and Fine. Songs and ballads of Dundee. Springthyme SPR 1017

II F1. Folk Songs of Britain Volume 1.
II F2. Folk Songs of Britain Vol. 2. Songs of Seduction Topic 12T158
II F3. Folk Songs of Britain Vol. 3. Jack of All Trades Topic 12T159
II F4. Folk Songs of Britain Vol. 4. Child Ballads 1 Topic 12T160
II F5. Folk Songs of Britain Vol. 5. Child Ballads 2 Topic 12T161
II F6. Folk Songs of Britain Vol. 6. Sailormen and Servingmaids Topic 12T194

II F7. Folk Songs of Britain Vol. 7.
II F8. Folk Songs of Britain Vol. 8. A Soldier's Life for Me. Topic 12T196
II F9.
II F10.
II F11. Folk Songs Topic Sampler No. 1. Topic TPS 114
II F12. Folk Songs Topic Sampler No. 2. Topic TPS 145
II F13.
II F14.
II F15.
II F16. Folk Songs Topic Sampler No. 6. Topic TPS 201
II F17. Fergusson's Auld Reekie. Iona IR003

II I1. The Iron Muse. Topic 12T86

II M1. Music In Trust. Temple TP022
II M2. Music In Trust. 2 Temple CTP029

II S1. Scottish Tradition 1 Bothy Ballads. Tangent TNGM 109
II S2. Scottish Tradition 2 Music from the Western Isles. Tangent TNGM 110
II S3. Scottish Tradition 3 Waulking Songs from Barra. Tangent TNGM 111
II S4. Scottish Tradition 4 Shetland Fiddle Music. Tangent TNGM 117
II S5. Scottish Tradition 5 The Muckle Sangs. Tangent TNGM 119/D
II S6. Scottish Tradition 6 Gaelic Psalms From Lewis. Tangent TNGM 120
II S7. Scottish Tradition 7 Calum Ruadh-Bard from Skye. Tangent TNGM 128
II S8. Scottish Tradition 8 James Campbell of Kintail. Tangent TNGM 140
II S9. Scottish Tradition 9 The Fiddler and His Art. Tangent TNGM 141

II T1. Treasures Of Scotland (NTS). Lismor LICS 5113
II T2. Thomson/Napier/Beethoven/Haydn. Scottish Folk Songs. EMI ASD 3167

II U1. Unity Creates Strength. Nevis NEV R007

III SCOTS ARTIST/GROUP/TITLE

III B1. Back O' Benachie Topic 12T180
III B2. The Battlefield Band. At The Front. Topic 12TS381
III B3. Battlefield Band. Home Is Where The Van Is. Temple TP005
III B4.
III B5.
III B6. Beck, Jack. O Lassie, Lassie. Greentrax TGRAX027
III B7. Boys of the Lough. Open Road. Topic 12TS433
III B8. Boys of the Lough. In The Tradition. Topic 12TS422
III B9. Boys of the Lough. The Boys Of The Lough. Shanachie 79002
III B10. Boys of the Lough. Boys Of The Lough Regrouped. Topic 12TS409
III B11. Boys of the Lough. Far From Home. Auk001

III C1. Campbell, Alex. Alex Campbell Sings Folk. SAGA SOC960
III C2. Campbells, The Singing Campbells. Topic 12T120
III C3. Carthy, Martin. Topic 12TS340
III C4. Capercaillie. Cascade. Five Records SRI 4KL 178
III C5. Clutha
III C6. The Corries. BBC. Fontana 6309 004

III F1. Fisher, Archie. Will Ye Gang Love. Topic 12TS277
III F2. Fisher, Archie. Archie Fisher. Celtic Music CM 007
III F3. Fisher, Archie. The Fate O' Charlie. Trailer LER
III F4. Fisher, Archie. The Man With A Rhyme. Folk-Legacy FSS–61
III F5.
III F6. Fisher, Cilla. Songs Of The Fishing Kettle KOP–11

III H1. Heather and Glen. Tradition TLP 1047
III H2. Heritage. Some Rantin' Rovin' Fun No Bad Records NBLP 01
III H3. Heritage Two. When the Dancin' It's A' Done. No Bad Records NBLP–2
III H4. Higgins, Lizzie. Princess of the Thistle (SMIC C–WY146 Cassette copy) Topic 12T185
III H5. Higgins, Lizzie. Up and awa' wi' the Laverock Topic 12TS260
III H6. Higgins, Lizzie. What A Voice. Lismor LIFL 7004
III H7. Hunter, Andy. King Farewel, Lismor LIFL 7002

III H8. Hom Bru. Obadeea Celtic Music CM009

III J1. Jackson, Billy. The Misty Mountain. Iona IR005
III J2. Jackson, Billy. The Wellpark Suite. Mill Records MR001

III K1 Kennedy, Norman. Scots Songs And Ballads. Topic 12T178

III L1. Lloyd, A.L. and MacColl English and Scottish Folk Ballads Topic 12T103
III L2. Lloyd, A.L. and MacColl A Sailor's Garland Prestige/Transatlantic
III L3. Laggan, The. I am The Common Man. Klub KLP 16

III M0. See L1. & L2 MacColl, Ewan and Lloyd, A.L.
III M1. MacColl, Ewan. The Jacobite Rebellions Topic 12T79
III M2. MacColl, Ewan. Solo Flight Argo ZFB12
III M3. MacColl, Ewan and Seeger, Peggy. Classic Scots Ballad XTRA 1054
III M4.
III M5. MacColl, Ewan and Seeger, Peggy. Blood and Roses Vol. 2. Blackthorne ESB 80
III M6. MacColl, Ewan and Seeger, Peggy. Blood and Roses Vol. 3. Blackthorne ESB 81
III M7. MacColl, Ewan and Seeger, Peggy. Blood and Roses Vol. 4. Blackthorne ESB 82
III M8. MacColl, Ewan and Seeger, Peggy. Blood and Roses Vol. 5. Blackthorne ESB 83
III M9.
III M10. MacColl, Ewan and Seeger, Peggy. Bothy Ballads of Scotland. Folkways FW 8759
III M11. MacColl, Ewan. Songs of Robert Burns. Folkways FW 8758
III M12. MacColl, Ewan and Seeger, Peggy. The Amorous Muse. Argo (Z)DA 84?
III M13. McCalmans, The. The Ettrick Shepherd. Greenwich Village GVR 209

III O1. Ossian. Seal Song. Iona IR002
III O2. Ossian. Dove Across The Water. Iona IR004
III O3. Ossian. Ossian. Springthyme Records SPR1004
III O4. Ossian. St Kilda Wedding. Iona IR 001
III O5. Ossian. Borders. Iona IR 007

III R1. Redpath, Jean. Frae My Ain Countrie. Folk-Legacy FSS–49
III R2. Redpath, Jean. There Were Minstrels. Trailer LER2106
III R3. = IV F2. Redpath, Jean. The Scottish Fiddle The Music And The Songs. Lismor LIFL 7009
III R4.
III R5.
III R6.
III R7.
III R8. Robertson, Jeannie. Jeannie Robertson. Topic Topic 12T96
III R9. Robertson, Jeannie. Jeannie Robertson. Lismor Lismor LIFL 7001
III R10. Reilly, John. The Bonny Green Tree. Topic 12T359

III S1. St Clair, Isla. Isla St Clair. Tangent TGS 112
III S2. Sprangeen. Sprangeen. Springthyme SPR 1013
III S3.
III S4. Stewarts of Blair. The Stewarts of Blair. Topic (and SMICC–WY146 cassette)
III S5. Stewarts of Blair. The Stewarts of Blair. Lismor LIFL 7010
III S6. The Travelling Stewarts. Topic 12T179
III S7. Stewart, Davie. Davie Stewart. Topic 12T293
III S8.
III S9.
III S10. Sutherland, Isabel. Vagrant Songs of Scotland. Topic 12T151
III S11. Seeger, Peggy. Peggy Alone. Argo(?) ZFB 63

III W0. Whistlebinkies, The. Amiga 8 45 127
III W1. Whistlebinkies, The. Claddagh CC22
III W2. Whistlebinkies, The. Claddagh CC31
III W3. Whistlebinkies, The. 3 Claddagh CC34

III W4. Whistlebinkies, The. 4 Claddagh CC43
III W5. Whistlebinkies, The. 5 Claddagh CC50
III W6.

IVA ACCORDION

(There are very many recordings in this category, easily obtained, only three are listed here).

IVA S1. Shand, Jimmy. A Tribute To Jimmy Shand. Waverley GLN 1017
IVA S2. Shand, Jimmy. Scotland My Home. Waverley EMI OC 058–07 546
IVA S3. Shand, Jimmy. Happy Hours With Jimmy Shand. Music For Pleasure MFP 41 5751 1

IVB BAGPIPES HIGHLAND

IVB B1. Brown, Robert. The Pipes of Balmoral. Master MALP–330
IVB B2. Burgess, John D. Pipe-major John Burgess. Lismor LILP 5125
IVB B3. Burgess, John. King of Highland Pipers. Topic

IVB C1. A Controversy of Pipers. Temple TP0081

IVB H1. Henderson, Murray. The World's Greatest Pipers Vol. 4. Lismor LILP 5159

IVB Mc1. MacCallum, Hugh. The World's Greatest Pipers Vol. 2. Lismor LILP 5147
IVB Mc2. MacDonald, Angus. The World's Greatest Pipers Vol. 1. Lismor LILP 5143
IVB Mc3. MacFadyen, Iain. Ceol Mor Ceol Beag. Temple TP018
IVB Mc4. MacPherson, Donald. Donald MacPherson. Master Records MALPS–374

IVB P1. Piobaireachd (MacNeill & MacFadyen) BBC REB 48M
IVB P2. Pibroch 1. Waverley. Waverley ZLP 2034
IVB P3. Pibroch 2. Waverley. Waverley ZLP 2035
IVB P4. Piper in The Nave 1. Piobaireachd and Light Music P–M Donald MacLeod. Scotsoun SSC 034
IVB P5. Piper In The Nave 2. Six Piobaireachd P–M Donald MacLeod Scotsoun SSC 046
IVB P6. Piping Championship. Lismor LILP 5134

IVB S1. Scottish Tradition. Cassette Series No. 1 Pibroch. Pipe-major William MacLellan. Tangent TGMMC 501
IVB S2. Scottish Tradition. Cassette Series No. 2 Pibroch. Pipe-major Robert Brown. Tangent TGMMC 502
IVB S3. Scottish Tradition. Cassette Series No. 3 Pibroch. Pipe-major Robert Nicol. Tangent TGMMC503
IVB S4. Stoddart, G.N.M. The World's Greatest Pipers Vol. 3. Lismor LILP 5151

IVB W1. Wallace, Rab. Chance Was A Fine Thing. Claddagh CC38

IVBB BAGPIPES (BELLOWS)

IVBB M1. Mooney, Gordon. O'er the Border. Temple TP 031
IVBB M2. Moore, Hamish. Cauld Wind Pipes Dunkeld DUN 003

IVC CLARSACH

IVC K1. Kinnaird, Alison. The Harp Key. Temple CSH 001
IVC K2. Kinnaird, Alison & Heymann, Ann. The Harper's Land. Temple CTP 012
IVC K3. Kinnaird, Alison. The Harper's Gallery. Temple CTP 003

IVC Mc1. MacKay, Rhona. Ceol na Clarsach. Lismor LILP 5130

IVC N1.Napier, Marie-Louise. Sweet Harping. Cairngorm Music CM 3544

IVC S1. Sileas. Delighted With Harps. Lapwing LAP 113C

IVC S2.
IVC S3.
IVC S4. Stivell, Alan. Renaissance of the Celtic Harp. Philips 6416 406

IVC W1. Williamson, Robin. Legacy of the Scottish Harpers. Claddagh CCF 12

IVF FIDDLE

IVF C1. Cape Breton Scottish Fiddle. Topic 12TS354
IVF C2. Curlew. Topic 12TS435
IVF C3. Cameron, Angus. Bow To The Fiddle. Beltona Sword SBE 180

IVF D1. James F. Dickie's Delights. Topic 12T279

IVF F1. The Fiddler and His Art Tangent TNGM 141
IVF F2. The Fiddler's Companion. Waverley-EMI GLN 1023 (Bain, Grant, Hardie, Stewart, Anderson, Hardie, MacAndrew)
IVF F3. The Fiddle Tradition of the Shetland Isles. Cambridge Studies in Ethnomusicology

IVF G1. Grant, Angus. Highland Fiddle. Topic 12TS 347

IVF H1. Hunter, Willie. Willie Hunter Celtic Music CM 010

IVF M1. Music To Measure (Dillon-Alburger). Music To Measure MtoM 1

IVF R1. Ringing Strings. Topic 12TS429

IVF S1. The Scottish Fiddle The Music And The Songs. Jean Redpath Lismor LIFL 7009
IVF S2. Scott Skinner. The Strathspey King. Topic 12T280
IVF S3.
IVF S4. Shetland Folk Fiddling Vol. 2 Topic 12TS379

IVFC FIDDLE CLASSICAL

IVFC F1. Fiddle Pibroch and Other Fancies. Scotland's Cultural Heritage SCH 002

IVFC M1. Music of Classical Edinburgh. Scotland's Cultural Heritage SCH 001

IVFC S1. Scots Fiddle High Style. Scottish records 33 SR 117

IVT TRUMP (JEW'S HARP)

IVT P1. How to play and Have Fun with the Jew's Harp. Lindsay Porteous TW002
IVT P2. Lindsay Porteous and friends. Greentrax CTRAX 022

V CHRONOLOGICAL/HISTORICAL

(Codes are for other sections)

V III M1. MacColl, Ewan. The Jacobite Rebellions Topic 12T79
V III F3. Fisher, Archie. The Fate o' Charlie. Trailer LER
V II F11. Fergusson's Auld Reekie Iona IR003
V III M11. MacColl, Ewan. Songs of Robert Burns. Folkways FW 8758
V III M10. McCalmans, The Ettrick Shepherd. Greenwich Village GVR 209
V III M10. MacColl, Ewan and Seeger, Peggy. Bothy Ballads of Scotland. Folkways FW 8759
V II I1. The Iron Muse Topic 12T86

VI GEOGRAPHICAL ALPHABETICALLY BY PLACE

(Codes are for other sections)

VI Cape Breton IVF C1
VI Shetland IVF C2
VI Shetland IVF S4
VI Dundee II C2

LIBRARIES AND ARCHIVES

The single most comprehensive reference library, music library, sound archive and provider of relevant material and information is *The Scottish Music Information Centre*, 1 Bowmont Gardens, Glasgow G12 (tel. 041-334 6393). This institution is open to the public and contains a huge collection, including most of the important manuscripts from a variety of libraries on microfilm. It is the only Scottish music sound archive with innumerable rare recordings of classical and traditional music, many recorded from radio programmes and including talks and ancillary material. It is the only library which starts with the basic classification of Scottish and therefore saves an immense amount of time for the browser. The reference library is excellent and easy to use.

The Scottish Music Information Centre is the proper starting point for almost any line of investigation. Its services are free, except for photocopying, tape dubbing and music hire.

The National Library of Scotland in Edinburgh houses a vast collection of music which includes most of the manuscripts and publications of Scottish origin or interest. However, relevant material is not always classified under a Scottish heading so you have to know what you are looking for or else rely on the excellent staff of the music and manuscript rooms. It is open to the public.

The School of Scottish Studies (part of the University of Edinburgh) has a unique collection of archive material and recordings of traditional music as well as a useful reference library. For the researcher interested in traditional music it is the most important centre for study. Admission by application.

The Mitchell Library in Glasgow has a good collection (including the Kidson collection with much eighteenth-century material) and is open to the public.

The Dundee Central Library houses the Wighton collection which has much rare and some unique Scottish music publications of the eighteenth century. Open to the public.

Edinburgh Central Library has some useful material and is open to the public.

The University Libraries of Edinburgh, Glasgow, Aberdeen and St Andrews can be used on application with a suitable recommendation. Edinburgh and Glasgow have particularly strong collections. The Reid Library in the music school in Edinburgh University contains most of Thomson's music; the *Inchcolm Antiphoner* is in the main library. Glasgow has the extensive Euing and Farmer collections with much rare material.

The Royal Scottish Academy of Music and Drama library has a good folk song collection as well as a certain amount of Scottish music. Admission by application.

The British Library contains a number of important manuscripts, especially the Scottish anonymous treatise from the sixteenth century, and is a vital source of rare publications. Admission by application.

The libraries of the Royal College and Royal Academy of Music in London, have manuscripts of MacKenzie and Wallace respectively. Admission by application.

There are manuscripts in the Bodleian Library (Oxford) and the Cambridge University Library. American University libraries and the Wheeler Institute in Washington have some material.

The Irish Traditional Music Archive in Merrion Square in Dublin has an excellent library and sound archive with much material relevant to Scotland, and a knowledgeable staff.

Sound Archives
Scottish Music Information Centre. Open to the public.
School of Scottish Studies. Admission by application.
National Sound Archives. Open to the public.
BBC archives in Edinburgh, Glasgow and London.
BBC Record libraries in Glasgow and London. Not open to the public.

National Library of Scotland. Open to the public.
Cecil Sharpe House. Open to the public.
Irish Traditional Music Archive. Open to the
   public.

Museums with Instrument Collections
The Royal Museum of Antiquities possesses the
Lamond and Queen Mary harps, early bagpipes of
various kinds, early Christian bells, the bronze-
age horn fragment, Roman trumpet mouthpieces,
the carnyx, and a number of other minor items.
The Reid School of Music in Edinburgh has a
particularly fine collection of early instruments,
some of Scottish manufacture.

The St Cecilia's Hall collection of keyboard
instruments (in Edinburgh) is outstanding, as
is the collection of musical instruments at Dean
Castle in Kilmarnock, but Scottish instruments
scarcely feature.
Glasgow Art Gallery and Museum has a good
little collection of instruments of relevance; so
too does the Horniman Museum in south-east
London. The Ulster Museum in Belfast and the
National Museum of Ireland (in Dublin) also
have some relevant holdings, especially from the
Bronze Age.

GLOSSARY OF SCOTTISH MUSICAL TERMS

Bagpipes, Highland   Single enclosed reed instrument with three drones and a conical open chanter fed with air from the mouth via a bag held under the arm. The most powerful and rich-toned of all bagpipes and used for Laments, Gatherings and Marches as well as dance music and slow airs.

Lowland   Bellows-blown bagpipe with cylindrical chanter producing a sweet tone, similar to the Northumbrian pipes.

Border   Bellows-blown pipes with three drones and conical bore chanter used by town pipers for reveilles and curfews.

Cauld-Wind   Literally 'cold wind', referring to the fact that air from a bellows is cold, unlike air from the mouth via a bag, is a term now applied to a variety of bellows-blown pipe.

Ballad   Story told in song.

Bard   Originally a poet/musician inferior to the *Filidh*, but latterly assuming those functions and responsible for the composition and performance of eulogies, satires, and laments.

Bothy Ballad   Song or ballad associated with farm work and created by the men who communally occupied the bothies, or cottages provided on the farms.

Bothy Band   A group of instrumentalists playing in the bothy style, usually involving fiddle and accordion. Bothy bands often played for dances.

Brosnachadh   Gaelic poetic incitement to battle, probably sung or intoned.

Canntaireachd   Unique syllabic notation for bagpipe music, sung and written.

Cant Organe   Sixteenth-century term thought to refer to a technique of free improvised polyphony.

Caoine   (Keen) Gaelic lament for the dead.

Ceilidh   Gaelic word, but used widely outwith the Gaelic-speaking area, describing an informal gathering involving story-telling, song, dancing, music-making or simply neighbourly chat. Formalised versions of the *ceilidh* are perpetrated by the media and for tourists, but a true *ceilidh* has elements of familiarity and spontaneity difficult to capture and impossible to organise.

Ceol   Gaelic for music.

Ceol Mor   Literally 'big music' and applied exclusively to *piobaireachd*.

Ceol Beg   Literally 'little music' and applied to dance music on the bagpipes.

Clarsach   Scottish harp. The term is applied to a variety of triangular framed harps of varying size, but all basically smaller than the modern concert harp. The number of strings can be thirty or more, but was certainly less in the early history of the instrument. Recent discussion tends to use the word to imply a gut-strung instrument, as opposed to the wire-strung harp more frequently, but not exclusively, associated with Ireland. Early instruments in central and southern Scotland may have been strung with horse-hair. In Scotland the instrument rests on the floor and the right shoulder; in Ireland, on the floor and the left shoulder. The assumption that Celtic harps were always tuned diatonically is no longer secure.

Clarsair   Player of the *Clarsach*.

Coronach   Scottish Gaelic term for the chorus of the *caoine* or lament. See *Goll*.

Crotals   Bronze-age rattles.

Dewar   Hereditary guardian of a holy relic, in particular early Christian bells.

Double-tonic   Harmonic progression (or melodic progression based on it) in which two chords a tone apart alternate. See Introduction for an example.

Duan   Gaelic word for a text delivered in a declamatory pitched vocal line, defined by some scholars as being more chant-like than the *Laoidh*.

Ecossaise   French dance of obscure origin assumed to be Scottish and popular in the eighteenth century. In the nineteenth century it was speeded up and possibly superseded by the *Schottische*.

Filidh or *Fili*   Member of a class of poets superior to bards with responsibility for genealogies, prophecies and eulogies. They probably sang or recited but were not instrumentalists.

Flyting   Abusive poetic contest between bards or makars, satirical, mostly good-humoured and frequently ribald. Traditional in Gaelic and Scots cultures.

Gaelic Psalm-singing   Used to refer to a specific kind of singing in the Gaelic church in which the psalm tune is 'lined-out' by a precentor, and is sung slowly with much decoration and with no attempt to produce a uniform choral result. Its nearest parallels are in the Middle East.

Gathering   Form of *piobaireachd* used to summon the clans.

Goll   Irish Gaelic term for the chorus section of the *caoine* or lament. See *Coronach*.

Gue   Type of fiddle known to have existed in Shetland, thought to have had two horse-hair strings and to have been played on or between the knees.

Hardanger or *Harding*   A type of Norwegian fiddle and/or a style of playing which imitates the effect of 'ringing strings' created by the sympathetic strings and frequent use of double-stopping on the Norwegian instrument. The style is imitated in Shetland.

Hornpipe   A dance form similar to the jig but with a different metre for the music, sometimes with three, sometimes two beats to the bar. Mattheson writing in the eighteenth century is probably right in declaring it to be Scottish in origin.

Iorram   Song intended to accompany rowing. Examples exist in different rhythms and speeds, implying different rates of rowing according to weather and vessel.

Jig   A lively dance form, high-stepping and usually with six quavers and two beats to the bar. The word as applied to dance makes its first appearance in Scottish literature in the sixteenth century. It also applies to a satirical type of song which may have involved dance or action also with strong Scottish associations in its early history. It is now accepted that the French *Gigue* is derived from the Jig.

Laoidh   Gaelic equivalent to English 'Lay', suggested by some scholars to be a more song-like form of melodic declamation than the *Duan*.

Lorica   Literally 'breastplate'. Refers to a Celtic verse prayer in Latin or Gaelic, probably sung or intoned, containing pagan elements invoking protection for the various parts of the body. By extension, any Celtic prayer the saying or singing of which was believed to give protection.

Makar   Scots word for a poet.

Moothie   Mouth-organ.

Mouth-music   See *Port-a-beul*.

Musick Fyne   Sixteenth-century term for any complex part music.

Oran Basaidh   Gaelic for a 'clapping song'.

Oran Luadhaidh   Gaelic for *Waulking Song*.

Oran Mor   Literally, 'big song'. Gaelic phrase describing traditional ballad-type songs.

Piobaireachd (Pibroch)   Literally 'pipe music', it is taken exclusively to mean *Ceol Mor* (big music). This term refers to a set of variations for Highland bagpipes, based on an *Urlar* (literally 'ground', meaning theme). In modern practice these variations increase in decorative complexity without interruption and end with a repeat (usually partial) of the opening urlar. Originally the *urlar* was almost certainly repeated in the middle of the *piobaireachd*, and the complexity of the *Throws* (decorations) was even greater than it is today. See Index for details in main text.

Port-a-beul   Instrumental-style music sung to words which are usually nonsense syllables, for the purpose of dance as well as entertainment, and involving very rapid articulation and intake of breath. Also known as *Mouth-music*.

Quern Song   See *Work Song*.

Reel   Scottish dance form incorporating a setting step and a travelling figure, at various times danced by three, four, six or eight dancers. The oldest patterns may have been circular but the figure of eight is the norm. The music is characterised by even and rapid quaver motion, with eight quavers and two beats to the bar. The American Hoe-down is derived from the reel.

Row   A dance form associated with the Borders and possibly based on child's play.

Schottische   Dance form. Origins obscure. Possibly derived from the *Ecossaise* by the incorporation of waltz steps in a two-crotchet-to-the-bar time signature. It evolved in the nineteenth century.

Scotch Snap   Rhythmic device in which a short accented note on the beat precedes a longer note. It is associated particularly with Scotland though it is not exclusive to it.

Strathspey   Scottish dance form similar to a slow reel and assumed to have originated in Strathspey. The music features strongly emphasised dotted rhythms and *Scotch snaps*.

Tiompan   Plucked stringed instrument similar to the lyre, possibly three-stringed. It was reputed to be sweet-toned and the strings were probably made of metal.

Trump   Jew's or jaws harp.

Urlar   Literally means ground and refers to the theme announced at the start of a *piobaireachd*

and on which the subsequent variations are based, sometimes loosely.

Waulking Song   A song of alternating chorus and solo lines (the latter frequently improvised) sung by women in the West Highlands when 'waulking' (shrinking) cloth. The custom no longer survives as modern methods have overtaken the tweed industry. The original method was to soak the tweed in human urine and thump it on a board or table rhythmically with feet or hands, the cloth being passed round as it was worked on. This could take up to half an hour. The quality of the cloth was much better preserved by this method, as was the quality of the wool on the old hand looms.

Work Song or *Labour Song*   A term applied to songs used to accompany and encourage various tasks, with the implication that the rhythm of the song fitted the rhythm of the work. Milking song, quern song (for accompanying the turning of a rotary hand-mill), lullaby, rowing song or *Iorram*, sea shanty, *Waulking Song* and others belong to this class.

LIST OF COLOUR PLATES

LIST OF BLACK AND WHITE PLATES

LIST OF MUSIC EXAMPLES

All titles are by Anon. unless otherwise stated. Authors' names are not given. Many items consist only of tiny excerpts of works. Those asterisked are musically complete. Titles are given in the order in which they appear in chapters. Music illustrations which take the form of plates are indicated.

INTRODUCTION

1   *Pentatonic Scale and My Ladie Laudians Lilt
2   *The Blythsome Bridal
3   *Air Faillirinn
4   *Lovely Molly
5   *Scotts Man
6   Fiddle figures
7   *Niel Gow: Lady Lucy Lesslie Melville's Reel

CHAPTER I

1   Redshank calls
2   *The Caoine or Pill-il-il-iu
3   The Nameless Lament
4   Crunluath and Barludh bagpipe cuttings
5   *Range of Caprington Horn

CHAPTER II

1   *Arthurian Lay (Am Bron Binn)
2   *Welsh Lullaby (Hwi hwi)
3   *Welsh Wren Song
4   *Shetland Lullaby/Wren Song
5   *Fairy Song (A Phiutrag 's a Phiuthar)
6   *The Bressay Lullaby (Baloo balilly)
7   *Charm against a hail shower (Clach mhin)
8   Peat-fire smooring prayer (Righ na Dul)
9   *Quern song ('S i mo bhra)
10 *Altus Prosator
11 Gaelic and Coptic chant
12 *Rowing song

CHAPTER III

1   *Mediae Noctis
2   *Pitches of Scottish Bronze Bells
3   *Ibunt Sancti
4   *Crucem Sanctam
5   *Salve Splendor
6   *O Columba Insignis Signifer
7   *Os Mutorum
8   *Sanctorum Piissime Columba
9   *Pater Columba
10 *O Mira Regis
11 *Rex Caeli

CHAPTER IV

1   *Parallel Organum
2   *Hymn To St Magnus (Nobilis Humilis)
3   *Free Organum
4   Vir Perfecte
5   *Qui Liber Est Scriptus
6   *In Rama Sonat Gemitus
7   *Kyrie Virginitatus Amator
8   Haec Dies
9   Hac In Anni Janua
10 Sanctus Ierarchia
11 Agnus Dei

CHAPTER V

1   *King Orfeo
2   *Thomas the Rhymer
3   *Ex Te Lux Oritur
4   *Sir Patrick Spens
5   *Hey Tutti, Tatti
6   *The Gowans are Gay
7   *Greysteil
8   The Pleughsang
9   Trip and Go Hey

CHAPTER VI

1   *Manus (Fenian lay)
2   *Laoidh Mhanuis (Fenian lay)
3   *Laoidh Fhraoich (Fenian lay)
4   *Deirdre's Lament
5   *Laoidh Dhiarmad
6   *Harlaw Brosnachadh
7   Battle o' the Harlaw and Lament for Red Hector of the Battles
8   *Battel of Harloe
9   *Tuning Prelude for Clarsach
10 The Ogham Alphabet
11 Ap Hyw ms and The Men Went to Drink
12 *Da Day Dawis
13 Scale and tuning methods of Clarsairs

CHAPTER VII

1   All Sons of Adam
2   *I Long for the Wedding
3   *Woe Worth the Time
4   *Into a Mirthful May Morning
5   *Robert Carver* Gaude Flore
6   *Robert Carver* O Bone Jesu
7&8 *Robert Carver* Six Part Mass
9   *Robert Carver* Missa L'Homme Armé
10 *Robert Carver* Ten Part Mass
11 *The Flowers of the Forest
12&13 *Robert Carver* Five Part Mass
14 Salva Festa Dies
15&16 Ave Gloriosa

CHAPTER VIII

1   Johnnie Armstrong
2   *John Fethy* O God Abufe
3   Song to Venus
4   *Robert Johnston* Dicant Nunc Judei
5&6 *Robert Johnston* Benedicam Domino
7   *Robert Johnston* Deus Misereatur Nostri
8   Descendi in Hortuum Meum
9   *David Peebles* Si Quis Diliget Me

CHAPTER IX

1   Untitled
2   Gallyard Queen Scotte
3   *Two Scottish Branles
4   The Scottish Huntsupe
5   Wo Betyde Thy Wearie Bodie
6   *Glenlogie
7   *Port Jean Lindsay
8   *The Four Maries
9   *Mary Beaton's Row
10 *Lauder* The Golden Pavan
11&12 *William Kinloch* Battel of Pavie
13 *William Kinloch* Ground
14 *John Fethy* The Time of Youth

CHAPTER X

1   *Nou Let Us Sing
2   *The Nyntene Canon
3   *The Saxt Canon
4   *Andro Blackhall* Adieu o Daisie of Delight
5   *As I Me Walked
6   *The Bonny Earl of Murray
7   *Rory Dall's Port
8   *John Black?* Report on Psalm 50 and 'When Shall My Sorrowful Sighing Slack?'
9   Walking I Chanc'd
10 *Tobias Hume* Harke, Harke
11 *Tobias Hume* A Souldiers Resolution
12 *Tobias Hume* The Passion of Music
13 *Tobias Hume* Cease Leaden Slumbers
14 *Aderneis Lilt
15 *Duncan Burnett* Pavan
16 * Kilt Thy Coat, Maggie

17 *Lady Cassilis Lilt
18 *The Gypsies' Lilt

CHAPTER XI

1   *Rinn Mi Mocheirigh
2   *Grigor Criodhal
3   * A Mhic Iain 'ic Sheumais
4   *Oran Na Comhachaig
5   *Cumha Do Iain Garbh
6   *Cumha Do Iain Garbh (different tune)
7   *Give Me Your Hand
8   *The Royal Lament
9   *Hilliu-an, Hilleo-an
10 *Latha Inbhir Lochaidh
11 *Cumha Lachlainn Daill
12 *Faill Nan Crann
Plate 29. Piobaireachd Dhonuil Dubh
13 The MacGregors' Gathering
14 *Pentatonic scales on bagpipes
15 Crunluath a-mach and McLeod's Salute
16 *Duntroon's Warning
17 Canntaireachd
18 Lament for Mary McLeod
19 *Patrick Mor MacCrimmon* Lament for the Children
20 McIntosh's Lament
21 *Iseabail Nic Aoidh

CHAPTER XII

1   *Babbity Bowster
2   *Put Up Thy Dagor Jamie
3   *The Bonnie Hoose o' Airlie
4   *Old Pots and Pans — Street Cries
5   *The Scotch Trumpet Tune
6   *Dainty Davie
7   *Mill o' Tiftie's Annie
8   *The Reveille
9   *The Gathering
10 *The Retreat
11 *The Scots March
12 *Pate Birnie: The Auld Man's Mare's Deid
Plate 34. For Our Long Biding Here
13 *Kishmul's Galley
14 *Alasdair MacMaster* Moch Sa Mhadainn
15 *The Celebrated Trumpet Tune
16 *Mo Run Geal Og
17 Tha Do Rioghachd Lan Do Ghloir

CHAPTER XIII

1   *The Duch Man
2   *John Abell* The Fifth Song
3   *John Abell* The Third Song
4   *John Abell* A Song on Queen Anne's Coronation
5   *John Abell* Birthday Ode to Queen Anne
6&7 *John Clerk* Cantata – Eheu, Eheu!
8&9 *John Clerk* Cantata – Dic Mihi Saeve Puer
10,11&12 *John Clerk* Cantata – Odo Di Mesto Intorno
13&14 *John Clerk* Cantata – Leo Scotiae Irritatus

CHAPTER XIV

1   *James Oswald?* Roslin Castle
2   The Reel of Tulloch
Plate 37. The Drummond Manuscript
3   *Alexander Munro* Sonata on Bonnie Jean of Aberdeen
4   *William McGibbon* Sonata in C Minor
5   *David Foulis* Sonata Number II
6   *James Oswald* Sonata on Scots Tunes
7   *James Oswald* The Freemason's Anthem
8   *James Oswald* The Narcissus (Airs for the Seasons)
Plate 39. *James Oswald* The Sneezwort
9   *James Oswald* The Marvel of Peru (Airs for the Seasons)
10 *James Oswald* The Rapture (Colin's Kisses)
    James Oswald The Stolen Kiss (Colin's Kisses)
11 *James Oswald* The Meeting Kiss (Colin's Kisses)

I am grateful for permission to quote from copyright works as detailed below:

Chapter XVIII
   Examples 5, 6 and 7 – Bayley and Ferguson.
   Example 8 – Dunedin Publications.
   Example 9 – Theodore Presser Company.
   Example 10 – Novello.
   Example 13 – Bardic Edition.

Chapter XIX
   Example 2 – Scottish Music Publishing.
   Examples 3 and 4 – Novello.
   Example 5 – Edward McGuire.
   Examples 6 and 7 – Scottish Music Publishing.
   Example 8 – Bardic Edition.

INDEX

Note: Musical examples are indicated by *italic page references* followed by *(ex.)*. **Bold** references are to plate numbers. Notes are indexed only when the name or subject does not appear in the text relating to the referent.

McArthur, Piper to Ranald Macdonald Esquire of Staffa, BY JOHN KAY